EQUITY AND ADMINISTRATION

Each generation of lawyers in common law systems faces an important question: what is the nature of equity as developed in English law and inherited by other common law jurisdictions? While some traditional explanations of equity remain useful – including the understanding of equity as a system that qualifies the legal rights people ordinarily have under judge-made law and under legislation – other common explanations are unhelpful or misleading. This volume considers a distinct and little noticed view of equity. By examining the ways in which courts of equity have addressed a range of practical problems regarding the administration of deliberately created schemes for the management of others' affairs, modern equity can be seen to have a strongly facilitative character. The extent of and limits on this characterisation of equity are explored in chapters covering equity's attitude to administration in various public and private settings in common law systems.

P.G. TURNER is a University Lecturer and a Fellow of St Catharine's College at the University of Cambridge.

EQUITY AND ADMINISTRATION

Edited by

P.G. TURNER

Faculty of Law, and St Catharine's College, University of Cambridge

CAMBRIDGE
UNIVERSITY PRESS

CAMBRIDGE
UNIVERSITY PRESS

University Printing House, Cambridge CB2 8BS, United Kingdom

Cambridge University Press is part of the University of Cambridge.

It furthers the University's mission by disseminating knowledge in the pursuit of education, learning and research at the highest international levels of excellence.

www.cambridge.org
Information on this title: www.cambridge.org/9781107142732

First published 2016

A catalogue record for this publication is available from the British Library

Library of Congress Cataloguing in Publication data
Turner, P. G. (Peter G.), editor.
Equity and administration / edited by P. G. Turner.
New York : Cambridge University Press, 2016.
LCCN 2015042972 | ISBN 9781107142732 (hardback)
LCSH: Equity – Great Britain. | Equity. | BISAC: LAW / Civil Law.
LCC KD674 .E68 2016 | DDC 346.41/004–dc23
LC record available at http://lccn.loc.gov/2015042972

ISBN 978-1-107-14273-2 Hardback

This volume is dedicated to the memory of
S.K.O.T.

CONTENTS

CONTRIBUTORS

Catherine Addy is a barrister at Maitland Chambers, Lincoln's Inn.

John F. Avery Jones is a retired judge of the Upper Tribunal (Tax and Chancery Chamber).

Matthew Conaglen is a Professor of Equity and Trusts at the University of Sydney.

Timothy Endicott is a Professor of Legal Philosophy in the University of Oxford.

David Feldman QC (Hon.), FBA, is the Rouse Ball Professor of English Law in the University of Cambridge.

William Gummow AC is a former Justice of the High Court of Australia, a Professor of Law at the University of Sydney and at the Australian National University and a Non-Permanent Judge of the Hong Kong Court of Final Appeal.

J.D. Heydon AC, QC is a former Justice of the High Court of Australia and a Visiting Professor in the University of Oxford.

Look Chan Ho is an Attorney-at-Law, a Solicitor-Advocate and the Head of Restructuring and Insolvency for Asia at Freshfields Bruckhaus Deringer, Hong Kong.

John H. Langbein is the Sterling Professor of Law and Legal History at Yale University.

Mark Leeming is a Judge of Appeal in the Supreme Court of New South Wales and the Challis Lecturer in Equity at the University of Sydney.

Michael Lobban is a Professor of Legal History at the London School of Economics.

Mike Macnair is an Associate Professor of Law in the University of Oxford.

Paul Matthews is a Deputy Master in the Chancery Division of the High Court of Justice of England and Wales and an honorary Professor of King's College, London.

Patricia I. McMahon recently completed a JSD at the Yale Law School.

Guy Newey is a Judge of the High Court of Justice of England and Wales.

R.C. Nolan is a Professor of Law at the University of York.

Nicholas Patten is a Lord Justice of Appeal of the Court of Appeal of England and Wales.

Philip Sales is a Lord Justice of Appeal of the Court of Appeal of England and Wales.

Henry E. Smith is the Fessenden Professor of Law and Director of Project on the Foundations of Private Law in the Harvard Law School.

Richard Snowden is a Judge of the High Court of Justice of England and Wales.

Chantal Stebbings is a Professor of Law and Legal History and Director of the Bracton Centre for Legal History Research at the University of Exeter.

Alan Steinfeld QC is a barrister at XXIV Old Buildings, Lincoln's Inn, and sits as a Deputy Judge of the High Court.

P.G. Turner is a University Lecturer and a Fellow of St Catharine's College in the University of Cambridge.

Robert Walker is a former Lord of Appeal in Ordinary and a former Justice of the Supreme Court of the United Kingdom.

Adrian Zuckerman is a Professor of Civil Procedure in the University of Oxford.

ACKNOWLEDGEMENTS

The conception of this book has its origins in a seminar of the same title held in Cambridge in January 2014. The seminar drew together, as it was designed to do, lawyers of a wide range of experience. Naturally they included English lawyers. But they also included lawyers from Australia, Canada and the United States. Naturally the gathering was scholarly. Yet it was made up of learned judges and practising lawyers as well as lawyers of the academy. The seminar was borne of a conviction that each of these groups had a deal to learn from all the others; and, at the seminar's conclusion, those from each group professed to have done so.

It was only possible to gather those lawyers together, and it is only now possible to offer this published collection, with the support of the Cambridge Centre for Private Law. Through its directors, Professor Graham Virgo and Professor Sarah Worthington, the Centre gave vast support. In turn, full thanks are due to the Centre's supporters – especially the Cambridge University Press, Clifford Chance LLP, the Faculty of Law in the University of Cambridge, Lord Grabiner QC, South Square Chambers and Trinity College, Cambridge.

Ms Kim Hughes of the Cambridge University Press was a most constructive and accommodating commissioning editor. The skill of Mr Peter Illidge, and a grant from the Yorke Fund administered by the Faculty of Law in the University of Cambridge, made the final stages of preparing the manuscript considerably simpler.

TABLE OF CASES

TABLE OF LEGISLATION

Acts

s. 150 445
s. 151 445
s. 152 445
s. 226 260
Sch. B 466
Common Law Procedure Act 1854, 17 & 18 Vict. c. 125 425, 442, 456, 468
s. 1 457
s. 4 457
s. 22 457
s. 23 457
s. 24 457
s. 46 457
s. 47 457
s. 50 456, 457
s. 51 457
s. 52 457
s. 53 457
s. 56 457
s. 57 457
s. 58 457
s. 59 457
s. 68 460, 468
s. 69 468
s. 70 460, 468
s. 71 460, 468
s. 72 468
s. 73 468
s. 74 468
s. 75 468
s. 76 468
s. 77 468
s. 78 468
s. 79 468
s. 82 460
s. 83 460, 468
s. 84 460
s. 85 460
s. 88 460
Common Law Procedure Act 1860, 23 & 24 Vict. c. 126 426, 442
s. 2 460
s. 12 460
s. 19 448

Statutory instruments

Conventions

United States

Federal

New York State

Australia

Uniform legislation

Commonwealth

New South Wales

Queensland

South Australia

Tasmania

Victoria

Western Australia

Canada

Ontario

India

1

Equity and administration

P.G. TURNER

Introduction

Each generation of lawyers in common law systems encounters the question: what is the nature of the source of law known by lawyers as equity? Long-standing opinions offer partial answers. Most speak of equity as being, and having been, founded in the justice of sometimes qualifying and dispensing with rules of the standing legal order. In this way most opinions on the nature of equity in common law systems liken equity in common law systems to general notions of equity. However, in England and jurisdictions whose legal systems derive from the English legal system, descriptions of equity also contain some historical element. For, in England and many jurisdictions descended from the English legal system, the dispensation of justice by equitable methods came to occur successively through the Sovereign, the Lord Chancellor, the Court of Chancery and hence courts of equity. To speak of equity in common law systems is therefore to speak of a jurisdiction, in a core sense of the word.[1] It is to speak of a source of law that continues to qualify and dispense with elements of the standing legal order, where settled principles so permit or require.

The problem addressed in this collection of essays is how to advance the understanding of modern equity from this basic position. In particular, how can the understanding of equity be advanced by means of the terms, concepts and habits of thought familiar to lawyers today?

One way is to understand equity as a body of doctrine that operates negatively. Non-legal as well as legal notions of equity support this understanding, which will be discussed later in this chapter and in other chapters

[1] Cf. C.C. Langdell, *A Brief Survey of Equity Jurisdiction* (Cambridge, Mass.: Harvard Law Review Association, 1908), 22–3.

of this collection. Even before equity became established as a system of principles, doctrines and remedies that were recognised, applied and granted by the English courts, it was settled that equity could operate by qualifying the ordinary legal rights of persons according both to the judge-made common law and, sometimes, parliamentary legislation. It was also recognised early that equity could require the consequences of otherwise lawful transactions to be undone, where the circumstances offended equitable principles. Such operations are negative: they prevent, restrain and undo proscribed actions and their consequences. And these negative operations of equity were prominent not only in historical English equity: a negative role for equity continues to be recognised in English law and all the national legal systems that possess a system of equity as part of their common law inheritance from England. However, it is inadequate to perceive equity as operating negatively only. It also operates in other ways. Yet these other important qualities of equity jurisprudence are little understood.

Among these qualities is the facilitative nature of equity. Many uniquely equitable principles, doctrines and remedies have the purpose of aiding and regulating the performance of practical tasks of administration. Rather than hinder desirable action and its consequences, equity commonly promotes it. Thus, when equity qualifies a person's ability to enforce his or her strict legal rights – a negative operation – on most occasions equity positively aids the performance of administrative processes, rather than obstructs the performance of legal responsibilities. How that is done is explored by the various essays in this collection. At times, equity does not positively and explicitly aid the performance of practical administrative tasks. However, where that is the case, equity often facilitates practical action in a different way. By abstaining where it might otherwise intervene, equity declines to interfere in the performance of administrative tasks. For example, where the performance of practical tasks might be hindered, equity often qualifies its general principles so as to facilitate practical action. In modern English legal jargon, equity often 'disapplies' its general principles where to do so assists administration.

Because administrative tasks are practical, equity's facilitative character ought to be clearest from its attitude towards administration. A wide variety of administrative tasks is to be found. They range from the administration of the assets of trusts, through the administration of insolvent estates and of solvent and insolvent business associations, and to the administration of the affairs of the legislative, executive and judicial branches of government. The concept of administration is accordingly wide. However, to define administration in this way for the purpose of the present enquiry is not to define it so widely as to become meaningless. The most telling situations in which equity's facilitative character can be seen are those where equity facilitates deliberately created schemes, transactions and sets of legal relations, especially where ongoing management of a state of affairs is required. Hence the examination of how equity operates upon settlements created deliberately by private transactions, as well as upon schemes established by parliamentary legislation and otherwise. At base, the variety of situations to be encountered are either (1) situations in which private persons are responsible for performing the practical tasks of administration envisaged or required by a private transaction, and in which equitable doctrines and remedies aid the proper performance of those persons' responsibilities, or (2) situations in which the responsibility of administration rather lies with the courts, in the exercise of equitable jurisdiction to administer certain legal relations. In the case of express trusts, for example, the categories overlap. The arrangement can be privately created and require the administration of the trust by private persons; yet courts of equity have administrative jurisdiction in respect of express trusts.

Wherever disputes over practical administrative tasks are justiciable, the law applied to decide those disputes can itself become an object of controversy. At the simplest, the law might be attacked for intervening too little or too much – and in either case hampering practical activity. It should not be surprising, then, to find that some instances in which equity assumes a facilitative role are controversial. For example, specific relief can facilitate the administration of a legislative scheme: properly granted, an injunction can keep a responsible person to the performance of his or her obligations under the scheme. However, what begins as facilitation can end as disruption. If an equitable doctrine is overly strengthened to further the attainment of desirable ends, other valuable activities may at the same time be stifled by equity's efforts to aid administration. Does this falsify the assertion that equity possesses a facilitative character? It is suggested not. Disagreements over how to delimit particular equitable remedies and doctrines are disagreements on a level of detail. While important, they should not be allowed to distract attention from more enduring and general features of equity. One such feature is the facilitative character of equity. The essays in this book have been collected together in the view that this role is basic to equity, and ought to be better understood.

The chapters that follow seek to better the current understanding of modern equity by studying its facilitative role. The chapters methodically examine a range of areas in which persons may or must conduct tasks and processes of practical kinds, and in which equity aids the satisfactory completion of those practical activities. The areas of conduct are ones in which the tasks and processes arise in relation to arrangements deliberately created by transacting parties or an individual acting alone or even by the legislative or executive branches of government. Examples are the schemes and arrangements established by declaring a trust, forming a partnership, forming a registered company, enacting parliamentary legislation, making subordinate legislation, devising an administrative scheme for implementation by the executive branch of government or a public authority and establishing procedures for the administration of justice by courts. Hence the title of this chapter and of this book: equity and administration. Some of the chapters directly address the nature of equity, either examining its historical development towards the system of equity known today, or by focusing on modern equity as such. Some chapters concentrate on present controversies regarding how, and how far, equity properly applies in aiding administration. While the emphasis of the chapters differs, all reveal, whether directly or indirectly, the strength of equity's facilitative nature. A later section of this chapter will suggest how each other chapter does so.

This chapter focuses less on controversial matters of doctrine arising in each area where equity aids administration and more on what those controversies indicate about the general characteristics of equity today. It outlines the types of activity that equity aids and the ways in which equity provides that assistance. The chapter also indicates the importance of taking a long view when pursuing these questions. Little investigation is needed before the value of a long perspective becomes apparent. Over short and long intervals, lines of equitable doctrine that aid administration in one area of activity have been extended to other areas and adjusted in recognition of the peculiar set of considerations – of principle and practicality – that exist in a given area. That is particularly seen in the extension of doctrines and remedies from the law of trusts to other areas, including constitutional and administrative law. However, before addressing the points just set out, something should first be said of other perspectives on modern equity and why a need exists to appreciate equity specifically as law that facilitates practical action.

Other perspectives on equity

The question of how contemporary lawyers ought to view equity within common law systems is complicated by at least two influences. Both depend on the fact that equity is a complex system, like all large systems of doctrines and rules.

The first complicating influence is that equity can be seen variously. Complex systems have many features. How the system is viewed and understood depends on which of its features are examined. The nature of the system can appear to change as first one set of features is examined and then another. The apparent variation creates a dilemma as to how the system ought to be viewed and portrayed.

Also complicating the matter is the influence of contemporary interests and needs. According to the interests and concerns of the day, radically different accounts of equity have been offered at different times. In the eighteenth century it was fashionable to view Chancery equity through maxims. The perspective on equity afforded by equitable maxims was desired so much that the maxims were propagated with an intensity that now seems curious. A more structured perspective of equity was reached through the trichotomy favoured by Mr Justice Story, borrowing from Fonblanque and Jeremy.[2] According to this, equity divides into the exclusive, concurrent and auxiliary jurisdictions. The exclusive is the jurisdiction in which equity supplies a remedy while the common law supplies none; the concurrent jurisdiction is that in which equity provides a remedy that could also be obtained at law; while the auxiliary jurisdiction of equity is that in which both equity and the common law supply a remedy, but the common law remedy is deficient in some way that is overcome by the equitable remedy.

Both these perspectives are instructive, and even important,[3] to an understanding of modern equity. However, modern equity is usually viewed otherwise. The view that equity operates negatively has already been mentioned. An understanding of equity based on that or certain other current perspectives on equity is likely to be inaccurate unless accompanied by perspectives that convey what appears from other

[2] D.E.C. Yale, 'A Trichotomy of Equity' (1985) 6 J.L.H. 194; M. Macnair, 'Equity and Conscience' (2007) 27 O.J.L.S. 659, 664–5. See also W. Blackstone, *Commentaries on the Laws of England* (Oxford: Clarendon Press, 1772), vol. 3, 438, 439, 441 (referring to the concurrent and exclusive jurisdictions of equity).

[3] See J.D. Heydon, M.J. Leeming and P.G. Turner, *Meagher, Gummow and Lehane's Equity: Doctrines and Remedies*, 5th ed. (Sydney: LexisNexis Butterworths, 2015), [25–075]–[25–095] (on rescission).

dominant features of equity. However, modern portrayals of equity tend towards stereotypes. To adjust and correct these other perspectives on equity, concentration on equity's facilitative nature is needed.

Four perspectives

Probably the commonest perspective on modern equity is that it is straightforwardly discretionary, largely unconstrained by boundaries or rules. Historically, this seems to have been particularly true of the justice administered by the Lord Chancellor before courts of equity, so called, had come into being.[4] In modern times, Lord Denning liked to apply this view of equity.[5] More recently again, it is evident in a case of relief against forfeiture, *Çukurova Finance Ltd* v. *Alfa Telecom Ltd (No. 4)*.[6] Three members of the Privy Council there said that when relief is granted from forfeiture, the relationship of the parties is restored not on terms earlier agreed by the parties themselves but on terms set by equity. Their Lordships stressed equity's 'free discretion' to set these terms, and spoke of the breadth, flexibility and greatness of equitable discretion.[7] Though not commonly applied in modern judicial decisions, such a view of equity is often encountered both in litigation and legal writing.[8] Ironically, it has a robust existence as a straw man.

From a second position, equity is seen as an 'alibi'[9] for non-compliance with ordinary legal obligations and rules. Thus, equity has been criticised for holding that, where a disposition of property is not completed, a party who was intended to gain certain common law proprietary rights upon

[4] Macnair, 'Equity and Conscience', 670–1; M. Macnair, 'Arbitrary Chancellors and the Problem of Predictability', in E. Koops and W.J. Zwalve (eds.), *Law and Equity: Approaches in Roman Law and Common Law* (Leiden: Martinus Nijhoff, 2014), 81–94.

[5] See A. Denning, 'The Need for a New Equity' [1952] C.L.P. 1; *Hussey* v. *Palmer* [1972] 1 W.L.R. 1286, 1289; *Eves* v. *Eves* [1975] 1 W.L.R. 1338, 1341.

[6] [2015] 2 W.L.R. 875; [2013] UKPC 20.

[7] [2015] 2 W.L.R. 875, [22]–[24], transposing certain statements in cases on the construction of statutory provisions for relief from forfeiture to the jurisdiction under the judge-made law. Although their Lordships said this free discretion could only be exercised in 'exceptional' cases, it is submitted that that constraint is unreal given (1) the nature of the discretion as stated by their Lordships (see also at [97]–[98]) and (2) that modern equity does not possess such a free discretion (nor the asserted 'exceptional' one).

[8] For a recent example, see J.W. Carter, W. Courtney, E. Peden, A. Stewart and G.J. Tolhurst, 'Contractual Penalties: Resurrecting the Equitable Jurisdiction' (2013) 13 J.C.L. 99, 109.

[9] B. Rudden, 'Equity as Alibi', in S. Goldstein (ed.), *Equity and Contemporary Legal Developments* (Hebrew University of Jerusalem, 1992), 30–46.

completion nevertheless has equivalent rights in equity.[10] A variant position is that equity operates through 'subterfuge' of ordinary legal obligations and rules. In *Yeates* v. *Line*,[11] the court held that an agreement with the effect but not the purpose of disposing of an interest in land was outside a statutory provision that '[a] contract for the sale or other disposition of an interest in land can only be made in writing and only by incorporating all the terms which the parties have expressly agreed in one document or, where contracts are exchanged, in each'.[12] Although the court's reasoning made no '[overt] ... appeal to "equity"',[13] an implicit appeal to equity is said to have involved the court in ignoring the words of the legislation 'on the basis of an all-encompassing subterfuge'.[14] The view of equity as alibi or subterfuge is summed up in the statement that equity cases 'never come close to dealing with the principled question of *why* equity can act [as equity acts]: it just *does*'.[15]

A third view is that equity obscures truth and normal modes of rational thinking.[16] While this overlaps in part with the previous view, it also exists independently. It holds that equity obscures truth and rationality by being expressed in diffuse and contradictory principles, thus violating a principle that like cases are to be treated alike. Thus, equity is said to violate, or at least undermine, the rule of law.[17] The fact that some equitable doctrines can be stated in words that have more than one meaning, and meanings that operate 'at different levels of generality', has been noted and criticised for undermining rational thinking.[18] Such equitable language is said to put rational analysis of the law beyond grasp.[19]

[10] See, for example, *Curtis* v. *Pulbrook* [2011] 1 B.C.L.C. 638, [47]; [2011] EWHC 167 (Ch); W. Swadling, 'The Vendor-Purchaser Constructive Trust', in S. Degeling and J. Edelman (eds.), *Equity in Commercial Law* (Sydney: Lawbook Co., 2005), 480–1.

[11] [2013] Ch. 363, [29]–[35]; [2012] EWHC 3085 (Ch).

[12] Law of Property (Miscellaneous Provisions) Act 1989 (UK), s. 2(1).

[13] M. Dixon, 'To Write or Not to Write?' [2013] Conv. 1, 1. [14] *Ibid.*, 1.

[15] *Ibid.*, 1 (italics original). Similarly, P. Birks, 'Equity in the Modern Law: An Exercise in Taxonomy' (1996) 26 U.W.A. L. Rev. 1, 22, 99.

[16] P. Birks and A. Pretto, 'Preface', in P. Birks and A. Pretto (eds.), *Breach of Trust* (Oxford: Hart Publishing, 2002), xi.

[17] Birks, 'Equity in the Modern Law: An Exercise in Taxonomy', 16–17; A. Burrows, 'We Do This at Common Law but That in Equity' (2002) 22 O.J.L.S. 1, 4–5 and *passim*. Cf. H.E. Smith, 'Property, Equity, and the Rule of Law', in L.M. Austin and D. Klimchuk (eds.), *Private Law and the Rule of Law* (Oxford University Press, 2014), ch. 10.

[18] Birks, 'Equity in the Modern Law: An Exercise in Taxonomy', 48.

[19] W. Swadling, 'The Fiction of the Constructive Trust' (2011) 64 C.L.P. 399, 433.

The fourth view to be considered is that equity is compulsory. Equity can ordain legal results that surprise transacting parties who thought they would achieve some other legal result; it can even directly contradict what the parties intended. The 'imposition' of fiduciary duties on joint venturers who did not believe they were in fiduciary relations with one another, and equity's refusal to enforce penal stipulations, are illustrations of this view.

By combining such perspectives on equity together, greater rhetorical force has been gained. Developing the argument that the language of equity places rational analysis of the law beyond grasp, it has been said that '[a]ll forms of appeal to very broad ideas tend to allow intuition to operate unrestrained by an analysis anchored in authority'.[20] That suggests a link with the first and second views of equity outlined earlier. It suggests that because equity employs broad language, it is unclear what the language denotes. The language is said to allow a court to decide a case unconstrained by prior judicial decisions. Broad language and language with meanings on several levels of generality are said to become alibis for an unconstrained equitable discretion.

Four views evaluated

These rhetorical claims about equity have little of substance behind them. Nevertheless, each of the four views has enough currency for it to be tendered in argument – adversarial, scholarly or otherwise – in the twenty-first century. Each is more prominent in legal discussion and argument than the view that much of equity has a facilitative nature. To show why a study of equity and administration is valuable to one who seeks to understand the nature of the modern law, it is therefore necessary to evaluate those four views of equity on their own terms and to suggest where corrections are necessary.

Discretionary equity

The first of these views may be briefly discussed. Any support for the view that equity is straightforwardly discretionary, unconstrained by boundaries and rules, must be very limited. When counsel have asserted that modern equity is widely discretionary in something like the way it once was historically, the courts have denied counsel's assertions.[21] Similarly,

[20] Birks, 'Equity in the Modern Law: An Exercise in Taxonomy', 22.

[21] *Re Telescriptor Syndicate Ltd* [1903] 2 Ch. 174, 195; *Re Diplock's Estate* [1948] Ch. 465, 481–2; *Bridge* v. *Campbell Discount Co. Ltd* [1961] 1 Q.B. 445, 449; Denning, 'The Need for a New Equity', 8. See also *Australian Broadcasting Corporation* v. *Lenah Game Meats*

when the courts have asserted a widely discretionary equitable jurisdiction, decisions based on those opinions have often been queried, qualified and overruled.[22] Those denials, queries, qualifications and over-rulings can leave scant support for the view that modern equity is strongly discretionary in the way that the Lord Chancellor's powers were, early in equity's history.[23] Decisions in which equitable discretion has been asserted or applied with no or few constraints are unorthodox. Equity in modern common law jurisdictions is not equity dispensed outside the system of law.[24]

Equity as alibi or subterfuge

The weaknesses of the view that modern equity is an alibi can also be shortly stated. To take its extreme variant – that equity is subterfuge – where a court exercising equitable jurisdiction delivers its reasons for judgment without offering a normative explanation for its application of a particular rule it is difficult to see this as subterfuge. A judge discharges his or her duty to give reasons by explaining how the relevant rules apply on the facts of the case, and with what results. Regardless of whether the case concerns common law, statutory or equitable rights and entitlements, the judge has no duty to give a normative explanation of the rules applied.[25] The absence of such a duty is not attributable to equity.

That conclusion points to a general problem with arguments that equity is an alibi or a subterfuge. Labelling equity as an alibi discourages the labeller and others from examining equitable doctrines on their own terms. Without being so examined, the principles that underlie an

Pty Ltd (2001) 208 C.L.R. 199, [16]; [2001] HCA 63; *Tanwar Enterprises Pty Ltd* v. *Cauchi* (2003) 217 C.L.R. 315, [20]–[26]; [2003] HCA 57; *Twentieth Century Fox Corp.* v. *Harris* [2014] Ch. 41; [2013] EWHC 159 (Ch).

22 See the discussion of Lord Denning's innovations by D.J. Hayton, 'Equity and Trusts', in J.L. Jowell and J.P.W.B. McAuslan (eds.), *Lord Denning: The Judge and the Law* (London: Sweet and Maxwell, 1984), ch. 3 and J. Glister and J. Lee, *Hanbury and Martin: Modern Equity*, 20th ed. (London: Sweet and Maxwell, 2015), [12–026].

23 See S. Worthington, *Equity*, 2nd ed. (Oxford University Press, 2006), 331–3; G. Virgo, 'Restitution through the Looking Glass: Restitution within Equity and Equity within Restitution', in J. Getzler (ed.), *Rationalizing Property, Equity and Trusts: Essays in Honour of Edward Burn* (London: LexisNexis, 2003), 110.

24 At earlier periods, the opposite was the case: Macnair, 'Arbitrary Chancellors and the Problem of Predictability', in Koops and Zwalve (eds.), *Law and Equity: Approaches in Roman Law and Common Law*, 91–4. Cf. J.M. Nolan-Haley, 'The Merger of Law and Mediation: Lessons from Equity Jurisprudence and Roscoe Pound' (2004) 6 Cardozo J. Conflict Resol. 57, 58 ('[E]quity . . . offer[s] a form of "individualized justice" unavailable in the official legal system').

25 Cf. H. Dagan, *Property: Values and Institutions* (Oxford University Press, 2011), ch. 1.

equitable doctrine invoked by litigants and applied by a court cannot be understood. The reasons and decision in *Yeates* v. *Line* were summarised earlier. If – undiscouraged by the 'subterfuge' label – a lawyer were to investigate *Yeates* v. *Line* for evidence of legal principle, what would the lawyer find? There is clear evidence that the court was interpreting the relevant statute purposively, not applying equitable doctrines or a free equitable discretion.[26] Purposive interpretations of statutes are not typically criticised as involving the subterfuge of legal method. Indeed, purposive interpretations are not the exclusive domain of equity. Such interpretations are 'equitable' only in the limited sense that, in times past, courts of equity sometimes interpreted a statute purposively where a court of common law would interpret the statute literally.[27] Labelling the decision in *Yeates* v. *Line* as an equitable subterfuge seems to have discouraged analysis of what the court's reasoning was – thus placing a plausible explanation of the case beyond reach. Equivalent arguments based on different examples share the same difficulty.

Equity as obscurity

The portrayal of modern equity as obscuring[28] truth and the possibility of analysis is also problematic but requires a longer response. Writers have said that the language of equity obscures real similarities between the common law and equity. The suggested similarities of law and equity as regards 'wrongs', 'damages' and 'compensation' have been stressed.[29]

26 See *Birmingham* v. *Renfrew* (1937) 57 C.L.R. 666, 678, 690–1; and J.D. Heydon, 'Equity and Statute', Chapter 12 of this volume, text to nn. 139ff. See also J. Cartwright, 'Equity's Connivance in the Evasion of Legal Formalities', in Koops and Zwalve (eds.), *Law and Equity: Approaches in Roman Law and Common Law*, 112–21 who, while not addressing statutory interpretation, discussed other principles animating equity's doctrines in this area. It should be noted that, notwithstanding its title, Professor Cartwright's chapter does not argue that equity as such connived in the evasion of legal formalities: the argument is only that this was 'the effect' of certain equitable doctrines (e.g. at 108, 113).

27 See Blackstone, *Commentaries on the Laws of England*, vol. 3, 430–1; R.S. French, 'The Interface between Equitable Principles and Public Law' (unpublished paper available at www.hcourt.gov.au/assets/publications/speeches/current-justices/frenchcj/frenchcj29oct10.pdf), 3–5; N. Duxbury, *The Elements of Legislation* (Cambridge University Press, 2013), ch. 6.

28 See, for example, J. Beatson, 'Unfinished Business: Integrating Equity', in J. Beatson (ed.), *The Use and Abuse of Unjust Enrichment* (Oxford: Clarendon Press, 1991), 246–8; P. Birks, 'Definition and Division: A Meditation on Institutes 3.13', in P. Birks (ed.), *The Classification of Obligations* (Oxford: Clarendon Press, 1997), 14–15, 33 and Burrows, 'We Do This at Common Law but That in Equity' (critiquing parts, but not all, of equity).

29 See, for example, J. Edelman and S. Elliott, 'Money Remedies against Trustees' (2004) 18 T.L.I. 116; Burrows, 'We Do This at Common Law but That in Equity'.

However, so long as the detailed rules for such things as wrongs, damages and compensation are different – as they currently are – the only commonality among these ideas at law and in equity will be on a very general level. The gravity of the truth 'hidden' by different equitable language is not strong if the common terminology is only shared on a very general level.

There is also the question of how to identify the similarities between law and equity said to be obscured by different equitable language. It has been seen that the language and doctrines of modern equity have been criticised for weakening the rule of law by failing to treat like cases alike – specifically by producing consequences different from those produced by applying the common law to the same set of facts. However, as Lady Hale J.S.C. has said in another context: 'The Aristotelian injunction that like cases be treated alike depends upon which characteristics are seen as relevant for the particular purpose'.[30] Since equity corrects, qualifies and fulfils the common law, it is a category error to say that when one set of facts yields different outcomes according to legal and equitable rules, equity fails to treat like cases alike. The charge that the language of equity obscures real similarities between equity and the common law is not made out simply by noting that equity and law can apply to the one set of facts and yield different results.

Equity and the common law are not needlessly different. The very fact that equity and common law often yield different outcomes indicates that the different language leading to those outcomes expresses differences of substance. It is useful to recall Mr Justice Story's tripartite division of equity into the exclusive, auxiliary and concurrent jurisdictions. Most equity jurisprudence is found in the exclusive and auxiliary jurisdictions. Because the exclusive jurisdiction of equity is concerned with conduct not recognised and remedied by the common law, the exclusive jurisdiction of equity can be expected to operate through concepts that differ from the concepts of the common law. And so it does. In the exclusive jurisdiction, equity starts with the fact that the common law does not relevantly address some injustice; the concepts and methods of equity that are deployed in order to reverse or prevent that injustice are therefore distinctive. In equity's auxiliary jurisdiction, there is another starting point. It is that, though the common law may supply some remedy (e.g. damages for breach of contract) to address some injustice, the common

[30] *Seldon* v. *Clarkson Wright & Jakes (a partnership)* [2012] 3 All E.R. 1301, [2]; [2012] UKSC 16.

law remedy is inadequate to do justice. The occasion for equity to intervene (e.g. by decreeing specific performance of a contract) is a deficit of the common law. In the auxiliary jurisdiction, equity's concepts and methods can again be expected to differ from those of the common law. And so they do.[31]

It is inherent in the nature of rules whose purpose is to overcome the deficiencies of other rules that the former work differently from the latter. Lest there be legal chaos, the former, higher-order, rules must not be coextensive with the more basic rules whose operation the former qualifies. In short, equity cannot be allowed to operate crudely and without qualification, whether in the exclusive or the auxiliary jurisdiction. Crude language, concepts and methods would tend to undo the common law in respects in which the common law is entirely sound, requiring no correction or supplement. The functions of equity make it almost inevitable that its concepts will have certain subtleties and complications that are less prevalent in the common law. That is simply because in the exclusive and auxiliary jurisdictions, equity only ever intervenes where the common law supplies no remedy, or an inadequate one, and in every part of the exclusive and auxiliary jurisdictions equity needs to take precautions not to undo all the justice done by the common law. The different equitable language relates to the different techniques and principles that need to be applied cautiously in order to protect the virtues of the common law.

Do all appeals to very broad ideas tend to allow intuition to operate unrestrained by analysis anchored in authority, as some have asserted? It is submitted that they do not.[32] The assertion assumes that whenever a word is used that denotes a very broad idea, but also narrower ideas, a reader or listener will understand the writer or speaker to have used the word in its broadest sense. That is contrary to the experience of users of the English language, as can be seen from the usage of the word 'equity' itself. 'Equity' is a word denoting a very broad idea. 'Equity' also denotes narrower ideas. It can denote particular principles, doctrines and remedies within common law legal systems. Those who read and hear the word 'equity' normally give it a wider or narrower meaning according to the context of the communication. Lincoln's Inn is one of numerous places where the word 'equity' is understood in ways that disprove the

[31] Cf. Blackstone, *Commentaries on the Laws of England*, vol. 3, 441.

[32] See further *Bofinger* v. *Kingsway Group Ltd* (2009) 239 C.L.R. 269, [92]–[94]; [2009] HCA 44.

suggestion that all appeals to very broad ideas tend to allow intuition to operate unconstrained by analysis. The existence of a body of law called 'equity' in common law systems where judges applying equity do not apply unconstrained intuition also points to the difficulties with the suggestion.

The last aspect of the view that equity obscures truth and rationality to be discussed here is the attempt to cast doubt on equity because, in equity, certain terms are used on different levels of generality. Such an attempt is unsustainable. It can be accepted that the more levels of generality with which a term is used, the greater the risk of confusion; and great risks of confusion are undesirable. However, the existence of a heightened risk itself points to no consistently reliable solution. Many words, in legal language and beyond, have wider and narrower meanings and yet successful communication constantly occurs. Falsity and irrational thinking are not the inevitable corollaries of an equitable vocabulary. Further, in ordinary conversation it is common experience that the most familiar words are used with different degrees of narrowness and width, precision and vagueness. A usage of terms is not invalid merely because the terms are used on different levels of generality. When the ordinary incremental processes of legal development – including the gradual forging of new rights and remedies over extended periods through long series of hard-fought cases – have led certain words in legal language to be used on different levels of generality, the argument that equity should have no distinctive language appears in substance to be an argument for the removal of some substantive content from the legal system.[33] On occasion that may be desirable. On many occasions it will not.

These doubts remove a deal of the support from the view of equity as obscuring the similarities between law and equity and otherwise obscuring reason and foreclosing analysis.

Compulsory equity

Finally, the view that equity is compulsory in over-riding parties' expectations and lawfully expressed intentions. This view is salient in the (typically unsuccessful) arguments of counsel in cases on the duties of joint venturers and on the enforceability of penal stipulations.[34] When

[33] An exception is Swadling, 'The Fiction of the Constructive Trust', 400.

[34] It is also salient in discussion of constructive trusts: for example *Muschinski* v. *Dodds* (1985) 160 C.L.R. 583, 614; *Westdeutsche Landesbank Girozentrale* v. *Islington London Borough Council* [1996] A.C. 669, 705, 708, 716 (but cf. at 706); *Air Jamaica Ltd*

litigation arises from joint ventures, it is not uncommon for one venturer to assert that the other owed the one fiduciary obligations. Even where they did not at the time appreciate it, a court of equity can find after the event that the joint venturers created fiduciary relations between themselves. Observers can be heard to say that the court thus 'imposed' fiduciary duties on parties who thought nothing of fiduciary doctrine.[35] Indeed, courts can be heard to speak of 'imposing' fiduciary duties on one or both of the joint venturers.[36]

However, it is a mistake to see this as illustrating an equitable will to over-ride parties' expectations and lawfully expressed intentions. The only sense in which fiduciary obligations are 'imposed' in such a case is that fiduciary obligations are recognised to apply to one or both parties even though they did not consciously bargain to create fiduciary duties. Equity 'imposes' these obligations only when their imposition furthers the performance of parties' duties in a proper manner.[37] Where the imposition of fiduciary obligations would be contrary to the terms or purposes of the parties' arrangements, fiduciary obligations will not be 'imposed'.

Nor does equitable relief against penal stipulations reveal that the nature of equity is to over-ride parties' lawfully expressed intentions except very limitedly.[38] When the penalty doctrine applies, either at common law or in equity, it applies on the basis that objectively speaking the parties are found to have intended that a secondary stipulation should punish one party for the failure of a primary stipulation, or alternatively should give the obligee security for the possible failure of the primary

v. *Charlton* [1999] 1 W.L.R. 1399, 1412; C. Mitchell, *Hayton & Mitchell: Commentary and Cases on the Law of Trusts and Equitable Remedies*, 13th ed. (London: Sweet & Maxwell, 2010), ch. 15 *passim* and esp. [15–01], [15–137]–[15–151]. However, see now B. McFarlane and C. Mitchell, *Hayton & Mitchell: Text, Cases and Materials on the Law of Trusts and Equitable Remedies*, 14th ed. (London: Sweet & Maxwell, 2015), [15–213]–[15–215].

35 See, for example, A. Whiteley, 'Non-Contractual Duties of Joint Venturers in Canada' (1993) 4 I.C.C.L.R. 148, 149, 152; J. Birchall, 'Duties of Good Faith in Commercial Joint Ventures? Contractual Duties, Fiduciary Duties, and Shareholder Remedies' [2005] J.B.L. 268, 269, 274, 275. See also J. Uguccioni, 'Buyer Beware: Failed Joint Venture Negotiations and Involuntary Business Partnerships' [2011] J.B.L. 160, 160, 161, 169.

36 See, for example, *Lac Minerals Ltd* v. *International Corona Resources Ltd* [1989] 2 S.C.R. 574.

37 See M. Conaglen, *Fiduciary Loyalty: Protecting the Due Performance of Non-Fiduciary Duties* (Oxford: Hart Publishing, 2010). On the 'imposition' of fiduciary duties more generally, see P.D. Finn, *Fiduciary Obligations* (Sydney: Law Book Co., 1977), [22]–[24].

38 Cf. *Elsley* v. *J.G. Collins Insurance Agencies Ltd* [1978] 2 S.C.R. 916, 937.

stipulation. To an extent, the penalty doctrine – including the doctrine in equity, where that still exists[39] – is compulsory: a secondary stipulation meant to punish the obligor will not be enforced according to its terms. However, where the secondary stipulation was meant as punishment, a court of equity with jurisdiction to grant relief does not rewrite the contract as such or find the secondary stipulation void: it enforces it to the extent that it is not penal.[40] Even less does equity over-ride the parties' bargain where a secondary stipulation was not intended to punish as such, but rather to be security for the failure of the primary stipulation. There, relief is given on the basis of what the parties in substance objectively intended: the court does not find the substance of the parties' agreement and then over-ride it. Unnatural straining is needed to see this as over-riding the parties' true intentions, given that the parties' true intentions are the basis of relief.[41]

A more general evaluation

The four views of equity stated earlier are therefore problematic. At best they reveal little of the general nature of modern equity.

It is not suggested that there is no truth in any of the four views. Instances of each view being enacted by a twentieth- or twenty-first-century court or writer can be found with minimal effort. There are decisions in which courts of one common law system or another actually or arguably spoke of equity as widely discretionary, or applied it as such in order to reach particular results. Also found in the law reports are cases in which courts have applied equity effectively as an alibi – that is, effectively to say that a result ought to be so but without convincing reasoning – or obscurely.[42] It accords with conventional principles to

[39] The status of the equitable jurisdiction to relieve against penal stipulations is doubtful, but unclear, for England since *Cavendish Square Holding BV* v. *Makdessi* [2015] 3 W.L.R. 1373; [2015] UKSC 67.

[40] *Jobson* v. *Johnson* [1989] 1 W.L.R. 1042, 1045–6 (a good authority in Australia, though heavily damaged in England by *Cavendish Square Holding BV* v. *Makdessi* [2015] 3 W.L.R. 1373); *Andrews* v. *Australia and New Zealand Banking Group Ltd* (2012) 247 C.L.R. 205, [10]; [2012] HCA 30.

[41] Blackstone, *Commentaries on the Laws of England*, vol. 3, 434–5. See also Lord Evershed, 'Reflections on the Fusion of Law and Equity after 75 Years' (1954) 70 L.Q.R. 326, 329 (on the 'complementary function' of equity seen where the maxim applies that equity follows the law).

[42] See, for example, Heydon, Leeming and Turner, *Meagher, Gummow and Lehane's Equity: Doctrines and Remedies*, 5th ed. [24–085] discussing *Giller* v. *Procopets* (2008) 24 V.R. 1; [2008] VSCA 236.

recognise that various equitable doctrines are compulsory in not simply giving way to the parties' expressed intentions and hopes. However, those instances are either unorthodox[43] or, while orthodox, do not convey the features of a wide range of areas in modern equity. A theory cannot be erected only on the basis of exceptional facts about the theorised subject. An understanding of modern equity cannot be erected on the basis of heterodox 'equity' while ignoring orthodox equity. Hence the need to consider orthodox equity to supplement and correct views such as the four considered earlier, where they are found.

From critical endeavours attention now turns to constructive ones. In what ways does equity aid administration? The following chapters in this book all bear on that question. A preliminary sketch may be useful immediately.

Types of administration

Administration in ordinary language refers to the management of affairs.[44] The management of a business is administration: typically it is the management of the collective commercial interests of individuals through a partnership of some type, or through a corporate form. The management of government and public affairs are types of administration. The management of government is done by the executive branch: the rules and doctrines as to the lawfulness and legal propriety of the actions of the executive form administrative law. In the United States, the term 'administration' is more widely used in respect of governments and public affairs than in some other jurisdictions. A president's period in office is referred to as the president's administration. In a different sense of the word, a member of the president's staff may also be said to form part of the president's administration.

The essays in this book discuss most of these, and other, types of administration. A shared feature of all types of administration is that each concerns a practical process or a practical task. In relation to the types of administration to be examined, each concerns tasks in some way related to other persons. The particular task or process may involve practical steps affecting the rights of others, such as those with claims on a fund of assets. Or the administrative process or task may involve the application of governmental power for public purposes. Thus, a public

[43] P.V. Baker, 'The Future of Equity' (1977) 93 L.Q.R. 529, 537.

[44] *Crociani* v. *Crociani* [2014] W.T.L.R. 975, [17]; [2014] UKPC 40.

Act may establish a scheme which, while conferring no entitlements directly on individuals, is to be administered by the executive branch for the benefit of an indefinite number of persons. The very exercise of equitable jurisdiction is administrative in ways that the jurisdiction derived from old common law courts is not.[45] Other aspects of administration are the application and implementation of power, whether in the form of a decision, or an instrument – including parliamentary legislation – or a body of doctrine, such as equity. These involve practical steps similar to those involved in the types of administration mentioned so far.

Many acts and processes can accordingly be described as administration. While the meanings of some words are so wide that they lose meaning by encompassing all, administration is not such a word. It relates to a practical process or task such as management or another application of authority or power. And that authority or power derives from intentionally created arrangements. Private parties may establish an arrangement recognised by equity as an express trust. They may adopt another legal form, such as a partnership or company. Other schemes and relationships that give rise to administration, which equity then aids, are established by parliamentary legislation or schemes devised by the executive. All this is done deliberately and calls for administration which equitable doctrines and remedies aid, or which courts of equity, exercising equitable jurisdiction, themselves conduct.

For an enquiry into the nature of modern equity, it is revealing to study administration. That is because administration is practical. Where equity aids administration, equity assists practical action and processes. It does not obstruct them. Studying administration and equity's attitude towards it thus shows the facilitative nature of much of equity. Indeed, it shows that equity's assistance strongly tends to promote objectives that are desired, since the assistance of equity is directed to the management of deliberately established schemes, relationships, transactions and legal forms.

It is appropriate now to outline how this assistance by equity is provided.

The assistance of equity

Equity promotes administration by a range of means. These bridge a distinction mentioned earlier between, on the one hand, administration

[45] Langdell, *A Brief Survey of Equity Jurisdiction*, ch. 2, esp. 23–6; J. Dickinson, *Administrative Justice and the Supremacy of Law in the United States* (Cambridge, Mass.: Harvard University Press, 1927), 23–4.

by courts of equity in the exercise of administrative equitable jurisdiction, and, on the other hand, administration by individual legal actors that is in some way supported by equity. Seven examples will be mentioned to demonstrate the variety of legal techniques by which equity promotes administration, followed by a fuller consideration of examples under the next subheading.

The first technique to mention is administration by courts of equity. This grew from the historical adoption of inquisitorial methods by equity courts but not common law courts. How are these methods seen in the law of today? Modern courts of equitable jurisdiction have declared their supervisory jurisdiction over trusts in general, not narrow, terms. The modern supervisory jurisdiction of equity courts to administer trusts is not confined to the arguments of the party or parties before the court.[46] Common law litigation of common law rights, in contrast, remains adversarial and largely confined to the litigants' arguments. Courts of equity hold administrative jurisdiction not found in common law jurisdiction as traditionally understood.

Secondly, instead of an equity court undertaking the administrative task, courts of equity can order litigants to perform or carry on administration. This is founded in equity's *in personam* jurisdiction which empowered Chancellors and the Court of Chancery to order parties to perform specific acts, including administrative acts, or suffer imprisonment for contempt.[47] Orders in the exercise of equity's supervisory jurisdiction over trusts represent the most intense form of administration at the behest of equity courts. Nevertheless, this administrative jurisdiction is manifested more widely over, for example, deceased estates, insolvencies and windings up.[48] Equitable doctrines articulate what must and must not be done by a person with administrative responsibilities for the affairs of others; courts of equity can coerce such a person to act accordingly.

A third technique is a corollary of the first and second: by assuming supervisory jurisdiction to administer and to order administration, particularly by trustees and other fiduciaries, equity has created entitlements

[46] *Schmidt* v. *Rosewood Trust Ltd* [2003] 2 A.C. 709, [51]; [2003] UKPC 26.

[47] Langdell, *A Brief Survey of Equity Jurisdiction*, 23–6.

[48] See Finn, *Fiduciary Obligations*, ch. 2; J. Baker, 'Equity and Public Law in England', in *Collected Papers on English Legal History* (Cambridge University Press, 2013), vol. II, 949–50. On the Chancery's assumption of jurisdiction over deceased estates, at the expense of the ecclesiastical and common law courts, see Langdell, *A Brief Survey of Equity Jurisdiction*, 125–90.

allowing particular persons to seek to have a deliberately created scheme or plan administered by obtaining equitable relief.

These techniques betray certain basic characteristics of equitable jurisdiction. Further techniques are found in the structure and operation of equitable doctrines and remedies. To adapt a phrase, these are 'ways of doing things with equitable rules'[49] with the purpose or effect of furthering administrative tasks.

Thus – continuing the list – a fourth technique is to provide an enforceable foundation for administrative tasks in equitable doctrines, principles and rules where such a foundation is not supplied by statute or the common law. Taking the express trust once again, the enforceability in law of the terms of a trust depends not as such on the common law or on statute but on the principles, doctrines, procedures and remedies of courts of equity. In recognising and enforcing trusts, equity gives effect to deliberately established regimes for the management of assets. It makes administrative tasks possible where the common law and statute do not.

Administration can require series of formal steps to be taken. A fifth way in which equity aids administration is by treating a failure to take a series of formal steps utterly correctly as still having some effect, even though by other measures – the requirements of statute, the judge-made common law or a voluntary instrument – the steps would not have their full potential effect. As will be seen, equity's upholding of trustees' defective execution of trust powers can be taken in illustration; other instances are where an informal conveyance of property has effect in equity though it lacks its intended effect at law because a required formality has not been completed.[50]

Sixthly, equity facilitates practical action through so-called default rules and principles. In more traditional terms, these are rules and principles with a presumptive effect that can be avoided through expression of an appropriate intention. A default rule at odds with the practical aims of a deliberately created scheme of legal relations may be displaced by a stipulation that promotes the scheme's objects and thus its administration. For example, a private scheme to found a company or a trust can displace 'default' rules concerning resulting trusts. The presumptive application of fiduciary doctrines can frequently be displaced by a suitable expression of intention to do so. Examples are common.

[49] Cf. W. Twining and D. Miers, *How to Do Things with Rules*, 5th ed. (Cambridge University Press, 2010).

[50] See text to nn. 55–6 and text between nn. 72 and 76 below.

Seventhly, administration is helped where widely stated equitable doctrines are constrained by equity itself. Equity often operates through widely phrased principles.[51] Like widely stated rules of all kinds, widely stated equitable doctrines can disrupt and undermine other parts of the legal system and the interests served by the legal system's constituent parts. The judge-made common law tends to avoid that difficulty by operating through tightly stated rules. In contrast, equity avoids the same problem by operating through open-textured principles which, while widely stated, are only applied once a thorough evaluation of the facts has occurred, and where that evaluation shows that the animating concerns of the relevant principle arise in the particular case. Thus, widely stated notions of equitable fraud are constrained by the requirements of the particular doctrines, such as undue influence, by which equitable fraud is redressed. The existence of discretion to refuse equitable relief where a prima facie entitlement to relief is made out can also be used to constrain wide equitable doctrines, as where a prima facie entitlement to an injunction is defeated on discretionary grounds.

Are these techniques too subtle or obscure to furnish good evidence that equity has a facilitative nature? If aiding administration is a salient feature of modern equity, the argument might go, the supporting evidence should be plain. However, the objection puts store in mere appearances at the expense of the substance of things. All evidence of equity's real character is good evidence. Good evidence may be plain or only apparent once the superficial appearance of other facts is analysed. Even hidden evidence is good evidence once it is brought to light. Hence the force of the various techniques by which equity operates. The true character of modern equity depends on accurate description of its substance as found by analysis both of the techniques by which equity aids administration and the high frequency with which it does so.

Doctrinal illustrations

To illustrate equity's various techniques more fully, the express trust may be further considered – especially since many of equity's facilitative principles across the areas of private and public law considered in this volume have an ancestry in the doctrines concerning the administration of express trusts.

[51] *Australian Broadcasting Corp.* v. *Lenah Game Meats Pty Ltd* (2001) 208 C.L.R. 199, [350]; [2001] HCA 63; *Paciocco* v. *Australia and New Zealand Banking Group Ltd* (2015) 321 A.L.R. 584, [264]–[271]; [2015] FCAFC 50.

Administration is a familiar heading in the trust law treatises, where it is used in a narrower sense than that employed so far in this chapter. Strictly, trust administration involves the exercise of powers and performance of duties that apply at stages logically prior to the exercise of powers (and performance of duties) to distribute trust assets to those entitled to them under the terms of the trust. Although the administrative processes and tasks are facilitated by equity in fields far beyond the law on express trusts, the law on express trusts is of special significance: all of the ways in which equity aids (or indeed conducts) administration, as listed earlier, operate in the law of trusts. And from the law of trusts certain doctrines have been adopted to aid administration elsewhere, including in public law. Those extensions are discussed in several of the following chapters. It is appropriate at this stage, then, to indicate points at which the techniques just listed operate in the law of trusts before moving to other examples.

At the most basic level, equity makes trust administration possible simply by recognising and enforcing trusts. The significance of this facility of equity cannot be overemphasised, though the point itself requires no further elaboration for the present purpose. What of the other ways in which equity facilitates trust administration? One is to recognise and enforce equitable powers of administration. The means by which this amounts to facilitation by equity include all seven of the techniques listed earlier. For example, a 'default rule' of trust law is that a trustee must not use any of the trustee's common law powers, as the owner of an asset. That reflects a passive and static notion of the trust as a property-holding relationship. However, the default position can be overcome by conferring 'equitable powers'[52] on the trustee (the sixth technique). Although the trustee could at law exercise the trustee's legal rights and powers without any equitable powers, the presence of equitable powers allows the trustee's legal powers to be exercised in permitted ways without thereby committing a breach of trust. The terms of the trust will be the source of these equitable powers.[53] Applied to these powers is a body of rules specifically addressed to trust administration which the

[52] See R.C. Nolan, 'Property in a Fund' (2004) 120 L.Q.R. 108; J. McGhee (gen. ed.), *Snell's Equity*, 33rd ed. (London: Sweet and Maxwell, 2015), [10–003]–[10–006]. The concept of 'equitable' power found in some older authorities, and explained in G. Farwell, *Farwell on Powers*, 3rd ed., C.J.W. Farwell and F.K. Archer (eds.) (London: Stevens and Sons Ltd, 1916), 1–3 is narrower than that invoked here.

[53] Legislation can confer functionally identical powers on trustees: for example Trustee Act 2000 (UK).

court itself may undertake where required (the first technique) or order other persons to do (the second technique).

Under these rules, equity sees to it that if any equitable power is exercised at all, the exercise is proper. Improper exercise of equitable powers can attract negative relief. A purported exercise of power may be void or voidable; an improper disposition of trust assets may be reversed through equitable relief. But the negative quality of such relief is fully compatible with equity's doctrines on trust administration being facilitative. The relief merely holds the trustee to that which the creator of the trust actually intended, or is taken to have intended. The only intentions that are thwarted are those of the trustee who maladministers the trust – and that thwarting aids the administration of the trust. So much is clear, for example, from the treatment of discretionary trusts and mere powers. The court may order the trustee to consider re-exercising the trustee's discretion where the purported exercise failed or was improper (the second technique).[54] However, the court will 'not normally' compel a trustee to exercise a mere power. If the power is a trust power, the court in a proper case 'will go further by exercising the discretion itself. When it does, the court will do so in the manner best calculated to give effect to the settlor's or testator's intentions' (the first technique).[55]

The exercise of dispositive powers has a strong administrative quality, in the sense of administration used in this chapter, although dispositive powers are outside the strict definition of trust administration found in some cases and trust law treatises. Failure to exercise a dispositive power with perfect correctness can be overlooked in some circumstances in equity. An appointment in substantial accordance with the expressed purpose of a power will be good in equity, even where it does not strictly accord with the form of the power (the fifth technique).[56] Further, an actual attempt at execution that is defective may, though not itself good in equity, be made good by obtaining equitable relief. If there is a good consideration, and if compelling the person entitled in default of execution to make good the defect would execute the intentions of the donor of the power, equity will interfere (the fifth technique).[57] Generally, the exercise of a trustee's powers is always subject to fiduciary prohibitions on placing a trustee's interest in conflict with the trustee's duty and on the

[54] *Re Hay's Settlement Trusts* [1982] 1 W.L.R. 202, 209.

[55] *Re Baden's Deed Trusts* [1971] A.C. 424, 457.

[56] Farwell, *Farwell on Powers*, 3rd ed., 366–72. [57] *Ibid.*, 376–83, 385–99.

trustee's making of an unauthorised profit. These widely expressed principles have a correspondingly wide application to trustees. But their application is controlled by findings that particular acts that are prima facie within the wide prohibition have been authorised (the seventh technique). When relief is awarded for breach of a fiduciary prohibition it is tailored to the specific facts in order to meet, not to exceed, the purpose of the fiduciary prohibitions.

A deliberately created scheme involving practical tasks and processes could not be administered if its terms were thwarted. In this respect, an attitude of equity towards express trusts has general application. In equity's approach to express trusts, a general policy is seen of staying out of areas in which there exist plans, schemes, arrangements and other lawfully expressed intentions as to how future events shall unfold. The policy is seen, for example, in discretionary trusts where equity is generally unwilling to exercise a discretion that was vested in a trustee. As Maitland saw, this desire on the part of equity judges to leave well alone was applied by equity to other legal relations.[58] From the attitude and doctrines developed in the law of trusts, analogous equitable doctrines have been applied to those other legal relations in ways of which the courts today are increasingly aware.

In corporate, constitutional and administrative law, the analogies are evident. As Maitland described, equity's policy of not encroaching upon deliberately created schemes for governing how future events shall unfold was adopted as regards municipal corporations and joint stock companies.[59] He said there was a common source for these ideas, an 'atmosphere of trust' associated with the doctrines of equity.[60] The judges adapted equity to promote this policy of non-interference while also applying equitable doctrines and granting equitable relief where equitable relief was proper. It became possible (subject to standing requirements) to obtain equitable relief by way of injunction in various areas in which the defendant's conduct stood to hinder the due administration of a trust[61] or a trading company[62] or later,[63] a municipal corporation,[64] or

[58] F.W. Maitland, 'Trust and Corporation', in D. Runciman and M. Ryan (eds.), *F. W. Maitland: State, Trust and Corporation* (Cambridge University Press, 2003), ch. 5.

[59] *Ibid.*, 118–27. [60] *Ibid.*, 126–7.

[61] *Marshall* v. *Sladden* (1849) 7 Hare 428; 68 E.R. 177; (1851) 4 De G. & Sm. 468; 64 E.R. 916.

[62] *Nelson* v. *Anglo-American Land Mortgage and Agency Co. Ltd* [1897] 1 Ch. 130.

[63] Baker, 'Equity and Public Law in England', in *Collected Papers on English Legal History*, vol. II, 952–6.

[64] *A.-G.* v. *Tynemouth Corp.* [1899] A.C. 293.

some other statutory authority[65] or even of the executive powers of a government minister,[66] as well as the administration of insolvencies.[67] To differing degrees, other sorts of equitable relief for breach of trust – monetary remedies and tracing among them – were adapted to afford relief in other areas, so as to promote the management of affairs.[68] The record of equity's developments in aid of administrative processes extended further still.

Can equity cut down or extend the operation of an administrative scheme? Do equitable doctrines permit the words of a scheme for the management of affairs to be given lesser or greater effect than the meaning of the words of a scheme as found by the normal processes of construction? The general policy of equity, of not interfering with deliberately established administrative regimes, might suggest not. In fact these questions do not have simple answers. Equity has sometimes extended the operation of statutes with analogies from the statute. In the law of set-off, one type of equitable set-off is a set-off of an equitable against a legal claim, or of two equitable claims, which if they were both legal claims could be set off under the Statutes of Set-off or equivalent modern legislation.[69] In equity, the effects of limitation statutes have been extended to circumstances not strictly within the terms of the statutes. Equitable claims have been barred on the ground that an analogous common law claim is directly limited by the statute.[70] Such measures extend the implementation of parliamentary legislation beyond

[65] *Auckland (Lord)* v. *Westminster Local Board of Works* (1872) L.R. 7 Ch. App. 597, 603–4, discussed in W. Gummow, 'Equity in the Modern Administrative State', Chapter 16 of this volume, text following n. 41.

[66] *In re M* [1994] 1 A.C. 377.

[67] *Stichting Shell Pensioenfonds* v. *Krys* [2015] A.C. 616, [18]–[24]; [2014] UKPC 41. See also H.W. Kroeger, 'The Jurisdiction of Courts of Equity to Administer Insolvents' Estates, Considered in Relation to Historical Antecedents' (1924) 9 St Louis L. Rev. 87 (Pt 1), 94; (1924) 9 St Louis L. Rev. 179 (Pt 2), 198; W.J. Jones, 'The Foundations of English Bankruptcy: Statutes and Commissions in the Early Modern Period' (1979) 69 Trans. Amer. Phil. Soc. 5, 49.

[68] See *Wood* v. *Dummer*, 3 Mason 308, 30 F.Cas. 435 (1824) (Story J.); *Buchler* v. *Talbot* [2004] 2 A.C. 298, [28]; [2004] UKHL 9; H.G. Hanbury, 'Equity in Public Law', in H.G. Hanbury, *Essays in Equity* (Oxford: Clarendon Press, 1934), 80ff; J. Barratt, 'Public Trusts' (2006) 59 M.L.R. 514. Cf. *Bathurst City Council* v. *PWC Properties Pty Ltd* (1998) 195 C.L.R 566, [44]–[51]; [1998] HCA 59; J.L. Sax, 'The Public Trust Doctrine in Natural Resource Law: Effective Judicial Intervention' (1970) 68 Mich. L. Rev. 471; D.T. Rave, 'Politicians as Fiduciaries' (2013) 126 Harv. L. Rev. 672.

[69] R. Derham, *Derham on the Law of Set-off*, 4th ed. (Oxford University Press, 2010), [3.07]–[3.09].

[70] *Knox* v. *Gye* (1872) L.R. 5 H.L. 656, 674–5.

its intended scope. Yet the operation of other statutes, such as the Statute of Frauds, has been narrowed in equity. For example, the doctrine of part performance (now abolished in England[71]) can fairly be said to have cut down the operation of the Statute of Frauds. It is (or was, in England) a uniquely equitable doctrine. Similarly, the doctrine associated with *Rochefoucauld* v. *Boustead*[72] – to the effect that, other things apart, a trust of land cannot be denied simply because writing evidencing the trust was not made – weakens the relevant Statute of Frauds provision.[73]

Since the implementation of the will of the legislature as expressed in statute is a species of administration, such problems – controversies over extending and shortening the effect of parliament's schemes – are difficult to resolve. However, not all equitable measures with respect to the implementation of legislation are as problematic. That can be seen from a further apparent instance of the equitable subversion of statutes. This is the doctrine by which equity recognises certain acts as having effect according to equitable doctrine even though some further act must be done before the acts taken will have their intended effect at common law. Where a conveyance is to be made by deed before the parties thereto will hold certain common law rights and liabilities as against one another, failure to comply with the statutory requirement will leave the parties without the common law liabilities and rights they would enjoy had the required deed been executed. However, failure to make the required deed will not necessarily prevent equity from giving effect to the parties' dealings in equity. If the parties contract for a disposition which, if made, would confer on the promisee a power of sale, for example, then equity may consider the promisee to have that power even though the deed has not been made. The proviso is that the parties' contract must be specifically enforceable. Systems of registration have sometimes attracted a similar treatment in equity, by means of a related doctrine. Ownership of debentures may require the holder's name to be entered on the register. The same can be said, in general terms, of shares in many limited liability companies, as well as of land in many jurisdictions – and of the holding of units in a unit trust. In each case, registration typically has beneficial consequences for the person registered. Those consequences vary from one situation to another and depend on the precise terms of the statute, debenture deed and so on, that provides for registration. But often equity forgives non-registration in that it will confer certain rights on an unregistered person provided certain other conditions are met.

[71] Law of Property (Miscellaneous Provisions) Act 1989 (UK), s. 2(8).

[72] [1897] 1 Ch. 196.

[73] In England, see now Law of Property Act 1925 (UK), s. 53(1)(b).

In overlooking certain imperfections, each of these doctrines enacts the maxim that equity considers as done that which ought to be done.[74] On analysis, that maxim is not a case of equity being an alibi for discernible principle and clear reasons for equitable intervention. First, when equity operates, it only gives rise to equitable rights, liabilities and so on, not to legal ones. Even a promisee under a contract who thereby holds an equitable lease under the doctrine in *Walsh* v. *Lonsdale*[75] only has the 'equivalent of a lease' as against the promisor; as against third parties, the position is much different from that of one who holds a legal demise. Secondly, where construction of the statute or other instrument reveals an intention that until the outstanding formality is completed the disponee shall have no rights at all, at law or in equity, then equity will not contradict that intention.[76]

The long view

When pursuing enquiries into the nature of modern equity, complete answers cannot be found in recent court decisions and recent commentaries alone. For all who wish to understand the subject, a longer view is necessary. That is true of all laws to the extent that a lawyer, when confronted with an existing law, is thereby confronted also with the law's past and the past that preceded that law.[77] An existing law may continue or may modify the reason of an earlier iteration of the particular law. Whether there is continuity or change will indicate much about the nature of the modern form of the law in question. The prevailing circumstances immediately before the given law was first created will often say much about the reason for its creation. In a case in which the history of the common law action for money had and received was closely examined, it was said that '[t]he point is not to look back to "an assumed

[74] *Simultaneous Colour Printing Syndicate* v. *Foweraker* [1901] 1 Q.B. 771 (unregistered registrable debentures); *Musselwhite* v. *C.H. Musselwhite & Co. Ltd* [1962] Ch. 964 (unregistered registrable share transfer); *Chan* v. *Cresdon Pty Ltd* (1989) 168 C.L.R. 533 (unregistered registrable lease); *Jerome* v. *Kelly* [2004] 1 W.L.R. 1409; [2004] UKHL 25 (unregistered registrable transfer of an estate in fee simple).

[75] (1882) 21 Ch. D. 9.

[76] Contrast, on the one hand, *Hibbert* v. *Rolleston* (1792) 3 Bro. C.C. 571; 29 E.R. 705 and *Chasteauneuf* v. *Capeyron* (1871) 7 App. Cas. 127, 131, with, on the other hand, *Cuthbertson* v. *Swan* (1877) 11 S.A.L.R. 102, 111–12; *Mascall* v. *Mascall* (1985) 50 P. & C.R. 119, 124–6, 128; and *Corin* v. *Paton* (1990) 169 C.L.R. 540, 559–60, 570, 582, 590.

[77] Hedley, 'Rival Taxonomies within the Law of Obligations: Is There a Problem?', in Degeling and Edelman (eds.), *Equity in Commercial Law*, 84.

golden age" but rather "to help us to see more clearly the shape of the law of to-day by seeing how it took shape"'.[78] The same is true of historical enquiries pursued to explain the nature of modern equity. Nostalgia ought to be foreign to such historical enquiries. Antiquarianism is a different endeavour.[79]

While all this is as true of equity as of other sources of law in common law systems,[80] two further observations may be made of equity in particular. One relates to the remark of Sir Henry Maine:

> So great is the ascendancy of the Law of Actions in the infancy of Courts of Justice, that substantive law has at first the look of being gradually secreted in the interstices of procedure; and the early lawyer can only see the law through the envelope of its technical form.[81]

Maine's insightful remark describes the development of large portions of the substantive law as it developed in common law systems. The observation to be made here, however, is that Maine's insight is truer of the law developed in the old courts of common law than of the law developed in courts of equity. The common law writs tended to obscure the substantive reasons for particular rules and their development.[82] Once equity came to possess stable doctrines and rules, the form of pleading and the prayer for relief tended to reveal the substantive reasons for equitable intervention. Because of its different procedures, in equity the reasons for particular rules and their development were much more often revealed. Less of equity was generated interstitially in Maine's sense.[83]

[78] *Australian Financial Services and Leasing Pty Limited* v. *Hills Industries Ltd* (2014) 253 C.L.R. 560, [107]; [2014] HCA 14. See also J. Getzler, 'Patterns of Fusion', in Birks (ed.), *The Classification of Obligations*, 167; A. Mason, 'Fusion', in Degeling and Edelman (eds.), *Equity in Commercial Law*, 12–13. Cf. *Federal Commerce & Navigation Co. Ltd* v. *Molena Alpha Inc. (The Nanfri)* [1978] 1 Q.B. 927, 974; Burrows, 'We Do This at Common Law but That in Equity', 4.

[79] Mason, 'Fusion', in Degeling and Edelman (eds.), *Equity in Commercial Law*, 12.

[80] Cf. Birks, 'Equity in the Modern Law: An Exercise in Taxonomy', 1; K. Mason, 'Fusion: Fallacy, Fusion or Finished?', in Degeling and Edelman (eds.), *Equity in Commercial Law*, 60 (although a different view is expressed at 70).

[81] H.S. Maine, *Dissertation on Early Law and Custom* (London: Jordan Murray, 1901), 389.

[82] J.H. Baker, 'Lecture Two: Legal Fictions', in *The Law's Two Bodies* (Oxford University Press, 2001), 33ff. Cf. Birks and Pretto, 'Preface', in Birks and Pretto (eds.), *Breach of Trust*, xi.

[83] Given that the common law writs dispensed with the need to expose important reasons for a decision, it is ironic that equity should have been criticised as providing an alibi from reason. See text between nn. 8 and 15, and text between nn. 24 and 28 above.

That observation leads to a second. Since enquiries into the history of equitable principles are relatively free of the obstacles posed by the common law forms of action, the history of an equitable principle – its origins and adaptation over time – is often plainer to see.[84] In a famous passage, Sir George Jessel M.R. said:

> It must not be forgotten that the rules of Courts of Equity are not, like the rules of the Common Law, supposed to have been established from time immemorial. It is perfectly well known that they have been established from time to time – altered, improved, and refined from time to time. In many cases we know the names of the Chancellors who invented them. No doubt they were invented for the purpose of securing the better administration of justice, but still they were invented. Take such things as these: the separate use of a married woman, the restrain on alienation, the modern rule against perpetuities, and the rules of equitable waste.[85]

Equally important is that a long view shows certain equitable principles to have continued with relatively little change for centuries. At a time when all can seem utterly new, it can seem remarkable that the fundamental features of the modern equitable doctrines of relief against forfeiture and penalties, for example, were firmly in place by at least the late seventeenth century.[86] Where modern doctrines have ancient roots, it can accordingly be necessary for lawyers to return to these in order to relearn the past and thereby to understand the present. Occasional claims that there is 'no reason'[87] for an established rule of equity are normally inaccurate and deliberately ignores the rule's antecedents.

It is appropriate to elaborate these thoughts in order to support the suggestion made throughout in this chapter, that a prominent feature of modern equity is its facilitative nature.

The very term 'equity' has come to have several meanings through legal developments over time.[88] Although it is not clear whether equity

[84] W.M.C. Gummow, *Change and Continuity: Statute, Equity, and Federalism* (Oxford University Press, 1999), 41–2.

[85] *Re Hallett's Estate* (1879) 13 Ch. D. 696, 710. See also Macnair, 'Arbitrary Chancellors and the Problem of Predictability', in Koops and Zwalve (eds.), *Law and Equity: Approaches in Roman Law and Common Law*, 101–3 and P. Sales, 'Equity and Human Rights: A Commentary', Chapter 21 of this volume, n. 6.

[86] Heydon, Leeming and Turner, *Meagher, Gummow and Lehane's Equity: Doctrines and Remedies*, 5th ed. [18–005]–[18–020].

[87] See, for example, *Simpson* v. *Norfolk & Norwich University Hospital NHS Trust* [2012] Q.B. 640, [7]; [2011] EWCA Civ 1149; *National Westminster Bank plc* v. *Kapoor* [2012] 1 All E.R. 1201, [29]; [2011] EWCA Civ 1083.

[88] J.C. Campbell, 'When and Why a Bribe is Held on a Constructive Trust: The Method of Reasoning towards an Equitable Remedy' (2015) 39 Aust. Bar Rev. 320, 325–7.

was ever used to describe the Chancellor's jurisdiction in times when his powers were widely discretionary, and completely or largely unconstrained by principles and rules, the justice granted in that period of equity's history has come to be referred to as 'equity' in the sense of fairness and justice administered without confining principles or rules. Turning to the modern law, wide notions of equity form the basis upon which certain statutory provisions are administered. Thus, a ground for the winding up of a registered company is that a court considers it 'just and equitable' to order as much. A court responsible for deciding whether the just and equitable ground is made out is not confined to enquiring into particular categories of facts. Nor is the court required to exclude any particular category of evidence from account, provided that the evidence is relevant and satisfies the other requirements of admissibility. Lord Wilberforce said, '[i]t would be impossible, and wholly undesirable, to define the circumstances in which these circumstances' – equitable considerations of a personal character arising between one individual and another, which may make it unjust or inequitable to insist on legal rights – 'may arise'.[89] Thus, 'equity' in the wide sense is used to describe the Chancellor's methods of adjudication in the Chancery's earliest days – before it was known as equity at all – and is current in the law of today. But between equity's early times and today, circumstances have changed. The just and equitable ground for winding up depends on equity of a type that is atypical of the modern system of equity. By and large, equitable discretion now operates within closely drawn lines. A long view of equity shows that the early equity akin to fairness became extensively systematised, particularly through Lord Nottingham's insistence on the maxim that equity follows the law.[90] To point out that 'equity' is important to the application of the statutory just and equitable ground is not to suggest that modern equity as a whole is equity in that same sense – and therefore to be feared.[91]

Similarly, it is one thing to point out that injunctive relief has come to be applied to those who administer public authorities through an extension of equitable concepts. A claimant who seeks an injunction is no longer required to show that the injunction is needed to protect the

[89] *Ebrahimi* v. *Westbourne Galleries Ltd* [1973] A.C. 360, 379.

[90] See generally McGhee (gen. ed.), *Snell's Equity*, 33rd ed. [1–06]–[1–14]. On the extent to which Lord Nottingham adhered to fixed equitable rules, see D. Klinck, 'Lord Nottingham's "Certain Measures"' (2010) 28 Law and Hist. Rev. 711.

[91] Cf. R. Snowden, 'Equitable Doctrines in Business Associations: A Commentary', Chapter 9 of this volume.

claimant's proprietary interest, as was formerly required.[92] A long view shows that this does not expose administrators who are part of the executive branch of government to unwieldy, unprincipled equity and equitable relief. The claimant must show 'an equity'.[93] That which amounts to 'an equity' is a matter of established doctrine. It is quite another thing to draw on 'equity' in support of a new form of regulation of government in the twenty-first century, to supplement or over-ride administrative law as it developed especially in the twentieth century. Whether or not such a new form of government regulation would have merit – which is open to doubt – the proposals therefor clearly call on a normative order different from the one called 'equity' in common law systems today. Thus, the mere mention of equity in public law discourse is not a cause for fear. A recommendation that equity of a widely discretionary form should operate in public law would justifiably elicit concerns: the same concerns as would exist if it were recommended that widely discretionary equity should take over from statute or the judge-made common law. A longer view of the legal development within common law systems can give relief from unnecessary concerns by clarifying precisely what is meant by the various uses of the word 'equity'.

This collection

The continuation of equity as a source of principles, doctrines and remedies in common law systems is a sign that those systems enjoy relative stability. Unconstrained equity has the capacity to disrupt the standing legal order. For that reason, *unconstrained* equity – as distinct from the system of equity found in actual common law systems – poses a risk to the rule of law.[94] The fact that there continue to be stable common law systems of which equity is a vital part suggests that the jurisdiction of equity, as it developed first in England and then elsewhere, has not been a mainspring of obstruction and interference. Since equity could have been eradicated for the lesser offence of being obstructive or unsatisfactory, its health and vitality today suggest that there is no meaningful sense in which equity had or has those characteristics. On the contrary: equitable principles, doctrines and remedies are habitually relied on by, for example, transacting parties and litigants who wish to

[92] See *A.-G.* v. *Sheffield Gas Consumer Co.* (1853) 3 De G.M. & G. 304, 320; 43 E.R. 119, 125.
[93] See Gummow, 'Equity in the Modern Administrative State', text after n. 51.
[94] See L.B. Solum, 'Equity and the Rule of Law', in I. Shapiro (ed.), *The Rule of Law* (New York University Press, 1994), 124–9.

protect their own interests or the interests of others on whose behalf they litigate. The habitual reliance on equity is entirely due to equity's nature. Of all the things that might accurately be said regarding equity's nature, among the most important is that the continued relevance and vitality of equitable principles depends on equity's facilitative nature.

The following chapters address this quality of equity. The chapters are grouped schematically. A group of five full-length chapters on equity's involvement in aiding the administration of private affairs, and shorter accompanying chapters of commentary, is followed by groups of chapters and accompanying commentaries on equity's involvement in aiding the administration of public affairs: two full-length chapters and two commentaries considering the implementation of the 'will' of the legislative branch of government, three full-length chapters and three commentaries on the management of affairs of the executive branch and then two full-length chapters and two commentaries on the judicial branch. The reason for beginning with the administration of private affairs has been mentioned: important precepts of equity were first worked out in that area – especially in the law of trusts – only later to be adapted for use in contexts including the administration of public affairs. Thus the sequence of the chapters reflects that process of legal development. The full-length chapters, and particularly the comparisons and contrasts between those and their shorter commentaries, are richer than it is possible to express here, especially given the purpose of this chapter to explain the reasons for studying equity and administration. It may nevertheless be useful to indicate how each of the full-length chapters addresses the facilitative nature of equity. The chapters of commentary, which limits of space prevent from individual mention here, add further sophistication to the treatment.

The opening chapters on the management of private affairs start from the position that equity facilitates practical action. As seen earlier,[95] evidence of that is found in the simple fact that it is equity that recognises and enforces the powers of trustees. Otherwise, there would be no occasion to consider the extent to which the exercise by trustees of their powers ought to be constrained. Yet Mr Justice Newey shows that consideration of that question is indeed necessary. Equity's facilitation of trust administration has led to the development of peculiarly equitable doctrines to do with funds of assets. In Chapter 4, Professor Nolan persuasively argues that these equitable doctrines as to how a trust fund

[95] See text before n. 52 above.

ought to be administered are reflected in the type and extent of proprietary relief available upon a breach of trust. The facilitative nature of equity can also be seen from more detailed equitable rules that apply, for example, in insolvency and in the law on general law partnerships and registered corporations. Examples are analysed in Chapter 6 by Mr Ho[96] and a further chapter (Chapter 8) by the editor. The facilitative aspect of equity in this area is thrown into relief by the so-called rule in *Saunders* v. *Vautier*,[97] by which the beneficiaries and objects of an express trust can on occasion halt the administration of a trust by terminating it before its execution or administration is complete. Starting from the premise that trust law is to facilitate the lawfully expressed intention of the creator of a trust, Professor Langbein argues – perhaps as persuasively as can be done – that this doctrine, found in English law but largely rejected in the United States, ought to be abandoned by jurisdictions where it remains.

What of the bearing of those chapters grouped around the idea of the administration of public affairs? The implementation of the legislative 'will' by applying parliamentary legislation is a task of daily importance in most common law jurisdictions. Equity aids this process generally by applying the maxim that equity follows the law: the meaning and force of a statute in equity and at common law are not different. But that is only generally so. On occasion equity has actually or apparently contradicted statute. On occasion equity has also implemented a statute farther than its terms, as properly construed, go. Situations can even be found in which public administrators – rather than the courts – have applied 'equitable' notions when implementing the legislation of parliament. Hence the question of equity's proper role in the implementation of parliamentary enactments, to which the chapters by Mr Heydon and Professor Stebbings (Chapters 12 and 14) are addressed.

The chapters grouped around the administration by the executive branch of government address the assistance provided by equity in several ways. Owing to the shortcomings – in that sense, the inadequacy – of the prerogative writs in keeping public officers to their duties, equitable doctrines and remedies have been extended from the law on express trusts to the area now known as administrative or public law. The premise of the chapter by Professor Gummow (Chapter 16) is, once again, that equity here sets out to facilitate rather than hinder the

[96] See further Mr Justice Clyne, 'The Commonwealth Bankruptcy Act' (1948–50) 1 Res Jud. 65, 67–8.

[97] *Saunders* v. *Vautier* (1841) Cr. & Ph. 240; 41 E.R. 482.

management of the relevant affairs, this time affairs of a public character. The differences to which Professor Gummow points in how these developments have been accepted in Australia, Canada, the United Kingdom and the United States go to the proper boundaries of equity. The strength of the facilitative nature of equity is demonstrated by how far it is assumed. The starting point of the chapter by Professor Smith (Chapter 18) on equity and administrative behaviour in the United States is that widened notions of technical equity were incorporated into the US statutory administrative law regime. His argument that there is scope to augment the role of equitable techniques of the regulation of administrative power in the United States is an argument of degree for the improved use of equitable methods to aid administration by limiting how far an administrative power can be abused so as to thwart the proper management of public affairs.

In England, the Human Rights Act 1998 requires any 'public authority' to act in accordance with the rights stated therein.[98] That obligation affects much of what a public authority does to implement the will of the legislative branch and otherwise in the management of public affairs. Here, Lord Walker suggests, equity traditionally did little. But Lord Walker finds in modern human rights law in England some of the features of equity.[99] A reading of *R* v. *Waya*[100] is consistent with that thesis. In that case, the Supreme Court had to decide whether the Human Rights Act constrained the Crown Court to ignore the justice of the case when exercising its power to make an order confiscating the assets of a person under the Proceeds of Crimes Act 2002 (UK). The statutory provision[101] empowered the court to conduct a type of tracing exercise, although it was said that the provision was not 'intended to bring in the whole panoply of the rules as to tracing in equity'.[102] Where equitable doctrines of tracing are applied, then although the process has been said to involve hard-nosed property rights,[103] there exists discretion to do justice by granting relief on terms.[104] Since the Crown Court lacked discretion of that sort in *R* v. *Waya*, only the Human Rights Act stood

98 See also the Charter of Human Rights and Responsibilities 2006 (Vic.).

99 See also Lord Neuberger of Abbotsbury, 'Developing Equity – A View from the Court of Appeal' (unpublished, London: Chancery Bar Association Conference, 20 January 2012), 5 (available at www.judiciary.gov.uk/wp-content/uploads/JCO/Documents/Speeches/mr-speech-chancery-bar-assoc-lecture-jan12.pdf).

100 [2013] 1 A.C. 294; [2012] UKSC 51.

101 Proceeds of Crime Act 2002 (UK) s. 80(3).

102 *R* v. *Waya* [2013] 1 A.C. 294, [58].

103 *Foskett* v. *McKeown* [2001] 2 A.C. 102, 109.

104 *Stephenson Nominees Pty Ltd* v. *Official Receiver* (1987) 16 F.C.R. 536, 558.

to lessen the harshness of the order sought. Lord Walker's chapter (Chapter 20) is a reminder that traditionally equity has been, as Lehane J. observed,[105] primarily concerned with financial interests and interests in respect of property. To the extent that the Human Rights Act requires the application of techniques and principles analogous to those of traditional equity, it is notable that a statute was necessary to make that so.

Finally, attention is turned to aspects of equity and the judicial branch of government. In contrast with the jurisdiction developed in the courts of common law, it has been seen that the jurisdiction of equity is administrative.[106] How that jurisdiction ought to be administered has itself been a controversial question. Dr McMahon revisits the debates of Victorian England and New York State on whether equity ought to be administered by separate courts of equity or by courts invested with the jurisdiction of equity and the common law. She suggests that the administrative 'fusion' associated in England with the statutory reforms of the 1870s is better understood as having occurred through piecemeal reforms of the procedure of the Chancery and the common law courts in the 1850s: reforms inspired, McMahon goes on to suggest, by earlier procedural reforms in New York State which sought to combine the best of common law and equitable procedure together, and to discard undesirable legal and equitable procedures.[107] Both common law and equitable methods are therefore prominent in modern procedural rules for the administration of justice. The operation of those rules can be troubled by an excess of development in their legal or their equitable ingredients. In the last full chapter (Chapter 24), Professor Zuckerman argues that the administration of justice through legal advice privilege need not be supplemented by equitable doctrine. Equitable procedures may have shaped modern civil procedure law,[108] but legal advice privilege can deliver justice, Zuckerman argues, without the intervention of equity.

Conclusion

What would follow if the view of equity commended in this chapter – that much of equity has a facilitative nature – should come to be generally appreciated? There would continue to be room for other perspectives on

[105] *Paramasivam* v. *Flynn* (1998) 90 F.C.R. 489, 505. [106] Text to n. 44ff above.

[107] See Lord Neuberger of Abbotsbury, 'Developing Equity – A View from the Court of Appeal', 9.

[108] See the argument of N.H. Andrews, 'The Influence of Equity upon the Doctrine of Legal Professional Privilege' (1989) 105 L.Q.R. 608.

equity. Indeed, other perspective would be important. The probability that one perspective on a complex subject could afford a view of all that needs to be seen is low. In the case of the complex subject of equity, allowance needs to be made for accounts that frankly describe other aspects of the nature of modern equity – especially modern equity as applied by the courts using established judicial methods. Equity does not merely facilitate the implementation of intentions and the management of states of affairs: a fair view of the subject requires attention to be given to the other operations of equity.

If the facilitative nature of modern equity should come to be generally appreciated, it would also remain possible and necessary to examine equity on different levels. Some of equity's principles – including the notion of 'conscience' – operate with relative generality, across several fields. Those principles must be examined on that general level. They may also need to be examined on a more detailed level, in order to show how a general concept comes to be applied to resolve individual concrete disputes between litigating parties. Rules and doctrines that are in their nature detailed would still require to be examined at the level on which they reside if the facilitative nature of equity came to be better understood.

In that way, the materials on equity and administration in this volume are offered not as a final or exhaustive statement of how modern equity might be understood but as a much needed means of bettering the understanding of modern equity and its place in common law systems today.

2

Constraints on the exercise of trustees' powers

GUY NEWEY

Introduction

Discretion plays a central part in trusts. The trustees of a trust will almost invariably have administrative powers, permitting them to choose, for example, how trust assets are invested. They will very often have dispositive powers as well, enabling them to make decisions as to who should benefit from the trust.

The courts are not, of course, equipped to second-guess every exercise by a trustee of a power. Nor could it possibly be right for them to do so. The powers have been conferred on the trustees, not the court.

On the other hand, there need to be some safeguards against incompetence, indolence and abuse. Were trustees' decisions entirely unregulated, settlors' wishes could be frustrated and beneficiaries left without proper protection.

The cases contain some general summaries of relevant legal principles. In *Dundee General Hospitals Board of Management* v. *Walker*,[1] for example, Lord Reid said:

> If it can be shown that the trustees considered the wrong question, or that, although they purported to consider the right question they did not really apply their minds to it or perversely shut their eyes to the facts or that they did not act honestly or in good faith, then there was no true decision and the court will intervene.[2]

In *Scott* v. *National Trust for Places of Historic Interest or Natural Beauty*,[3] Robert Walker J. said:

> Trustees must act in good faith, responsibly and reasonably. They must inform themselves, before making a decision, of matters which are relevant to the decision. These matters may not be limited to simple matters of fact but will, on occasion (indeed, quite often) include taking advice from

[1] [1952] 1 All E.R. 896. [2] *Ibid.*, 905. [3] [1998] 2 All E.R. 705.

> appropriate experts . . . It is however for advisers to advise and for trustees to decide: trustees may not (except in so far as they are authorised to do so) delegate the exercise of their discretions, even to experts.[4]

Robert Walker J. (as Lord Walker of Gestingthorpe) recently had to revisit, in *Pitt* v. *Holt*,[5] the circumstances in which the courts will intervene in relation to the exercise of trustees' powers. *Pitt* v. *Holt* was concerned with what had been termed (erroneously, as it transpired[6]) the rule in *Hastings-Bass*,[7] which was understood to allow the exercise of a power by trustees to be impugned on the basis that the trustees had not taken account of the correct considerations when making their decision.

This chapter seeks to review, with the benefit of the Supreme Court's decision in *Pitt* v. *Holt*, some of the principles that operate to constrain the exercise of trustees' powers. As will be seen, the principles are in part concerned with *objective* factors and in part with the trustees' *subjective* intentions. A distinction can also be drawn between, on the one hand, matters relating to the *scope* of the relevant powers and, on the other, those bearing on *how* powers are exercised. Sometimes the focus is not on how a decision was in *fact* made, but on whether there was a *risk* that it would not be taken in a disinterested way. The remedies sought may include the *invalidation* of a decision or *financial redress*.

One problem with the law in this area is that the courts have not always been consistent in their use of language. The expressions 'good faith' and 'bad faith' illustrate the point. Millett L.J. saw the requirement to act in 'good faith' as an aspect of a fiduciary's 'obligation of loyalty'.[8] The expression 'good faith' has also, however, been used to refer to the need to give genuine consideration to the exercise of a power.[9] In *Gailey* v. *Gordon*,[10] O'Regan J. gave 'bad faith', the counterpart of 'good faith', a much wider meaning: he took it to extend to 'a decision for an ulterior motive, taking into account relevant considerations and acting capriciously'.[11]

Trust law is obviously not the only context in which the courts have to grapple with the limits to discretion and the grounds on which the

[4] *Ibid.*, 717. See also *Pitt* v. *Holt* [2013] 2 A.C. 108, [10]; [2013] UKSC 26 (Lord Walker).

[5] *Pitt* v. *Holt* [2013] 2 A.C. 108, [10].

[6] Since the 'rule in *Hastings-Bass*' was found not to be derived from the case of that name: see *Pitt* v. *Holt* [2013] 2 A.C. 108, [32].

[7] After *Re Hastings-Bass* [1975] Ch. 25.

[8] See the text to n. 137, below.

[9] As to which, see the text to nn. 15–17 below.

[10] [2003] 2 N.Z.L.R. 192.

[11] *Ibid.*, [89].

exercise of a power can be impugned. Administrative lawyers habitually have to address such issues. They can also arise in relation, for instance, to contractual powers, to fiduciaries other than trustees and to when decisions of courts and tribunals can be appealed.[12] Questions arise as to how far it is helpful to compare the approaches that the courts adopt in different contexts.[13]

I should perhaps identify some of the things which this chapter does not attempt to address. It does not consider *when* trustees must exercise their powers or consider doing so. Nor do I try to deal with specific rules that apply to particular powers. The chapter focuses on principles of general application.

Genuine consideration

A first point is that a trustee must give genuine consideration to the exercise of a power. Trustees are to exercise their discretions 'with a fair consideration of the subject'.[14] A discretion must be exercised 'upon real and genuine consideration'.[15]

Where trustees executed deeds of appointment without realising that they had any discretion to exercise or understanding the effect of the documents they were signing, the deeds were set aside. Mervyn Davies J. said that if appointors 'fail altogether to exercise the duties of consideration', 'there is no exercise of the power and the purported appointment is a nullity'.[16] Lord Walker has referred to the case in question as one of 'equitable *non est factum*'.[17]

[12] As to which, see, for example, *Roache* v. *News Group Newspapers Ltd* [1998] E.M.L.R. 161, 172 where Stuart-Smith L.J. said as regards review of a judge's exercise of discretion:

> The court must not be tempted to interfere with the judge's order merely because we would have exercised the discretion differently from the way in which the judge did. Before the court can interfere it must be shown that the judge has either erred in principle in his approach, or has left out of account, or taken into account, some feature that he should, or should not, have considered, or that his decision is wholly wrong because the court is forced to the conclusion that he has not balanced the various factors fairly in the scale.

[13] See W. Gummow, 'Equity in the Modern Administrative State', Chapter 16 of this volume.

[14] *Re Beloved Wilkes' Charity* (1851) 3 Mac. & G. 440, 448; 42 E.R. 330, 333.

[15] *Karger* v. *Paul* [1984] V.R. 161, 164 (McGarvie J.).

[16] *Turner* v. *Turner* [1984] Ch. 100, 111.

[17] *Pitt* v. *Holt* [2013] 2 A.C. 108, [43].

Construction and the general law

Trustees are of course constrained by the terms in which their powers have been conferred and by the general law.

As to the former, the scope of a power is a function of the provision conferring it. If, say, a clause empowers trustees to appoint in favour of the children or remoter issue of X, the trustees plainly will not be entitled to appoint in favour of a person not within that class. Were they to try to do so, the purported exercise of the power would be void. They would have acted outside their powers (or 'ultra vires').

The position is similar where trustees purport to do something that the general law prohibits. Suppose, for example, that trustees seek to create interests in such a way that the rule against perpetuities is infringed. There may be a question as to whether the exercise of the power is wholly nugatory or can be saved in part, as regards elements that would not of themselves offend perpetuity principles.[18] There is no doubt, however, that it will be void in so far as the interests for which it provides are precluded by the rule against perpetuities.

Improper purposes

> It is trite law that a power can be exercised only for the purpose for which it is conferred, and not for any extraneous or ulterior purpose.[19]

This principle is manifested in the trust context in the 'fraud on a power' doctrine.[20] As has often been pointed out, the name of the doctrine is misleading. It has 'little, if anything, to do with fraud', at least in the common law's sense.[21] While the cases to which it applies can involve true fraud, they do not necessarily do so. There need not have been 'any conduct on the part of the appointor amounting to fraud in the common law meaning of the term or any conduct which could be properly termed dishonest or immoral'.[22] The doctrine applies where a power 'has been exercised for a purpose, or with an intention, beyond the scope of or not justified by the instrument creating the power'.[23]

18 See, for example, *Pitt* v. *Holt* [2013] 2 A.C. 108, [13]–[15].

19 *In re Courage Group's Pension Schemes* [1987] 1 W.L.R. 495, 505 (Millett J.).

20 Very similar principles apply in company law; see, for example, *Howard Smith Ltd* v. *Ampol Petroleum Ltd* [1974] A.C. 821 and, now, section 171(b) of the Companies Act 2006 (UK) (a company director must 'only exercise powers for the purposes for which they are conferred').

21 *Medforth* v. *Blake* [2000] Ch. 86, 103 (Scott V.-C.).

22 *Vatcher* v. *Paull* [1915] A.C. 372, 378 (Lord Parker of Waddington).

23 *Ibid.*

As that quotation suggests, identification of 'the purpose for which [a power] was conferred' depends to an extent on the wording of the particular instrument. It is also influenced by the general principle that a trust exists for the benefit of its beneficiaries.[24]

The expression 'fraud on a power' has traditionally been applied in relation to powers of appointment.[25] The same principles operate, however, in relation to other powers.

Wellesley v. *Earl of Mornington*[26] provides an old-fashioned example of fraud on a power. In that case, a father made an appointment in favour of his son, 'then in a state of mental and bodily disease', with a view to inheriting it as the son's next of kin on the son's death. Page Wood V.-C. held that the father had made the appointment 'not for the benefit of his son but for his own benefit' and that there had been a fraud on the power.

Hillsdown Holdings plc v. *Pensions Ombudsman*[27] illustrates the principles in a more modern context. There, trustees of a pension scheme, under which there was no power to return any surplus to the employer, exercised a power to transfer funds to another scheme with a view to such a return being effected. Knox J. held the transfer to be a fraud on the power.

Fraud on a power has conventionally been considered to render an exercise of the power void. As already mentioned, if an instrument gives trustees power to appoint in favour of one person, then a purported exercise in favour of someone else will be void: the appointment will be outside the scope of the power and nugatory. Fraud on a power has long been taken to have the same result in equity. Authority for that can be found in *Cloutte* v. *Storey*.[28] The position may be logically justified on the basis that the purported exercise of the power is beyond its true scope. Viewing matters in this way, there is no real difference between (say) (a) appointing in favour of X when the power is to appoint in favour of Y and (b) making an appointment nominally in favour of Y but with the intention of benefiting X rather than Y.

[24] Compare the definition of a trust provided by Maitland (see F.W. Maitland, *Equity: A Course of Lectures*, 2nd ed., by A.H. Chaytor and W.J. Whittaker, rev. by J. Brunyate (Cambridge University Press, 1936), 44):

> I should define a trust in some such way as the following – When a person has rights which he is bound to exercise upon behalf of another or for the accomplishment of some particular purpose he is said to have those rights in trust for that other or for that purpose and he is called a trustee.

[25] *Walker* v. *Stones* [2001] Q.B. 902, 932. [26] (1855) 2 K. & J. 143; 69 E.R. 728.

[27] [1997] 1 All E.R. 862. [28] [1911] 1 Ch. 18.

In recent times, however, various judges have expressed doubts about *Cloutte* v. *Storey*. In *Abacus Trust Co (Isle of Man)* v. *Barr*,[29] Lightman J. described the judgment of Farwell L.J. in *Cloutte* v. *Storey* as 'problematic'. In *Pitt* v. *Holt*, Lloyd L.J. said that he shared Lightman J.'s reservations about Farwell L.J.'s judgment and observed that '[i]n principle, cases where an act done by trustees which appears to be within their powers can be held to be void ought . . . to be kept to a minimum'.[30] In the Supreme Court, Lord Walker said in the same case that *Cloutte* v. *Storey* 'may have to be revisited one day'.[31]

Caprice, reasonableness and rationality

It is well established that the exercise of a power for capricious reasons can be impugned. In *Pilkington* v. *Inland Revenue Commissioners*,[32] Viscount Radcliffe referred to the courts' ability to restrain or correct a purported exercise of a power that could be shown to be 'merely wanton or capricious and not to be attributable to a genuine discretion'.[33] In *Re Manisty's Settlement*,[34] Templeman J. spoke of the court being willing to intervene where trustees have acted 'capriciously': for reasons that could be said to be 'irrational, perverse or irrelevant to any sensible expectation of the settlor'.[35]

The courts have used rather comparable language when considering the exercise of discretions conferred by contracts. In *Paragon Finance plc* v. *Nash*,[36] for instance, the Court of Appeal concluded that a mortgagee's power to set interest rates was not completely unfettered: it could not be exercised dishonestly, for an improper purpose, capriciously, arbitrarily or 'in a way that no reasonable lender, acting reasonably, would do'.[37] Similarly, in *Socimer International Bank Ltd* v. *Standard Bank Ltd*,[38] Rix L.J., borrowing the language of 'decision-maker' from public law to refer generally to contract parties who have a contractual discretion to exercise, said:

> [such] a decision-maker's discretion will be limited, as a matter of necessary implication, by concepts of honesty, good faith, and genuineness, and the need for the absence of arbitrariness, capriciousness, perversity and irrationality.[39]

29 [2003] Ch. 409, [31]; [2003] EWHC 114 (Ch).
30 [2012] Ch. 132, [98], [101]; [2011] EWCA Civ 197.
31 *Pitt* v. *Holt* [2013] 2 A.C. 108, [62].
32 [1964] A.C. 612.
33 *Ibid.*, 641.
34 [1974] Ch. 17.
35 *Ibid.*, 26.
36 [2002] 1 W.L.R. 685; [2001] EWCA Civ 1466.
37 [2002] 1 W.L.R. 685, [41].
38 [2008] Bus. L.R. 1304; [2008] EWCA Civ 116.
39 [2008] Bus. L.R. 1304, [66].

Having referred to *Socimer* and other authorities,[40] Jackson L.J. said in *Mid Essex Hospital Services NHS Trust* v. *Compass Group UK and Ireland Ltd*:[41]

> An important feature of the above line of authorities is that in each case the discretion did not involve a simple decision whether or not to exercise an absolute contractual right. The discretion involved making an assessment or choosing from a range of options, taking into account the interests of both parties. In any contract under which one party is permitted to exercise such a discretion, there is an implied term. The precise formulation of that term has been variously expressed in the authorities. In essence, however, it is that the relevant party will not exercise its discretion in an arbitrary, capricious or irrational manner.[42]

The courts have stressed that, in this context, the concern is whether the decision was one that the decision-maker could reasonably have made rather than what would reasonably have been decided. In *Clark* v. *Nomura International plc*,[43] Burton J. said:

> I do not consider it is right that there be simply a contractual obligation on an employer to act reasonably in the exercise of his discretion, which would suggest that the court can simply substitute its own view for that of the employer. My conclusion is that the right test is one of irrationality or perversity (of which caprice or capriciousness would be a good example) *i.e.* that no reasonable employer would have exercised his discretion in this way.[44]

In *Socimer*, Rix L.J. said:

> Reasonableness and unreasonableness are also concepts deployed in this context, but only in a sense analogous to *Wednesbury* unreasonableness, not in the sense in which that expression is used when speaking of the duty to take reasonable care, or when otherwise deploying entirely objective criteria: as for instance when there might be an implication of a term requiring the fixing of a reasonable price, or a reasonable time. In the latter class of case, the concept of reasonableness is intended to be entirely mutual and thus guided by objective criteria.[45]

[40] Namely, *Abu Dhabi National Tanker Co.* v. *Product Star Shipping Ltd (The 'Product Star') (No. 2)* [1993] 1 Lloyd's Rep. 397; *Horkulak* v. *Cantor Fitzgerald International* [2005] I.C.R. 402; [2004] EWCA Civ 128; and *JML Direct Ltd* v. *Freestat UK Ltd* [2010] EWCA Civ 34.

[41] [2013] B.L.R. 265, [83]; [2013] EWCA Civ 200.

[42] [2013] B.L.R. 265, [83].

[43] [2000] I.R.L.R. 766.

[44] *Ibid.*, [40].

[45] *Socimer International Bank Ltd* v. *Standard Bank London Ltd* [2008] Bus. L.R. 1304, [66]. See also the *Paragon* case, in which Dyson L.J. said (at [41]):

'*Wednesbury* unreasonableness' derives, of course, from the Court of Appeal's decision in *Associated Provincial Picture Houses Ltd* v. *Wednesbury Corp.*[46] There Lord Greene M.R. said:

> It is true the discretion must be exercised reasonably. Now what does that mean? Lawyers familiar with the phraseology commonly used in relation to exercise of statutory discretions often use the word 'unreasonable' in a rather comprehensive sense. It has frequently been used and is frequently used as a general description of the things that must not be done. For instance, a person entrusted with a discretion must, so to speak, direct himself properly in law. He must call his own attention to the matters which he is bound to consider. He must exclude from his consideration matters which are irrelevant to what he has to consider. If he does not obey those rules, he may truly be said, and often is said, to be acting 'unreasonably'. Similarly, there may be something so absurd that no sensible person could ever dream that it lay within the powers of the authority. Warrington L.J. in *Short* v. *Poole Corporation*[47] gave the example of the red-haired teacher, dismissed because she had red hair. That is unreasonable in one sense. In another sense it is taking into consideration extraneous matters. It is so unreasonable that it might almost be described as being done in bad faith; and, in fact, all these things run into one another.[48]

> It is one thing to imply a term that a lender will not exercise his discretion in a way that no reasonable lender, acting reasonably, would do. It is unlikely that a lender who was acting in that way would not also be acting either dishonestly, for an improper purpose, capriciously or arbitrarily. It is quite another matter to imply a term that the lender would not impose unreasonable rates. It could be said that as soon as the difference between the claimant's standard rates and the Halifax rates started to exceed about two percentage points the claimant was charging unreasonable rates. From the defendant's point of view, that was undoubtedly true. But, from the claimant's point of view, it charged these rates because it was commercially necessary, and therefore reasonable, for it to do so.

46 [1948] 1 K.B. 223. 47 [1926] Ch. 66, 90, 91.

48 *Associated Provincial Picture Houses Ltd* v. *Wednesbury Corp.* [1948] 1 K.B. 223, 229. Speaking in *Equitable Life Assurance Society* v. *Hyman* [2002] 1 A.C. 408, [20], while Lord Wilberforce was still alive, Lord Woolf M.R. remarked on the Chancery background of Lord Greene, observing that the 'similarity between the role of the courts on judicial review and in relation to a fiduciary duty should cause no surprise when it is remembered that Lord Greene MR . . . was a distinguished Chancery lawyer, as is Lord Wilberforce, one of the patriarchs of English administrative law'. Professor Matthew Conaglen has pointed out that the relevant principles have much older origins. He suggests that some connection might possibly be found 'in the fact that fiduciary conflict doctrine began to solidify into its modern form around the time of Lord Eldon's period as Lord Chancellor, which was also the period in which the courts began to give effect to the notion of a public trust, also under Lord Eldon's leadership': M. Conaglen, 'Public-

In *Council of Civil Service Unions* v. *Minister for the Civil Service*,[49] Lord Diplock termed '*Wednesbury* unreasonableness' 'irrationality'.[50] It applies, he said, to 'a decision which is so outrageous in its defiance of logic or of accepted moral standards that no sensible person who had applied his mind to the question to be decided could have arrived at it'.[51]

The Supreme Court has recently confirmed that rationality is not to be equated with (mere) reasonableness. The question arose in *Hayes* v. *Willoughby*,[52] which concerned the construction of the Protection from Harassment Act 1997. That Act makes it both a criminal offence and a civil wrong for a person to pursue a course of conduct which amounts to harassment. The Act does not, however, apply to a course of conduct if the person shows that it was pursued 'for the purpose of preventing or detecting crime'. The Supreme Court held, by a majority of four to one, that the word 'purpose' connotes a subjective state of mind, but that an alleged harasser who acts irrationally will not be regarded as having the relevant purpose. Lord Sumption, with whom Lord Neuberger and Lord Wilson agreed, said:

> Before an alleged harasser can be said to have had the purpose of preventing or detecting crime, he must have sufficiently applied his mind to the matter. He must have thought rationally about the material suggesting the possibility of criminality and formed the view that the conduct said to constitute harassment was appropriate for the purpose of preventing or detecting it. If he has done these things, then he has the relevant purpose. The court will not test his conclusions by reference to the view which a hypothetical reasonable man in his position would have formed. If, on the other hand, he has not engaged in these minimum mental processes necessary to acquire the relevant state of mind, but proceeds anyway on the footing that he is acting to prevent or detect crime, then he acts irrationally.[53]

Private Intersection: Comparing Fiduciary Conflict Doctrine and Bias' [2008] P.L. 58, 65. See also Gummow, 'Equity in the Modern Administrative State', text after n. 41.

49 [1985] A.C. 374 (the *GCHQ* case).

50 *Council of Civil Service Unions* v. *Minister for the Civil Service* [1985] A.C. 374, 410–11.

51 *Ibid.*, 410. Lord Diplock grouped the grounds on which administrative action is subject to control by judicial review under irrationality, so defined, and two further heads: 'illegality' and 'procedural impropriety'. By 'illegality' he referred (at 410) to the principle that 'the decision-maker must understand correctly the law that regulates his decision-making power and must give effect to it'. 'Procedural impropriety' was used (at 411) to encompass failure to observe the rules of natural justice but also 'failure by an administrative tribunal to observe procedural rules that are expressly laid down in the legislative instrument by which its jurisdiction is conferred'.

52 [2013] 1 W.L.R. 935; [2013] UKSC 17.

53 [2013] 1 W.L.R. 935, [15].

One consequence is that

> the law will not regard [the alleged harasser] as having had the relevant purpose at all. He has simply not taken the necessary steps to form one.[54]

Lord Sumption considered the relationship between rationality and reasonableness. He said there:

> Rationality is a familiar concept in public law. It has also in recent years played an increasingly significant role in the law relating to contractual discretions, where the law's object is also to limit the decision-maker to some relevant contractual purpose ... Rationality is not the same as reasonableness. Reasonableness is an external, objective standard applied to the outcome of a person's thoughts or intentions. The question is whether a notional hypothetically reasonable person in his position would have engaged in the relevant conduct for the purpose of preventing or detecting crime. A test of rationality, by comparison, applies a minimum objective standard to the relevant person's mental processes. It imports a requirement of good faith, a requirement that there should be some logical connection between the evidence and the ostensible reasons for the decision, and (which will usually amount to the same thing) an absence of arbitrariness, of capriciousness or of reasoning so outrageous in its defiance of logic as to be perverse. For the avoidance of doubt, I should make it clear that, since we are concerned with the alleged harasser's state of mind, I am not talking about the broader categories of *Wednesbury* unreasonableness ..., a legal construct referring to a decision lying beyond the furthest reaches of objective reasonableness.[55]

Lord Reed, dissenting, said that he would be slow to infer that criminal liability was intended to turn on 'the subtle distinction between what is unreasonable and what is irrational'. He observed:

> I have to confess that I am not sure that I understand the distinction drawn at para 14 between on the one hand 'rationality [as] a familiar concept in public law', which 'is not the same as reasonableness', and on the other hand 'the broader categories of *Wednesbury* unreasonableness'; or the statement that there should be 'an absence of arbitrariness, of capriciousness or of reasoning so outrageous in its defiance of logic as to be perverse', but that the court is not referring to 'a decision lying beyond the furthest reaches of objective reasonableness ...'[56]

I find it easy to sympathise.

A few months before *Hayes* v. *Willoughby* was decided, the Court of Appeal had touched on the relationship between '*Wednesbury* unreasonableness' and perversity in *Bramston* v. *Haut*.[57] At first instance, the judge

[54] *Ibid.*, [15]. [55] *Ibid.*, [14]. [56] *Ibid.*, [28].
[57] [2013] 1 W.L.R. 1720; [2012] EWCA Civ 1637.

had taken the view that a trustee in bankruptcy's refusal to make or sanction an application by the bankrupt to suspend his discharge from bankruptcy had been '*Wednesbury* unreasonable'. The Court of Appeal said that the judge had fallen into error by adopting the *Wednesbury* unreasonableness test when he 'ought to have asked himself whether the trustee had acted perversely'.[58] The court clearly did not consider that a person who had acted unreasonably in a *Wednesbury* sense would necessarily have acted perversely. It also noted that in *In re Edennote Ltd*[59] the Court of Appeal had questioned whether it was helpful to introduce a *Wednesbury* test in relation to decisions made by liquidators. Nourse L.J., with whom Millett L.J. agreed, observed in *Edennote* that 'it is unnecessary, rather it may be confusing, to introduce into the court's control of the acts and decisions of liquidators the language of its control of administrative action'.[60]

The courts have taken somewhat differing views as to how far it is helpful to refer to public law in relation to the exercise of contractual discretion and trustees' powers. In *Abu Dhabi National Tanker Co.* v. *Product Star Shipping Ltd (The 'Product Star') (No. 2)*,[61] Leggatt L.J. said that 'the exercise of judicial control of administrative action is an analogy which must be applied with caution to the assessment of whether a contractual discretion has been properly exercised'.[62] That did not prevent Dyson L.J. from concluding in *Paragon Finance plc v. Nash* that in the *Product Star* case the word 'unreasonably' had been used 'in a sense analogous to unreasonably in the *Wednesbury* sense'.[63] As mentioned above, Burton J. drew an analogy with public law in *Clark* v. *Nomura International plc*, as did Rix L.J. in the *Socimer* case. In contrast, in *Lymington Marina Ltd* v. *Macnamara*[64] the Court of Appeal was critical of a first instance judge for having used public law principles when considering whether a party had been entitled to refuse consent under a contract. Pill L.J. said:

> While I accept that unreasonableness, in the sense used by Leggatt and Mance L.JJ.[65] is analogous to the use of the word in the *Wednesbury* case, it appears to me unnecessary, and undesirable, to introduce expressions

[58] See *Bramston* v. *Haut* [2013] 1 W.L.R. 1720, [71]. [59] [1996] 2 B.C.L.C. 389.
[60] *Ibid.*, 394. [61] [1993] 1 Lloyd's Rep. 397.
[62] *Abu Dhabi National Tanker Co.* v. *Product Star Shipping Ltd (The 'Product Star') (No. 2)* [1993] 1 Lloyd's Rep. 397, 404.
[63] *Paragon Finance plc* v. *Nash* [2002] 1 W.L.R. 685, [38]; [2001] EWCA Civ 1466.
[64] [2007] 2 All E.R. (Comm.) 825; [2007] EWCA Civ 151.
[65] In, respectively, the *Product Star* case and *Gan Insurance Co. Ltd* v. *Tai Ping Insurance Co. Ltd (No. 2)* [2001] 2 All E.R. (Comm.) 299; [2001] EWCA Civ 1047.

> appropriate to public law challenges, of which reasonableness is only one, into the construction of commercial contracts. I agree with Arden L.J. that it was inappropriate to use the expression 'Wednesbury sense' in the order made in this case, particularly when Wednesbury is misquoted in that the word 'reasonable' is replaced by the word 'rational'. It does not lead to clarity.[66]

Turning to trust cases, in *Scott* v. *National Trust for Places of Historic Interest or Natural Beauty*, Robert Walker J. remarked on the 'obvious though not exact parallel between charity proceedings aimed at an alleged misuse of decision-making by a statutory charity and judicial review proceedings aimed at an alleged misuse of decision-making power by a public officer or body'.[67] A couple of years later, Chadwick L.J., delivering the judgment of the Court of Appeal in *Edge* v. *Pensions Ombudsman*,[68] thought it 'no coincidence that courts, considering the exercise of discretionary powers by those to whom such powers have been entrusted (albeit in different contexts), should reach similar and consistent conclusions; and should express those conclusions in much the same language'.[69] In *Abacus Trust Co. (Isle of Man)* v. *Barr*,[70] Lightman J. noted that there are 'critical differences between public, or administrative, law and private law proceedings' as regards, first, 'the discretion vested in the court in public law proceedings whether or not to grant relief', secondly, 'the distinction between what is "void" and what is "voidable"' and, thirdly, 'the strict time limits insisted upon for commencement of proceedings for judicial review'.[71] In *Pitt* v. *Holt*, Lloyd L.J. said that he wished to discourage reference to public law principles in relation to trust law, 'since trust law has plenty of satisfactory means of dealing with the issues that arise under trusts, and those issues are inherently different from those arising in public law'.[72] When the case reached the Supreme Court, Lord Walker referred to the 'superficial similarities between what the law requires of trustees in their decision-making and what it requires of decision-makers in the field of public law', but said that the analogy 'cannot . . . be pressed too far'.[73]

[66] *Lymington Marina Ltd* v. *Macnamara* [2007] 2 All E.R. (Comm.) 825, [69].

[67] *Scott* v. *National Trust for Places of Historic Interest or Natural Beauty* [1998] 2 All E.R. 705, 715–16.

[68] [2000] Ch. 602. [69] *Ibid.*, 628. [70] [2003] Ch. 409. [71] *Ibid.*, [29].

[72] [2012] Ch. 132, [77].

[73] *Pitt* v. *Holt* [2013] 2 A.C. 108, [11]. See Gummow, 'Equity in the Modern Administrative State'.

There has been debate in New Zealand over the extent, if any, to which *Wednesbury* unreasonableness has a role to play in the context of trustees' decisions. In *Craddock* v. *Crowhen*,[74] Tipping J. said:

> [I]t is generally understood that beneficiaries cannot complain about the exercise by trustees of a discretionary power unless they have acted ultra vires or in bad faith ... However an ostensibly intra vires exercise of a discretionary power can, in my judgment, be impugned on a basis somewhat wider than what is conventionally understood by bad faith in this field. If trustees exercise their discretionary powers in a manner which, although formally intra vires, is unreasonable, the court should be able to intervene ... Unreasonableness in this context is analogous to unreasonableness in administrative law: cf. the *Wednesbury* Concept. Those exercising public powers are usually required to exercise them reasonably. I can see no good reason why those exercising private powers should be free of similar control, subject always of course to the terms of their empowering instrument. But, it must be emphasised, a decision in the present field, as in the public law area, will not be regarded as unreasonable unless it is such that no reasonable trustee could rationally have made it in all the circumstances. The court will not intervene simply because it would or might have made a different decision. To be impugned the decision must be one that can fairly be said to be beyond the bounds of reason.[75]

Tipping J.'s remarks have been followed or quoted in several subsequent cases, but they were doubted in *Gailey* v. *Gordon*.[76] In that case, O'Regan J. said:

> That approach involves some relaxation of the normal reluctance of the [c]ourts to intervene, except where a decision has been exercised in bad faith or is ultra vires. Bad faith in this context has been recognised as including a decision for an ulterior motive, taking account of irrelevant considerations, and refusal to take into account relevant considerations and acting capriciously. However, the potential for the [c]ourt to intervene in the exercise of discretion by trustees where the discretion has been exercised unreasonably involves some extension of the [c]ourt's supervisory role. In the absence of any Court of Appeal authority mandating that approach, I prefer the limited approach which recognises the traditional reluctance of the [c]ourts to intervene in the exercise of a discretion by trustees unless it is in bad faith (as broadly defined above), or ultra vires.[77]

More recently, Asher J. said in *DNZ Property Fund Ltd* v. *Argosy Property Management Ltd*:[78]

[74] (1995) 1 N.Z.S.C. 40,331. [75] *Ibid.*, 40,337. [76] [2002] 2 N.Z.L.R. 192.
[77] *Ibid.*, [89]. [78] [2011] NZHC 1334.

> A decision so unreasonable that no reasonable trustee could have rationally made it in all the circumstances (the narrow original *Wednesbury* notion of unreasonableness) can be seen as equating to an irrational or capricious decision.[79]

Perhaps public law should, at most, be seen as providing trust lawyers with interesting analogies. The direct importation of public law concepts such as '*Wednesbury* unreasonableness' into trust law may be more likely to generate confusion than clarity. That said, I should have thought that the courts should be prepared to intervene if a decision made by trustees lacked any rational basis. That conclusion is borne out by Templeman J.'s reference to intervention where trustees have acted for reasons that could be said to be 'irrational, perverse or irrelevant to any sensible expectation of the settlor'.[80]

Care and skill

Trustees are expected to take care when exercising their powers.[81] Judge-made equity requires trustees to exercise the same standard of diligence and care as an ordinary prudent man of business would exercise in the management of his own affairs. It was also said that, when investing, a trustee must

> take such care as an ordinary prudent man would take if he were minded to make an investment for the benefit of other people for whom he felt morally bound to provide.[82]

Nowadays, a statutory duty of care applies in relation to the exercise of most administrative powers.[83] Section 1(1) of the Trustee Act 2000 (UK) states that, where the duty for which it provides is applicable, a trustee must

> exercise such care and skill as is reasonable in the circumstances, having regard in particular –
>
> (a) to any special knowledge or experience that he has or holds himself out as having, and

[79] *Ibid.*, [56]. [80] See text to n. 35 above.

[81] Lloyd L.J. noted the existence of a duty of care in *Pitt* v. *Holt*: see [2012] Ch. 132, [107].

[82] See *Re Whiteley, Whiteley* v. *Learoyd* (1886) 33 Ch. D. 347, 355 (Lindley L.J.), and *Cowan* v. *Scargill* [1985] Ch. 270, 289.

[83] Trustee Act 2000 (UK), Sch. 1 (although this may be excluded 'if or in so far as it appears from the trust instrument that the [statutory] duty is not meant to apply': Sch. 1 para. 7).

> (b) if he acts as trustee in the course of a business or profession, to any special knowledge or experience that it is reasonable to expect of a person acting in the course of that kind of business or profession.

The 2000 Act provides for the statutory duty of care to apply to trustees *when exercising* a range of powers.[84] It does not therefore operate in relation to decisions as to *whether* powers should be exercised at all.[85] Nor is it in point as regards the exercise of powers of appointment, maintenance and advancement.

The statutory and non-statutory duties seem little different. The Law Commission (together with the Scottish Law Commission) expressed the view that its proposals for a new statutory duty of care probably represented 'no more than a codification of the existing common law duty'.[86]

More is expected of a paid professional than of, say, a public-spirited volunteer with no relevant expertise serving as a trustee of a small charity.[87] This makes obvious sense.

Taking the correct matters into consideration

Edge v. *Pensions Ombudsman*[88] illustrates that a trustee exercising a power must do so 'giving proper consideration to the matters which are relevant and excluding from consideration matters which are

[84] See the 2000 Act, s. 1 and Sch. 1.

[85] The Law Commission and the Scottish Law Commission explained in their joint report, *Trustees' Powers and Duties* (Law Com. No. 260, Scot Law Com. No. 172) (1999), [3.12] (omitting references):

> The decision *whether* to exercise a discretion will remain, as it is now, a matter for the trustees to determine. That decision will *not* be subject to the new duty of care. However, once trustees have decided to exercise a discretionary function which is subject to the new duty, the *manner* in which they exercise it will be measured against the appropriate standard of care.

[86] See Law Commission and the Scottish Law Commission, *Trustees' Powers and Duties* (1999), [2.35]; see also *Pitt* v. *Holt* [2012] Ch. 132, [107]. That said, the Law Commission decided against merely requiring trustees to act 'with the care of the ordinary prudent person of business'. It considered that, in formulating the new statutory duty, 'express regard should be had to the particular skills and position of the trustees, and to the circumstances of the trust'; see *Trustees' Powers and Duties* (1999), [3.24].

[87] See Trustee Act 2000 (UK), s. 1 and, for the non-statutory position, *Re Waterman's Will Trusts* [1952] 2 All E.R. 1054, 1055 and *Bartlett* v. *Barclays Bank Trust Co. Ltd* [1980] Ch. 515, 525.

[88] [2000] Ch. 602.

irrelevant'.[89] This principle lies at the heart of the rule in *Hastings-Bass*, as now re-interpreted in *Pitt* v. *Holt*.

Cases in which the *Hastings-Bass* rule has been invoked have typically involved the exercise of dispositive powers. However, I find it difficult to see a logical reason for confining the duty to take the correct matters into consideration to dispositive powers. It has been taken to extend to the exercise of administrative powers in both Jersey and the Cayman Islands.[90]

What is relevant will depend on the purpose of the power being exercised. A power of advancement can be exercised only 'if it is for the benefit of the child or remoter issue to be advanced or . . . it is thought to be "a good thing" for the advanced person to have a share of capital before his or her due time'.[91] A matter will therefore be relevant if it bears on whether the proposed advancement is for the benefit of the relevant individual. A power of investment must usually be exercised so as to yield the best financial return for the beneficiaries,[92] so matters relating to the possible rewards and risks will be relevant when considering how the power should be exercised.

In *Pitt* v. *Holt*, Lloyd L.J. observed that it is 'not possible to lay down any clear rule as to the matters which trustees ought to take into account when considering the exercise of a power of advancement or some other dispositive discretionary power'.[93] Perhaps it will tend to be easier to specify the matters relevant to the exercise of an administrative power than a dispositive one. For example, trustees deciding how funds should be invested should clearly have regard to the potential rewards and risks of different investments. There may be more room for argument as to quite what is relevant to the exercise of, say, a power of appointment in favour of a wide class.[94]

Unsurprisingly, the authorities confirm that the wishes, circumstances and needs of beneficiaries can be relevant.[95] So can the settlor's wishes[96]

[89] *Ibid.*, 627.

[90] See especially *Seaton Trustees Ltd* v. *Morgan* [2008] W.T.L.R. 553, [16] (an *obiter dictum*) (not reported in the Jersey Law Reports: see *In the Matter of the Seaton Trustees Ltd* 2009 J.L.R. *N.* [15]) and *Wang* v. *CIBC Bank and Trust Co. (Cayman) Ltd* [2013] W.T.L.R. 129, [19]. Compare D. Hayton, P. Matthews and C. Mitchell, *Underhill and Hayton: Law Relating to Trusts and Trustees*, 18th ed. (London: LexisNexis, 2010), [57.24].

[91] *Re Pauling's Settlement Trusts* [1964] Ch. 303, 333.

[92] *Cowan* v. *Scargill* [1985] Ch. 270, 287.

[93] [2012] Ch. 132, [118].

[94] Some guidance can, however, be derived from *McPhail* v. *Doulton* [1971] A.C. 424 (especially at 449) and *Re Hay's Settlement Trusts* [1982] 1 W.L.R. 202, 209–10.

[95] *Pitt* v. *Holt* [2012] Ch. 132, [114].

[96] *Abacus Trust Co. (Isle of Man)* v. *Barr* [2003] Ch. 409, 419; *Pitt* v. *Holt* [2012] Ch. 132, [114]; [2013] 2 A.C. 108, [65].

and fiscal considerations.[97] Legitimate expectations can be material as well. In *Scott* v. *National Trust for Places of Historic Interest or Natural Beauty*, Robert Walker J. said that he was 'inclined to think that legitimate expectation may have some part to play in trust law as well as in judicial review cases'.[98] The example he gave related specifically to procedure: to whether it would be reasonable for trustees to discontinue payments to an elderly, impoverished beneficiary 'without any warning, and without giving the beneficiary the opportunity of trying to persuade the trustees to continue the payment, at least temporarily'.[99] I should have thought, however, that a beneficiary's legitimate expectations could be relevant to substance as well as procedure: the fact that an elderly, impoverished beneficiary was dependent on payments he had long been receiving should surely be considered when deciding whether to discontinue the payments at all, not merely in relation to whether the payments should be stopped without affording him an opportunity to persuade the trustees otherwise.

A decision made without taking the correct matters into consideration can potentially be set aside. Whereas, however, the exercise of a power of appointment in favour of a person who is not an object of the power is void, a decision tainted by failure to have regard to the correct considerations is merely voidable. The difference reflects 'the very important distinction between an error by trustees in going beyond the scope of a power ... and an error in failing to give proper consideration to relevant matters in making a decision which is within the scope of the relevant power'.[100] If trustees purport to do something that they simply have no power to do, it is nugatory. Where, on the other hand, the complaint is that trustees have failed to have regard to the correct considerations, the court will intervene, if at all, on the basis that the trustees have acted in breach of duty. 'Breach of duty is essential (in the full sense of that word) because it is only a breach of duty on the part of the trustees that entitles the court to intervene'.[101]

The fact that trustees did not have regard to a relevant matter when making a decision will not necessarily mean that they acted in breach of

[97] *Pitt* v. *Holt* [2012] Ch. 132, [115]; [2013] 2 A.C. 108, [65].

[98] [1998] 2 All E.R. 705, 718. [99] *Ibid.*

[100] *Pitt* v. *Holt* [2013] 2 A.C. 108, [60]. In this connection, Lord Walker referred (at [1]) to an article by Professor Richard Nolan, 'Controlling Fiduciary Power' [2009] C.L.J. 293.

[101] *Pitt* v. *Holt* [2013] 2 A.C. 108, [73] (apart perhaps from 'the special case of powers of maintenance of minor beneficiaries, where the court was in the past more interventionist').

duty. Trustees who act with reasonable care will not be guilty of breach of duty even if they fail to identify something relevant to their decision-making. In *Pitt* v. *Holt*, Lord Walker observed that 'it would be contrary to principle and authority to impose a form of strict liability on trustees who conscientiously obtain and follow, in making a decision which is within the scope of their powers, apparently competent professional advice which turns out to be wrong'.[102] In similar vein, Lloyd L.J. had said in the Court of Appeal:

> [I]f the trustees, aware of the need to consider relevant matters, seek advice . . . as to the position while considering what, if anything, to do under their discretionary powers, then unless the process of taking and acting on the advice is itself open to challenge in some way, I do not see that the trustees can be said to be in breach of their duty if they proceed to address the exercise of their discretionary power on the basis of the advice given to them as to, for example, tax consequences.[103]

A little earlier, Lloyd L.J. had said:

> [T]he extent of the proper consideration on the part of the trustees would be affected by the nature and circumstances of what was proposed. It might be different if what was proposed was the release from the trust of a relatively modest sum of capital to meet an extremely urgent need of one of several beneficiaries. In such a case it might not be necessary to undertake the same degree of inquiry and examination as it would be if the proposed transaction affected a very large proportion of the trust fund, or was not required as a matter of extreme urgency.[104]

Lord Walker made the point more than once in *Pitt* v. *Holt*, that, for inadequate deliberation on relevant matters to give rise to breach of duty,

[102] [2013] 2 A.C. 108, [80]. [103] [2012] Ch. 132, [124].

[104] *Ibid.*, [117]. See also *Prudential Staff Pensions Ltd* v. *The Prudential Assurance Co. Ltd* [2011] Pens. L.R. 239, [235]; [2011] EWHC 960 (Ch), where I said:

> It is doubtless incumbent on a trustee to familiarise himself, in general terms, with his powers. However, there can be no absolute rule that a trustee must be aware of every possibility inherent in his powers. How far a trustee should go to ensure that he understands the scope of his powers must . . . depend on the duty to exercise reasonable skill and care and vary according to the circumstances. If it is desirable that a trustee should be able to act in a particular way, and the trustee appreciates that his powers could potentially allow him to do so, it may well be his duty to clarify the extent of his powers . . . If, at the other end of the spectrum, the trustee neither knows, nor ought reasonably to know, of any uncertainty of practical importance, he can be under no obligation to obtain advice on the precise scope of his powers; in fact, spending money on an unnecessary exercise of that kind might itself be in breach of duty.

'the inadequacy must be sufficiently serious as to amount to a breach of duty'.[105] As Lord Walker explained:

> It is not enough to show that the trustees' deliberations have fallen short of the highest possible standards, or that the court would, on a surrender of discretion by the trustees, have acted in a different way.[106]

In this area,

> the law has to balance the need to protect beneficiaries against aberrant conduct by trustees . . . with the competing interests of legal certainty, and of not imposing too stringent a test in judging trustees' decision-making.[107]

In *Pitt* v. *Holt*, culpable failure to have regard to correct considerations was characterised as breach of fiduciary duty. In the Supreme Court, Lord Walker said that 'for the rule to apply the inadequate deliberation on the part of the trustees must be sufficiently serious as to amount to a breach of *fiduciary* duty' and that 'only breach of *fiduciary* duty justifies judicial intervention'.[108] In the Court of Appeal, Lloyd L.J. had similarly said:

> If the act of the trustees which purports to alter or bring to an end the interest of a beneficiary is affected by a breach of *fiduciary* duty, then the beneficiary is entitled to restrain the trustees from acting on it, and to have it set aside, subject always to equitable defences and discretionary factors.[109]

The references to 'fiduciary' duty may be the subject of debate. In *Bristol & West Building Society* v. *Mothew*,[110] Millett L.J. observed that the expression 'fiduciary duty' is 'properly confined to those duties which are peculiar to fiduciaries and the breach of which attracts legal consequences differing from those consequent upon the breach of other duties'.[111] The 'distinguishing obligation of a fiduciary', Millett L.J. said, 'is the obligation of loyalty'.[112] He went on:

> Breach of fiduciary obligation . . . connotes disloyalty or infidelity. Mere incompetence is not enough. A servant who loyally does his incompetent best for his master is not unfaithful and is not guilty of a breach of fiduciary duty.[113]

[105] [2013] 2 A.C. 108, [68]. See also [39]. [106] [2013] 2 A.C. 108, [73]. [107] *Ibid.*, [83].
[108] *Ibid.*, [73] (italics added). [109] [2012] Ch. 132, [99] (italics added).
[110] [1998] Ch. 1. [111] *Ibid.*, 16. [112] *Ibid.*, 18. [113] *Ibid.*, 18.

In the same vein, Millett L.J. remarked that it is 'inappropriate to apply the expression ["fiduciary duty"] to the obligation of a trustee or other fiduciary to use proper skill and care in the discharge of his duties'.[114]

There are doubtless cases in which a trustee's failure to have regard to the correct considerations is a consequence of disloyalty. The trustee may have taken the relevant decision for reasons other than the interests of the beneficiaries. A trustee need not, however, have been disloyal to have acted in breach of duty. Failure to have regard to the correct considerations will typically have arisen from lack of care rather than want of loyalty. Carelessness is thus being termed 'breach of fiduciary duty' in *Pitt* v. *Holt*.

Professor Lionel Smith has in the past remarked that 'it is commonplace for decisions to be set aside when they are made in breach of the duty of loyalty' but that it has 'never been understood to be the law that a fiduciary's decision can be avoided retroactively because it was made in breach of the duty of care, skill and diligence'.[115] That view cannot stand without qualification now. It is apparent from *Pitt* v. *Holt* that, in this jurisdiction at least, the fact that a decision was made without due care can justify rescission.

The ability of beneficiaries to complain that trustees have failed to have regard to the correct considerations is in practice very much curtailed by the fact that trustees do not usually have to give reasons for their decisions.[116] Prior to *Pitt* v. *Holt*, it had become common for trustees

[114] *Ibid.*, 16. See also *Hilton* v. *Barker Booth & Eastwood* [2005] 1 W.L.R. 567; [2005] UKHL 8, where Lord Walker said (at [29]):

> The relationship between a solicitor and his client is one in which the client reposes trust and confidence in the solicitor. It is a fiduciary relationship. But not every breach of duty by a fiduciary is a breach of fiduciary duty: see the observations of Millett L.J. in *Bristol and West Building Society* v. *Mothew* ... If a solicitor is careless in investigating a title or drafting a lease, he may be liable to pay damages for breach of his professional duty, but that is not a breach of a fiduciary duty of loyalty; it is simply the breach of a duty of care. This may have practical consequences, for instance in relation to causation, as in the *Mothew* case.

Similarly, in *Spread Trustee Co. Ltd* v. *Hutcheson* [2012] 2 A.C. 194; [2011] UKPC 13, Lord Clarke referred (at [61]) to 'the fundamental distinction between the fiduciary duties owed by the trustee on the one hand and the duty to exercise care and skill owed by the trustee on the other'.

[115] L. Smith, 'Can I Change My Mind? Undoing Trustee Decisions' (2008) 27 Est. Tr. & Pensions J. 284, 302.

[116] See, for example, L. Tucker, N. Le Poidevin and J. Brightwell, *Lewin on Trusts*, 19th ed. (London: Sweet and Maxwell, 2015), [29–234]–[29–239], and *Breakspear* v. *Ackland* [2009] Ch. 32; [2008] EWHC 220 (Ch), especially at [53]–[57].

themselves to assert and rely on 'their own failings, or those of their advisers, in seeking the assistance of the court'.[117] Applications by trustees are, however, bound to be far less common in the future. In *Pitt* v. *Holt*, Lord Walker agreed with Lloyd L.J. that 'in general it would be inappropriate for trustees to take the initiative in commencing proceedings of this nature'.[118]

Procedural fairness

Discussion of the need for trustees to 'inform themselves, before making a decision, of matters which are relevant to the decision' (to use words of Robert Walker J. in *Scott* v. *National Trust for Places of Historic Interest or Natural Beauty*[119]) leads on to the question of whether public law principles of procedural fairness operate in the context of trusts. The short answer is that, in general at least, they do not. The rules of natural justice, which obviously play a key role in public law, do not apply as such to trustees. In *Karger* v. *Paul*,[120] McGarvie J. (in the Supreme Court of Victoria) said:

> I see no good reason for importing rules of natural justice into the exercise of discretion by the trustees of the will. Such an implication is not necessary. The trustees of the will did not exercise their power in a type of situation where a right to make representations upon its exercise is normally afforded.[121]

Trustees need to inform themselves of matters relevant to a decision,[122] but they are 'not under any general duty to give a hearing to both sides'.[123] In *R* v. *Charity Commissioners, Ex p. Baldwin*,[124] Mr Jack Beatson Q.C. (sitting as a Deputy High Court Judge) encapsulated the difference between the public and trust law in this way:

> The difference between the public law and the trust approach is that the former focuses on the individual's opportunity to be heard before a decision, whereas the trust concept focuses on the information available to the person making the decision.[125]

117 [2013] 2 A.C. 108, [69]. 118 *Ibid.*, [69]. 119 [1998] 2 All E.R. 705, 717.
120 [1984] V.R. 161. 121 *Ibid.*, 166.
122 *Scott* v. *National Trust for Places of Historic Interest or Natural Beauty* [1998] 2 All E.R. 705, 717.
123 *Ibid.*, 718. 124 (2001) 33 H.L.R. 48.
125 *R* v. *Charity Commissioners, Ex p. Baldwin* [2001] W.T.L.R. 137, [49]; see also [59]. Compare, however, *Finch* v. *Telstra Super Pty. Ltd* (2010) 242 C.L.R. 254, [66]; [2010] HCA 36, where the High Court of Australia spoke of the duty of trustees to inform

Prophylaxis

Trustees, like other fiduciaries, are subject to the 'no conflict' and 'no profit' rules. The effect of these was summarised in these terms by Deane J. in the High Court of Australia in *Chan* v. *Zacharia*:[126]

> Stated comprehensively in terms of the liability to account, the principle of equity is that a person who is under a fiduciary obligation must account to the person to whom the obligation is owed for any benefit or gain (i) which has been obtained or received in circumstances where a conflict or significant possibility of conflict existed between his fiduciary duty and his personal interest in the pursuit or possible receipt of such a benefit or gain or (ii) which was obtained or received by use or by reason of his fiduciary position or of opportunity or knowledge resulting from it.[127]

The 'no conflict' and 'no profit' rules exist at least in part to ensure that fiduciaries are not influenced by their own interests when exercising their discretions. In *Bray* v. *Ford*,[128] Lord Herschell said:

> It is an inflexible rule of a Court of Equity that a person in a fiduciary position . . . is not, unless otherwise expressly provided, entitled to make a profit; he is not allowed to put himself in a position where his interest and duty conflict. It does not appear to me that this rule is . . . founded upon principles of morality. I regard it rather as based on the consideration that, human nature being what it is, there is danger, in such circumstances, of the person holding a fiduciary position being swayed by interest rather than by duty, and thus prejudicing those whom he was bound to protect.[129]

Equity's 'inflexible rule' is reflected in the self-dealing rule. The self-dealing rule is (in the words of Megarry V.-C. in *Tito* v. *Waddell (No. 2)*,[130]) that

> if a trustee sells the trust property to himself, the sale is voidable by any beneficiary *ex debito justitiae*, however fair the transaction.[131]

themselves being 'more intense in superannuation trusts in the form of the Deed than in trusts of the *Karger* v. *Paul* type', namely, wholly voluntary trusts.

126 (1984) 154 C.L.R. 178.

127 *Ibid.*, 199, cited with approval in *Don King Productions Inc.* v. *Warren* [2000] Ch. 291, 341.

128 [1896] A.C. 44.

129 *Ibid.*, 51. See also *Murad* v. *Al Saraj* [2005] W.T.L.R. 1573; [2005] EWCA Civ 959, especially at [107].

130 [1977] Ch. 106.

131 *Tito* v. *Waddell (No. 2)* [1977] Ch. 106, 241. *Earl of Cardigan* v. *Moore* [2012] W.T.L.R. 931; [2012] EWHC 1024 (Ch), provides a recent illustration of the operation of the rule.

The rule 'is based, not only upon the consideration that a trustee cannot be both seller and buyer . . . but also on the wider principle that a trustee must not put himself in a position where there is a conflict or possible conflict between his interest and duty'.[132] The rule is 'a severe one which applies however honest the circumstances, even though the price is fair and irrespective of whether any profit is made by the trustee'.[133]

A public law analogy to the 'no conflict' and 'no profit' rules can be found in the rule against apprehended bias. An arbiter will be treated as biased where a 'fair-minded and informed observer, having considered the facts, would conclude that there was a real possibility that the tribunal was biased'.[134] The principle 'admits of the possibility of human frailty' and 'requires the identification of what it is said might lead a judge (or juror) to decide a case other than on its legal and factual merits'.[135] As has been pointed out, this language is reminiscent of that used by Lord Herschell in *Bray* v. *Ford*.[136] I doubt, however, whether comparison with the rule against bias is likely to give any real guidance as to the proper ambit of the 'no conflict' and 'no profit' rules. The contexts are too different. Apart from anything else, the relationship between a fiduciary and his principal (trustee and beneficiaries, for example) will be quite unlike that of an arbiter and those affected by his decisions.

Loyalty (or good faith)

That brings me to the duty of loyalty (or good faith).

As mentioned above, Millett L.J. pointed out in *Bristol & West Building Society* v. *Mothew* that the 'distinguishing obligation of a fiduciary is the obligation of loyalty'.[137] He explained that '[t]he principal is entitled to the single-minded loyalty of his fiduciary' and accordingly a fiduciary 'must act in good faith' and 'may not act for his own benefit or the benefit of a third person without the informed consent of his principal'.[138]

In the law of trusts, the duty of loyalty is fundamental. The 'duty of the trustees to perform the trusts honestly and in good faith for the benefit of

[132] Tucker, Le Poidevin and Brightwell, *Lewin on Trusts*, 19th ed. [20–105]; see also, for example, *Wright* v. *Morgan* [1926] A.C. 788, 797 and *In re Thompson's Settlement* [1986] Ch. 99, 115.

[133] Tucker, Le Poidevin and Brightwell, *Lewin on Trusts*, 19th ed. [20–105].

[134] *Porter* v. *Magill* [2002] 2 A.C. 357, [103]; [2001] UKHL 67.

[135] *Ebner* v. *Official Trustee in Bankruptcy* (2000) 205 C.L.R. 337, [8]; [2000] HCA 63.

[136] Conaglen, 'Public-Private Intersection: Comparing Fiduciary Conflict Doctrine and Bias', 71.

[137] *Bristol & West Building Society* v. *Mothew* [1998] Ch. 1, 18.

[138] *Ibid.*, 18.

the beneficiaries is the minimum necessary to give substance to the trusts'.[139]

It is necessary to distinguish in this context between administrative and dispositive powers. With administrative powers, 'the trustee must exercise the power (or not) in what he perceives to be the best interests of the beneficiaries'.[140] A dispositive power, however, can authorise a trustee to benefit someone who is as yet not a beneficiary at all. There, 'you must be motivated by the fulfilment of what you perceive to be the purpose for which the power was given'.[141]

The focus is on the trustee's subjective intentions. That is apparent from the quotations from the judgments in *Mothew* and *Armitage* v. *Nurse*. The position is similar with company directors, who are also of course fiduciaries. In *Regentcrest plc* v. *Cohen*,[142] Jonathan Parker J. explained:

> The duty imposed on directors to act bona fide in the interests of the company is a subjective one ... The question is not whether, viewed objectively by the court, the particular act or omission which is challenged was in fact in the interests of the company; still less is the question whether the court, had it been in the position of the director at the relevant time, might have acted differently. Rather, the question is whether the director honestly believed that his act or omission was in the interests of the company. The issue is as to the director's state of mind. No doubt, where it is clear that the act or omission under challenge resulted in substantial detriment to the company, the director will have a harder task persuading the court that he honestly believed it to be in the company's interest; but that does not detract from the subjective nature of the test.[143]

The distinction between want of good faith and negligence was eroded in *Walker* v. *Stones*.[144] That case involved a clause which exempted trustees

[139] *Armitage* v. *Nurse* [1998] Ch. 241, 253–4 (Millett L.J.). *Armitage* v. *Nurse* was endorsed by the Privy Council (by a majority) in *Spread Trustee Co. Ltd* v. *Hutcheson* [2012] 2 A.C. 194.

[140] L. Smith, 'The Motive, Not the Deed', in J. Getzler (ed.), *Rationalizing Property, Equity and Trusts: Essays in Honour of Edward Burn* (London: LexisNexis, 2003), 69. See also *Cowan* v. *Scargill* [1985] Ch. 270, 286–7, where Megarry V.-C. described the duty of trustees 'to exercise their powers in the best interests of the present and future beneficiaries of the trust, holding the scales impartially between different classes of beneficiaries' as 'paramount'. Megarry V.-C. went on to explain that 'the best interests of the beneficiaries are normally their best financial interests'.

[141] Smith, 'The Motive, Not the Deed', in Getzler (ed.), *Rationalizing Property, Equity and Trusts: Essays in Honour of Edward Burn*, 73 n. 86.

[142] [2001] 2 B.C.L.C. 80.

[143] *Regentcrest plc* v. *Cohen* [2001] 2 B.C.L.C. 80, [120].

[144] [2001] 2 Q.B. 902.

from liability for anything 'other than wilful fraud or dishonesty on the part of the trustee whom it is sought to make liable'. At first instance, the judge had considered it 'impossible to call a trustee's conduct "dishonest" in any ordinary sense of that word, even if he knew he was acting in breach of the terms of his trust, if he so acted in a genuine (even if misguided) belief that what he was doing was for the benefit of his beneficiaries'.[145] On appeal, Sir Christopher Slade (with whom the other members of the court agreed) said:

> At least in the case of a solicitor-trustee, a qualification must in my opinion be necessary to take account of the case where the trustee's so-called 'honest belief', though actually held, is so unreasonable that, by any objective standard, no reasonable solicitor-trustee could have thought that what he did or agreed to do was for the benefit of the beneficiaries.[146]

The exemption clause would therefore

> not exempt the trustees from liability for breaches of trust, even if committed in the genuine belief that the course taken by them was in the interests of the beneficiaries, if such belief was so unreasonable that no reasonable solicitor-trustee could have held that belief.[147]

Whatever the merits of this approach in the context of trustee exemption clauses,[148] I do not think that it should be applied in the context of the duty of loyalty/good faith. Negligence, however gross, is not disloyalty. Failing to act as a reasonable person would act may provide evidence that the defendant acted in bad faith. However, a failure to act as a reasonable person would act is not as such an act of bad faith.[149]

145 *Walker* v. *Stones* [2000] W.T.L.R. 79, 99 (Ch.D.).

146 *Walker* v. *Stones* [2001] 2 Q.B. 902, 939 (C.A.). 147 [2001] 2 Q.B. 902, 941.

148 *Walker* v. *Stones* was the subject of an appeal to the House of Lords, but it was compromised shortly before it was due to be heard. In *Spread Trustee Co. Ltd* v. *Hutcheson* [2012] 2 A.C. 194, Lord Mance left open the correctness of *Walker* v. *Stones*. He said (at [107]) that it was 'unnecessary on this appeal to go into the question of the standard of dishonesty discussed in *Walker* v. *Stones*, where the Court of Appeal concluded that it could include an objective element, embracing conduct such that no reasonable person could have believed it honest'.

149 See further *Spread Trustee Co. Ltd* v. *Hutcheson* [2012] 2 A.C. 194, where Sir Robin Auld said (at [117]):

> Gross negligence, like negligence not so qualified, may be committed in good faith and, therefore, without dishonesty or wilfulness. Indeed, dishonesty – an inherent ingredient of fraudulent or wilful misconduct – is the antithesis of negligence, an inadvertent falling short of a duty to take reasonable care in all the circumstances.

The need to distinguish negligence and bad faith was brought out in a case concerning receivers appointed by a mortgagee, *Medforth* v. *Blake*.[150] In that case, Scott V.-C. said:

> I do not think that the concept of good faith should be diluted by treating it as capable of being breached by conduct that is not dishonest or otherwise tainted by bad faith. It is sometimes said that recklessness is equivalent to intent. Shutting one's eyes deliberately to the consequences of what one is doing may make it impossible to deny an intention to bring about those consequences. Thereapart, however, the concepts of negligence on the one hand and fraud or bad faith on the other ought, in my view, to be kept strictly apart.[151]

That reasoning is equally cogent when applied to trustees.

The relationship between the duty of loyalty and that to act for proper purposes merits comment. Clearly, there is at least an overlap between the two: the father who committed a fraud on a power in *Wellesley* v. *Earl of Mornington*[152] could also be said to have acted in breach of his duty of loyalty. To my mind, however, it is helpful to recognise that trustees, in common with other fiduciaries, have a core obligation of loyalty that manifests itself in the 'no conflict' and 'no profit' rules as well as the requirement not to act otherwise than 'in good faith for the benefit of the beneficiaries'. In so far as the fraud on a power doctrine deals with the exercise of powers in the interests of persons other than beneficiaries, it can be seen as a reflection of the duty of loyalty.

Impartiality

Another limitation on trustees' decision-making is to be found in the principle that trustees must act impartially. In *Re Tempest*,[153] Turner L.J. observed:

> [I]t is of the essence of the duty of every trustee to hold an even hand between the parties interested under the trust. Every trustee is in duty bound to look to the interests of all, and not of any particular member or class of members of his *cestuis que trusts*.[154]

Rather more recently, Dillon L.J. said in *Nestle* v. *National Westminster Bank plc*:[155]

[150] [2000] Ch. 86. [151] *Ibid.*, 103. [152] (1855) 2 K. & J. 143; 69 E.R. 728.
[153] (1866) L.R. 1 Ch. App. 485. [154] *Re Tempest* (1866) L.R. 1 Ch. App. 485, 487–8.
[155] [1993] 1 W.L.R. 1261.

> The obligation of a trustee is to administer the trust fund impartially, or fairly (I can see no significant difference), having regard to the different interests of beneficiaries.[156]

The need for impartiality can be seen as an aspect of one or more of the duties discussed above. In *Edge* v. *Pensions Ombudsman*, Chadwick L.J. analysed matters in this way:[157]

> Properly understood, the so-called duty to act impartially . . . is no more than the ordinary duty which the law imposes on a person who is entrusted with the exercise of a discretionary power: that he exercises the power for the purpose for which it is given, giving proper consideration to the matters which are relevant and excluding from consideration matters which are irrelevant.[158]

Taxonomy

Public lawyers do not need to distinguish between void and voidable decisions. All invalid administrative acts are void in law. As Wade and Forsyth's treatise, *Administrative Law*, explains:[159]

> In several decisions the House of Lords made it clear that 'there are no degrees of nullity' and that errors such as bad faith, wrong grounds, and breach of natural justice all necessarily involve excess of jurisdiction and therefore nullity.[160]

In practice, 'theoretically void administrative acts' may be 'functionally voidable'[161] because they are treated as valid unless and until the court pronounces to the contrary. What is significant in this context, however, is that the various grounds on which decisions can be impugned can all be allowed to 'run into one another' (to use words of Lord Greene M.R. in the *Wednesbury* case).[162]

156 *Nestle* v. *National Westminster Bank plc* [1993] 1 W.L.R. 1261, 1279. At first instance, Hoffmann J. had criticised the 'traditional image of holding the scales equally between tenant for life and remainderman' because it suggested not only a 'weighing of known quantities whereas investment decisions are concerned with predictions of the future' but also 'a more mechanistic process than . . . the law requires' (see (1988) [2000] W.T.L.R. 795n, 803).

157 [2000] Ch. 602. 158 *Ibid.*, 627.

159 H.W.R. Wade and C.F. Forsyth, *Administrative Law*, 11th ed. (Oxford University Press, 2014). Compare, however, Lord Woolf, J. Jowell and A. Le Sueur, *De Smith's Judicial Review*, 7th ed. (London: Sweet & Maxwell, 2013), [4–059].

160 Wade and Forsyth, *Administrative Law*, 11th ed., 247. 161 *Ibid.*, 249.

162 *Associated Provincial Picture Houses Ltd* v. *Wednesbury Corp.* [1948] 1 K.B. 223, 229.

Trust lawyers are not so fortunate. The decision of the Supreme Court in *Pitt* v. *Holt* confirms that it is necessary to differentiate between matters going to the scope of a power and those concerned with how it is exercised. An attempt to exercise a power outside its true scope will be void. In contrast:

> [I]f an exercise by trustees of a discretionary power is within the terms of the power, but the trustees have in some way breached their duties in respect of that exercise, then (unless it is a case of a fraud on a power) the trustees' act is not void but it may be voidable at the instance of a beneficiary who is adversely affected.[163]

There is room for argument as to how some matters should be classified. I have already referred to the doubts that have been expressed as to whether fraud on a power should continue to be treated as rendering an exercise of the power void. Some or all of the doctrine could, alternatively, be treated as going to *how* a power is exercised rather than its *scope*. If, however, a fraud on a power is still to be considered void, the exercise of a power in breach of the duty of loyalty is itself presumably void, since the trustee could equally be said to have committed fraud on the power. What about the exercise of a power for capricious reasons or without any rational basis? In each case, the trustee could be argued to have acted otherwise than for the purposes for which the power was conferred and so outside it.

Another point relates to the requirement to take the correct matters into consideration. There is clearly overlap between this principle and other concepts described in this chapter. As already noted, a failure to have regard to the correct considerations may be attributable to either disloyalty or want of care or both; it might also mean that the trustee had exercised the relevant power for an improper purpose. There may be a case for absorbing the obligation to take account of the correct considerations into other duties. It is instructive to compare the directors' duties set out in the Companies Act 2006 (UK). Section 171 provides for duties comparable to those mentioned above: a director is required to 'act in accordance with the company's constitution' and 'only exercise powers for the purposes for which they are conferred'. Section 172 contains a duty to act in the way the director 'considers, in good faith, would be most likely to promote the success of the company'; this corresponds to the trustee's duty of loyalty. Section 174 stipulates that a director, like

[163] [2012] Ch. 132, [99] (Lloyd L.J.) (endorsed by Lord Walker: [2013] 2 A.C. 108, [93]).

a trustee, must exercise reasonable care, skill and diligence. Sections 175 and 176 give statutory form to the 'no conflict' and 'no profit' rules. What the 2006 Act does not contain is a distinct duty to take the correct considerations into account when making decisions. Perhaps trust law should also dispense with any separate duty to take relevant matters into account.

The impact of exemption clauses

The protection that the various rules discussed in this chapter could afford to beneficiaries is, in practice, reduced by the existence of exemption clauses.[164] The trustees of whom the most could reasonably be demanded, that is paid professionals, are particularly likely to have the benefit of such clauses. A typical clause will provide that a trustee is not to be liable for any loss or damage unless it was caused by fraud on his part. The validity of clauses of this type was upheld by the Court of Appeal in *Armitage* v. *Nurse*, a decision which was endorsed by the Privy Council in *Spread Trustee Co. Ltd* v. *Hutcheson*.[165] The Law Commission considered recommending changes in the law, but ultimately decided not to do so.[166]

Concluding comments

Various legal principles serve to impose constraints on the exercise of powers by trustees. While, however, *Pitt* v. *Holt* has clarified the law helpfully in important respects, there remain obscurities in relation to the scope of some of the principles and, especially, their interrelationship. Further, the availability of relief is in practice limited to a considerable extent by the fact that trustees do not generally have to give reasons for their decisions and by the existence of exemption clauses.

[164] The existence of an exemption clause will typically, however, affect the availability of financial redress as against a trustee rather than whether the validity of the relevant transaction can be challenged.

[165] [2012] 2 A.C. 194. [166] See *Trustee Exemption Clauses*, Law Com. No. 301.

3

Constraints on the exercise of trustees' powers

A commentary

ALAN STEINFELD

Introduction

The topic of Sir Guy Newey's chapter (Chapter 2) is a fundamentally important one as it is central to the whole existence of a trust. For, unless the court is able to enforce the trust, there cannot be a trust – and this in turn must entail the court having at least some measure of control over the exercise by the trustees of their powers. It is certainly from the practitioner's point of view the topic upon which he or she is most liable to be engaged. When consulted by the trustees the most frequent matter upon which we are asked to advise is whether the trustees can properly take certain actions in exercise or purported exercise of their powers. When consulted by beneficiaries, the most frequent matter raised is whether there is any basis for challenging the exercise by the trustees of their powers. And most hostile trust litigation is concerned with complaints raised by beneficiaries as to the exercise by the trustees of their powers.

For this reason, Sir Guy's chapter is hugely, in my opinion, helpful and illuminating. I pay especial tribute to the depth of his research and to the manner in which in a relatively short span he has managed to deal with virtually the whole breadth of this complex topic. If I were to attempt to deal with and comment upon every facet of the material dealt with by Sir Guy, I would well exceed the length which has been allowed for this commentary.

So what I shall do is to attempt merely to deal with the following matters arising from or touched upon in Sir Guy's chapter which especially interest me.

Fraud on the exercise of the power

Sir Guy deals with this under the heading 'Improper purposes'.[1] I think that his heading is the correct one. A purported exercise of a power which goes beyond that which on its true construction the power permits is beyond the scope of the power altogether and will be void. So, a power to appoint in favour of A cannot be exercised so as to appoint to B, as Sir Guy points out.[2] However, here we are dealing with an entirely different point, namely the exercise of a power which on its face is within what is permitted by the power but for a purpose which is both improper and beyond what the power was intended to achieve. Millett L.J. called it an 'extraneous or ulterior purpose'.[3] If by that is meant some *improper* purpose, there can be no quarrel. I would question, however, whether the mere fact that a power is exercised for a purpose which goes beyond what that particular power contemplated necessarily entails that there has been a fraud on the power.[4] Surely the fundamental point is that all the powers conferred on trustees are intended to be exercised for the benefit of the beneficiaries, as Sir Guy points out.[5] So if, say, a power of investment (to which the doctrine applies[6]) is exercised for a purpose which goes beyond the mere investment of the assets for the best return but which is nevertheless for the benefit of the beneficiaries, I question whether it is correct to stigmatise this as a fraud on the power.

A recent example of this is, in the context of so-called pensions liberation, the exercise by the trustees of a defined contribution pension scheme of their powers of investment for the purpose of enabling part of a member's 'pension pot' to be lent to that member on terms that it is only repayable out of the capital sum to which that member will become entitled on reaching the relevant age (currently fifty-five), so accelerating the ability of the member to access that sum. In *Dalriada Trustee Ltd* v. *Faulds*[7] two such schemes had entered into a reciprocal arrangement whereby they each lent to the other at a rate of interest the requisite sum

[1] G. Newey, 'Constraints on the Exercise of Trustees' Powers', Chapter 2 of this volume, text to nn. 19–31.

[2] *Ibid.*, text between nn. 17 and 18.

[3] *In Re Courage Group's Pension Schemes* [1987] 1 W.L.R. 495, 505.

[4] See *Bank of New Zealand* v. *Board of Management of New Zealand Officers' Provident Association* [2004] 1 N.Z.L.R. 577, [26]; [2003] UKPC 58; *Pitt* v. *Holt* [2012] Ch. 132, [97]; [2011] EWCA Civ 197.

[5] Newey, 'Constraints on the Exercise of Trustees' Powers', text to n. 24.

[6] *Cowan* v. *Scargill* [1985] Ch. 270, 287–8.

[7] [2012] 2 All E.R. 734; [2011] EWHC 3391 (Ch).

on the basis that it was to be lent on to the relevant member in the other scheme.[8] Bean J. (sitting as an additional judge of the Chancery Division) went along with and approved the agreement of counsel that this was a fraud on the power of investment and was as such 'void in equity'.[9] I question whether this is correct given that lending money at interest was within the power and that the purpose of the loan (albeit extraneous to a mere investment) was to benefit the beneficiary (i.e. the member who alone was entitled to the money) and so was not improper.

For the same reason I further question whether on analysis we are dealing here with a separate topic at all or merely an exercise of a power made in breach of trust (which we now know from *Pitt* v. *Holt* renders the exercise voidable rather than void).[10]

The standard required for the proper exercise of the power

This the most important topic takes up by far the majority of Sir Guy's chapter. Although he deals with it under various different headings, the fundamental one, as I see it, is what he calls 'Caprice, reasonableness and rationality'. His analysis of the authorities dealing with it is, if I might be permitted to say so, masterly, indeed 'remarkable', to borrow the word used by Lord Walker in *Pitt* v. *Holt* to describe the judgment of Lloyd L.J. in the Court of Appeal.[11] The fundamental starting point, of course, is that the exercise of any trust power is within the discretion of the trustees and it is not for the court to substitute its own judgment for that of the trustees. So, the question is in what circumstances should the court interfere with the exercise by the trustees of their powers. It is, as Sir Guy points out, a problem that arises in many different areas of the law, notably in the exercise of statutory powers by a public body, and there has been a strong degree of cross fertilisation in the authorities between the approaches of the Court in these different areas.

In many, if not most, cases the exercise by the trustees of their powers is expressed in the trust instrument to be in the trustees' 'absolute discretion' and sometimes the words 'and uncontrolled' are added after 'absolute'. In days gone by these words were held to entail that the only

[8] It was done in this way to avoid the tax charge that would otherwise be imposed on the member.

[9] [2012] 2 All E.R. 734, [57], [80].

[10] *Pitt* v. *Holt* [2012] Ch. 132, [99] (Lloyd L.J.), endorsed on appeal: [2013] 2 A.C. 108, [93]; [2013] UKSC 26.

[11] *Pitt* v. *Holt* [2013] 2 A.C. 108, [5].

fetter on the trustees' discretion was that it must be exercised 'in good faith', meaning honestly.[12] However, the law has, as Sir Guy points out, moved on essentially, as equity has often done in the past, by giving the words 'in good faith' an extended meaning going beyond mere honesty. Sir Guy points out the many different and varied tests that have been adopted in the authorities in an attempt to mark out quite at what point the court can and should intervene.

The more I read Sir Guy's exposition, the more I think that perhaps all that we are here dealing with is a semantic quibble and that the true and only real test is that the trustees must not exercise their powers capriciously, meaning 'for reasons which could be said to be irrational, perverse or irrelevant to any sensible expectation of the settlor'.[13]

I am not convinced that the *Wednesbury* test adopted in *Hastings-Bass* and subsequent authorities, namely the duty to take into account all relevant matters and not to take into account irrelevant matters, is by itself a sufficient basis for the court to intervene. In a public law context, it plainly is because in that context the court is often as much concerned with the manner in which a decision has been reached as with the decision itself. That is not the same as dealing with the exercise of trustee powers. In *Hastings-Bass* itself and subsequent authorities, the question that was posed was whether, had the trustees not taken into account irrelevant matters or failed to take into account relevant matters, they would not have acted in the way that they did. Viewed now in the light of what Lord Walker has said in *Pitt* v. *Holt*, what this appears to entail is that the exercise of the power will not be regarded as a breach of trust simply because the trustee failed to take account of a relevant matter unless he would have acted differently otherwise. I would suggest that the true test must be that, even if the trustee says he would have acted in the same way, the exercise of the power will be set aside if it is regarded as capricious in the light of the matter which the trustee failed to take into account or wrongly took into account. That may be the explanation for *Stannard* v. *Fisons*,[14] where the Court of Appeal set aside the exercise of a power by the trustees of a pension scheme (to determine the amount to go for the benefit of a group of departing members) for failing to take into

[12] See, for example, *Gisborne* v. *Gisborne* (1877) 2 App. Cas. 300, 305 (Lord Cairns L.C.): 'Their discretion . . . always supposing there is no *mala fides* with regard to its exercise, is to be without any check or control from any superior tribunal'.

[13] L. Tucker, N. Le Poidevin and J. Brightwell, *Lewin on Trusts*, 19th ed. (London: Sweet and Maxwell, 2015), [29–153].

[14] [1992] I.R.L.R. 27.

account a highly relevant matter even though the trustees had said that they would have acted in the same way even had they taken that matter into account.

The provision of information relevant to the exercise of the power

Of course, whatever test is adopted to determine whether a trustee has properly exercised a power, a disappointed beneficiary is potentially bereft of a remedy if he is deprived of the ability to force the trustee to divulge to him the basis on which he has done so. In some cases, the exercise might be on the face of it so apparently perverse that the court would be inclined to set it aside unless the trustee is able to provide convincing reasons to justify it. In those circumstances, the beneficiary is able to commence proceedings against the trustee and obtain disclosure in those proceedings of the documents containing the relevant information.

However, in other cases this may not be so clear and, without disclosure of the relevant information, it may be difficult for the beneficiary to be able to plead a sustainable case. This problem is lightly touched upon by Sir Guy.[15] The traditional view is that trustees are not bound to disclose to beneficiaries material which bears upon the exercise by them of their discretions.[16] The justification for the rule was said to be that without it people would be reluctant to become trustees,[17] a reason that can hardly be applied aptly to a corporate trustee whose business is to act as a trustee.

It seems to me, as it does to the editors of *Lewin*,[18] that this rule may need to be re-examined in the light of *Schmidt* v. *Rosewood Trust Ltd.*[19] In that case, the Privy Council held that the entitlement of a beneficiary or object of a power to be provided with trust information and documentation was 'best approached as one aspect of the court's inherent jurisdiction to supervise, and where appropriate intervene in, the administration of trusts'.[20] In reaching its conclusion, the Judicial Committee cited with approval the judgment of Kirby P. in the Court of Appeal of New South Wales in *Hartigan Nominees Pty Ltd* v. *Rydge*,[21] which made reference to

15 Newey, 'Constraints on the Exercise of Trustees' Powers', text to nn. 116–18.

16 *Re Londonderry's Settlement* [1965] Ch. 918.

17 See *Ibid.*, 928, 937; *Finch* v. *Telstra Super Pty Ltd* (2010) 242 C.L.R. 254, [59]; [2010] HCA 36.

18 Tucker, Le Poidevin and Brightwell, *Lewin on Trusts*, 19th ed. [29–234].

19 [2003] 2 A.C. 709; [2003] UKPC 26. 20 [2003] 2 A.C. 709, [66].

21 (1992) 29 N.S.W.L.R. 405.

the beneficiary's 'right of access [to trust documents] which the courts will enforce to uphold the cestui que trust's entitlement to a reasonable assurance of the manifest integrity of the administration of the trust by the trustees'.[22] That must surely extend to material relevant to how the trustees have exercised their powers.

The extent to which the settlor's wishes are to be taken into account in the exercise of a power

Sir Guy has but a single reference to this factor,[23] albeit that in relation to the exercise of dispositive powers, it is generally the most important factor which trustees take into account. In the offshore trust industry, it is sometimes regarded as the only factor to take into account, such that the judges of the Family Division regard an offshore discretionary trust set up by a husband from which he is capable of benefiting as being no more than a colourable device by the husband to evade on divorce his financial obligations to his wife.

Traditionally, the rule is that the trustees should take the settlor's wishes into account but should not slavishly follow them.[24] The rule is often more honoured in its breach than in its observance in that trustees, particularly offshore trust companies, will almost inevitably comply with wishes of the settlor whom they regard as their client. Indeed, in a case which I dealt with in Gibraltar, a professional trustee asserted memorably in cross examination that he regarded the wishes of the settlor as overriding the terms of the trust instrument itself!

That attitude is perhaps understandable. The feeling of these trustees is that their exercise of their powers is less likely to be challenged if they do what the settlor wishes them to do than if they do not. I am not sure that they are right. In my experience, the most likely cause of trust litigation these days is the dissatisfaction by beneficiaries with the actions of their trustee in slavishly, as they see it, following the wishes of the settlor.

This is, I feel, an area where there needs to be more guidance from the courts. It is questionable how far, if the settlor has entrusted the exercise of the discretions wholly to his chosen trustees, the trustees should continue to have regard to his wishes. In particular, it is questionable to what extent they should pay any regard to anything other than his

[22] *Ibid.*, 421.
[23] Newey, 'Constraints on the Exercise of Trustees' Powers', text following n. 94.
[24] Tucker, Le Poidevin and Brightwell, *Lewin on Trusts*, 19th ed. [29–162]–[29–167].

original wishes when the settlement was established. Furthermore, in circumstances where the exercise of a power is apparently justified, if at all, only by the wishes of the settlor, I can see no justification for the trustees' withholding from their beneficiaries production of the settlor's letter of wishes. In my view, the decision of Briggs J. (as he then was) in *Breakspear* v. *Ackland*[25] needs to be re-examined.

25 [2009] Ch. 32; [2008] EWHC 220 (Ch).

4

The administration and maladministration of funds in equity

Making a coherent set of choices

R.C. NOLAN

Introduction

The creation, definition and administration of funds constitute some of the most useful contributions of equity to English private law. Maitland remarked that the trust was 'perhaps . . . the most distinctive achievement of English lawyers';[1] yet the trust would be of very limited utility if its range of application were limited merely to the passive holding of title for another, rather than the active management of a fund of assets. The floating charge, another innovation of equity in the administration of funds, likewise still has great utility in English law, though it has been superseded by statutory systems in many other common law jurisdictions. How a fund is created, ascertained and administered and what is the distribution of rights and interests in a fund of assets are therefore important issues in themselves, but they are not the main focus of this chapter.[2] This chapter is principally concerned with the implications of these matters for remedying the maladministration of a fund: it considers the implications of duly administering a fund for tracing, that is, the process of identifying the assets which may be the subject of a proprietary claim following a breach of trust or equivalent duty.

The key to a proper theoretical understanding of tracing is the notion of exchange, as understood in the administration of funds. This chapter

The author would like to thank Professor Matthew Conaglen, Professor Eilís Ferran, Dr David Fox, Professor Simon Halliday and Dr Peter Turner for comments on drafts of this chapter. The usual disclaimers apply.

1 F.W. Maitland, *Equity: A Course of Lectures*, ed. by A.H. Chaytor and W.J. Whittaker, rev. by J. Brunyate (Cambridge University Press, 1936), 23.

2 The author has addressed these issues before in R.C. Nolan, 'Property in a Fund' (2004) 120 L.Q.R. 108.

argues that the existing law of tracing seeks to mimic, so far as possible, the due administration of the fund, rather than directly to reverse unjust enrichment. In other words, tracing has its theoretical basis in the law relating to fund management, not the law of restitution or unjust enrichment. The distinction is much more than mere semantics. Allowing the capture of exchange products through a combination of tracing and claims founded on the equitable property rights that are the result of tracing may very often overlap with the reversal of unjust enrichment, but they are not necessarily and always the same. The distinction matters crucially from the perspective of timing. Exchanges do not have to be simultaneous. The relative timing of the individual dispositions which comprise an exchange is not the key issue: what is crucial is the presence or absence of a nexus of exchange, as exchange is understood in law and society. Where such a nexus is present, tracing adheres to its basic conceptual principles. As a matter of policy, that in turn keeps the effects of tracing within some bounds. Where there is no such nexus, to allow tracing would be inconsistent with the well-established and accepted equitable principles of administering a fund. If there is to be a coherent approach to the administration and maladministration of funds, where rights and remedies form a consistent set of choices, tracing of that sort is neither necessary nor appropriate.

Such a proper theoretical understanding of tracing matters in the law of trusts. It is particularly important in the debate about so-called 'backwards tracing'. And it also matters crucially in the application of tracing beyond its origins in the law of trusts.

The chapter begins by considering the administration of a trust fund as offering the paradigm case of due administration of a fund in equity and examines the principles and concepts used to describe and establish what amounts to due administration of the fund. It then goes on to consider what implications this correct way of proceeding has for one particular response to the maladministration of a fund – that is, what implications it has for the consequences which follow on from depletion of the fund through a breach of trust or equivalent duty. The chapter focuses on the proprietary rather than personal liabilities which may result from misapplication of assets in breach of trust – and in particular the rules – the tracing rules, which are used to identify the assets which may be the subject of a proprietary claim with a view to restoring the fund. It makes an argument for consistency between the basic right – the right to due administration of a fund – and not just the remedies which vindicate that right but also the procedures, such as tracing, whose purpose is to facilitate some of those remedies. Finally, it considers the implications of the argument for circumstances beyond the paradigm case of the trust fund *stricto sensu*. If there is to be departure in these circumstances from the approach taken in the paradigm case, those departures are neither minor nor trivial.

The due administration of assets in a trust fund

The rules which define what is a trust fund – what assets fall within the fund and why – are obviously vital to the law of trusts. It is axiomatic that the subject matter of a trust must be certain if the trust is to be validly established.[3] The trustees, beneficiaries and the court need to know what assets are subjected to the trust. This matters for the purposes of defining the extent of obligations – the trustees' duties – and the correlative rights of the beneficiaries; and it matters for the purposes of defining the extent of the beneficiaries' proprietary rights, and the correlative extent to which assets owned by a trustee do not form part of his beneficial estate.[4] The rules which define a trust fund also ensure that the collection of assets subject to a trust continues to be identifiable at any point in the future as the individual assets change when the trustees exercise any powers they have (or fulfil their duty) to exchange a trust asset for another asset. Such a continuing ability to identify assets matters for the same reasons that it is vital to identify trust assets in the first place.

These points can be expressed in more general terms in the language of organisational theory:[5] the rules which define a trust fund are necessary for the purposes of asset partitioning and asset management. These rules define which assets are partitioned and subjected to a specific regime of property rights, and priorities amongst those rights. Once the partitioned fund is identified, the fund manager can apply the rules governing its administration.

A very common way of creating a defined fund of assets is to use the concept of legal personality. A corporation is treated as a legal person and 'its' assets – the fund that is to be managed as a separate pool of assets – are determined by application of the general law which governs the allocation and transfer of assets among persons, subject to some glosses

[3] *Knight* v. *Knight* (1840) 3 Beav. 148; 49 E.R. 58.

[4] R.C. Nolan, 'Equitable Property' (2006) 122 L.Q.R. 232.

[5] See, for example, H. Hansmann and U. Mattei, 'The Functions of Trust Law: A Comparative and Economic Analysis' (1998) 73 N.Y.U. L. Rev. 434; H. Hansmann and R. Kraakman, 'The Essential Role of Organizational Law' (2000) 110 Yale L.J. 387.

and modifications to reflect the fact that a corporation is not a natural person. The most important glosses are rules of attribution, through which the behaviour of human beings can, in law, be treated as that of the corporation, an artificial person.[6] Only by application of such rules can a corporation be said to acquire, keep or dispose of assets. An example of the modification of the generally applicable law is the doctrine of *ultra vires* which can preclude a corporation from undertaking an act which a natural person could have done.[7] Another example of modification is the law regulating consideration for the issue of shares by a company. But the use of corporations to create funds of assets basically draws on the ordinary rules governing the allocation of assets between persons, however those rules are glossed and modified. And the most common example of a corporation used to create and manage a distinct fund of assets is a registered company limited by shares.

A trust, however, is not a corporation: the law does not attribute legal personality to a trust, so the use of personality to constitute a fund of assets is not possible. Instead, a specific set of rules is used to determine what constitutes a trust fund. Rules require the identification of the initial fund, and further rules determine what goes into and what comes out of that fund. The scope and operation of these rules are largely unproblematic. Crucial to them is the notion of exchange, as explained below.[8] But it is worth dwelling on these rules for a moment for the sake of clarity before considering the more controversial question of their implications for what happens when the due administration of a trust breaks down.

The trust fund developed out of the settlement of specific assets. The original and basic principle is that assets settled on trust are to be retained for the use and enjoyment of the beneficiaries *in specie*.[9] This primary duty was subject to some exceptions, even in equity, though all these exceptions yielded to any contrary intent expressed in the relevant trust instrument.[10] Some of these exceptions have themselves now been modified by statute law, but again subject to any contrary provision in the trust instrument.[11] Furthermore, trustees were obviously to realise trust

[6] See, for example, *Meridian Global Funds Management Asia Ltd* v. *Securities Commission* [1995] 2 A.C. 500.

[7] *Ashbury Railway Carriage and Iron Co.* v. *Riche* (1879) L.R. 7 H.L. 653. As regards companies formed under the Companies Acts, see now Companies Act 2006 (UK), s. 31.

[8] See the text following n. 42 below.

[9] See, for example, *Pickering* v. *Pickering* (1839) 4 My. & Cr. 289, 298–9; 41 E.R. 113, 116.

[10] Such exceptions include, for example, the rule in *Howe* v. *Earl of Dartmouth* (1802) 7 Ves. Jun. 137; 32 E.R. 56.

[11] See, for example, the Trusts (Capital and Income) Act 2013 (UK).

assets where the settlement directed them to do so, for example where assets were settled on a trust for sale which did not include a power to postpone sale. For present purposes, however, the key exception to the general principle of retaining trust assets *in specie* was that the trustees might lawfully realise trust assets where the settlement authorised them to do so.

When trustees lawfully use such administrative powers to dispose of a trust asset to a purchaser, there are consequences both for the purchaser and for the beneficiaries of the trust.[12] Unless statute provides to the contrary,[13] the purchaser will acquire a derivative title to the asset, or a derivative interest in it, from the trustees: the trustees had some title to the asset and could accordingly pass that title to the purchaser, or confer on him some interest granted out of it. So long as the trustees acted lawfully within their powers, the beneficiaries can have no complaint about this: the beneficiaries' rights are limited *ab initio* by the trustees' powers, so the beneficiaries simply do not have sufficient title to sue the trustees. Furthermore, where the trustees dispose of a trust asset without any breach of trust, the beneficiaries have no grounds for any claim against the purchaser either, so he can enjoy the title he acquired from the trustees free of the beneficiaries' equitable interests or claims. The trustees do not dispose of the beneficiaries' rights, nor do they infringe the principle of *nemo dat quod non habet*. The trustees deal with their property in an asset, and the beneficiaries' property or other interest in that asset is simply so limited that it does not affect a purchaser from the trustees.[14]

In fact, a purchaser's immunity from the beneficiaries' claims may be wider than the trustees' immunity. If the terms of a trust provide that a purchaser is not to be affected by some breach of trust committed in the

[12] The qualification 'lawfully' indicates that the trustees must respect any implicit limitation on their explicit power: for example, they must not use it in bad faith or for an improper purpose. See, generally, R.C. Nolan, 'Controlling Fiduciary Power' [2009] C.L.J. 293 and G. Newey, 'Constraints on the Exercise of Trustees' Powers', Chapter 2 of this volume.

[13] See, for example, Settled Land Act 1925 (UK), s. 18.

[14] Note that sometimes a purchaser will be affected by the beneficiaries' rights because other distinct principles apply to the facts. For example, if Trustees A and B sell an asset to Trustee B within the terms of the trustees' administrative powers, that sale is valid at law (Law of Property Act 1925 (UK), s. 72(4)) and the purchaser (B) is no longer a trustee of the asset, but the sale to him is *voidable* at the instance of the beneficiaries because Trustee B has engaged in self-dealing: *Campbell* v. *Walker* (1800) 5 Ves. Jun. 678; 31 E.R. 801; *Guinness plc* v. *Saunders* [1990] 2 A.C. 663, 697–8 (Lord Goff). See also M. Conaglen, *Fiduciary Loyalty: Protecting the Due Performance of Non-Fiduciary Duties* (Oxford: Hart Publishing, 2010), 77–9, and M. Conaglen, 'Fiduciary Duties and Voluntary Undertakings' (2013) 7 J. Eq. 105, 119–22.

course of the disposition by which he receives a trust asset,[15] then the purchaser will still get good title to the asset even if such a breach of trust has been committed. The trustees, as owners of a trust asset, can still alienate that asset to a purchaser, even though they commit a breach of trust by doing so. The purchaser still has immunity from the beneficiaries' claims, although in this case the trustees do not enjoy a similar immunity. In other words, though the beneficiaries might sue the trustees, the beneficiaries still have insufficient title under the terms of the trust to sue the purchaser. Consequently, the purchaser will acquire title to the asset free of the beneficiary's rights.[16] Again, there is no infringement of the *nemo dat* principle: the trustees still deal with their property in an asset, albeit wrongfully, but the beneficiaries' property or other interest in that asset is still so limited that it does not affect the purchaser from the trustees.

Where trustees act so as to overreach their beneficiaries' rights in an asset, as described above, the beneficiaries will typically get something else, *quid pro quo*. If the trustees do in fact acquire any proceeds from a lawful dealing with a trust asset, the beneficiaries will acquire rights in those proceeds equivalent to their rights in the original asset, unless the terms of the trust in question provide otherwise. Such rights to substitutes depend on a development of English jurisprudence which was, and remains, of great practical importance. In equity, beneficiaries can automatically take proprietary rights in assets which are the proceeds of the trustees' lawful dealing with a trust asset, without the need for any further act by the trustees or the beneficiaries to generate such rights.

What assets shall form part of the fund may be stated explicitly. It has long been very common to provide expressly in trust instruments that beneficiaries shall have equivalent rights in both the initial trust assets and their proceeds, direct and indirect. The form of words used to achieve this end may vary, but the substance is the same.[17] In fact, and

15 See, for example, Trustee Act 1925 (UK), s. 17, Trusts of Land and Appointment of Trustees Act 1996 (UK), ss. 10(1), 16(1), (2) and Lord Millett et al., *The Encyclopaedia of Forms and Precedents*, 5th ed. (London: Butterworths, 2001), vol. 40(1), 291, clause 5.

16 See, generally, D. Fox, 'Overreaching', in P. Birks and A. Pretto (eds.), *Breach of Trust* (Oxford: Hart Publishing, 2002), 99–100. For completeness, it should be remembered that there are some (generally statutory) limitations on how far the terms of a trust may exonerate a purchaser from the effects of a breach of trust: see, for example, Law of Property Act 1925 (UK), ss. 2 and 27(2) as regards the payment to trustees of capital proceeds from land.

17 So, for example, the Society of Trust and Estate Practitioners' standard provisions (2nd ed.) use the following definitions: '"Trust Fund" means the property comprised in the Trust for the time being' and '"Trust Property" means any property comprised in the

though lawyers still tend to draft trusts which expressly entitle beneficiaries to such rights, express words are rarely strictly necessary, whatever comfort they give to the lawyers concerned. Where trustees lawfully dispose of a trust asset, and in exchange acquire some other asset, equity has long recognised that beneficiaries who had an interest in the original asset may prima facie claim an equivalent interest in the substitute.[18]

A beneficiary's right to assets lawfully acquired by trustees in substitution for other assets always depends on the terms of the relevant trust, however: the beneficiary would not have such a right if the trust instrument provided to that effect, which very occasionally it might. For example, if a trust provided that realty should be held for X, personalty for Y, and the trustees exercised a power conferred on them to sell land and turn it into money, then Y, not X, would take an interest in what had become personalty.[19]

Trust Fund'. The *Encyclopaedia of Forms and Precedents* is a little more expansive: '"the Trust Fund" means the sum of £ . . . cash paid by the Settlor to the Original Trustees as recited above, all assets at any time added to it by way of further settlement accumulation of income capital accretion or otherwise and all property from time to time representing the same': Millett et al., *The Encyclopaedia of Forms and Precedents*, 5th ed., vol. 40(1), 283.

18 See, for example, *Burdett* v. *Willett* (1708) 2 Vern. 638; 23 E.R. 1017 (a factor held goods as trustee for the plaintiff, lawfully sold them, and was likewise a trustee of the proceeds for the plaintiff, which therefore did not form part of the factor's estate in bankruptcy) and *Ex p. Chion* (1721) 3 P. Wms. 185, 187, n(2); 24 E.R. 1023 (a trader held money for another and used it to buy South-sea stock in his own name but for the account of that other; the trader held the stock on trust for the other, and so the stock did not form part of the trader's estate in bankruptcy). Indeed, this right to lawfully acquired substitutes was so well established by the early nineteenth century that it formed common ground between the parties in *Taylor* v. *Plumer* (1815) 3 M. & S. 562; 105 E.R. 721.

19 *Rich* v. *Whitfield* (1866) L.R. 2 Eq. 583, but note the Settled Land Act 1925 (UK), s. 75(5). See also J.S. Vaizey, *A Treatise on the Law of Settlements of Property* (London: Sweet & Sons, 1887), vol. 1, 424. A trust which obliged (rather than merely permitted) trustees to convert realty into personalty, or *vice versa*, was until recently treated differently from a power to effect such conversion. For the purpose of determining equitable entitlements under a trust, interests under a trust for sale of land were treated *ab initio* as interests in personalty, and likewise personalty which was to be used to buy land, or was to be sold and the proceeds used to buy land, was itself treated as land: Vaizey, *A Treatise on the Law of Settlements of Property*, 425; Maitland, *Equity: A Course of Lectures*, ed. by Chaytor and Whittaker, rev. by Brunyate, 215ff; R.E. Megarry and H.W.R. Wade, *The Law of Real Property*, 5th ed. (London: Stevens, 1984), 431–4. This was a consequence of the 'doctrine of conversion', which was abolished on 1 January 1997 by section 3 of the Trusts of Land and Appointment of Trustees Act 1996 (UK), subject to minor transitional savings. Even before its abolition, however, the doctrine did not apply for all purposes: see, for example, *Williams & Glyn's Bank Ltd* v. *Boland* [1981] A.C. 487.

Trustees might also acquire assets by way of further settlement,[20] or from someone who is obliged for value to settle such assets on them.[21] In the former case, the beneficiaries' interests must attach to the assets in question when the trustees receive them, because '[p]roperty which is not presently owned cannot be impressed with a trust any more than it can be effectively assigned'.[22] In the latter case, the beneficiaries' interests attach to an asset within the scope of the obligation once the obligor must and can deliver the asset to the trustees – normally, that is, when he receives it.[23]

All this means that an expressly created trust fund will be something quite particular. It will be the product of a particular bargain or undertaking to which equity gives effect, not the direct result of some rule of law. That particular bargain or undertaking subjects the trustees' property in a class of assets to whatever equitable proprietary rights a beneficiary may have, but in turn gives the trustees limited powers to deal with the assets free of the beneficiary's rights. In addition, the bargain or undertaking almost invariably grants the beneficiary rights in any product of such a dealing which are equivalent to the rights he enjoyed in the original assets. The general law then gives effect to the bargain or undertaking and supplements it where necessary. Express terms are supreme, save where they contravene some mandatory provision of law, and implied terms deal with issues where express terms have no effect.

This analysis also explains what happens to property in a trust fund when things go wrong. When trust assets are misapplied, equitable proprietary rights in those assets are not overreached. The rights continue to affect the assets until the assets reach the hands of someone who is, by operation of law, immune from the rights, such as a *bona fide* purchaser of a legal interest in the assets for value without notice of the rights. Consequently, the beneficiary can assert his right in the asset in accordance with normal rules of priority. There is no need to explain the rights as only having proprietary effect following the misapplication.[24]

20 See, for example, the language commonly used to define a trust fund in the text to n. 17: this envisages further settlement.

21 For an exposition of the complicated law relating to covenants to settle property, see D. Hayton, P. Matthews and C. Mitchell, *Underhill and Hayton: The Law Relating to Trusts and Trustees*, 18th ed. (London: LexisNexis, 2010), [9.76]–[9.121].

22 *Williams* v. *Commissioners of Inland Revenue* [1965] N.Z.L.R. 395, 401 (Turner J.).

23 *Pullan* v. *Koe* [1913] 1 Ch. 9.

24 The view put forward by the author here, and previously in 'Property in a Fund' (2004) 120 L.Q.R. 108, has been adopted in the D.J. Hayton and C. Mitchell, *Hayton & Marshall: Commentary and Cases on the Law of Trusts and Equitable Remedies*, 12th ed. (London:

The beneficiary will also be able to trace into substitutes for the misapplied asset and claim an interest in such a substitute, subject to any defences available to other people who have an interest in the substitute.[25] However, such rights to substitutes are generated by mandatory rules of law, rather than by voluntary undertakings to which the law gives effect.[26]

The administration of assets derived improperly from a trust fund

The question for this chapter is, therefore: what is the relevance of the rules governing the due administration of a trust fund – a body of rules founded primarily on consensual agreement and implications into such an agreement, given effect by law – on the rules of mandatory law which identify the assets in which a beneficiary may assert a proprietary right following a breach of trust? The core argument of this chapter is that the former set of rules must have significant implications for the latter set of rules, or else various absurdities result. This is because the tracing rules are purposive. They do not exist in a vacuum. They are rules that exist to identify assets for the purposes of restoring due administration of a trust fund. They are not Platonic universals.

Sweet & Maxwell, 2005), [1–58] and C. Mitchell, *Hayton & Mitchell: Commentary and Cases on the Law of Trusts and Equitable Remedies*, 13th ed. (London: Sweet & Maxwell, 2010), [1–52]; but contrast previous editions of *Hayton & Marshall*. The situation described in the text is not the only one in which a person interested in a trust may reclaim misapplied assets. For example, the beneficiaries of a discretionary trust may not have a right in the fund which can reasonably be called proprietary, because it fails to satisfy the commonly accepted *indicia* of such a right. (See n. 19 and the texts cited there.) Nevertheless, such beneficiaries can reclaim misapplied assets: see generally Hayton, Matthews and Mitchell, *Underhill and Hayton: Law Relating to Trusts and Trustees*, 18th ed. [2.9]–[2.15], and J.D. Heydon, M.J. Leeming and P.G. Turner, *Meagher, Gummow & Lehane's Equity: Doctrines & Remedies*, 5th ed. (Sydney: LexisNexis, 2015), [4–060], [4–170]–[4–085]. In that regard, their respective interests share features with an equitable proprietary interest under a trust, even though in other regards those interests are so significantly different as not to warrant the epithet 'proprietary'.

25 See *Foskett* v. *McKeown* [2001] 1 A.C. 102.

26 The right of a beneficiary following an *authorised* disposition of trust property is a right to the substitute asset(s), if there are any, and unless the trust provides otherwise. Following an *unauthorised* disposition of trust assets, the beneficiary may have a similar interest in the substitute asset(s), but that will depend on his election: purely personal relief aside, he could, in the alternative, elect to claim a lien over those substitute asset(s) to secure due reinstatement of the trust fund. See generally, Fox, 'Overreaching', in Birks and Pretto (eds.), *Breach of Trust*, ch. 4.

Tracing is about identifying one asset as a substitute, in whole or in part, for another. What amounts to a 'substitute' asset is a matter of positive law, not a fact of nature: tracing is in that sense a matter of attribution. Rules of attribution – including the tracing rules – exist for a purpose, and their content is informed by that purpose. The core purpose of the equitable tracing rules is to identify assets for the purposes of a claim to redress a breach of trust. The claim may be proprietary, for example the assertion of a beneficial interest in,[27] or a charge over,[28] the asset in question, or it may be a personal claim founded on a proprietary right, for example a claim for knowing receipt (or unconscionable retention) of an asset in which such a proprietary right subsisted.[29]

Tracing must therefore reflect the rules governing how a breach of trust should be redressed. So, for example, the principle that a wrongdoing trustee may not take advantage of his own wrong is reflected in presumptions against a trustee in the allocation of a mixed fund derived from both his own assets and the trust fund.[30] Another crucial principle of trust law which must be reflected in the tracing rules is the principle that beneficiaries are entitled to respond to a breach of trust, if they so wish, by treating the trustee's wrongful acts as done for their benefit.[31] This means that the beneficiaries can claim rights in an asset the trustee acquired by wrongful use of trust funds (whether directly or through a chain of transactions), because the trustee can be treated as acting for their benefit.

But the beneficiaries cannot do more: they cannot have access to more assets in the hands of the trustee than they would have had if the trustee's actions had been undertaken for their benefit. As so often, the point has been made by Maitland.

> Observe that metaphor of 'investment'. We conceived that the 'trust fund' can change its dress, but maintain its identity. To-day it appears as a piece of land; tomorrow it may be some gold coins in a purse; then it will be a sum of Consols; then it will be shares in a Railway Company, and then Peruvian Bonds. When all is going well, changes of investment may often

[27] *Foskett* v. *McKeown* [2001] 1 A.C. 102. [28] *Re Hallett's Estate* (1879) 13 Ch. D. 696.

[29] *El Ajou* v. *Dollar Land Holdings plc* [1994] 2 All E.R. 685.

[30] *Lupton* v. *White* (1808) 15 Ves. Jun. 432; 33 E.R. 817; *Re Hallett's Estate* (1879) 13 Ch. D. 696; *Re Oatway* [1903] 2 Ch. 356, 359 (Joyce J.); *Re Tilley's Will Trusts* [1967] Ch. 1179, 1183 (Ungoed-Thomas J.).

[31] See, for example, D. Hayton, 'The Development of Equity and the "Good Person" Philosophy in Common Law Systems' [2012] Conv. 263, 265–7; P. Millett, 'Proprietary Restitution', in S. Degeling and J. Edelman (eds.), *Equity in Commercial Law* (Sydney: Lawbook Co., 2005), ch. 12.

> be made; the trustees have been given power to make them. All along the 'trust fund' retains its identity. 'The price of takes the place of the object' we might say, 'and the object takes the place of the price'. But the same idea is applied even when all is not going well. Suppose that a trustee sells land meaning to misappropriate the price. The price is paid to him in the shape of a bank-note which is now in his pocket. That bank-note belongs 'in equity' to the destinatories [*sc.* beneficiaries]. He pays it away as the price of shares in a company; those shares belong 'in equity' to the destinatories. He becomes bankrupt; those shares will not be part of the property that is divisible among his creditors; they will belong to the destinatories. And then, again, if the trustee mixes 'trust money' with his own money, we are taught to say that, so long as this is possible, we must suppose him to be an honest man and to be spending, not other people's money, but his own.[32]

The tracing rules are thus framed by reference to the rules which determine what assets are comprised within a duly administered trust fund. As Viscount Radcliffe noted, 'Equity in fact calls into existence and protects equitable rights and interests in property only where their recognition has been found to be required in order to give effect to its doctrines.'[33]

This conceptualisation of tracing, derived from the cases, has significant theoretical implications: while the notion of replenishing a fund to its proper state as if it had been duly administered may often overlap with the notion of reversing unjust enrichment, it is not the same thing, and it explains the cases and their reasoning more accurately. If there is to be a departure from this conceptualisation to a conceptualisation based on unjust enrichment theory, that change would amount to much more than just a minor exercise in tidying up: it would either produce results that are inconsistent with the law of trusts and fiduciary fund management or else necessitate different tracing rules for different purposes, creating complexity rather than simplicity. In neither case is the change minor or insignificant. The rest of this section shows why.

The tracing rules are a process, but they are a process directed towards an end – identifying assets for the purposes of claims. Claims for breach

[32] F.W. Maitland, 'Trust and Corporation', in D. Runciman and M. Ryan (eds.), *F.W. Maitland: State, Trust and Corporation* (Cambridge University Press, 2003), 94–5. The point was made at least as long ago as Lord Ellenborough's judgment in *Taylor* v. *Plumer* (1815) 3 M. & S. 562, 574; 105 E.R. 721, 725–6, where he explicitly rejects the arguments of Mr Marryat, counsel for the plaintiff, reported at (1815) 3 M. & S. 562, 567; 105 E.R. 721, 723.

[33] *Commissioner of Stamp Duties (Qld)* v. *Livingston* [1965] A.C. 694, 712 (Viscount Radcliffe).

of trust, naturally, reflect the obligations of a trustee. A trustee must perform his office. A trustee cannot claim to act for his own benefit in breach of trust, subject only to the payment of compensation for loss caused by his action. To put the point in more generalised terms, trust law does not admit of an 'efficient breach of trust': a trustee is not an economic actor who is independent of the beneficiary and may divest himself of his obligations to the beneficiary, subject to the payment of compensation for loss caused thereby. The beneficiary is not, therefore, obliged to acknowledge the wrong and seek compensation for it, though of course he may do so. The beneficiary can, in the alternative and at his election, claim to take the benefit of what the defaulting trustee has done, notwithstanding that it amounts to a wrong. In short, the basic approach to remedying a breach of trust is founded on the idea that a trustee cannot be heard to say he has done wrong.[34] This is very different from the position of someone who breaches a contract. In the vast majority of cases, a contract breaker is not required to do right, or to account for whatever he has done on the (counterfactual) basis that he did it in performance of the contract. All he has to do is to pay damages for the loss which in law results from the breach;[35] and if he has, as a result of his wrongdoing, made a profit which exceeds that loss, he may keep the excess.[36]

The next question is, therefore, how do the tracing rules serve to facilitate this approach to remedying a breach of trust? After all, if the tracing rules truly are just a process, then the principles governing actions for breach of trust – the principles which govern how a beneficiary's rights may be vindicated – must inform the rules, not *vice versa*.

Claims on (or regarding) substitute assets constitute one example of a claim where the beneficiary seeks to take benefit from what the trustee has done: any such claim relies on what the trustee has done to give the beneficiary rights in an asset that he would not otherwise have. The beneficiary's claim, whatever it may be, is founded on those rights. The beneficiary might be able to claim an equitable ownership interest in that asset.[37] He might be able to make a personal claim to vindicate an equitable ownership interest in that asset, such as a claim for knowing

[34] See, for example, the texts cited at n. 24 above.

[35] *Hadley* v. *Baxendale* (1854) 9 Ex. 341; 156 E.R. 145 as interpreted in *Transfield Shipping Inc.* v. *Mercator Shipping Inc. (The Achilleas)* [2009] 1 A.C. 61; [2008] UKHL 48.

[36] The exception to the general rule, where 'gain based damages' may be recovered, is very limited, whatever the arguments about its precise extent: *A.-G.* v. *Blake* [2001] 1 A.C. 268.

[37] *Foskett* v. *McKeown* [2001] 1 A.C. 102.

receipt (or unconscionable retention).[38] He might be able to claim a security interest in the asset, either directly[39] or via subrogation.[40] Where more than one such claim is possible, the facts, or, if needs be, the beneficiary's election, will govern which is pursued and awarded. Indeed, the beneficiary's election (where it is available) between an ownership interest and a security interest also reflects the ability of the beneficiary either to take the benefit of what the trustee has done, and claim that the asset is held for the beneficiary, or to repudiate what the trustee has done and hold the asset as security for the trustee's obligation to make 'compensation' for his wrongdoing in the *Re Dawson* sense of replenishing the trust fund.[41] But the key point, for present purposes, is that any claim on the asset, or on a person in respect of an interest in the asset, is a claim where the beneficiary seeks to take benefit from what the trustee has done in acquiring the asset: the beneficiary in every such claim necessarily treats, and is allowed to treat, the trustee's actions in acquiring the asset as if they were something done for his benefit, even though that is contrary to the facts.

In summary, therefore, the position is this. When a trustee wrongfully deals with trust assets, the beneficiary can assert that the trustee's actions are to be treated as if they were undertaken for his (the beneficiary's) benefit. When a trustee deals with the wrongfully acquired substitutes for trust assets, the beneficiary can make the same assertion. But it is implicit in any such assertion that the beneficiary cannot claim *more* than if the trustee had acted rightfully.

The same principles apply to tracing into or through the hands of anyone whose conscience is affected. The principle is still that the beneficiary can seek to have that person's actions treated as if they had been undertaken properly and for his (the beneficiary's) benefit. And as before, the applicable tracing rules mirror this. There is an entirely separate, and for present purposes irrelevant, debate to be had about whether the rules determining who is a wrongdoer are too wide and draw too many into their ambit. But that does not affect the points about tracing once it is accepted, at least for present purposes, that such people are wrongdoers.

Tracing against innocent volunteers is different and does not follow the paradigm explained above.[42] That is entirely consistent with the basic

[38] *El Ajou* v. *Dollar Land Holdings plc* [1994] 2 All E.R. 685.

[39] *Re Hallett's Estate* (1879) 13 Ch. D. 696. [40] *Boscawen* v. *Bajwa* [1996] 1 W.L.R. 328.

[41] [1966] 2 N.S.W.R. 211.

[42] *Re Diplock* [1948] Ch. 465; *Barlow Clowes International Ltd (in liq.)* v. *Vaughan* [1992] 4 All E.R. 22.

thesis that the tracing rules are informed by the purposes of the claims they facilitate. When tracing against a trustee, or someone who is in no better position than a trustee, the rules are modelled to identify assets as if the trustee's (or similar person's) actions had occurred in the due administration of the trust, given that the very notion of tracing involves relying on the trustee's (and possibly the third party's) actions. The innocent volunteer, *ex hypothesi*, is not under the managerial obligations of a trustee and cannot be treated as so obliged: his conscience is not affected by the obligations of a trustee, even though he cannot (being a volunteer) claim priority to the interests of the beneficiaries. The rules have to reflect that. But crucially, for present purposes, the rules applied to an innocent volunteer are *less* stringent than those applicable to trustees and wrongdoers, *not more* stringent. In short, the core case, and the case by which the rules applicable to others are measured – and measured more leniently, where innocent volunteers are concerned – is the case of the trustee. And the tracing rules as they apply to a trustee are modelled on the due administration of a trust for reasons given above, namely to give the beneficiaries access to assets which they would have had if the trustee's actions had been rightful, but no more.

This brings the focus of attention back to the question of how trust assets are identified when administered properly. The answer, where the constitution of the fund is in the hands of the trustee, and not the result of further settlement, lies, as has been seen earlier, in the concept of exchange. Two points should be mentioned here, before going on. First, exchange means expenditure of trust funds in return for some interest in an asset, not necessarily in exchange for the acquisition of full title to the asset. Secondly, exchange is only used to identify the asset in which an interest is sought; it does not dictate what interest is then asserted in that asset, which depends on the transaction in question, whether a purchase, a lease, a charge or some other disposition.

Now, once it is said that the key notion is *exchange*, as understood and defined in the law relating to the administration of trusts, the question becomes what that means. In order to answer that question, it is necessary to look in trust doctrine, to examine some examples, to see what is meant by exchange.

Take the example of buying a particular, ascertained, book. Assume title to the book passes on contract, in accordance with Sale of Goods Act 1979 (UK), section 18, rule 1, and in advance of payment for the book. If the purchaser were a trustee, seeking to use trust funds lawfully to buy the book, how would we characterise his actions? It would be necessary to do so, for example, in order to ascertain whether the trustee had acted within his powers under the terms of the trust to deal lawfully with the trust fund. To answer that question requires both a correct understanding (construction) of the trustee's powers and also correct characterisation of what the trustee has done, to see whether the trustee's action was permitted by his powers. In the scenario outlined above, the transaction would be characterised as a purchase (exchange of money for a chattel) using trust funds, lawfully made by the trustee if he had power to purchase a book.

This example also shows the importance of understanding characterisation correctly as a purposive activity. The juridical characterisation of facts is always (and inevitably) undertaken from a perspective and for a purpose. In general terms, there is no one single 'correct' characterisation of facts; and to suggest otherwise is bizarre. A single individual can be categorised quite correctly, for different purposes, as a man, a human being, English, a lawyer and so on and so forth. Categorisation is purposive, not absolute.

So, the characterisation of the above transaction from the perspective of the parties and for the purposes of determining their rights and liabilities *inter se* at any given moment may perfectly well be as follows. First, the purchaser of the book (the trustee) gains title to the book, by reason of the unrebutted presumption of Sale of Goods Act 1979, section 18, rule 1. Secondly, the book shop advances credit to the purchaser (trustee) for a short period, credit that could be satisfied by the transfer of cash, and in the meantime holds the rights of an unpaid seller under sections 38(1)(a) and 39 of the Sale of Goods Act 1979. Thirdly, the period of credit is terminated by the purchaser's (trustee's) delivery of the cash to the book shop with the intention that the shop should become owner of it, thereby transferring title to the cash and discharging the purchaser's (trustee's) outstanding contractual obligations.

But that is not the way to characterise the same facts from the perspective of the trustee's beneficiary for the purposes of determining whether the trustee acted within the scope of his powers and duties.[43] The transaction would not be characterised for those purposes as an acquisition on credit and discharge of that credit. There would be no investigation of the terms of the trust to discover whether the trustee could borrow or take credit. This transaction would undoubtedly be permitted if the trustee had power to purchase chattels but did not

[43] Cf. L. Smith, 'Tracing into the Payment of a Debt' [1995] C.L.J. 290.

have power to borrow or take credit. That is very simply because the transaction is characterised in context and in its entirety for the purposes of deciding what the trustee may and may not do: equity looks to substance not form. The transaction is not broken down into the constituent steps of contractual performance for those purposes; and there is no reason why it should be, because what matters for the purposes of trust administration is the nature of the transaction as a whole, by which its lawfulness as between trustee and beneficiary is to be judged.

If the trustee did the same thing, but this time had no power to buy a book and so acted in breach of trust, how would we characterise the transaction? Again, as exchange, and for the same reasons, but this time for the purposes of tracing. However, the fact that, when tracing, a beneficiary is addressing actions which are *ex hypothesi* wrongful (in breach of trust) is reflected in the fact that he is offered elections: first, the beneficiary may choose whether or not to trace at all (i.e. whether or not to assert any sort of remedy that relies on the trustee's albeit wrongful action); secondly, even when the beneficiary does decide to trace assets, and does so successfully, he may assert a right to claim the asset (or a share in it) if the trust funds were used to acquire it, or else hold the asset as security for the monetary restoration of the trust fund. This is where the wrongfulness of the trustee's actions is accommodated: in the decision whether or not to trace, and in the choice of remedies a beneficiary may assert, not by warping notions used to identify assets in respect of which he may assert a remedy.

The very recent decision of the Privy Council in *Brazil* v. *Durant*[44] is entirely consistent with – indeed, it applies – this thesis. The Mayor of São Paulo had taken bribes in breach of his duty to the City. São Paulo, together with the Brazilian Federal authorities, claimed that the Mayor therefore held the bribes on constructive trust for the City.[45] The bribes were paid away to other people in the process of money laundering. The Brazilian authorities alleged that monies in the hands of the defendant, Durant, represented the traceable proceeds of those bribes, and therefore argued that Durant held those monies subject to a constructive trust in favour of São Paulo. Durant resisted this claim by arguing, *inter alia*, that some of the monies were not the traceable proceeds of the bribes. The monies had been paid to the defendant from an account in

[44] [2015] 3 W.L.R. 599; [2015] UKPC 35.

[45] Though *Brazil* v. *Durant* was a case from Jersey, the law concerning bribes was taken to be the same as English law, as re-stated in *FHR European Ventures LLP* v. *Cedar Capital Partners LLC* [2015] A.C. 250; [2014] UKSC 45.

New York controlled by the Mayor's son. However, three of the payments into the New York account – payments which had been identified as the proceeds of the bribe – were in fact made after the payment of monies from the account to the defendant. Hence, the defendant argued that those three payments into the New York account could not be traced on into its hands, as that would amount to 'backwards tracing' and there was no sound doctrinal basis for such 'backwards tracing'.[46] The Privy Council rejected that argument and held that the monies were the traceable proceeds of the original bribes.

Does that give the green light to all 'backwards tracing'? Quite properly, and consistently with principle, it appears not. Lord Toulson, giving the advice of the Privy Council, was very careful to emphasise that in general:

> Whether it [*sc.* an asset] can properly be traced into another asset depends on whether there is a sufficient transactional link. In considering that question the court should concentrate on the substance of the transaction and not the form;[47]

and that:

> The Board therefore rejects the argument that there can never be backward tracing, or that the court can never trace the value of an asset whose proceeds are paid into an overdrawn account. But the claimant has to establish a coordination between the depletion of the trust fund and the acquisition of the asset which is the subject of the tracing claim, looking at the whole transaction, such as to warrant the court attributing the value of the interest acquired to the misuse of the trust fund. This is likely to depend on inference from the proved facts, particularly since in many cases the testimony of the trustee, if available, will be of little value.[48]

On the facts, the Privy Council held that the Jersey courts, whose judgments were under appeal, had been entitled to conclude that there was a single transaction which, as a matter of law, warranted tracing into its proceeds, and that therefore the Privy Council should uphold their decision allowing such tracing and the claims based on it.

In other words, the law recognised that the parties to the payments had sought, and had achieved, the effect of exchanging a credit at a New York bank for a credit standing to the account of the defendants. And the defendant was not allowed, as a matter of positive law, to resist the

46 [2015] 3 W.L.R. 599, [10].
47 *Ibid.*, [32], considering *Foskett* v. *McKeown* [2001] 1 A.C. 102.
48 [2015] 3 W.L.R. 599, [40].

claimant's assertion that the latter was entitled to the benefit and proceeds of that exchange. The fact that the characterisation of facts as an exchange can sometimes be difficult or contestible is neither here nor there. Characterisation is unavoidable for the purposes of applying legal rules couched in general terms. Given the extensive legal and social understanding of what is meant by an 'exchange', this making characterisation should not be so difficult as to cast doubt on its practical utility. Equally, the fact that the events could (and would) be analysed differently as between the paying and receiving banks is, for reasons stated earlier, immaterial.[49] The juridical characterisation of facts is always undertaken from a perspective and for a purpose. Indeed, that is inevitable.

The examples given above can be contrasted with an example of 'true' backwards tracing. The case law does not admit of such backwards tracing.[50] And there are very good reasons for that, namely the need for consistency of claims founded on tracing with the due administration of a trust. Suppose an individual took out a bank loan, bought a car with the loan monies and then used monies he held on trust to repay the loan. If the trustee were to seek to justify his action as lawful, within the terms of the trust, he would have to show both that the terms of the trust permitted him to borrow for the purposes of buying a car, so that the loan monies became part of the trust fund, and the trustee correspondingly had authority to use trust funds in repayment of the loan, and also that the terms of the trust permitted him to buy a car using trust monies. Both authorities must be shown. If the trustee did not have power to borrow, then whatever his intentions, the trustee would be personally liable for the debt he incurred, but he could not look to the trust fund to repay the loan, whilst the loan monies would be his beneficially and would not constitute trust monies. Their use in buying the car, therefore, would not give the beneficiaries any rights in the car: in that case, the trustee's own monies were paid in exchange for the car, not trust monies. Why should a breach of trust in using trust monies to repay the trustee's own personal indebtedness give the beneficiaries greater rights? Why should this sort of 'backwards tracing' be the means through which the beneficiaries can acquire any greater rights? There is no reason whatsoever.[51] It is one thing to say that a beneficiary may elect to take the benefit of his trustee's misadministration of trust

[49] See the text to and preceding n. 43 above.

[50] See M. Conaglen, 'Difficulties with Tracing Backwards' (2011) 127 L.Q.R. 432.

[51] See *Bishopsgate Investment Management Ltd (in liq.)* v. *Homan* [1995] Ch. 211, 220 (Leggatt L.J.).

assets;[52] but it is quite another to allow the beneficiary to claim some benefit from the trustee's use of what are undoubtedly the trustee's own assets.[53] That said, the trustee may well have been enriched. So naturally the beneficiaries should have personal remedies against the trustee, and quite possibly the right to be subrogated to any security for the loan. But whatever the matter of enrichment, the nexus of exchange is not present so as to warrant proprietary rights in the car.

One more example might be useful. The following argument has been made.

> [I]t would seem that 'backward tracing' must be accepted if one is to explain tracing into and through 'in credit' bank accounts. This is because if one is tracing funds into a bank account, the account is often credited before the bank has received the relevant funds. In other words, the debt owed by the bank to the customer, which is treated as a substitute for the funds, exists in advance of the funds being received.[54]

In fact, there is no need for so-called backwards tracing to explain what happens in these circumstances. A credit is only applied to the account because the crediting bank has been informed that it will receive funds debited from another account which constitutes, or through a prior process of tracing, represents, trust monies. If that information turns out to be wrong, the credit will be reversed. Just as in the earlier example of buying a book where the book is delivered before the tender of cash in payment, there is an exchange. The concept of exchange does not necessarily entail simultaneous performance, though a particular contractual term in a particular contract may do so. And the concept of exchange does not necessarily entail that one particular side perform before the other. In other words, the new credit is perfectly properly described and characterised as the exchange product of the misapplied funds, notwithstanding that the credit was raised in anticipation of receiving the funds, assuming that the funds were subsequently received. And if those funds are not subsequently received, there will be no exchange, and the credit will be reversed.[55]

Exchange is the concept that warrants the beneficiaries' acquisition of proprietary rights in substitute assets in the course of the due

[52] See n. 26 above. [53] Cp. *James Roscoe (Bolton) Ltd* v. *Winder* [1915] 1 Ch. 62.

[54] A. Burrows, *The Law of Restitution*, 3rd ed. (Oxford University Press, 2011), 142.

[55] See now *Relfo Ltd (in liq.)* v. *Varsani* [2015] 1 B.C.L.C. 14, [60]–[64]; [2014] EWCA Civ 360 (Arden L.J., with whom Gloster and Floyd L.JJ. agreed at [101] and [106] respectively).

administration of a trust fund. It would be perverse if a wider notion than exchange were used to warrant their acquisition of such rights following a breach of trust: otherwise the process of tracing would enable the remedy to become greater than right. This is quite aside from the practical consideration of the untoward effect of such unprincipled tracing on the holders of unsecured claims. An unsecured creditor can only look for satisfaction of his claim to the debtor's beneficially owned assets after discharge of encumbrances on them. That pool of available assets would be further depleted by allowing tracing in the absence of exchange: that would increase the number of assets against which a proprietary claim might lie, having priority to the creditor's unsecured claim.

As it happens, though it is not the main point of this chapter, the notion of exchange also underlies some, but not all, of the remedies which may follow a successful exercise in tracing. It is exchange that warrants a beneficiary's election, where such an election is possible after tracing, to assert a beneficial ownership of an asset or a beneficial undivided share in an asset, thus capturing for the trust fund uplift in value of the asset. When one asset is exchanged for a beneficial interest in another, it is axiomatic in our system of law that acquisition of that interest carries with it the fruits of that interest and any uplift in its value, *absent* some specific provision to the contrary like provision for overage payments. Tracing is based in the concept of exchange; and the remedies consequent on it admit the normal consequences of that concept, though these consequences are not mandated, given that the relevant exchange was, from the perspective of the beneficiaries, improper. The result in *Foskett* v. *McKeown*[56] is entirely consistent with principle; though in *Foskett*, what rights were exchanged for what others was a matter of contention and difficulty. That does not affect the principle. It is often possible that reasonable people may differ in the application of the principle to difficult facts.[57] Equally, the evidence may be such that the principles are difficult to apply, and consequently some indulgence may be shown towards

[56] [2001] 1 A.C. 102.

[57] A well-known example is the occasional difficulty in applying the principle governing conflicts of duty and interest. 'The division in the House of Lords in *Phipps* v. *Boardman* respecting the application of principle to the facts in that case indicates that different minds may reach different conclusions as to the presence or absence of a real or substantial possibility of conflict between duty and interest or between duty and duty': *Pilmer* v. *Duke Group Ltd (in liq.)* (2001) 207 C.L.R. 165, [79]; [2001] HCA 31 (McHugh, Gummow, Hayne and Callinan JJ.).

claimants who suffer a lack of information which makes application of the principles difficult.[58] But that too does not affect the principle.

Finally, there are some well-known but difficult cases that may at first sight appear to test the notion of exchange used in tracing; but they are perfectly consistent with it. In some cases, misapplied trust monies are used to discharge a secured debt, and the beneficiaries of the trust may be granted a new charge over the asset which formerly stood as security for the debt discharged with the trust funds.[59] In other cases, the misapplied trust monies may be used to improve existing property, and it is possible for the beneficiaries to be granted a charge over the property.[60] In yet other cases, misapplied trust assets may be destroyed by their use in the manufacture of a new asset; and it is arguable that the beneficiaries can acquire a charge over that asset.[61] In all these cases, there is no item of property constituting the exchange product of the misapplied trust funds. There simply is no asset resulting from the transaction which the beneficiaries could claim, or in which they could share: were beneficiaries to try and treat the transaction as if undertaken on their behalf, they would be entitled to nothing. So there is no tracing into the asset. Yet there can be a proprietary remedy for the beneficiaries by way of charge. In such a case, the beneficiaries gain no rights in the asset itself. Instead, a charge may be imposed *de novo* by way of remedy, founded on the distinct principles of subrogation.

Summary

The principle which informs remedies for breach of trust is not to reverse unjust enrichment, but to restore the due administration of the trust, whether by compensating losses caused to the trust fund or capturing

[58] For example, Buckley L.J. said 'it is a fundamental feature of the doctrine of tracing that the property to be traced can be identified at every stage of its journey through life': *Borden (UK) Ltd* v. *Scottish Timber Products Ltd* [1981] Ch. 25, 46F. Yet, as Millett J. noted in *El Ajou* v. *Dollar Land Holdings plc* [1993] 3 All E.R. 717, 734–6, presumptions may be used against a wrongdoer in the absence of evidence, and in other circumstances the court may well draw inferences as to identification based on limited positive evidence. Millett J.'s views were accepted and applied by the Court of Appeal in *Relfo Ltd (in liq.)* v. *Varsani* [2015] 1 B.C.L.C. 14, [60]–[64].

[59] *Boscawen* v. *Bajwa* [1996] 1 W.L.R. 328.

[60] *Re Diplock* [1948] Ch. 465, 547–8 where the possibility was admitted but defeated on the facts by a defence of 'unconscionability'.

[61] *Re Bond Worth Ltd* [1980] Ch. 228, though the charge in that case was rendered void as against the company's liquidator for want of registration under Companies Act 1948 (UK), s. 95.

benefits that should be in the fund. Tracing may be a process, not a remedy, but it is a process directed towards these remedies and consequently it does, and should, mimic the due administration of a trust in taking its key concept as *exchange*. Now, allowing the capture of exchange products may very often overlap with the reversal of unjust enrichment, but they are not necessarily and always the same.

Failure to realise or acknowledge this may reflect a pre-Judicature Act common law mindset, where all litigation involves two parties and (more or less) straightforwardly correlative rights and liabilities. This may accommodate an 'event/response' analysis of restitution. But two points should be made. Any attempt to fit all litigation into a conceptual structure based on two-party actions before 1875 cannot survive the general application of the post-Judicature Act procedural rules. Nor does that conceptual framework accommodate equitable procedures with a different structure: trust administration, the administration of deceased estates, partnership dissolution, the (now largely historical) jurisdiction over infants and lunatics, and many others. The two-party way of looking at things is entirely adequate for many purposes, but not others. Any attempt to make everything fit such a paradigm is bound to end in distortion.

Beyond trust funds

Tracing within the context of the law of trust provides no warrant for tracing in the absence of exchange. However, tracing is used well outside the context of the law of trusts. Do these other contexts warrant acceptance of a wider notion of tracing? More generally, should the exercise of tracing to locate property rights be approached differently outside the context of the law of trusts?

It might be argued that when an action is directed towards reversing unjust enrichment, tracing should not be limited by reference to the rules developed in the context of the law of trusts. This claim must be considered carefully. The response to it is in parts. But throughout it must be borne in mind that the argument is not concerned with the question of when title does or should pass in compromised transactions: when title does or should pass is a matter for the law of property. The only question at issue is the extent of any proprietary response in a situation where title has passed.

The first important, but partial, response to the suggestion that a wider notion of tracing might be used outside the context of the law of trusts is to check the facts. Many proprietary claims commonly described as claims in unjust enrichment are in fact about the restoration of a fund (e.g. claims to restore misapplied corporate property). In those contexts, the analogy with trust law is compelling, because these cases are concerned with the restoration of a fund, just like trust law. It is the need to restore the integrity of a fund of assets that warrants the proprietary claim. The notion of restoring a fund, being the primary and governing concept in these cases, should determine the nature and scope of remedies following unlawful depletion of the fund, and processes such as tracing which are directed towards achieving such remedies.

The above argument is only a partial response, however. If we assume, for the sake of argument, that there are claims in unjust enrichment which generate a proprietary response, what then? The argument might be made that the equitable interests raised to reverse unjust enrichment should not be limited in their vindication by reference to principles developed in the context of express trusts. What else could the law do? One possibility is that it could identify assets that the holder would not have but for the enrichment – an approach based on causation – and allow the claimant a proprietary interest in such assets. There are at least two responses to this possibility.

The first is that causation alone is too weak a notion to be the basis of remedial property rights: where is the normative basis for allowing causation to generate property rights, rather than exchange? Exchange is at least a well-founded and accepted justification for property rights in substitute assets – though no justification of property is entirely watertight. Causation is a much broader and weaker notion than exchange. The natural justice of allowing a proprietary right to a claimant in the exchange product of an asset in which the claimant had a proprietary right is clear, but not beyond criticism. But any such criticism applies with much greater force to any proprietary claim based merely on the fact that he can show that the defendant is wealthier than he would be but for the facts alleged. This is, in substance, the 'swollen assets theory' revisited. The swollen assets theory suggested that a court should be able to award a proprietary remedy over any of the assets of someone who had been enriched by the receipt of misapplied trust assets (or, possibly, their proceeds). But this theory of tracing and consequent proprietary remedies has not been accepted; nor should it be now. Whatever the strength of exchange as a basis for claiming proprietary rights in substitute assets, causation is a much weaker justification, quite aside from further arguments that it would cast the net of proprietary claims too widely, particularly in the context of insolvency.

Another response is to focus on the bizarre result of using a different set of tracing rules to identify assets that the holder would not have but for the enrichment. If such rules were accepted and applied in the context of proprietary claims that respond to unjust enrichment, the result would be to give greater scope for vindication to restitutionary equitable rights (i.e. equitable rights created following the transfer or loss of express property rights) than would be given using the current tracing rules to expressly created equitable property rights under trusts. That is self-evidently wrong. And it cannot be put right by the suggestion that expressly created equitable property rights should be vindicated using tracing rules that are founded on causation. The reasons why the tracing rules applicable to trusts should be grounded in the notion of exchange are set out earlier: remedies, and processes such as tracing which are directed towards achieving a remedy, must reflect rights. Exchange is the key concept underlying and explaining the due administration of a trust fund. It must therefore be the key concept underlying the process of identifying assets which may be used to restore the trust fund following its unlawful depletion.

A more radical proposal would be to sever the link between equity and proprietary responses to unjust enrichment. This would involve establishing proprietary rights generated in response to unjust enrichment, which can form the basis for tracing, as entirely separate and distinct species of rights than equitable interests. Of course, this is emphatically not the law: it forms at most an argument for radical law reform. But that argument seems unconvincing, because, as above, it would lead to the perverse result that these proprietary rights (again, *ex hypothesi* rights created following the transfer or loss of express property rights) would be given greater scope for vindication than expressly created rights under trusts. Again, this is perverse: simply and self-evidently wrong.

In summary, some of the 'strain' pulling against the current exchange-based view of tracing results from the fact that the right to trace extends well beyond the law of trusts *stricto sensu*, so that any explanation of tracing based on trusts may seem less convincing the further away the explanation is used from the paradigm case of the rights of a beneficiary to trace following a misapplication of assets subject to an express trust. But as shown above, there are good reasons not to allow 'wider' tracing rules in other contexts.

What may well provide a more promising route for the development of the law is to recognise, albeit cautiously, incrementally and in appropriate cases, *personal* rather than proprietary claims in unjust enrichment against indirect recipients of some benefit, claims which are not founded on proprietary reasoning, and so do not involve the use of tracing. Indeed, there is evidence that the law may be developing in this way.[62] Such claims focus openly and immediately on issues of enrichment which warrant a personal, not a proprietary, claim, and so avoid the risk of distorting rules about property rights – the tracing rules – into rules about enrichment or the receipt of benefits.

Conclusion

The due administration of funds in equity has clear implications for the equitable consequences of maladministration of a fund. Tracing is one of those consequences. Tracing is a purposive activity, whose content is informed by its purpose and context. The paradigm purpose of tracing is as one technique to allow the restoration of a trust fund following depletion of the fund through a breach of trust. It follows that tracing is not concerned exclusively with identifying enrichment or value. It is concerned with the value inherent in specific assets, and those assets are identified by reference to the notion of exchange. Indeed, if tracing were purely about value, surely a proprietary claim should lie where no trust property as such had necessarily been removed from the trust fund, but where something had been done by the trustee in breach of trust which had the effect of enhancing somebody's wealth. Yet that is clearly not the law. Nor should it be, given the effect of proprietary claims on third parties.

A notion of tracing properly based on the concept of exchange reflects the current law. The law, quite property, seeks consistency between tracing following the maladministration of a fund and the principles governing the due administration of the fund. Any alteration of that position will entail either incoherence or more significant change to the law than might be supposed: the change would not be minor, trivial or insignificant.

This conclusion is itself indicative of a wider phenomenon, deserving more attention: the distorting effect of over-inclusive theory. What has often seemed to happen is evident in the subject matter of this chapter. Legal rules, principles and doctrines may have a certain effect, in the present case, 'locating value' in the hands of a defendant. But that is only

[62] See now the *obiter dicta* in *Relfo Ltd (in liq.)* v. *Varsani* [2015] 1 B.C.L.C. 14, [69]–[99] (Arden L.J.), [103]–[104] (Gloster L.J.), [107]–[123] (Floyd L.J.).

part of the story, and a part told without context. The rules, doctrines and principles 'locate value' in certain assets identified by reference to certain criteria chosen for certain purposes. If the effect of the rules is translated into broad, theoretical terms, but the context is not, the result is too often distortion in the description of what has happened and in the prescriptions offered for what should happen: such theory 'may distort well settled principles in other fields, including those respecting equitable doctrines and remedies, so that they answer the newly mandated order of things'.[63]

The law of trusts and equitable rules for the administration of funds embody well and long settled principles which facilitate the due administration of a fund. The equitable rules which address the consequences of maladministration must vindicate those principles and reflect how they were meant to operate. Looking at the effect of remedies, and procedures through which a remedy may be claimed, should not obscure the fact that they exist to vindicate particular rights.

[63] *Roxborough* v. *Rothmans of Pall Mall Australia Ltd* (2001) 208 C.L.R. 516, [74]; [2001] HCA 68 (Gummow J.).

5

The administration and maladministration of funds in equity

A commentary

NICHOLAS PATTEN

Professor Nolan's chapter (Chapter 4) seeks to explore the relevance of the rules governing the due administration of a trust to those which identify the assets in which a beneficiary may claim to have a proprietary interest following a breach of trust. There has, he argues, to be consistency between the two in order to restore the trust to what it should have been but at the same time to avoid over-compensation of the beneficiaries. They are entitled to choose to take any substitute assets acquired by the defaulting trustee in satisfaction of the trustee's duty to re-constitute the fund just as they will have their beneficial interests transferred to substitute assets acquired by the trustee in the lawful exercise of his powers of sale and investment. But in both cases they will not be entitled to see the original trust assets replaced with anything more than they are or would be entitled to under the due administration of the trust.

This process of substitution is examined first by reference to the proper exercise of the trustee's powers of sale and disposal. The beneficiaries' interests are automatically transferred into the newly acquired assets which become part of the corpus of the fund. Correspondingly, the original assets are transferred to third parties free of any title or claim which the beneficiaries would otherwise have. But these principles are also relied on to explain what happens when things go wrong. In such cases, the rights of the beneficiaries in the original assets are not overreached. They remain enforceable against all third parties except bona fide purchasers for value without notice and holders of statutory defences (such as under land registration statutes). Subject to that, the beneficiaries can continue to assert a proprietary interest in the misapplied assets and may take those assets or their derivatives in substitution for the original assets, provided that they give credit for them in relation to the trustee's obligation to re-constitute the fund. In so doing, the fund is restored in much the same way as it would have been, had the disposal been a lawful one.

The question for the chapter is how the rules of tracing fit into all of this. Since the purpose of tracing is to identify the assets against which the beneficiaries can assert a proprietary claim, it follows, Professor Nolan argues, that the rules of tracing must reflect the rules which dictate how a breach of trust should be remedied. This includes the principle that beneficiaries can claim rights in an asset which the trustee has acquired by his breach of trust, but cannot recover by this process more assets in the hands of the trustee than if his actions had been undertaken for their benefit. In this sense, the tracing rules are therefore shaped by the same rules which govern the proper administration of the trust.

The other important question raised in the chapter is how the relevant assets should be identified. Professor Nolan suggests that the key notion is that of exchange: that is, the replacement of one asset by another based on an analysis of the transaction and the rights and liabilities it creates. The rules of tracing are not intended to provide a general remedy based on the unjust enrichment of the trustee. Based on the criterion of exchange, the beneficiaries are entitled to acquire an interest in the substitute assets but no wider rights. If, for example, trust monies are wrongfully applied to repay a loan to the trustee taken out to buy a car, the beneficiaries have a claim against the trustee for repayment but no claim to the car which was not acquired with their money. The concept of exchange prohibits backward tracing of this kind.

I have no real quarrel with much of this but I pose the question as to how much of it really matters. In particular, I doubt whether the application of similar rules to the due administration of a trust and the steps available to the trustees to cure the breach tell us much more than that the latter are obviously intended to restore the trust fund to the position it would have been in but for the breach of trust. Nothing more but hopefully nothing less. Looked at in these terms, it is hardly surprising that there are parallels between what a trustee should have done and what the court will allow a beneficiary to recover in order to restore what he has lost.

I also have my doubts about the utility of the concept of exchange as the touchstone by which any attempt to identify a derivative falls to be judged. Exchange is said to underpin or be central to a legitimate change in the identity of the trust asset – for example, the sale and replacement of investments – because it provides both a justification and an explanation of why and how the property of the beneficiaries in the existing trust assets comes to be replaced by a similar interest in the newly acquired trust assets. The proper exercise of the trustee's powers of sale and investment permits this replacement of assets and frees the trust assets disposed of from any claims by the beneficiaries to that property in the hands of its recipients. If by exchange one is describing a process by which the trustee replaces existing assets with assets of a comparable or greater value, then it provides a useful shorthand for the criteria by which any dealing with trust property by a trustee falls to be judged. But I am not sure that it tells us anything more than that. Professor Nolan says that when trustees lawfully dispose of a trust asset and in exchange acquire another, equity recognises that the beneficiaries with an interest in the original asset may prima facie claim an equivalent interest in the substitute. But the cases he refers to seem to me to do no more than to confirm (as he mentions earlier in his chapter) that all that a beneficiary is entitled to is the proper execution of the trust in accordance with the terms of the trust instrument and the general law. The trust assets as defined will therefore comprise both the original assets and any additions to the fund through the lawful exercise of the trustee's powers. By the same token, they will not include assets lawfully disposed of, and the beneficiaries will have no choice but to accept the substitute assets. This is simply giving effect to the terms of the trust. The trust deed gives them no greater rights. I would not, therefore, myself regard this process of change in the identity of the fund as comparable in terms of legal theory to the situation which exists when a trustee has unlawfully disposed of trust assets and the beneficiary does have a real choice as to how he requires the loss to be made good.

In these circumstances, as Professor Nolan explains in his chapter, the rights of the beneficiaries are not overreached or automatically transferred to the replacement assets. The trustee comes under a duty to restore the fund to the status quo ante either by replacing the lost assets in specie or by making financial compensation in an amount which will enable that to be done. If the newly acquired asset is such that it occasions no loss to the trust although unauthorised, then the beneficiaries may have no claim for compensation against the trustee at all; but they are entitled to choose to take the benefit of the unauthorised purchase and any profit with it.

These options assume, however, that the breach of trust has resulted in an identifiable, although illegitimate, acquisition of an alternative asset and that the trustee is solvent and therefore at least able to put matters right. In such cases, it is no surprise that there is an element of similarity between the process which has to be gone through to rectify the effects of the breach of trust and the position which would obtain if there had been no breach of trust. In both cases, the trustee remains under a personal duty to the beneficiaries to secure the proper administration of the trust and his duty to restore the fund can be regarded as one aspect of this. If the trustee replaces the lost assets in specie or the beneficiaries accept the unauthorised investment as a substitute, the duty is treated as performed and the breach of trust has no further consequences. But, in many cases where the breach of trust involves a deliberate misappropriation of trust property, that kind of genteel resolution is not possible. The trustee may retain control of the assets but they will often (if liquid) have been mixed with other funds or sold and replaced with other things. In other cases, the assets (or their substitutes) will have passed to third parties who may or may not be able to claim the protection of being bona fide purchasers or the holder of a statutory defence. The beneficiaries' right to follow or trace these assets is likely in many of these cases to be their only effective means of obtaining any form of recovery for their loss.

Tracing, as we all know, is not a remedy in itself but rather a means of identifying assets against which the beneficiaries' equitable title can be asserted in priority to other claims. Professor Nolan says that it can be characterised as a process of identifying one asset as a substitute for another, which it can; and that the rules of tracing (e.g. into a mixed fund) reflect the rules governing how a breach of trust should be redressed by employing a series of presumptions against the defaulting trustee. The beneficiaries (as in any case of breach of trust) can elect to take the assets acquired by the trustee in whole or partial satisfaction of their claim; but cannot in turn claim more than they would have been entitled to had the trustee's actions been undertaken for their benefit. None of this is controversial. But it is not in my view a particularly fertile ground for the creation of a global theory linking tracing rules with the principles of due administration. Tracing is not of itself concerned with the ultimate measure of recovery as between beneficiary and trustee. It has a much narrower focus and purpose which is simply to identify assets (or their substitutes) against which the beneficiaries' title remains effective. It serves, therefore, to facilitate the vindication of the beneficiaries' proprietary claim to those assets and its limits are set by equity's recognition that these rights of property continue to subsist against assets acquired with trust property regardless of the identity of any recipient bar one who has given value without notice of the beneficiaries' prior rights or who holds a statutory defence.

For much the same reason, I am also doubtful whether it is right that tracing is based on the concept of exchange which according to the thesis in the chapter underlies the proper exercise of a trustee's power of sale. The beneficiaries' subsequent claim to the identifiable assets will of course require choices to be made. They are likely in practice to be limited choices governed by what Lord Millett in *Foskett* v. *McKeown*[1] described as a mixture of advantage and circumstance in the form of the value and recoverability of the available assets. But they are in essence choices between identified assets in respect of which the beneficiaries could assert a subsisting claim in equity based on their derivation from the original trust assets. I am not, therefore, convinced that the concept of exchange helps very much in establishing any principled basis of recovery. The answer to the claim to trace the trust monies into the car is essentially one of timing. So long as the beneficiaries' claim to the assets remaining in the trustee's hands is based on a chronological analysis of what was acquired with what, and not on a more general theory of unjust enrichment, the answer should in most cases be straightforward. There will of course be difficult cases like *Foskett* v. *McKeown* in which the issue was whether payment of some insurance premiums with trust money gave the beneficiaries an interest in the policy itself as opposed to a lien to secure repayment of the money. But I find it difficult to see how the concept of exchange helps to solve problems of this kind.

[1] [2001] 1 A.C. 102, 129–33, 140.

6

Equity and insolvency

LOOK CHAN HO

Introduction

Equity and insolvency intersect in countless ways. This is no doubt due to the distinct and overlapping functions performed by equity and insolvency law. Indeed the US Supreme Court has repeatedly said that bankruptcy courts are courts of equity and apply the principles and rules of equity jurisprudence.[1]

This chapter considers how equity and insolvency influence each other's developments and at the same time restrict each other's sphere of operation.

Overview of the nature of insolvency law and equity's role

The corpus of insolvency law concerns in essence how an asset deficit is to be managed in a way fair to all participants:

> Insolvency is the factual situation that arises when a debtor is unable to pay creditors ... Certain legal proceedings become available upon insolvency, which typically allow a debtor to obtain a court order staying its creditors' enforcement actions and attempt to obtain a binding compromise with creditors to adjust the payment conditions to something more realistic. Alternatively, the debtor's assets may be liquidated and debts paid from the proceeds according to statutory priority rules. The former is usually referred to as reorganization or restructuring while the latter is termed liquidation ...
>
> While insolvency proceedings may be governed by different statutory schemes, they share some commonalities. The most prominent of these is the single proceeding model. The nature and purpose of the single proceeding model are described by Professor Wood in *Bankruptcy and Insolvency Law*:[2]

[1] For example, *Young* v. *United States*, 535 U.S. 43, 50 (2002).

[2] R.J. Wood, *Bankruptcy and Insolvency Law* (Toronto: Irwin Law, 2009), 2–3.

> 'They all provide a collective proceeding that supersedes the usual civil process available to creditors to enforce their claims. The creditors' remedies are collectivized in order to prevent the free-for-all that would otherwise prevail if creditors were permitted to exercise their remedies. In the absence of a collective process, each creditor is armed with the knowledge that if they do not strike hard and swift to seize the debtor's assets, they will be beat out by other creditors'.
>
> The single proceeding model avoids the inefficiency and chaos that would attend insolvency if each creditor initiated proceedings to recover its debt. Grouping all possible actions against the debtor into a single proceeding controlled in a single forum facilitates negotiation with creditors because it places them all on an equal footing, rather than exposing them to the risk that a more aggressive creditor will realize its claims against the debtor's limited assets while the other creditors attempt a compromise.[3]

Similarly, in a decision affirmed by the Singapore Court of Appeal, Vinodh Coomaraswamy J.C. said:

> Insolvency proceedings are not about individual benefit. Indeed, one of the fundamental objectives of insolvency proceedings is to preclude action for individual benefit. Where an entity's liabilities exceed its assets or where it is unable to pay its debts in full as they fall due, it is insolvent. It is then in the collective interest of all of the insolvent's creditors to substitute for piecemeal individual action an orderly process for conserving, collecting, realising and distributing its assets *pari passu*. Insolvency law comprises the legal rules applicable to initiate and carry out that orderly process.[4]

An essential limb of the corpus of insolvency law is the distribution of assets among the claimants, while respecting as much as possible the claimants' pre-insolvency entitlements. As the US Supreme Court has held, '[c]reditors' entitlements in bankruptcy arise in the first instance from the underlying substantive law creating the debtor's obligation, subject to any qualifying or contrary provisions of the Bankruptcy Code'.[5] Once the pre-insolvency entitlements are established, the

[3] *Century Services Inc.* v. *Canada (A.-G.)* [2010] 3 S.C.R. 379, [12], [22]; 2010 SCC 60.

[4] *Chimbusco International Petroleum (Singapore) Pte Ltd* v. *Jalalludin bin Abdullah* [2013] 2 S.L.R. 801, [36]; [2013] SGHC 55, aff'd *sub. nom. Mohd Zain bin Abdullah* v. *Chimbusco International Petroleum (Singapore) Pte Ltd* [2014] 2 S.L.R. 446; [2014] SGCA 8. See also *Lee Sai Nam* v. *Li Shu Chung* [2013] HKEC 732, [159]; [2013] HKCFI 801 ('Bankruptcy and insolvency proceedings are collective in nature, brought to enforce a compulsory administration of the debtor's assets for the benefit of those with claims on them . . .'); *Stichting Shell Pensioenfonds* v. *Krys* [2015] A.C. 616, [32]; [2014] UKPC 41 ('Liquidation is a mode of collective enforcement of claims arising under the general law.').

[5] *Raleigh* v. *Illinois Dept. of Revenue*, 530 U.S. 15, 20 (2000). See also *Travelers Casualty & Surety Co. of America* v. *Pacific Gas & Electric Co.*, 549 U.S. 443, 450 (2007).

claimants' rights to payment from the insolvent estate are solely a matter of insolvency law, primarily a matter of legislative policy informed by such normative standards as equality, fairness, liberty and efficiency. Mummery L.J. pointed out in *Re Polly Peck International plc (in admin.) (No. 2)*[6] that Parliament has sanctioned a scheme for distribution of assets designed to achieve a fair distribution of the insolvent company's property among the unsecured creditors. The essential characteristic of the statutory scheme is that the insolvency officeholder is bound to deal with the assets of the company as directed by statute for the benefit of all creditors.

While equity is relevant to many aspects of an insolvency process, equity's involvement may be divided into three broad categories, namely, the distribution of the estate's assets, insolvency expenses and the integrity of the insolvency process, to be explained in turn below.

Insolvency distribution

It is trite law that 'property held subject to a trust is not available in a liquidation, or in any other scenario where creditors of a trustee company attempt to have access to the assets of the company',[7] for central to the distribution of an insolvent estate's assets is the concept of beneficial ownership. Beneficial ownership comprises a bundle of rights and some incidental limitations such as the liability to execution, namely the liability of the owner's interest to be taken away from him for debt.[8] One of the strands in the bundle of rights is the ability to use the property to discharge a debt.

Equity consists of a large body of rules (in particular trusts) dealing with the allocation of beneficial interest among different claimants:

> [A]bsolute owners (in the Honoré sense) are entitled to the benefit of the thing owned, but it would be wrong to say that they have an equitable interest in the thing: it is their legal interest in the thing that entitles them to beneficial enjoyment, and will continue to do so unless and until either they transfer it to someone else by a legal disposition, or equity steps in and allocates it elsewhere, by recognising someone other than a legal interest holder as the person entitled to beneficial enjoyment.[9]

6 [1998] 3 All E.R. 812, 826–7.

7 *Independent Trustee Co. Ltd* v. *Registrar of Companies* [2015] IEHC 12.

8 T. Honoré, *Making Law Bind* (Oxford: Clarendon Press, 1987), ch. 8.

9 A. Clarke and P. Kohler, *Property Law: Commentary and Materials* (Cambridge University Press, 2005), 314.

That description was echoed to striking effect in a Singapore case, where it was said:

> The presumption is that an owner of a legal estate in land is absolutely entitled to every incident of ownership of that land to the extent reflected in the legal title. At this point in the inquiry, there are no equitable interests in the land to speak of. Equitable interests are not inherent in property, created and existing automatically and in parallel with legal interests . . . An equitable interest in property comes into existence only when one of a limited number of sets of events takes place which are legally significant in that equity attaches consequences to them which have proprietary effect.[10]

Thus the natural consequence of the application of equity is also the distribution of an insolvent estate's assets. A British Columbia court observed:

> Trust claims to property, if proven, have long been acknowledged within the bankruptcy and insolvency context and result in the debtor having no beneficial interest in such property. It has been a fundamental principle of insolvency law that only property owned by the insolvent person can be subject to payment of that person's debts.[11]

And in *Pearlman* v. *Reliance Insurance Co.*, the US Supreme Court said:

> Property interests in a fund not owned by a bankrupt at the time of adjudication, whether complete or partial, legal or equitable, mortgages, liens, or simple priority of rights, are of course not a part of the bankrupt's property and do not vest in the trustee. The Bankruptcy Act simply does not authorize a trustee to distribute other people's property among a bankrupt's creditors.[12]

Five areas of equitable intervention that merit some discussion are set-off in insolvency, specific performance, *Quistclose* trusts, remedial constructive trusts and company directors' duty to creditors.

Set-off

Set-off may be divided into solvent set-off and insolvency set-off. Solvent set-off refers to the legal bases for set-off at common law and in equity that are available outside formal insolvency proceedings. Solvent set-off

10 *Buthmanaban s/o Vaithilingam* v. *Krishnavanny d/o Vaithilingam* [2015] SGHC 35, [62].
11 *Re TLC the Land Conservancy of British Columbia*, 2014 BCSC 97, [175].
12 *Pearlman* v. *Reliance Insurance Co.*, 371 U.S. 132, 135–6 (1962).

may take various forms such as independent set-off, transaction set-off, banker's set-off and contractual set-off.

Insolvency set-off is available only in formal insolvency proceedings in circumstances prescribed by the insolvency legislation, principally rule 4.90 and rule 2.85 of the Insolvency Rules 1986 (UK) and section 323 of the Insolvency Act 1986 (UK).[13] 'Insolvency set-off arises when there are mutual debts or other mutual dealings between an insolvent person and a creditor. The amount due by one to the other is set off against the debt due by that other and only the difference can be claimed.'[14]

As a general principle, set-off should not be permitted where one person uses another person's claim to discharge his own liability, for one should use one's own property to discharge one's own liability. Hence, the requirement of mutuality of cross-claims.[15] Mutuality requires commensurable cross-claims between the same people[16] in the same capacity; each party should be debtor and creditor in the same capacity.[17]

In determining mutuality, the focus is on the beneficial ownership of claim and cross-claim, rather than the mere legal title.[18] Thus equity

[13] 'Legislation of this type goes back to the time of Queen Anne': *Finnigan* v. *He* [2010] 2 N.Z.L.R. 668, [16]; [2009] NZHC 2156. See Bankrupts Act 1705, 4 & 5 Anne c. 4.

[14] *Re Opes Prime Stockbroking Ltd* (2008) 171 F.C.R. 473, [8]; [2008] FCA 1425.

[15] *Good Property Land Development Pte Ltd (in liq.)* v. *Société-Générale* [1996] 1 S.L.R. (R.) 884, [18]; [1996] SGCA 25.

[16] Note that the Crown is one and indivisible: *Secretary of State for Trade & Industry* v. *Frid* [2004] 2 A.C. 506; [2004] UKHL 24; *Commissioner of Inland Revenue* v. *Wright* [2013] NZHC 476.

[17] *RPG Receivables Purchase Group Inc.* v. *Krones Machinery Co. Ltd*, 2010 ONSC 2372, [14] ('mutuality . . . requires that the debts be between the same parties and that the debts be in the same right'). Thus a claimant's proprietary claim to money or other assets cannot be set off against any personal liabilities in debt: *Williams* v. *Bateman* [2009] B.P.I.R. 973, [15]; [2009] EWHC 1760 (Ch); *Blue Sky One Ltd* v. *Mahan Air* [2010] EWHC 631 (Comm), [118]; *Re Lehman Brothers International (Europe)* [2010] 2 B.C.L.C. 301, [331]; [2009] EWHC 3228 (Ch), reversed on appeal on other issues: *Lehman Brothers International (Europe) (in admin.)* v. *CRC Credit Fund Ltd* [2012] Bus. L.R. 667; [2012] UKSC 6; *E-Clear (UK) plc* v. *Elia* [2012] EWHC 1256 (Ch), [37]–[38], [47]; *Re Guidezone* (unreported, Chancery Division, 27 June 2014), [18].

[18] *Good Property Land Development Pte Ltd (in liq.)* v. *Société-Générale* [1996] 1 S.L.R. (R.) 884, [18] ('Mutuality sees through to the real beneficial ownership, regardless of who is the legal, nominal, titular or procedural holder of the claim or procedurally the appropriate plaintiff.'); *Secretary of State for Trade & Industry* v. *Frid* [2004] 2 A.C. 506, [19], [26]; *Collected Mind Investments Ltd* v. *Shebo Trading Co. Ltd* [2012] HKEC 1339, [18]; [2012] HKCFI 1518.

> Mutuality means that the demands must be between the same parties, and that they must be held in the same capacity, or right, or interest . . .

often determines the availability of solvent set-off and insolvency set-off. For example, a claim by a trustee on behalf of a beneficiary cannot be set off against a debt owing by the trustee personally. Similarly, a bank may not set off funds held in a special-purpose trust account against the depositor's independent liabilities to the bank.[19]

At the same time, insolvency may restrict the applicability of set-off that is otherwise available in equity. For example, it is debatable whether equitable set-off may continue to apply after liquidation. It has been said: 'Once a company has gone into liquidation, the rules of insolvency set-off, where relevant, come into play and are mandatory, displacing all other forms of set-off not exercised prior to the winding-up'.[20] *Re Bank of Credit and Commerce International SA (in liq.) (No. 8)*[21] supports the proposition that there does not exist a non-statutory equitable right of set-off in insolvency which is wider than liquidation set-off. This is also the position in New Zealand, where Heath J. said:

> In some circumstances a party to a contract will be entitled to off-set moneys owing by the other contracting party to an associated entity. However, that principle has two important restrictions. The first is that there must be a considerable degree of interdependence between the two arrangements. The second is that this type of set-off is not available when one of the parties to the contract is subject to a formal collective insolvency regime.[22]

At any rate, the position should not be regarded as settled.[23] Indeed in *Mulkerrins* v. *PricewaterhouseCoopers (a firm)*,[24] Lord Millett remarked as follows:

> It means no more than that the same two parties were involved, and that each of the parties who is liable to the other must be beneficially interested in a cross claim against that other.

> (L. Gullifer (ed.), *Goode on Legal Problems of Credit and Security*, 5th ed. (London: Sweet & Maxwell, 2013), 345.)

19 *Barclays Bank Ltd* v. *Quistclose Investments Ltd* [1970] A.C. 567. Cf. *In re KD Builders*, 382 B.R. 1 (Bankr. D. Mass. 2008).

20 R. Goode, *Principles of Corporate Insolvency Law*, 4th ed. (London: Sweet & Maxwell, 2011), 286–7 (footnotes omitted).

21 [1996] Ch. 245.

22 *Nylex (New Zealand) Ltd (in rec. & in liq.)* v. *Independent Timber Merchants Co-operative Ltd* (2010) 20 P.R.N.Z. 41, [24]; [2010] NZHC 1829.

23 R. Derham, *Derham on the Law of Set-Off*, 4th ed. (Oxford University Press, 2010), [6.25]–[6.32].

24 [2003] 1 W.L.R. 1937; [2003] UKHL 41.

> The reason that the debtor's consent is not required to an assignment of a debt is that the assignment cannot prejudice him. The assignment is subject to equities, which means that any set-off which the debtor may have against the assignor can be asserted against the assignee. On bankruptcy the trustee is in no better position than his bankrupt; a creditor's right to sue his debtor vests in his trustee subject to equities.[25]

These remarks suggest that if a debt is assigned to a corporate assignee which thereafter becomes subject to liquidation thereby triggering insolvency set-off, any solvent set-off which the debtor may have against the assignor can be asserted against the liquidator of the assignee despite the operation of insolvency set-off.

Specific performance

As a general rule, if a person may be ordered specifically to perform a contract (such as a contract for sale of land), he remains liable to an order for specific performance despite his insolvency.[26] The justification is that an order for specific performance does not prejudice the general body of creditors because a specifically performable contract already confers on the counter-party, via a constructive trust, a beneficial interest in the subject-matter of the contract. In general terms, as Professor McKendrick writes:

> An agreement to transfer ownership, provided that it was of such a kind as to be enforceable by specific performance, [is] given effect in equity as if the transfer had already been executed, so that while legal title remained in the intended transferor, beneficial ownership was held to vest immediately in the intended transferee.[27]

Nourse L.J. addressed the topic in some detail:

> [W]here company A enters into an unconditional contract to sell shares in company B to company C[,] [s]hares in company B not being readily obtainable in the market, such a contract is specifically enforceable at the suit of company C. By parity with contracts for the sale of land, it has long been held that the right to specific performance gives company C the equitable interest in the shares, company A becoming a qualified trustee in the sense that it must preserve the shares for company C while remaining entitled to any dividends accruing before completion. In that state of

25 [2003] 1 W.L.R. 1937, [15].

26 *Bristol Alliance Nominee No. 1 Ltd* v. *Bennett* [2014] 1 E.G.L.R. 9; [2013] EWCA Civ 1626.

27 E. McKendrick (ed.), *Goode on Commercial Law*, 4th ed. (London: Penguin, 2010), 42 (footnotes omitted).

> affairs in which of the two companies is the beneficial ownership of the shares vested pending completion of the contract? It cannot be doubted that it is vested in company C.[28]

The same justification had earlier been adopted by Oliver J., who took it as obvious that:

> Of course, specific performance of existing contracts for the sale of land can be decreed against the liquidator or a trustee in bankruptcy of the vendor, but that is based on the existence of the equitable proprietary interest created by the contract for sale.[29]

However, sometimes insolvency law may operate to curtail the availability of specific performance. It is established that the court will not normally order specific performance of a contract entered into by an insolvent person to pay money in order to protect the general body of creditors. Oliver J. was of the view that:

> In the ordinary way the court does not . . . decree specific performance against a trustee in bankruptcy or a liquidator where the obligation is simply to pay money, as, for instance, in the case of the insolvent purchaser of land . . . The reason is not . . . far to seek. The effect would be in fact that the other party to the contract would be receiving payment otherwise than *pari passu* with the other creditors.[30]

Moreover, a specifically performable contract may conceivably be compromised by a scheme of arrangement under Part 26 of the Companies Act 2006 (UK). Consider a property company that has contracted to sell land to investors and, as part of a restructuring exercise, would like to compromise via a scheme the investors' equitable right to the land arising from specifically enforceable contracts. An immediate objection to the feasibility of such a scheme would be the decision in *Re Lehman Brothers International (Europe) (in admin.) (No. 2)*[31] holding that Part 26 did not include a scheme of arrangement with proprietary claimants. The *Lehman* case concerned a proposed scheme intended to achieve a resolution of certain trust claims in the administration of Lehman Brothers International (Europe) (LBIE) after its sudden collapse and entry into administration in September 2008. In outline, the scheme provided for any client who had both a pecuniary claim against LBIE and a proprietary or beneficial interest in assets held or controlled by

[28] *J. Sainsbury plc* v. *O'Connor* [1991] 1 W.L.R. 963, 978.

[29] *In re Dynamics Corp. of America (in liq.)* [1976] 1 W.L.R. 757, 774.

[30] *Ibid.*, 774.

[31] [2010] Bus. L.R. 489; [2009] EWCA Civ 1161.

LBIE to be treated as a scheme creditor and have both its pecuniary and its property interest dealt with by an 'arrangement' under the scheme. While there was much to be said generally for the certainty and simplicity of what was proposed, the question was whether property rights could be dealt with in such a way under a scheme. The court answered in the negative.

The court reasoned that clients *qua* trust beneficiaries holding proprietary claims against LBIE (thus in their capacity as beneficial owners of property) were not LBIE's creditors within Part 26. The court had no power to sanction the proposed scheme even though the clients had at least contingent claims for damages or equitable compensation against LBIE for breach of trust and were thus LBIE's creditors within Part 26 in respect of those claims. This is because a creditor scheme could only be proposed with creditors of a company in their capacity as creditors.[32]

On one reading, *Lehman* has firmly excluded trusts from the scheme jurisdiction. The following passage sounds categorical:

> [A]n arrangement between a company and its creditors must mean an arrangement which deals with their rights inter se as debtor and creditor. That formulation does not prevent the inclusion in the scheme of the release of contractual rights or rights of action against related third parties necessary in order to give effect to the arrangement proposed for the disposition of the debts and liabilities of the company to its own creditors. But *it does exclude from the jurisdiction rights of creditors over their own property which is held by the company for their benefit* as opposed to their rights in the company's own property held by them merely as security.[33]

A clear implication of *Lehman* is that a bare corporate trustee would not be able to promote a scheme to compromise trust beneficiaries' *in rem* rights.

However, it is suggested that *Lehman* does not prevent a scheme from compromising beneficial *in rem* rights in all circumstances. That a scheme may compromise a constructive trust arising from a specifically enforceable contract should follow from the following steps.

In the first place, there is little doubt that purchasers of land are creditors for scheme purposes as the seller's failure to convey land will entitle the purchasers to damages.

[32] *Re T & N Ltd (No. 4)* [2007] Bus. L.R. 1411, [45]; [2006] EWHC 1447 (Ch).

[33] *Re Lehman Brothers International (Europe) (in admin.) (No. 2)* [2010] Bus. L.R. 489, [65] (italics added).

The next issue would be whether a scheme may compromise specifically enforceable contracts. It is instructive to consider some Australian authorities. There is a long line of authorities concerning companies that had granted share options and wished to rid themselves of the obligations to issue shares. The companies promoted schemes of arrangement between themselves and the option-holders on the basis that the latter were creditors, rather than members. The Australian courts have consistently upheld such schemes compromising the option-holders' rights to share allotment, treating the option-holders as contingent creditors because if the companies failed to honour their obligations to issue shares, the option-holders would have damages claims.[34]

A share allotment contract in respect of shares in a private company may be specifically enforced.[35] Although the Australian authorities did not mention the issue of specific performance, they are consistent with the proposition that a specifically enforceable contract may be compromised by a scheme.

As the *Lehman* decision does not concern issues of specific performance, the court remains free to sanction a scheme that compromises specifically enforceable contracts.

Using the example above in *J. Sainsbury plc* v. *O'Connor*, if a scheme compromised the contract between company A and company C, it would logically also compromise company C's equitable right to the shares (under a constructive trust) pending completion.

Just as a scheme could compromise rights of contingent members by characterising them as contingent creditors under the option contracts, so a scheme could compromise rights of constructive trust beneficiaries by characterising them as contingent creditors under the sale contracts. This argument no doubt requires a slight extrapolation of the Australian cases like *Re MIA Group Ltd* because the option-holders there did not have any proprietary interest in unissued shares.

The equitable interest triggered by a specifically enforceable contract is different in kind from the equitable interest under a bare trust. The former is premised on the notion that equity treats as done that which ought to be done. '[E]quity considers that because the contract

[34] See, for instance, *Re Asia Oil & Minerals Ltd* (1986) 5 N.S.W.L.R. 42; *Re MIA Group Ltd* (2004) 50 A.C.S.R. 29; [2004] NSWSC 712; *Re Sino Gold Mining Ltd (ACN 093 517 579)* (2009) 74 A.C.S.R. 647; [2009] FCA 1277; and *Re Coventry Resources Ltd* [2012] FCA 1252.

[35] *Sri Lanka Omnibus Co.* v. *Perera* [1952] A.C. 76.

requires transfer of title then transfer of title must be deemed to have taken place automatically.'[36]

In other words, in the case of a specifically enforceable contract, the equitable interest is premised on the *in personam* right under the contract to call for title transfer which in equity is treated as having taken place. The equitable interest created by a specifically enforceable contract is not an unconditional, vested property right, unlike the equitable interest under a bare trust. As Lord Walker has explained:

> It would therefore be wrong to treat an uncompleted contract for the sale of land as equivalent to an immediate, irrevocable declaration of trust (or assignment of beneficial interest) in the land. Neither the seller nor the buyer has unqualified beneficial ownership. Beneficial ownership of the land is in a sense split between the seller and buyer on the provisional assumptions that specific performance is available and that the contract will in due course be completed, if necessary by the court ordering specific performance. In the meantime, the seller is entitled to enjoyment of the land or its rental income. The provisional assumptions may be falsified by events, such as rescission of the contract (either under a contractual term or on breach). If the contract proceeds to completion the equitable interest can be viewed as passing to the buyer in stages, as title is made and accepted and as the purchase price is paid in full.[37]

Once the purchaser's contractual, *in personam* right under the contract to call for title transfer is compromised by a scheme, the contract would no longer be specifically enforceable. Once the contract is no longer specifically enforceable, then the equitable interest disappears.

The position is in fact analogous to schemes compromising secured creditors' rights to secured assets.[38] Schemes may compromise secured creditors' *in rem* rights for this reason:

> [T]he security is an incident of the debt; to put the point another way, it is parasitic on the debt. If there is no longer any debt, there is no security . . . Accordingly, as section 895 [of the Companies Act 2006] enables a scheme which varies the debt, then it must follow that the variation must, as it were, be followed through to the security.[39]

[36] G.W. Thomas and A. Hudson, *The Law of Trusts*, 2nd ed. (Oxford University Press, 2010), [28.02] (footnote omitted).

[37] *Jerome* v. *Kelly* [2004] 1 W.L.R. 1409, [32]; [2004] UKHL 25. See also *Golden Mile Property Investments Pty Ltd (in liq.)* v. *Cudgegong Australia Pty Ltd* (2015) 319 A.L.R. 151; [2015] NSWCA 100, [98]–[106].

[38] For example, *Re Empire Mining Co.* (1890) 44 Ch. D. 402; *Re Alabama, New Orleans, Texas and Pacific Junction Railway Co.* [1891] 1 Ch. 213.

[39] *Re Lehman Brothers International (Europe) (in admin.) (No. 2)* [2010] Bus. L.R. 489, [82].

It is not far-fetched to say a purchaser's equitable interest under a constructive interest triggered by a specifically enforceable contract is an incident of and parasitic on the contract. If section 895 enables a scheme to vary the contract, then the variation must be followed through to the purchaser's equitable interest. To use Patten L.J.'s phraseology, the constructive trust element in these sale arrangements ought to be merged into the general contractual framework and treated merely as ancillary when considering the limits of the scheme jurisdiction.[40]

Quistclose trust

A *Quistclose* trust[41] is one whereby one party, A, pays money to another party, B, on terms that B will hold the money in trust for A subject to a power for B to apply the money for a stated purpose.[42] Such an arrangement has the effect that A's beneficial interest in the money will remain unless and until the money is applied in accordance with the stated purpose of the power.[43] By reason of the fact that the money is always the subject of a trust (although the beneficiaries of the trust change), beneficial title to the fund never passes to the trustee or holder of the funds.[44]

[40] *Ibid.*, [68].

[41] The trust gets its name from the case of *Barclays Bank Ltd* v. *Quistclose Investments Ltd* [1970] A.C. 567.

[42] *Gore* v. *Mishcon de Reya* [2015] EWHC 164 (Ch), [32]:

> [T]he classic form of *Quistclose* trust which has been recognised by the courts concerns moneys that have been loaned to a recipient for one particular purpose and which are to be returned if that purpose is not achieved; but provided the terms can be established by evidence, such a trust can come into existence whenever parties enter into a commercial arrangement which permits one party to have a limited use of the other's money for a stated purpose, is not free to apply it for any other purpose, and must return it if for any reason the purpose cannot be carried out. Moreover such terms need not be set out or accepted in writing.

[43] *Bieber* v. *Teathers Ltd (in liq.)* [2013] 1 B.C.L.C. 248, [14]–[15]; [2012] EWCA Civ 1466; *Harlequin Property (SVG) Ltd* v. *O'Halloran* [2013] IEHC 362, [98]; *Ontario (Training, Colleges and Universities)* v. *Two Feathers Forest Products LP*, 2013 ONCA 598, [9]–[22]; *Coolbrew Pty Ltd* v. *Westpac Banking Corp.* [2014] NSWSC 1108, [44]–[55], affirmed [2015] NSWCA 135; *Craigcare Group Pty Ltd* v. *Superkite Pty Ltd* [2014] NSWSC 326, [199]–[212]; *Bellis* v. *Challinor* [2016] W.T.L.R. 43, [63]; [2015] EWCA Civ 59; *A.-G.* v. *Aljunied-Hougang-Punggol East Town Council* [2015] SGHC 137, [114].

[44] *Ying* v. *Song* [2010] NSWSC 1500, [246], affirmed *Ying* v. *Song* [2012] NSWCA 362; *Westgem Investments Pty Ltd (receivers and managers) (administrator appointed)*

It follows that, if the trust purpose fails, the subject funds would not be available to the creditors of the borrower (or grantee). From the perspective of the funds provider, a *Quistclose* trust performs essentially a security function.[45]

An issue that remains to be decided is whether the fund provider, by virtue of his status as a trust beneficiary, would be able to revoke the trust pursuant to *Saunders* v. *Vautier*.[46] The Court of Appeal[47] has approved the following statement of this rule:

> Although the beneficiaries cannot[,] in general, control the trustees while the trust remains in being, or commit them to a particular dealing with the trust property, they can, if *sui juris* and together entitled to the whole beneficial interest, put an end to the trust and direct the trustees to hand over the trust property as they direct; and this is so even if the trust deed contains express provisions for the determination of the trust. This principle also applies where there is an absolutely vested gift made payable on a future event, with a direction to accumulate the income in the meantime and pay it with the principal.[48]

In terms more sceptical of the traditional understanding of the rule, the New South Wales Court of Appeal has said:

> [T]he 'rule' [in *Saunders* v. *Vautier*] is best described as a *power* on the part of the beneficiaries, with a correlative *liability* on the part of the trustees . . . The exercise of the power does not involve the performance by the trustees of any part of their office as active trustees; instead, it brings their office to an end . . . Anglo-Australian law has taken the course of giving primacy to adult beneficiaries who enjoy an absolute vested and

v. *Saracen Project Management Pty Ltd [No. 2]* [2012] WASC 358, [47]: "A Quistclose trust typically involves a loan of money to be used by the borrower solely for the purpose of making a payment to a particular person or class of persons (although the reasoning in Quistclose Investments has since been applied to transfers of money other than by way of loan). The borrower does not receive and hold the money absolutely prior to payment to the third party and is it [sic] obliged in equity to return the money to the lender if the purpose of the loan cannot be fulfilled for any reason. Consequently, a debt will only be created between the lender and the borrower once the trust has been discharged".

45 *Ontario (Training, Colleges and Universities)* v. *Two Feathers Forest Products LP*, 2013 ONCA 598, [23].

46 *Saunders* v. *Vautier* (1841) Cr. & Ph. 240; 41 E.R. 482.

47 *Thorpe* v. *Revenue and Customs Commissioners* [2010] S.T.C. 964, [22]; [2010] EWCA Civ 339.

48 J. McGhee (gen. ed.), *Snell's Equity*, 31st ed. (London: Sweet & Maxwell, 2005), [27–025] (footnotes omitted). See now J. McGhee (gen. ed.), *Snell's Equity*, 33rd ed. (London: Sweet & Maxwell, 2015), [29–030].

> indefeasible interest in trust property, such that the power overrides restrictions imposed by testators and settlors in the trust instrument.[49]

Imagine that a debtor, as part of a restructuring exercise and in exchange for certain stakeholders' consent to the restructuring plan, transfers a sum of money to a trustee for the purpose of discharging liabilities to certain third-party creditors. If the restructuring plan is unsuccessful and the debtor goes into liquidation, the liquidator might be tempted to rely on *Saunders* v. *Vautier* to terminate the *Quistclose* trust so that the funds would be available to all creditors. The reliance on *Saunders* v. *Vautier* would be on the basis that, pending payment to the intended payees, the debtor is the only beneficiary of the *Quistclose* trust. The point is thus whether a *Quistclose* trust fund provider could invoke *Saunders* v. *Vautier* to revoke the trust, notwithstanding that the trust purpose could still be implemented.

The rule in *Saunders* v. *Vautier* may be excluded by contract and other appropriate forms of stipulation.[50] Absent appropriate stipulation, the fund provider would nevertheless not be able to revoke the trust if the intended payees had acquired a beneficial interest in the trust fund. That is because:

> [W]here trustees are directed at their absolute discretion to pay or apply the whole or any part of the income of the fund to or for the benefit of A, and are told to pay or apply to or for the benefit of B any part of the income not applied for A's benefit, A and B, if both *sui juris*, can together compel the trustees to pay the whole income as they direct, for they are the sole owners of each slice of income. But the rule does not apply if other persons have possible interests in the income, so that A and B alone could not control the trustees' application of the income.[51]

[49] *Beck* v. *Henley* [2014] NSWCA 201, [33]–[34] (italics original; citations omitted).

[50] *Don King Productions Inc.* v. *Warren* [2000] Ch. 291, 321:

> The rule in *Saunders* v. *Vautier* . . . (which enables the sole beneficiary or beneficiaries to give directions to the trustee) only applies if the beneficiary is entitled to wind up the trust and require the trustee to assign to him the subject matter of the trust. If the trust cannot be determined because the trustee has under the contract held as a trust asset outstanding obligations and has no power to transfer the trust asset to the beneficiary or his order, the rule does not apply.

[51] McGhee (gen. ed.), *Snell's Equity*, 31st ed. [27–025] (footnotes omitted), quoted with approval in *Thorpe* v. *Revenue and Customs Commissioners* [2010] S.T.C. 964, [22]. See now McGhee (gen. ed.), *Snell's Equity*, 33rd ed. [29–030].

The intended payees may gain a beneficial interest in at least two situations identified by the Deputy Judge in *Re Margaretta*[52] as being:

> a. where the obvious intention of the transaction would be frustrated if the donor were to retain a power of revocation of the trust;
> b. where the existence of the trust arrangements is communicated to the intended payee and the latter gains a beneficial interest in the money either because of the creation of an estoppel in his favour or because communication perfects an assignment of the donor's equitable interest to him.[53]

Even if the intended payees were not informed of the trust arrangement, it seems that the trustee's insolvency could prevent the application of *Saunders* v. *Vautier*. In the hypothetical above, revocation of the *Quist close* trust could frustrate the intention of the arrangement, namely to afford insolvency protection to the third-party creditors.

Remedial constructive trust

'[T]he courts of England and Wales do not recognise a remedial constructive trust as opposed to an institutional constructive trust.'[54] This is in part due to the concerns about its impact on insolvency law:

> The insolvency road is blocked off to remedial constructive trusts, at least when judge driven in a vehicle of discretion . . . To a trust lawyer and, even more so[,] to an insolvency lawyer, the prospect of a court imposing such a trust is inconceivable and, in my judgment, even the most enthusiastic student of the law of restitution would be forced to recognise that the scheme imposed by statute for a fair distribution of the assets of an insolvent company precludes the application of the equitable principles manifested in the remedial constructive trust.[55]

In jurisdictions that allow a remedial constructive trust, its availability is sensitive to insolvency considerations. For example, in Canada it is said:

> Constructive trust is a discretionary remedy. In a bankruptcy there are other interests to consider besides those of the defrauder and the

[52] [2005] S.T.C. 610; [2005] EWHC 582 (Ch).
[53] [2005] S.T.C. 610, [24] (citations omitted).
[54] *Sinclair Investments (U.K.) Ltd* v. *Versailles Trade Finance Ltd (in administrative receivership)* [2012] Ch. 453, [37]; [2011] EWCA Civ 347. See also *FHR European Ventures LLP* v. *Cedar Capital Partners LLC* [2015] A.C. 250, [47]; [2014] UKSC 45.
[55] *Re Polly Peck International (in admin.) (No. 2)* [1998] 3 All E.R. 812, 827.

> defraudee: there are other creditors. Thus, the exercise of remedial discretion must be informed by additional considerations than in a civil fraud trial.[56]

In the United States, where courts often speak of the constructive trust as an equitable remedy for certain claims in restitution, the Court of Appeals for the Seventh Circuit developed its concerns over the use of the remedial constructive trust in insolvency as follows:

> We ... recognize that the constructive trust can subvert bankruptcy's distribution scheme if courts lose sight of the fact that it is an extraordinary equitable remedy, to be used sparingly ...
>
> When a restitution claim is made against a bankruptcy estate, the key question to ask is whether the estate – not the now-defunct debtor – would be unjustly enriched by keeping the claimant's property ... The court should focus its attention on the equities of the unauthorized transfer of the claimant's property to the debtor's creditors ...
>
> One question remains: How could the debtor's creditors (that is, the debtor's bankruptcy estate) gain an equitable interest when the debtor itself had none? To answer it, we must remember what, in substance, the constructive trust is designed to do ... The question is not whether the debtor had a legitimate ownership interest in the disputed property. The question is whether the law should presume that the debtor was holding the property for the benefit of another. If so, then the rightful owner has a claim in restitution against the bankruptcy estate. The remedy for that claim, if proven, is return of the property, unless a good defense exists ...
>
> If the issue were only the statutory scope of the debtor's property, the debtor's creditors would always lose in a contest with a claimant who had a valid restitution claim against the debtor. But if the constructive trust is understood as the remedy for a restitution claim against the estate, the estate may be able to invoke certain defenses that were not available to the debtor ...
>
> Viewing constructive trust in bankruptcy for what it is – the remedy for a claim in restitution where the estate possesses property belonging to another – allows these defenses to be available to the estate.
>
> We need not explore every nook and cranny in the complex area of constructive trust in bankruptcy. It is enough to say that, in bankruptcy, a restitution claimant must at a minimum prove its interest in specific property in the estate's possession to warrant the remedy of constructive trust. The estate, acting on behalf of the debtor's general creditors, may have state-law defenses against the restitution claim that the debtor did not have.[57]

[56] *Credifinance Securities Ltd* v. *DSLC Capital Corp.* (2011) 74 C.B.R. (5th) 161, [44]; 2011 ONCA 160.

[57] *In re Mississippi Valley Livestock Inc.*, 745 F.3d 299, 304–7 (7th Cir. 2014).

In jurisdictions where constructive trusts have remedial qualities, the advent of insolvency can thus affect whether a constructive trust is recognised or enforced at all. But even in England, insolvency law informs the decision whether constructive trusts exist.

Directors' duty to creditors and transaction avoidance

The statutory insolvency scheme is buttressed by provisions allowing the reversal of antecedent transactions that are deemed to violate the policies underlying the statutory scheme, such as fraudulent conveyances and unlawful preferences.[58]

The insolvency transaction avoidance regime must maintain an appropriate balance between commercial certainty and insolvency policy.[59] In this regard, equity plays a significant role in promoting the objectives of insolvency law, in particular in regulating directors' conduct. The Singapore Court of Appeal has said:

> It is trite that directors have a duty to act in the best interest of the company as a whole. When a company is solvent, the company's directors owe no duty to creditors . . . However, it is now also settled law that when a company is insolvent, or even in a parlous financial position, directors have a fiduciary duty to take into account the interests of the company's creditors when making decisions for the company. This fiduciary duty requires directors to ensure that the company's assets are not dissipated or exploited for their own benefit to the prejudice of creditors' interests. In this regard, the purpose of this duty mirrors that of the avoidance provisions in seeking to preserve the company's assets for distribution to the company's creditors through the mechanism of insolvency.[60]

[58] *Singularis Holdings Ltd* v. *PricewaterhouseCoopers* [2015] 2 W.L.R. 971, [11]; [2014] UKPC 36.

[59] *Allied Concrete Ltd* v. *Meltzer* [2015] NZSC 7, [1], [138]:

> Parliament has long accepted that creditors who enter into transactions with companies which have reached the point of insolvency are entitled to protection in some circumstances. This acknowledges that considerations of fairness to individual creditors are engaged in this context and that there are risks to commercial confidence if what appear to be normal, everyday commercial transactions are re-opened long after the event ... Maintaining an appropriate balance between not disrupting settled commercial dealings when insolvency is not suspected and upholding the system of distribution on insolvency has been the long-standing fixed policy of voidable transaction legislation.

[60] *Liquidators of Progen Engineering Pte Ltd* v. *Progen Holdings Ltd* [2010] 4 S.L.R. 1089, [48]; [2010] SGCA 31. See also *National Westminster Bank plc* v. *Lucas* [2014] B.P.I.R.

Accordingly, a director responsible for a voidable transaction (such as an unlawful preference) may also be in breach of his duty to have regard to the interests of the creditors as a class.[61]

Equity also has a role in moderating the application of statutory transaction avoidance rules. A notable example concerns section 550 of the US Bankruptcy Code.[62] Section 550(a) provides that, to the extent that a transfer is avoided under, among others, sections 544, 545, 547, 548 549 and 553(b),[63] the trustee may recover, for the benefit of the estate, the property transferred, or, if the court so orders, the value of such property, from (1) the initial transferee of such transfer or the entity for whose benefit such transfer was made; or (2) any immediate or mediate transferee of such initial transferee.

The Bankruptcy Code does not define 'initial transferee', and the legislative history is silent on the issue as well. It is generally accepted that the first entity in physical possession of funds is not necessarily a transferee. 'Transferee' is not a self-defining term; it must mean something different from possessor or holder or agent. Case-law suggests 'transferee' must have legal dominion or dispositive control over the assets at issue.[64] Thus 'initial transferee' does not include those who are not beneficial owners.[65] For example, when A gives a cheque to B as agent for C, then C is the 'initial transferee'; the agent may be disregarded.[66]

Accordingly, the majority of courts apply the 'dominion and control' test to determine whether an entity qualifies as the 'initial transferee'. Under the dominion and control test, an initial transferee must (1) have legal dominion and control over the property – for example, the right to

551, [71]; [2014] EWHC 653 (Ch) (when 'a company . . . faces a real risk of being unable to pay its creditors . . . the directors are bound to consider the interests of the creditors and not simply those of the shareholders . . .'); *Moulin Global Eyecare Holdings* v. *Olivia Lee Sin Mei* (2014) 17 H.K.C.F.A.R. 466, [57]; [2014] HKCFA 63.

61 *Re Cityspan Ltd* [2007] 2 B.C.L.C. 522; [2007] EWHC 751 (Ch); *GHLM Trading Ltd* v. *Maroo* [2012] 2 B.C.L.C. 369, [168]; [2012] EWHC 61 (Ch).

62 5 U.S.C.

63 These provisions deal, inter alia, with unlawful preference and fraudulent conveyance.

64 *CNB International Inc. Litigation Trust* v. *Lloyds TSB Bank plc (In re CNB International Inc.)*, 440 B.R. 31 (W.D.N.Y. 2010); *Bonded Financial Services* v. *European American Bank*, 838 F.2d 890, 893 (7th Cir. 1988) ('Although the Bankruptcy Code does not define "transferee", and there is no legislative history on the point, we think the minimum requirement of status as a "transferee" is dominion over the money or other asset, the right to put the money to one's own purposes.')

65 *Weisfelner* v. *Fund 1 (In re Lyondell Chemical Co.)*, 503 B.R. 348, 382 (Bankr. S.D.N.Y. 2014).

66 *Bonded Financial Services* v. *European American Bank*, 838 F.2d 890, 893 (1988).

use the property for its own purpose – and (2) exercise this legal dominion and control.[67] Thus when a debtor's cheque transfers money to a current account, the 'initial transferee' is the bank's customer, who possesses control over the funds, rather than the bank that holds money subject to its customer's orders.[68]

The rationale behind the 'dominion and control' test is equitable:

> [T]his Court carved out an *equitable* exception to the literal statutory language of 'initial transferee,' known as the mere conduit or control test, for initial recipients who are mere conduits with no control over the fraudulently-transferred funds ... In doing so, this Court has adopted a flexible, pragmatic, *equitable* approach of looking beyond the particular transfer in question to the circumstances of the transaction in its entirety ... The mere conduit or control test is a judicial creation that is not based in statutory language, but is an exception based on the bankruptcy courts' *equitable* powers ... *Equitable* considerations play a major role in the mere conduit or control test because it would be inequitable to hold an initial recipient of the debtor's fraudulently-transferred funds liable where that recipient could not ascertain the transferor debtor's solvency, lacked any control over the funds, or lacked knowledge of the source of the funds ... The conduit or control test is based on, and defined by, *equity* and requires good faith to escape 'initial transferee' liability. In effect, we have tempered literal application of § 550(a)(1), examining all the facts and circumstances surrounding a transaction to prevent recovery from a transferee innocent of wrongdoing and deserving of protection.[69]

The parallel with the equitable doctrine of ministerial receipt as it is known in various common law jurisdictions will be apparent.[70]

Insolvency expenses

Insolvency expenses are post-insolvency entitlements which by statute generally have priority over creditors' pre-insolvency entitlements.

[67] *Grayson Consulting Inc.* v. *Wachovia Securities Inc. (In re Derivium Capital LLC)*, 716 F.3d 355, 362 (4th Cir. S.C. 2013); *In re Allen*, 2014 Bankr. LEXIS 1302 (Bankr. D.N.J., 26 Mar. 2014).

[68] *Bonded Financial Services* v. *European American Bank*, 838 F.2d 890 (1988).

[69] *Martinez* v. *Hutton (In re Harwell)*, 628 F.3d 1312, 1322–3 (11th Cir. 2010) (emphasis added).

[70] For example, *Jeremy D. Stone Consultants Ltd* v. *National Westminster Bank plc* [2013] EWHC 208 (Ch), [244]–[245]; *Chua Kwee Sin* v. *Venerable Sek Meow Di* [2013] SGHC 265, [54].

In liquidation terminology, pre-insolvency debts are provable, while post-insolvency claims are payable in full (though not provable).

There is, however, an equitable exception. Certain pre-insolvency debts would become payable as expenses if they fell within the principle in *In re Lundy Granite.*[71] The principle 'permits, on equitable grounds, the concept of a liability incurred as an expense of the liquidation to be expanded to include liabilities incurred before the liquidation in respect of property afterwards retained by the liquidator for the benefit of the insolvent estate'.[72] Sometimes it is seen as the salvage principle.[73]

The Supreme Court of Victoria, after a careful review of the English authorities,[74] accurately summarised the operation of the *Lundy Granite* principle in respect of rent as follows:

> First, prima facie claims under pre-liquidation leases are provable; they are not payable as expenses of the winding-up, the importance of preserving *pari passu* distribution being emphasised. Second, although rent is not incurred by the liquidator (the obligation existing in the pre-liquidation lease) the ambit of the administration expense is expanded where the liquidator actively retains (as opposed to passively holds) or uses the premises for the purposes of the winding-up. In those circumstances rent accruing during that period of retention or use will be an expense of the winding-up. Third, the rent will not be an expense of the winding up where the retention or use is agreed to or acquiesced in by the landlord so as to secure mutual benefits for both the purposes of the winding-up and the landlord.[75]

The *Lundy Granite* principle does not mean that whether debts should count as insolvency expenses is a matter for the discretion of the court. The principle serves only to illuminate the process of statutory construction.[76] Accordingly, in context of liquidation expenses, Lord Hoffmann said:

[71] (1871) L.R. 6 Ch. App. 462.

[72] *Re Toshoku Finance UK plc (in liq.)* [2002] 1 W.L.R. 671, [29]; [2002] UKHL 6.

[73] *Jervis* v. *Pillar Denton Ltd* [2015] Ch. 87; [2014] EWCA Civ 180.

[74] Including, *In re Progress Assurance Co.* (1870) L.R. 9 Eq. 370; *In re Bridgewater Engineering Co.* (1879) 12 Ch. D. 181; *In re South Kensington Co-operative Stores* (1881) 17 Ch. D. 161; *In re Oak Pits Colliery Co.* (1882) 21 Ch. D. 322; *In re Lancashire Cotton Spinning Co.* (1887) 35 Ch. D. 656; *Shackell & Co.* v. *Chorlton & Sons* [1895] 1 Ch. 378; *In re ABC Engineering Co. (No. 3)* [1970] 1 W.L.R. 702; *In re Downer Enterprises* [1974] 1 W.L.R. 1460.

[75] *Ansett Australia Ground Staff Superannuation Plan Pty Ltd* v. *Ansett Australia Ltd* (2002) 174 F.L.R. 1, [321]; [2002] VSC 576.

[76] *Jervis* v. *Pillar Denton Ltd* [2015] Ch. 87, [77].

> [The *Lundy Granite* principle] was not . . . a general test for deciding what counted as an expense of the liquidation. Expenses incurred after the liquidation date need no further equitable reason why they should be paid. Of course it will generally be true that such expenses will have been incurred by the liquidator for the purposes of the liquidation. It is not the business of the liquidator to incur expenses for any other purpose. But this is not at all the same thing as saying that the expenses will necessarily be for the benefit of estate. They may simply be liabilities which, as liquidator, he has to pay. For example, there will be the fees payable to fund the Insolvency Service, ranking as paragraph (c) in rule 4.218(1) [of the Insolvency Rules 1986 (UK)], where the benefit to the estate may seem somewhat remote . . .
>
> Rule 4.218 determines what counts as expenses, subject only to the limited discretion under section 156 of the [Insolvency Act 1986 (UK)] to re-arrange the priorities of expenses *inter se*. The court will of course interpret rule 4.218 to include debts which, under the *Lundy Granite Co.* principle, are deemed to be expenses of the liquidation. Ordinarily this means that debts such as rents under a lease will be treated as coming within paragraph (a), but the principle may possibly enlarge the scope of other paragraphs as well. But the application of that principle does not involve an exercise of discretion any more than the application of any other legal principle to the particular facts of the case.[77]

The application of the *Lundy Granite* principle is not limited to rent. For instance, a liquidator's election not to disclaim an ongoing contract for services may result in the charges for those services being liquidation expenses.[78] Thus it has been said that the *Lundy Granite* principle applies where, before the commencement of the insolvency process, the company entered into a contract with a third party which continued to operate after the insolvency process and the insolvency officeholder elected to retain the benefit of the contract for the purposes of the insolvency process.[79]

The *Lundy Granite* principle may be contrasted with the *Berkeley Applegate* principle. When the former does not apply, the latter may.[80] The former does not confer a discretionary jurisdiction to award insolvency expenses, but the latter does:

[77] *Re Toshoku Finance UK plc (in liq.)* [2002] 1 W.L.R. 671, [30], [38].

[78] *Grapecorp Management Pty Ltd (in liq.)* v. *Grape Exchange Management Euston Pty Ltd* (2012) 93 A.C.S.R. 1, [89]; [2012] VSC 112.

[79] *Re Portsmouth City Football Club Ltd (in liq.)* [2013] Bus. L.R. 374, [95]; [2012] EWHC 3088 (Ch).

[80] *Thackray* v. *Gunns Plantations Ltd* (2011) 85 A.C.S.R. 144, [58]; [2011] VSC 380.

> The authorities establish . . . a general principle that where a person seeks to enforce a claim to an equitable interest in property, the court has a discretion to require as a condition of giving effect to that equitable interest that an allowance be made for costs incurred and for skill and labour expended in connection with the administration of the property. It is a discretion which will be sparingly exercised; but factors which will operate in favour of its being exercised include the fact that, if the work had not been done by the person to whom the allowance is sought to be made, it would have had to be done either by the person entitled to the equitable interest . . . or by a receiver appointed by the court whose fees would have been borne by the trust property . . .; and the fact that the work has been of substantial benefit to the trust property and to the persons interested in it in equity. [81]

Although the jurisdiction is to be exercised in respect of property in which an equitable interest subsists and is to be enforced, it is not one which is to be exercised only in favour of someone standing in the position of trustee in relation to that property. The claim for an allowance is a claim made by a person who has done work or incurred expenditure which benefits the beneficiary.[82] Thus in *Berkeley Applegate* itself, the court allowed a liquidator to be paid his proper expenses and remuneration incurred in connection with the administration of assets held by a company on trust where the company's own assets were insufficient to meet those expenses and remuneration.

The principle's rationale is in essence practicality and fairness:

> The *Berkeley Applegate* principles were built on the equitable principle that he who seeks equity has to do equity. If work has been done by the trustee in respect of the trust property, without which work it would be impossible for the beneficiary to actualise or claim the trust property and that work has to be done either by the beneficiary or a receiver appointed by the court, the beneficiary has to give recognition to the skill and labour of the trustee incurred in making his claim possible. In other words, the question is whether the work done by the trustee is reasonably necessary to enable the beneficiary to claim his beneficial interest over the trust property. If yes, the court has jurisdiction to award an allowance to the trustee for his skill and labour and to order it be paid out of the trust property.[83]

In *Re Performance Investment Products Corp.*,[84] the Hong Kong Court of First Instance returned to first principles in addressing a claim that the

[81] *Re Berkeley Applegate (Investment Consultants) Ltd (in liq.)* [1989] Ch. 32, 50–1.

[82] *Green* v. *Bramston* [2011] B.P.I.R. 44, [18]; [2010] EWHC 3106 (Ch).

[83] *Re Lehman Brothers Securities Asia Ltd* [2011] HKEC 567, [48]; [2011] HKCFI 265.

[84] [2014] HKEC 465; [2014] HKCFI 481.

Berkeley Applegate principles applied to the costs a liquidator incurred in identifying and locating the assets of the debtor company. The court said:

> The underlying logic of the *Berkeley Applegate* principle is straightforward. There will be cases in which it is difficult, and sometimes impossible, to identify what part of a group of disparate assets held in the name of an insolvent company are assets which other people have entrusted to the company and which part are assets which form part of a company's own estate. A liquidator faced with liquidating such a company will have to undertake tasks necessary to locate all assets and assess whether it is possible to identify if some of them belong to third parties who are asserting claims as beneficial owner to assets held by the company. The costs of undertaking those tasks are generally fairly attributable to both the assets held on trust and those of the company. It would be artificial and probably impossible to apportion them precisely between the two. It would also be very expensive. In such circumstances the court proceeds on the basis that the fairest and most practical way to proceed is to apportion the costs between the two interest groups in proportion to the total value of their respective claims.[85]

Later, the court continued:

> The principle extends to identifying and locating assets. The reason is practical. A liquidator is appointed over a Hong Kong company to collect in assets in which it appears to a liquidator it has a proprietary interest. An obvious example would be a bank account opened in the name of a company. It may become apparent during the course of a liquidation that some of those assets may be held on trust for third parties. The liquidator may discover this from his own investigations or because claims are asserted by third parties; as in the present case. To continue with the example of the bank account, a third party may assert a beneficial interest in funds derived from transfers made to a subsidiary of the company in liquidation, and the liquidator is in a position to know that the subsidiary transferred parts of its receipts from third parties over time to a bank account of the company in Hong Kong. He will need to investigate the flow of transfers and the liquidator and lawyers will need to consider whether or not any part of the money in the company's account, as a matter of Hong Kong law, is properly treated as money in which the third party has a beneficial interest. Those tasks do not add to or maintain the value of the asset, but they are tasks which it is necessary and proper for the liquidator to carry out. The *Berkeley Applegate* principle provides that the cost of such work is payable out of trust assets. This of itself does not prejudice the third party. Without the assistance of the liquidator he would probably find it impossible to demonstrate that he

[85] [2014] HKEC 465, [56].

> had a beneficial interest in any part of the assets of the company in liquidation.[86]

It follows from these general and specific statements of the principle's rationale that the *Berkeley Applegate* discretion will not normally be exercised in favour of a person pursuing, or investigating whether to pursue, an interest adverse to that of the beneficiary. That is, the discretion normally will not be exercised in favour of a person who maintains that the beneficiary is not entitled to the property from which the allowance is sought. It is a different matter where the allowance is sought in respect of work done for the purposes of advancing, enforcing and giving effect to the beneficial interests of those entitled to the trust property.[87] In that situation, the *Berkeley Applegate* discretion may be exercised. Thus it has been said that the *Berkeley Applegate* principle can apply only where the beneficiary needs the assistance of the court to secure his rights.[88]

While the court's power to allow a trustee – or the administrator or liquidator of a corporate trustee – recourse to trust assets for remuneration and expenses is to be sparingly exercised,[89] it is generally established that a liquidator is entitled to be paid from the trust account in priority to other claimants his reasonable remuneration and reimbursement or exoneration for reasonable expenses incurred in administering the trust property, including handling and determining claims of creditors necessary to determine who is entitled to the moneys in the account.[90]

It also applies to assets subject to a statutory charge created by the insolvency legislation. Although it is unclear whether the beneficiaries of

[86] *Ibid.*, [58]. See also *Custom House Capital Ltd (in liq.)* v. *Companies Acts 1963–2009* [2012] IEHC 382; *Re Home Payments Ltd (in liq.)* [2013] IEHC 507; *Re MF Global Hong Kong Ltd* [2015] HKEC 1089, [31]; [2015] HKCFI 972 ('*Berkeley Applegate* recognises that it is equitable for fiduciaries tasked with collecting in and administering trust property held by the company which they supervise, to recover their costs of so doing out of the trust assets. It is inherent in this reasoning that there is at the material time no practical nor fair alternative.').

[87] *Re Lehman Brothers Securities Asia Ltd* [2014] HKEC 465, [58]; *Credit and Mercantile* v. *Kaymuu* [2014] B.P.I.R. 1127, [223]–[224]; [2014] EWHC 1746 (Ch).

[88] *Re Birchall* [2015] B.P.I.R. 751, [19]; [2015] EWHC 1541 (Ch).

[89] *Trio Capital Ltd (administrator appointed)* v. *ACT Superannuation Management Pty Ltd* (2010) 79 A.C.S.R. 425, [26]; [2010] NSWSC 941; *Re Home Payments Ltd (in liq.)* [2013] IEHC 507; *Re Dungowan Manly Pty Ltd (in liq.)* [2015] NSWSC 491, [107].

[90] *Re All Class Insurance Brokers Pty Ltd (in liq.)* [2014] NSWSC 475, [29]; *Re AAA Financial Intelligence Ltd (in liq.) (No. 2)* [2014] NSWSC 1270.

the statutory charge have an equitable interest in the assets, Briggs J. (as he then was) said:

> [T]he *Berkeley Applegate* principle applied to the position of administrators who, when taking office after the cessation of former administrators, find that they are, whether they realised it previously or not, in the position of having to administer and execute the terms of the statutory charge created by schedule B1, para. 99(4) [of the Insolvency Act 1986 (UK)]. It seems to me, as a matter of common sense, justice and equity, only right that the beneficiaries of that charge should have to pay collectively a reasonable sum towards the cost of having it executed in their favour against the company's assets.[91]

Analogous to the *Berkeley Applegate* fact pattern is an insolvency office-holder's application for directions which necessitates the joinder of representative parties. Who should bear the costs incurred by such representative parties?

It is instructive first to consider the usual practice in cases involving the court's determination of a question arising in connection with the administration of an estate. Costs ordinarily follow the event. The winner receives his costs. The loser pays them. However:

> Special costs rules have been devised in the Equity jurisdiction to guide parties to trusts-related litigation. Costs in such cases remain at the discretion of the Court. But subject to that overriding discretion, the cases provide litigants with some guidance as to how that discretion is likely to be exercised, all other things being equal. The 'classic statement' is that of Kekewich J. in *Re Buckton*[92] ... In *Re Buckton*, Kekewich J. divided trust litigation into three broad categories: (a) The first category involves proceedings brought by trustees to obtain the Court's guidance on the construction of the trust deed or some aspect of the trust's administration. In such cases, the costs of all parties necessarily participating are treated as incurred for the benefit of the estate and ordered to be paid out of the trust fund.
>
> (b) The second category involves a similar application, but by someone other than a trustee (such as a beneficiary). However, it is a case which would have justified application by a trustee. The same approach is taken to costs in the second category as to the first.
>
> (c) The third category, however, is where a beneficiary is making a 'hostile claim' against the trustees, or another beneficiary. The claim may still involve a point of construction, or administration. It will often involve a claim to a beneficial interest or entitlement to a part of the trust fund. In the third category, involving a hostile claim against trustees or

[91] *Re Sports Betting Media Ltd (in admin.)* [2008] 2 B.C.L.C. 89, [11]; [2007] EWHC 2085 (Ch).

[92] [1907] 2 Ch. 406.

> another beneficiary, the usual principles as to costs apply. Ordinarily they will follow the event.[93]

To what extent is this usual procedure affected by the English Civil Procedure Rules? Referring to the applicable practice direction, in *Re Savile (dec'd)*,[94] Patten L.J. said:

> C.P.R. 46 PD.1 preserves the rule that a trustee or personal representative is entitled to an indemnity out of the trust fund or estate for costs properly incurred but makes no express provision for the costs of the other parties to an application for directions falling within the first two classes described in *Re Buckton*. But there is no doubt that the costs of any necessary parties to such an application will ordinarily be paid out of the fund or estate. The application is designed to allow the trustee or personal representative to obtain the sanction or guidance he needs for the proper administration of the estate and the Court's determination of that issue necessarily involves a consideration of the position of those affected (beneficiaries or creditors as the case may be) taking into account any objections or other submissions which they make . . .
>
> There can, of course, be exceptions to this general rule. Even in the context of an application which is necessary for the proper administration of the estate, the Court retains the power to disallow particular items of costs where the party in question has, for example, launched an unjustified personal attack on one of the other parties or has raised issues which make its conduct of the litigation deserving of moral condemnation. The Court has in such cases to distinguish between genuine points pursued in argument which are germane to the issue under consideration but which ultimately fail and points taken or applications made for no good or proper reason or which are motivated out of animosity towards the other parties. Applications for directions in relation to the administration of a trust or an estate should be critical but also constructive.[95]

His Lordship concluded:

> In my judgment, opposition by a beneficiary to a proposed course of action by a trustee or personal representative is not, without more, sufficient to justify a departure from the general rule that the costs of all necessary parties to a *Buckton* class 1 or class 2 application should be borne by the trust fund or estate. Strong opposition is often encountered, in my experience, in applications for directions by, for example, the trustees of pension funds particularly where the proposed course of action

[93] *Woodward* v. *Smith* [2014] 3 N.Z.L.R. 525, [21]–[23]; [2014] NZHC 407 (citations omitted). See also *Singapore Airlines Ltd* v. *Buck Consultants Ltd* [2012] Pens. L.R. 1, [67]; [2011] EWCA Civ 1542; *Perpetual Trust Ltd* v. *Capital + Merchant Finance Ltd (in receivership and in liq.)* [2013] NZHC 2320, [13]–[15].

[94] [2015] W.T.L.R. 635; [2014] EWCA Civ 1632.

[95] [2015] W.T.L.R. 635, [108]–[109].

> will either cast additional financial burdens on the employer or reduce the fund available to a particular class of member.[96]

The court's usual approach in the trust administration context has no doubt informed the judicial approach to insolvency officeholders' application for directions. As much as evident from the following remarks of Sir Nicolas Browne-Wilkinson V.-C., which may be quoted at length in order clearly to show the developing influence of the *Buckton* principles:

> If a trustee, liquidator or receiver, or any other person in a neutral capacity is holding moneys which belong to others but it is not known who is beneficially entitled, the court frequently makes orders that the costs of determining who is beneficially entitled to those moneys are to be paid out of the moneys held . . . I was initially surprised to discover that there is no general practice in the Companies Court as to the correct order for costs in cases where receivers or liquidators have taken out summonses to determine questions arising in the course of their administration. In some cases the order is made that the costs follow the event and the unsuccessful claimant pays, in others the costs come out of the fund . . . The range of summonses which can be issued and are heard raise such a wide range of issues that there can be no fixed rule. However, in my judgment the proper approach is as follows. In general, claims arising for determination in such cases are . . . hostile claims in which one or more parties are in dispute as to the ownership of property. It is litigation between rival claimants. In those circumstances one would expect that the costs would normally follow the event, the unsuccessful claimant paying not only his own costs but also the other side's. However, there are many cases in which it is essential for the due administration of the liquidator's or receiver's duties to obtain a decision from the court. In such cases there are often large classes of creditors, contributories or other claimants, the exact membership of which class is often not easily established or even known, who will be affected by such decision. In such a case the liquidator or receiver joins a representative respondent to argue the point on behalf of the class. Frequently the sum at stake for the individual respondent joined does not justify him incurring the costs involved in litigating the matter. As a result, in order to ensure that the matter is properly determined the costs of the representative respondents are frequently paid out of the fund. An agreement to that effect is often made before the proceedings are heard; indeed on occasion the court orders it before trial. But in my judgment those are special cases in which it is necessary for the proper execution of the duties of the receiver or liquidator to have the matter determined and a pre-emptive order as to costs is a necessary prerequisite to that determination being obtained.

[96] *Ibid.*, [112].

> This is not a rule applicable in all cases; it is simply in my judgment the right general approach to costs in these cases.[97]

That the trust law principle is now established in insolvency cases can be seen from *Re Equilift Ltd*,[98] where the court said:

> Ordinarily, where there is real doubt over whether a liquidator is holding monies as liquidator or as trustee, the Court will join the necessary parties (and, where there are a large number of them, representatives of recognised classes of potential beneficiaries) so that the matter may be resolved conclusively. Either way, the liquidator will usually be entitled to his costs out of the property (whatever its character). Often, but not always, the representative parties will be likewise entitled in respect of their costs, and a pre-emptive costs order will sometimes be made so as to ensure their effective participation. Nevertheless, it has to be borne in mind that any claim to treat what is ostensibly the Company's property as someone else's is, from the Company's perspective, hostile litigation, as to which the normal costs order is that the losing party pays.[99]

Some courts have indeed applied *Buckton* to determine the representative parties' liability for costs.[100]

In *Pearson* v. *Lehman Brothers Finance SA*, in the context of an application for directions by the administrators of LBIE, the court gave a reserved judgment because 'the submissions which have been made give rise to a question of potentially wide application upon which there is little direct authority'.[101] The court applied the general costs rule because the proceedings were a straight adversarial fight between LBIE and five of its affiliates, in relation to the beneficial ownership of certain classes of securities held by LBIE. For present purposes, the court's pertinent remarks are these:

> The line of authority [concerning the costs of a contentious probate action] is of course applicable, if at all, only by analogy to litigation about insolvent estates ... [A]lthough there are features of insolvency litigation which, by analogy with litigation about deceased's estates, may justify a departure from the general rule, the court should nonetheless

[97] *Re Westdock Realisations Ltd* [1988] B.C.L.C. 354, 359–60. 'Although [*Re Westdock Realisations*] did not concern trusts, Browne-Wilkinson V.-C. followed the same approach that Kekewich J. had in *Re Buckton*': *Woodward* v. *Smith* [2014] 3 N.Z.L.R. 525, [31].

[98] [2010] B.C.C. 860; [2009] EWHC 3104 (Ch).

[99] [2010] B.C.C. 860, [8]. See also *Denis MPC Ho* v. *Chan Kam Tim* [1999] 2 H.K.L.R.D. 102.

[100] For example, *Adams* v. *Sun* [2014] NZHC 1395.

[101] *Pearson* v. *Lehman Brothers Finance SA* [2010] EWHC 3044 (Ch), [1].

> approach any particular case for a departure with real caution, and litigants ought to expect to have to justify such a departure by reference to the facts about their alleged predicament, rather than merely by recourse to some supposed general principle.[102]

With respect, the court's reasoning seems slightly tortuous; seems to have discounted the fact that the *Buckton* principle applies to probate litigation;[103] and seems to have overlooked the clear judicial assimilation of insolvency litigation to trust litigation in costs matters. In fact, the court could have simply concluded that the proceedings there were essentially a *Buckton* category 3 case.[104]

Integrity of the insolvency process

Equity may serve to strengthen and preserve the objectives of insolvency proceedings and the insolvency process itself. Two examples are the anti-suit injunction and the rule in *Ex p. James*.[105]

As mentioned above, insolvency proceedings are a form of collective enforcement of claims. Thus it is well-established that the effect of a winding up order is to create a statutory trust of the world-wide assets of the company to be dealt with in accordance with English statutory rules of distribution.[106]

The statutory insolvency scheme is buttressed by provisions allowing the reversal of antecedent transactions that are deemed to violate the policies underlying the statutory scheme.[107] For instance, the preference

[102] *Ibid.*, [11], [13].

[103] *Cheung Pui Yuen* v. *Worldcup Investments Inc.* (2009) 12 H.K.C.F.A.R. 31, [56]–[59].

[104] See also *Kong Colin Chung Ping* v. *Kong Wing On* [2015] HKEC 968; [2015] HKCFI 883.

[105] (1874) L.R. 9 Ch. App. 609.

[106] *Singularis Holdings* v. *PricewaterhouseCoopers* [2015] 2 W.L.R. 971, [10]; *Stichting Shell Pensioenfonds* v. *Krys* [2015] A.C. 616, [14]. Cf. *Commissioner of Taxation* v. *Linter Textiles Australia Ltd (in liq.)* (2005) 220 C.L.R. 592; [2005] HCA 20.

[107] Such avoidance rules are ubiquitous in all insolvency systems; *Rubin* v. *Eurofinance SA* [2013] 1 A.C. 236, [94]; [2012] UKSC 46:

> Systems of insolvency law use avoidance proceedings as mechanisms for adjusting prior transactions by the debtor and for recovering property disposed of by the debtor prior to the insolvency. Thus under the Insolvency Act 1986 (UK) an administrator, or liquidator, or trustee in bankruptcy may, where there has been a transaction at an undervalue, or amounting to an unlawful preference, apply for an order restoring the position to what it would have been had the transaction not taken place: sections 238 et seq and 339 et seq. Other systems of law have similar mechanisms, but they will differ in matters such as the period during which such transactions are at risk of reversal and the role of good faith of

avoidance provisions serve to adjust the rights of creditors among themselves in such a way as to eliminate the effects of favourable treatment afforded to one or more creditors, to the exclusion of others, in the period immediately before an insolvent administration commences.[108]

In this connection, equity has an established role in the context of cross-border insolvency. The court may issue an anti-suit injunction against a creditor seeking to use foreign proceedings to gain an advantage over other creditors. For instance, the court may prevent a creditor from taking advantage of a foreign attachment.[109] The rationale for such injunction has been described thus:

> Where a company is being wound up in the jurisdiction of its incorporation, other interests are engaged. The court acts not in interest of any particular creditor or member, but in that of the general body of creditors and members … [T]here is a broader public interest in the ability of a court exercising insolvency jurisdiction in the place of the company's incorporation to conduct an orderly winding up of its affairs on a worldwide basis, notwithstanding the territorial limits of its jurisdiction. In protecting its insolvency jurisdiction, … the court is not standing on its dignity. It intervenes because the proper distribution of the company's assets depends upon its ability to get in those assets so that comparable claims to them may be dealt with fairly in accordance with a common set of rules applying equally to all of them. There is no jurisdiction other than that of the insolvent's domicile in which that result can be achieved. The alternative is a free-for-all in which the distribution of assets depends on the adventitious location of assets and the race to grab them is to the swiftest, and the best informed, best resourced or best lawyered.[110]

The emphasis in this passage on protecting the insolvency jurisdiction of the insolvent entity's domicile or incorporation is a rather old-fashioned

the parties to the transaction. While the precise elements of each avoidance provision differ from jurisdiction to jurisdiction, the differences merely reflect the local insolvency and commercial policies; *Rubin* v. *Eurofinance SA* [2013] 1 A.C. 236, [15] ('there is no international unanimity or significant harmonisation on the details of insolvency law, because to a large extent insolvency law reflects national public policy, for example as regards priorities or as regards the conditions for the application of avoidance provisions').

108 For example, *New Cap Reinsurance Corp. Ltd* v. *A.E. Grant* (2009) 257 A.L.R. 740, [21]; [2009] NSWSC 662.

109 *Harms Offshore Aht 'Taurus' GmbH & Co. Kg* v. *Bloom* [2010] Ch. 187; [2009] EWCA Civ 632.

110 *Stichting Shell Pensioenfonds* v. *Krys* [2015] A.C. 616, [24]. The same insolvency policy may also justify an anti-anti-suit injunction: for example, *Carlyle Capital Corp. Ltd (in liq.)* v. *Conway* [2013] 2 Lloyd's Rep. 179.

way of seeing things. Nowadays, the most pertinent jurisdiction is in fact the place of the insolvent entity's centre of main interests.[111]

While from a financial point of view insolvency proceedings are carried out for the benefit of creditors, insolvency proceedings are also a public act or process in which the public has an interest.[112] Thus a winding-up order has much wider consequences than a judgment *inter partes* because of its numerous statutory effects.[113]

Equity again has a role in maintaining the public nature of insolvency proceedings. Pursuant to *Ex p. James*, though sometimes described as an anomalous principle,[114] the court has power to control the actions of a trustee in bankruptcy. However, the power exists only in circumstances where it is necessary for directions to be issued by the court to ensure that the trustee, as the court's own officer, behaves as honestly as other people and in an honourable and high-minded way. In such cases, a court will issue directions controlling what a trustee in bankruptcy does, even if this means overriding rights which interested persons might otherwise be entitled to claim on a strict application of the rules of law and of equity in the technical sense.[115]

The actual decision in *Ex p. James* had an equitable origin and concerned a payment by a creditor to a trustee in bankruptcy under a mistake of law. The court ordered the trustee to repay the money and said:

> I think that the principle that money paid under a mistake of law cannot be recovered must not be pressed too far, and there are several cases in which the Court of Chancery has held itself not bound strictly by it. I am of opinion that a trustee in bankruptcy is an officer of the Court. He has inquisitorial powers given him by the Court, and the Court regards him as its officer, and he is to hold money in his hands upon trust for its equitable distribution among the creditors. The Court, then, finding that he has in his hands money which in equity belongs to some one else, ought to set an example to the world by paying it to the person really entitled to it. In my opinion the Court of Bankruptcy ought to be as honest as other people.[116]

[111] *Kemsley* v. *Barclays Bank plc* [2013] B.P.I.R. 839; [2013] EWHC 1274 (Ch); *Re HIH Casualty and General Insurance Ltd* [2008] 1 W.L.R. 852, [31]; [2008] UKHL 21.

[112] *Gamlestaden Fastigheter AB* v. *Baltic Partners Ltd* [2007] Bus. L.R. 1521, [32]; [2007] UKPC 26.

[113] *Re Intermain Properties Ltd* (1985) 1 B.C.C. 99555; *Interocean Holdings Group (BVI) Ltd* v. *Zi-Techasia (Singapore) Pte Ltd* [2014] 2 S.L.R. 485, [16]; [2014] SGHC 9.

[114] *Re Alitalia Linee Aeree Italiane SpA* [2011] 1 W.L.R. 2049, [47]; [2011] EWHC 15 (Ch).

[115] *Bank of Baroda* v. *Patel* [2009] B.P.I.R. 255, [45]; [2008] EWHC 3390 (Ch); *Re Nortel GmbH (in admin.)* [2014] A.C. 209, [122]; [2013] UKSC 52.

[116] *Ex p. James* (1874) L.R. 9 Ch. App. 609, 614. Cf. *O'Neill* v. *Phillips* [1999] 1 W.L.R. 1092, 1098 ('One of the traditional roles of equity, as a separate jurisdiction, was to restrain the

The present scope of the rule in *Ex p. James* has been described variously:

> The rule, . . . which at best is exercised as a discretionary power by the court, appears to have been exercised only in cases where there has been some form of enrichment of the assets of a bankrupt or insolvent company at the expense of the person seeking recoupment.[117]

More recently, David Richards J. said:

> [T]he principle may be confined to cases where the assets available for distribution are increased as a result of a mistake of law or fact or where advantage is taken of payments made by a third person without giving credit for them, *i.e.* an unjust enrichment of the company. [118]

And in another High Court case, there was said to be 'no basis on which the court could or should intervene to alter the terms expressly agreed at arm's length between commercial parties'.[119]

The application of *Ex p. James* resulting in a liquidator's repayment of a mistaken payment to the payor may incidentally achieve the economic effect of a remedial constructive trust.[120]

Conclusion

The brief survey in this chapter shows that equity's role in insolvency law is pervasive, and its relationship with insolvency law is complex. Three levels of equity–insolvency interaction may be detected. First, some equitable rules enlighten and shape insolvency law and practice. Secondly, some equitable rules are subordinated to insolvency law and policy. And thirdly, some equitable rules are developed specifically to promote insolvency objectives.

For ease of exposition, this chapter has sought to delineate equity's role into three categories, namely insolvency distribution, insolvency expenses and the integrity of insolvency proceedings. But the truth remains that '[t]he principles on which a court of equity acts are not

exercise of strict legal rights in certain relationships in which it considered that this would be contrary to good faith. These principles have, with appropriate modification, been carried over into company law.').

117 *Government of India* v. *Taylor* [1955] A.C. 491, 513.

118 *Re T & N Ltd* [2004] Pens. L.R. 351, [18]; [2004] EWHC 1680 (Ch). See also *Turner* v. *Avis* [2008] B.P.I.R. 1143.

119 *Amble Assets LLP (in admin.)* v. *Longbenton Foods Ltd (in liq.)* [2012] 1 All E.R. (Comm.) 764, [99]; [2011] EWHC 3774 (Ch). *Lomas* v. *Burlington Loan Management Ltd* [2015] B.P.I.R. 1162, [183]; [2015] EWHC 2270(Ch).

120 *Strategic Finance Ltd (in rec. and in liq.)* v. *Bridgman* [2013] N.Z.L.R. 650; [2013] NZCA 357.

divided into watertight compartments but form a seamless whole, however necessary it may be for the purposes of exposition to attempt to set them out under distinct headings'.[121]

If one were to attempt a summary of equity's engagement with insolvency, it would seem apt to say mutual fertilisation.

[121] *Re Berkeley Applegate (Investment Consultants) Ltd (in liq.)* [1989] Ch. 32, 51.

7

Equity and insolvency

A commentary

CATHERINE ADDY

Introduction

In his chapter on equity and insolvency (Chapter 6), Look Chan Ho explores 'how equity and insolvency influence each other's developments and at the same time restrict each other's sphere of operation'. For the purposes of that exploration he submits that whilst equity is relevant to many aspects of insolvency processes, its involvement may be divided into three broad categories: the distribution of an insolvent estate's assets, insolvency expenses and the integrity of the insolvency process. His survey leads him to conclude that equity's role in insolvency law is pervasive and that the relationship between the two is complex. Nevertheless, he considers that three types of insolvency–equity interaction may be detected:

> First, some equitable rules enlighten and shape insolvency law and practice. Secondly, some equitable rules are subordinated to insolvency law and policy. And thirdly, some equitable rules are developed specifically to promote insolvency objectives.[1]

Whilst there is no doubt that the three types of insolvency–equity interaction exist, a survey of the categories identified by Mr Ho also suggests that equity (alongside the application of the common law) can more appropriately be viewed as part of the rich and textured canvas upon which the largely statutory insolvency law has been painted: the weave and finish of the canvas both informing and affecting the colour, density and composition of the legislative paint required and, ultimately, its subsequent appearance.

[1] L.C. Ho, 'Equity and Insolvency', Chapter 6 of this volume, text after n. 120.

The result, it is submitted, is a work of art constantly evolving as the brushwork of the legislature makes deliberate changes – sometimes delicate, occasionally resembling the whitewash technique – to a continually developing overall picture.

Insolvency distribution

In addressing the first of his three categories, namely 'the distribution of the [insolvent] estate's assets', Look Chan Ho correctly notes that it is trite law that property which is held by an insolvent estate subject to a trust in favour of another is not available to the debtor's creditors and that, at least in the common law world, the concept of beneficial ownership is central to the distribution of the estate's assets.

As Mr Ho recognises with reference to authority, this reflects the fact that, ordinarily, a debtor cannot use that which he does not beneficially own in order to discharge his personal liabilities. Indeed, although expressly recognised by the UK legislature in bankruptcy,[2] in the sphere of corporate insolvency law it is simply an assumed matter of basic principle.[3] Its elementary nature is evidenced by the fact that it is rarely expressly stated.[4]

The equitable canvas upon which the insolvency law is painted naturally delimits the sphere of the latter's operation. Equity's involvement in this respect is not really concerned with the issue of the orderly *distribution* of the insolvent estate's assets but with the logically prior issue of the *identification* of those assets which may (and in the case of those assets

[2] See Insolvency Act 1986 (UK), s. 283(3), which provides that a bankrupt's estate (defined as all property belonging to or vested in the bankrupt at the commencement of the bankruptcy: sub-s. (1)) does not include any 'property held by the bankrupt on trust for any other person'. This section repeats similar provision which was previously to be found in the Bankruptcy Act 1914 (UK), s. 38(b).

[3] Parts IV–VII of the Insolvency Act 1986 (UK), which apply to corporate insolvency, contain no equivalent of the bankruptcy provision in section 283(3). However, the position stated in the text has long been accepted in corporate insolvency: for example, *Heritable Reversionary Co. Ltd* v. *Millar* [1892] A.C. 598.

[4] See, for example, *Lehman Bros International (Europe) (in admin.)* v. *CRC Credit Fund Ltd* [2012] Bus. L.R. 667; [2012] UKSC 6, termed the 'Client Money litigation'. The proceedings – an application by the administrators for directions – were premised upon the notion that identifiable money which was held by LBIE on trust for its clients was necessarily excluded from the estate available for distribution to creditors. It was evidently thought that such an elementary proposition did not require express judicial decision. Similarly, see *Re BA Peters plc (in admin.)* [2010] 1 B.C.L.C. 142, [21]; [2008] EWCA Civ 1604.

beneficially owned by others, may not) legitimately be collected for distribution.

Mr Ho concentrates on five areas of 'equitable intervention' as meriting discussion: set-off in insolvency, specific performance, *Quistclose* trusts, remedial constructive trusts and company directors' duties to creditors. However, are these areas not so much examples of 'equitable intervention' in the field of insolvency but rather examples of the ordinary application of equitable principles for the purposes of identifying those assets which fall within, and those assets which fall outside of, the relevant insolvent estate and are available to creditors? Brief consideration of the five areas suggests the latter and that each forms an integral part of the equitable backdrop to the insolvency legislation and, therefore, to the administration of insolvent estates. A number of interesting, novel ideas also arise.

Specific performance

From a practical perspective, the issues raised by specific performance and the specific enforceability of agreements are perhaps the most important of the five areas to be considered.

In *Re Lehman Brothers International (Europe) (in administration) (No. 2)*,[5] Patten L.J. explained why a scheme of arrangement pursuant to Part 26 of the Companies Act 2006 (UK) could not be sanctioned in respect of claimants' proprietary interests. Might it be possible to navigate a way out of the otherwise strict consequences of the language of Part 26 in circumstances where the equitable interests concerned arise from specifically enforceable contracts? With impressive ingenuity, Mr Ho argues that it might. Using the example of a landholding company which has contracted to sell land to investors, he suggests that a scheme of arrangement may indeed compromise the investors' constructive trust interests arising under specifically enforceable contracts.

Whilst its ingenuity is admirable, it is debatable whether the argument would survive judicial scrutiny. As the Court of Appeal concluded in the *Lehman Brothers* case, the court's jurisdiction under Part 26 of the Companies Act 2006 is circumscribed by the requirement that the scheme should be an arrangement with its creditors (or its members), reflecting the fact that it is only such persons who have claims against the company's estate (i.e. property which is beneficially owned by the

[5] [2010] Bus. L.R. 489; [2009] EWCA Civ 1161.

company). There is no provision which permits the court to vary compulsorily the existing proprietary *ownership* interests of others in assets which do not therefore form part of the insolvent estate.[6] Necessarily, such a beneficiary is not a creditor of the company in respect of his proprietary interest.

The position of a beneficial owner of an asset held by the company is also to be contrasted with the position of creditors who have proprietary interests pursuant to security over the *company's* own assets.[7] As Patten L.J. noted in the *Lehman Brothers* case, a secured creditor's position is 'wholly different' because the property over which such security is granted is never owned beneficially by the creditor but remains that of the company and is only ever held by the creditor as security for the debt.[8] The nature of the equitable interest of a purchaser under a specifically enforceable contract for the sale of land is that of an *existing beneficial owner* and is not one which falls within the same category as a *secured creditor*. In *Mountney* v. *Treharne*,[9] a case in which it was necessary for the Court of Appeal to identify the nature of the equitable interest of a purchaser under a specifically enforceable contract, Jonathan Parker L.J.[10] referred to authorities including *Howard* v. *Miller*,[11] in which Lord Parker of Waddington explained the position thus:

> It is material to consider what this interest – i.e. the interest of the purchaser under a contract for the sale of land – really was. It is sometimes said that under a contract for the sale of an interest in land *the vendor becomes a trustee for the purchaser of the interest contracted to be sold subject to a lien for the purchase-money*; but however useful such a statement may be as illustrating a general principle of equity, it is only true if and so far as a court of equity would under all the circumstances of the case grant specific performance of the contract. The interest conferred by the agreement in question was an interest commensurate with the relief which equity would give by way of specific performance . . .[12]

6 This could of course be achieved consensually, with the proprietary claimant voluntarily relinquishing such right in favour of the company and in return for creditor status. However, the court could not sanction a scheme which would have the effect of imposing this outcome upon those who were unwilling to consent to it.

7 As Look Chan Ho notes, these rights are capable of being compromised by a scheme of arrangement because it is the creditor's claim in *debt* which is varied or extinguished.

8 *Re Lehman Brothers International (Europe) (in administration) (No. 2)* [2010] Bus. L.R. 489, [60].

9 [2003] Ch. 135, [68]–[73]; [2002] EWCA Civ 1174.

10 Aldous and Laws L.JJ. agreed with Jonathan Parker L.J.

11 [1915] A.C. 316.

12 *Ibid.*, 326 (italics added).

Similarly, reference was made in *Mountney* v. *Treharne* to the following extract from *Fry on Specific Performance*:

> Where such a contract [*sc.* a contract for the sale of real property] is entered into, the legal estate in the property passes, not by the contract, but only upon and by virtue of the execution of a subsequent formal deed of conveyance. The *equitable estate or beneficial ownership, however, passes, as between the contracting parties, by the contract itself*, but only sub modo, or, in other words, conditionally upon the contract being one of which the court would decree specific performance, and also being ultimately completed by the fulfilment by vendor and purchaser respectively of the mutual obligations imposed on them by the contract.[13]

Accordingly, the Court of Appeal concluded that 'equity treats the personal contractual rights of a purchaser under a specifically enforceable contract for the sale of land as conferring on the purchaser a proprietary right enforceable against the land'.[14] In so doing, their Lordships expressly adopted the rationale of the judge at first instance in *Swiss Bank Corp.* v. *Lloyds Bank Ltd*,[15] where Browne-Wilkinson J. said:[16]

> [U]nder a specifically enforceable contract for the sale of land, the purchaser is treated in equity as the owner of the property whether or not an order for specific performance has been made. Again, in the law of trusts the beneficiary is treated as immediately entitled to his interest in the trust property whether or not an order for the execution of the trust has been made against the trustee. In this way the plaintiff's rights, although founded upon the ability of the court to make an order in *personam* against the other contracting party or the trustee, become an interest in the property itself, an equitable interest. Once the position is reached that an order for specific performance could have been made against the legal owner if the matter had been brought before the court, thereafter the legal owner holds the property shorn of those rights in the property which the courts of equity would decree belong to another.[17]

Mr Ho considers that there is little doubt that purchasers of land are creditors for the purposes of schemes of arrangement, since the seller's subsequent failure to convey the land would entitle the purchasers to

[13] E. Fry, *A Treatise on the Specific Performance of Contracts*, 6th ed., ed. by G.R. Northcote (London: Stevens, 1921), § 1392 (italics added).

[14] *Mountney* v. *Treharne* [2003] Ch. 135, [71]. [15] [1979] Ch. 548.

[16] Although, as noted by Jonathan Parker L.J., the decision in the *Swiss Bank Corp.* case was reversed by the Court of Appeal (whose decision was upheld by the House of Lords, both decisions being reported at [1982] A.C. 584), no doubt was cast on the accuracy of Browne-Wilkinson J.'s quoted analysis.

[17] *Swiss Bank Corp.* v. *Lloyds Bank Ltd* [1979] Ch. 548, 565–6.

damages. However, it is respectfully submitted that this is to fall into the same trap as did the administrators in the *Lehman Brothers* case. On the authorities identified above, if the purchaser has paid the entire purchase price for an identifiable piece of land pursuant to an enforceable contractual agreement for its sale, then he will already be the beneficial owner of such land. The only monetary claim, in respect of which the purchaser is properly a contingent creditor, is his claim in respect of the costs that he might incur in securing transfer of the legal title. Moreover, even if part of the agreed consideration remains outstanding prior to completion, if the contract is specifically enforceable, then it is the *seller* who is more aptly to be described as a creditor – in respect of his monetary claim against the purchaser for the relevant balance. Accordingly, if the vendor should subsequently become the subject of formal insolvency proceedings, the land will never form part of the estate available for distribution amongst its unsecured creditors. The Australian authorities which have allowed rights pursuant to share-option contracts to be compromised under a relevant scheme do not assist.[18] Whilst such a contract might be specifically enforced, prior to the compulsory allotment of shares, there are no identifiable issued shares in respect of which the option-holder could be said to be the existing beneficial owner pursuant to a constructive trust. Unlike the purchasers of land, such option-holders are therefore truly contingent creditors.

Time will tell which line of reasoning is to be judicially preferred. But in any event, the equitable doctrine of specifically enforceable contracts is not an example of equity 'intervening' in the application of Part 26 of the Companies Act regarding schemes of arrangement. Rather, it is an example of the legislation (as judicially construed) simply respecting the pre-existing equitable interests of others. If and to the extent that the legislature should wish to override the pre-existing equitable interests of third parties as a matter of insolvency law, it could no doubt do so with further brushwork.

Quistclose *trust*

Quistclose trusts can be of special importance in insolvency. They may be entered into to guard against the otherwise adverse consequences of potential formal insolvency proceedings. However, their creation and observance depend upon general laws – equitable principles of trusts and

[18] Ho, 'Equity and Insolvency', text to n. 34.

powers, and common law rules of contract – rather than on special insolvency laws. In his discussion concerning the operation of *Quistclose* trusts, Look Chan Ho poses an interesting question as to whether the rule in *Saunders* v. *Vautier*[19] might be applied so as to enable a fund-provider to revoke the original trust. This appears not to have been considered in the decided cases on *Quistclose* trusts. There are foreseeable difficulties with this where the relevant purpose of the *Quistclose* trust is to provide potential security for another. The nature of the latter's contingent interest in the fund (as an object of a mere power) as well as the interest of the fund-holder (or other person in whom a relevant directive power may be vested, if the fund-holder is a third party) will obviously require detailed further consideration before any attempt is made to rely upon the rule by the fund-provider (whether solvent or acting by its insolvency office-holder). However, rather than depending on insolvency laws as such, these are underlying issues of general equitable doctrine (subject of course to the provision of the fund being separately unwound pursuant to any applicable transaction avoidance legislation).

Remedial constructive trust

It is well known that remedial constructive trusts are not a feature of English law. Mr Ho's account of remedial constructive trusts poses a question: Is the firm stance taken against remedial constructive trusts by English courts founded in real or merely apparent concerns? According to Ho's exposition, even in those jurisdictions where remedial constructive trusts are an available form of discretionary relief, their imposition follows judicially recognised principles which will result in a consistent application of the remedy in circumstances where the target of the remedy is insolvent. Moreover, assuming the remedy operates retrospectively from the time at which the equity to the relief arose,[20] it will therefore operate in a reasonably predictable fashion to determine those assets which fall outside of the insolvent estate (and are to be regarded, retrospectively, as having always done so).

[19] (1841) Cr. & Ph. 240; 41 E.R. 482.

[20] See J.C. Campbell, 'When and Why a Bribe is Held on a Constructive Trust: The Method of Reasoning Towards an Equitable Remedy' (2015) 39 Aust. Bar Rev. 320, 330–2. By contrast, the issues raised by Campbell concerning the differing decision in *Muschinski* v. *Dodds* (1985) 160 C.L.R. 583 exemplify concerns which lie behind the stance of the English courts.

Also notable are the circumstances in which the US Court of Appeals for the Seventh Circuit anticipate that the remedy would be applied to a restitution claim. In *Re Mississippi Valley Livestock Inc.*,[21] the Court of Appeals said that such a claim would lead to relief in the form of a remedial constructive trust where the court considers that the estate 'would be unjustly enriched by keeping the claimant's property' and 'the question is whether the law should presume that the debtor was holding the property for the benefit of another'.[22] Though English law disclaims the remedial constructive trust, it is notable that the circumstances in which a constructive trust will be found to exist, as recently stated by the UK Supreme Court in *FHR European Ventures LLP* v. *Cedar Capital Partners LLC*,[23] seem to mirror the conditions for relief as stated in the *Mississippi Valley Livestock* case.

Set-off in insolvency

In his discussion of set-off in insolvency, Mr Ho refers to the distinction between solvent set-off and insolvency set-off, the latter being a feature of the statutory artwork currently found in rules 2.85[24] and 4.90[25] of the Insolvency Rules 1986 (UK) and section 323[26] of the Insolvency Act 1986 (UK). He notes that in the application of the self-executing statutory set-off, it is necessary to focus on the beneficial ownership of (rather than merely the legal title to) the relevant claims and thus, rightly, concludes

[21] 745 F.3d 299 (7th Cir. 2014).

[22] *Ibid.*, 304–7. This doctrine is subject to any state-law defences against the restitution claim which might be available to the creditors of the estate as a matter of insolvency law.

[23] [2015] A.C. 250; [2014] UKSC 45. The Supreme Court there overruled prior English authority to the effect that a beneficiary of a fiduciary's duties could not claim a proprietary interest, but was only entitled to an equitable account, in respect of any money or assets acquired by a fiduciary in breach of his duties to the beneficiary, unless the asset or money was or had been beneficially the property of the beneficiary or the trustee acquired the asset or money by taking advantage of an opportunity or right which was properly that of the beneficiary: see *Sinclair Investments (UK) Ltd* v. *Versailles Trade Finance Ltd* [2012] Ch. 453, [88]; [2011] EWCA Civ 347. Instead, the Supreme Court ruled that all unauthorised benefits obtained by a fiduciary in breach of his duties to his principal are held by the fiduciary upon constructive trust for his principal – the law presuming that the fiduciary received those benefits for his principal. See also *A.-G. for Hong Kong* v. *Reid* [1994] 1 A.C. 324 and Sir Terence Etherton, 'The Legitimacy of Proprietary Relief' (2014) 2 Birkbeck L. Rev. 59, 60.

[24] This rule takes effect only once triggered by the administrators giving notice, pursuant to the Insolvency Rules 1986 (UK), r. 2.95, of their intention to make a distribution: see r. 2.85(1).

[25] Which applies in liquidation.

[26] Which applies in personal bankruptcy.

that equity often determines its availability. However, that is not peculiar to insolvency set-off. The same is true of equitable set-off between solvent parties, and, recognising appropriate boundaries of legal personality and property ownership, unsurprisingly the legislation has not sought to widen the scope of insolvency set-off so as to enable the claims of one to be set off against those owed by another. It may be that insolvency set-off has peculiar features. For instance, it has been said that whereas mutuality is probably not strictly required of substantive equitable set-off, it is strictly required of insolvency set-off.[27] Assuming that those differences exist, however, the distinctive features of insolvency set-off result not so much from equitable doctrines as from the properties of the insolvency legislation.

Company directors' duties to creditors

Equity plays a significant role in promoting the objectives of insolvency law, including, as Mr Ho notes, through equity's regulation of company directors' conduct. Although now partially a matter of statutory codification in the UK,[28] it has long been accepted in common law jurisdictions that when a company is insolvent, of doubtful solvency or on the verge of insolvency, in exercising their fiduciary duties the directors must consider and act in the best interests of the creditors of the company.[29]

Furthermore, the objectives of insolvency law and relevant responsibilities of directors are promoted by other general equitable doctrines that have been the subject of recent development in English law. The Supreme Court's decision in *FHR European Ventures LLP* v. *Cedar Capital Partners LLC*, that all benefits obtained by a fiduciary in breach of his duties are subject to equitable proprietary claims in favour of his principal, renders the English legal position consistent with the position

[27] See R. Derham, *Derham on the Law of Set-off*, 4th ed. (Oxford University Press, 2010), [6.25]–[6.33].

[28] Section 172 of the Companies Act 2006 (UK), which codifies a duty to act, in good faith, in a way which is most likely to promote the success of the company, provides (by subsection (3)) that the duty imposed by this section 'has effect subject to any enactment or rule of law requiring directors, in certain circumstances, to consider or act in the interests of creditors of the company'.

[29] See *West Mercia Safetywear Ltd* v. *Dodd* [1988] B.C.L.C. 250, 252–3 (Dillon L.J.); *Colin Gwyer & Associates Ltd* v. *London Wharf (Limehouse) Ltd* [2003] 2 B.C.L.C. 153, [74]; [2002] EWHC 2748 (Ch), both citing *Kinsela* v. *Russell Kinsela Pty Ltd (in liq.)* (1986) 4 N.S.W.L.R. 722, 730 (Street C.J.).

in other Commonwealth countries.[30] It may well be used to swell the coffers available to creditors of an insolvent company where a director – who, as is often the case, is himself insolvent, so that personal claims against him have no real value – has become accountable for what is now clearly to be regarded, in equity, as the company's property.

Accordingly, it can be seen that each of the five issues considered in Ho's treatment of the distribution of an insolvent estate's assets forms an integral part of the equitable backdrop to the insolvency legislation.

Insolvency expenses

In the second of the main sections of his chapter, Mr Ho considers the operation of two distinct equitable principles which both admit of the recovery of certain expenses from an insolvent estate or fund in priority to other unsecured claims. They are respectively known as the *Lundy Granite* (or 'salvage') principle[31] and the *Berkeley Applegate* principle.[32]

The former serves to inform the process of statutory construction concerning what will constitute an insolvency expense pursuant to the prescribed legislative regime, and what will accordingly be payable out of the assets of the insolvent estate with corresponding priority. Strictly speaking, the *Lundy Granite* principle is not therefore an 'equitable exception' to the statutory insolvency regime, but, by a process of interpreting the legislation against the relevant equitable background, it is instead to be regarded as an integral part of the statutory insolvency regime. As Lewison L.J. explained in *Jervis* v. *Pillar Denton Ltd*,[33] where the claimed expense was rent:

> [W]hether rent is payable as an administration expense is not a question of an exercise of the court's discretion. Either it counts as an expense, or it does not.[34]

He adopted the following statement of Lord Hoffmann in *Re Toshoku Finance UK plc*:[35]

> The court will of course interpret rule 4.218 [of the Insolvency Rules 1986 (UK)] to include debts which, under the *Lundy Granite* principle, are

[30] Namely Australia, New Zealand, Singapore, US jurisdictions and Canada.

[31] After *In re Lundy Granite Co.* (1871) L.R. 6 Ch. App. 462.

[32] After *Re Berkeley Applegate (Investment Consultants) (in liq.)* [1989] Ch. 32.

[33] *Jervis* v. *Pillar Denton Ltd* [2015] Ch. 87; [2014] EWCA Civ 180.

[34] *Jervis* v. *Pillar Denton Ltd* [2015] Ch. 87, [8].

[35] [2002] 1 W.L.R. 671, [38]; [2002] UKHL 6.

> deemed to be expenses of the liquidation. Ordinarily this means that debts such as rents under a lease will be treated as coming within paragraph (a) [of Rule 4.218], but the principle may possibly enlarge the scope of other paragraphs as well.[36]

'Thus', held Lewison L.J., 'the salvage principle will apply to the interpretation of rule 2.67' of the Insolvency Rules,[37] which had subsequently been enacted (for administrations) in terms which broadly mirrored the provisions of rule 4.218 (applicable in liquidation) upon which Lord Hoffmann had ruled.[38]

Accordingly, Lewison L.J. concluded:

> [W]hether the salvage principle applies is not a matter of discretion. As Lord Hoffmann explained in *In re Toshoku Finance UK plc* it is a principle that informs the interpretation of the rules which contain the complete list of what could rank as expenses of the relevant insolvency process . . . Thus in order to rank as an expense a liability must fall within the rules as interpreted in the light of the salvage principle . . . [T]he rationale is a judge-made deeming provision under which the office holder is deemed to have incurred the liability in the course of the winding up or administration. The foundation of the principle is the application of equity.[39]

By contrast, the *Berkeley Applegate* principle operates on an entirely free-standing basis and, as Mr Ho identifies, the court's ordinary[40] equitable discretion in this regard may usefully be called upon by an appointed insolvency office-holder in order to seek to recover from the fund (which is held by, but does not belong to, the insolvent estate) fees and expenses which have been incurred by the office-holder in its management. In view of the existence of such equitable jurisdiction of the courts – as a part of the underlying canvas upon which the legislation is drawn – there was no need for the legislature to make similar statutory provision. It was sufficient for the ambit of insolvency legislation to extend only to the assets beneficially owned by the insolvent estate. Moreover, it might be said that such fees and costs are not really insolvency expenses properly so called but are expenses of the administration of the relevant asset or fund which

36 *Jervis* v. *Pillar Denton Ltd* [2015] Ch. 87, [16]. 37 *Ibid.*, [17].

38 Rule 2.67 of the Insolvency Rules 1986 (UK) was brought into force after the publication of Lord Hoffmann's judgment in *Re Toshoku.*

39 *Jervis* v. *Pillar Denton Ltd* [2015] Ch. 87, [77].

40 Meaning, for these purposes, applicable irrespective of any relevant insolvency. Thus, 'ordinary equitable discretion' is not an insolvency specific issue but is an application of equitable principles developed in the sphere of property and trust law and which continue to apply in an insolvency context.

falls outside of the insolvent estate. In other words, they are the expenses recoverable for administration generally, not only where the administration is of an insolvent estate.

Integrity of the insolvency process

Finally, under this heading Mr Ho addresses the positive influence of both the anti-suit injunction and the application of the principle known as the rule in *Ex p. James.*[41] There is no doubt that both of these, which exist independently of statutory insolvency law and might be described as part of the courts' inherent judicial armoury, have served to strengthen and preserve the objectives of insolvency proceedings. It is, however, debatable whether they are to be regarded as being of purely equitable (rather than having at least some common law) foundation: in particular, the origins and ambit of the rule in *Ex p. James* – which concerns the court's control over its own officers[42] – are issues which are perhaps worthy of a chapter in their own right.

Nevertheless, the subject of 'integrity of the insolvency process' does provide further support for the existence of an equitable canvas which informs and affecting the insolvency legislation drawn upon it. In particular, it has long been established that, although they are principally creatures of statute, appointed insolvency office-holders are nevertheless regarded in equity as fiduciaries for the estates in respect of which they are appointed; thus, such statutory appointees owe corresponding fiduciary duties as a matter of equity – a proposition which has recently been confirmed in *Brook* v. *Reed*[43] and in *Re MK Airlines Ltd.*[44] Although such fiduciary obligations are supplemented (and can be varied) by specific statutory provisions,[45] the equitable backdrop remains.

[41] Derived from *Ex p. James* (1874) L.R. 9 Ch. App. 609.

[42] See *In re Nortel GmbH (in admin.)* [2014] A.C. 209, [122]; [2013] UKSC 52 (Lord Neuberger of Abbotsbury P.S.C.): 'As to the common law, there are a number of cases, starting with *Ex p. James; In re Condon* . . . in which a principle has been developed and applied to the effect that "where it would be unfair" for a trustee in bankruptcy "to take full advantage of his legal rights as such, the court will order him not to do so".'

[43] [2012] 1 W.L.R. 419; [2011] EWCA Civ 331.

[44] [2013] Bus. L.R. 169; [2012] EWHC 1018 (Ch).

[45] See, for example, the various provisions in the Insolvency Rules 1986 (UK) dealing with the authorised recovery of profit-based remuneration from the estate.

Conclusion

It is impossible to take issue with any of the three specific threads drawn out by Look Chan Ho in his chapter on equity and insolvency: that some equitable rules enlighten and shape insolvency law and practice, some equitable rules are subordinated to insolvency law and policy, and some equitable rules are developed specifically to promote insolvency objectives. Nevertheless, a survey of the relations between equity and insolvency law additionally suggests the alternative conclusion anticipated earlier: that equity might be viewed more appropriately as part of the rich and textured canvas upon which the largely statutory insolvency law has been painted, the composition of such fabric both informing and affecting the colour, density and constitution of the legislative paint required and, ultimately, its overall quality and appearance.

8

Equitable doctrines in business associations

P.G. TURNER

Introduction

The conjunction of equity and business activity can be a sensitive one. A business must be able to derive enough profit from its commercial activities in order to be a sustainable organisation. The success of a business association also requires that the allocation of power among those involved in its operation be stable and clear. And in the daily operation of business associations, it is necessary that decisions as to how the business ought to proceed can be adhered to or departed from so as to allow an organisation to find business success in circumstances where the activities of rivals and the wants of customers may quickly change. Flexibility and certainty are both necessary. However, these various requirements can be hampered by equity. Equitable doctrines and remedies can be applied incorrectly or mechanically in ways that handicap acceptable activity by business associations. Equity can be misapplied by applying its doctrines to facts literally within the scope of a doctrine, but where the reason or purpose of the doctrine is not present. Such concerns have often been expressed in the decisions of the courts.[1]

Common law systems, of which equity is a part, nonetheless allow business associations to be formed and profitable commercial activities to be conducted in economically sustainable ways. This suggests several possible conclusions. The number of business associations and the extent of their activities in common law jurisdictions support the inference that the administration of equity by the courts of those jurisdictions is not anathema to the requirements of business associations and their

[1] For example, *Barnes* v. *Addy* (1874) L.R. 9 Ch. App. 244, 251, 255; *Scandinavian Trading Tanker Co. AB* v. *Flota Petrolera Ecuatoriana* [1983] 2 A.C. 694, 703–4; *Westdeutsche Landesbank Girozentrale* v. *Islington London Borough Council* [1996] A.C. 669, 704–5; *Cobbe* v. *Yeoman's Row Management Ltd* [2008] 1 W.L.R. 1752, [81]; [2008] UKHL 55. See also P. Millett, 'Equity's Place in the Law of Commerce' (1998) 114 L.Q.R. 214, 214.

activities. Particular equitable doctrines – or misapplications of equitable doctrines – may curtail the requirements of business, but so may provisions of parliamentary legislation, the actions of regulators, and particular rules and decisions of the judge-made common law. The *system* of equity inherited from the English Court of Chancery does not as such retard business activity. In this chapter, a further hypothesis is ventured. Doctrines of equity have promoted the development of modern laws on business associations to a substantial degree. The establishment and maintenance of business associations today continue to be assisted by equitable doctrines, and statutory extensions of equitable doctrines. Because the conjunction of equity and business activity is sensitive, these conclusions are not trivial. On the contrary, to see that equitable doctrines facilitate the conduct of business through business associations is to find that many equitable doctrines promote the practical processes and tasks of administration of such bodies[2] – notwithstanding that the prevailing views of equity today suggest otherwise.[3]

The focus of this chapter will be on business associations, particularly on unincorporated partnerships and companies incorporated by registration, with a view to identifying doctrines by which equity has facilitated and does facilitate the establishment of these business structures and their administration. Since some of the equitable doctrines and attitudes to be discussed have counterparts in the laws applicable to other types of organisations – most obviously express trusts and statutory bodies – it may be instructive to consider the doctrines relevant to business associations in terms also familiar in areas of law considered in other chapters in this volume. As such, the chapter will in turn address the role of equitable doctrines in the constitutional arrangements of business associations and the administration of the executive organs of business associations.

Constitutional arrangements

In certain features, a business association resembles a nation state. Both have 'rather definite patterns' of government.[4] The patterns typically

[2] See P.G. Turner, 'Equity and Administration', Chapter 1 of this volume; J. Getzler and M. Macnair, 'The Firm as Entity before the Companies Acts', in P. Brand, K. Costello and W.N. Osborough (eds.), *Adventures of the Law: Proceedings of the Sixteenth British Legal History Conference, Dublin, 2003* (Dublin: Four Courts Press, 2005), 267–88.

[3] See Turner, 'Equity and Administration', text to nn. 4–44.

[4] A.B. DuBois, *The English Business Company after the Bubble Act 1720–1800* (New York: The Commonwealth Fund, 1938), 287 (speaking of companies).

include an aggregate of persons who are subject to, and entitled to the benefit of, the peculiar laws of the association or state. As members of the association or state, those persons in law give – or in political theory are seen to give – power and authority to a designated body of persons within the association or state. The body which donates these powers and the executive body that receives them may be distinct from one another to a great or minor degree. In companies and representative democracies, the distinction is great; in partnerships and direct democracies, it is small. These features have had marked effects on the involvement of equitable doctrines and remedies in business associations. Equitable principles have been adjusted to suit these patterns of government, and indeed to allow these patterns to be formed at all. Illustrations will be found throughout this chapter.

The role of 'legal' equity descended from the Court of Chancery has also been influenced by the fact that the structural resemblances between business associations and a nation state such as the United Kingdom are not complete. For example, registered companies have organs corresponding to the executive and legislature of a nation state – respectively, the directors and the company in general meeting – but nothing very like a judiciary. Partnerships are less similar again to the state: the partnership, which is the partners themselves, both legislates for and exercises the power of the partnership. It no more has an organ corresponding to a judiciary than has a registered company. If disputes among those involved in the company or partnership are to be resolved according to the laws of the business association itself, rather than an external judiciary supplied by the nation state to whose general laws the association is subject, they must be resolved in either of two ways. The dispute may be put to a general meeting of the company or a meeting of partnership. Alternatively, it may be sent to arbitration if all the members or partners so agree or instead under a provision in the company or partnership articles to which the members or partners have agreed[5] or are taken to have agreed.[6] Unlike modern trading corporations, companies incorporated by a special Act of Parliament often had

[5] For example, *Fortress Value Recovery Fund I LLC* v. *Blue Skye Fund Special Opportunities Fund LP* [2013] 1 W.L.R. 3466, [9]; [2013] EWCA Civ 367 (limited partnership under the Limited Partnerships Act 1907).

[6] DuBois, *The English Business Company after the Bubble Act 1720–1800*, 125–7, 221. As to the possibility of arbitrating disputes concerning trusts, see M. Conaglen, 'The Enforceability of Arbitration Clauses in Trusts' [2015] C.L.J. 450.

or have something closer to a judicial avenue available to settle controversies in the form of a visitor.[7] But while traditional conceptions of the judicial function include some proceedings of an inquisitorial rather than adversarial character, the fact that visitatorial jurisdiction is largely confined to resolving disputes inquisitorially by keeping the corporation to the wishes of its founder means that visitation does not correspond closely with a fully elaborated concept of adjudication as understood in common law countries. Indeed, visitation is meant as an alternative to the jurisdiction of the courts.

On the detailed level of doctrines and rules, the similarities between the position of business associations and nation states are less prominent than the structural resemblances. The call for equitable intervention and the propriety of affording it accordingly differ between business associations and the nation state. Among the reasons is that the character of business organisations and that of the state are in other respects[8] antithetical. The constitution of the nation state is seen inherently as a matter of national politics and what has come, especially in England, to be known as 'public law'. In contrast, the constitution of a company or partnership is primarily seen as a matter of private governance and 'private law'.

These ideas must be qualified to maintain accuracy; however, they are useful in explaining certain aspects of the technical law which might otherwise be hard to explain. First, the position of the Crown and its servants meant that the laws now located under the headings of contract, equity, restitution and tort did not come to apply as extensively, or in the same ways, to the Crown and Crown servants and to other legal persons. Secondly, the laying down of important features and principles of modern company law occurred in a period in which business associations were deliberately conducted out of the sight of the state itself. Once the Bubble Act had prohibited the acting or presuming to act as a corporate body, the raising of a transferable stock, the transferring of such stock and so on without authority of Parliament or the Crown,[9] business

[7] R. Pound, 'Visitatorial Jurisdiction over Corporations in Equity' (1936) 49 Harv. L. Rev. 369; *Bateman's Bay Local Aboriginal Land Council v. Aboriginal Community Benefit Fund Pty Ltd* (1998) 194 C.L.R. 247, [26]; [1998] HCA 49.

[8] And in matters of detail: for example, *O'Neill* v. *Phillips* [1999] 1 W.L.R. 1092, 1102 (regarding legitimate expectations in public law and company law).

[9] 6 Geo. I c. 18 (1720), ss. 18–20. In the *Statutes at Large*, 6 Geo. I c. 18 is dated 1719, and concerns marine insurance and the lending of money upon bottomry to two corporations to be established by royal charter; the Bubble Act appears as 7 Geo. I c. 1 (1720).

associations could not safely be seen to do these things. This affected the law of business organisations. 'Since the unincorporated company' that needed to stay wide of the Bubble Act 'was definitely not "the creature of the state"', unlike statutory and chartered corporations, 'the state in its turn was less accessible to such a unit'.[10] The beginnings of the modern law of business organisations were put in place by 'a body of office law and practice, built up by the counsel of business corporations and their opinions'[11] – a very private sort of law, administrative in character – and later by the Court of Chancery, 'which by closing its eyes to the irregularity of the unincorporated group with a joint stock, adhered to its well-established practice of welcoming new litigants' in days when the courts of common law, among others, 'did not see fit to occupy themselves with the problems of the unincorporated company, which was more tolerated than encouraged'.[12] Whereas the law on government administration was statute law, the common law and the prerogative writs, business administration in the main became subject to the Chancellor's equity.[13]

While the structural or constitutional similarities referred to above are persistent features of equity's involvement in business associations, an account of equity's involvement must likewise accommodate the dissimilarities between business associations and entities such as the nation state.

Private law of the association

Both similarities and differences are seen in the first area in which equity has been significantly involved in the establishment of a 'private law' of the business association. Like (for example) the English legal system, each of the company and the partnership establishes a 'private law' for those directly involved in each body. On a general level, the same is true of statutory corporations[14] and corporations founded by charter, and even of trusts. When Lord Cross of Chelsea spoke of 'the common law of the company', this was the notion he invoked. The common law of the company was 'to be found in the memorandum and articles' thereof.[15]

[10] DuBois, *The English Business Company after the Bubble Act 1720–1800*, 227.

[11] *Ibid.*, 126. [12] *Ibid.*, 227.

[13] See S. Watson, 'The Significance of the Source of the Powers of Boards of Directors in UK Company Law' [2011] J.B.L. 597.

[14] J. Grant, *A Practical Treatise on the Law of Corporations* (London: Butterworths, 1850), 289–90.

[15] *Ebrahimi* v. *Westbourne Galleries Ltd* [1973] A.C. 360, 384. See R.C. Nolan, 'The Continuing Evolution of Shareholder Governance' [2006] C.L.J. 92.

The corresponding 'common laws' of a partnership or a trust are to be found respectively in the partnership articles or the terms of the trust. Rather than see this as a private law, one might see this as law local to the particular organisation. The metaphor of locality remains current. Early companies legislation borrowed the language of the municipal corporations to give companies the power to pass bye-laws, invoking the idea of laws of the borough[16] – language that is still used in parts of Canada and the United States. Lord Sumption J.S.C. has spoken in cognate terms when referring to 'the constitutional distinction between the respective *domains* of the board and the shareholders' of a registered company.[17]

The provision of such a private or local law is not a peculiarly equitable function. Equity may further its attainment. However, a law of this sort may be attained without equity, as where a statutory corporation is founded. It may be attained by any rules which lay down obligations and liabilities that bind the participants in an association, and to which those not participating in the association may safely remain oblivious.[18] A court recently described a unit trust as being 'Janus-like, having both a legal and an equitable face as well as a public and a private face'.[19] Similarly, the participants in a company or partnership may be subject to one set of 'laws' that govern the interior of the association; externally, the company or the partners (or the trustee and beneficiaries, in the case of a trust) may be subject to quite different laws in their relations with outsiders. Equity creates this dichotomy in the trust, but it may be created in other ways – and without equity.

However, legal transactions are historically contingent. The fact a particular business structure might conceivably have been obtained without equity does not say much about how and why equitable doctrines have actually been used, as they have, to set up particular business structures. Indeed, legal systems themselves are historically contingent. The fact that the laws of business associations found in England and other

[16] F.W. Maitland, 'Trust and Corporation', in D. Runciman and M. Ryan (eds.), *F.W. Maitland: State, Trust and Corporation* (Cambridge University Press, 2003), 124.

[17] *Eclairs Group Ltd* v. *JKX Oil & Gas plc* [2015] Bus.L.R. 1395, [37]; [2015] UKSC 71 (italics added).

[18] See also P. Sales, 'Equity and Human Rights: A Commentary', Chapter 21 of this volume, text between nn. 39 and 40 ('legislation' by transacting parties through the law of trusts and the law of contract).

[19] *Australian Securities and Investments Commission* v. *Wellington Capital Ltd* (2013) 94 A.C.S.R. 293, [66]; [2013] FCAFC 52 (appeal dismissed without affecting this point, *sub. nom. Wellington Capital Ltd* v. *Australian Securities and Investments Commission* (2014) 254 C.L.R. 288; [2014] HCA 43), adapting H.A.J. Ford and W.A. Lee, *Principles of the Law of Trusts* (Thomson Lawbook Co., 2010), [12.020].

common law jurisdictions might have developed otherwise – in ways that gave equity a greater or lesser role – is factually uninformative. It does not explain what in fact is the case.

There are more informative observations to make about the connection between equity jurisprudence and the attainment of business structures with these basic features. One such observation is that equitable doctrines and remedies were central to the development and operation of deed of settlement companies and partnerships after the Bubble Act. The law of the equity courts was therefore central to the developing body of company law from which the Companies Acts of the 1850s and 1860s were made, and in the exegesis of those Acts. The calls on equity were various. Trusts were often used to hold a company's assets for the convenience of holding assets indirectly[20] and in an attempt to circumvent the procedural problems of actions brought and defended by the members of the association.[21] Those with executive power were held to equitable standards of conduct: like trustees, in the case of company directors;[22] or like fiduciary agents, in the case of partners. Relief to restrain breaches of duty and to undo the consequences of wrongdoing and dereliction of duty was much more meaningful than the thin forms of relief available at common law.[23] Equitable procedures were also needed. A partner might wish to sue the partnership of which he was a partner, or a member of a company might wish to sue the company of which he was a member. The appearance of the plaintiff on both sides of the record forced the common law courts to say that the action was impossible, because no one could be both plaintiff and defendant.[24] Equity was able to see past the problem.[25] The favourable response of equity to the various calls made on it over a long period has given equity

20 DuBois, *The English Business Company after the Bubble Act 1720–1800*, 115–16.

21 *Ibid.*, 217, 220–2.

22 *Charitable Corp. v. Sutton* (1742) 2 Atk. 400, 405–6; 26 E.R. 642, 644–5; DuBois, *The English Business Company after the Bubble Act 1720–1800*, 125, 203 n. 284.

23 The common law writs of *quo warranto* and *mandamus* issued on appropriate occasions respectively to question a corporation's powers and control the actions of a corporation's officials: DuBois, *The English Business Company after the Bubble Act 1720–1800*, 123–4. However, they were little used in respect of unincorporated companies, and were ill adapted for use generally. See *Hazell* v. *Hammersmith & Fulham London Borough Council* [1990] 2 Q.B. 697, 716–21, 769–76 (C.A.); [1992] 2 A.C. 1, 39–43 (H.L.).

24 N. Lindley and S. Dickinson, *A Treatise on the Law of Partnership including its Application to Companies*, 4th ed., ed. by M.D. Ewell (Chicago: Callaghan & Company, 1881), 872–6.

25 *Ibid.*, 872–7; DuBois, *The English Business Company after the Bubble Act 1720–1800*, 220–2; *Carnie* v. *Esanda Finance Corp. Ltd* (1995) 182 C.L.R. 398, 427–9.

a 'deep and persistent' involvement in modern business associations and enterprises and in their evolution.[26]

It is informative to notice more particular equitable developments which accentuated the structural features already mentioned. The differentiation of the executive and legislative organs of the company – the directors and the members in general meeting[27] – was largely done by the drafting for deed of settlement companies. Equity's treatment of these arrangements further differentiated their respective positions. To what constraints were participants subject in equity when exercising their rights as participants in the association? According to Lord Lindley, partnership law formed the model.[28] Partners owe a duty of 'good faith' to one another. A partner who disrupts the usual process for making decisions among the partners may in principle be restrained from doing so if the disruption occurs in bad faith.[29] In contrast, the members of joint stock companies and, later, companies incorporated under the general Acts of incorporation did not and generally do not owe fiduciary obligations to one another. The doctrine that developed is that members may vote in their several interests provided they do so in good faith. Members who vote with a desire to oppress a minority of their number are seen by equity to act in bad faith. Otherwise, the members – like parliamentary legislators – are essentially free to act as they wish. The different constitutional positions of a company's directors and its members in a general meeting are such that the powers of the former are watched more closely by equity than are the powers of the latter. Added to that is a general equitable disinclination to interfere in matters of internal regulation in an attempt 'to settle all . . . squabbles' and to redress 'mere passing improprieties, arising from infirmities of temper' and the like.[30]

[26] *Elders Trustee & Executor Co. Ltd* v. *E. G. Reeves Pty Ltd* (1987) 78 A.L.R. 193, 229 (Gummow J.).

[27] The members in general meeting were often termed the 'general court' in deed of settlement companies, in contradistinction to the 'court of directors' or assistants in whom vested executive power: DuBois, *The English Business Company after the Bubble Act 1720–1800*, 287.

[28] Lindley and Dickinson, *A Treatise on the Law of Partnership including its Application to Companies*, 4th ed., 895–902.

[29] R. I'A. Banks, *Lindley and Banks on Partnership*, 18th ed. (London: Sweet & Maxwell, 2010), [23–142].

[30] Lindley and Dickinson, *A Treatise on the Law of Partnership including its Application to Companies*, 4th ed., 895. See also DuBois, *The English Business Company after the Bubble Act 1720–1800*, 227.

The greatest equitable accentuation of the differences between the 'owners' and 'managers' of the company came with the equity case, *Foss* v. *Harbottle*.[31] Although the procedural delicacy of litigation involving partnerships suppressed litigation involving them, it was established that the partners were both owners and managers. Questions about whether mere owners without managerial powers might sue on behalf of the partnership did not arise. However, such questions arose in the company case of *Foss* v. *Harbottle*, when two of the members of a company incorporated by statute brought a bill on behalf of themselves and all other members except the defendant directors and one member who was not a director. The bill in effect charged the defendants with engaging in a dishonest and fraudulent design with regard to the company.[32] It is possible to leave aside the difficulties surrounding the exceptions to the 'rule' in this case[33] and to focus wholly on the basic constitutional points made by the Vice-Chancellor, Sir James Wigram: that the members of the company are not as such entitled to sue in the name of the company; '[i]n law the corporation and the aggregate members of the corporation are not the same thing for purposes like this'; and prima facie, the corporation 'should sue in its own name and in its corporate character' or through an appointed legal representative.[34] Maladministration by the directors does no wrong to the company members in their several capacity so as to entitle them to sue in the manner attempted by the plaintiffs in *Foss* v. *Harbottle*. Speaking of the Vice-Chancellor's decision, Professor Lobban has said: 'In effect, companies were regarded as little democracies, so that minority shareholders could not ask for the intervention of the courts.'[35] Legislation has since outgrown the Vice-Chancellor's decision but maintains the structural distinctions that the Vice-Chancellor drew.[36] As will be seen, these constitutional features attract further attention from equity, including through the grant of relief for inadequate and improper action by a company's directors.

31 (1843) 2 Hare 461; 67 E.R. 189. 32 See *Ibid.*, 468–84; 193–200.

33 As to which, see K.W. Wedderburn, 'Shareholders' Rights and the Rule in *Foss* v. *Harbottle*' [1957] C.L.J. 194; D.A. DeMott, 'Shareholder Litigation in Australia and the United States: Common Problems, Uncommon Solutions' (1987) 11 Syd L.R. 259.

34 *Foss* v. *Harbottle* (1843) 2 Hare 461, 490–1; 67 E.R. 189, 202.

35 M. Lobban, 'The Politics of English Law in the Nineteenth Century', in P. Brand and J. Getzler (eds.), *Judges and Judging in the History of the Common Law and Civil Law: From Antiquity to Modern Times* (Cambridge University Press, 2012), 127.

36 See the Companies Act 2006 (UK), ss. 260–4; *Universal Project Management Services Ltd* v. *Fort Gilkicker Ltd* [2013] Ch. 551, [44]–[49]; [2013] EWHC 248 (Ch) (Briggs J.).

The stability of the structure

The constitution of business associations finds stability in the courts' unwillingness to allow the parties' decision to adopt a given sort of business association for the running of their business to be outflanked by other legal principles. Equity has a greater range than the common law of doctrines and remedies which, if wrongly applied, might be used to destabilise the adopted structure. The coercive relief available in equity, and the principles to do with equitable fraud and constructive trusts, could be deployed with especially disruptive effect. So may other equitable doctrines. In one case, an attempt to rely on the equitable doctrine of contribution was likened to an application for idiosyncratic justice.[37] The plaintiff sought to render his alleged partner or joint venturer liable to contribute towards the repayment of a loan taken out by the plaintiff. Their business had been conducted through a registered company. The loan terms did not declare the plaintiff and the defendants jointly and severally liable to repay the loan. The High Court of Australia held that there was no coordinate liability of the sort that contribution requires in equity[38] (and, in slightly different language, the English model of contribution legislation[39]) and that the plaintiff's allegations sought 'to outflank the consequences of the selection by the parties of the corporate structure', which brought with it corporate legal personality and limited liability.[40] Although the courts' unwillingness to permit other rules to outflank the parties' decision to adopt a particular business structure applies to attempts to use common law[41] and equitable principles alike,[42] the attitude of restraint is more noticeable when it is shown by equity because of equity's greater ability to disrupt states of affairs.

[37] *Friend* v. *Brooker* (2009) 239 C.L.R. 129, [47]; [2009] HCA 21, echoing the language of Deane J. in *Muschinski* v. *Dodds* (1985) 160 C.L.R. 583, 615–16, which was quoted approvingly by Lord Walker in *Cobbe* v. *Yeoman's Row Management Ltd* [2008] 1 W.L.R. 1752, [17].

[38] *Friend* v. *Brooker* (2009) 239 C.L.R. 129, [50], [67]–[83].

[39] Civil Liability (Contribution) Act 1978 (UK), s. 1(1).

[40] *Friend* v. *Brooker* (2009) 239 C.L.R. 129, [88].

[41] See *Bratton Seymour Service Co. Ltd* v. *Oxborough* [1992] B.C.L.C. 693, 696–8 (term imposing liability on a member to contribute towards the upkeep of the amenity areas of a development of flats owned by the company could not be implied into the articles of association).

[42] *Prest* v. *Petrodel Resources Ltd* [2013] 2 A.C. 415, [16], [28], [35]–[36]; [2013] UKSC 34 (unsuccessful assertion of a resulting trust over company assets).

While the principles expounded in *Ebrahimi* v. *Westbourne Galleries Ltd*[43] give force to deliberate decisions whose terms sit behind the corporate form in fact adopted, the statutory equities so important in that case did not outflank the participants' decision to adopt a corporate legal form for their business association. The 'equities' operated otherwise. The director who had been removed by an ordinary resolution was entitled to have the company wound up on the just and equitable ground. He had joined in forming the company on the understanding that he would continue to be entitled to participate in the company's management.[44] To wind up the company was not as such to weaken the structure adopted. The winding up instead brought that strong structure to an end by keeping those involved in it to the earlier underlying decision that the company should operate on a particular basis: a basis that had come to an end. Unlike the decision from which the High Court of Australia allowed an appeal in *Friend* v. *Brooker* – which would have made company directors liable to action during the subsistence of the company – the non-observance of standards of 'justice' and 'equity' as defined in the *Ebrahimi* case did not as such make the directors liable to action during the company's subsistence. Rather, the consequence of not observing those standards was that the company was liable to be wound up on the just and equitable ground.

Of the several ways in which equity aids administration,[45] the adoption of the corporate structure for the conduct of business is aided by the fact that generally stated principles of equity – principles of the law of trusts, principles of contribution and others – are not applied where a close examination of the facts shows the rationale of those principles to be absent.[46] The operation of business associations is assisted by equity withholding its doctrines and relief where the reasons therefor are not found in the facts of the case. A further example is expressed in the statement that there is no equity to rectify company articles. On the ground of mistake, rectification may be ordered of an instrument, the terms of which do not embody the true intentions of the parties to it. On this basis, conveyances and written contracts have often been rectified where the mistake is mutual. The fact that companies legislation declares there to be a 'contract' between the members of a company for the time being[47] (just as there is a contract between partners) might be

[43] [1973] A.C. 360. [44] *Ibid.*, 380–1, 386–7.

[45] See Turner, 'Equity and Administration', text after n. 44. [46] *Ibid.*, text after n. 50.

[47] Companies Act 2006 (UK), s. 33; Corporations Act 2001 (Cth), s. 140(1).

thought to mean that an equity to rectify company articles could in principle arise. However, although the companies legislation does not in terms say that a court exercising equitable power may not order the rectification of the constitutional documents of a company, the invitation to assert such a power has been firmly declined. The English Court of Appeal has held that equity has 'no jurisdiction' to rectify company articles, even though they 'do not accord with what is proved to have been the concurrent intention of all the signatories therein at the moment of signature'.[48] The court said that rectification of a deed *inter partes* or a deed poll alters the form in which the relevant intention is expressed, not the constitution of the intention itself. In contrast, to rectify a company's memorandum or articles would be to alter the only legally recognised means of constituting the company: it is not possible to say there is some separate legally constitutive act by which the company was truly created, to which the memorandum and articles give incorrect or inadequate expression.[49] The purpose of the equitable doctrine of rectification therefore did not exist. That conclusion was reinforced by the fact that the statute otherwise left 'no room . . . for the application . . . of the principles upon which a Court of Equity permits rectification of documents whether *inter partes* or not'.[50]

For similar reasons, there appears to be no equity to rescind a company's memorandum or articles for mistake or undue influence.[51] On the other hand, the rationale of rectification can exist where a business is run under partnership articles or through an express trust. An instrument purporting to express the partnership agreement or the terms of the trust can be rectified where the necessary requirements are met, just as much as those types of instrument can be rescinded in equity for undue influence, and so on.

48 *Scott* v. *Frank F. Scott (London) Ltd* [1940] Ch. 794, 801. See *Bailey* v. *New South Wales Medical Defence Union Ltd* (1995) 184 C.L.R. 399, 435.

49 *Scott* v. *Frank F. Scott (London) Ltd* [1940] Ch. 794, 802. See also *Wambo Coal Pty Ltd* v. *Sumiseki Materials Co. Ltd* (2014) 290 F.L.R. 1, [258]; [2014] NSWCA 326.

50 *Scott* v. *Frank F. Scott (London) Ltd* [1940] Ch. 794, 801. The statutory provisions that 'filled the room' are discussed at [1940] Ch. 794, 801–4. Considerations that persuaded the court that there was no remaining space therein included that third parties would rely on the register, and that the companies legislation itself provided a means for altering the company articles. The same statutory provisions evidently confine the principles of contractual construction associated, in English law, with *Investors Compensation Scheme Ltd* v. *West Bromwich Building Society* [1998] 1 W.L.R. 896: see *A.-G. of Belize* v. *Belize Telecom Ltd* [2009] 1 W.L.R. 1988; [2009] UKPC 10.

51 *Bratton Seymour Service Co Ltd* v. *Oxborough* [1992] B.C.L.C. 693, 698 (Steyn L.J.).

Winding up

Though equity is unwilling to interfere in the constitution of business associations, it is willing to effect their deconstitution through winding up. Equity developed a leading role in the winding up of business associations which continues largely unmodified today, under the Partnership Act 1890, and in legislative enactments 'developed . . . from the general principles of the law of partnership' for application to companies.[52] The general principles of partnership law recognise that the partners may themselves wind up the partnership either by agreement or under a term of the partnership agreement. Equitable relief will issue to give effect to such an agreement or term, especially through the taking of accounts. Where no such agreement or term is found, a court of equity may decree a dissolution and winding up on the happening of certain types of events, such as where the partnership can operate only at a loss. Where winding up is an act of the parties, the only equity to relief is to relief that implements the parties' deliberately adopted agreement. However, where no agreement to a winding up is reached by the parties, there may be both an equity to wind up a partnership and an equity to consequential relief. What is the basis and nature of those forms of equitable relief?

Where the partnership articles stipulate for a winding up in circumstances that have occurred, there will be an equity to consequential relief where the partners cannot agree on partnership accounts. Equity will order a taking of accounts to bind all the parties. In practice, this form of relief can easily be obtained because equity is ready – perhaps overly ready – to find that by the act of the parties the partnership has been dissolved. The partners' obligations of good faith towards one another are vital. Since each partner is generally the agent of all the other partners, each partner needs to have trust and confidence in all the others.[53] Any act by one partner that removes or harms that trust and confidence is in equity readily viewed as dissolving the partnership – following which an equity to consequential relief will easily be found. For example, the death of a partner and the sale of a partner's share would prima facie terminate the partnership

[52] Lindley and Dickinson, *A Treatise on the Law of Partnership including its Application to Companies*, 4th ed., 1042–3.

[53] It is not suggested that this is always or even commonly the case, especially in the case of large partnerships. But that tends to support the point in the text, for it is in situations where such good faith is wanting that strife and discontent are likeliest to occur.

and prompt equity to order a winding up. When a partnership is found to be so dissolved, the decision rests on a finding, inference or presumption that the partners intended the partnership to dissolve in the events that have happened. If it is the case that these principles allow for dissolution too readily – so readily that commercial expectations are unacceptably disrupted – then the principles may require adjustment. However, the presently relevant feature of these principles is their objective of furthering the partners' intentions.

If the partners came together on terms that make their respective shares freely transferable, a transfer of one partner's share cannot be seen to jeopardise the partners' trust and confidence in one another. The transfer would not warrant dissolution. This is why, before the Companies Act 1862 (UK), a deed of settlement company with freely transferable shares could not be wound up as easily as a partnership in which the transfer of a partner's share removed the trust and confidence among the partners. Legislative intervention was needed to extend the equitable grounds as they had developed for partnerships. The statutory grounds for the winding up of registered companies re-express for modern-day registered companies the equitable principles originally developed for partnerships.

Other matters affecting the constitution of business associations are the subjects of equitable doctrines. Examples are the maintenance of the register of members of a company; the transfer of shares among the members of a company or a partnership; the forfeiture of shares; the distinction between capital and business; and so on. Because those matters tend to arise from the exercise of executive power by company directors or the partners acting executively, they will be discussed in the following section.

Administration

The administration of the affairs of a company or partnership occurs through the exercise of the directors' or the partners' executive powers. Powers of some width will often be needed in order to assess and, where proper, take commercial risks for the benefit of the business. Since power is accompanied by the danger of its abuse, the routine administration of business affairs is accompanied by the risk of maladministration. Equity places controls on the powers of fiduciaries, including directors and partners, in ways now to be considered. As will be seen, these are further ways in which equitable doctrines assist in administering executive power in business associations – ways that expand the variety already considered.

Controls on fiduciary power

The 'private law' of a corporation or partnership – that is, those legally enforceable provisions deliberately adopted in order for business to be pursued and to regulate the relations of those interested in and responsible for the business[54] – covers a large area of the activities of business associations. It reserves extensive liberty to those conducting the business to pursue commercial aims largely as they desire, without equitable or other legal interference. In developing modern company and partnership law, the courts were astute to avoid the dilemma that too extensive a set of controls on the exercise of discretions would be self-defeating, in that it would undermine the discretion initially given.[55] One form of control thus established is the principle of law and equity that an agent may not act outside its authority. Beyond that the controls are equitable only.[56] The developments leading to these modern principles were summarised by Professor Sealy:

> It was natural and, indeed, inevitable that those seeking redress against defaulting directors should go to the courts of Chancery, which had long had a monopoly of the jurisdiction in partnership matters. There were the advantages of better accounting facilities, of discovery, the representative suit (virtually developed for this purpose) and the general superiority of equitable remedies. As events proved, the range and flexibility of the principles of fiduciary obligation were adequate to cope with most of the problems which arose.[57]

In a practical sense, the controls equity places on the exercise of fiduciary power by those who hold it – company directors, partners, trustees, boards of managers and so on – are such that equity's role is auxiliary.[58] Equity does not dictate that a fiduciary power should be

[54] See text to nn. 14–15 above.

[55] R.C. Nolan, 'Controlling Fiduciary Power' [2009] C.L.J. 293.

[56] See Lindley and Dickinson, *A Treatise on the Law of Partnership including its Application to Companies*, 4th ed., 590–1.

[57] L.S. Sealy, 'The Director as Trustee' [1967] C.L.J. 83, 86. Professor Sealy's article contains valuable discussion of the adaptation of equitable doctrines from trust law for use in relation to companies.

[58] The description of equity as 'auxiliary' here is to be distinguished from the 'auxiliary jurisdiction' of equity, which has a more technical definition: Turner, 'Equity and Administration', text to nn. 2–3 and text between nn. 30 and 32.

exercised for one commercial purpose or another. Equity does not dictate how the business ought to be run. Its controls on executive power in business associations are auxiliary in that they are largely negative. Thus, while equity will not require a director's discretionary power to be exercised in just one of the many ways permitted by the terms of the power, equitable doctrine does allow a director to be prevented from exercising such a power for purposes outside the purposes for which the power was given. Similarly, the principles of equity allow a partner to decide how best to exercise the partner's authority and powers, except if there is a want of good faith. The need to avoid entering into a position in which a person's interest conflicts with that person's duty as a holder of fiduciary power, or in which the person makes an unauthorised 'profit' by reason of a fiduciary position, is a significant further control. While the equitable controls are auxiliary in this practical sense, their importance is not therefore marginal. Whenever the holders of executive power in a business association freely exercise their discretion, they do so subject to the negative controls supplied by equitable principles.

A less direct type of control derives from the possibility that the company or partnership will be wound up on the 'just and equitable' ground.[59] The just and equitable ground is not focused as such on the fiduciaries' exercise of their power. However, it is rational of directors or partners to avoid exercising their powers in ways that would warrant an order for a winding up. Thus, the remote prospect of a winding up can control executive behaviour. The factors relevant to winding up on the 'just and equitable' ground need not reach the heights of 'proved cases of mala fides',[60] nor prove that the defendant committed a breach of fiduciary duty or exercised an executive power for improper purposes. Lord Wilberforce explained that the just and equitable ground

> does, as equity always does, enable the court to subject the exercise of legal rights to equitable considerations; considerations, that is, of a personal character arising between one individual and another, which may make it unjust, or inequitable, to insist on legal rights, or to exercise them in a particular way.[61]

The unfair prejudice ground in company law also controls the directors' powers indirectly. Under statute, the actual or proposed conduct of a company's affairs with unfair prejudice to the interests of some or all

[59] For registered companies, Insolvency Act 1986 (UK), s. 122(1)(g); Corporations Act 2001 (Cth), s. 461(k).

[60] *Ebrahimi* v. *Westbourne Galleries Ltd* [1973] A.C. 360, 381.

[61] *Ibid.*, 379.

of the company's members may lead a court to grant relief to regulate the future conduct of the company's affairs.[62] Practically speaking, the unfair prejudice doctrine confines the exercise of strict legal powers of those who conduct the affairs of the company.[63] The directors are confined to 'using the rules [in the company articles which vest powers in them] in a manner which equity would regard as [not] contrary to good faith'.[64]

As already seen, winding up as a process of company law is an outgrowth of the equitable doctrines developed for partnerships. Lord Wilberforce observed that the words 'just and equitable' in the list of grounds for a court to order the winding up of a company 'provide a bridge' between the company law cases and 'the principles of equity developed in relation to partnerships'.[65] How far the equitable principles as to partnerships extend is therefore significant. For example, are these equitable principles defiant of the law of contract? If they are, then they hinder administration, in that they may hinder the implementation of a deliberately adopted scheme for the performance of practical processes and tasks.

Discussion of this point has been stirred by the House of Lords' indications in *Hurst* v. *Bryk* of the extent of the equitable doctrines as to winding up partnerships.[66] In *obiter dicta* of Lord Millett adopted by the House, their Lordships said that parties who enter into a partnership agreement remove themselves from the normal rules of contract law, by which a repudiation accepted by a counterparty discharges the parties thereto from any future obligations towards one another. Lord Millett's reasoning has been criticised for contradicting the proposition that contracts may generally be determined *in futuro* by the acceptance of a repudiation of the contract.[67]

Supposing, for the sake of argument, that Lord Millett exaggerated the extent to which equity displaces the common law of contract in respect of partnership agreements, it would be wrong to over-correct. Little in fact turns on whether the doctrine of termination *in futuro* applies to partnership agreements. When a partnership is dissolved, the liabilities of the

62 Companies Act 2006 (UK), ss. 994–6, formerly Companies Act 1985 (UK), ss. 459–61.

63 *O'Neill* v. *Phillips* [1999] 1 W.L.R. 1092, 1098; also 1100–1.

64 *Ibid.*, 1099. Regarding unit trusts, see M. May, 'Oppression in the Context of Corporate Trustees' (2013) 87 A.L.J. 271.

65 *Ebrahimi* v. *Westbourne Galleries Ltd* [1973] A.C. 360, 375.

66 *Hurst* v. *Bryk* [2002] 1 A.C. 185.

67 E. Peden and J.W. Carter, 'The Bonds of Partnership' (2000) 16 J.C.L. 277. See *Ryder* v. *Frohlich* [2004] NSWCA 472, [127]–[133].

partnership must be discharged and the partnership assets sold in order to satisfy each partner's share. The partners' affairs cannot be automatically disentangled by stipulating that, when the partnership is dissolved, the liabilities of the partnership shall not be discharged and that the partnership assets shall not be sold in order to satisfy each partner's share. An arrangement lacking those features is not a partnership. Where a partnership exists, there must be some person able to give effect to these essential features of partnership. If the partners have not agreed to wind up the partnership voluntarily, then the person able to give effect to these essential features of partnership may be identified from the terms of a new contract between the parties. Where the former partners have taken initial steps towards winding up the business and liquidating its assets, an agreement appointing such a person may readily be implied. Even if the former partners cannot agree on a winding up among themselves, it is difficult to suppose that equity will withhold its relief to leave gains and losses where they fall. It is likely that a court of equity would appoint a receiver with power to bind the partners for the purpose of winding up the business.

Thus, if the doctrine of termination *in futuro* applies to true partnerships, it is unimportant. Since the equitable principles on the winding up of partnerships fulfil the rights of a partner, the principles in *Hurst* v. *Bryk* do not hinder the implementation of any regime deliberately adopted by the partners. The opposite is the case for partnerships and, so far as the principles on the winding up of partnerships apply by analogy to the winding up of companies, also in the case of registered companies.

Joint stock

A company's directors, like the partners of a partnership, have control of the assets of the company or the partnership. In significant respects, the assets of a company and a partnership are seen as a fund. In common law systems, the notion of a fund as applied to companies and partnerships depends on elements which themselves depend on equitable principles and on developments which occurred in courts of equity that were sometimes then followed by the courts of common law. Thus, the administration of a company's and a partnership's assets depends on doctrines of equity. It also depends on a tradition of equitable adjudication which has facilitated the implementation of deliberately adopted schemes with administrative features. The legal recognition of the joint stock idea so fundamental to the modern companies is a consequence thereof.[68]

One of the elements of the fund notion as applied to companies and partnerships in common law systems is that the relevant parties intend to establish an aggregation of assets distinct from their personal assets and designed to have a semi-autonomous status. For example, the parties may particularly intend that their liabilities be limited to the value of their share in the aggregation. In the law of business associations, this first element of the fund idea is seen in the concept of the joint stock. Each participant in the regulated trading companies of the sixteenth and seventeenth centuries traded on his own account and kept his own stock. The stock was a several stock. It was distinct from the company's joint stock, from which no participant had a claim to a conveyance or to delivery of any particular asset.[69] In England, men of business particularly sought to employ the joint stock mechanism from the eighteenth century onwards.

The second feature of the fund notion entails that no participant in the fund can claim any portion of the fund property as such. This notion applies differently to companies and partnerships, on the one hand, and to trusts, on the other hand. One who holds a share in a company or in a partnership is entitled only to a share representing the proceeds upon a winding up of the entity; economically, each participant has only a residual claim on the assets. While this can be a feature of express trusts, and thus of the fund notion as applied to trusts, it is not an essential feature of express trusts. The drafting of a trust instrument may give a participant the right at some point to subtract a particular asset from the trust fund.

This recalls an important development in the law of companies and partnerships. At first, the notion of a fund, as applied to companies and partnerships, possessed this feature only in that the constitutive documents provided for it. The courts of common law did not recognise it, for they did not recognise a joint stock. At common law, the stock was identified with the individual participants' liability. However, the Court of Chancery was willing to recognise the new idea. The Chancery developed the partners' 'lien' on the property of the firm 'to have the property of the partnership applied in payment of the debts and liabilities of the

[68] See Watson, 'The Significance of the Source of the Powers of Boards of Directors in UK Company Law', 606.

[69] DuBois, *The English Business Company after the Bubble Act 1720–1800*, 114.

firm' and in satisfaction of each partner's share.[70] The law later followed equity to recognise the joint stock as well.[71] Both at law and in equity, it eventually became settled that, as between partners, no proceeding in debt or in the nature of debt lay during the continuance of the relationship, nor after its determination. 'The amount owing to a partner by his fellow partners is recoverable only by the taking of an account in equity after the partnership has been dissolved.'[72]

A third element of the notion of a joint stock or fund is curial relief, giving the notion practical effect. The common law's refusal to entertain an action in debt between partners gives the notion some effect. But the notion receives much greater effect through equitable remedies and doctrines, which give the fund some of its most distinctive legal qualities. In particular, while a fund lacks legal personality in English law, the measure and kind of relief available to enforce claims for the benefit of a fund – whether in company law, partnership law or the law of trusts – are different from the relief recoverable by any one or more persons who are responsible for the fund, or who combine together to participate in a business.[73]

The impersonal qualities of a fund may be illustrated by the express trust. First, on those occasions[74] when a beneficiary sues on behalf of a trust, the rights enforced are not the mere rights of the claimant severally. Thus, a beneficiary who sues in trespass for damage done to land held on trust sues on common law rights vested in the trustee.[75] Secondly, when a beneficiary sues on behalf of a trust, the rights enforced by the beneficiary are not merely the aggregate of the claimant's own rights and those of any or all other beneficiaries or objects of the trust. For example, beneficiaries may have acquired their rights under their trust as an investment, yet if they recover the traceable proceeds of misappropriated trust assets, they recover a measure and type of relief different from what the law of contract affords them. Thirdly, when proceedings are brought to recover trust property, the measure and type of relief can differ from the measure and type of relief that the claimants – be they

[70] Lindley and Dickinson, *A Treatise on the Law of Partnership including its Application to Companies*, 4th ed., 679.

[71] See *Hallett* v. *Dowdall* (1852) 21 L.J. Q.B. 98.

[72] *Hurst* v. *Bryk* [2002] 1 A.C. 185, 194.

[73] See also M. Conaglen and R. Nolan, 'Contracts and Knowing Receipt: Principles and Application' (2013) 129 L.Q.R. 359.

[74] See, for example *Alexander* v. *Perpetual Trustee WA Ltd* (2004) 216 C.L.R. 109, [55]–[56]; [2004] HCA 7; *Roberts* v. *Gill* [2011] 1 A.C. 240; [2010] UKSC 22.

[75] *Young* v. *Murphy* [1996] 1 V.R. 279.

trustees or beneficiaries – could recover if suing to enforce a personal interest. Thus, when proprietary relief is sought under equitable doctrines of tracing and following,[76] the claimant trustees or beneficiaries recover a measure and type of relief different from that which they could recover if enforcing their individual rights apart from what the law of trusts affords them.

Accordingly, the fund in trust law has person-like characteristics even without limiting the beneficiaries' liability. As Maitland observed, these features have been achieved by equitable doctrine without needing formally to personify the trust.[77] Courts of equity also applied these principles to partnerships, joint stock companies and, in due course, limited liability corporations. Today the notion of a fund retains common features where it applies to corporations, partnerships and trusts. In all these situations, the fund depends on a notion of continuity that Maitland thought 'one of the most remarkable ideas developed by modern English jurisprudence': that a 'fund' may continue to exist even while the elements of which it consists undergo change.[78] As this notion was developed by courts of equity, it took support from the equitable doctrines of tracing and following already mentioned above. Under these doctrines, it became possible to say that a particular asset removed from the fund – whether that of a company, partnership or trust – remains 'part of' or 'in' the fund, and that some asset that was never in the fund, but was acquired with an asset that was removed from the fund, or some other asset acquired with an asset from the fund (and so on), can be treated as part of the fund. These and other features are shared, notwithstanding the fact that different procedural rules apply to the bringing of claims for the benefit of a company, partnership or trust by those respectively interested in the due administration of each form of association.[79] Indeed, some doctrines apparently peculiar to one of these fields are, upon examination, not peculiar at all. The company law doctrine of reflective loss – according to which a shareholder cannot recover for a loss to the shareholder individually where the claimed loss

[76] *Ibid.*, 281–7. See also *Montrose Investments Ltd* v. *Orion Nominees Ltd (No. 2)* [2004] W.T.L.R. 1133, [23]–[25]; [2004] EWCA Civ 1032.

[77] F.W. Maitland, 'The Unincorporate Body', in Runciman and Ryan (eds.), *F. W. Maitland: State, Trust and Corporation.*

[78] *Ibid.*, 55–6. See R.C. Nolan, 'The Administration and Maladministration of Funds in Equity: Making a Coherent Set of Choices', Chapter 4 of this volume, text after n. 31.

[79] For the principles as applied to partnerships, see Lindley and Dickinson, *A Treatise on the Law of Partnership including its Application to Companies*, 4th ed., 682.

merely 'reflects' a loss suffered by the company[80] – applies equally to partnerships and trusts as a result of the equitable doctrines applied uniformly to the notion of a fund or joint stock.

Capital v. business

Among other things, the notion of a joint stock and the notion of a fund allow all the assets of a company, partnership or trust to be identified: the assets identified as part of the joint stock or fund are the assets to be administered subject to the 'private law' of the particular company, partnership or trust. However, the executive duties of directors and partners may require them to distinguish different elements of a fund. Most directors are responsible for managing the company in order to generate profit. Under general partnership law, all partners are responsible for managing the partnership in order to generate profits. In doing so, these holders of executive power will have to distinguish capital from business in order to identify distributable profits. The legal force of the distinction derives from changes both in the common law and in equity.

For example, modern company shares are personal property as a result of statutory provisions that restate the outcome of developments in equitable doctrine. In law, the now basic distinction between capital and business only became clear for companies and partnerships in the nineteenth century, although in eighteenth-century accountancy practice the distinction was already seen. On the assets side of the account was placed the business: its land, buildings, stock, cash, goodwill and profits. On the liability side of the account was placed the capital: called and uncalled subscriptions of shareholders.[81] Did holding a share in a business which held land as an asset confer on the shareholder an interest in realty or personalty? At first, the shareholder's interest was an interest in realty. In a deed of settlement company, the deed of settlement certainly conferred on a shareholder some equitable interest in the stock. Under general trust notions, it was initially held that where the company held land, a conveyance of the member's share was required to comply with the Statute of Frauds formalities for conveyances of interests in land. For the share to be devised, it was necessary that the corresponding formalities for the passing of an interest in land by will be fulfilled.

[80] See *Johnson* v. *Gore Wood & Co.* [2002] 2 A.C. 1, 54–5.
[81] B. Rudden, *The New River: A Legal History* (Oxford: Clarendon Press, 1985), ch. 10.

Later, the courts are said to have been 'forced' away from treating the shareholders in land-holding companies, on the one hand, as owning 'fractions of real estate' and, on the other hand, as owning rights in the business conducted on that land 'as personal property'; the force pushed the courts towards treating shares as personal property only, even where the company owned land.[82] This change, which occurred both at law (in questions of inheritance) and in equity (in questions of the administration of deceased estates), bore out the purposive construction of the Statute of Frauds that had originated in equity,[83] which harboured a 'bias ... against a too literal construction of the statute'.[84] The cases reached the position that an assignment of a share in a land-owning company was required to comply with section 4 of the statute if the purpose of the company was to give the shareholder a right to a conveyance of some or all of the land of the company. Usually, however, the company's purpose was simply to conduct its business upon the land and to generate profits for distribution as dividends to its members. That was the purpose of a joint stock. Hence, company shares and shares in partnerships came to be seen as personalty. This 'equitable' position was cemented for companies by the legislation of 1856 and 1862[85] and for partnerships later, in 1890.[86]

It can be no coincidence that equity had a habit, formalised into several doctrines, of treating land to be sold as already being personalty, for the purposes of descent upon death, and as treating money to be invested in land as realty to the same end.[87] The maxim applied that equity considers as done that which ought to be done. That habit of treating a contemplated investment or sale as changing the character of the property prior to its sale no doubt makes it simpler to see land held by

[82] C.A. Cooke, *Corporation, Trust and Company* (Manchester University Press, 1950), 70–1.

[83] W.S. Holdsworth, *A History of English Law* (London: Methuen, 1924), vol. VI, 393–5.

[84] *Ibid.*, 393. See Turner, 'Equity and Administration', text between nn. 25 and 28.

[85] Joint Stock Companies Act 1856 (UK), 19 & 20 Vict. c. 47, s. 15; Companies Act 1862 (UK), 25 & 26 Vict. c. 89, s. 22. See now Companies Act 2006 (UK), s. 541 and Corporations Act 2001 (Cth), s. 1070A.

[86] Partnership Act 1890 (UK), s. 22 (repealed by the Trusts of Land and Appointment of Trustees Act 1996 (UK), Sch. 4).

[87] See especially S. Anderson, 'The Proper Narrow Scope of Equitable Conversion in Land Law' (1984) 100 L.Q.R. 86, 100–9. The equitable experience of monitoring trustees to ensure that the equitable life tenant and equitable remainderman were treated fairly, and the detailed rules on the allocation to capital and income in trust law, may have been another influence in the development of the legal distinction between a company's capital and business. See J.D. Heydon and M.J. Leeming, *Jacobs' Law of Trusts in Australia*, 7th ed. (Sydney: LexisNexis Butterworths, 2006), ch. 19.

a company or partnership as having the character of personalty for the purpose of *inter vivos* transactions and statutory conveyancing formalities. Indeed, the character of a share – today, most importantly, a share in a partnership or a share or unit in a trading trust – as personalty has been attributed to the doctrine of equitable conversion.[88] Strictly, the processes are distinct. Whether land should go to the person entitled to a deceased's real estate or the person entitled to the deceased's personal estate is one thing. Quite another thing is whether the land would have needed to be conveyed in writing compliant with the Statute of Frauds during the deceased's life.[89]

However, through the equitable doctrine of conversion equity did carry the distinction between capital and business further.[90] Shares in a company or partnership that held land were subjected to the doctrine of equitable conversion. As between the deceased's real and personal representatives, a share in a company was (and is) treated as personalty. Partnership shares were treated in the same way in England until the doctrine of conversion was abolished in 1996.[91] Since then, no case appears to have decided whether partners' shares will be treated as personalty even now, for purposes other than succession. Yet it would be curious if the character of partners' shares were now to be treated as realty or personalty depending on what assets the partnership holds.

The character of distributions

The adjustment of equitable doctrines for use in business settings is seen in a second example of an equitable development of accounting ideas. Periodically, a profitable company must decide whether to distribute profits; partnership articles generally require a periodic distribution of profits to the partners; and under a trust used for business, the trust terms may be drafted to require a distribution of profits, be that an absolute duty or one qualified by a discretion given to the trustees. There had been a doctrine that when a company makes a distribution of profits and one

[88] Lindley and Dickinson, *A Treatise on the Law of Partnership including its Application to Companies*, 4th ed., 672.

[89] J.D. Heydon, M.J. Leeming and P.G. Turner, *Meagher, Gummow and Lehane's Equity: Doctrines and Remedies*, 5th ed. (Sydney: LexisNexis Butterworths, 2015), [35–005], [35–135].

[90] See also P. Ireland, 'Capitalism Without the Capitalist: The Joint Stock Company Share and the Emergence of the Modern Doctrine of Separate Corporate Personality' (1996) 17 J.L.H. 41, 50–3.

[91] Trusts of Land and Appointment of Trustees Act 1996 (UK), Sch. 4.

of the members is a trustee under a settlement creating successive interests, the way that distribution fell to be treated as between an equitable life tenant and an equitable remainderman was controlled by the company's decision: if the directors had discretion to declare a dividend[92] and resolved to pay one, the distribution had the character of income under the settlement, while if the directors issued shares, the trustee was to treat the distribution as capital. However, the doctrine was later revised by courts of equity.

The revised doctrine more clearly distinguishes between the company's actions, as between itself and its members, and the position of the members and anyone to whom a member may owe trust obligations. The reason is that

> [t]he company does not know and does not care whether a shareholder is a trustee of his shares or not. It is of no concern to a company which is parting with moneys to a shareholder whether that shareholder (if he be a trustee) will hold them as trustee for A absolutely or as trustee for A for life only.[93]

This relieves the company of having to look into the proper application of the distribution. The revised doctrine also means that the company's own actions in deciding in what form to make the distribution cannot control the terms of the (external) trust. That is for the settlor of the trust to do in the trust's terms or, absent trust terms, then for equity to do through further default (trust law) rules as to apportionment.

Status as shareholder

The commercial activities of a business association all assume a proper record of who holds a stake in the business. Doctrines of equity serve the need for a proper record. Various circumstances can impinge on the accuracy of such records, which include registers of companies' shareholders, deeds of partnership and other forms of record. Because of that variety, the doctrines of equity that serve the need for a proper record are also various. Claims to have the record altered by means of equitable relief may be grounded on there having been fraud, a forfeiture or an assignment of shares. Each of those situations will be considered, as will the applicability of the equitable doctrine of rectification.

92 *Wambo Coal Pty Ltd* v. *Sumiseki Materials Co Ltd* (2014) 290 F.L.R. 18, [73]–[84].
93 *Hill* v. *Permanent Trustee Co. of NSW* [1930] A.C. 720, 731.

Rescission of fraudulent issuance of shares

The treatment of claims to rescind a contract by which a person became a member of a company, or entered into a partnership, shows a way in which relief on the basis of general equitable doctrines can be refused where some administrative scheme would be unjustifiably disrupted by the grant of equitable relief. The withdrawal of equity there aids administration.

The 'rule' is that a contract by which a person bought shares or entered into a partnership cannot be rescinded for fraud in a winding up. Common law rules do not permit rescission of such contracts in any circumstances: the machinery to restore the *status quo ante* is wanting at common law. Equity has the required machinery. What, then, bars equitable relief? The bar cannot depend on the judge-made principles of equity to the exclusion of all statutory considerations, for creditors' and shareholders' rights are affected by statutory provisions whose effect begins with the winding up.[94] Statutory considerations must somehow be taken into account. Nor can the bar depend exclusively on the statutory provisions barring rescission wholly apart from considerations of equitable doctrine, for the statutory provisions do not purport to exclude equitable relief by rescission.[95] The bar must depend on the interaction of statute and equity. Precisely how it does so requires further examination.

The authors of an important book on rescission criticise simplistic justifications of the bar, although they apparently support the bar itself. They closely analyse the explanation that rescission is barred on equitable grounds in a winding up due to the fact that it would defeat or prejudice the creditors' rights upon a winding up. This explanation is found lacking: rescission 'is ... permitted' before a winding up even though that is prejudicial to creditors,[96] yet 'insolvency is not alone sufficient' to bar rescission even though it too prejudices the rights of creditors. Instead, the authors argue that the 'real objection' to affording rescission to a defrauded shareholder or partner in a winding up is that the winding up 'materially changes the creditors' rights' by conferring on them, '[i]n place of a claim against the company[,] ... a claim against its assets, which include all funds paid or payable by the shareholders'.[97]

Those views arguably depend on too bounded a view of the cases. Though the cases indicate that rescission may occur before a winding up,

[94] D. O'Sullivan, S. Elliott and R. Zakrzewski, *The Law of Rescission*, 2nd ed. (Oxford University Press, 2014), [25.30]–[25.31], [25.37]–[25.39].

[95] *Ibid.*, [25.30]–[25.32], [25.35]. [96] *Ibid.*, [25.33]. [97] *Ibid.*, [25.34].

even though that could in a sense prejudice the company's creditors, the cases do not suggest that rescission of a fraudulent contract to subscribe for shares or to enter a partnership is necessarily barred wherever rescission would occasion prejudice to creditors' and shareholders' rights. In other words, the juristic change to the nature of a creditor's claim upon a winding up is not alone the reason why equitable relief is effectively barred. More depends on the facts and on the requirements of equitable relief in aid of rescission.

So much is seen from *Tennent* v. *City of Glasgow Bank*: a Scottish appeal to the House of Lords, in which Lord Cairns L.C. spoke in terms that require some adaptation to common law jurisdictions with a system of equity, but terms which once adapted nonetheless demonstrate that the bar to equitable relief depends on more than the juristic change in the nature of the creditor's claim upon a winding up. His Lordship compared and contrasted the position of someone seeking rescission of a fraudulent contract to enter a partnership and a fraudulent contract to take up shares. Of the former, he said:

> In an ordinary partnership, not formed on the joint stock principle, it is impossible, *as a general rule*, for a partner at any time to retire from or repudiate the partnership *without satisfying*, or remaining bound to satisfy, the liabilities of the partnership. He may have been induced by his co-partners by fraud to enter into the partnership, and that may be a ground for relief against them, but it is no ground for getting rid of a liability to creditors. This is the case whether the partnership is a going concern, or whether it has stopped payment or become insolvent.[98]

The general rule therefore did not always apply. It might or might not apply in a winding up. In terms of equitable doctrine, the general rule would seem not to apply if the plaintiff had complied with the maxim that those who seek equity must do equity. The plaintiff could then have done equity by satisfying the liabilities of the partnership. Alternatively, the plaintiff could have given an undertaking to do so. This may have been burdensome for the plaintiff to do; indeed, it may have been impossible for the plaintiff. However, that is beside the point. To fail to offer equity, or to decline to do so, is in principle fatal to a claim for equitable relief wherever the maxim applies.[99]

[98] *Tennent* v. *City of Glasgow Bank* (1879) L.R. 4 H.L. 615, 621 (italics added). See also *Houldsworth* v. *City of Glasgow Bank* (1889) L.R. 5 H.L. 317, 324–5.

[99] *Langman* v. *Handover* (1929) 43 C.L.R. 334.

It follows that the bar to rescission of a fraudulent issue of shares in a company or partnership in a winding up depends on the inability or unwillingness of the claimant to do equity by satisfying the extant liabilities of the company or partnership, namely the liabilities of shareholders and creditors as affected by legislation upon the commencement of the winding up. Taken alone, the affectation or change does not justify the bar. That explanation is consistent with the further analysis of Lord Cairns L.C. in *Tennent's* case addressing joint stock companies specifically.[100]

The consequence is that, while equitable doctrines serve the need for a proper record of shareholders in a company or a partnership, equity's demands of reciprocal justice effectively bar rescission in equity where the correction of the record of shareholders would be to the prejudice to others with rights under the statutory winding up scheme.

Relief against forfeiture of shares

The same consequence ensues where equitable relief is sought against a forfeiture of shares brought about by company directors' exercise of a power to forfeit the share of a member.[101] A partner's share cannot be forfeited.[102] However, because the complaint differs from the complaint of a party who seeks rescission in equity of a fraudulent contract, the reasons for equitable relief being denied also differ between the two situations.

Forfeitures occur for a range of reasons and in several ways. Using the term in its ordinary legal sense, 'forfeiture' always involves the determination of one person's property rights as the direct result of the action of another, or the automatic exertion of legal force through an instrument (such as a statute or contract) whose force on the property owner's rights is not immediately within the property owner's control. The harshness of forfeitures rests in the combination of (1) the loss of (*ex hypothesi* desirable) proprietary rights and (2) the immediate cause of that loss being the act of another, or some automatic event.[103]

[100] *Tennent* v. *City of Glasgow Bank* (1879) L.R. 4 H.L. 615, 621–2. See also *Sons of Gwalia Ltd* v. *Margaretic* (2007) 231 C.L.R. 160, [58]; [2007] HCA 1.

[101] Company articles may include provision for forfeiture of shares: see Companies Act 2006 (UK), ss. 617(5)(c), 659(2)(c), 662(1)(a), 668(1)(a); Model Articles for Public Companies, arts 50(8), 57–61: see n. 111 below.

[102] Dissolution is the only way in which a partner may be got rid of against his or her will: Lindley and Dickinson, *A Treatise on the Law of Partnership including its Application to Companies*, 4th ed., 744.

[103] Thus, the Companies Act 2006 (UK) distinguishes forfeiture from surrender: for example, section 662(1)(a). See generally Heydon, Leeming and Turner, *Meagher, Gummow*

A forfeiture of a member's shares by a company's directors displays these features. Nevertheless, equitable relief will generally not go in aid of a shareholder whose shares are properly forfeited. The rationale of equitable relief here demands that the party benefiting from the forfeiture be 'compensated' by being put back in the position the party would have held had the forfeiture not occurred. The basic rule of equitable doctrine is only to relieve against a forfeiture if compensation is able to be made to the person or persons who would otherwise benefit from the forfeiture.[104] Though compensation in the form of damages can be awarded for types of loss not truly susceptible of calculation in the law of torts, in this area of equity money will not necessarily overcome the prejudice a party entitled to the benefit of a forfeiture would suffer if the forfeiture were undone. The acts leading to the forfeiture of a member's shares are typically unable to be compensated in the relevant sense: by the member's default, the company suffers irremediable prejudice.[105] Equity stays its hand out of deference to the community of interest and the need for the scheme governing that community properly to be administered.

Equitable claims to shares

If the preceding examples – of rescission and relief against forfeiture – suggest that a proper record of who has a stake in a business is not necessarily a record including all persons with some equitable claim, then that suggestion receives further support from the rules as to the priority of claims to dealings with particular shares in a company or partnership. A share might be transferred first to one transferee and then purportedly transferred a second time to another transferee. A priority contest may follow between the two transferees. Reliance may also be placed on rules of priority where a transferee takes a share that is held on an express trust or is subject to a constructive trust. Conceivably, equitable priority rules could be applied to identify who ought to be recorded as the holder of the relevant stake in a particular business. The equitable priority rules would further the transaction under which the successful claimant's claim is made. However, equity allows these rules to be displaced (as they often are) by appropriate expressions of intention in a company's articles of association or constitution; the rules may also be displaced by

and Lehane's Equity: Doctrines and Remedies, 5th ed. [18–210]–[18–245]; cf. *Cavendish Square Holding BV* v. *Makdessi* [2015] 3 W.L.R. 1373; [2015] UKSC 67.

104 *Peachy* v. *Duke of Somerset* (1721) 1 Str. 447, 453; 93 E.R. 626, 630.

105 *Sparks* v. *Liverpool Waterworks Co.* (1807) 13 Ves. 428, 434–5; 33 E.R. 354, 356–7.

parliamentary legislation. The displacing of these equitable rules allows for superior administrative arrangements.

This can be seen from the treatment by equity of an assignment of a partner's share. General law partnerships have legal features that inhibit the application of ordinary priority rules to dealings with a partner's share. Notice of an equitable assignment normally binds the obligor or holder of a fund in which an interest is assigned. The notice causes the obligor or fund-holder to have an equitable liability towards the assignee. However, partners acquire no equitable liability when they receive notice that one of their partners has assigned a share to a third party. The partnership depends on good faith existing between the partners. The partners cannot be taken to be willing to trust strangers in the same way. It would go against the nature of the intended relationship of partnership to find that notice of the assignment binds the partners in equity towards the outsider. The ordinary position that notice of an equitable assignment of a chose in action binds the obligor does not apply because, in the circumstances, the reason for that general rule does not apply. The partners, as fund-holders, are relieved of the obligation to take notice of trusts and equities in favour of assignees.[106]

The case of registered companies is different. In a modern registered company, as in the old joint stock company, the members typically do not owe fiduciary obligations towards one another. While the fiduciary relations between partners are at the root of why partners acquire no equitable liability when they receive notice that one of their partners has assigned a share, the company will not necessarily be bound in equity by notice that a share in the company has been assigned merely because the relations between its members are not fiduciary. The effect of notice depends on the circumstances. The relevant circumstances must include not only the apparent nature of the parties' relations – including any fiduciary qualities the relations may have – but also on what terms the relations are created, whether those terms involve fiduciary elements or not. Thus, joint stock companies could be created on terms that the company was not to be bound by particular equities, or equities of any kind.[107] However, since the Joint Stock Companies Act 1856, companies

[106] Cf. *Federal Commissioner of Taxation* v. *Everett* (1980) 143 C.L.R. 440, 448 (assignee 'may be entitled to receive payments from partnership profits direct from the partnership').

[107] *Société Générale de Paris* v. *Tramways Union Co. Ltd* (1884) 14 Q.B.D. 424, 439–40, 443–8, 450–8, aff'd *sub. nom. Société Générale de Paris* v. *Walker* (1886) 11 App. Cas. 20;

legislation has provided that a company is not to be attached with 'Notice of any Trust, expressed or implied or constructive'.[108]

Consequently, a dividend payable on a share may generally be paid only to the person registered as the holder of the share at the record date; an equitable assignee of the right to payment of the dividend cannot gain rights directly against the company. Further, for any right cognisable at law that is subject to such provisions, it cannot be assigned effectively in equity so as to bind the obligor. It cannot be converted into a 'legal' assignment under the statutory provisions for the assignment of legal title to choses in action.[109] The statutory rule introduced in the 1862 legislation 'is no longer absolute'.[110] In England, statute merely provides that no notice of any trust shall be entered on the register of members or be receivable by the registrar; provisions entitling the company to disregard equities must come, if at all, from the company articles.[111] In Australia, the rule in the 1862 legislation does not apply to unlisted companies, or to a trustee, executor or administrator of a deceased estate, or to bankrupts or infirm persons.[112]

These variations allow administrative efficiency to be gained for the business association by allowing the record of who holds a stake in the association to be kept relatively clear, thus simplifying the internal administration of the company as against its members and holders of derivative claims under its members.[113]

see at 30–1 (Lord Selborne L.C.). Policies of insurance were issued on similar terms: for example, *Re Turcan* (1888) 40 Ch. D. 5, 6, 10–11.

108 Joint Stock Companies Act 1856 (UK), s. 19; Companies Act 1862 (UK), s. 30; Companies Act 2006 (UK), s. 126; Corporations Act 2001 (Cth), s. 1072E(10).

109 In England, the Law of Property Act 1925 (UK), s. 136, which derives from section 25(6) of the Judicature Act 1873 (UK). See *Bluebottle UK Ltd* v. *Deputy Commissioner of Taxation* (2007) 232 C.L.R. 598, [52]–[70]; [2007] HCA 54.

110 *Bluebottle UK Ltd* v. *Deputy Commissioner of Taxation* (2007) 232 C.L.R. 598, [56].

111 See K.W. Mackinnon and R. Buchanan-Dunlop (eds.), *Palmer's Company Precedents*, 17th ed. (London: Sweet & Maxwell, 1956), Pt 1, 418–21 and, in relation to the Companies Act 2006 (UK), the Model Articles for Private Companies Limited by Shares, art. 23 (as prescribed by the Companies (Model Articles) Regulations 2008 (S.I. 2008/3229) (UK), Sch. 1), and Model Articles for Public Companies, art. 45 (as prescribed by the Companies (Model Articles) Regulations 2008 (UK), Sch. 3). The relevant model articles apply by default in the events detailed in section 20 of the 2006 Act. On the 'remarkable exception' contained in Part 22 of the Companies Act 2006 (UK), see *Eclairs Group Ltd* v. *JKX Oil & Gas plc* [2014] Bus. L.R. 835, [36]; [2014] EWCA Civ 640 (appeal allowed on grounds not affecting this point: *Eclairs Group Ltd* v. *JKX Oil & Gas plc* [2015] Bus. L.R. 1395).

112 Corporations Act 2001 (Cth), s. 1072E(2)–(7). This is not a 'replaceable rule' within the meaning of section 135.

113 *Salomon* v. *Salomon & Co. Ltd* [1897] A.C. 22, 55. See also Companies Act 2006 (UK), ss. 145–53 (exercise of members' rights).

Rectification of the record

The Joint Stock Companies Act 1856 for the first time conferred on superior courts of law and equity a power to order the company to rectify the register of members.[114] Rectification of this sort and the rectification of instruments (such as written contracts) proceed differently. The rectification of instruments involves the redrawing of an instrument to ensure that its terms reflect the parties' true agreement, rather than an agreement expressed by mistake. Rectification of a share register effectively involves a mandatory injunction ordering the company to alter the register.

Before that statutory procedure was introduced, courts of equity had inherent jurisdiction to grant such relief. On occasion, a mandamus would issue at common law to the same end.[115] The succession of that equitable power by statute changes its source and the nature of the power. Except where statute requires otherwise, however, there must be inherent equitable jurisdiction to order the correction of a record of those with interests in a business association, such as a trading trust in which participants hold units. As Fullagar J. said of a register of company members, 'the power of a court of equity to order rectification is no more and no less than a part of its general jurisdiction to "act *in personam*" in aid of a legal right, and it must be subject to the same principles which apply generally to equitable remedies'.[116]

Debt financing

Extending outside the structures and workings of business associations themselves, the 'company charge', associated with the issue of debentures, is a major equitable contribution to company financing.[117] A charge by a natural person over the person's assets, present and future, suffers the hurdles of compliance with the Bills of Sale legislation and the risk that it will be seen as a transaction in fraud of creditors. It is therefore

114 Joint Stock Companies Act 1856 (UK), s. 25. See Companies Act 1862 (UK) s. 35 (extending the power to the Vice Warden of the Stannaries in the case of companies subject to his jurisdiction) and now the Companies Act 2006 (UK), s. 125 and Corporations Act 2001 (Cth), s. 175. On the operation of those provisions, see *Nilon Ltd* v. *Royal Westminster Investments SA* [2015] 3 All E.R. 372, [35]–[53]; [2015] UKPC 2.

115 *Ward* v. *South-Eastern Railway Co.* (1862) 2 El. & El. 812; 121 E.R. 304.

116 *Grant* v. *John Grant & Sons Pty Ltd* (1950) 82 C.L.R. 1, 51.

117 See the essays collected in J. Getzler and J. Payne (eds.), *Company Charges: Spectrum and Beyond* (Oxford University Press, 2006).

impracticable for one sort of business association: the partnership. But the same legal mechanics[118] enable the company to use the floating charge effectively because the company is free of the requirements of the Bills of Sale Acts. That the doctrines on which the floating charge are based are largely equitable – if not exclusively so – is not open to doubt. Be that as it may, the commonality of function between the floating charge and the 'partner's lien' would not have been lost on the Victorian Chancery judges.[119] Both the floating charge and the partner's lien had some proprietary effect; the enforcement of both typically required the assets to which it applied to be sold; and each typically applied to a 'fund' of assets the elements of which would change as trading activities were undertaken by the company or partnership respectively.[120] However, while the partners' lien applies to those within the partnership – for the benefit of the partners as residual claimants – the floating charge applies externally for creditors.

The equities involved in a fixed or floating charge largely service the parties' agreed terms. They extend the agreed terms somewhat where, for example, there is merely a specifically enforceable contract to grant debentures with floating charge security.[121] The would-be debenture holders will have 'a charge equivalent to that of actual debentures'; execution against secured assets will be subject to the would-be debenture holders' equities.[122]

Of a different sort are the new interpretive 'equities' to be seen in the latter day company charge cases decided in England. Faced with drafting which, it appears, was assumed to disrupt the statutory order of priority of claims on the assets subject to a company charge that was floating 'as created', the Privy Council[123] and then the House of Lords[124] variously interpreted the company charge itself, or the insolvency legislation, in a manner perceived to reach equity.[125] The judicial experience seems to have been like that in anti-avoidance tax cases such as *W. T. Ramsay Ltd*

[118] Analysed by R.C. Nolan, 'Property in a Fund' (2004) 120 L.Q.R. 108, 117–30.

[119] Nolan, 'Property in a Fund', 118–19.

[120] Lindley and Dickinson, *A Treatise on the Law of Partnership including its Application to Companies*, 4th ed., 679–83.

[121] See also Companies Act 2006 (UK), s. 740 (enforcement of contract to subscribe for debentures).

[122] *Simultaneous Colour Printing Syndicate* v. *Foweraker* [1901] 1 Q.B. 771, 773–4.

[123] *Agnew* v. *Commissioner of Inland Revenue* [2001] 2 A.C. 710; [2001] UKPC 28.

[124] *In re Spectrum Plus Ltd (in liq.)* [2005] 2 A.C. 680; [2005] UKHL 41.

[125] The starting assumption is arguably false: P.G. Turner, 'Charge Characterisation in English Law: A Settled Debate?' [2006] Sing. J.L.S. 200, 210.

v. *Inland Revenue Commissioners*.[126] In the outcome, a similarity between the company charge cases and the tax cases is that both groups subject commercial instruments to a type of mandatory equity distinct from the sorts of equity so far considered. Depending on how it is approached, this mandatory equity may demand the 'reinterpretation' of the parties' intentions[127] or of applicable statute.[128] That species of 'equity' requires careful feeding.

Conclusion

A legal account of the reasons for the success of the registered companies and unincorporated partnerships as means of conducting business in common law jurisdictions contains much on equity. Significant developments in the law of companies and the law of partnerships occurred in equity courts. At a time when the basic elements of these bodies of law were being laid down, after the enactment of the Bubble Act, resort to all courts, including the Chancery, was eschewed. Even then significant developments occurred through the jurisprudence of the courts of equity. The 'equitable trust'[129] was used to create a structure for business associations. The structure allowed basic features of incorporation to be attained without incorporation. These features remain apparent in the business associations of today. A 'private law' for governing the participants in the association was able to be created. This law of the company or partnership was distinct from the general laws of England and was something to which outsiders were neither entitled nor subject. In the case of joint stock companies, the trust device enabled a constitutional separation to be made between the holders of the executive power (the directors) and the holders of legislative power (the company in general meeting). For partnerships no such division was sought. What was sought for both companies and partnerships, however, was a joint stock or fund. When curial recognition of the unincorporated companies and partnership was eventually desired, the common law courts declined to recognise the joint stock. Equity recognised it and, through its distinctive procedures and relief, gave the joint stock fund practical effect.

Rather than prove a handicap, these developments show equity to have promoted business associations by supplying much of the law applicable

[126] [1982] A.C. 300.
[127] *In re Spectrum Plus Ltd (in liq.)* [2005] 2 A.C. 680, [141] (Lord Walker).
[128] *Ibid.*, [98], [107], [111] (Lord Scott).
[129] Cooke, *Corporation, Trust and Company*, 86.

to them. However, equity's facilitation of the conduct of business through business associations was extended further. Apart from providing the structural means for establishing unincorporated business associations, equity aided the workings of the entities so created. Some of the aid was given through the application of equitable doctrines and equitable relief. Some of the aid was given otherwise, especially by declining to apply equitable doctrines which, if applied inflexibly, would be intolerably disruptive. The inaptness of the equitable remedy of rectification to alter the terms of a company's articles of association is but one example.

All sources of law in common law systems are capable of being misapplied or incautiously extended so as to hamper legitimate business activity. While that risk will never be a risk merely in theory, such hampering is relatively uncommon. In particular, it rarely occurs at the hands of a judge applying the principles and doctrines of equity. Indeed, the illustrations in this chapter support the conclusion that doctrines of equity have to a substantial degree promoted modern laws on business associations through a 'deep and persistent involvement . . . in the evolution of modern commercial institutions and enterprises'.[130] In this area, as in others, equity facilitates the practical processes and tasks of administration.

[130] *Elders Trustee & Executor Co. Ltd* v. *E. G. Reeves Pty Ltd* (1987) 78 A.L.R. 193, 229. See also *O'Neill* v. *Phillips* [1999] 1 W.L.R. 1092, 1098; Cooke, *Corporation, Trust and Company*.

9

Equitable doctrines in business associations

A commentary

RICHARD SNOWDEN

Dr Turner's chapter (Chapter 8) illustrates and rationalises the contribution the courts of equity have made to the development and operation of business associations. The thesis of the chapter is that equitable doctrines and remedies have assisted the common law and statute where they were found wanting, and that they have been withheld where there was no reason for their application. The result, it is argued, is that the law's hypothetical businessman, who prefers bright lines and certainty (not to mention speed and efficiency), need have no reason to fear that equity will muddy the otherwise clear waters of commerce.

The chapter focuses on unincorporated partnerships and companies incorporated by registration. The early influence of equity is still seen strongly in the law of unincorporated partnerships. But that business model is on the decline in favour of incorporated partnerships and companies with limited liability. It is, therefore, to the more ubiquitous area of company law that one should primarily look for a rigorous test of equity's continuing utility and role in a modern business setting.

The tentative analogy drawn in the first section of Dr Turner's chapter between the constitutional structure of a business association and a nation state will not be readily recognisable to the equity lawyer. There are of course some similarities: there is an executive management ultimately responsible to an electorate in both, and, as the chapter points out, in common with the electorate of a democratic nation state, members of a company are free to vote in their own interests in general meeting. But as the chapter rightly recognises, none of that requires or illustrates the involvement of equity.

The equity lawyer will more readily identify with the chapter's description of how familiar doctrines from the law of trusts and partnerships were adapted and applied to the new joint stock companies of the nineteenth century. Dr Turner demonstrates how company law was founded upon the equitable concept of management of a fund of assets for the benefit of those who have collective interests in it but who do not own any of the individual assets. Moreover, although the duties of directors are now codified in English law, statute has expressly retained the principles of equity as an aid to interpretation and application of those duties and in defining the remedies for their breach.[1] Similarly, the role of equity in the development of the floating charge as a means of securing flexible debt finance for trading companies in the late nineteenth and early twentieth centuries is well known, and equitable principles are still capable of being developed and applied to deal with modern financing techniques in this regard.[2]

It is also entirely appropriate for the chapter to draw attention to the fact that there are areas of company law where the courts have chosen not to apply equitable doctrines. But it is perhaps an overstatement to regard these as examples of equity choosing to 'withhold' its doctrines, or to suggest that equity has actively 'assisted' the development of business associations by finding reasons not to apply its doctrines in various situations. The reality might be thought to be rather more prosaic.

For the most part, the enlarged statutory framework for companies and the common law doctrines of contract operate tolerably well on their own in the modern business environment. They neither need nor benefit from any equitable correction or enhancement. The courts and practitioners of equity in the corporate sphere should be content with equity's traditional role of being a means by which identifiable deficiencies in the application of statute and contract law can be ameliorated where considerations of an essentially personal nature so require.

The point can be illustrated by several of the examples given in the chapter. Take, for example, the fact that the courts have not sought to apply the equitable doctrine of rectification to the articles of association of a company limited by shares. The reason for this is the same as the reason why the courts, when applying the common law, have modified the conventional principles of contractual interpretation so as to exclude recourse to the matrix of background facts against which the incorporators agreed the articles. An essential feature of the limited company is that persons can adhere to the collective statutory contract by buying shares without any need for interaction of a personal nature with the continuing

[1] Companies Act 2006 (UK), ss. 170(4), 178.

[2] See *In re Spectrum Plus Ltd (in liq.)* [2005] 2 A.C. 680; [2005] UKHL 41.

members or management. That business model works well: it simply would not work if the rules had a different meaning than might appear from their words as a result of facts known to some but not all of the members.[3]

Likewise, it is important not to overstate the role that equitable principles have in regulating the relations between members of a company *inter se* and the exercise of power by those who are appointed to manage the affairs of the company by the majority. In contrast to the Roman law *societas*, or the unincorporated partnership, which equity has long regarded as a personal contract of good faith between all partners, equity has not intervened with the same broad brush in company law.

So, for example, the general principle is that shareholders of a company are free to exercise their votes in their own interests,[4] and it is only in limited circumstances that equity restricts that freedom. One such circumstance is where shareholders are given a power, by a majority, to amend the articles of association. Such alteration has the ability to affect the contractual rights and obligations by which members have agreed to be bound and thereby directly to affect the rights and interests of the minority against their wishes. It is one of the features of democracy that minorities agree to be bound by a majority vote provided that the change can reasonably be thought to operate for the greater good of the whole body. It is quite another to hold that a minority have agreed to be bound by a majority who do not seek to advance the greater good but seek simply to benefit themselves at the expense of the minority.

That, rather than some overarching equitable requirement of good faith, is the reason why the power of amendment has long been thought to be subject to an implied limitation, classically explained by Lindley L.J. in *Allen* v. *Gold Reefs of West Africa*:[5]

> The power ... conferred on companies to alter the regulations contained in their articles is limited only by the provisions contained in the statute and the conditions contained in the company memorandum of association. Wide, however, as the language of [the] section ... is, the power conferred by it must, like all other powers, be exercised subject to those general principles of law and equity which are applicable to all powers conferred on majorities and enabling them to bind minorities. It must be exercised, not only in the manner required by law, but also bona fide for

[3] *Bratton Seymour Service Co. Ltd* v. *Oxborough* [1992] B.C.L.C. 693; *A.-G. of Belize* v. *Belize Telecom Ltd* [2009] 1 W.L.R. 1988; [2009] UKPC 10.

[4] *Burland* v. *Earle* [1902] A.C. 83, 94.

[5] [1900] 1 Ch. 656.

> the benefit of the company as a whole, and it must not be exceeded. These conditions are always implied, and are seldom, if ever, expressed.[6]

It will be seen that Lindley L.J. did not specifically identify the restriction on the exercise of power as an equitable restraint, and in *Assenagon Asset Management SA* v. *Irish Bank Resolution Corp.*,[7] Briggs J. was inclined to see this restriction not as a principle of equity at all but as a species of implied term arising by operation of law in the sense described in *Liverpool City Council* v. *Irwin*.[8]

So also, when considering the role of equitable doctrines in the statutory 'just and equitable' winding up jurisdiction, the much-quoted dictum of Lord Wilberforce in *Ebrahimi* v. *Westbourne Galleries Ltd*,[9] to the effect that equity may enable the court to subject the exercise of legal rights to equitable considerations, must not be applied too liberally and without bearing in mind the qualification that preceded it. It is worth repeating the relevant passage from Lord Wilberforce's speech in full:

> The words ['just and equitable'] are a recognition of the fact that a limited company is more than a mere legal entity, with a personality in law of its own: that there is room in company law for recognition of the fact that behind it, or amongst it, there are individuals, with rights, expectations and obligations inter se which are not necessarily submerged in the company structure. *That structure is defined by the Companies Act [1948] and by the articles of association by which shareholders agree to be bound. In most companies and in most contexts, this definition is sufficient and exhaustive, equally so whether the company is large or small. The 'just and equitable' provision does not, as the respondents [sc. the company] suggest, entitle one party to disregard the obligation he assumes by entering a company, nor the court to dispense him from it.* It does, as equity always does, enable the court to subject the exercise of legal rights to equitable considerations; considerations, that is, of a personal character arising between one individual and another, which may make it unjust, or inequitable, to insist on legal rights, or to exercise them in a particular way.[10]

As Lord Wilberforce indicated, the default position is the statutory and contractual regime, and in most cases that regime is sufficient and exhaustive. It will work perfectly well without the need for equitable intervention. There will only be a need to have recourse to equitable doctrines where considerations of a personal character between members make the operation of the statutory and contractual regime unjust.

6 *Ibid.*, 671–2. 7 [2013] Bus. L.R. 266; [2012] EWHC 2090 (Ch). 8 [1977] A.C. 239.
9 [1973] A.C. 360. 10 *Ibid.*, 379 (italics added).

This also leads to the conclusion, as Lord Hoffmann has made clear in the parallel statutory context of the unfair prejudice remedy contained in section 994 of the Companies Act 2006, that in most cases a member cannot complain unless there has been some breach of the statute or of the contractual terms upon which he agreed that the affairs of the company should be conducted. Moreover, building on Lord Wilberforce's lead, Lord Hoffmann emphasised that any recourse to equity could only be on the basis of established principles, rather than some generalised sense of fairness.[11]

A final, and recent, example of a limitation on the application of equity in the modern corporate setting relates to the long-standing statutory jurisdiction to rectify a company's register of members. Although the jurisdiction is expressed in wide terms, the companies legislation proceeds upon the basis that membership is determined by entry on the register, and the company is concerned only with the *legal* entitlement of its members to be entered there. As Dr Turner observes, this promotes efficiency and simplicity in the administration of a company, or to put it another way, '... the companies legislation proceeds on that basis and would be unworkable if that were not so'.[12] This has the result that the statutory jurisdiction to rectify the register of members cannot apply to determine disputes about beneficial ownership or equitable claims to shares. The applicant for an order for rectification must have a right to registration by virtue of a valid transfer of legal title. A person claiming to have an equitable interest in shares should seek to establish his rights in ordinary litigation.[13]

In conclusion, one must acknowledge, as Dr Turner does, the enormous influence that equity has had on the historical development of the business association in various forms and recognise also that equitable principles still have a significant role to play today in regulating the conduct of company directors and in supplementing statute and contract law in the case of the archetypal small private company which is the result of the incorporation of an earlier partnership or individual joint venture. However, care must be taken not to overplay equity's hand. There are many areas in which statutory and contractual principles are sufficient for the efficient conduct of the affairs of the modern business association, and the intervention of equity is neither necessary nor welcome.

[11] *O'Neill* v. *Phillips* [1999] 1 W.L.R. 1092, 1098.

[12] *Enviroco Ltd* v. *Farstad Supply A/S* [2011] 1 W.L.R. 921, [38]; [2011] UKSC 16.

[13] *Nilon Ltd* v. *Royal Westminster Investments SA* [2015] 3 All E.R. 372; [2015] UKPC 2, holding that *Re Hoicrest Ltd* [2000] 1 W.L.R. 414 was wrongly decided.

10

Why the rule in *Saunders* v. *Vautier* is wrong

JOHN H. LANGBEIN

Introduction

The leading English trust case of *Saunders* v. *Vautier*[1] stands for a principle that is not well articulated in the judgments in the case, but that the judgments are thought to evidence or presuppose. The rule in *Saunders* v. *Vautier* is that an adult beneficiary of a trust who is alone entitled to the beneficial interest may require the trustee(s) to terminate the trust and distribute the trust property to the beneficiary despite an express term of the trust directing that distribution be postponed to a later time.[2]

The case involved a testamentary trust of East India stock valued at £2,000. The trust was created under the will of Richard Wright for the benefit of his nephew, Daniel. At the time of Richard's death, Daniel was twelve years old. The trust terms directed the trustees to hold the stock, accumulate the income until Daniel reached age twenty-five, and then terminate the trust by transferring the stock and accumulated income to Daniel. In 1841, when Daniel turned twenty-one (then the age of majority), he petitioned for immediate termination. The Chancery courts (Lord Cottenham L.C., affirming Lord Langdale M.R.) held for Daniel. The rule was thereafter extended to trusts having more than one beneficiary, in cases in which all of them are *sui juris* and agree on termination.[3]

I acknowledge with gratitude suggestions from Robert Sitkoff, Peter Turner and Lawrence Waggoner.

[1] (1841) Cr. & Ph. 240; 41 E. R. 482 (L.C.), affirming (1841) 4 Beav. 115; 49 E.R. 282 (M.R.).

[2] See, for example, D.J. Hayton, P.B.J. Matthews and C.C.J. Mitchell, *Underhill and Hayton: Law Relating to Trusts and Trustees*, 18th ed. (London: LexisNexis, 2010), [66.1]–[66.2]; G. Thomas and A. Hudson, *The Law of Trusts*, 2nd ed. (Oxford University Press, 2010), [7.05].

[3] Hayton, Matthews and Mitchell, *Underhill and Hayton: Law Relating to Trusts and Trustees*, 18th ed. [66.1] (termination with the assent of 'all those who may possibly benefit under a trust, whether concurrently or successively').

The protective purpose

The rule in *Saunders* v. *Vautier* has been a part of English trust law for so long that one can overlook how counterintuitive it is. The reason that a transferor such as Richard Wright wishes to postpone distribution of the trust property to a youthful beneficiary such as Daniel Vautier is protective. The trust provision requiring Daniel to wait four years into adulthood before obtaining control of the property reflected Richard's judgment that further life experience would help Daniel use the property more wisely. Richard imposed the condition of postponed enjoyment for the purpose of benefiting the beneficiary, by protecting him from the dangers of youthful improvidence.[4] (The trend in recent decades in many jurisdictions to lower the age of majority from twenty-one to eighteen has heightened the danger of allowing persons so inexperienced in the conduct of wealth management to have complete dominion over substantial assets.)

The trust form is an ideal device for implementing such a protective purpose. In Bernard Rudden's succinct account, 'the normal private trust is essentially a gift, projected on the plane of time and so subjected to a management regime'.[5] Richard, the donor in *Saunders* v. *Vautier*, sought just that – to project his gift to Daniel on the plane of time by arranging for trustees, acting under fiduciary obligations, to hold and manage the property for Daniel until he reached twenty-five. Had Richard not had the misfortune to die when Daniel was twelve, but instead lived to see Daniel turn twenty-one and then twenty-five, Richard could have carried out his plan by refraining from making his gift to Daniel until Daniel reached age twenty-five. Sadly, Richard was unable to survive until Daniel's twenty-fifth year, but he undertook to achieve a comparable result by having trustees stand in for him, to hold the property for Daniel's benefit until Daniel turned twenty-five.

Why refuse to enforce a protective term that is so evidently benign? The judgments in *Saunders* v. *Vautier* do not answer that question, that

[4] One of the several Canadian provincial law revision commission reports that criticise the rule in *Saunders* v. *Vautier* observes that '[i]n modern cases, the motive for postponement is usually a reservation about the maturity and responsibility of the beneficiary. This is a legitimate concern that would be respected by the courts in other contexts': Law Reform Commission of Saskatchewan, *The Rule in Saunders* v. *Vautier and the Variation of Trusts*, Consultation Paper on the Law of Trusts No. 1 (1994), 3. The Canadian reports are further discussed, below text at nn. 13–15, 40.

[5] B. Rudden, Book review (of J.P. Dawson, *Gifts and Promises: Continental and American Law Compared* (New Haven: Yale University Press, 1980)) (1981) 44 M.L.R. 610, 610.

is, they offer no functional justification for the result.[6] The rationale for the rule in *Saunders* v. *Vautier* is that the sole beneficiary of an interest in trust is entitled to immediate possession, because there is no other owner of the interest. This rationale is essentially doctrinal or legal-conceptual, as opposed to purposive or functional. The rule that defeated Richard's intent corrects no wrong, it prevents no harm. The idea is that because the trust bestowed 'equitable ownership'[7] of the trust property on the sole beneficiary, that ownership must have included every component of ownership, including the component that the settlor in *Saunders* v. *Vautier* attempted to have postponed, that is, the right to present control and enjoyment during the years before the beneficiary turned twenty-five. Because no one else owned that component of the equitable ownership of the trust property, Daniel's ownership rights must have included the right to present control and enjoyment, despite the express condition of postponed enjoyment.

Ease of evasion

A transferor can easily impose an age restriction that will be effective despite the rule in *Saunders* v. *Vautier*, by wording the provision a little differently. Had Richard's trust provided that, in the unlikely event that Daniel were to die before reaching age twenty-five, the trust property should revert to Richard's residuary devisees, or be given to some alternative taker (a gift over), then Daniel's interest would have been contingent rather than vested,[8] he would not have been the sole 'equitable

[6] Had *Saunders* v. *Vautier* been decided oppositely, the protection afforded the beneficiary's interest would not have been complete; a creditor of the beneficiary could still have attached the interest. But lack of ready access to the trust asset would have restrained the beneficiary from many forms of improvident consumption, and the beneficiary would have been kept from management of the asset (and hence from investment blunders) during the protective period. (Under the American rules discussed below, text to nn. 31–39 and n. 34, the combination of the *Claflin* doctrine and a spendthrift provision in the trust defeats creditor claims.)

[7] M.R. Chesterman, 'Family Settlements on Trust: Landowner and the Rising Bourgeoisie', in G.R. Rubin and D. Sugarman (eds.), *Law, Economy and Society, 1750–1914: Essays in the History of English Law* (Abingdon: Professional Books, 1984), 124, 154, quoting J.W. Harris, *Variation of Trusts* (London: Sweet and Maxwell, 1975), 2.

[8] Daniel's interest in a trust so worded could also be characterised as vested in interest but not in possession, hence subject to a condition of defeasance in favour of the taker of the gift over in default should Daniel die before reaching the age of 25. As with a contingent interest, Daniel would not in such a case have been the sole 'equitable owner' of the property, and the condition of postponed enjoyment would have been enforced.

owner' of the property, and the condition of postponed enjoyment would have been enforced.[9] That construction was not available in *Saunders* v. *Vautier* because, as the trust was worded, if Daniel failed to survive to age twenty-five, the trustees were to transfer the trust property to Daniel's executors or administrators, thus precluding any reversion or gift over.[10]

The ease with which the rule in *Saunders* v. *Vautier* can be evaded by expressing an age condition as a contingent interest[11] underscores that what motivated the rule was not hostility to the protective purpose of a condition of postponed enjoyment but rather simply the supposed doctrinal logic of 'equitable ownership'. Across the decades since *Saunders* v. *Vautier*, trust drafters have devised and the courts have sanctioned a variety of protective regimes turning on determinable interests, including one facilitated under the Trustee Act 1925 (UK).[12] Accordingly, the principal practical effect of the rule in *Saunders* v. *Vautier* is to function as a trap for the unwary, that is, for the transferor who has the misfortune to engage an insufficiently skilled drafter. Several Canadian provincial law revision commissions have emphasised this aspect of the rule in *Saunders* v. *Vautier* among the reasons for rejecting the rule. The Alberta report, observing ways that a transferor 'who wants to avoid *Saunders* v. *Vautier* can do so by careful drafting', concluded that this attribute of the rule 'actually invalidates any rationale for it. There is no point to a rule which merely penalises

[9] For discussion, with citation to the case law, see, for example, P. Matthews, 'The Comparative Importance of the Rule in *Saunders* v. *Vautier*' (2006) 122 L.Q.R. 266, 268.

[10] The trustees were directed 'to pay or transfer the principal of such East India stock, together with such accumulated interest and dividends, unto the said Daniel Wright Vautier, his executors, administrators, or assigns absolutely': *Saunders* v. *Vautier* (1841) Cr. & Ph. 240, 240; 41 E.R. 482, 482. The Chancellor pointed to this feature of the trust and concluded, '[t]here is no gift over': at 248; 485.

[11] 'The most effective method of avoiding a *Saunders* v. *Vautier* termination is for the instrument to create a gift over on the death of [the beneficiary] under the required age' which 'has the effect of making it clear that [the beneficiary] has not acquired the whole beneficial interest': D.M. Waters, M.R.P. Gillen and L.D. Smith, *Waters' Law of Trusts in Canada*, 4th ed. (Toronto: Carswell, 2012), 1241.

[12] Trustee Act 1925 (UK), s. 25; see, for example, G. Moffat, G. Bean and R. Probert, *Trusts Law: Text and Materials*, 5th ed. (Cambridge University Press, 2009), 275–6, describing the 'tripartite structure' of the provision: determinable interest, forfeiture provision, and 'a discretionary trust springing up at forfeiture'.

poor drafting'.[13] Similar views are expressed in the Manitoba[14] and Saskatchewan[15] reports.

Dead hand?

The rule in *Saunders* v. *Vautier* is not needed to police the dead hand, that is, to prevent enforcement of conditions that offend public policy or are harmful to the interests of trust beneficiaries. The anti-dead-hand policy is achieved by means of the rules against perpetuities[16] and against illegal[17] or capricious purposes,[18] as well as the power of a court to modify a trust under the Variation of Trusts Act 1958 (UK) and by means of non-statutory change-of-circumstances doctrines.[19]

[13] Alberta Institute of Law Research and Reform, *The Rule in Saunders* v. *Vautier*, Report No. 9 (1972), 5. The report also remarked upon the tendency of courts to engage in strained construction of a 'disposition in a way that will leave it outside the rule': at 6, citing Canadian cases.

[14] Manitoba Law Reform Commission, *Report on the Rule in Saunders* v. *Vautier*, Report No. 18 (1975), 23–4.

[15] Law Reform Commission of Saskatchewan, *The Rule in Saunders* v. *Vautier and the Variation of Trusts*, Consultation Paper on the Law of Trusts No. 1 (1994), 12–13, concluding that the rule is 'capricious in its application': at 13.

[16] See generally C. Harpum, S. Bridge and M. Dixon, *Megarry and Wade: The Law of Real Property*, 8th ed. (London: Sweet and Maxwell, 2012), [9-012]–[9-146]. The 'lives-in-being' feature of the rule against perpetuities strikes a balance that permits the transferor considerable control over the transfer of property to persons whom the transferor might know, but not persons more remote. The rule in *Saunders* v. *Vautier*, by contrast, interferes with the transferor's effort to benefit (by means of a protective restriction) a person whose weaknesses the transferor may know well.

[17] See Hayton, Matthews and Mitchell, *Underhill and Hayton: Law Relating to Trusts and Trustees*, 18th ed. [11.1]ff.

[18] The American Uniform Trust Code (UTC) expresses the rule against capricious terms as the requirement that '[a] trust and its terms must be for the benefit of its beneficiaries': UTC § 404 (2000); to the same effect, *Restatement (Third) Trusts* § 27(2) (2003). UTC § 404 is mandatory: UTC § 105(b)(3) (2000). I have discussed the UTC for English and Commonwealth readers in J.H. Langbein, 'The Uniform Trust Code: Codification of the Law of Trusts in the United States' (2001) 15 T.L.I. 69.

[19] For example, *Re Jackson* (1882) 21 Ch. D. 786 (variation from trust terms ordered to permit repairs on endangered buildings). The American Uniform Trust Code codifies several deviation-type rules: see UTC §§ 411–12, 414, 416–17 (2000), subject in most respects to the material purpose doctrine discussed below in this essay, below text at nn. 38–40; to the same effect, *Restatement (Third) Trusts* §§ 65–6, 68 (2003).

Trusteeship

The most problematic aspect of the rationale of the rule in *Saunders* v. *Vautier* is that the rationale neglects the role of trusteeship in mediating between the interests of settlor and beneficiary. *Saunders* v. *Vautier* transposed into trust law a pre-existing rule regarding legacies, that is, legal interests in personalty passing by will, as opposed to equitable interests in trust. The ecclesiastical courts, which administered estates of personalty, had refused to enforce conditions of postponed enjoyment on legacies.[20] Lord Langdale M.R. based his judgment in *Saunders* v. *Vautier* on that rule.[21] There is, however, a notable difference between a legacy and an interest in trust, namely, trusteeship.

When the trust form is used to make a gift that is subject to a condition of postponed enjoyment, trustees[22] are intermediated between legal and equitable title. The trustees are required to act under fiduciary obligations in administering the trust property for the sole benefit of the beneficiary. In this way, the beneficiary's equitable ownership of the interest in trust is fully recognised, even though subjected to the condition imposed by the donor for the benefit of the beneficiary. The treatise, *Underhill and Hayton*, remarks that on account of the rule in *Saunders* v. *Vautier*, 'the

[20] In 'the practice of the ecclesiastical courts, . . . an adult legatee whose interest in the legacy was vested could demand payment of the capital sum even though the testator had stipulated that income should be accumulated and the capital withheld for some specified period': Chesterman, 'Family Settlements on Trust: Landowner and the Rising Bourgeoisie', 153, citing *Lord Pawlet's Case* (1685) 2 Vent. 366; 86 E.R. 489; accord, Matthews, 'The Comparative Importance of the Rule in *Saunders* v. *Vautier*', 8–10. *Pawlet's Case* is not well reported, and the rationale is cryptic. The principal modern justification for the rule against a so-called disabling restraint on a legal interest is that such a restraint impairs marketability of the asset: *Restatement (Second) Property: Donative Transfers* § 4.1, cmt. a (1983).

[21] He said:

> I think that principle has been repeatedly acted upon; and where a legacy is directed to accumulate for a certain period, or where the payment is postponed, the legatee, if he has an absolute indefeasible interest in the legacy, is not bound to wait until the expiration of that period, but may require payment the moment he is competent to give a valid discharge.
>
> (*Saunders* v. *Vautier* (1841) 4 Beav. 115, 116; 49 E.R. 282, 282)

Looking back on the rationale of *Saunders* v. *Vautier* half a century later, Lord Herschell observed that it 'seems . . . to have been rather assumed than decided': *Wharton* v. *Masterman* [1895] A.C. 186, 193.

[22] I speak of 'trustees' in the plural, the common practice evidenced in *Saunders* v. *Vautier*, but a settlor may choose to use a single trustee.

trustee's raison d'être ceases to exist, and consequently, he himself becomes merely a person in possession of another person's estate'.[23] But that account is conclusory; it states an outcome without a reason. The contrary view is that the fiduciary obligation inherent in trusteeship is centrally important in distinguishing an interest in trust from an attempted restraint on non-trust property. The trust form enables trustees to preserve both the property interest of the beneficiary and the protective purpose of the donor's condition of postponed enjoyment.

The trustees' fiduciary obligations are enforceable by the beneficiary, and the beneficiary's right to remedy any wrongdoing by the trustees evidences the beneficiary's underlying property right. To illustrate, suppose that *Saunders* v. *Vautier* had been decided oppositely, and Daniel had been restrained from control and enjoyment of the trust property until he turned twenty-five, as Richard intended. Suppose further that when Daniel was, say, twenty-three, he learned that the trustees were misappropriating trust property in violation of their fiduciary duties of loyalty and prudent administration. Despite the condition of postponed control and enjoyment, Daniel's equitable ownership of the trust property would have allowed him immediate standing to seek remedies such as injunctive relief, surcharge, and trustee removal.[24]

The notion that a person who owns an asset may nevertheless be restrained from present control and enjoyment over the asset for protective reasons is hardly controversial. Indeed, the rule in *Saunders* v. *Vautier* as it is commonly expressed presupposes beneficiaries who are *sui juris*.[25] During the decade that Daniel was a minor, there was no objection to the trustees having enforced the settlor's condition of postponed enjoyment. The trustees recognised Daniel's sole property interest by administering the trust asset for Daniel's sole benefit.

[23] Hayton, Matthews and Mitchell, *Underhill and Hayton: Law Relating to Trusts and Trustees*, 18th ed. [66.2], and cases there cited.

[24] See generally Thomas and Hudson, *The Law of Trusts*, 2nd ed. [22.33]–[22.37] (trustee removal), [31.15], [31.18] (injunctive relief), ch. 32 (compensatory and restitutionary relief).

[25] For example, A. Hudson, *Equity and Trusts*, 8th ed. (London: Routledge, 2013), 182 (stating the rule as permitting 'all the beneficiaries, constituting 100% of the equitable interest in a trust fund, provided that they are all *sui juris* and acting together, can direct the trustees').

The donor

Perhaps the most striking feature of the rule in *Saunders* v. *Vautier* is its disregard for the intent of the donor, even though 'donative intent is the essence of a gift'.[26] As an English court remarked in a modern case, the rule in *Saunders* v. *Vautier* permits the beneficiary 'to overbear and defeat the intention'[27] of the donor who gave the trust property. This result is said to follow from the beneficiary's ownership of the property. 'The underlying principle is that a man may deal with his own property as he wishes and the court will not enforce any restraint on his absolute ownership and enjoyment.'[28] But this view of the matter neglects a crucial question: Which is the 'man [who] may deal with his own property as he wishes'? Is it the donee, as the quoted passage presupposes, or the donor?

Return to Rudden's helpful image of the donative trust as 'a gift, projected on the plane of time and so subjected to a management regime'.[29] At the outset of the transfer in *Saunders* v. *Vautier*, Richard, the donor, was the sole owner of the property that he intended to transfer to Daniel. Concerned about the risk that Daniel was then too young to use the property well, Richard decided to implement his gift on a plane of time by employing the management regime of the trust. Richard's intent was to transfer ownership of what was then his property in a phased way, using the trust device to postpone Daniel's control and enjoyment of the property for a few years after the time that Richard transferred the property to the trustees. As previously discussed, there is no satisfying functional account of why Richard, as owner of his property, should not be able to release his ownership in this phased manner, consistent with his protective purpose.

It is on this question – whether to recognise the property rights of the donor at the time of transfer – that American trust law has diverged from English. Across the nineteenth century, the Americans absorbed most of the conceptual structure and terminology of the English law of trusts,[30]

[26] *Restatement (Third) Property: Wills and Other Donative Transfers* § 6.1, cmt. b (2003). Speaking of the English law of wills, a prominent treatise says: 'The first and great rule to which all others must bend is that effect must be given to the intention of the testator': R.F.D. Barlow, R.A. Wallington, S.L. Meadway and J.A.D. MacDougald, *Williams on Wills*, 10th ed. (London: LexisNexis, 2014), vol. 1, § 49.1.

[27] *Goulding* v. *James* [1997] 2 All E.R. 239, 247.

[28] Thomas and Hudson, *The Law of Trusts*, 2nd ed. [7.05].

[29] Rudden, Book review, 610.

[30] The two most prominent jurists of the early national period, James Kent and Joseph Story, were particularly influential in encouraging this absorption, Story in his treatises on equity, Kent as chancellor of the New York court of chancery. See J. Story,

but in 1889 in *Claflin* v. *Claflin*,[31] the Massachusetts Supreme Judicial Court, which has been the most influential American court in trust matters, declined to follow the rule in *Saunders* v. *Vautier*. The facts in *Claflin* were quite comparable to those in *Saunders* v. *Vautier*. *Claflin* concerned a testamentary trust for the sole benefit of the testator's son, directing the trustees to pay the son $10,000 at age twenty-one, a further $10,000 at age twenty-five, and the balance of the fund at age thirty. The son, after having turned twenty-one, collected the first payment, but before reaching age twenty-five he demanded immediate distribution of the remainder of the fund. The Massachusetts court rejected his claim, endorsing the settlor's protective purpose[32] and emphasising that 'the restriction upon the [beneficiary's] possession and control is . . . one that the testator had a right to make; . . . and we see no good reason why the intention of the testator should not be carried out'.[33] In concluding that the settlor 'had a right' to restrict the beneficiary's 'possession and control' of the trust property, the court was focusing on the settlor's ownership of the property at the outset of the transfer. The logic of *Claflin* is that the settlor's 'right' to condition his gift as he did was an incident of his ownership of the property that he was transferring in trust.[34]

Commentaries on Equity Jurisprudence as Administered in England and America (Boston: Hilliard, Gray and Co., 1836) (fourteen editions to 1918); J. Story, *Commentaries on Equity Pleadings and the Incidents Thereof According to the Practice of the Courts of Equity of England and America* (Boston: Little and Brown, 1838) (ten editions to 1892). Regarding Kent's role in entrenching English law, and especially English equity, during the formative period of American legal institutions, see J.H. Langbein, 'Chancellor Kent and the History of Legal Literature' (1993) 93 Colum. L. Rev. 547, 566–84.

31 149 Mass. 19; 20 N.E. 454 (Mass. 1889).

32 The court observed that on account of the provision for postponed distribution, 'there is not the same danger that he will spend the property while it is in the hands of the trustees as there would be if it were in his own': *ibid.*, 23; 456.

33 *Ibid.*, 24; 456.

34 In the years before *Claflin*, American courts voiced a similar rationale in support of spendthrift trusts, that is, a trust containing a term that prohibits the beneficiary from alienating the beneficial interest, and that forbids the trustees from paying the beneficiary's creditors. In *Brandon* v. *Robinson* (1811) 18 Ves. Jun. 429; 34 E.R. 379, Lord Eldon refused to enforce such terms. Deciding oppositely in 1882, the Massachusetts court explained its reasoning: the settlor of the trust 'was the absolute owner of his property. He had the entire right to dispose of it, either by an absolute gift to [the beneficiary], or by a gift with such restrictions or limitations, not repugnant to law, as he saw fit to impose': *Broadway National Bank* v. *Adams*, 133 Mass. 170, 173 (1882). Although *Claflin* and *Adams* share a common basis in the property rights of the transferor, they are distinguishable on policy grounds. Unlike the rule in *Claflin*, which permits a condition of postponed enjoyment, the rule allowing spendthrift trusts impairs the rights of creditors of the beneficiary.

Thus, both the rule in *Saunders* v. *Vautier* and the opposite *Claflin* rule are property rules, rules that respect ownership. The difference is one of timing: the *Claflin* rule frames the relevant property rights at the time that the property is still in the hands of the donor, whereas the rule in *Saunders* v. *Vautier* ignores rights claimed to have arisen at that time, waits for the transfer to have taken place, and then reckons the property in the hands of the donee as the sole source of property rights. As the trust scholar Austin W. Scott observes in his treatise, the choice between these competing views 'is not one of logic, but one that involves broad considerations of policy'.[35] Scott continues:

> It is the view of the American courts that the directions of the settlor should be carried out unless they can be shown to be against public policy, and it is difficult to say that the postponement of enjoyment of the principal of the trust fund by the sole beneficiary of the trust is against public policy.[36]

What has come to be known as the *Claflin* doctrine prevails in virtually all American jurisdictions. As codified in the first *Restatement of Trusts* in 1935, the rule is that '[i]f the continuance of the trust is necessary to carry out a material purpose of the trust, the beneficiaries cannot compel its termination'.[37] Applying the material purpose standard is not without challenges,[38] but there is now long experience with the rule, and deep acceptance of the principle that it embodies, which the *Third Restatement* describes as 'respect for serious objectives that appear to have motivated the settlor in creating the trust'.[39]

[35] A.W. Scott and W.F. Fratcher, *Scott on Trusts*, 4th ed. (Boston: Little, Brown, 1989), vol. 4, § 337.3.

[36] *Ibid.*, § 337.3. This tension between the interests of donor and donee is developed in G.S. Alexander, 'The Dead Hand and the Law of Trusts in the Nineteenth Century' (1985) 37 Stan. L. Rev. 1189.

[37] *Restatement (First) Trusts* § 337(2) (1935), continued in *Restatement (Second) Trusts* § 337(2) (1959). The Uniform Trust Code § 411 (2000), now in force in over half the states (with some state-specific modifications) substantially codifies the rule. The Third Restatement endorses a broader power in the court to approve termination or modification if the court 'determines that the reason(s) for termination or modification outweigh the material purpose': *Restatement (Third) Trusts* § 65(2) (2003).

[38] 'The line is not always easy to draw between a "material purpose" on the one hand and, on the other, specific intentions that are deemed less important so that the *Claflin* doctrine does not protect them ... Sometimes, of course, the very nature or design of a trust suggests its protective nature or some other material purpose': *Restatement (Third) Trusts* § 65(2), cmt. d (2003).

[39] *Restatement (Third) Trusts* § 65(2), cmt. d (2003). Because the rule in *Saunders* v. *Vautier* is mandatory, the settlor of an English trust 'cannot opt for the American or any other'

The two Canadian jurisdictions that have abrogated the rule in *Saunders* v. *Vautier* – Alberta in 1973 and Manitoba in 1983 – replaced it with expanded judicial authority under the Variation of Trusts Acts, in preference to the American material purpose rule.[40] The case law under the Canadian legislation has taken into account whether variation from the trust terms would be 'in the best interests of the beneficiaries', as well as what the transferor 'wanted to achieve'.[41]

The contractarian dimension

I think that the critique of the rule in *Saunders* v. *Vautier* thus far assembled from English, American, and Canadian sources suffices to show why the rule is mistaken. I wish to conclude by directing attention to a further basis for questioning the rule.

I have elsewhere developed the view that the trust in its prevailing modern form as a management regime for financial assets is best understood as a hybrid of contract and property, a deal between settlor and trustee(s) 'about how the trust assets are to be managed and distributed'.[42] Because modern trust law consists so heavily of default terms that the settlor is free to modify, subject to the acceptance by the trustees[43] of the trust so configured, the trust device exhibits the defining features of contract, consensual formation, and consensual terms. This point is hardly novel. Maitland observed a century ago that the trust 'generally ha[d] its origin in something that we cannot but call an

rule, whereas, because the *Claflin* doctrine is a default rule, the American settlor is free to choose the English regime: R.H. Sitkoff, 'An Agency Costs Theory of Trust Law' (2004) 89 Cornell L. Rev. 621, 663.

40 For discussion of the Alberta and Manitoba legislation and case law, see Waters, Gillen and Smith, *Waters' Law of Trusts in Canada*, 4th ed., 1258–62. The Ontario report also 'recommend[ed] that the rule known as the rule in *Saunders* v. *Vautier* should be severely limited' by amending the Ontario Variation of Trusts Act, R.S.O. 1990. c. V. 1: Ontario Law Reform Commission, Report on the Law of Trusts (1984), vol. II, 416. Legislation has not resulted.

41 Waters, Gillen and Smith, *Waters' Law of Trusts in Canada*, 4th ed., 1261.

42 J.H. Langbein, 'The Contractarian Basis of the Law of Trusts' (1995) 105 Yale L.J. 625. The discussion in this and the next paragraph of this chapter derive from that article.

43 Apart from the constructive trust, which is an equitable remedy as opposed to a conventional donative trust, service as a trustee is voluntary. The requirement that trusteeship be accepted parallels the requirement of acceptance in contract law. Regarding the modes of acceptance in English trust law, see Hayton, Matthews and Mitchell, *Underhill and Hayton: Law Relating to Trusts and Trustees*, 18th ed. [35.1]–[35.11].

agreement'.[44] '[The] trust was originally regarded as an obligation, in point of fact a contract though not usually so called.'[45] F.H. Lawson, writing in 1953 in a celebrated work of modern comparative law, pointed out that 'the three-cornered relation of settlor, trustee, and [beneficiary is] . . . easily explained in the modern law in terms of a contract for the benefit of a third party'.[46]

English contract law was long impoverished by its refusal to recognise third-party-beneficiary contracts. Like the rule in *Saunders* v. *Vautier*, this is a subject about which English and American law diverged in the second half of the nineteenth century. *Lawrence* v. *Fox*,[47] the landmark New York decision recognising third-party-beneficiary contracts in 1859, was based on the notion that trust exemplifies contract. The court reasoned that '[t]he duty of the trustee to pay the [beneficiaries], according to the terms of the trust, implies his promise to the latter to do so'.[48] The court reasoned that the principle of enforcing third-party claims 'has been applied to trust cases, not because it was exclusively applicable to those cases, but because it was a principle of law, and as such applicable to those cases'.[49]

There are important differences between trust and contract,[50] notably in the circumstance of trustee insolvency.[51] For present purposes, one need not resolve the question of how closely trust and contract correspond. The present point is simply that trust and contract are close functional substitutes for many purposes. The deal-like or contractarian dimension of the trust invites comparison with the third-party-beneficiary contract. In a jurisdiction that enforces such contracts,

[44] F.W. Maitland, *Equity: A Course of Lectures*, ed. by A.H. Chaytor and W.J. Whittaker, rev. by J. Brunyate (Cambridge University Press, 1936), 28.

[45] *Ibid.*, 110.

[46] F.H. Lawson, *A Common Lawyer Looks at the Civil Law* (Ann Arbor: University of Michigan Law School, 1953), 200.

[47] 20 N.Y. 268 (1859). For an intriguing account of the origins of the case, see A.J. Waters, 'The Property in the Promise: A Study of the Third Party Beneficiary Rule' (1985) 98 Harv. L. Rev. 1109, 1116–46.

[48] 20 N.Y. 268, 274 (1859). [49] *Ibid.*, 274.

[50] See P. Matthews, 'From Obligation to Property, and Back Again? The Future of the Non-Charitable Purpose Trust', in D. Hayton (ed.), *Extending the Boundaries of Trusts and Similar Ring-Fenced Funds* (The Hague: Kluwer Law, 2002), 210, 219–21.

[51] *Ibid.*, 221; Hudson, *Equity and Trusts*, 8th ed., 70–1; Langbein, 'The Contractarian Basis of the Law of Trusts', 667–8. Statutes, such as those in some American states that authorise life insurance company separate accounts, can provide for contract-based accounts that achieve trust-like insolvency protection for beneficial interests. See Langbein, 'The Contractarian Basis of the Law of Trusts', 668–9.

contract terms that embody the intent of the promisee can be enforced, either by the beneficiary or the promisee.[52] The promisee-equivalent figure in trust law is the settlor,[53] the person whose intent the rule in *Saunders* v. *Vautier* ignores.[54] In English law, the rule in *Saunders* v. *Vautier* mirrored the rule against third-party-beneficiary contracts, the two rules defeating alike the intent of contract promisee and trust settlor. The question is invited whether the 1999 legislation finally recognising third-party-beneficiary contracts in English law[55] may stimulate reconsideration of the mistake in *Saunders* v. *Vautier*. The donative trust is a contract-like transfer in which the intent of the transferor, like the intent of a contract promisee, should be entitled to recognition.

Conclusion

In this chapter I have emphasised that the rule in *Saunders* v. *Vautier* was ill-considered in its inception, the judgments in the case having assumed the result rather than reasoned to it. The case transposed into trust law a rule that had developed to deal with disabling restraints on legal

52

> The promisee of a promise for the benefit of a beneficiary has the same right to performance as any other promisee ... If the promisee has no economic interest in the performance, as in many cases involving gift promises, the ordinary remedy of damages for breach of contract is an inadequate remedy, since only nominal damages can be recovered. In such cases specific performance is commonly appropriate.

(*Restatement (Second) Contracts* § 305, cmt. a (1981))

53 I have expressed the view that the settlor should in some circumstances have standing to enforce a trust. See Langbein, 'The Contractarian Basis of the Law of Trusts', 664. American law has been inching in that direction by providing for settlor standing to enforce charitable trusts. See *Restatement (Third) Trusts* § 94(2) (2012); UTC § 405(c) (2000); *Smithers* v. *St. Luke's-Roosevelt Hospital Center*, 723 N.Y.S. 2d 426 (App. Civ 2001). The baseline rule against settlor standing to enforce private trusts remains in effect: *Restatement (Third) Trusts* § 94(1) (2012). For the suggestion that the spread of trust protector regimes functions in some circumstances as a proxy for settlor standing, see M.R. Houston, '*Estate of Wall* v. *Commissioner*: An Answer to the Problem of Settlor Standing in Trust Law?' (2005) 99 Nw U. L. Rev. 1723, 1743.

54 The question of whether the acceptance of third-party-beneficiary contracts in American law from 1859 onward (rooted as noticed above in the analogy to trusts) influenced the subsequent trend away from the rule in *Saunders* v. *Vautier* has not to my knowledge been studied in the case law.

55 Contracts (Rights of Third Parties) Act 1999 (UK). The legislation is examined in E. Peel, *Treitel on the Law of Contract*, 14th ed. (London: Sweet and Maxwell, 2015), [14–090]–[14–122].

interests in legacies, failing to take account of the fundamental difference between a restraint on a legal interest that interferes with the marketability of the asset and a restraint on an interest in trust that does not have that effect. The rationale for the rule in *Saunders* v. *Vautier* is syllogistic ('legal theology'[56] in the view of the Alberta Institute of Law Research and Reform): the sole beneficiary of an interest given in a donative trust is entitled to immediate control and enjoyment of the trust property, despite a contrary condition, because there is no other owner of the interest. I have emphasised that this rationale is doctrinal or legal-conceptual as opposed to functional. It defeats the settlor's benign protective purpose without any offsetting gain. The rule is mistaken conceptually, because it fails to take account of the role of fiduciary obligation in evidencing and protecting the ownership interest of the beneficiary. The rule is easy to evade by apt drafting, which means that it mostly victimises transferors who do not find their way to competent lawyer-drafters. The proprietary theory on which the rule rests is tautologous, providing no basis for favouring the property rights of the donee over those of the donor. Sensitivity to the contractarian character of the trust, although hardly necessary to explain why the rule is mistaken, provides a further basis for rethinking the rule.

[56] Alberta Institute of Law Research and Reform, *The Rule in Saunders* v. *Vautier*, Report No. 9 (1972), 5.

11

Why the rule in *Saunders* v. *Vautier* is wrong

A commentary

PAUL MATTHEWS

> '"Dad, is it true that I absolutely can't get at any of my money?"
> "Only the income, fortunately, my love."
> "How perfectly beastly! Can't it be done somehow?"'[1]

Professor Langbein's elegantly written, closely argued chapter (Chapter 10) argues that the rule of English trust law known as the rule in *Saunders* v. *Vautier*[2] ('the Rule') is wrong and that English trust law should apply the doctrine laid down in *Claflin* v. *Claflin*[3] and applied in most of the states of the United States, or at any rate some approximation to that doctrine. In my view, this view is in itself mistaken, and English trust law should continue to apply the Rule. I make no claim that it should also apply in the United States. Different folks need different strokes, not one trust law under God.

The Rule, as expressed by Professor Langbein, is that 'an adult beneficiary of a trust who is alone entitled to the beneficial interest may require the trustee(s) to terminate the trust and distribute the trust property to the beneficiary despite an express term of the trust directing that distribution be postponed to a later time'. This is narrower than usually found in the English cases, but the distinctions are not now material. The *Claflin* doctrine rejects the Rule and holds that '[if] the continuance of the trust is necessary to carry out a material purpose of the trust, the beneficiaries cannot compel its termination'.[4]

[1] J. Galsworthy, *The Forsyte Saga* (London: Penguin Classics, 2001), vol. 1, 'In Chancery', 487.

[2] (1841) Cr. & Ph. 240; 41 E. R. 482 (L.C.), affirming (1841) 4 Beav. 115; 49 E.R. 282 (M.R.).

[3] 149 Mass. 19; 20 N.E. 454 (Mass. 1889).

[4] *Restatement (First) Trusts* § 337(2) (1935); *Restatement (Second) Trusts* § 337(2) (1959). *Cf. Restatement (Third) Trusts* § 65(2) (2003).

Criticising the judges for not having thought out the Rule, Langbein's chapter assumes (1) that the Rule was newly made in *Saunders* v. *Vautier* and (2) that it was later extended to cases where there was more than one beneficiary. Neither assumption is correct. Reported cases embodying this principle go back at least to 1685,[5] and there are cases of two or more beneficiaries combining to demand the transfer of the trust property at least from 1822.[6] The Rule was well known to judges and counsel at the date of the decisions in *Saunders* v. *Vautier*, and no doubt they saw no need to re-invent the wheel.[7]

In its first section, 'The protective purpose', Langbein's chapter argues that it is counter-intuitive to refuse to enforce a term of a trust postponing enjoyment and thereby make it difficult for the settlor to protect a prodigal. It complains that the Rule 'corrects no wrong, [and] prevents no harm'.[8] You might as well say that the rule that the common law owner of a thing is prima facie entitled to possession of it 'corrects no wrong, [and] prevents no harm'. Yet it does, at least prophylactically. A person whose property is in another's hands is at risk, and such a rule enables him to minimise that risk, if he chooses to do so.

The second section is called 'Ease of evasion', though any tax lawyers reading this might consider that it would perhaps be more accurate to refer to avoidance rather than evasion.[9] It accepts that, if the gift had been contingent on the beneficiary attaining a specified age in the future (which it coyly describes as 'wording the provision a little differently'), the Rule would not have applied, and the beneficiary would not have been able to call for a transfer before the age was attained. But it says that its practical effect is to act as a trap for the unwary and his unskilled draftsman. However, in a subject as complex as trust law, there will be fine lines to be crossed (or not), and it is sometimes hard to know when this has happened. Skilled advice will be needed. The idea that all the rules of the law of trusts should be simple enough for the average layman to operate on his own is unrealistic. This is not the *Code Napoléon*, after all.

[5] *Lord Pawlet's Case* (1685) 2 Vent. 366; 86 E.R. 489.

[6] *Barton* v. *Briscoe* (1822) Jac. 605; 37 E.R. 978.

[7] Matters are made worse by the procedural tangle into which the case had fallen.

[8] J.H. Langbein, 'Why the Rule in *Saunders* v. *Vautier* is Wrong', Chapter 10 of this volume, text before n. 7.

[9] 'Avoidance' is generally used in England to mean arranging matters such that a given rule does not apply. Evasion, on the other hand, means arranging matters such that, although the rule in fact applies, the consequences that should follow from this do not (e.g. because lies have been told, and the truth of the matter is not known).

More importantly, however, it misstates why using a contingent gift produces a different result. It is not the consequence of 'the supposed doctrinal logic of "equitable ownership"',[10] but instead that of fidelity to the settlor's intention. It is the settlor's property before the trust is created, and he may – within public policy limits – choose how to deal with it, expressing the choice in the trust terms.

In English law, the settlor has three options. First, he may give the entire equitable interest in the property to the beneficiary. In that case, the beneficiary (being of full age and sound mind) may do what he likes with it, and the settlor cannot restrict the uses to which the beneficiary may put it.[11] Any fetter on the enjoyment of a person otherwise absolutely entitled is void for public policy, at law as in equity.[12] Secondly, he may give to the beneficiary less than one hundred per cent, retaining the rest. The retained rights may give him more or less control over the thing. Thirdly, he may give the entire equitable interest to the beneficiary *and others*, so that he himself no longer has any claim on it and has no control over it. But then the beneficiary is not the complete master of the thing, as others may have rights which prevent his doing what he likes. The result in practice is the same as the second possibility, except that, if the beneficiary can agree with the others, he can put an end to the trust and take whatever share is agreed to fall to him.

However, Professor Langbein suggests that, even if the settlor makes clear that the trust is *not* contingent, and that the beneficiary is the *only* person who can ever enjoy the property, *but* the settlor wishes to postpone enjoyment until a future time, the court should ignore his choice of absolute interest and enforce the postponement clause. What will the English court do? It must decide what *was* the settlor's intention, as expressed in the trust terms. It will take full account of the postponement clause, suggesting that the gift was intended to be contingent. But if, ultimately, the court is satisfied that the settlor's intention was not to create a contingent trust, but to give the entire beneficial interest immediately to the beneficiary, it will disregard the postponement clause, because it is repugnant to the settlor's intention.[13] In English law at least, no settlor may provide in his trust that two plus two equal five.

In the third section ('Dead Hand?'), the chapter argues that the Rule is not needed to police the public policy objection to the 'dead hand', that is,

[10] Langbein, 'Why the Rule in *Saunders* v. *Vautier* is Wrong', text after n. 11.

[11] *Re Lipinski's Will Trusts* [1976] Ch. 235.

[12] *Re Rosher* (1884) 26 Ch. D. 801.

[13] *Corbett* v. *Corbett* (1889) 14 P.D. 7.

past settlors controlling present beneficiaries. There are other doctrines that help to achieve this. This is certainly true with regard to the rules against perpetuities (mentioned) and the rule against non-charitable purpose trusts (not mentioned), at any rate to some extent. It is however not true of (1) the rules against illegal and capricious purposes and (2) the court's power under the Variation of Trusts Act 1958 (both mentioned). The first concerns whether the court may properly execute the trust if the trustee fails to do so. And the second actually relies on the Rule to be effective.[14] The chapter also refers to non-statutory change-of-circumstances doctrines, but these are limited in practice,[15] and in any event are derived not so much from anti-'dead hand' theology as from presumed settlors' intentions in changed circumstances.

Nevertheless, the Rule assists in policing the dead hand. It prevents settlors from reserving the right to control property in which they have no sufficient interest. And it incentivises beneficiaries to release trust property from the dead hand when they think they can do better than the trustees.

The fourth section is headed 'Trusteeship'. It says that '[t]he most problematic aspect of the rationale of [the Rule] is that [it] neglects the role of trusteeship in mediating between the interests of settlor and beneficiary'.[16] While in my view there is no mistake here, I certainly agree that this is the real heart of the matter. Professor Langbein is, however, wrong to assert that the Rule took a pre-existing rule from legacies and transposed it into trust law. The earliest reported case[17] applying the Rule was actually not a legacy case, but instead one where capital sums for the absolute benefit of certain beneficiaries were charged on real estate by an *inter vivos* trust, yet stipulated to be paid only at a certain future date.[18]

Nevertheless, the important point is this. If the common law says you cannot give a thing to someone absolutely and then tell him how to deal (or not to deal) with it, does it make any difference if you give it to him not at common law, but via a trust? In such a case, the gift to the trustee is absolute. So there is an owner who has every right to deal with the assets

[14] *Re Holt's Settlement* [1969] 1 Ch. 100. [15] *Chapman* v. *Chapman* [1954] A.C. 429.

[16] Langbein, 'Why the Rule in *Saunders* v. *Vautier* is Wrong', text after n. 19.

[17] *Lord Pawlet's Case* (1685) 2 Vent. 366; 86 E.R. 489.

[18] The deed gave the settlor the power of revocation by will, but in fact his will confirmed the gift. The Lord Keeper expressly refuted the argument that it was just a legacy, saying that it was 'a trust charged upon lands, and trusts are governed by the intention of the party': *Lord Pawlet's Case* (1685) 2 Vent. 366, 367; 86 E.R. 489, 490.

as he wishes, without any flaw in his ownership. It is only the beneficiary who is subject to that flaw. The common law is satisfied. Why should equity care?

Langbein cites Austin Scott to give the American answer to this question:

> [I]t is difficult to say that the postponement of enjoyment of the principal of the trust fund by the sole beneficiary of the trust is against public policy.[19]

He also argues that 'the fiduciary obligation inherent in trusteeship is centrally important in distinguishing an interest in trust from an attempted restraint on non-trust property'.[20] Even if the beneficiary were restrained from enjoyment and control of the trust property until the specified age, he would still have had standing to seek remedies for an actual or even threatened breach of trust before he reached that age. This is true, but nothing to the point. A person with no actual rights to enjoyment, such as the object of a discretionary trust or power, equally has such standing. It tells us nothing about the case at hand. If it is against public policy to give a thing outright to a donee and yet to seek to restrict his use or disposal of it, why is it not against public policy to give an outright equitable interest to a trust beneficiary coupled with such a restriction?

No answer is made explicitly at this stage. But later on (in the conclusion) it is argued that there is a difference between disabling legal owners and disabling trust beneficiaries. In the latter case, the asset itself is still marketable by the trustee as legal owner. However, marketability is not ensured just because the trustee owns it. Until the late nineteenth century, trustees of land rarely had the power to sell it as against the beneficiary.[21] So the trustee's ability to sell at common law was in practice meaningless. Secondly, in any event, the economic value of the trust assets could not be consumed (as opposed to exchanged). Thirdly, the economic value could not be invested in speculative investments: in effect it was withdrawn from the pool of available risk capital. These are all reasons why English public policy should apply the same rule to absolute

[19] A.W. Scott and W.F. Fratcher, *Scott on Trusts*, 4th ed. (Boston: Little, Brown, 1989), vol. 4, § 337.3.

[20] Langbein, 'Why the Rule in *Saunders* v. *Vautier* is Wrong', text after n. 23.

[21] Indeed, only in 2000 was the default position in English trust law altered so that trustees would have general power to sell and buy trust assets as if they were beneficially entitled: Trustee Act 2000 (UK), s. 3.

equitable interests that it applied to absolute legal ones. What the English cases show is that the mere interposition of a trust does not enable a settlor to sidestep the rules of public policy. English and American public policy differ significantly here.

In the next section, 'The donor', Professor Langbein argues that '[p]erhaps the most striking feature of [the Rule] is its disregard for the intent of the donor . . .'[22] This is because, in saying that 'a man may deal with his own property as he wishes',[23] the English court does not consider that the donor having created the trust retains any sufficient right in the assets given. If a settlor wishes to give property in stages, he should be able to transfer the assets to trustees, on terms that the onward transfer to the beneficiary be postponed for a limited period. The settlor should 'be able to release his ownership in this phased manner'.[24]

English law agrees. But there is a corollary. If the settlor releases his ownership in stages, then at each stage what the settlor does not release he must retain.[25] So if, for example, he gives away the whole interest contingent on some event occurring, he retains the interest if it should *not* occur. As we have seen, this is sufficient in English law to prevent the Rule from applying.

Professor Langbein says that, in considering what right the settlor has to control the release of the assets to the beneficiary, the *Claflin* doctrine looks at the question of the settlor's rights immediately before the transfer into trust. Before the transfer, the settlor had all the rights in the assets, whereas afterwards the settlor had only what he did not give away.

To me this seems the wrong way to look at the matter. I do not see how a settlor can be entitled to exercise any control over a thing by virtue of a right at a time when *ex hypothesi* he no longer has that right. The correct approach is to consider the position immediately after the transfer and ask what rights the settlor then has, and whether such rights count as property rights for this purpose, as distinct from, say, personal rights (such as those arising by way of contract only). In English law, A may have a right that B not do something with B's property. However, without more that right cannot be a property right. If the right concerns land, and is for the benefit of A's own retained land, rather than in gross,[26] then it

22 Langbein, 'Why the Rule in *Saunders* v. *Vautier* is Wrong', text to n. 26.
23 *Goulding* v. *James* [1997] 2 All E.R. 239, 247.
24 Langbein, 'Why the Rule in *Saunders* v. *Vautier* is Wrong', text after n. 29.
25 *St Aubyn* v. *A.-G.* [1952] A.C. 15, 27, 49.
26 *London County Council* v. *Allen* [1914] 3 K.B. 642.

can be a restrictive covenant. The *Claflin* doctrine however does not confer a property right known to English law. The settlor has to have something more, for example an interest in the asset contingent on the beneficiary's not satisfying the condition for benefit.

The last section of Professor Langbein's chapter, 'The contractarian dimension', advances a different argument against the Rule, based on his earlier treatment of the trust as a 'deal' between settlor and trustee about managing and distributing trust assets.[27] It argues that (1) trust and contract are functional substitutes for many purposes, (2) the Rule 'mirrored' the common law contract rule that a third-party beneficiary cannot enforce it, and therefore (3) the change in English contract law made in 1999 to allow the third party to enforce it[28] may require reconsideration of the Rule in trust law.

In my view, the argument does not hold at any of the three stages. As to (1), this may be factually correct in the United States, but it is scarcely so in England. Most trusts in English law today are not in any sense 'deals', let alone contractual deals, but gifts. All the reported cases I have found involving the Rule are of this kind. As to (2), Professor Langbein says that the two rules mirrored each other because they '[defeat] alike the intent of contract promisee and trust settlor'.[29] Even if so, it does not make them similar in any other way. Moreover, these two parties occupy different places in each structure. The contract promisee is like the beneficiary in the trust, and may not even know that something has been promised him, and therefore – unlike the contracting parties – may have no relevant intention. The settlor, however, is like a contracting party in the contract. But a settlor in English trust law has no standing to enforce a trust[30] and cannot be treated as in any way comparable to a contracting party.

As to (3), the 1999 Act does not seem to have much changed English contract behaviour. At an anecdotal level, in most contracts purporting to confer any benefit on a third party which I see in a professional capacity, the benefit of the Act is expressly excluded. But in any event, it is hard to see why allowing any relevant intent of a third-party beneficiary to prevail should have any effect on the public policy rule that holds that you cannot give someone an absolute beneficial interest in

[27] J.H. Langbein, 'The Contractarian Basis of the Law of Trusts' (1995) 105 Yale L.J. 625.

[28] Contracts (Rights of Third Parties) Act 1999 (UK).

[29] Langbein, 'Why the Rule in *Saunders* v. *Vautier* is Wrong', text after n. 54.

[30] *Re Astor's Settlement Trusts* [1952] Ch. 534, 542; *Bradshaw* v. *University College of Wales* [1988] 1 W.L.R. 190, 194; *Murphy* v. *Murphy* [1999] 1 W.L.R. 282, 295; *Twinsectra Ltd* v. *Yardley* [2002] 2 A.C. 164, [96]; [2002] UKHL 12.

property and then restrict what they can do with it. Contracts are simply not property rights. Trusts are.

Reading Professor Langbein's analysis and argument, one is struck once again by the lighter, more contractual feel to the American trust, in its language, its context and its functions, and also by the very different approach taken to the nature of rights and public policy. In the light of these features, I am not surprised that the Rule did not hold in America. But America is not England.

12

Equity and statute

J.D. HEYDON

It is trite to stress the importance of statutes. It is less common to remember the late Lord Bingham of Cornhill's unflattering reference to the 'legislative hyperactivity' of the modern scene.[1] Statutes grow each year in bulk. Often they lack any apparent point. They are far too numerous. They can be excessively complex. Frequently they are evanescent. They tend repeatedly and frequently to be amended. Sometimes they are repealed and replaced. All this is even truer of delegated legislation. In New South Wales the legislature, frightened, apparently, by the consequences of its own fecklessness and fecundity, has given up the task of producing statutes in paper versions – a grave threat to the rule of law as enunciated by Hayek.[2]

There are now many relationships between these voluminous and complicated modern legislative provisions and equity. But there have been relationships between equity and statute for a long time. For equity is far from comprising an entirely judge-made collection of principles, defences and remedies which operate by themselves, in isolation from the wider legal world to which statute contributes so much. 'Legislation and the common law [including equity] are not separate and independent sources of law; the one the concern of parliaments, and the other the concern of courts. They exist in a symbiotic relationship.'[3] Further, in some usages the expression 'equity' includes those statutes which are closely related to the application of non-statutory principles or which have triggered the creation of equitable principles, such as various statutes descended from the Statute of Frauds 1677 (Eng.),[4] Lord Cairns' Act 1858 (UK)[5] and nineteenth-century trust legislation.

I am indebted to the editor for the numerous improvements he has suggested.

1 'The Rule of Law' [2007] C.L.J. 67, 70.

2 F.A. Hayek, *The Road to Serfdom* (University of Chicago Press, 1944), 54.

3 *Brodie* v. *Singleton Shire Council* (2001) 206 C.L.R. 512, [31]; [2001] HCA 29 (Gleeson C.J.).

4 29 Car. II, c. 3. 5 21 & 22 Vict. c. 27.

It is convenient to divide the subject into two broad categories. The first comprises statutory reactions to equity. The second comprises equity's reactions to statute. In each category it is proposed to proceed through various sub-categories in ascending order of the intensity which can be generated by the seeming collisions between statute and equity. No claim is made that the examples given within each sub-category, and the sub-categories and categories themselves, are exhaustive.

Statutory reactions to equity

Statute can facilitate the development of equity

Some statutory provisions have led to considerable curial activity in developing equitable principle without much, or any, stipulation by the legislature of the relevant criteria. An example is section 165 of the Companies Act 1862 (UK).[6] It provided liquidators, creditors and contributories with the right to recover monies misapplied by 'misfeasance or breach of trust'.[7] Section 165 did not define what 'misfeasance' was. It did not define what 'breach of trust' was. It left it to the courts to identify the separately existing rights corresponding to those wrongs. It created a method by which the courts, after identifying them, and perhaps developing them, could enforce them. Section 165 was a much-used method. It has had many successors.[8]

Another illustration of a court contributing to general equitable learning can arise where it is exercising a statutory power which corresponds with the equitable powers existing before the statute. One instance may be statutory provisions about relief against the forfeiture of leases.[9]

A further illustration arises where a specific statutory requirement compels a reconsideration of general principle which might not

[6] 25 & 26 Vict. c. 89.

[7] See *Re B. Johnson & Co. (Builders) Ltd* [1955] Ch. 634, 645; *Cohen* v. *Selby* [2001] 1 B.C.L.C. 176, 183; *Angas Law Services Pty Ltd (in liq.)* v. *Carabelas* (2005) 226 C.L.R. 507, [47] n. 29; [2005] HCA 23. See also F. Oditah, 'Misfeasance Proceedings Against Company Directors' [1992] L.M.C.L.Q. 207; W.M. Heath, 'The Director's "Fiduciary" Duty of Care and Skill: A Misnomer' (2007) 25 C. & S.L.J. 370, 386–93.

[8] For the United Kingdom, see Companies (Winding-Up) Act 1890 (UK), s. 10; Companies (Consolidation) Act 1908 (UK), s. 215; Companies Act 1929 (UK), s. 276; Companies Act 1948 (UK), s. 333 and Insolvency Act 1986 (UK), s. 212. See also, for example, Companies Act 1961 (NSW), s. 367B; Companies (New South Wales) Code 1981 (NSW), s. 542; Corporations Act 2001 (Cth), s. 598.

[9] *Çukurova Finance International Ltd* v. *Alfa Telecom Turkey Ltd (No. 4)* [2015] 2 W.L.R. 875, [22]; [2013] UKPC 20; cf. at [91].

otherwise have been necessary. One example is cases on the specific performance of contracts to sell Crown lands where statute requires Ministerial consent.[10] Another example arises where a claim for relief on a statutory ground is an equitable claim requiring the claimant to do equity: if this does not stimulate the development of equity, it can at least stimulate a more precise analysis of it.[11]

Finally, statements in the Preamble to the Statute of Charitable Uses 1601 (Eng.)[12] have been used by the courts as a technique for developing and organising the law of charity.[13]

Statutory codification of equitable doctrines, defences and remedies

There do not appear to be any general statutes codifying the whole of equity. In England, a bill codifying the law relating to trusts was drafted in 1907 and introduced into Parliament, but after it was referred to a select committee it did not proceed further.[14]

In India, specific performance is put on a statutory footing by the Specific Relief Act 1963, ss. 9–25, and the Contract Act 1872, ss. 37–67.[15] There are trust codes in India and Sri Lanka. But these enactments are only seen as non-exhaustive statements of the relevant law.

What of the United States? Some jurisdictions have enacted a trust code drafted by David Dudley Field. Others have enacted a Uniform Trust Code. There are other Uniform Acts on particular parts of the law of trusts.[16] And particular fiduciary duties are often created by legislation.[17]

To some extent that last proposition is true in other places also. In general, much of the law of trusts is statutory. So is the law of partnership. But in Australia, for example, calls for the law of trusts to be reduced

[10] *McWilliam* v. *McWilliams Wines Pty Ltd* (1964) 114 C.L.R. 656; *Brown* v. *Heffer* (1967) 116 C.L.R. 344.

[11] *Langman* v. *Handover* (1929) 43 C.L.R. 334. [12] 43 Eliz. I c. 4.

[13] *Income Tax Special Purposes Commissioners* v. *Pemsel* [1891] A.C. 531.

[14] See S. Tofaris, 'Trust Law Goes East: The Transplantation of Trust Law in India and Beyond' (2015) 36 J.L.H. 299, which discusses the background to the 1907 bill and its fate.

[15] See A. Singh, *Textbook on Law of Contract and Specific Relief*, 5th ed. (Lucknow: Eastern Book Co., 2009), ch. 12.

[16] A.W. Scott, W.F. Fratcher and M.L. Ascher, *Scott and Ascher on Trusts*, 5th ed. (New York: Aspen Publishers, 2006), vol. 1, § 1.11. An example is the Uniform Trustees' Powers Act 1964.

[17] T. Frankel, *Fiduciary Law* (New York: Oxford University Press, 2011), 183–93.

to statutory language and made uniform across all jurisdictions have not yet been answered positively.

Statutory amendment to equitable rules

Despite the non-codification of equity, many statutes supplement or modify the judge-made rules.

For example, statutes have often widened the powers of trustees beyond those conferred by the trust instrument in important ways. One instance concerns powers to invest.[18] Another concerns the variation of trusts.[19]

Statute can also offer a general means of tempering the extreme outcomes which a given equitable rule might produce. In 1899, Sir Nathaniel Lindley M.R.[20] said that the principles applied in the nineteenth century to breach of trust reflected 'a very hard state of the law, and one which shocked one's sense of humanity and of fairness'. The law, he said, was 'relaxed . . . deliberately'[21] by section 3 of the Judicial Trustees Act 1896 (UK).[22] That provision conferred on the courts power to grant relief to a trustee in breach of trust provided that the trustee had acted 'honestly and reasonably' and 'ought fairly to be excused for the breach of trust and for omitting to obtain the direction of the court in the matter on which the trustee committed the breach'. That was a reference to the court's power to give an opinion, advice or direction on any question respecting the management or administration of the trust property, or respecting the interpretation of the trust instrument.[23]

It may be that the inherent jurisdiction of a court of equity extends to a power of that kind.[24] But the immediate origins of section 3 lie in

18 Law of Property Amendment Act 1859 (UK), 22 & 23 Vict. c. 35, s. 32; Trustee Act 1893 (UK), s. 1; Trustee Act 1925 (UK), s. 1; Trustee Investments Act 1961 (UK); see now Trustee Act 2000 (UK), Part II.

19 Early modest instances can be found in the Trustee Act 1925 (UK), s. 57 and its equivalents, like Trustee Act 1925 (NSW), s. 81. Much wider powers came later: Variation of Trusts Act 1958 (UK); Trustee Act 1958 (Vic), s. 63A.

20 *Perrins* v. *Bellamy* [1899] 1 Ch. 797, 800. See also *Maguire* v. *Makaronis* (1997) 188 C.L.R. 449, 473–4. Sir Nathaniel's view was common: see C. Stebbings, *The Private Trustee in Victorian England* (Cambridge University Press, 2002), ch. 6.

21 *Perrins* v. *Bellamy* [1899] 1 Ch. 797, 800.

22 59 & 60 Vict. c. 35. See now Trustee Act 1925 (UK), s. 61; and see Trustee Act Amendment Act 1902 (NSW), s. 9, replaced by Trustee Act 1925 (NSW), s. 85.

23 See Trustee Act 1925 (NSW), s. 63.

24 *Macedonian Orthodox Community Church St Petka Inc.* v. *His Eminence Petar the Diocesan Bishop of the Macedonian Orthodox Diocese of Australia and New Zealand*

legislation introduced by Lord St Leonards – Law of Property Amendment Act 1859 (UK), s. 30[25] and Law of Property Amendment Act 1860 (UK), s. 9.[26] The court's power to advise trustees before the fact and its power to excuse them after the fact are interlinked. This was recognised by Lord St Leonards, who had intended to introduce a provision empowering the court to excuse trustees at the same time as he introduced the power to advise them in the 1850s.[27] But this was not done until section 3 was enacted in 1896.[28] The legislation introduced by Lord St Leonards was swiftly and widely followed. For example, it was enacted in the Trust Property Act 1862 (NSW), s. 30.[29] This legislative history reveals a tendency for gradual development in legislation modifying, or guarding against the harsh development of, equitable doctrine. It is a tendency evident in other fields in which statute has modified or supplemented equitable rules as well.

A little while after 1896, in 1907, the jurisdiction to excuse trustees was used as a model for a provision to assist company directors.[30] It has steadily been extended. In Australia, it now exists in relation to the officers and employees of corporations; their auditors, experts, receivers, receivers and managers, and liquidators; and other persons appointed by the court to carry out a duty in relation to corporations.[31] In Australia,

(2008) 237 C.L.R. 66, [34] n. 47; [2008] HCA 42. See also Stebbings, *The Private Trustee in Victorian England*, 185.

25 22 & 23 Vict. c. 35.

26 23 & 24 Vict. c. 38. There were even earlier statutory precursors for charities: Charities Procedure Act 1812 (UK), 52 Geo. III c. 101 (Sir Samuel Romilly's Act) and the Charitable Trusts Act 1853 (UK), 16 & 17 Vict. c. 137, s. 16.

27 *Macedonian Orthodox Community Church St Petka Inc.* v. *His Eminence Petar the Diocesan Bishop of the Macedonian Orthodox Diocese of Australia and New Zealand* (2008) 237 C.L.R. 66, [35].

28 Judicial Trustees Act 1896 (UK).

29 It was replaced by the Trustee Act 1898 (NSW), s. 20, which in turn was replaced by the Trustee Act 1925 (NSW), s. 63.

30 Companies Act 1907 (UK), s. 32. For the history thereafter, see *Australian Securities and Investments Commission* v. *Vines* (2005) 65 N.S.W.L.R. 281, [10]–[18]; [2005] NSWSC 1349. The provision is now section 1157 of the Companies Act 2006 (UK) replacing section 727 of the Companies Act 1985 (UK).

31 Section 1318(1) of the Corporations Act 2001 (Cth) provides:

> If, in any civil proceeding against a person to whom this section applies for negligence, default, breach of trust or breach of duty in a capacity as such a person, it appears to the court before which the proceedings are taken that the person is or may be liable in respect to the negligence, default or breach but that the person has acted honestly, and that, having regard to all the circumstances of the case, including those connected with the person's appointment, the person ought fairly to be excused for the negligence,

unlike England, there is no express requirement of reasonableness, but it remains a relevant factor.[32]

Statutory provisions partially overlapping with equitable rules

Sometimes statutory provisions partially overlap with equity. They may extend further in some respects. They may operate more narrowly in other respects.

Thus, equitable injunctive relief for passing off may be compared with statutory injunctive relief against the wrong of misleading and deceptive conduct created by section 52 of the Trade Practices Act 1974 (Cth) (now section 18 of the Australian Consumer Law, which is Schedule 2 to the Competition and Consumer Act 2010 (Cth)). Equity will permit an account of profits and in that respect is wider than the statute. On the other hand, injunctive relief under the statute is probably wider than that available in equity.[33]

Another example concerns the equitable duty of trustees to 'exercise their powers in the best interests of the . . . beneficiaries'.[34] A similar duty is often imposed by statute. Thus, section 14B(2)(a) of the Trustee Act 1925 (NSW) provides:

> a duty imposed by any rules and principles of law or equity includes . . .
> (a) a duty to exercise the powers of a trustee in the best interests of all present and future beneficiaries of the trust[.][35]

Section 1 of the Trustee Act 2000 (UK) creates a duty on trustees to exercise reasonable care and skill. It reflects a general law duty which is equitable and, some think, fiduciary.

> default or breach, the court may relieve the person either wholly or partly from liability on such terms as the court thinks fit.

This had predecessors: Companies Act 1961 (NSW), s. 365; Companies Code 1981, s. 535; Corporations Law 1989, s. 1318.

32 *Australian Securities and Investments Commission* v. *Vines* (2005) 65 N.S.W.L.R. 281, [23]–[41].

33 See *Truth About Motorways Pty Ltd* v. *Macquarie Infrastructure Investment Management Ltd* (2000) 200 C.L.R. 591, [66]–[68]; [2000] HCA 11. See also text following n. 48 below.

34 *Cowan* v. *Scargill* [1985] Ch. 270, 286. See also *Buttle* v. *Saunders* [1950] 2 All E.R. 193.

35 See also Superannuation Industry (Supervision) Act 1993 (Cth), s. 52(2)(a) and the statutes cited by G.W. Thomas, 'The Duty of Trustees to Act in the "Best Interests" of Their Beneficiaries' (2008) 2 J. Eq. 177, 180–1.

Other examples may be found in company law. Independently of statute, it is often said that directors must act bona fide in the best interests of the company as a whole.[36] As Starke J. stated: 'Directors in the exercise of their powers are in a fiduciary position and must exercise those powers for the benefit of the company.'[37] There are now related statutory duties. Directors and officers are under a statutory duty to exercise their powers and discharge their duties in good faith in the best interests of the corporation and for a proper purpose. This development began in 1958. In that year the Victorian legislature introduced the following provision as section 107 of the Companies Act:

> (1) A director shall at all times act honestly and use reasonable diligence in the discharge of the duties of his office.
> (2) Any officer of a company shall not make use of any information acquired by virtue of his position as an officer to gain an improper advantage for himself or to cause detriment to the company.
> (3) Any officer who commits a breach of the foregoing provisions of this section shall be guilty of an offence against this Act and shall be liable to a penalty of not more than [f]ive hundred pounds and shall in addition be liable to the company for any profit made by him or for any damage suffered by the company as a result of the breach of any of such provisions.
> (4) Nothing in this section shall prejudice the operation of any other enactment or rule of law relating to the duty or liability of directors or officers of a company.

This was adopted in section 124 of the uniform Companies Acts in Australia in 1961. It has been re-enacted with elaborations subsequently.[38] Similar provisions exist in the United Kingdom.[39]

Over the years both the English and the Australian statutory positions have become elaborate – perhaps over-elaborate. Thus, section 180 of the Australian Act provides:

> (1) A director or other officer of a corporation must exercise their powers and discharge their duties with the degree of care and diligence that a reasonable person would exercise if they:

36 *Richard Brady Franks Ltd* v. *Price* (1937) 58 C.L.R. 112, 135.

37 *Mills* v. *Mills* (1938) 60 C.L.R. 150, 175.

38 Companies Code 1981 s. 229; Corporations Law 1989 s. 232; Corporations Act 2001 (Cth), s. 181.

39 Companies Act 2006 (UK), ss. 170–7. See D. Ahern, 'Directors' Duties, Dry Ink and the Accessibility Agenda' (2012) 128 L.Q.R. 114.

(a) were a director or officer of a corporation in the corporation's circumstances; and
(b) occupied the office held by, and had the same responsibilities within the corporation as, the director or officer.

(2) A director or other officer of a corporation who makes a business judgment is taken to meet the requirements of subsection (1), and their equivalent duties at common law and in equity, in respect of the judgment if they:

(a) make the judgment in good faith for a proper purpose; and
(b) do not have a material personal interest in the subject matter of the judgment; and
(c) inform themselves about the subject matter of the judgment to the extent they reasonably believe to be appropriate; and
(d) rationally believe that the judgment is in the best interests of the corporation. The director's or officer's belief that the judgment is in the best interests of the corporation is a rational one unless the belief is one that no reasonable person in their position would hold.

(3) In this section *business judgment* means any decision to take or not take action in respect of a matter relevant to the business operations of the corporation.

This section provokes, and the succeeding sections reiterate, a question: What, if any, is the effect of these provisions on the courts' formulations of the equitable doctrines applying to directors and other officers? Section 181 provides:

(1) A director or other officer of a corporation must exercise their powers and discharge their duties:

(a) in good faith in the best interests of the corporation; and
(b) for a proper purpose.

(2) A person who is involved in a contravention of subsection (1) contravenes this subsection.

The meaning of 'involved' appears in section 79:

A person is involved in a contravention if, and only if, the person:
(a) has aided, abetted, counselled or procured the contravention; or
(b) has induced, whether by threats or promises or otherwise, the contravention; or
(c) has been in any way, by act or omission, directly or indirectly, knowingly concerned in, or party to, the contravention; or
(d) has conspired with others to effect the contravention.

Section 182(1) provides:

(1) A director, secretary, other officer or employee of a corporation must not improperly use their position to:
   (a) gain an advantage for themselves or someone else; or
   (b) cause detriment to the corporation.

Section 183(1) provides:

(1) A person who obtains information because they are, or have been, a director or other officer or employee of a corporation must not improperly use the information to:
   (a) gain an advantage for themselves or someone else; or
   (b) cause detriment to the corporation.

Section 184 provides:

(1) A director or other officer of a corporation commits an offence if they:
   (a) are reckless; or
   (b) are intentionally dishonest;

   and fail to exercise their powers and discharge their duties:
   (c) in good faith in the best interests of the corporation; or
   (d) for a proper purpose.
(2) A director, other officer or employee of a corporation commits an offence if they use their position dishonestly:
   (a) with the intention of directly or indirectly gaining an advantage for themselves, or someone else, or causing detriment to the corporation; or
   (b) recklessly as to whether the use may result in themselves or someone else directly or indirectly gaining an advantage, or in causing detriment to the corporation.
(3) A person who obtains information because they are, or have been, a director or other officer or employee of a corporation commits an offence if they use the information dishonestly:
   (a) with the intention of directly or indirectly gaining an advantage for themselves, or someone else, or causing detriment to the corporation; or
   (b) recklessly as to whether the use may result in themselves or someone else directly or indirectly gaining an advantage, or in causing detriment to the corporation.

And section 185 provides:

> Sections 180 to 184:
> (a) have effect in addition to, and not in derogation of, any rule of law relating to the duty or liability of a person because of their office or employment in relation to a corporation; and
> (b) do not prevent the commencement of civil proceedings for a breach of a duty or in respect of a liability referred to in paragraph (a).

Sections 182(2) and 183(2) are equivalent, *mutatis mutandis*, to section 181(2). There is no equivalent to section 181(2) for section 180 or section 183.

The disgraceful barbarism of the prose is striking. The Holy Roman Emperor Sigismund remarked, after an adviser drew attention to a grammatical mistake: '*Ego sum Rex Romanorum, et supra grammaticam*'.[40] The Commonwealth legislature seems to see itself similarly. But there are two points of legal significance in this structure. Their significance is interrelated.

First, like section 107(4) of the Victorian Act of 1958, section 185 preserves other rules relating to the duty or liability of persons holding an office or employment in relation to a corporation. This stands in contrast to the United Kingdom sections which operate in substitution for corresponding equitable duties.[41]

The second point concerns the accessorial and civil liability created by sections 79, 181(2), 182(2) and 183(2) read with section 79. The statutory regime does not provide for accessorial liability for failure to exercise care and diligence. But two questions might be asked: 'Should equity, for that reason alone, abstain from doing so? And even where the statutory regime does provide for accessorial liability, should equity abstain from intervening on any basis which differs from the

[40] 'I am king of the Romans and above grammar.'

[41] Companies Act 2006 (UK), s. 170(3), provides that the general duties in sections 171–7 have effect 'in place of' common law rules and equitable principles. Section 170(4) provides that the general duties 'shall be interpreted and applied in the same way as common law rules or equitable principles, and regard shall be had to the corresponding common law rules and equitable principles in interpreting and applying the general duties'. As Matthew Conaglen has pointed out, some of the statutory duties are different from those created by equitable principles and it is thus difficult to apply them 'in the same way': M. Conaglen, 'Interaction between Statutory and General Law Duties Concerning Company Director Conflicts' (2013) 31 C. & S.L.J. 403, 412.

statutory one?'[42] One possible answer to the second question might be: Yes, because otherwise the law runs the risk of becoming incoherent and over-complex. Another answer might be: No, because section 185 preserves whatever equitable intervention would otherwise exist at any point of time after it was enacted, equitable principles have an inherent capacity to develop over time, and section 185 recognises and does not nullify that capacity. Coherence has high claims. But so does richness. An enactment can only be amended by the legislature, not the courts. But unenacted law can be developed by the courts in the light of experience. Even where there is no equivalent to section 185, why should the law hold that after statutory language is allowed to have its full effect, it has an additional function restricting the principled development of non-statutory rules of common law and equity not in terms affected by it? If the legislature wants 'coherence' at the expense of those possibilities, its legislation should make it clear, as section 170(3)–(4) of the Companies Act 2006 (UK) did. Some general factors affecting the answer to both questions are touched on below.[43]

Statutory adoption of equitable rules

Under the third heading, 'Statutory amendment to equitable rules', there was discussion of legislation which, however radical it might be, took as its starting point the existing body of equitable principle and, while adding to or modifying it, left that body of principle as the primary legal regime. Under the fourth heading, 'Statutory provisions partly overlapping with equitable rules', there was discussion of statutes which set up regimes which were new but closely related to the equitable regimes on which they drew. The present section examines statutes which select concepts, doctrines and remedies from equity and incorporate them within complex statutory machinery operating entirely independent of general equity principles. This may happen for a variety of reasons.

One example is the statutory career of unconscionable conduct, and related doctrines, in the United Kingdom and Australia.

[42] See W.M.C. Gummow, 'The Equitable Duties of Company Directors' (2013) 87 A.L.J. 753, 757.

[43] See text between nn. 74 and 116 below.

The Money-Lenders Act 1900 (UK), s. 1(1), gave the court power to reopen a money-lending transaction if it were 'harsh and unconscionable or . . . otherwise such that a court of equity would give relief'. That was repealed by the Consumer Credit Act 1974 (UK). Sections 137–40 of that Act provided that the court could reopen a credit agreement if it were 'extortionate', that is, if the payments were 'grossly exorbitant' or the bargain otherwise 'grossly' contravened 'ordinary principles of fair dealing'. These provisions were replaced by the Consumer Credit Act 2006 (UK), ss. 140A–140D. Those sections permit intervention against contracts which are 'unfair to the debtor'. With that language, the legislature has drifted quite some distance from any equitable conception of an unconscionable bargain. What is more, it is uncertain language. Hayek regarded it as essential to the rule of law that the governed be able to foresee with fair certainty the outcomes of the relevant rules. He thought that this ideal had been attained in the West. And he thought that this was the greatest contribution to the prosperity of the West.[44] If he was correct, legislation in this form derogates from the rule of law, and its existence is likely to be damaging to prosperity. In Australia, various submissions to the Swanson Committee had asked it to recommend a prohibition on 'unfair methods of competition in or affecting commerce, and unfair or deceptive acts or practices in or affecting commerce'. The Swanson Committee opposed this quite 'strongly' because it could 'result in a considerable degree of uncertainty in commercial transactions'.[45]

In New South Wales, in 1959, section 88F was introduced into the Industrial Arbitration Act 1940. Section 88F gave power to the Industrial Commission of New South Wales to avoid 'any contract or arrangement or any condition or collateral arrangement relating thereto whereby a person performs work in any industry' if it was 'unfair' or 'harsh and unconscionable' or 'against the public interest'. The provision continues to this day after numerous legislative amendments to, much re-ordering of, and the replacement of the Industrial Arbitration Act.[46] No doubt the same power exists in courts of general equitable jurisdiction (e.g. the Supreme Court of New South Wales). But the point of the enactment was to confer the power on the Industrial Commission. That is a court with

[44] Hayek, *The Road to Serfdom*, 54, 208.

[45] Trade Practices Act Review Committee, *Report to the Minister for Business and Consumer Affairs* (Canberra: A.G.P.S., 1976), [9.56], [9.58].

[46] See now section 106 of the Industrial Relations Act 1996 (NSW). See *Stevenson* v. *Barham* (1977) 136 C.L.R. 190.

specialist expertise. It is not a court of general equitable jurisdiction, though it is a court with a strong emphasis, which, some think, perhaps over time became unduly strong, on protecting employees against employers.

Similar statutory controls of unconscionable conduct can be found in state legislation dealing with hire purchase.[47]

In 1980, the Contracts Review Act (NSW) was enacted. It empowers a court to grant relief where it finds that a contractual provision was 'unjust in the circumstances relating to the contract at the time it was made' (s. 7(1)).

Then significant developments took place in Commonwealth legislation. In 1986 and 1998, two new sections were introduced into the Trade Practices Act 1974 (Cth). That Act is now known as the Competition and Consumer Act 2010 (Cth). As its title and bulk suggest, it is a substantial piece of legislation. It regulates anticompetitive behaviour and misconduct in trade in many detailed respects. Sections 21 and 22 of Schedule 2 to the Act (the 'Australian Consumer Law') correspond with the two new sections introduced in 1986 and 1998. Section 21 prohibits unconscionable conduct in trade or commerce in connection with the supply or acquisition of goods or services. The Swanson Committee, which recommended it in 1976, said it based the recommendation on 'a standard which historically developed under the equitable jurisdiction of the courts'.[48]

In 1993, the equitable approach was explicitly taken over by a third new section, which is now section 20(1) of the Australian Consumer Law. It provides: 'A person must not, in trade or commerce, engage in conduct that is unconscionable, within the meaning of the unwritten law from time to time.'[49] Why did the legislature adopt the general law in this way instead of leaving it to operate outside the Australian Consumer Law? Perhaps because the Australian Consumer Law has a large range of remedies which are in some respects more claimant-friendly than the general law. Examples include 'compensation orders' (sections 237–45)

[47] See D.W. Greig and J.L.R. Davis, *The Law of Contract* (Sydney: Law Book Co., 1987), 981, legislation in Western Australia (Hire Purchase Act 1959 (W.A.), s. 24) and Queensland (Hire Purchase Act 1959 (Qld), s. 28) and the National Credit Code (Schedule 1 to the National Consumer Credit Protection Act 2009 (Cth)).

[48] Trade Practices Act Review Committee, *Report to the Minister for Business and Consumer Affairs*, [9.60].

[49] Section 20(1) may impermissibly depart from a constitutionally mandated separation of powers.

and injunctions (section 232). The power to grant an injunction conferred by section 232 (and, in relation to competition law, under section 80 of the Act itself) is another instance of equity contributing a model to the legislature. First, the legislature works changes on the model. Then it uses the model as a cog in a new statutory regime. Thus section 232 is more liberal than equitable injunctions in relation to standing. It requires no threat, or past misconduct, or any imminent danger of substantial damage. And section 234 is more liberal than the general law in relation to undertakings as to damages or costs when an interlocutory injunction is applied for.[50] These provisions may be compared with sections 380–1 of the Financial Services and Markets Act 2000 (UK).

One final example within this category occurs where a statute takes conduct in breach of equitable duty and criminalises it.[51]

The deference of statute to equity

In *Aid/Watch Inc.* v. *Federal Commission of Taxation*,[52] a majority of the High Court of Australia said:

> Where a statute picks up as a criterion for its operation a body of the general law, such as the equitable principles respecting charitable trusts, then, in the absence of a contrary indication in the statute, the statute speaks continuously to the present, and picks up the case law as it stands from time to time.[53]

In areas where this doctrine applies, the structure of the statute may begin to creak and groan if the body of law which supplies the relevant criteria ceases to remain static and goes beyond foreseeable development towards a radical reformulation.

Taxation statutes commonly pick up key equitable conceptions. This is not surprising, since private transactions, whether commercial or not, naturally follow many existing structures created largely in accordance with equitable ideas. And legislation providing that certain equitable charges were void against a liquidator was construed so that 'equitable charge' had its ordinary meaning[54] and did not include trusts.[55]

[50] The Supreme Court reached a similar result without equivalent statutory backing: *Financial Services Authority* v. *Sinaloa Gold plc* [2013] 2 A.C. 28; [2013] UKSC 11.

[51] Stebbings, *The Private Trustee in Victorian England*, 182–3.

[52] (2010) 241 C.L.R. 539; [2010] HCA 42.

[53] (2010) 241 C.L.R. 539, [23] (French C.J., Gummow, Hayne, Crennan and Bell JJ.).

[54] See *In re Bank of Credit and Commerce International SA (in liq.)* [1998] A.C. 214, 226.

[55] *Associated Alloys Pty Ltd* v. *ACN 001 452 106 Pty Ltd* (2000) 202 C.L.R. 588, [5]–[6]; [2000] HCA 25.

Statutory receivers are often treated as having the same characteristics as non-statutory ones, save to the extent that the statute provides otherwise.[56] And other concepts in proceeds of crime legislation have equitable sources, for example equitable tracing, third-party defences analogous to the bona fide purchaser for value without notice defence and property which 'vests in equity' but not 'at law'.[57]

These phenomena are not confined to equity. In similar fashion, legislative reference to a common law doctrine can incorporate that doctrine both as it exists and as it changes.[58]

Equity's reactions to statute

Statutory analogy: general

Equity frequently moulds its doctrines and remedies by reference to statute. It can add to the content of equitable rules, defences and remedies by drawing on the common law (including statute law) and applying it by analogy.

Equitable applications of statutes of limitation by analogy

For example, equity applies statutes of limitation by analogy. It draws a distinction between two types of limitation statutes. Statutes in the first category in their terms operate directly to bar equitable claims. Statutes in the second category, though they do not operate directly to bar equitable claims, are applied by analogy so as to have the effect of barring equitable claims. Application of the statute of limitation by analogy, naturally, depends on the existence of a common law analogue to the equitable relief claimed. Thus, in *Cohen* v. *Cohen*,[59] Dixon J. had to consider three claims made by a wife against a husband. The first was to recover 9,000 marks which she had lent to him so that he could buy goods for his business. The second was to recover the proceeds of sale of some

[56] *Capewell* v. *Revenue and Customs Commissioners* [2007] 1 W.L.R. 386, [18], [21]–[25]; [2007] UKHL 2.

[57] Proceeds of Crime Act 2002 (Cth), ss. 67(1)(a), 97(1)(a), 202, 330(4). See also Proceeds of Crime Act 2002 (UK); *R* v. *Waya* [2013] 1 A.C. 294, [55]–[61]; [2012] UKSC 51; and *Director of the Serious Fraud Office* v. *Lexi Holdings plc (in admin.)* [2009] Q.B. 376; [2008] EWCA Crim 1443.

[58] *Peters (WA) Ltd* v. *Petersville Ltd* (2001) 205 C.L.R. 126, [30]; [2001] HCA 45 (discussing the restraint of trade doctrine).

[59] (1929) 41 C.L.R. 91.

furniture which the wife had entrusted to the husband for sale. The third was to recover money from the husband which was paid by an insurer to the husband in respect of loss to his wife's property. Dixon J. said that an analogy with the statute of limitations was found

> in the case of constructive trusts, where the equity is fastened upon the trustee not because he intended to become the fiduciary of property but because of the character of his dealings and in spite of his intention to take the property for himself. But [c]ourts of equity have refused to see any analogy when a person, intending to act in a capacity which is fiduciary, has received, as and for the beneficial property of another, something which he is to hold, apply or account for specifically for his benefit.[60]

Dixon J. held that the second and third claims were not barred by analogy to the statute of limitations.[61] That was because the husband was accountable specifically for the proceeds of the sale and the insurance. 'He was not merely to take the money, mix it with other funds as his own and treat his wife simply as his creditor whose debt, like other debts, was to be met out of his general resources.'[62] But Dixon J. held that the first claim was barred by analogy. That was because the husband 'was not accountable specifically for the money he received nor the goods into which it was transformed or the proceeds of those goods'.[63]

Analogies have been found where equitable compensation was claimed in circumstances in which a common law action for damages for breach of contract[64] or for fraud[65] was also available.

But there are limits to equity's application of statutes by analogy. At common law, there is a rule that a creditor who sues on a debt just before the limitation period expires stops the limitation period from running. It does not matter that the creditor only recovers outside the limitation period so long as the action commences before the limitation period ends. In *Motor Terms Co. Pty Ltd* v. *Liberty Insurance Ltd*,[66] a majority of the High Court of Australia (Barwick C.J., Taylor J. and Menzies J.) said that an order for the winding up of a company could be made on the petition of a creditor whose debt had become statute-barred between the date when the petition was presented and the date when the

[60] *Ibid.*, 100. To the same effect is *Paragon Finance plc* v. *D.B. Thakerar & Co.* [1999] 1 All E.R. 400, 415–16. See also *Williams* v. *Central Bank of Nigeria* [2014] A.C. 1189, [54]–[64]; [2014] UKSC 10.

[61] Mercantile Law Amendment Act 1856 (UK), 19 & 20 Vict. c. 97, s. 9.

[62] *Cohen* v. *Cohen* (1929) 42 C.L.R. 91, 101.

[63] *Ibid.*, 102.

[64] *Companhia de Seguros Imperio* v. *Heath (REBX) Ltd* [2001] 1 W.L.R. 112.

[65] *Coulthard* v. *Disco Mix Club Ltd* [2000] 1 W.L.R. 707.

[66] (1967) 116 C.L.R. 177.

winding up order was made.[67] They reached that view as a matter of statutory construction. Kitto J.[68] uttered dicta reaching the contrary view. He too reached that view as a matter of statutory construction. But he also rejected reasoning employed in the court below which relied on the use of statutes of limitation in equity by analogy. He said:

> [T]he analogy of the statute is used in a suit for equitable relief as affording a prima facie proper standard by which to decide whether the relief should be refused on the ground of the staleness of the claim. In winding up proceedings under the Companies Act [1961 (NSW)] the analogy has no relevance, except that where a person claims to be a 'creditor' in respect of an equitable debt it is necessary to consider at the hearing whether his petition is not that of a 'creditor' because on ordinary equitable principles, including the analogy of the Statute, a Court of Equity would refuse him an order for payment.[69]

'Equity follows the law'

The 'law' which equity follows is not just the non-statutory law. It is the 'law' comprised by both non-statutory and statutory law. And the 'law' which is to be followed need not be 'law' which is precisely applicable to the circumstances.

Independently of legislation, where land is conveyed to two or more persons, a joint tenancy of the legal estate is created. That is at least if the four unities are present and there are no words of severance. Equity followed the law in this respect, at least where the purchase money had been provided by the purchasers in equal shares. Where the shares were unequal, the purchasers took the beneficial interests as tenants in common. What, however, was the impact of legislation providing that, in an instrument, a disposition of the beneficial interest in property 'to or for two or more persons together beneficially shall be deemed to be made to or for them as tenants in common, and not as joint tenants'?[70] And what was its impact where there was a disposition to only one person but that person and another had contributed equally to the purchase price without stipulating whether they were to hold the equitable interest as joint tenants or tenants in common? Section 26 had no direct application, because there had been no instrument disposing of the beneficial interest in property to two or more persons. But the common law rule which

[67] *Ibid.*, 179, 189–92, 194–7. [68] *Ibid.*, 180–5. [69] *Ibid.*, 184–5.
[70] Conveyancing Act 1919 (NSW), s. 26(1).

equity followed in order to conclude that there was a joint tenancy had ceased to exist. The High Court of Australia said:

> It would indeed be surprising if the rules of equity required the courts to follow a rule of the common law that no longer existed and in doing so to reach a result which equity generally tried to avoid. However the doctrines of equity are not so inflexible. If equity follows the law, it will follow the rules of law in their current state. Where, as a result of following the law, a beneficial joint tenancy would formerly have been created, now a beneficial tenancy in common will (in New South Wales) come into existence. In other words, although s. 26 . . . has no direct application to the present case, its indirect effect is to require it to be held that there was a resulting trust for the purchasers in an interest of the same kind as that which would have resulted if the land had been conveyed to them at law, ie as tenants in common.[71]

Further, where equity follows the law, it need not follow it exactly. Equity follows the law in requiring restitution as a condition of rescission where the contract has been wholly or partly executed. But it allows greater flexibility in the basis upon which restitution and accounting between the parties may be ordered. It does not require complete restitution of the position which existed before the contract but allows its remedies, particularly an order for monetary accounts, to be utilised to achieve practical restitution and justice.[72] Thus, in *Alati* v. *Kruger*,[73] Dixon C.J., Webb, Kitto and Taylor JJ. said:

> If the case had to be decided according to the principles of the common law, it might have been argued that at the date when the respondent issued his writ he was not entitled to rescind the purchase, because he was not then in a position to return to the appellant *in specie* that which he had received under the contract, in the same plight as that in which he had received it . . . But it is necessary here to apply the doctrines of equity, and equity has always regarded as valid the disaffirmance of a contract induced by fraud even though precise *restitutio in integrum* is not possible, if the situation is such that, by the exercise of its powers, including the power to take account of profits and to direct inquiries as to allowances proper to be made for deterioration, it can do what is practically just between the parties, and by so doing restore them substantially to the *status quo*.[74]

[71] *Delehunt* v. *Carmody* (1986) 161 C.L.R. 464, 473 (Gibbs C.J.). For examples of equity following the law where property is placed in joint names, see *Stack* v. *Dowden* [2007] 2 A.C. 432, [33]; [2007] UKHL 17; *Jones* v. *Kernott* [2012] 1 A.C. 776, [22], [51], [68]; [2011] UKSC 53.

[72] *Vadasz* v. *Pioneer Concrete (SA) Pty Ltd* (1995) 184 C.L.R. 102, 111.

[73] (1955) 94 C.L.R. 216. [74] *Ibid.*, 224–5.

Statutes as the source of 'values' relevant to equitable doctrines

The Supreme Court of New South Wales has found an estoppel against Papua New Guinea on the basis of a statement which was unconscionable. An element in its unconscionable character was that it was misleading or deceptive. The court held that it was permissible to take that into account even though a statute prohibiting misleading and deceptive conduct did not apply because it did not bind a foreign government.[75] Young J. said, in purported but rather extreme reliance on the 'equity of a statute' doctrine propounded by Sir Edmund Plowden,[76] 'that courts of equity do mould their application of principles of unconscionability and other doctrines depending on changes in statute law'.[77]

Another example of that point arises in Australia in relation to the federal statutory prohibition on unconscionable conduct which was derived from equitable doctrine and which was discussed above.[78] The Full Federal Court recently reasoned as follows. What is unconscionable depends on the norms and values of the community. Key values include honesty and fairness. Those values may be illuminated, elaborated and developed by legislatures, including state legislatures, which set standards through their legislation.[79] Thus, the content of federal law stated by reference to equitable doctrines is modified by the standards reflected in state legislation.

Statutory analogy: inhibitions on equitable development?

There has been much recent interest in the question whether the common law ought to adapt itself by reference to the content of, and in particular to changes in, statute law. Obviously, legislation which is in terms inconsistent with a potential path for the common law prevents that path from being trodden. But silence in legislation does not necessarily create inconsistency. In some circumstances it may be 'a myth to imagine that the enactment of certain provisions represents a considered rejection by Parliament of other provisions'.[80] The instant question arises

75 *Tasiba Pty Ltd* v. *Sovereign State of Papua New Guinea* (1994) 34 N.S.W.L.R. 691, 701–2.

76 *Eyston* v. *Studd* (1574) 2 Plow. 459, 466–7; 75 E.R. 688, 698.

77 *Tasiba Pty Ltd* v. *Sovereign State of Papua New Guinea* (1994) 34 N.S.W.L.R. 691, 702.

78 See text to nn. 49–50 above.

79 *Australian Competition and Consumer Commission* v. *Lux Distributors Pty Ltd* [2013] A.T.P.R. 42–429, [23]; [2013] FCA 47.

80 A. Burrows, 'The Relationship between Common Law and Statute in the Law of Obligations' (2012) 128 L.Q.R. 232, 244–5.

in a more refined way. It can arise in relation to that part of the common law which is equity. In *Erven Warnink BV* v. *J. Townend & Sons (Hull) Ltd*,[81] Lord Diplock enunciated what will be called below for short 'Lord Diplock's doctrine':

> Where over a period of years there can be discerned a *steady trend* in legislation which reflects the *views of successive Parliaments* as to *what the public interest demands in a particular field of law*, development of the common law in that part of the same field which has been left to it *ought to proceed* upon a parallel rather than a diverging course.[82]

One response to this call in a context which included equity took place in *Moorgate Tobacco Ltd* v. *Philip Morris Ltd (No. 2)*.[83] In that case the High Court denied the existence of an action for 'unfair competition'. Deane J. referred to 'the traditional and statutory causes of action which are available to a trader in respect of damage caused or threatened by a competitor'.[84] He said those causes of action had 'established limits'.[85] He said the limits defined 'the boundary between the area of legal or equitable restraint and protection and the area of untrammelled competition'.[86] He said that the limits 'increasingly reflect what the responsible Parliament or Parliaments have determined to be the appropriate balance between competing claims and policies'.[87] He concluded:

> Neither legal principle nor social utility requires or warrants the obliteration of that boundary by the importation of a cause of action whose main characteristic is the scope it allows, under high-sounding generalizations, for judicial indulgence of idiosyncratic notions of what is fair in the marketplace.[88]

Similarly, it has been said in relation to a largely non-equitable field (restraint of trade) that in deciding 'what development, if any, there should be of the common law', the court could have regard to the Trade Practices Act 1974 (Cth), Pt IV, and to 'the appropriate balance between competing claims and policies'.[89]

[81] [1979] A.C. 731.

[82] *Erven Warnink BV* v. *J. Townend & Sons (Hull) Ltd* [1979] A.C. 731, 743 (italics added).

[83] (1984) 156 C.L.R. 414. [84] *Ibid*., 445–6. [85] *Ibid*., 445. [86] *Ibid*., 445.

[87] *Ibid*., 445. [88] *Ibid*., 445–6.

[89] *Peters (WA) Ltd* v. *Petersville Ltd* (2001) 205 C.L.R. 126, [33] (Gleeson C.J., Gummow, Kirby and Hayne JJ.), quoting Deane J. in *Moorgate Tobacco Ltd* v. *Philip Morris Ltd (No. 2)*, *ibid*., 445.

The language used in the *Moorgate* case indicates that the court thought there was more than one reason for rejecting the claim that there was a doctrine of 'unfair competition' in the common law.

The force of Lord Diplock's doctrine varies directly with the novelty of the cause of action, defence or remedy which it may seek to preclude. The supposed action for 'unfair competition' was very novel, and thus Deane J.'s reasoning had strength. Lord Diplock's doctrine has less force for analogical or other modest changes in the law.

In *Esso Australia Resources Ltd* v. *Federal Commissioner of Taxation*[90] Gleeson C.J., Gaudron and Gummow JJ. quoted four questions raised by P.S. Atiyah:

> [Is it] possible for the courts to take account of statute law, in the very development of the common law itself? Can the courts, for instance, use statutes as analogies for the purpose of developing the common law? Can they justify jettisoning obsolete cases, not because they have been actually reversed by some statutory provision, but because a statute suggests that they are based on outdated values? Could the courts legitimately draw some general principle from a limited statutory provision, and apply that principle as a matter of common law?[91]

They also quoted the next three sentences:

> It must be clear that using statutes in this way is fundamentally different from any process of construction, however benevolent or liberal that might be. Construction, as a matter of theory at least, requires the court to give effect to what it thinks the legislation actually enacts. Using statutes by way of analogy quite clearly involves using them to produce results which the legislation does *not* enact.[92]

Atiyah's questions are directed to what might be called positive developments in the law: developments which might follow advances already made by statute. The *Moorgate* case illustrates rather the use of statute to prevent development which is, if not incipient, at least possible.

One set of short answers to Atiyah's questions might be as follows. To use the language which Atiyah employed in each question, the courts *could* do these things. Whether in any particular circumstances they *will* do these things is a matter for individual judgment in the particular case.

90 (1999) 201 C.L.R. 49; [1999] HCA 67.

91 *Esso Australia Resources Ltd* v. *FCT* (1999) 201 C.L.R. 49, [20], quoting P.S. Atiyah, 'Common Law and Statute Law' (1985) 48 M.L.R. 1, 6.

92 *Esso Australia Resources Ltd* v. *FCT* (1999) 201 C.L.R. 49, [20], quoting Atiyah, 'Common Law and Statute in Law', 6 (italics original).

But, to answer a question Atiyah did not ask, they are not *obliged* to do these things. Yet proponents of Lord Diplock's doctrine sometimes speak as though its application was obligatory. Lord Diplock himself spoke of how common law development 'ought to proceed'.[93] To treat Lord Diplock's doctrine as creating an obligation rather than a choice may at first sight increase predictability. But the assessment of what trends are 'steady', what the 'views of successive Parliaments' are as to what the 'public interest demands' and what courses are 'parallel rather than ... diverging' involves examination of imponderable and indeterminate criteria. Predictability of outcome is important for the rule of law, but there is no improved predictability here. Is it not more desirable to leave it to the legislature to provide by clear words what the law is and what it is not than to leave it to the courts to essay these murky inquiries? In a world which is dominated by statutes – a world warmly welcomed by many lawyers – is it unreasonable to ask that those statutes comply with standards of clarity? And is it unreasonable to see pursuing the necessarily vague reasoning of Lord Diplock's doctrine as something antithetical to key rule of law criteria? Lord Diplock's doctrine provokes two questions: Where the legislature has enacted a statute abstaining from modifying, or denying the possibility of, an existing equitable principle, defence or remedy, why should a court of equity decline to embark on a development not in terms precluded by that statute? And why should it not do so where the statute specifically preserves certain equitable rules, in the manner of section 185 of the Corporations Act 2001 (Cth)?

The reach of Lord Diplock's doctrine is both obscure and controversial. There is a statement doubting whether it is 'possible for a court to go beyond what a statute actually enacts and to draw from it some principle to be applied by way of analogy in fashioning the common law'.[94] And Lord Diplock's doctrine is less suitable for federations than it is for classical Westminster-type legislatures: uncommanded commanders free of federal constitutional constraints and not surrounded by the legislatures of other polities each pursuing the course it thinks best. Hence, Lord Diplock's doctrine has not often been applied in Australia because Australia is a federation. It can be difficult to detect 'a steady trend' or a considered legislative view of a 'consistent pattern of

[93] Another example is given below: *Adelaide Steamship Co. Ltd* v. *Spalvins* (1998) 81 F.C.R. 360, 373 ('must now adapt itself').

[94] *Lamb* v. *Cotogno* (1987) 164 C.L.R. 1, 11 (Mason C.J., Brennan, Deane, Dawson and Gaudron JJ.).

legislative policy' where some legislatures move in a particular way but others do not.[95]

Lord Diplock's doctrine is potentially far-reaching. If it is sound for what Lord Diplock called the 'development of new law', why is it not sound for what Atiyah called the 'jettisoning of old law'? Take the statutory requirements for the assignment of choses in action. They were introduced in 1873 and have been re-enacted.[96] They call for writing and notice to the debtor. The requirements of equity for equitable assignments do not. The equitable criteria for validity are thus laxer.[97] Does it follow that equitable assignments should no longer be recognised because they have laxer criteria than the statutes? Why does equity not infer from the policy underlying the 'steady trend in legislation which reflects the views of successive Parliaments' imposing those statutory requirements – from 'what the public interest demands in a particular field of law' – that it should no longer recognise assignments which are not in writing and of which no notice was given to the debtor? Why should the courts not apply Isaacs J.'s reasoning in *Anning* v. *Anning*[98] in preference to that of Griffith C.J.[99] and refuse to recognise any title in an assignee whose assignor has not fully complied with statutory requirements? There are various arguments for negative answers.[100] But the simplest answer is Lord Macnaghten's:

[95] For an example in relation not to equity but to the common law, see *Esso Australia Resources Ltd* v. *FCT* (1999) 201 C.L.R. 49, [25]. For an example of equity's refusal to act in conformity with statutory provisions permitting apportionment for contributory negligence, see *Pilmer* v. *Duke Group Ltd (in liq.)* (2001) 207 C.L.R. 165, [86], [165]–[173]; [2001] HCA 31. See also *CSR Ltd* v. *Eddy* (2005) 226 C.L.R. 1, [54]; [2005] HCA 64 (on the question of whether state legislation rested on any particular assumption as to the common law).

[96] Judicature Act 1873 (UK), 36 & 37 Vict. c. 66, s. 25(6); see now Law of Property Act 1925 (UK), s. 136 and, in Australia, the Conveyancing Act 1919 (NSW), s. 12 and its equivalents.

[97] Unless there is a disposition of an equitable interest, in which case there is a statutory requirement that it be in writing. See Law of Property Act 1925 (UK), s. 53(1)(c) and Conveyancing Act 1919 (NSW), s. 23C(1)(c) and their equivalents.

[98] (1907) 4 C.L.R. 1049, 1062–76.

[99] *Ibid.*, 1057, approved in *Corin* v. *Patton* (1990) 169 C.L.R. 540, 559 by the dicta of Mason C.J. and McHugh J., and at 571 and 582 per Deane J. See also *Mascall* v. *Mascall* (1984) 50 P. & C.R. 119. The approach is criticised in *Curtis* v. *Pulbrook* [2011] 1 B.C.L.C. 638, [47]; [2011] EWHC 167 (Ch).

[100] J.D. Heydon, M.J. Leeming and P.G. Turner, *Meagher, Gummow and Lehane's Equity: Doctrines and Remedies*, 5th ed. (Sydney: LexisNexis, 2015), [6–040]; P.G. Turner, 'Legal Assignment of Rights of Restricted Assignability' [2008] L.M.C.L.Q. 306, 316–19.

> Why that which would have been a good equitable assignment before the statute should now be invalid and inoperative because it fails to come up to the requirements of the statute, I confess I do not understand. The statute does not forbid or destroy equitable assignments or impair their efficacy in the slightest degree.[101]

Lord Macnaghten did not seem to think that Lord Diplock's doctrine was a matter to be taken into account.

Statutory analogy: 'gravitational pull'

Lord Diplock's doctrine is sometimes encapsulated in a metaphor – the 'gravitational pull' of statutes.[102] In *Adelaide Steamship Co. Ltd* v. *Spalvins*,[103] the statute which was said to be exerting the pull enacted a 'dominant purpose' test for legal professional privilege in relation to the tender of evidence. The question was whether the common law as stated in Australia should be changed so as to make that test applicable to the different fields of claims for privilege at common law in relation to documents to be inspected on discovery or after production on subpoena. The Full Court of the Federal Court of Australia (Olney, Kiefel and Finn JJ.) said that the advent of the legislation 'has created an entirely new setting to which the common law *must now adapt itself*, and adapt itself in such a way as to "include [the Act] as a fundamental part of its fabric"'.[104] The Full Court then changed the common law to conform with the statute, thus purporting to overrule authority in the High Court of Australia by which it was bound.[105] Of course, a court could and should do this by applying a subsequently enacted statutory change. But the Full Court's decision seems to treat a change in the common law developed by analogy with a subsequently enacted statute as equivalent to a statutory change. This confuses the role of courts and legislatures. And it annihilates the doctrine of precedent. For that reason, the decision to treat Lord Diplock's doctrine as compelling 'gravitational pull' by the statute to draw the common law towards it was impermissible for an intermediate appellate court. The High Court, in overruling that case,

101 *William Brandt's Sons & Co.* v. *Dunlop Rubber Co. Ltd* [1905] A.C. 454, 461.

102 The expression is used in *South Pacific Air Motive Pty Ltd* v. *Magnus* (1998) 87 F.C.R. 301, 317 (Beaumont J.). Its sources seem to be R. Dworkin, *Taking Rights Seriously* (London: Duckworth, 1977), 111 and G. Calabresi, *A Common Law for the Age of Statutes* (Cambridge, Mass.: Harvard University Press, 1982), 85–6.

103 (1998) 81 F.C.R. 360.

104 *Ibid.*, 373 (italics added) quoting Calabresi, *A Common Law for the Age of Statutes*, 86.

105 *Grant* v. *Downs* (1976) 135 C.L.R. 674.

declined to take the step for itself on the ground that it would not be justified in changing the common law of legal professional privilege for the whole country in the light of statutory changes in some, but not all, of its jurisdictions.[106]

There are many forces to which one can be subject without being aware of them. One is gravitational force. An example of unconscious, or perhaps only semi-conscious, subjection to forces of that kind may be the decision of the High Court of Australia in *Vadasz* v. *Pioneer Concrete (SA) Pty Ltd.*[107] A supplier of goods to a financially troubled company had issued invoices for payment. On 7 August 1992, a surety entered a guarantee to the supplier that all its invoices, whether dating from before or after 7 August, would be paid. The supplier procured this guarantee by misrepresentation. The misrepresentation was that the document guaranteed only the payment of future invoices, whereas in truth it applied to past invoices as well. The High Court was not prepared to find that the misrepresentation was fraudulent but dealt with the appeal on the assumption that it was. The High Court held that the guarantee was valid, but only as to future invoices. This has been viewed as a case of partial rescission, and thus heterodox. That is because instead of restoring the parties to their pre-contractual positions or leaving the bargain on foot, the court rewrote the bargain.[108] It was not thought possible to do this in relation to equitable rescission. But it was possible under section 87(2)(b) of the Trade Practices Act 1974 (Cth).[109]

The High Court's reasoning is couched in the language of equity. It did not assert that it was relying on section 87(2)(b). There is little to suggest that it was relying on section 87(2)(b). But before the trial judge, reliance had been placed on section 87(2)(b). The trial judge had made an order referring to it. An appeal against that order was dismissed by the Full Court of the Supreme Court of South Australia. And the appeal to the High Court failed. That undisturbed order of the trial judge may have influenced the High Court, with sleepwalker-like confidence,

[106] *Esso Australia Resources Ltd* v. *FCT* (1999) 201 C.L.R. 49, [23]–[28].

[107] (1995) 184 C.L.R. 102.

[108] For severe criticism, see D. O'Sullivan, S. Elliott and R. Zakrzewski, *The Law of Rescission*, 2nd ed. (Oxford University Press, 2014), [13.19]–[13.25], [19.34]–[19.37], [19.39]: the authors assembled numerous articles discussing the case.

[109] Section 87(2)(b), permits 'an order varying such a contract or arrangement in such manner as is specified in the order and, if the Court thinks fit, declaring the contract or arrangement to have had effect as so varied on and after such date before the date on which the order is made as is so specified'. The applicable legislation is now section 243(b) of the Australian Consumer Law: Competition and Consumer Act 2010 (Cth), Sch. 2.

subconsciously to incorporate into its reasoning on equitable rescission section 87(2)(b) considerations as being relevant factors modifying equitable principle.[110]

Despite the attention it has attracted, the case is in truth not a very significant one. There is less in it than meets the eye. That is because the judgment sum was 'calculated on the basis that the guarantee is rescinded or set aside as regards past indebtedness'.[111] The supplier accepted this.[112] The surety contended that the guarantee should be set aside qua future indebtedness as well.[113] It was thus common ground that the trial judge's orders should be upheld so far as they reflected the surety's liability in relation to post-7 August supplies. The only controversy was whether they should reflect liability in relation to pre-7 August supplies. Thus, the High Court's reasons were directed not to justifying the orders made (and upheld) as far as they went. They were directed to explaining why the orders should not be wider. So far as there was 'partial rescission', it resulted from acceptance of what was common ground between the parties. The court said that enforcing the guarantee to the extent of future indebtedness was to do no more than hold the surety to what he was prepared to undertake independently of any misrepresentation. It was in that context that the court, after referring to a case under the Contracts Review Act 1980 (NSW), mentioned in a footnote a case decided under section 52 of the Trade Practices Act.[114] That case did deal with section 87. But it is hard to see how it dealt with section 87 because it is only reported as a summary.[115] The court offered no explicit analysis of what impact section 87 could have on equitable rescission. At all events, what the court said was a dictum, not ratio, and it was not a very significant dictum. The ratio lies in the court's rejection of the surety's submission that there should have been more extensive rescission. Its reasons for that rejection included reasoning which may be open to criticism, but it included some other reasoning which was less open to criticism; for example, the surety's refusal to do equity by paying for the value of the goods supplied in reliance on the guarantee.

[110] O'Sullivan, Elliott and Zakrzewski, *The Law of Rescission*, 2nd ed. [13.18] n. 30 referred to 'the long shadow' which the Competition and Consumer Act 2010 (Cth) casts over commercial litigation in Australia.

[111] (1995) 184 C.L.R. 102, 108. [112] *Ibid.*, 110. [113] *Ibid.*, 111.

[114] *Money* v. *Westpac Banking Corporation* [1988] A.T.P.R. (Digest) 46–034.

[115] (1995) 184 C.L.R. 102, 116 n. 47.

Statutes 'reformed' by equity: the 'equity of a statute'

This expression is used in at least two senses.

In the first sense, the 'equity of a statute' is the mischief it is dealing with. Thus, Byles J. said: 'I suppose "within the equity", means the same thing as "within the mischief" of the statute'.[116] However, Byles J.'s approach, though related to that adopted by Edmund Plowden in his celebrated note on *Eyston* v. *Skidd*,[117] is perhaps narrower than it.

The second sense of the 'equity of a statute' can be seen in the following statement by Plowden in that note:

> [I]t is not the words of the law, but the internal sense of it that makes the law, and our law (like all others) consists of two parts, viz. of body and soul; the letter of the law is the body of the law, and the sense and reason of the law is the soul of the law . . . And it often happens that when you know the letter, you know not the sense, for sometimes the sense is more confined and contracted than the letter, and sometimes it is more large and extensive. And equity . . . enlarges or diminishes the letter according to its discretion.[118]

Plowden then said:

> [E]xperience shews us that no law-makers can foresee all things which may happen, and therefore it is fit that if there is any defect in the law, it should be reformed by equity, which is no part of the law, but a moral virtue which corrects the law . . . From whence the reader may observe how convenient a thing this equity is, and the wise [j]udges of our law deserve great commendation for having made use of it where the words of the law are rigorous, for thereby they have softened the severity of the text, and have made the law tolerable.[119]

In this way, the equity of a statute extends its provisions to problems not foreseen by its makers. Plowden is thus expounding a theory of statutory interpretation. He continued:

> And in order to form a right judgment when the letter of a statute is restrained, and when enlarged, by equity, it is a good way, when you peruse a statute, to suppose that the law-maker is present, and that you have asked him the question you want to know touching the equity[;] then you must give yourself such an answer as you imagine he would have done, if he had been present . . . And if the law-maker would have followed

[116] *Shuttleworth* v. *Le Fleming* (1863) 19 C.B. (N.S.) 687, 703; 144 E.R. 956, 962.

[117] (1574) Plow. 459, 465–7; 75 E.R. 688, 695–9. See C.K. Allen, *Law in the Making*, 7th ed. (Oxford: Clarendon Press, 1964), 451–6.

[118] (1574) Plow. 459, 465; 75 E.R. 688, 695.

[119] *Ibid.*, 466; 698 (citations omitted).

> the equity, notwithstanding the words of the law . . . you may safely do the like . . .[120]

This 'equity of a statute' doctrine came to be generally understood to permit the court to extend the statute to instances not covered by its express words and to narrow the statute so that it did not apply to some instances which were covered by its express words.

The 'equity of a statute' doctrine began to decline in the seventeenth century. Lord Mansfield said that the expression was 'synonymous to the meaning of the legislator'.[121] The doctrine came under increasing criticism in the nineteenth century.[122] In the twentieth century Griffith C.J. said it was 'open to the grave objection that the adaptation or extension of the words of a statute to a case not within its actual provisions is the function of the legislature and not of the court'.[123] He also said:

> [I]t may well be that, if the legislature had applied its mind to the subject, it would have refused to make the suggested adaptation or extension, or would have made it subject to conditions, of which the court can have no knowledge, and on which it has no right to speculate.[124]

Griffith C.J. set out[125] Coke's statement of the doctrine:

> '*Equitie*' is a construction made by the judges, that cases out of the letter of a statute, yet being within the same mischiefe, or cause of the making of the same, shall be within the same remedie that the statute provideth; and the reason hereof is, for that the law-makers could not possibly set down all cases in expresse terms.[126]

But Griffith C.J. then said: 'this doctrine is no longer followed'.[127]

Modern lawyers no longer commonly use the phrase 'the equity of a statute'. But they know the thing. The doctrine survives in at least two ways. First, authorities decided in reliance on it continue to stand.[128]

120 *Ibid.*, 467; 699. 121 *R* v. *Williams* (1759) 1 W. Bl. 94, 95; 96 E.R. 51, 52.

122 *Brandling* v. *Barrington* (1827) 6 B. & C. 467, 475; 108 E.R. 523, 526–7; *Miller* v. *Salamons* (1852) 21 L.J. (Ex.) 161, 197; *A.-G.* v. *Sillem* (1863) 2 H. & C. 431, 532; 159 E.R. 178, 223; *Swindell* v. *Bulkeley* (1886) 18 Q.B.D. 250, 255.

123 *Commonwealth* v. *Baume* (1905) 2 C.L.R. 405, 415–16.

124 *Ibid.*, 416. This point is an effective criticism of Lord Diplock's doctrine discussed at 31–42 above.

125 *Commonwealth* v. *Baume* (1905) 2 C.L.R. 405, 416.

126 E. Coke, *First Part of the Institutes of the Laws of England*, 19th ed., ed. by C. Butler, rev. by F. Hargrave and C. Butler (London: J. & W. Clarke *et. al.*, 1832), vol. I, 24b.

127 *Commonwealth* v. *Baume* (1905) 2 C.L.R. 405, 416.

128 *Nelson* v. *Nelson* (1995) 184 C.L.R. 538, 553–4.

Secondly, the doctrine survives under another name so far as it corresponds with modern theories of interpretation which are styled 'purposive'. C.K. Allen said:

> Plowden's grandiloquent principles crystallize merely into a general doctrine of liberal and intelligent interpretation, having the double aspect that a 'remedial' statute is to receive an 'equitable interpretation', while a penal statute, or a statute in derogation of the Common Law, is to be construed strictly.[129]

C.K. Allen's use of the word 'equitable' must be understood in a special sense. Plowden's doctrine does not appear to have been generated out of any specific equitable doctrines recognisable in the modern law. However, there are no doubt general conceptions of justice underlying both the modern principles of equity and the doctrine of statutory construction which Plowden advocated.

In construing a statute, the condition of the law at the time of enactment is a relevant matter. But it is, of course, wrong to rely unduly heavily on it – whether it be common law or equity, with whatever statutory elements are intermixed with either field. There is also a principle of legality. Legislation will not be interpreted as abrogating or contracting fundamental rights and freedoms in the absence of clear words. But there is not any equivalent presumption or principle that the common law (including equity) is not to be affected save by clear words, unless the part which may be affected creates a fundamental right or freedom. The position was probably different in earlier decades. Appeal is still made to it, but usually unsuccessfully. When the prohibition in section 52 of the Trade Practices Act 1974 (Cth) against misleading and deceptive conduct in trade or commerce, and the right to damages for breach of section 52 conferred by section 82, were introduced, attempts were made to read them down. It came to be understood that 'trade or commerce' was a broad expression and that section 52 created a norm of strict liability. The cry, however, went up: 'But you can't get damages for innocent misrepresentation!' That attempt to make sections 52 and 82 conform to a (not fully understood) equitable rule did not prevail.

129 Allen, *Law in the Making*, 7th ed., 453 (citation omitted). See also *Nelson* v. *Nelson* (1995) 184 C.L.R. 538, 553 (Deane and Gummow JJ.): 'cases within the terms of the statute but not within its mischief might be placed outside its operation'.

'Trusts' created by an enactment but not enforceable in equity

When the expression 'trust' is used in an enactment an issue of construction arises. It was explained by Lord Selborne L.C. in *Kinloch* v. *Secretary of State for India in Council.*[130] The word 'trust' can refer to 'higher matters, such as might take place between the Crown and public officers discharging, under the directions of the Crown, duties or functions belonging to the prerogative and to the authority of the Crown'.[131] Or the word 'trust' can refer to 'those matters which are the proper subjects for an equitable jurisdiction to administer'.[132] Trusts in the higher sense do not fall within equitable jurisdiction. The language creating them is to be read as if it created trust or fiduciary powers, not as actually doing so.[133] Some 'trusts' in the higher sense may not be enforceable at all. Some may be enforceable by administrative law remedies (including injunctions) employed for administrative law purposes, but they are not trusts in the equitable sense of that expression.[134]

In contrast to that state of affairs, sometimes legislation which does not contain express references to trusts is described as creating a 'statutory trust'. An example is legislation dealing with the winding up of companies, described as 'a statutory trust for the administration of the company's assets'.[135] But in truth the 'process is statutory and does not ... invite analogy with an administration suit: nor ... are the statutory duties

[130] (1882) 7 App. Cas. 619. See also *New South Wales* v. *Commonwealth (No. 3)* (1932) 46 C.L.R. 246, 260–1, 268; *Tito* v. *Waddell (No. 2)* [1977] Ch. 106, 211, 226–31; *Town Investments Ltd* v. *Department of the Environment* [1978] A.C. 359; *Aboriginal Development Commission* v. *Treka Aboriginal Arts and Crafts Ltd* [1984] 3 N.S.W.L.R. 502; *Registrar of the Accident Compensation Tribunal* v. *FCT* (1991) 178 C.L.R. 145, 162–3.

[131] *Kinloch* v. *Secretary of State for India in Council* (1882) 7 App. Cas. 619, 626.

[132] *Ibid.*, 625.

[133] *Equitable Life Assurance Society* v. *Hyman* [2002] 1 A.C. 408, 416. See P. Finn, 'Public Trusts, Public Fiduciaries' (2010) 38 Fed. L. Rev. 335, 339–40.

[134] *Bathurst City Council* v. *PWC Properties Pty Ltd* (1998) 195 C.L.R. 566, [65]; [1998] HCA 59. For the expressions 'trust' and 'trust property' in liquidation legislation, see *Ayerst (Inspector of Taxes)* v. *C & K (Construction) Ltd* [1976] A.C. 167; cf. *Commissioner of Taxation* v. *Linter Textiles Australia Ltd (in liq.)* (2005) 220 C.L.R. 592, [111]–[130]; [2005] HCA 20 (McHugh J.). For a discussion of the trusts on which a solicitor's trust account is held under the Legal Profession Act 2004 (Vic.), see *Legal Services Board* v. *Gillespie-Jones* (2013) 249 C.L.R. 493; [2013] HCA 35. For arguments that the latter construction mentioned in the text should be favoured, see Finn, 'Public Trusts, Public Fiduciaries'. See also *Re Lehman Brothers International (Europe) (a co.) (in admin.)* [2012] Bus. L.R. 667; [2012] UKSC 6 (pooling of client money).

[135] *Motor Terms Co. Pty Ltd* v. *Liberty Insurance Ltd* (1967) 116 C.L.R. 177, 190 (Taylor J.); see also 191.

and obligations of the liquidator to be explained by reference to the laws relating to trusts'.[136]

Equity construes general statutory words cautiously

Lord Denning M.R. was of the opinion that an enactment providing for an injunction to be granted where it was 'just and equitable' to do so was to be construed as not limited by prior rules.[137] That view has generally not been accepted: the general language is construed as not doing away with settled principles under which injunctions only lay to protect a legal or equitable right.[138]

Equity defies statute

Section 4 of the Statute of Frauds 1677[139] provided:

> [N]o action shall be brought ... to charge any person ... upon any Contract for Sale of Lands, Tenements or Hereditaments, or any Interest in or concerning them ... unless the Agreement upon which such Action shall be brought, or some Memorandum or Note thereof, shall be in Writing, and signed by the Party to be charged therewith, or some other Person thereunto by him lawfully authorized.

Yet in fact ever since it was enacted, actions have been brought to 'charge' persons upon contracts for the sale of land which were not in writing and of which there was no note or memorandum. They were brought on the ground that there had been 'part performance'. This exception is not mentioned in the statute. Even before 1677, there were instances where equity would not decree specific performance of a parol agreement unless it had been performed in part.[140] That proposition recognises one barrier to specific performance, to be overcome by part performance. It does not explain how and why it was that the new statutory barrier to specific performance – the need for writing or evidence in writing – could be

136 *Ibid.*, 179 (Barwick C.J.). 137 *Chief Constable of Kent* v. *V* [1983] Q.B. 34, 42.

138 *Australian Broadcasting Corp.* v. *Lenah Game Meats Pty Ltd* (2001) 208 C.L.R. 199, [59]–[60], [88], [89], [97]; [2001] HCA 63.

139 29 Car. II, c. 3.

140 See D.E.C. Yale (ed.), *Lord Nottingham's Chancery Cases, vol. I*, 73 Selden Society (London: Bernard Quaritch, 1957), cii–ciii n. 2, discussed in *Khoury* v. *Khouri* (2006) 66 N.S.W.L.R. 241, [74]; [2006] NSWCA 184. See generally J. Williams, *The Statute of Frauds Section Four in the Light of Its Judicial Interpretation* (Cambridge University Press, 1932), ch. VII.

overcome in that way. M.R.T. Macnair has pointed out that the prohibition in section 4 on bringing an 'action' did not in terms affect English bills for specific performance, which were not 'actions'. However, he points out that just after the statute there was significant litigation in Chancery on what constituted part performance and proceeds to examine why this was so.[141] The examination has been on foot for a long time.

The doctrine of part performance has had a disputed paternity at all times up to the present day. In *J.C. Williamson Ltd* v. *Lukey and Mulholland*,[142] Evatt J. said:

> The *Statute of Frauds* must not, it was claimed, be used as an instrument of fraud. The consequence was a substantial alteration of the *Statute of Frauds* itself which, as Lord *Blackburn* pointed out in *Maddison* v. *Alderson*,[143] was interpreted by [c]ourts of equity as if it contained a positive exception – 'or unless possession of the land shall be given and accepted'. The judicial gloss on the statute was regarded by him as an unjustified interpolation. Its justification was historical, not logical. Indeed, the speech of the Earl of *Selborne* in the same case, which puts forward the doctrine from the point of view of Courts of Equity in the most effective and plausible way, has running through it, I fancy, an undercurrent which admits the force of Lord *Blackburn's* criticism. 'In a suit founded on such part performance', said the Lord Chancellor,[144] 'the defendant is really "charged" upon the equities resulting from the acts done in execution of the contract, and not (within the meaning of the statute) upon the contract itself. If such equities were excluded, injustice of a kind which the Statute cannot be thought to have had in contemplation would follow' . . .
>
> None the less, there is no escape from the truth of the comment of *Brett* L.J. in *Britain* v. *Rossiter*,[145] that the cases in the Court of [C]hancery, applying the doctrine of part performance to suits concerning land, although the evidence required by the statute was lacking, were 'bold decisions on the words of the statute'.[146]

Historical explanations have been offered to explain the boldness. It has been suggested that Lord Chancellor Jeffreys, in developing the doctrine very soon after the Statute of Frauds, in *Butcher* v. *Stapely*,[147] may have been relying on private knowledge that those responsible for the Statute

[141] M.R.T. Macnair, *The Law of Proof in Early Modern Equity* (Berlin: Duncker and Humblot, 1999), 160–4.

[142] (1931) 45 C.L.R. 282. [143] (1883) 8 App. Cas. 467, 489. [144] *Ibid.*, 475.

[145] (1879) 11 Q.B.D. 123, 129.

[146] *J.C. Williamson Ltd* v. *Lukey and Mulholland* (1931) 45 C.L.R. 282, 308–9.

[147] (1685) 1 Vern. 363; 23 E.R. 524.

never intended it to apply where there was part performance.[148] This is reminiscent of the patriarchal age of great judges in the early fourteenth century, when there were giants on the earth. It was the age in which paladins like Hengham J. commanded counsel: 'Do not gloss the statute for we know better than you; we made it';[149] in which Brabazon C.J. informed counsel: 'We will advise with our companions who were at the making of the statute';[150] in which Shareshulle J. told counsel that Herle J. said that the strongest argument he knew against a submission which he, Shareshulle J., had put as counsel was that 'Hengham who made the statute read it another way';[151] and in which Bereford C.J. applied a bold construction to the statute *De Donis*[152] on the ground that Hengham, who had drafted it, 'through negligence ... omitted to insert express words to that effect in the statute'.[153] But the approach to statutory construction in the late seventeenth century may have approximated more to the looser medieval attitude than to modern approaches. Further, according to Pound:

> When *Butcher* v. *Stapely* was decided, the air was full of ideas of natural law, on a higher plane than any human legislation, and the courts of law were about to decide that the king, in particular cases and 'on necessary and urgent occasions', could in his discretion dispense with penal statutes.[154] If for good reasons James II might dispense with the statute of Charles II requiring public officers to take a test oath, Lord Jeffreys might well feel that James's chancellor, for good reasons, could dispense

[148] G.P. Costigan, 'The Date and Authorship of the Statute of Frauds' (1913) 26 Harv. L. Rev. 329, 342–6. Yale said that it was 'a matter of assumption . . . that the Statute did not apply where the contract been executed in part': Yale (ed.), *Lord Nottingham's Chancery Cases, vol. I*, ciii. Costigan said: 'The judges who framed the Statute of Frauds were so anxious to tie the hands of juries and so possessed by the idea that the statute would not apply *ex proprio vigore* to chancery cases that they neglected to be as explicit in the wording of the statute as they should have been': at 344–5.

[149] *Aumeye* v. *Anon.* (1305) Y.B. 33–5 Edw. I, 79, 83 (on the Statute of Westminster II, 1285, 13 Edw. I).

[150] *Bygot* v. *Ferrers* (1307) Y.B. 33–5 Edw. I, 577, 585.

[151] *Ros* v. *Graa* (1341) Y.B. 15 Edw. III, 388, 394. [152] 13 Edw. I c. 1 (1285).

[153] *Belyng* v. *Anon.* (1312) Y.B. 5 Edw. II, printed in W.C. Bolland (ed.), *Year Books of Edward II 1311–1312*, 31 Selden Society (London: Bernard Quaritch, 1915), 176, 177. Except for the quotation from *Belyng* v. *Anon.*, which is translated by Bolland, the Year Book translations are by Plucknett: T.F.T. Plucknett, *Statutes and Their Interpretation in the First Half of the Fourteenth Century* (Cambridge University Press, 1922), 50–2.

[154] *Godwin* v. *Hales* (1686) Comb. 21; 90 E.R. 318, also reported *sub. nom. Godden* v. *Hales* (1686) 2 Show. K.B. 475; 89 E.R. 1050.

> with another statute of Charles II, requiring contracts for the sale of land to be in writing.[155]

It has also been suggested that, since taking possession of the land is the typical act of part performance, and since such a change of possession took place in the classical common law conveyance, feoffment with livery of seisin, the courts felt able to ignore the new statutory need for writing. Like the previous suggestion, whether or not this is historically correct, it cannot justify the modern law.

Judge Cardozo justified the modern law by reasoning that the purpose of the writing required by the Statute of Frauds is to prove certain facts; if those facts can be inferred from acts of part performance, the requirement of writing becomes superfluous and need not be complied with. He said:

> The peril of perjury and error is latent in the spoken promise. Such, at least, is the warning of the statute, the estimate of policy that finds expression in its mandate. Equity, in assuming what is in substance a dispensing power, does not treat the statute as irrelevant, nor ignore the warning altogether. It declines to act on words, though the legal remedy is imperfect, unless the words are confirmed and illuminated by deeds. A power of dispensation, departing from the letter in supposed adherence to the spirit, involves an assumption of jurisdiction easily abused, and justified only within the limits imposed by history and precedent. The power is not exercised unless the policy of the law is saved.[156]

This sonorous explanation can scarcely survive the decision in *Steadman* v. *Steadman*[157] that the acts of part performance need refer only to some contract and need not refer to the particular words of the contract.

Then the question has been asked: 'Since a purchaser in possession can use the oral contract as a defence to an action of trespass by the vendor, why can the purchaser not use possession to avoid the writing requirement for all purposes?'[158] The answer is this: when the purchaser raises the contract as a defence the purchaser is not infringing the Statute of Frauds, for it applies only to actions brought on a contract – when the defendant is 'charged' upon a contract. The position when the Statute of

155 R. Pound, 'The Progress of the Law, 1918–1919: Equity (Concluded)' (1920) 33 Harv. L. Rev. 929, 941–2.

156 *Burns* v. *McCormick*, 233 N.Y. 230, 234–5; 135 N.E. 273, 274 (1922) (citation omitted).

157 [1976] A.C. 536.

158 E.D. Re, *Chafee and Re's Cases and Materials on Equity* (Brooklyn, N.Y.: Foundation Press, 1975), 683 n. 57.

Frauds is not infringed cannot be used by way of analogy to suggest what should happen when it is infringed.

The law of part performance does not survive in England.[159] The standard modern justification for the law of part performance in the jurisdictions in which it does survive is Lord Selborne's. He said that the Statute of Frauds can be ignored because it applies only where the defendant is charged upon a contract, and under the doctrine of part performance the defendant is not charged on a contract but on the equities arising from the acts of part performance.[160] This is coupled with the theory that the Statute of Frauds cannot be construed so as to permit it to be used as an instrument of fraud. But if that justification is sound, why need the acts of part performance refer to any contract? If the Statute of Frauds is not to be used as an engine of fraud, why is not any evidence admissible which reveals that fraud?

In other areas, equity can intervene against a party who has received property on certain terms not recorded in compliance with legislation. Here equity does not require part performance. But what does it require? Where the execution of a document which would have satisfied the legislation is prevented by the fraud of the defendant, the defendant will be prevented from relying on the legislation.[161] Further, '[t]he repudiation by any person of the terms upon which he has been entrusted with the legal title to property is a fraudulent use of another's confidence, and the Statute is not intended to cover fraud'.[162] Equity gives relief in relation to secret trusts, half-secret trusts and mutual wills. It has never been universally agreed why. One common justification rests on a point of construction: statutes designed to prevent fraud cannot themselves be construed as permitting their use as an engine of fraud. On that approach, which is sometimes applied somewhat heroically, equity is not disobeying the statute on its true construction. However, the doctrine does not mean 'that equity will relieve against a public statute of general policy in cases admitted to fall within it'.[163]

159 Section 40(2) of the Law of Property Act 1925 (UK), preserving the law of part performance, was repealed by the Law of Property (Miscellaneous Provisions) Act 1989 (UK).

160 *Maddison* v. *Alderson* (1883) 8 App. Cas. 467, 475.

161 *Wakeham* v. *Mackenzie* [1968] 1 W.L.R. 1175; *Last* v. *Rosenfeld* [1972] 2 N.S.W.L.R. 923, 927–34.

162 *Cadd* v. *Cadd* (1909) 9 C.L.R. 171, 187 (Isaacs J.), citing *In re Duke of Marlborough; Davis* v. *Whitehead* [1894] 2 Ch. 133 and *Rochefoucauld* v. *Boustead* [1897] 1 Ch. 196.

163 *Maddison* v. *Alderson* (1883) 8 App. Cas. 467, 474.

What the consequences of failure to comply with such a statute are is a question which has been said to depend on 'the policy of the law'. It has been said that that is something distinct from express or implied statutory prohibition, but it has also been said to depend on 'the scope and purpose of the particular statute'.[164] Ascertaining the scope and purpose of a statute depends on discovering the meaning of its language. The question is whether that language penalises conduct or renders contracts to carry out that conduct void as well.[165] At this point, the answer depends on how the statute is construed, not on some overriding equitable or common law doctrine permitting disobedience to the statute.

The other celebrated example of curial sidestepping of a statute concerned the Statute of Uses 1536 (Eng.).[166] Unlike the doctrine of part performance, the courts' approach to the Statute of Uses was not one of complete defiance. Rather, in addition, it exploited gaps and silences. The technicality and gradualness of the process by which a statute that had the function of terminating uses led to the modern law of trusts preclude examination of it here.[167]

But the normal and correct reaction of courts of equity to statutes is to comply with them, not defy them. Thus estoppel, whether its common law or its equitable aspects are relied on, cannot operate against a statute. If the executive has a power or duty to act under a statute, it cannot 'disable itself from, or hinder itself in', performing it by binding itself, whether by representation or promise, not to exercise the power or perform the duty, or only to exercise the power in a particular way.[168] The conclusion can be supported on higher grounds still. Article 1 of the Bill of Rights 1689 (Eng.) provided: 'That the pretended Power of Suspending of Laws or the Execution of Laws by Regall Authority without Consent of Parlyament is illegall.'[169]

[164] *Nelson* v. *Nelson* (1995) 184 C.L.R. 538, 552 (Deane and Gummow JJ.).

[165] *Equuscorp Pty Ltd* v. *Haxton* (2012) 246 C.L.R. 498, [124]–[125]; [2012] HCA 7.

[166] 27 Hen. VIII, c. 10 (1536).

[167] See generally A.W.B. Simpson, *A History of the Land Law*, 2nd ed. (Oxford: Clarendon Press, 1999), ch. VIII; S.F.C. Milsom, *Historical Foundations of the Common Law*, 2nd ed. (London: Butterworths, 1981), ch. 9; J. Getzler, 'Duty of Care', in P. Birks and A. Pretto (eds.), *Breach of Trust* (Oxford: Hart Publishing, 2002), 63–4.

[168] *A.-G. (NSW)* v. *Quin* (1990) 170 C.L.R. 1, 17 (Mason C.J.).

[169] 1 Will. & Mar., st. ii, c. 2 (1689); *Singh* v. *Minister for Immigration and Citizenship* (2011) 190 F.C.R. 552, [47]; [2011] FCAFC 27.

Conclusion

The problems raised by the interrelationship between statute and equity are soluble if each source of law is kept within its proper field. Even though much of equity strictly so-called consists of statute law, the adherence of statute and equity to their proper fields depends on the legislature and the judiciary each remaining within their proper fields. On that basis there can be harmonious operation. Underlying the expression 'proper field' are two ideas. On the one hand, equity must give way to statute if statute expressly or impliedly changes equity principles. Statutes must be construed, and the courts must give effect to their construction, however little they like the outcome: there is no room for an appeal to an 'equity of the statute' which distorts the meaning. But for the legislature's role to be given legitimate operation there must be reasonable clarity in the legislation it enacts. On the other hand, to the extent that statute does not explicitly or implicitly change equitable principles, they should be allowed to survive and develop without hindrance from any wide appeal to the policy of statutes or the public interest underlying them.

13

Equity and statute

A commentary

MARK LEEMING

Dyson Heydon's magisterial survey of statutory reactions to equity, and equitable reactions to statute, demonstrates by its wealth of examples the complexity of the interrelationship between equity and statute. The first half of his survey illustrates how statutes may codify or amend or overlap with existing equitable doctrine, and, more interestingly, how statutes may facilitate the creation of equitable doctrine, or may in terms adopt or defer to existing equitable doctrine. The second half deals with the converse question: the response of equity to statute. A recurring theme in the modern cases is the choice between applying or otherwise drawing upon statute by analogy, or else concluding that there is no legitimate room for development, and hence following the law. One important truth is clear immediately. There can be no simple unifying analysis: the range of statutory modes of drafting (contrast the terse command that positively invites judicial creativity with the comprehensive code) and the legislative purposes and values they implement, not to mention the range of equitable doctrines, stand in the way of any such attempt. But that does not mean that the interplay between statute and equity is without interest or importance; far from it.[1]

[1] For recent work on this topic, see N. Duxbury, *Elements of Legislation* (Cambridge University Press, 2013); S. Gageler, 'Common Law Statutes and Judicial Legislation: Statutory Interpretation as a Common Law Process' (2011) 37 M.U.L.R. 1; M. Leeming, 'Theories and Principles Underlying the Development of the Common Law: The Statutory Elephant in the Room' (2013) 36 U.N.S.W.L.J. 1002; G. Postema, 'Law's System: The Necessity of System in Common Law' [2014] N.Z. L. Rev. 69; R. Walker, 'Developing the Common Law: Haw Far is Too Far?' (2013) 37 M.U.L.R. 232, and for a particular instance (the incorporation of fiduciary and trust principles in the regulation of superannuation and financial planning), see M.S. Donald, 'Regulating for Fiduciary Qualities of Conduct' (2013) 7 J. Eq. 142, 152–66.

This commentary focuses upon a single example: the transplantation of unconscionability into statute. As Dyson Heydon points out, section 20(1) of the Australian Consumer Law provides that: 'a person must not, in trade or commerce, engage in conduct that is unconscionable, within the meaning of the unwritten law from time to time'. This is sufficient for present purposes.[2] The basal idea is that if the norm of 'unconscionability' is breached by a contract within the purview of the Act (a contract whereby work is performed, a retail lease, etc.), then wide and largely discretionary statutory remedies are available.

The language of section 20(1) makes four things plain. First, as Gleeson C.J. has said, the reference to the unwritten law confirms that the legal meaning is the legal term, not the colloquial expression; in everyday speech, 'unconscionable' may be 'merely an emphatic method of expressing disapproval of someone's behaviour, but its legal meaning is considerably more precise'.[3]

Secondly, section 20(1) makes applicable the conventional legal meaning unmodified by further legislative considerations. (It may be contrasted with the New South Wales statutory formulations in, say, section 62B of the Retail Leases Act 1994, where regard may be had to an open-ended list of factors,[4] producing the result that the statutory

[2] Statutory proscriptions against unconscionable conduct are, of course, more elaborate. Focusing on legislation applicable in New South Wales, there is section 88F of the Industrial Arbitration Act 1940 (NSW) and its successors, the 'unjust' contract provisions in the Contracts Review Act 1980 (NSW) (which is 'An Act with respect to the judicial review of certain contracts and the grant of relief in respect of harsh, oppressive, unconscionable or unjust contracts') and legislation based on it (such as the Retail Leases Act 1994 (NSW)), and the federal legislation formerly known as the Trade Practices Act 1974 (Cth), now the Competition and Consumer Act 2010 (Cth). Some of the legislation is framed upon contracts which are 'unjust' or 'unfair', but all expressly employ, directly or indirectly, the word 'unconscionable': for example, a contract whereby a person performs work in an industry is 'unfair' if it is 'harsh, unjust or unconscionable': Industrial Relations Act 1996 (NSW), ss. 105 and 106.

[3] *Australian Competition and Consumer Commission* v. *C.G. Berbatis Holdings Pty Ltd* (2003) 214 C.L.R. 51, [7]; [2003] HCA 18.

[4] Namely,

> (a) the relative strengths of the bargaining positions of the lessor and the lessee, and (b) whether, as a result of conduct engaged in by the lessor, the lessee was required to comply with conditions that were not reasonably necessary for the protection of the legitimate interests of the lessor, and (c) whether the lessee was able to understand any documents relating to the lease, and (d) whether any undue influence or pressure was exerted on, or any unfair tactics were used against, the lessee or a person acting on behalf of the lessee by the lessor or a person acting on behalf of the lessor in relation to the lease, and (e) the amount for which, and the circumstances

evaluative conclusion of unconscionability bears the same name as, but has different context to, its judge-made law counterpart. This gives rise to 'some different concept of unconscionability from that established under the general law':[5] a new statutory amalgam.)

Thirdly, because it is a *federal* statute, a plaintiff who invokes it may approach different courts (i.e. federal courts), and even if the claim is adjudicated by a State or Territory court, that court will be exercising federal jurisdiction. That in turn may give rise to a different choice of law analysis[6] and may even give rise to different avenues of appeal.[7]

Fourthly, section 20(1) recognises in terms that the legal meaning of 'unconscionability' is ambulatory ('from time to time'), and so is apt to rise and fall in light of developments in judge-made law. All words change meaning from time to time; the (apocryphal) praise of St Paul's Cathedral as 'awful, artificial and amusing' is an example.[8] Whatever the state of equitable doctrine be at the relevant time, it is picked up, federalised, and used to define a federal norm of conduct, contravention of which engages a power to award a range of statutory remedies which in terms go (considerably) beyond what is available at general law.[9]

---

under which, the lessee could have acquired an identical or equivalent lease from a person other than the lessor, and (f) the extent to which the lessor's conduct towards the lessee was consistent with the lessor's conduct in similar transactions between the lessor and other like lessees, and (g) the requirements of any applicable industry code, and (h) the requirements of any other industry code, if the lessee acted on the reasonable belief that the lessor would comply with that code, and (i) the extent to which the lessor unreasonably failed to disclose to the lessee: (i) any intended conduct of the lessor that might affect the interests of the lessee, and (ii) any risks to the lessee arising from the lessor's intended conduct (being risks that the lessor should have foreseen would not be apparent to the lessee), and (j) the extent to which the lessor was willing to negotiate the terms and conditions of any lease with the lessee, and (k) the extent to which the lessor and the lessee acted in good faith.

[5] *Canon Australia Pty Ltd* v. *Patton* (2007) 244 A.L.R. 759, [4]; [2007] NSWCA 246 (Basten J.A.).

[6] See *Blunden* v. *Commonwealth* (2003) 218 C.L.R. 330; [2003] HCA 73; *Agtrack (NT) Pty Ltd* v. *Hatfield* (2005) 223 C.L.R. 251, [8]; [2005] HCA 38; and *Sweedman* v. *Transport Accident Commission* (2006) 226 C.L.R. 362, [33]; [2006] HCA 8.

[7] See M. Leeming, *Authority to Decide* (Sydney: Federation Press, 2012), 85.

[8] By which was meant awe-inspiring, highly artistic and thought-provoking: see A. Scalia and B.A. Garner, *Reading Law: The Interpretation of Legal Texts* (St Paul, Minn.: Thomson/West, 2012), 78.

[9] How those remedies apply – whether by analogy with principles of judge-made law, or despite those principles – is a large question, not unrelated to, but not addressed by, this paper.

That is a lot of work for twenty-five words to do! It immediately emphasises something long familiar about the process of statutory construction: the legal meaning of a statute is impossible to ascertain without first understanding the legal context in which it was enacted. This is trite, and ancient. Sir Edward Coke said that '[t]o know what the common law was before the making of any statute . . . is the very lock and key to set open the windowes of the statute'.[10] Or, as Joel Prentiss Bishop put it in 1882:

> A new statutory provision, cast into a body of written and unwritten laws, is not altogether unlike a drop of coloring matter to a pail of water . . . In every case, [a statute] is a thread of woof woven into a warp which before existed. It is never to be contemplated as a thing alone, but always as a part of a harmonious whole . . . obviously no statute can be understood except by him who understands the prior law.[11]

Plainly enough, if section 20(1) were enacted in the United Kingdom, it would have a different operation, which would be different again from its operation in the United States of America. Some of the divergences between those three common law jurisdictions are readily appreciated. The statements of regret made by Sir Peter Millett (as his Lordship then was) and Lord Hobhouse tend to confirm that a narrower approach to unconscientious conduct obtains in England and Wales than in Australia:

> We have substituted an inappropriate bright line rule for a proper investigation of the facts and have failed the vulnerable in the process. The Australians are turning to the jurisdiction to relieve against harsh and unconscionable bargains as an alternative, and there is much merit in this approach.[12]

It is speculation, but one plausible reason for the relative Australian innovativeness may be the familiarity gained by exposure to statutory formulations and modifications of unconscionability, which have been present in State and federal legislation now for more than seven decades, coupled with the process of seeking coherence within the legal system.[13]

[10] E. Coke, *The Second Part of the Institutes of the Laws of England* (London: E. and R. Brooke, 1797), 307.

[11] J.P. Bishop, *Commentaries on the Written Laws and their Interpretation* (Boston, Mass.: Little Brown and Co., 1882), §§ 4–6.

[12] P. Millett, 'Equity's Place in the World of Commerce' (1998) 114 L.Q.R. 214, 220. See also *Royal Bank of Scotland plc* v. *Etridge (No. 2)* [2002] 2 A.C. 773, [115]; [2001] UKHL 44 (Lord Nicholls).

[13] Gerald Postema (following Jeremy Waldron) uses the language of 'systematicity' to describe this aspect (or something akin to this aspect) of a legal system: see Postema, 'Law's System: The Necessity of System in Common Law', 80–1.

Unconscionability is even more expansive in at least some States in the United States of America. Again, why that is so is deeply interesting, albeit insufficiently analysed; it is possible that further work might tend to enhance an understanding of why aspects of those two federal legal systems are in fact only deceptively similar. For present purposes, I wish to note only that the broad doctrine of unconscionability enunciated by the Supreme Court of California has prompted an interesting and illustrative conflict between equity and a statute which prima facie *expressly* deferred to it.

AT&T Mobility LLC v. *Concepcion*[14] concerned a federal law which makes agreements to arbitrate 'valid, irrevocable, and enforceable, save upon such grounds as exist at law or in equity for the revocation of any contract'.[15] One might think that that would preserve 'generally applicable contract defenses, such as fraud, duress, or unconscionability', and indeed the Supreme Court had so held.[16] However, in very large measure, contract defences, such as unconscionability, are the product of the judge-made law of the States, which differs from State to State. (It follows that the same federal law will have different practical operation throughout the same country.)[17]

The California Supreme Court ruled that a class action waiver in consumer contracts was, at least in many circumstances, per se unconscionable.[18] Accordingly, the question arose whether unconscionability in its broad Californian formulation was available under the federal statute to invalidate an arbitration agreement. Scalia J. for a majority in the United States Supreme Court held that the

[14] 131 S.Ct. 1740 (2011). [15] Federal Arbitration Act, 9 U.S.C. § 2.

[16] *Doctor's Associates Inc.* v. *Casarotto*, 517 U.S. 681, 687 (1996).

[17] Australian federal examples are rarer, but one is the selective 'roll-back' of federal corporations law pursuant to section 5F of the *Corporations Act* 2001 (Cth): see *Loo* v. *Director of Public Prosecutions* (2005) 15 V.R. 665; [2005] VSCA 161.

[18]

> [W]hen the waiver is found in a consumer contract of adhesion in a setting in which disputes between the contracting parties predictably involve small amounts of damages, and when it is alleged that the party with the superior bargaining power has carried out a scheme to deliberately cheat large numbers of consumers out of individually small sums of money, then . . . the waiver becomes in practice the exemption of the party 'from responsibility for [its] own fraud, or willful injury to the person or property of another.' Under these circumstances, such waivers are unconscionable under California law and should not be enforced.

(*Discover Bank* v. *Superior Court,* 113 P. 3d 1100, 1110 (2005) (citation omitted))

Californian doctrine of unconscionability 'interferes with fundamental attributes of arbitration and thus creates a scheme inconsistent with the [Federal Arbitration Act]'[19] and was for that reason pre-empted by federal law. That is to say, the very law which subjects itself to 'unconscionability' as formulated by State courts was held, by bare majority,[20] to displace 'unconscionability' in its Californian formulation.

It is not the burden of this chapter to defend or criticise the outcome. My point is that even where statute expressly defers to judge-made law, there may nonetheless continue to be cases where it overrides it. That reflects the normative complexity of the legal system, involving 'the interaction between the rules of law, principles of equity, requirements of statute and between legal, equitable and statutory remedies';[21] the interaction is even more complex than a superficial reading of Dyson Heydon's various categories might suggest.

Then there are statutes and statutes. One drafting approach is detailed and prescriptive, seen in (say) the Australian corporations and taxation regimes. That technique is common in modern Australian statutes. (It suffices to contrast the size of the annual statute books of five decades ago with today's.) But the complaint that that technique is doomed, without judicial interpretation, to catch all conduct intended to be caught is far from new. Neil Duxbury quotes Montaigne complaining about Justinian's edict against the publication of 'interpretations, or rather perversions, of the laws'[22] in the introduction to the *Digest*, as follows:

> For legislators to try 'to rein in the authority of the judges' by drafting statutes which seek to deal with every likely instantiation of a particular legal problem is futile, moreover, because '[t]he multiplicity of our human inventions will never attain to the diversity of our cases'.[23]

On the other hand, some important statutes, perhaps especially in the United States, are very concise. The Sherman Act may be the best known. However, the most extreme example is possibly the vast body of judge-made law stemming from section 10(b) of the Securities Exchange Act

[19] *AT&T Mobility LLC* v. *Concepcion*, 131 S.Ct. 1740, 1748 (2011).

[20] Breyer, Ginsburg, Sotomayor and Kagan JJ. dissented.

[21] *Bankstown City Council* v. *Alamdo Holdings Pty Ltd* (2005) 223 C.L.R. 660, [27]; [2005] HCA 46.

[22] *Alias autem legum interpretations, immo magis perversiones eos iactare non concedimus.*

[23] Duxbury, *Elements of Legislation*, 136, quoting M. de Montaigne, *The Complete Essays* (London: Penguin, [1580–95] 2003), 1208.

1934[24] and rule 10b–5 made under that section.[25] Most of the law regulating insider trading is judge-made law based on that sparse language, and the succeeding eight decades have seen the rise and fall of competing theories, based either on the idea that there is a breach of trust or fiduciary obligation by the trader or else a 'misappropriation' of information. Hence decisions such as *Chiarell* and *Dirks*,[26] holding that there was no contravention in the absence of (respectively) a breach of a relationship of trust and confidence owed to those with whom the employee traded, and trading for the employee's personal benefit. However, more recent decisions have relied on a 'misappropriation' theory.[27]

There is very substantial scope for developing judge-made law where the statutory language is sparse; indeed, in a real sense, such language reflects a legislative purpose that that should occur. It is striking that the uncompromising common law notions of 'device, scheme or artifice to defraud', 'untrue statement of a material fact' and 'engage in any act,

[24] 15 U.S.C. § 78a:

> It shall be unlawful for any person, directly or indirectly, by the use of any means or instrumentality of interstate commerce or of the mails, or of any facility of any national securities exchange …
>
> b. To use or employ, in connection with the purchase or sale of any security … any manipulative or deceptive device or contrivance in contravention of such rules and regulations as the Commission may prescribe as necessary or appropriate in the public interest or for the protection of investors.

[25] Rules and Regulations Promulgated under the Securities Exchange Act of 1934, § 240.10b–5:

It shall be unlawful for any person, directly or indirectly, by the use of any means or instrumentality of interstate commerce, or of the mails or of any facility of any national securities exchange,

(a) To employ any device, scheme, or artifice to defraud,
(b) To make any untrue statement of a material fact or to omit to state a material fact necessary in order to make the statements made, in the light of the circumstances under which they were made, not misleading, or
(c) To engage in any act, practice, or course of business which operates or would operate as a fraud or deceit upon any person, in connection with the purchase or sale of any security.

[26] *United States* v. *Chiarell*, 445 U.S. 222 (1980); *Dirks* v. *Securities and Exchange Commission*, 463 U.S. 646 (1983).

[27] See *Carpenter* v. *United States*, 484 U.S. 19 (1987) and *United States* v. *O'Hagan*, 521 U.S. 642 (1997), and see R. Baxt, A. Black and P. Hanrahan, *Securities and Financial Services Law*, 8th ed. (Chatswood, NSW: LexisNexis, 2012), 690–2.

practice or course of business which operates . . . as a fraud or deceit upon any person' in federal laws have given rise to a body of law based very largely on *equitable* notions: of liability based on breach of an employee's fiduciary duty to his or her employer, and breach of confidence. It might well be of interest to survey the extent to which sparse statutory language has been filled by equitable, as opposed to common law, principles of judge-made law.

Those considerations lead to a large question: is there anything special about the relationship between *equity* and statute, as opposed to other bodies of judge-made law, notably common law and statute? There is scant scope in this comment to address that in detail, but the following is offered. First, it is one thing to construe a statutory text, and quite another to read a court's reasons for judgment and extract principle from them. In part, this is the difference between the general and the particular:

> Case law usually sets out reasons for the solution of a problem in a particular way, while statutory provisions tend to stipulate how a problem is to be negotiated in general terms.[28]

Neil Duxbury reminds us that judicial opinions are almost always authorial (indeed, they are said to be 'written') and 'challeng[e] the reader to follow and assess reasoned arguments',[29] whereas statutes (which are invariably 'drafted') often comprise a series of definitions and commands, not necessarily in a sensible order.[30] Hence the force of the familiar (and often ignored) command that a court's reasons for judgment are not to be read as if they were a statute. That is *particularly* inappropriate in the case of equity. For example, a recurring theme in the equitable notion of unconscionability is the inability to circumscribe the circumstances in which it could be invoked. An illustration is Fullagar J.'s statement in *Blomley* v. *Ryan* that the circumstances 'are of great variety and can hardly be satisfactorily classified'[31] and, as Kitto J.'s dissent in the same case illustrates, the divergent views which may be held of a 'serious disadvantage' sufficiently evident to the stronger party that it is unconscientious to take advantage of it. In short, as Lord Walker has emphasised, equitable principle often requires a broad evaluative judgment after

[28] Duxbury, *Elements of Legislation*, 59. [29] *Ibid.*, 60.

[30] *Ibid.*, 59–60. I have referred elsewhere to 'the focus on ideas and analogies and themes in judge-made law [being] far more attractive than the relentless verbalism of statutes': Leeming, 'Theories and Principles Underlying the Development of the Common Law: The Statutory Elephant in the Room', 1003.

[31] (1956) 99 C.L.R. 362, 405.

careful scrutiny of the facts,[32] and the fact that the decision-maker has invariably been a judge (as opposed to a common law jury), capable of granting relief which is discretionary and which may be on terms, is something quite different from a common law rule. Those principles may nonetheless be transplanted into statute, but to do so is quite different from, say, amending a common law rule that contributory negligence is a complete defence.

Secondly, to return to statutory unconscionability in Australia, is a different approach to be taken when the supple language of equity is transplanted to a statute? Courts are accustomed to identifying necessary and sufficient elements within statutory formulations; does the same approach hold when statute incorporates an equitable principle? In New South Wales, Spigelman C.J. once sought to distinguish between what was unconscionable and what was merely unfair or unjust, and held, for some years quite influentially,[33] that 'unconscionability is a concept which requires a high level of moral obloquy'.[34] But more recently, courts have returned to the text of the statute, as opposed to explanatory glosses upon it:

> [T]o treat the word 'unconscionable' as having some larger meaning, derived from ordinary language, and then to seek to confine it by such concepts as high moral obloquy is to risk substituting for the statutory term language of no greater precision in an attempt to impose limits without which the [c]ourt may wander from well-trodden paths without clear criteria or guidance. That approach should not be adopted unless the statute clearly so requires.[35]

Finally, it is hard to think of a more influential statutory incorporation of equitable doctrine than the modern appeal, which reflects the rehearing in Chancery. Sir George Jessel M.R. explained in *Re St Nazaire Co.*[36] that

[32] See R. Walker, 'Equity and Human Rights', Chapter 20 of this volume.

[33] See for example *Body Bronze International Pty Ltd* v. *Fehcorp Pty Ltd* (2011) 34 V.R. 536, [90]–[91], [96]; [2011] VSCA 196; *Violet Homes Loans Pty Ltd* v. *Schmidt* (2013) 300 A.L.R. 770, [58]; [2013] VSCA 56; *Canon Australia Pty Ltd* v. *Patton* (2007) 244 A.L.R. 759, [41]–[43]; [2007] NSWCA 246; but cf. at [4].

[34] *A.-G. of NSW* v. *World Best Holdings Ltd* (2005) 63 N.S.W.L.R. 557, [121]; [2005] NSWCA 261.

[35] *Canon Australia Pty Ltd* v. *Patton* (2007) 244 A.L.R. 759, [4]; [2007] NSWCA 246. See also *Director of Consumer Affairs Victoria* v. *Scully* (2013) 303 A.L.R. 168, [45]; [2013] VSCA 292; *Australian Competition and Consumer Commission* v. *Lux Distributors Pty Ltd* [2013] A.T.P.R. 42-447, [41]; [2013] FCAFC 90; see the discussion by Sackville A.J.A. in *PT Ltd* v. *Spuds Surf Chatswood Pty Ltd* [2013] NSWCA 446, [99]–[106].

[36] (1879) 12 Ch. D. 88.

the right of rehearing was in the nature of an appeal and was transferred to the Court of Appeal, which thereafter applied that process to all proceedings, common law, equitable, ecclesiastical and admiralty.[37] As Thesiger L.J. said in the same case, 'nothing can be clearer than that there was nothing analogous to that in the Common Law Courts'.[38] Hence, as Dixon J. explained, 'the jurisdiction and the power of the new Court of Appeal were conferred upon it in terms derived from Chancery'.[39] That appellate jurisdiction has, more than most other things, affected the legal systems of the United Kingdom and Australia, creating the familiar coherent bodies of law which in large measure we take for granted in the twenty-first century.

[37] *Ibid.*, 98. [38] *Ibid.*, 101.

[39] *Victorian Stevedoring and General Contracting Co. Pty Ltd* v. *Dignan* (1931) 46 C.L.R. 73, 108–9. See also *Builders Licensing Board* v. *Sperway Constructions (Syd.) Pty Ltd* (1976) 135 C.L.R. 616, 619–20 (Mason J.), 625–8 (Jacobs J.).

14

The equity of the executive

Fairness in tax law in nineteenth-century England

CHANTAL STEBBINGS

Introduction

To a lawyer of the common law tradition, equity is immediately understood as that system of law aimed at mitigating the rigours of the common law, founded on its own distinct principles and coming into discrete existence from the sixteenth century. It developed in England when the original legal system failed to provide for the needs of society. Equity developed as a system of supplementary rules, doctrines and procedures to rectify the deficiencies of the common law and address the injustices that were caused by its inflexible application.[1] It developed not into a self-contained code but piecemeal and as a complement to the common law: primarily, though not solely, the common law of property. Although it was derived from the imperatives of conscience, it came to contain a body of settled doctrines and rules, developed by judges who were constitutionally empowered to do so, and administered in what in constitutional terms were courts of law. As such, equity became an integral and legitimate part of the English legal system. 'Equity', therefore, referred to both (1), in a technical sense, a body of law and (2), in a wider sense, the underlying purpose of that body of law: to achieve fairness. These traditional meanings of equity still pervade English law. Outside the realm of law, however, the term has a different and less specialised meaning, though one which includes the original essence of what will be referred to as 'legal equity'. It encompasses, essentially, notions of fairness, equality, impartiality and even-handed dealing.[2]

This work was supported by the Wellcome Trust [WT095723MA].

[1] F.W. Maitland, *Equity: A Course of Lectures*, ed. by A.H. Chaytor and W.J. Whittaker, rev. by J. Brunyate (Cambridge University Press, 1936), 1–22.

[2] G. Watt, *Equity Stirring* (Oxford: Hart Publishing, 2012), 36–45. This work reflects a growing interest in how other disciplines regard equity: A. Hudson, *Equity and Trusts*, 8th ed. (London: Routledge, 2015), 1309–13.

In tax law, singular in so many ways within the British legal system, the primary perception of the term equity was traditionally in its original, wider, non-technical sense. Of course, tax law and tax lawyers had to deal with equity in the legal sense – the equity associated with the Court of Chancery – when addressing such matters as the taxation of equitable interests and the tax position of trustees, but it was not legal equity which pervaded the consciousness of the legal regime of tax in its formative period.[3] The rhetoric of tax in the eighteenth and nineteenth centuries reveals constant references to the equity of specific taxes or taxation in general. And in this context, equity meant, above all, fairness, quite distinct from Chancery equity.

In the long nineteenth century, when the legal foundations of the modern British tax system were constructed and refined, the formal legal methods, whereby it was sought to achieve this kind of non-technical equity, were found to be incapable of ensuring comprehensive fairness. As a result there developed – coeval with the enactment of all tax legislation – a discrete body of informal rules emanating from the revenue departments of the executive aimed at achieving the fair treatment of taxpayers within the intense formalism of the legal system of tax.[4] This body of rules is called 'executive equity' for the purposes of this chapter. This raft of discretionary decisions as to the application or meaning of statutory charging provisions arrived at exclusively in order to make the tax system operate fairly, namely to create a consistency of treatment within a specific taxable group and to ensure there was no individual hardship, was part of a wide body of rules and guiding principles which was known as 'practice'. The development of most revenue 'practice' was not motivated by considerations of fairness, but pragmatically driven by urgent administrative necessity to implement the tax laws and make the tax system workable on a daily basis so as to raise the anticipated public revenue and thereby to ensure the revenue authorities fulfilled their statutory duties. While both facets of revenue practice reveal the nature of the interface between the tax executive and formal law, executive equity is of particular interest not only because it is rarely addressed as a discrete element in revenue practice but also because

[3] This perception has proved enduring. A tax lawyer asked to discuss equity would probably immediately think in terms of 'vertical equity' and 'horizontal equity' in tax (explained in the text following n. 18 below) rather than in terms of traditional legal equity: see A.C. Infanti, 'Tax ~~Equity~~' (2008) 55 Buff. L. Rev. 1191.

[4] Cf. legal equity: Hudson, *Equity and Trusts*, 8th ed., 1306–23.

ultimately – unlike revenue practice driven purely by administrative necessity – it was found to be legally unacceptable.[5]

In exploring the nature of executive equity, this chapter aims to see why and how in the nineteenth century these informal practices rapidly came to have significant authority within the legal system of tax and how, by the end of that century, they had acquired a status and authority within that system analogous to the status of legal equity in the sense that executive equity was regarded by the revenue authorities and the taxpaying public as of equal importance to formal law. The chapter examines the legal and bureaucratic conditions of the nineteenth century, as well as contemporary views of fairness in tax, to assess why executive equity was necessary and why it became of such importance and authority in tax that it gave rise to profound legal questions as to its legitimacy and control to be addressed by judges and legal scholars in the following century. The chapter concludes with an assessment of how the place of executive equity in the legal framework of tax in the nineteenth century promoted and exacerbated the isolation of tax law within the British legal system.

Fairness in tax

Fairness in tax, a notion which is informed by contemporary culture and values and accordingly differently conceived at different periods, has been of constant and immense importance to the law and administration of tax. Fairness – however it was conceived – is crucial because of the fiscal imperative of compliance. Taxes have never been popular, but by the early nineteenth century a balance had been achieved between people's dislike of paying taxes and people's appreciation that they owe an underlying public duty to do so. The balance was, however, somewhat fragile. Although taxpayers had no unambiguous right to a 'fair' tax, if they perceived a tax as unfair according to the model of a fair tax accepted at the time, then there existed the very real danger of non-compliance. Non-compliance – namely outright refusal to pay on a widespread scale, the articulation of popular resentment, or widespread evasion – endangered the yield. Yield was the sole measure of the success or failure of a tax. Yield depended on compliance; compliance depended on popular

[5] In *R (Wilkinson)* v. *Inland Revenue Commissioners* [2003] 1 W.L.R. 2683; [2003] EWCA Civ 814, aff'd [2005] 1 W.L.R. 1718; [2005] UKHL 30, it was held that the revenue authorities could not legitimately exercise their powers so as to grant extra-statutory concessions on the basis of 'general equity between men and women' ([2005] 1 W.L.R. 1718, [21] (Lord Hoffmann)).

acceptance of a tax; and popular acceptance depended on the perception of a tax as fair.[6]

The meaning of fairness in tax was, and remains, fluid. By the end of the eighteenth century in Britain, however, the malleable notion of fairness in tax had acquired certain stable features which it continued to exhibit, and which were widely understood, well into the twentieth century. It related to a number of facets of taxation: tax as an institution; the characteristics of taxes; the substance of taxes; and the administration of taxes. John Locke had maintained that the concept of taxation was morally justifiable, constituting a fair contribution to the expenses of managing the state and a key element in the social contract.[7] Below this highest conception of fairness in taxation existed a number of general principles of good taxation, developed by Adam Smith and other classical economists, including the view that taxes should be as light a burden on production as possible, that they should be easy and as cheap as possible to collect and that they should be certain and equal.[8] These were the underlying broad tenets of a good – and, implicitly, a fair – tax,[9] and although the notion of fairness in taxation was to change in other ways, these tenets became central to the theory of modern taxation. A greater degree of specificity in the concept of fairness was provided by another tier of canons of taxation which gave British taxation its particular legal character. They required taxes to be voluntary and necessary in substance, and, in their implementation, non-inquisitorial and administered by agencies outside central government. Taxes were voluntary[10] if they were submitted to as a matter of choice, for example by choosing not to purchase a commodity which was subject to tax. As to the question of necessity, direct taxes were understood to be such a potent instrument in

[6] The Poll Tax of the 1980s is an example of a tax which was perceived as unfair and was rejected by the taxpaying public.

[7] For Locke's theory of social contract, see J. Frecknall-Hughes, 'The Concept of Taxation and the Age of Enlightenment', in J. Tiley (ed.), *Studies in the History of Tax Law. Vol. 2* (Oxford: Hart Publishing, 2007), 261–3.

[8] A. Smith, *An Inquiry into the Nature and Causes of the Wealth of Nations*, ed. by R.H. Campbell, A.S. Skinner and W.B. Todd (Oxford: Clarendon Press, 1976), vol. ii, bk V, ch. 2, 825–8; J.S. Mill, *Principles of Political Economy*, 6th ed., People's Edition (London: Longmans, Green & Co., 1896), bk V, 483–5. See too H. Lloyd Reid, *The British Tax-Payers' Rights* (London: T. Fisher Unwin, 1898), 210.

[9] Notions of fairness pervaded contemporary debate on taxation: A. Herald, *The Income Tax in Utopia* (Letchworth: Garden City Press Ltd, 1917), 5.

[10] See the speech of Sir William Pulteney in the debate on the income tax in 1798, *Parliamentary History of England* (22 December 1798), vol. 34, cols. 134–5; see too W. Phillips, 'The Origin of Income Tax' [1967] B.T.R. 113.

the hands of the central government that they had to be required by an extraordinary national emergency. A tax was non-inquisitorial if it respected deeply held notions of privacy by ensuring its administration did not require physical encroachment on private property or the exposure of private financial affairs. Finally, if direct taxes were assessed and collected by the local representatives of the taxpayers themselves – persons unconnected with the central government and free from its control or influence – the taxpayer would be protected from illegal encroachment by the Crown.

Once the fact of taxation was accepted, in the late eighteenth and early nineteenth centuries the canons of taxation comprehensively addressed the question of fairness in a tax. Objections to new taxes or the reform of established ones almost invariably reflected the undermining of one of the specific canons. For example, the 'triple assessment' of 1798[11] was vehemently resisted: being based entirely on past expenditure, it broke the principle of voluntarism. That criticism was equally directed at the new income tax introduced the following year.[12] Fierce resistance met all new taxes that were perceived as inquisitorial and invasive. The window and house taxes of the eighteenth century were regarded as excessively intrusive since government officers were permitted to enter houses and gardens for the purpose of taxation, and the principal objection to the income tax in 1799 was its unequivocally inquisitorial nature.[13] The reintroduction of the income tax in 1842 in a time of peace was condemned for breaching the canon of necessity. Excise duties had always been resented due to their administration entirely by officers of the central government,[14] and when in the later years of the nineteenth century the principle of localism in the administration of income tax was

[11] Taxation Act 1798, 38 Geo. III c. 16.

[12] Duties on Income Act 1799, 39 Geo. III c. 13. For the history of income tax, see B.E.V. Sabine, *A History of Income Tax* (London: George Allen & Unwin Ltd, 1966); P. Harris, *Income Tax in Common Law Jurisdictions* Cambridge Tax Law Series (Cambridge University Press, 2006); B.E.V. Sabine, 'Great Budgets: I. Pitt's Budget of 1799' [1970] B.T.R. 201; Thirteenth Report of the Commissioners of Inland Revenue on the Duties under their Management, *HCPP* 1870 (C. 82) XX.193, 326–7.

[13] C. Stebbings, 'The Budget of 1798: Legislative Provision for Secrecy in Income Taxation' [1998] B.T.R. 651. But see too W. Phillips, 'The Real Objection to the Income Tax of 1799' [1967] B.T.R. 177.

[14] M.J. Braddick, 'Popular Politics and Public Policy: The Excise Riot at Smithfield in February 1647 and Its Aftermath' (1991) 34 *The Historical Journal* 597; S. Matthews, 'A Tax Riot in Tewkesbury in 1805' [2002] B.T.R. 437.

being undermined by the officials of the central government, the objections were intense.[15]

In the nineteenth century, however, the traditional canons for ensuring fairness diminished in importance. The requirements that direct taxes should be necessary and voluntary were breached, with taxes that were not required directly to meet a national emergency and that were compulsory – notably the income tax – becoming accepted, albeit reluctantly, as a regular part of the tax system. It was necessary to do so to meet the increasing demands of the Exchequer. The requirements that a tax should be non-inquisitorial and locally administered, though eroded, were more robust and enduring. The battle to retain them was fought in the context of the income tax until well into the twentieth century. As taxation came to affect a greater proportion of the public, other, latent, concepts of fairness in tax were revealed. These perceptions of fairness, which had always existed alongside the orthodox canons but had been obscured by them, focussed to a greater extent on the taxpayer rather than the tax. Essentially they demanded not an examination of the fairness of the tax as such, in terms of the tax base for example, but rather the fairness of the position of the individual taxpayer in relation to his fellow taxpayers. They were based on whether taxation in general and individual taxes in particular ensured the equal treatment of taxpayers in two senses. The first was that one group within a tax should not pay more than another in proportion.[16] This public understanding of fairness emerged strongly in the middle years of the nineteenth century, when it became understood that the income tax was practically, if not theoretically, permanent. The introduction of estate duty in 1894[17] raised new challenges and also demanded a re-evaluation of the notions of fairness beyond those inherent in the orthodox canons.

The second of these two emerging notions of fairness based on equality forms the subject of this chapter. It was that the treatment of taxpayers within a taxable group should be consistent, and therefore predictable, with no extraordinary individual hardship. This concern was not new. It became more acute as tax legislation increased in volume and complexity in the nineteenth century. It was a notion of fairness that had always been felt keenly by individual taxpayers. Other 'higher' notions of fairness, though certainly having a material effect on anyone subject to tax

[15] See, for example, C. Stebbings, 'A Local Tax Rebellion: Popular Perceptions of Income Tax Law in the Nineteenth Century' (2001) 22(2) J.L.H. 45.

[16] See A.G. Davies, *Render Unto Caesar?* (London: Elek Books, 1966), 79–90.

[17] Finance Act 1894.

when they were ignored, lacked the directness of the imposition, by law, of extraordinary hardship on an individual. Such hardship would emerge at the administration stage of a tax, namely at assessment and collection. That stage of the taxation process was always the most sensitive it was the stage at which individuals first felt the real impact of a tax. This 'lowest' notion of fairness – the avoidance of extraordinary individual hardship – ultimately gave rise to executive equity: a body of rules developed by the executive in order to ensure that the enacted law operated justly and fairly.

Achieving fairness

Once the fact of taxation was accepted in the late eighteenth and early nineteenth centuries, fairness in tax could take any of three meanings: adherence to the orthodox canons of taxation; the equalising of the burden of taxation on all taxpayers; and consistency of treatment of taxpayers to ensure no taxpayer should suffer extraordinary individual hardship through the imposition of tax. The first and second elements were achieved through the substance of the tax law.

The taxes of the late eighteenth and early nineteenth centuries adhered to at least some of the canons in their very nature as expressed in the legislation. Most of the new taxes of the period could be ascribed directly to the exigencies of war. The triple assessment of 1798 and William Pitt's income tax of 1799 were both unequivocally introduced to meet the financial demands of the war against France and were accordingly necessary. Similarly, in the eighteenth century the tax base was carefully chosen. Most taxes then were deliberately and ostentatiously imposed on luxuries which did not need to be purchased if the taxpayer wished to avoid the tax. These taxes, it was argued, were therefore voluntary. The assessed taxes were imposed on the keeping of servants and on the purchase of such commodities as horses, carriages, windows, wigs, clocks, silver, hair powder and so on.[18] Necessities such as bread, soap and candles were carefully avoided. The raft of stamp duties introduced in the late eighteenth century was similarly voluntary in nature. Nearly all the assessed taxes were by their nature non-inquisitorial in that they could be assessed by external viewing. When Henry Addington recast the income tax in 1803, he took great pains to ensure that its structure

[18] For a history of these taxes see S. Dowell, *A History of Taxation and Taxes in England* (London: Longmans, Green & Co., 1884), vol. iv.

avoided the accusation of inquisition. He introduced the schedular system of income taxation, which endured for some 200 years. This ensured that no one official would ever know the entire income of any given taxpayer. Finally, the law placed the administration of the land tax, assessed taxes and income tax in the hands of local lay tribunals to ensure that, ostensibly, these imposts were not administered by the central government.

In the same way, the equalising of the burden of taxation throughout the taxpaying sector of society was achieved through policy choices as to the form and balance of taxes and the design of particular taxes. Both policy choices were expressed in legislation. A survey of the tax code from the eighteenth century to the present day reveals that the British system moved from a system dominated by indirect taxation to a more balanced one comprising both direct and indirect taxation. Individual taxes were increasingly designed to achieve internal equality. So generally, regarding tax policy, fairness came to be considered in terms of 'horizontal equity'. According to this notion, people in similar circumstances should pay the same amount of tax. Fairness was also considered in terms of 'vertical equity', which demands that people in different circumstances should pay a different amount; specifically, it demands that wealthier individuals pay proportionately more tax than poorer ones. Horizontal equity, which was advocated by Adam Smith in the eighteenth century, was and remains uncontroversial. Vertical equity was less readily accepted. Graduation at the lower end of the income scale had always formed part of the income tax, but the new estate duty of 1894 included a clear and comprehensive principle of graduation, with a scale of rates of the tax depending on the value of the estate.[19] In 1910, after more than fifty years of debate, the same principle of graduation was introduced into the income tax through the medium of super-tax.[20] Throughout the formative era of British tax, therefore, the substantive statutory law of tax was cast broadly in accordance with prevailing notions of fairness.

The formal law of tax could not, however, ensure comprehensive fairness. It was not inherently unfair in that it did not purport to treat individuals within a defined group differently. But the very nature of tax legislation undermined the third expression of fairness: the consistent treatment of taxpayers within a taxable group with no extraordinary individual hardship. Tax legislation had already, by the late eighteenth century, developed a unique character which was largely due to its

[19] Finance Act 1894. [20] Finance (1909–10) Act 1910, s. 66.

constitutional underpinning. The Bill of Rights 1689 provided that a tax could only be imposed with parliamentary authority, namely with the consent of the taxpayer through his representatives.[21] That became the exclusive legal basis of the right to levy tax and the liability to pay. It followed from this cardinal rule that not only were all taxes to be imposed by statute but also that an individual could only be taxed through clear explicit words in the legislation and never by implication. Legislators accordingly attempted expressly to provide for as many situations as it was possible to foresee, either through lengthy detailed provisions or through a very wide charging clause, in order to ensure that all the taxpayers whom the legislature had intended to catch were indeed brought within the statutory language. Inevitably, Parliament could not envisage every situation where tax might become payable as a result of a statutory provision. Or a wide provision might have unforeseen consequences, and so there would arise cases where taxpayers fell within the letter of a taxing Act but not within its spirit. Indeed, legislators and judges admitted that taxing provisions often had 'monstrous'[22] results which Parliament could never have intended.[23]

The judges of the regular courts could not address this unfairness. The constitutional requirement of taxation only by clear words was reflected in the attitude of the judiciary to the interpretation of tax statutes. For the whole of the formative period of British tax, and beyond, in interpreting the tax legislation to establish its scope, the judges could not look for the intendment of a tax Act and had to adopt a strict literal approach to its interpretation.[24] They could have recourse only to the words of the enactment, giving them their literal and natural meaning to reveal the intention of Parliament.[25] That meant that the judges could not be driven by considerations of practicality or equity, and so could not introduce any flexibility into the tax code. If a taxpayer came within the clear words of a legislative provision imposing a tax, he was liable even though common sense, or indeed common humanity, might suggest that the legislature had no intention of bringing such an individual in those particular circumstances into charge. These were usually cases at the

[21] 1 Will. & M. sess. 2 c. 2, s. 4 (1689).

[22] *Bates* v. *Inland Revenue Commissioners* [1968] A.C. 483, 516 (Lord Upjohn).

[23] *Ibid.*, 504 (Lord Reid).

[24] *Partington* v. *A.-G.* (1869) L.R. 4 H.L. 100, 122 (Lord Cairns).

[25] See generally Mr Justice Vinelott, 'Interpretation of Fiscal Statutes' [1982] Stat. L.R. 78; D.W. Williams, 'Taxing Statutes are Taxing Statutes: The Interpretation of Revenue Legislation' (1978) 41 M.L.R. 404.

fringes of the code.[26] The consequences of a literal interpretation were ignored. The clear words of the statute could be neither enlarged nor restricted to include or exclude any special case, even where their strict application led to hardship, absurdity or revealed a clear anomaly.[27] The judges were not 'to be led away by the equities of any case'[28] and, as Lopes L.J. remarked in 1894, 'we have nothing to do with whether the law may press hardly in certain cases; what we have to do is to administer the law as we find it'.[29] The judicial view was most famously expressed by Rowlatt J. in 1921 when he observed that 'there is no equity about a tax'.[30] Only where the words were ambiguous and had several meanings could nineteenth-century judges legitimately avoid a patent absurdity.[31] In tax legislation, therefore, neither the old common law doctrine of the equity of the statute nor its modern form of purposive statutory interpretation, whereby a statute was recognised as comprising both its letter and its 'sense',[32] had any role to play. Whereas judges could normally correct unacceptable legislative rigour or address unforeseen situations, and call on notions of justice and fairness to go beyond the words of a statute, the strictest and most intense formalism surrounded tax statutes: words were everything.

The nature of tax legislation led to further unfairness. As a result of its underlying constitutional requirements, tax statutes were traditionally among the most complex, and certainly the longest, known to English law.[33] And in the nineteenth century they became progressively more detailed and extensive as legislative adjustments were regularly made to close loopholes identified in earlier enactments, the income tax being the prime example. A code of such intricacy and volume inevitably led later draftsmen to adopt short cuts which added to its complexity and incoherence. Incorporation by reference, whereby an Act provided that it was to be read along with a series of other statutes as far as they were

[26] A. Johnston, *The Inland Revenue* (London: George Allen & Unwin Ltd, 1965), 68.

[27] See, for example, *Farr* v. *Price* (1800) 1 East 55; 102 E.R. 22.

[28] *R* v. *Winstanley* (1831) 1 C. & J. 434, 440; 148 E.R. 1492, 1495 (Lord Wynford).

[29] *Grainger and Son* v. *Gough* (1894) 3 T.C. 311, 321 (Lopes L.J.). (The corresponding, slightly differently worded, passage in the Law Reports is [1895] 1 Q.B. 71, 82; rev'd without affecting this point [1896] A.C. 325.) But see the modification of the strictness of the rule in *Colquhoun* v. *Brooks* (1889) 14 App. Cas. 493.

[30] *Cape Brandy Syndicate* v. *Inland Revenue Commissioners* [1921] 1 K.B. 64, 71.

[31] *A.-G.* v. *Hallett* (1857) 2 H. & N. 368, 375; 157 E.R. 152, 155 (Pollock C.B.).

[32] See J.D. Heydon, 'Equity and Statute', Chapter 12 of this volume, text to nn. 116–30.

[33] G.S.A. Wheatcroft, 'The Present State of the Tax Statute Law' [1968] B.T.R. 377; J. Clark, 'Statutory Drafting' [1980] B.T.R. 326.

consistent, was a common practice. The use of standard forms across the taxes was usual. Loose wording and lack of definition were equally typical features of tax legislation. These drafting practices resulted in provisions or combinations of provisions having unforeseen consequences. Loose drafting, in particular, led to ambiguous and uncertain provisions. This resulted in individuals or groups of individuals being brought into charge when, again, it appeared absurd or unjust to do so.

Instances of such unfairness are found throughout the tax regime of the nineteenth century. The legislative framework struggled to keep up with the astonishing pace of social and economic change which characterised that period in Britain's history. Nineteenth-century tax legislation, almost without exception, was antiquated, inconsistent, illogical, incoherent, complex and obscure. Stamp duties, excise duties, the land tax, assessed taxes and even the income tax were all essentially of an eighteenth-century character in their underlying structures and processes, and they suffered the deficiencies of all tax legislation.

Since it was the nature of tax legislation which gave rise to unfairness and individual hardship, the taxes that best reveal revenue practices specifically conceived to ensure fairness are those older taxes which remained unreformed during the dynamic tax developments which marked the nineteenth century. These were relatively few. Most of the taxes introduced in the eighteenth century were at least partially reformed during the nineteenth, but a striking example of a tax that was left virtually untouched in terms of reforming legislation was the medicine stamp duty. As a result, it was rife with antiquated and anomalous provisions; it reflected a lack of the fiscal sophistication that was to characterise later taxes; and it suffered the problems of being based on a species of tax which was itself already a century old and initially conceived with a very different tax base. This gave rise to widespread injustices and hardships on an individual basis, and as a result the tax became one dominated by revenue practice to an extraordinary degree.

As such, the medicine stamp duty provides a revealing model for the examination of the executive equity which pervaded the whole tax system. This was one of the many stamp duties on commodities – in this case, proprietary medicines – introduced to raise money in a time of severe financial exigencies in 1783.[34] Being of minor fiscal importance, it

[34] Stamp Duties Act 1783, 23 Geo. III c. 62. The tax was revised two years later to adopt its modern form (Medicine Duties Act 1785, 25 Geo. III c. 79) and re-enacted in 1812 (Medicines Stamp Act 1812, 52 Geo. III c. 150). The 1812 Act remained in force and almost entirely unreformed until the abolition of the tax in 1941.

was left almost entirely unreformed for the whole of its 160-year history. This, and the complexity of the statutory provisions, which resulted from the considerable challenges of definition in this field of activity, gave rise to unacceptable hardship or injustice where the legislation was to be strictly applied. The spirit of the legislation was to impose a duty at the point of sale on what were popularly called quack medicines, which were sold by unqualified and unscrupulous individuals to the detriment of the public good. However, the comprehensive letter of the legislation caught many products which were not medicines at all in the usual sense of the term, as well as some products that were regular medicines sold by qualified and responsible practitioners. The legislation also caused individual injustice and hardship among the body of sellers of proprietary medicines at which the Act was undeniably directed, with some individuals being liable, others not, for no apparently sound principle. The medicine stamp duty constitutes an extreme example of a tax that, applied strictly in accordance with constitutional norms, gave rise to widespread unfairness to the public and to the pharmaceutical profession.

The practice of the executive

The British constitution thus required any charge to tax to be imposed predictably, rigorously and by explicit legislative provision; no element of the taxing provision was to be left to implication. Flexibility, discretion, justice, intendment, conscience, equality: all these qualities that reflected the essential and original ethos of legal equity were the antithesis of the requirements of tax law. With their pragmatic appreciation that taxation is consensual and that compliance is crucial to the success of any tax, the revenue authorities understood that individual instances of unfairness had to be addressed as a matter of urgency in order to ensure the tax in question was acceptable to the wider public. The amendment of the substantive law by parliamentary process to address unfairness at the margins of the legislative code was then, as now, impracticable where perhaps only a very few taxpayers were affected or the difficulty in expressing the case of unfairness insuperable. And with the judiciary constrained primarily by constitutional imperatives, the only way that the unfairness caused by the special nature of tax legislation could be cured was through the modification of its practical implementation. This matter was the responsibility of the revenue departments of the executive. These were the organs of the central government charged with the administration of the different taxes. In the nineteenth century, they consisted of the various boards:[35] the boards of excise, customs, stamps and taxes. The various boards existed separately, at first, and subsequently underwent a variety of mergers culminating in 1849 in the creation of the Board of Inland Revenue, which held charge of the excise, stamps and taxes for the rest of the nineteenth century.[36] During this period, the fiscal demands of the central government grew in the new economic conditions of industrial and commercial transformation. As this was reflected in taxation of increasing scope and sophistication, the revenue authorities themselves became among the most powerful and influential of government departments, a development aided by their striking degree of independence and autonomy.[37] Fairness or equity in tax was thus achieved neither through parliament nor the courts. It was achieved in large measure by the revenue authorities of the executive who took it upon themselves to mitigate the strictness of the legislation where it worked unacceptable hardship. Only they could 'temper the wind to the shorn lamb'.[38] So, just as the judges in the regular courts recognised the need to give expression to the equity of statutes in other spheres and did so by conceiving the intention of the legislature, so the revenue authorities of central government stepped in to fill the judicial lacunae in tax legislation. When these officers of the executive intervened to modify the law, they drew on the equitable tradition, making their decisions on the basis of fairness,[39] as the term was conceived in relation to tax.

[35] See generally, J.H. Craig, *A History of Red Tape* (London: Macdonald & Evans Ltd, 1955), ch. 9.

[36] Inland Revenue Board Act 1849, 12 & 13 Vict. c. 1; see generally L.W. Griffith, *A Hundred Years: The Board of Inland Revenue 1849–1949* (London: Somerset House, 1949), 2–6. The excise was removed from the Board of Inland Revenue in 1909 and transferred to a Board of Customs and Excise.

[37] The members of the boards were appointed by the Crown: Johnston, *The Inland Revenue*, 21. See the Twentieth Report of the Commissioners of Inquiry (Excise Establishment), *HCPP* 1836 (22), XXVI.179, 303.

[38] M. Nolan, 'The Unsatisfactory State of Current Tax Law' [1981] Stat. L.R. 148, 150. On the exercise of discretion in revenue administration, see D.W. Williams, *A Mere Matter of Machinery* (Unpublished LL.M. thesis, University of Wales, 1975), 54–97. The shepherding impulse to temper the wind to the shorn lamb may be seen at work in cases of 'legal equity': for example, *Pennington* v. *Waine* [2002] 1 W.L.R. 2075, [54], [59]; [2002] EWCA Civ 227.

[39] A movement seen more generally in the developing administrative state: see H.E. Smith, 'Equity and Administrative Behaviour', Chapter 18 of this volume.

The principal means whereby the revenue authorities introduced a measure of flexibility into the tax code, in the interests of fairness, was where they ignored a statutory provision entirely or applied a beneficial administrative interpretation (or re-interpretation) of a clear statutory provision whose ordinary meaning would have brought the individual into the charge to tax. These were not instances of ambiguous or uncertain provisions. They were cases where an individual was clearly within the meaning of the statutory provision and accordingly liable to tax, or else excluded from a provision of tax relief, but where the revenue authorities took the view that to apply the law – either strictly or indeed at all – would cause unacceptable hardship. In such cases tax was legally payable, but the revenue authorities took it upon themselves to waive the payment.

The medicine stamp duty provides many examples. For instance, certain 'medicines' were undoubtedly within the charge to tax when sold, the statute clearly saying so. And yet the revenue authorities refused to tax them because to do so would be unfair. It was thus revenue practice not to tax products which in their view were not medicines at all. The authorities accordingly allowed peppermint and ginger lozenges, which were widely consumed in the nineteenth century and were undoubtedly within the letter of the legislation, to be sold free of duty. The authorities' view was that the lozenges were confectionary and not medicines, and so not within the spirit of the legislation.[40] Other articles whose sale was strictly within the charge, but to which the same revenue practice was applied, were the toiletries sold by hairdressers and perfumers.[41] Similarly, some perfumes and preparations, such as Eau de Cologne and Arquebusade Water, were expressly within the charge to tax. However, the revenue authorities decided not to tax them because, where customs duty had already been paid on perfumed spirits, it would have been unfair to tax them a second time. And again, the revenue authorities were mindful of the injustice of double taxation when they waived the payment of the medicine stamp duty on some beverages containing medicinal drugs, such as dandelion coffee, if the excise duty

[40] W. Chamberlaine, *History of the Proceedings of the Committee appointed by the General Meeting of Apothecaries, Chemists, and Druggists, in London, for the Purpose of obtaining Relief from the Hardships imposed on the dealers in Medicine, by certain Clauses and Provisions contained in the new Medicine Act, passed June 3, 1802, etc.* (London: Highley, 1804), 31–2. Lozenges were eventually removed from the charge by the Stamp Act 1815, 55 Geo. III c. 184, s. 154.

[41] (1848) 8 *Pharmaceutical Journal* (1st series) 155.

on coffee substitutes was also payable.[42] Another concession of the revenue authorities was to permit the breaking up of bulk packages of medicines (on which the duty had already been paid) and the selling of the contents in penny twists of paper. Although they could have insisted on the payment of the tax on the sale of the penny twists, they did not do so on two grounds: (1) that it would be unjust for the tax to be paid twice, and (2) that, as the duty strictly payable on the penny twists would be more than double the price of the medicine, to insist on the further tax would be to treat poorer customers unfairly. Revenue practice in this tax also shows that commercial fairness was equally valued. The authorities introduced a concession for foreign medicines, which were subject to the medicine stamp duty, when they were sold by a British wholesaler to a retail chemist for the purpose of making up prescriptions. The revenue authorities would not press for the tax in such cases, the reason for this so-called dispensing concession being to put British manufacturers on the same commercial footing as foreign manufacturers.[43] Similarly, the Board felt it was unjust to deny the 'known, admitted and approved remedies' exemption to limited companies where a qualified chemist was employed, though the legislation forbade it.[44]

The medicine stamp duty was an extreme example, but newer and quite different taxes equally needed their hard effects to be mitigated by the revenue authorities. For example, the authorities moderated the inequitable effect of a provision in the Succession Duty Act 1853 whereby the rate of tax was determined according to the chronology of succession rather than merit.[45] Succession duty provided another important instance of remission after the death in 1894 of Alexander III, the Emperor of Russia, though not a case of individual hardship in the conventional sense.[46] The revenue authorities, though reluctant at first, ultimately waived their right to collect death duties on certain bonds the emperor held in the Bank of England. There was no doubt that the property was legally liable. But on the grounds of 'international comity',

[42] Board of Customs and Excise and Predecessor: Private Office Papers, *The Medicine Stamp Duties 1783–1936*, The National Archives CUST 118/366, 37.

[43] *Ibid.*, 67–8; E.N. Alpe, *Handy Book of Medicine Stamp Duty* (London: Offices of 'The Chemist and Druggist', 1888), 110.

[44] Board of Customs and Excise and Predecessor, *The Medicine Stamp Duties 1783–1936*, 83, 89–90.

[45] 16 & 17 Vict. c. 51, s. 11; Second Report of the Commissioners of Inland Revenue, *HCPP* 1857–8 (2387), XXV.477, 502–3.

[46] J. Booth, *The Inland Revenue . . . Saint or Sinner?* (Lymington: Coracle Publishing, 2002), 167–75.

namely the treating of 'the foreigner and native as entitled to a like measure of justice',[47] special privileges were accorded to the emperor's estate and payment of the tax was not pressed for.[48] There was some precedent for this, as there had developed a practice of permitting the remission of certain customs duties for foreign ambassadors.[49]

These specific examples were just a few of dozens of remissions granted by the revenue authorities on the grounds of undue hardship throughout the nineteenth century across the tax regime. The remissions continued in force into the twentieth century, and increased in number.[50] At the same time, their purpose came more often to be expressly articulated. The remissions were designed to achieve fairness in the tax system by 'softening the rigour of the law'[51] – an invocation of Lord Ellesmere's famous pronouncement on legal equity, if ever there was one[52] – to work 'great justice between the Crown and the subject'.[53] They constituted 'an act of administrative mercy',[54] 'a discretionary forbearance',[55]

> a relaxation ... to deal with what are, on the whole, minor or transitory anomalies under the legislation and to meet cases of hardship at the margins of the code where a statutory remedy would be difficult to devise or would run to a length out of proportion to the intrinsic importance of the matter.[56]

In short, they were developed and maintained to ensure that the tax legislation operated fairly, and the historical evidence supports the view that they succeeded in doing so.

Remissions, or extra-statutory concessions, as they came to be known, were not the only instance where the revenue authorities made discretionary decisions on the grounds of fairness. They did likewise where they assigned a 'fair' meaning to a provision in the tax legislation. Where a provision was uncertain or ambiguous, the task of assigning a meaning

[47] Second Report and Minutes of Evidence before Committee of Public Accounts, *HCPP* 1897 (196), VIII.5, 42 q. 420.

[48] *Ibid.*, 10, 38–43 qq. 358–432.

[49] *Ibid.*, 42–3 qq. 423–6.

[50] See generally Johnston, *The Inland Revenue*, 67–8; D.W. Williams, 'Extra Statutory Concessions' [1979] B.T.R. 137.

[51] H.W.R. Wade, *Constitutional Fundamentals* (London: Stevens & Sons, 1980), 57.

[52] *Earl of Oxford's Case* (1615) 1 Ch. Rep. 1; 21 E.R. 485; and see D. Ibbetson, '*The Earl of Oxford's Case* (1615)', in C. Mitchell and P. Mitchell (eds.), *Landmark Cases in Equity* (Oxford: Hart Publishing, 2012), ch. 1.

[53] *Korner* v. *Inland Revenue Commissioners* [1969] 1 W.L.R. 554, 558 (Lord Upjohn).

[54] Wade, *Constitutional Fundamentals*, 57.

[55] (1848) 8 *Pharmaceutical Journal* (1st series) 212.

[56] www.hmrc.gov.uk/specialist/esc.pdf.

to it inevitably fell on the executive.[57] So numerous were such provisions that a great deal of the time of revenue officials was spent on this task. In most cases they had to do so simply to ensure the provision could be implemented at all. But in some instances the evidence reveals that the authorities actively preferred an interpretation because it would be perceived as fair and did not catch those cases on the fringe that it had never been intended to catch. Yet again, the medicine stamp duty provides clear examples. The tax applied to products which relieved 'ailments'. The authorities regarded it as unfair to include within this term conditions such as baldness, dandruff, freckles or chapped lips because to treat these conditions as ailments would catch too many products which came outside the spirit of the Act.[58] The charge applied only to 'preparations', which term the revenue authorities interpreted restrictively to require some element of active processing. For example, unprepared herbs were thus allowed to escape the charge.[59] The charge also applied to articles that were 'recommended', an immensely broad term encompassing advertisement and dosage instructions. Through the interpretation of this broad term, the revenue authorities were able to include or exclude medicines as they saw fit. Such examples are found in their hundreds and pervade the entire tax code: from the Excise Board interpreting the provision imposing a tax on every horse running for any kind of prize 'in its spirit rather than in its letter' so as to exempt all hunters and horses running for farmers' and yeomanry plates,[60] to a liberal interpretation of the income tax provisions for computing trading profits so as to permit deduction for wear and tear of machinery and plant.[61] By the practical expedients of granting remissions and applying beneficial administrative interpretations and re-interpretation to statutory provisions of uncertain meaning, the revenue authorities ensured that the complex, antiquated and rigid legislative framework of the tax code operated as fairly as possible.

[57] See M.S. Amos, 'The Interpretation of Statutes' [1934] C.L.J. 163.

[58] Board of Customs and Excise and Predecessor, *The Medicine Stamp Duties 1783–1936*, 48.

[59] TNA IR 83/61.

[60] Thirteenth Report of the Commissioners of Inland Revenue on the Duties under their Management, *HCPP* 1870 (C.82), XX.193, 255.

[61] Twentieth Report of the Commissioners of Her Majesty's Inland Revenue on the Inland Revenue, *HCPP* 1878 (C.1896), XXVI.593, 646–8; Twenty-first Report of the Commissioners of Her Majesty's Inland Revenue on the Inland Revenue, *HCPP* 1878 (C.2158), XXVI.717, 780; Income Tax Committee, *Appendix to the Report of the Departmental Committee on Income Tax, HCPP* 1905 (Cd. 2576), XLIV.245, 258–9.

Executive equity

Revenue practice, including executive equity, rapidly became a permanent feature of the tax system of immense importance. As early as the eighteenth century, it was universally recognised that an understanding of tax law was incomplete – indeed impossible – without a familiarity with tax practice. Though supplementary in nature, and engrafted upon the formal statutory code, it was perceived as an integral part of tax law. Commentaries of all kinds, popular and expert, on taxation matters rarely drew any distinction between the statutory provisions and the revenue practices adopted in their implementation. Indeed, it was sometimes difficult to tell in the nineteenth century what was law and what was practice. The inference was that revenue practice was nothing less than quasi-law in terms of substance and authority.[62] A number of factors were responsible for this growing status.

Because revenue practices were caused primarily by the nature of nineteenth-century tax legislation, they were copious. They began to develop from the moment a tax statute was enacted and, although, as far as it can be judged, practices that developed purely to ensure fairness formed only a small proportion of the whole, a huge body of revenue practice addressed the daily implementation of tax law for the purely practical end of effective implementation. Revenue practice was based on unsurpassed technical expertise and the authority of experience. Indeed, for most of the nineteenth century, until the emergence of a small tax bar, tax officials were the only experts in the field. Although many members of the revenue boards were appointed from other areas of public life, a proportion rose through the revenue service where over the years as revenue officers they had acquired, through competitive examination and special training, a profound and minute knowledge of tax law and an unrivalled experience in the practice of the revenue.[63] And all the boards and their officers had the support of their own specialist legal staff.[64] Not only did this expert knowledge give their numerous pronouncements authority, it gave the development of a body of quasi-law a measure of

62 R.E. Megarry famously described extra-statutory concessions, and indeed practice notes, as prime examples of 'quasi-legislation': R.E. Megarry, 'Administrative Quasi-Legislation' (1944) 60 L.Q.R. 125.

63 For the recruitment, training and promotion of surveyors, see D. Williams, 'Masters of All They Surveyed: 1900–14'; [2005] B.T.R. 142, 144–7.

64 See Minutes of Evidence before the Select Committee on Inland Revenue and Customs Establishments, *HCPP* 1862 (370), XII.131, 245 q. 2200.

inevitability and momentum and promoted the development of an executive jurisprudence.

The revenue authorities undoubtedly intended their interpretations, remissions and decisions to be acted upon and rigorously adhered to by their officers, and they achieved this. From the eighteenth century onwards, the decisions were included in the circulars, regulations, orders and instructions that the central boards in London constantly disseminated to their officers all over the country.[65] These instructions on how the taxes were to be administered were conclusive as far as the officers of the boards were concerned. The officers had to follow the central boards' instructions and implement them to the letter; indeed, to the same degree as Acts of Parliament and judicial decisions.[66] After all, the officers were subject to very close and rigorous control by the revenue boards. As a result, revenue practice had immense de facto legal force. As far as taxpayers were concerned, it was binding on them, and would remain so until it was declared illegal by the judges of the regular courts. It was a courageous and wealthy individual indeed who would challenge the revenue boards' interpretations of the law in the courts. This, and restricted rights of appeal in many tax matters, made any judicial engagement with tax law rare in the nineteenth century. It resulted in the revenue boards' enjoying a monopoly on the initial interpretation of tax legislation and ensured the relative endurance of their decisions.

Remissions and interpretations made on the grounds of fairness were taken on the basis of each individual case; a record of systematic practice in awarding remissions and offering beneficial administrative interpretations (and re-interpretations) of revenue statutes is absent. Nevertheless, there is clear evidence that not only was there a widespread reluctance to disturb established practices on the grounds of efficiency[67] but also that they had the force of precedent within the service. This was so even where a practice was subsequently found to be unsound. A famous exemption to the medicine stamp duty, for example, was that for 'known, admitted

[65] See for example, Precedents and Instructions, TNA IR 78/289 (1903); TNA IR 78/60.

[66] Board of Inland Revenue, *Instructions to Surveyors on that part of their Duty which relates to Taxes* (London: HMSO, 1855), 5; Inland Revenue Board Act 1849, 12 & 13 Vict. c. 1, s. 3; D. Williams, 'Surveying Taxes, 1900–14' [2005] B.T.R. 222.

[67] See for example the reluctance in 1905 to disturb the basis of assessment for Sch. D on the grounds that it 'will cause such a disturbance in the Income Tax practice which has grown up during the sixty years the tax has been in existence . . .': Income Tax Committee, *Appendix to the Report of the Departmental Committee on Income Tax, HCPP* (1905) (Cd. 2576), XLIV.245, 268.

and approved remedies' sold by a qualified person.[68] Having in practice disregarded this statutory provision for the whole of the nineteenth century as being merely declaratory in nature,[69] the revenue authorities were forced to recognise its legal force as a result of a judicial decision in 1903 to the effect that it was a material exemption.[70] Motivated by pragmatic imperatives rather than any ideals of fairness, the revenue authorities interpreted this decision in an extraordinary way, effectively disregarding it and giving the exemption such a wide scope that it could be claimed by any chemist disclosing the formula of his medicine.[71] Bearing so little relation to the letter of the statute, this concession was undoubtedly flawed, and the revenue authorities later admitted that it had continued only because there was an institutional reluctance to disturb the clear interpretation of the Board of Inland Revenue.[72] Furthermore, when in the last years of the nineteenth century some of the practices became more formalised – notably the reporting to the Public Accounts Committee[73] of those remissions granted to individuals 'from motives of equity or of compassion'[74] – the status of revenue practice as a body of quasi-law, 'a kind of code',[75] was reinforced.

Supporting these factors was the popular approval that the revenue practice enjoyed. It was developed with the best of motives. Other than in the deliberate undermining of the principle of localism in tax administration,[76] the intention of the revenue authorities in developing their body of practice was not to ensure control over the taxing process. Although it was early understood that the revenue authorities could go beyond the intention of Parliament and favour the state rather than the taxpayer in their zeal to raise the public revenue,[77] for most of the

[68] Medicines Stamp Act 1812, 52 Geo. III c. 150.

[69] Minutes of Evidence before the Select Committee on Patent Medicines, *HCPP* 1914 (414), IX.59, 62–3, q. 19; Board of Customs and Excise and Predecessor, *The Medicine Stamp Duties 1783–1936*, 56.

[70] *Farmer* v. *Glyn Jones* [1903] 2 K.B. 6.

[71] The National Archives IR 83/61; Board of Customs and Excise and Predecessor, *The Medicine Stamp Duties 1783–1936*, 84–6; Minutes of Evidence before the Select Committee on Patent Medicines, *HCPP* 1914 (Cd. 414), IX.1, 62–4, qq. 19–34.

[72] Board of Customs and Excise and Predecessor, *The Medicine Stamp Duties 1783–1936*, 88.

[73] Second Report from the Committee of Public Accounts, *HCPP* 1897 (196), VIII.5, 11–12.

[74] First Report from the Select Committee of Public Accounts, *HCPP* 1928 (35) I.8, 35, 99.

[75] Wade, *Constitutional Fundamentals*, 58.

[76] C. Stebbings, *The Victorian Taxpayer and the Law* (Cambridge University Press, 2009), 77–110, especially 103–5.

[77] See H.H. Monroe, 'The Constitution in Danger' [1969] B.T.R. 24, 30.

nineteenth century the popular consensus was that the authorities were not sinister in their development of their executive equity. While it may have been a symptom of the growing power of the central government, it was not a deliberate encroachment thereof, or 'officialism' as it was popularly known. On the contrary, the revenue authorities were simply trying to ensure the tax system was fair in those specific instances. Admittedly this was ultimately in the interests of compliance, but it was not in order to increase the authorities' control over the system. Indeed, the evidence confirms they would rather not have had to make these concessions and interpretations to ensure fairness, and that they recognised it as unsatisfactory to implement a tax on that basis. They wanted, above all, a sound legislative regime to apply.[78] In its absence they did what they could to ensure fairness. The system they developed was pragmatic, flexible, and provided substantial and procedural justice. And from the end of the nineteenth century, despite some concerns as to the extent of revenue practice in extreme cases such as the medicine stamp duty,[79] the revenue authorities were consistently praised for their 'extreme fairness and courtesy' in dealing with borderline cases[80] and for their common sense in making decisions in order to make the tax system work.[81]

It might be thought that the development of an executive equity, aimed at ensuring that the injustices which inevitably flowed from such a complex and technical legislative system of tax law were remedied, was as beneficial to the taxpayer as the development of 'legal equity' had been to ensure justice for the population subject to the common law. The growing authority of revenue practice, however, hid serious flaws. While arguably it ensured fairness for the individual directly subject to the decision, in terms of the wider body of taxpayers it introduced a greater and more widespread degree of unfairness. Unlike legal equity, executive equity in tax was unable to balance out the needs of certainty against individual fairness. Indeed, it undermined the classical canon which laid down that the instances where a subject was to be charged to tax should be, in the words of Lord Ellenborough C.J. in 1807, 'fairly

[78] See for example (1869) 10 *Pharmaceutical Journal* (2nd series) 625.

[79] See for example (1876) 6 *Pharmaceutical Journal* (3rd series) 780; (1889) 19 *Pharmaceutical Journal* (3rd series) 682.

[80] Minutes of Evidence before the Select Committee on Medicine Stamp Duties, *HCPP* 1936–37 (54), VIII.129, 220.

[81] Report of the Income Tax Codification Committee, *HCPP* (1935–36) (Cmd. 5131), XII.1, 15–16.

marked out'.[82] It has been seen that revenue practice bound a taxpayer de facto, and it followed that taxpayers should be able to access it in order to find out with some degree of certainty the nature of the charge to tax, and whether it applied to their own personal situation or not.

It was, however, almost impossible for a taxpayer to acquire any certainty, predictability or understanding of his fiscal position because revenue practice was utterly inaccessible. Physical and intellectual inaccessibility already permeated tax law, from an incomplete, piecemeal and uncodified constitution to vast and impenetrable formal statutory provisions and unrecorded tribunal decisions. Revenue practice made a serious situation intolerable. Although most revenue practices were recorded, it was not in any systematic way. They were scattered throughout the voluminous literature on the taxes, and found recorded in internal circulars and instructions published for the use of revenue officials; referred to in evidence given to Select Committees and Royal Commissions, sometimes in the formal minutes of the proceedings of the revenue boards; and articulated in correspondence between the revenue boards and their officers, the Treasury or taxpayers. Some remissions, such as the dispensing concession granted to pharmaceutical chemists under the medicine stamp duty, were not formally recorded at all. Even where there was some record, it was almost impossible for a taxpayer or his legal advisers[83] to access revenue practice other than with the willing cooperation of the revenue authorities. The official view was one of secrecy. The minutes, instructions and circulars which revealed the policies and practices of the central boards were regarded as strictly confidential. They were never made public for fear that they might bind the boards or be pleaded in litigation against them[84] or, equally, that they would be 'equivalent to an admission that they neglect their duty by not enforcing the law to the strict letter'.[85] The board of excise was an extreme example. While it published its thousands of general orders in one volume in 1829,[86] it consistently refused to allow them to be seen by the traders subject to the excise, or to publish any

82 *Warrington* v. *Furbor* (1807) 8 East 242, 245; 103 E.R. 334, 335–6.

83 Report of a Committee on Excise Establishment, *HCPP* 1837 (96), XXX.397, 595.

84 Twentieth Report of the Commissioners of Inquiry (Excise Establishment), *HCPP* 1836 (22), XXVI.179, 525. For the extent to which the revenue authorities are today bound by their informal decisions, see D. Sandler, 'The Revenue Giveth – The Revenue Taketh Away' [1994] C.L.J. 273.

85 (1848) 8 *Pharmaceutical Journal* (1st series) 212.

86 J. Owens, *Plain Papers relating to the Excise Branch of the Inland Revenue Department, from 1621 to 1878* (Linlithgow: [s.n.], 1879), 261.

guidance based on them.[87] It would not even allow a printed analysis of the excise laws to be made available outside the service.[88] And when the revenue authorities published explanatory pamphlets in relation to the different taxes, these tended to consist of a statement of the legislative provisions, a measure of clarification and only occasionally an explanation of their practice.[89]

Public discussion and reporting of revenue practices was very limited. While the annual reports of the revenue boards sometimes discussed them it was pure chance whether a taxpayer's particular situation would be mentioned, and as the century progressed, so the reports became increasingly brief and formulaic. Select Committees or Royal Commissions on taxation issues occasionally addressed revenue practice. The evidence and reports of these official inquiries were published and thereby made accessible to the public, at a price. With tens of thousands of questions in the minutes of evidence alone being commonplace, and some tax knowledge being necessary to identify the relevant subject matter and navigate the material, they were entirely impracticable for any taxpayer who sought to inform himself as to his own tax position.

The only secure way by which taxpayers could find out the practice applicable to their own fiscal situation was to ask the revenue authorities themselves. The public well understood that the revenue officers were the true experts in the complex and technical law of tax, and that only they would have any accurate knowledge of the practices and policies of the board. At a time when there was no tax profession and self-help associations were in their infancy, individuals necessarily relied on the advice of the officers of the revenue boards, from the local surveyors[90] to the members of the boards themselves. The evidence shows that the boards differed in their approachability. For example, the Board of Inland Revenue was widely appreciated as an accessible and helpful board,[91]

87 Twentieth Report of the Commissioners of Inquiry (Excise Establishment), *HCPP* 1836 (22), XXVI.179, 525.

88 Fourteenth Report of the Commissioners of Inquiry into the Excise Establishment (Paper), *HCPP* 1835 (16), XXXI.159, 181–2.

89 For the 'Instructions to Officers relating to the Medicine Stamp Duty', see (1848) 8 *Pharmaceutical Journal* (1st series) 153–62; (1909) 82 *Pharmaceutical Journal* 674–6.

90 Williams, 'Surveying Taxes, 1900–14', 229.

91 Minutes of Evidence before the Select Committee on Inland Revenue and Customs Establishments, *HCPP* 1862 (370), XII.131, q. 504; Twentieth Report of the Commissioners of Her Majesty's Inland Revenue, *HCPP* 1878 (C.1896), XXVI.593, 646. Occasionally the surveyor gave general advice through the medium of the local newspaper, as when in 1843 the Exeter surveyor published a letter in which he carefully

which willingly answered the queries of individual taxpayers as to their own personal assessments. In contrast, the Board of Excise was deliberately obscure and secretive, reluctant to respond to inquiries or disclose its practice.[92] Where the taxpayer was a member of a professional organisation, he could find out about revenue practice by that route. For example, the editors of the *Pharmaceutical Journal*, the official organ of the Pharmaceutical Society of Great Britain, not only printed their correspondence with the revenue authorities, but also the board's instructions to its own officers in which the law and the manner of its interpretation were set out.[93] But however accessible and helpful the revenue authorities were, it is clear that they entirely controlled the nature and volume of information as to their practice that was released to the public. Their position as the only authoritative source of this key element of tax administration served to reinforce the view that the tax legislation meant what the revenue authorities said it meant. Taxpayers had little choice but to accept it.

Certainty in tax affairs was further undermined because, as with any body of truly discretionary decisions, revenue practice lacked any obvious coherence. The practices that the revenue authorities developed to ensure fairness were occasional ad hoc decisions made in the course of the administration of tax to relieve hardship in extreme cases. Even when the practices were referred to in the formal day-to-day minutes of the boards' proceedings, the record was purely factual. Very rarely was the reasoning behind a decision explained. An allusion in the minutes to internal correspondence explaining the decision was usually the most that was found. As a result, revenue practices were almost invariably unexplained, with the unfairness they were purporting to address being implicit rather than explicit. A general trend of the executive trying to achieve fairness emerges, but the instances are haphazard and founded entirely on the merits of the individual case. Furthermore, any fairness which practice was intended to introduce was that decided upon by the revenue authorities. The judges of whether the treatment of an individual subjected to the letter of the tax code was unduly harsh were the commissioners of the board in question. They arrived at their decisions on the

explained the nature of income tax appeal proceedings: see *Trewman's Exeter Flying Post*, 12 and 19 January 1843. For the response of the board to chemists' inquiries, see for example (1878) 9 *Pharmaceutical Journal* (3rd series) 544.

92 Fourteenth Report of the Commissioners of Inquiry into the Excise Establishment (Paper), *HCPP* 1835 (16), XXX.159, 182; see too at 285.

93 (1854) 14 *Pharmaceutical Journal* (1st series) 147.

basis of their own experience, their understanding of the intention behind the legislation, the reports of their officials and the advice of their legal staff. The point was emphasised in the following century when a judge observed that the revenue authorities had 'worked out what they consider to be an equitable way of operating [the statutory provision in question] which seems to them to result in a fair system of taxation'.[94] The board's conception of fairness was not necessarily that perceived by the general taxpaying public. The bureaucratic view of fairness was inevitably tempered by practicality and encompassed the desire for efficiency and uniformity in tax administration – considerations the general public's view of fairness did not necessarily include.

To that extent, then, fairness was determined not by the length of the chancellor's foot but that of the chairman of the board. The interpretation of the 'known, admitted and approved remedies' exemption in the medicine stamp duty, for example, was the personal view of Sir Henry Primrose, the chairman of the Board of Inland Revenue in 1904.[95] This inaccessibility, and an uncertain provenance arising from a medley of pragmatic imperatives and equitable objectives, made revenue practice appear both random and irrational to the taxpaying public. They could find no predictability, no consistency and therefore no certainty in their relationship with the law of tax. One chemist observed in 1889 that 'the judgments of the Board of Inland Revenue as to liability to medicine stamp duty were uncertain and contradictory' and that the authorities seemed to be 'guided in their interpretation by expediency rather than by principle'.[96] Unable to tell conclusively and easily whether a medicine was dutiable or not, revenue practice caused 'a sense of insecurity' among chemists.[97]

Conclusion

By the end of the nineteenth century the only way to ensure fairness at the margins of the formal tax code was by executive equity. It had evolved into a body of quasi-law, a significant and, for all practical purposes, a binding set of increasingly formal rules and guidance supplementing the formal law administered by an organ of the executive. It had become

94 *Bates* v. *Inland Revenue Commissioners* [1968] A.C. 483, 516.
95 Board of Customs and Excise and Predecessor, *The Medicine Stamp Duties 1783–1936*, 88.
96 (1889) 20 *Pharmaceutical Journal* (3rd series) 405.
97 (1889) 19 *Pharmaceutical Journal* (3rd series) 651.

ingrained in the tax system in the crucial years of its development into a modern system as a gloss of complementary rules in response to an unacceptable though inevitable degree of formality, rigidity and complexity in the principal code of law with the objective of ensuring fairness between taxpayers. Despite its serious weakness of physical and intellectual inaccessibility – a practical problem of the interface of administration and law – it was largely accepted by the taxpaying public, the legislature and the revenue authorities, all of whom recognised that it was both necessary and effective. Any discomfort as to the legality of revenue practice was as yet hardly felt.[98] It was the growth of revenue practice into a substantial body of rules of evident authority reaching its zenith in the nineteenth century that would demand the resolution of such issues in the next.[99] Meanwhile, pragmatism was an acceptable imperative to the fiscal authorities in the nineteenth century as they sought to make an antiquated tax system function as efficiently as possible in the face of unprecedented government demands for public revenue. Revenue practice thus became, and remains, embedded in the modern fiscal landscape.

The context of executive equity, however, has changed significantly. Extra-statutory concessions continue, despite their being still regarded as a 'curiosity',[100] though they are fewer in number, more formally

[98] For the early discussion of such issues, see Second Report and Minutes of Evidence before Committee of Public Accounts, *HCPP* 1897 (196), VIII.5, 7–12, 38–45, 75–82, qq. 359–463, 878–1006.

[99] *Absalom* v. *Talbot (HM Inspector of Taxes)* [1943] 1 All E.R. 589, 598 (Scott L.J.) (rev'd [1944] A.C. 204); Johnston, *The Inland Revenue*, 67–8; *Inland Revenue Commissioners* v. *Frere* [1965] A.C. 402, 429 (Lord Radcliffe); *Vestey* v. *Inland Revenue Commissioners (No. 2)* [1979] Ch. 198, 203–4 (Walton J.); *Vestey* v. *Inland Revenue Commissioners (No. 1)* [1980] A.C. 1148, 1172–4 (Lord Wilberforce); G.S.A. Wheatcroft, 'Law, Justice and Equity in Tax', in R.H. Code Holland and G. Schwarzenberger (eds.) *Law, Justice and Equity* (London: Sir Isaac Pitman and Sons Ltd, 1967), 90; D.C. Potter, 'Extra-Statutory Concessions' [1980] B.T.R. 270; M. Gammie, '"Revenue Practice": A Suitable Case for Treatment?' [1980] B.T.R. 304; R. Baldwin and J. Houghton, 'Circular Arguments: The Status and Legitimacy of Administrative Rules' [1986] P.L. 239; Booth, *The Inland Revenue . . . Saint or Sinner?*, 17–20, 145–75. See now *R (Wilkinson)* v. *Inland Revenue Commissioners* [2003] 1 W.L.R. 2683; [2003] EWCA Civ 814, aff'd [2005] 1 W.L.R. 1718; [2005] UKHL 30, which clarified the scope of the revenue authorities' administrative discretion to make concessions which departed from the letter of the law. It resulted in the revenue authorities' reviewing of all their extra-statutory concessions. Where a concession exceeded their proper discretion the intention was either to give them statutory expression or to abolish them.

[100] D.W. Williams and G. Morse, *Davies Principles of Tax Law*, 4th ed. (London: Sweet & Maxwell, 2000), 34.

expressed and more specific and narrow in their operation than in the nineteenth century. Tax practice is now published, its reasoning explained and it is easily accessible.[101] Tax guidance leaflets, statements of practice, tax bulletins on revenue interpretations and even instruction manuals are available to the public in print or on the Internet.[102] The interpretation of tax statutes has become more purposive.[103] Because of the improvement in standards of legislative drafting, achieving fairness through the beneficial administrative interpretation and re-interpretation of uncertain provisions is no longer widespread and has reduced the volume of revenue practice considerably. Furthermore, taxpayers are better informed, independent expert tax advice is available and the revenue authorities are subject to a far greater degree of scrutiny and accountability.

The executive equity of the nineteenth century has two enduring legacies. The first lies in the nature of tax legislation. Executive equity resulted primarily from a flawed legislative regime. As late as 1921 a judge observed in relation to a taxing Act that '[m]ost of the operative clauses are unintelligible to those who have to pay the taxes'.[104] Complexity of expression was largely inevitable, but there is evidence to suggest that the embedding of a widespread and generally effective revenue practice in the administration of tax law made legislators lazy[105] and the revenue authorities arrogant. Certainly the revenue authorities took the view that they well knew the intention of Parliament, having been closely involved with the drafting of the legislation,[106] and that they were ensuring fairness where Parliament had intended, but failed, to do so. Executive equity therefore served to mask the effects of slack legislation and allowed unsatisfactory legislative practices to endure. There was less incentive

[101] Accessibility of revenue practice began to improve in the latter part of the twentieth century: Gammie, '"Revenue Practice": A Suitable Case for Treatment?', 306–9.

[102] www.hmrc.gov.uk/thelibrary/esc.htm.

[103] *W.T. Ramsay Ltd* v. *Inland Revenue Commissioners* [1982] A.C. 300, 323 (Lord Wilberforce); *Barclays Mercantile Business Finance Ltd* v. *Mawson (Inspector of Taxes)* [2005] 1 A.C. 684; [2004] UKHL 51.

[104] *Brown* v. *National Provident Institution* [1921] 2 A.C. 222, 257 (Lord Sumner). In 1948 Singleton J. famously advised a taxpayer thus: 'I hope you will not trouble your head further with tax matters, because you seem to have spent a lot of time in going through these various Acts, and if you go on spending your time on Finance Acts and the like, it will drive you silly': *Briggenshaw* v. *Crabb* (1948) 30 T.C. 331, 333.

[105] G.S.A. Wheatcroft, 'The Attitude of the Legislature and the Courts to Tax Avoidance' (1955) 18 M.L.R. 209, 221.

[106] Johnston, *The Inland Revenue*, 68.

for the legislature to address the intractable problems of legislative drafting in tax in the face of an established, and largely effective, system of bureaucratic solutions. As a result, tax legislation remained profoundly unsatisfactory. Obscure, ambiguous or antiquated language, an absence of definition or coherent structure and the need to read most tax Acts in conjunction with a number of others continued until well into the twentieth century. The unintelligibility and sheer bulk of tax legislation permeated tax law. Paradoxically, however, it was the sheer scope, depth and volume of revenue practice that highlighted the inadequacy of tax legislation, and the very existence of revenue practice revealed and confirmed the appalling state of tax legislation as opaque and antiquated, and totally impenetrable. As Scott L.J. observed in 1943, echoing the complaints of judges for over a hundred years, '[t]he fact that such extra-legal concessions have to be made to avoid unjust hardships is conclusive that there is something wrong with the legislation'.[107] This led to reforms in legislative drafting in tax and, ultimately, to the Tax Rewrite Project of the late 1990s, whose object was to recast the direct tax legislation in clearer language and in a logical structure.[108]

The second enduring legacy of revenue practice in general and executive equity in particular is less tangible. The key role which it played in the administration of tax law, and its influence on its substance, served to reinforce the isolation of tax law within the institutions, theory, practice and public perceptions of English law. Tax law was already different to other branches of law with which practitioners had to deal in that it had a strong political and constitutional context and its mastery required a certain ease with accounts and figures. But what rendered it most distinctive, to the extent that it was regarded as an irregular species of law, was that it lay at the interface of law and administration and came to acquire a strongly administrative character. This was largely due to the admixture of administrative and judicial functions given by the legislation to the revenue boards and their various organs in order to fulfil their overall executive function of implementing the legislative regime of tax. To do so, they were given functions which, had they stood alone, would have been judicial in nature. The administrative process of implementing the tax regime

[107] *Absalom* v. *Talbot (HM Inspector of Taxes)* [1943] 1 All E.R. 589, 598.

[108] For an insightful analysis of the problems relating to the nature of tax legislation, see J. Avery Jones, 'Tax Law: Rules or Principles?' (1996) 17 *Fiscal Studies* 63.

subsumed otherwise clearly judicial functions. This was very obvious where the revenue authorities, directly or indirectly, exercised judicial powers of adjudication of tax disputes, since they regarded those powers as no more than part of the administrative process of assessing individuals to tax. Revenue practice incorporated other judicial functions, such as statutory interpretation, and parliamentary functions, such as granting exemptions from statutory provisions, which made it difficult to isolate tax law from tax administration. In general, the executive implementation of tax law was so embedded into legal practices – adjudication, statutory interpretation and law making – that it obscured the usual boundaries between law and its administration and made it even more difficult to achieve any clarity of legal rights. The isolation of tax law due to its administrative character had profound consequences in that it undermined the authority of law and increased the power of the revenue authorities of the executive by lessening the controlling influence of legal norms.

Fairness is still at the centre of popular discourse as to tax policy, though the meaning is wider, including not only the traditional equality and consistency of treatment, but also simplicity, accessibility, neutrality in effect and competitiveness.[109] The removal of loopholes and incentives which place a burden on some sections of the taxpaying public while allowing other sections to have a lighter liability also form part of what is now called tax justice and has become a global political concern. This kind of substantive fairness is now ensured principally through substantive legislation and judicial decisions. But the need for executive equity remains because the constitutional underpinning of tax law remains as robust as ever. It is still the case that an individual cannot be taxed other than by clear words in an Act of Parliament. This principle continues to shape the form and content of tax legislation. Taxation is, by nature, complicated and reflects the growing sophistication of commercial affairs.[110] So, while a complex legislative framework is inevitable, it necessarily continues to give rise to unfairness at the margins of the code, which is addressed by adjusting its implementation through administrative action, namely through executive equity. It is clear that the judicial attitudes and practices developed in relation to the

[109] R. Baron, *Fairness and Justice in Tax Policy* (London: Institute of Directors, 2009: www.iod.com/influencing/policy-papers/taxation/fairness-and-justice-in-tax-policy); United Kingdom, H.C. Deb., 12 March 2013, vol. 568, cols. 162–215, 'Tax Fairness'.

[110] Report of the Royal Commission on Income Tax, *HCPP* 1920 (Cmd. 615), XVIII.97, 187.

construction of statutes in general, and those of bureaucrats in relation to tax legislation in particular, served the same useful purpose: to introduce flexibility into the statutory system, to cure defects, to remedy injustice. Whereas the former has given rise to legal equity, the latter evolved as a form of administrative equity.

15

The equity of the executive

A commentary

JOHN F. AVERY JONES

I am in substantial agreement with Professor Stebbings and should like to explore how several of her themes relate to each other: the nature of early tax legislation, practice that interprets the legislation, concessionary practice (or executive equity, in Professor Stebbings's terms), the role of the courts, and how the revenue kept a tight control over practice when income tax was administered by agencies outside central government. I shall describe each of these and then try to put them together.

The nature of early tax legislation

The original income tax legislation contained virtually no definitions. Take this example from Addington's 1803 Act defining part of the scope of Schedule D that is still in the legislation today:

> And upon the annual Profits or Gains arising or accruing to any Person or Persons whatever, whether Subjects of his Majesty or not, although not resident within Great Britain, from any . . . Trade . . . exercised in Great Britain.[1]

No further statutory elucidation was given about the meaning of profits, resident,[2] trade, or exercised *in*, leaving the scope for practice wide open to an extent that would be unthinkable in legislation today. On the first of

[1] Income Tax Act 1803, 43 Geo. III c. 122, Sch. D. The current equivalent is in Income Tax (Trading and Other Income) Act 2005 (UK), s. 6(2).

[2] Apart from sections dealing with British subjects who had departed Great Britain for occasional residence elsewhere, and for visitors for some temporary purpose and not with any view or intent of establishing residence: Income Tax Act 1803, 43 Geo. III c. 122, ss. 85, 86.

these items, profits,[3] the history of allowance for depreciation is particularly interesting in illustrating the scope of practice.[4] By 1805, the legislation, slightly inconsistently, prohibited any deduction for the diminution of capital employed in a trade, but permitted the deduction of sums usually expended in the supply or repairs or alterations of any implements, utensils, or articles employed for the purpose of a trade on the basis of the average of the preceding three years, which was the normal period for assessment.[5] Revenue practice was to construe the latter provision liberally to include renewals and replacements.[6]

This caused a problem for larger items, such as ships, which were not likely to be renewed within the three-year period. In giving an allowance for depreciation of ships, the revenue were granting a concession. However, the Law Officers gave an opinion in 1857 that the concession was permitted on the basis of the ordinary meaning of 'profit'; that opinion completely failed to consider that the depreciation was capital.[7] The law was brought into line with the practice and extended beyond ships in 1878. This allowed such deduction as the General Commissioners may think just and reasonable as representing the diminished value by reason of wear and tear during the year of any machinery or plant (another undefined term).[8]

Residence of individuals was essentially governed by practice until legislation in 2013 and provides a good example of changing fashions of legislation. By 1936, the Codification Committee said that relying on

[3] By the time of the Income Tax Act 1806, 46 Geo. III c. 65, there was a list of bizarre prohibitions on deductions that one is surprised that anyone might think could be deductible, such as capital withdrawn, sums employed as capital, debts (other than bad debts), and expenses of maintenance of the parties, their families or establishments: Sch. D Cases I and II r.1.

[4] For a detailed survey of this topic, see D. de Cogan, 'Law and Administration in Capital Allowances Doctrine: 1878–1950', in J. Tiley (ed.), *Studies in the History of Tax Law, Vol. 6* (Oxford: Hart Publishing, 2013), ch. 5. Professor Stebbings refers to it: C. Stebbings, 'The Equity of the Executive: Fairness in Tax Law in Nineteenth Century England', Chapter 14 of this volume, text to n. 61.

[5] Income Tax Act 1805, 45 Geo. III c. 49, s. 205 and Sch. D Case I r. 4 respectively. The second of these was not in the 1803 Act.

[6] Circular to General Commissioners of 4 June 1877 reproduced in the Twentieth Report of the Commissioners of Her Majesty's Inland Revenue on the Inland Revenue for the Year ended 31 March 1877, *HCPP* 1878 (C. 1896) XXVI.595, 647–8; de Cogan, 'Law and Administration in Capital Allowances Doctrine', 179.

[7] TNA:PRO IR98/13 item 14a referred to by de Cogan, 'Law and Administration in Capital Allowances Doctrine', 180.

[8] Customs and Inland Revenue Act 1878 (UK), 41 Vict. c. 15, s. 12.

revenue practice was 'intolerable and should not be allowed to continue'.[9] They proposed a statutory definition comprising 43 lines, but nothing was done. Ultimately, in 2013, we had legislation in a 66-page Schedule containing no fewer than 159 paragraphs about which HMRC has published detailed guidance notes running to 106 pages.[10] The more prescriptive the rules, the more likely it is that they will give the 'wrong' answer, particularly when there are arbitrary dividing lines.[11]

The role of the courts

Lawyers and the courts were excluded from the whole process. Neither the taxpayer nor the surveyor (the predecessor of the Inspector of Taxes) was allowed legal representation on an appeal to the General Commissioners, which was heard in private.[12] This rule was relaxed slightly in 1898 and 1903 but it was not until 1923 that the General Commissioners were required to permit legal representation,[13] in spite of the fact that they were required to hear only lawful evidence. No appeal lay from the decision of the General Commissioners until appeals to the courts were finally permitted in 1874. The unreformed versions of both of these rules reflected the original need to collect tax without any delaying process; the prospect of *Jarndyce* v. *Inland Revenue* was not attractive. And even when the courts became involved it was clear that the judges were not enthusiastic. As Hubert Monroe memorably said:

[9] Report of the Income Tax Codification Committee, *HCPP* 1935–36 (Cmd. 5131), XII.1, 37. Much later, failure to apply the practice became in principle subject to judicial review. The relationship between the law and the practice in relation to individual residence is explored in *R (Davies)* v. *Revenue and Customs Commissioners* [2011] 1 W.L.R. 2625; [2011] UKSC 47.

[10] Finance Act 2013 (UK), Sch. 45.

[11] I am indebted to Emma Chamberlain, barrister, for the example of a foreign academic who comes to Cambridge from September to January living in a rented house with her family while renting out her foreign home. For a consecutive period of ninety-one days, she has a UK home and is resident. If she had rented out her foreign home for fewer than ninety-one days, then one would have to judge UK residence under the 'sufficient ties' test.

[12] Taxes Act 1803, 43 Geo. III c. 99 s. 26 (an Act applying to the assessed taxes (carriages, wigs etc.) incorporated by reference into income tax); Taxes Management Act 1880 (UK), 43 & 44 Vict. c. 19, s. 57(9). The restriction on lawyers may be explained by the fact that assessed taxes did not normally raise points of law, but rather factual questions such as how many windows there were in a house or what was the type of some carriage.

[13] Finance Act 1898 (UK), s. 16; Revenue Act 1903 (UK), s. 13; Finance Act 1923 (UK), s. 25.

> How then did the judges fare when they entered the ring after 1874? As was said of the lion in the case of 'Albert and the Lion' you could see that the judge did not like it. Here was a topic of which few, if any, judges had professional experience, though all no doubt had disagreeable personal experience. The topic was entirely statutory, scattered in addition over a multitude of statutes, and apparently lacking in any discernible principles. What could a judge do but fall back on the words of so much of the statutory code as was brought to his attention?[14]

Almost by definition the courts never came to hear about the revenue granting concessions. In the rare exceptions, they disapproved it, but that had little effect other than giving rise to some famous sayings, such as Walton J.'s: 'One should be taxed by law, and not be untaxed by concession'.[15] The problem of concessions was put before the House of Lords in a way that could not be avoided in *Wilkinson*,[16] where the taxpayer was arguing that the Board of Inland Revenue should make a concession to extend to widowers a statutory provision giving relief for widows. Lord Hoffmann said:

> This discretion[17] enables the commissioners to formulate policy in the interstices of the tax legislation, dealing pragmatically with minor or transitory anomalies, cases of hardship at the margins or cases in which a statutory rule is difficult to formulate or its enactment would take up a disproportionate amount of parliamentary time.[18]

Following *Wilkinson*, the revenue had to take notice and started to enact concessions wherever possible, usually giving rise to detailed legislation with the possibility of the taxpayer falling outside its terms. The concession known as equitable liability provides an example where this may have been taken too far. Where (before self-assessment) an estimated assessment became final because it was not appealed in time, the revenue used the concession in appropriate cases to restrict collection

[14] H. Monroe, *Intolerable Inquisition? Reflections on the Law of Tax* (London: Stevens, 1981), 49.

[15] *Vestey* v. *Inland Revenue Commissioners (No. 1)* [1979] Ch. 177, 197. See Stebbings, 'The Equity of the Executive: Fairness in Tax Law in Nineteenth Century England', n. 99.

[16] *R (Wilkinson)* v. *Inland Revenue Commissioners* [2005] 1 W.L.R. 1718; [2005] UKHL 30.

[17] Conferred by section 1 of the Taxes Management Act 1970 (UK) (now as substituted by Commissioners for Revenue and Customs Act 2005 (UK)). Lord Diplock saw that discretion as 'a wide managerial discretion as to the best means of obtaining for the national exchequer from the taxes committed to their charge, the highest net return that is practicable having regard to the staff available to them and the cost of collection': *Inland Revenue Commissioners* v. *National Federation of Self-Employed and Small Businesses Ltd* [1982] A.C. 617, 636.

[18] *R (Wilkinson)* v. *Inland Revenue Commissioners* [2005] 1 W.L.R. 1718, [21].

of the tax to the right amount of tax rather than the (higher) estimated amount; the same applied under self-assessment where the revenue made a determination in the absence of a return against which there was no right of appeal. The existence of this concession was mentioned in a Tax Bulletin in 1995 and as far as I can see not earlier, although it certainly existed earlier. Following *Wilkinson*, it was put on a statutory footing, now called special relief, one of the terms of which was that 'it would be unconscionable for the Commissioners to seek to recover the amount'.[19] Suppose this concession continued in its original form and the matter ever came before the courts (although it is difficult to see how it could): would any court say to HMRC that they were acting illegally in collecting the right amount of tax, rather than an excessive amount, where the high amount strictly applied only because HMRC over-estimated the tax payable; the taxpayer had failed to appeal or make a return in time; and HMRC regarded it as unconscionable to collect the excess?

The revenue's tight control over practice and the administration of tax by agencies outside central government

There is an apparent conflict between the following passages in Professor Stebbings's chapter:

> The requirements that a tax should be non-inquisitorial and locally administered, though eroded, were more robust and enduring. The battle to retain them was fought in the context of the income tax until well into the twentieth century[20]

and:

> The revenue authorities undoubtedly intended their interpretations, remissions and decisions to be acted upon and rigorously adhered to by their officers, and they achieved this.[21]

[19] See the Taxes Management Act 1970 (UK), Sch. 1AB para. 3A(4) (income tax) and the Finance Act 1998 (UK), Sch. 18 para. 51BA(4) (corporation tax). The amendments were inserted into the 1970 and 1998 Acts by The Enactment of Extra-Statutory Concessions Order 2011 (UK) (S.I. 2011/1037), art. 2 and art. 3. On the use of the equitable language of 'unconscionability' in other legislation, see J.D. Heydon, 'Equity and Statute', Chapter 12 of this volume and the accompanying commentary by Justice Mark Leeming, 'Equity and Statute: A Commentary', Chapter 13 of this volume.

[20] Stebbings, 'The Equity of the Executive: Fairness in Tax Law in Nineteenth Century England', text after n. 15.

[21] *Ibid.*, text after n. 64.

There is no doubt that both statements were true and the facts in each statement were true at the same time. The short answer to the apparent conflict is that, from about the middle of the nineteenth century, the former statement reflects what the legislation said rather than the practice, while the latter statement reflected what happened in practice. The original legislation put the power to assess trading profits in the hands of the General Commissioners – an office similar to that of a Justice of the Peace, and which required the Commissioner to meet a substantial property qualification – giving the central government official, the surveyor, a right to object if he 'shall apprehend the Determination made by the [Additional] Commissioners to be contrary to the true Intent and Meaning of this Act',[22] which the General Commissioners would decide. By about the middle of the nineteenth century, this system no longer worked in practice; the surveyor fixed a figure which the General Commissioners generally rubber stamped. The legislation, however, remained essentially unchanged until 1964.

Fitting the factors together

Thus, the early legislation was silent about the details of almost everything. It left great scope for interpretation even where (as with the depreciation of ships) the limits of interpretation were reached; apparently concessionary practice was willingly adopted. All this occurred with legislation that was certainly not complex. Since the courts were excluded until 1874 and appeals to the General and Special Commissioners were heard in private, there was no mechanism for clarifying interpretation; full scope was thus left for revenue practice to flourish. As Professor Stebbings puts it, the revenue boards enjoyed a monopoly on interpretation of the legislation.[23] Even after the courts became involved, matters progressed in the usual leisurely common law fashion with, for example, the undefined residence of companies being settled over time between 1876 and 1928 in relation to various factual circumstances. Residence of individuals, being factually far more complex, never really became settled by the courts; the way was thus left open for the continuation of practice until 2013. Nor was there anyone to prevent the revenue from giving concessions; indeed, this did not really change even when the courts

[22] Income Tax Act 1803, 43 Geo. III, c. 122, s. 137.

[23] Stebbings, 'The Equity of the Executive: Fairness in Tax Law in Nineteenth Century England', text after n. 66.

became involved. Finally, although it looked from the administrative provisions of the legislation as if the revenue had little power, in practice they administered the system and were able to exercise a unifying influence over the interpretation of the legislation and the granting of concessions through instructions to their surveyors. Their influence over interpretation waned slightly when the courts came on the scene. But this was a slow process and some topics, like residence of individuals, continued to be governed largely by practice. Their influence over concessions continued unabated until very recently.

When there is no definition of a concept, as in the example of profits, resident, trade and exercised *in*, there is no definite boundary and so nothing is clearly inside or outside the boundary. There is no difference between practice that defines and concessionary practice. Perhaps this led to a frame of mind that was willing to adopt practice to achieve fairness whenever required. Only when the boundary is defined, as in the three-year rule for the replacement of plant and machinery, can something clearly be outside the boundary; therefore, practice going beyond the boundary is concessionary. When legislation became more detailed more boundaries were defined – and that in turn gave more scope for concessionary practice. This may be the inevitable result of detailed legislation rather than necessarily meaning that the legislation is flawed.

Finally, to take matters beyond the end of the nineteenth century, it took about one hundred years to shake off the judges' strict interpretation approach during which time 'tax law was by and large left behind as some island of literal interpretation'.[24] It is also extraordinary how recent the developments were to make revenue practice accessible: extra-statutory concessions were first published in booklet form in 1966, statements of practice from 1978, and manuals from 2000. It is sad to have to relate that unpublished concessions still exist; recently the First-tier Tribunal decided 'that as a matter of *Wednesbury* unreasonable[ness], it is unlawful to act as HMRC have done and give a concession but fail to publish it'.[25]

[24] *Inland Revenue Commissioners* v. *McGuckian* [1997] 1 W.L.R. 991, 999 (Lord Steyn).

[25] *L.H. Bishop Electrical Co. Ltd* v. *Commissioners for Her Majesty's Revenue and Customs* [2013] S.T.I. 3433, [510]; [2013] UKFTT 522 (TC).

16

Equity in the modern administrative state

WILLIAM GUMMOW

The focus of this chapter is not so much upon equitable doctrine in private law as upon equitable remedies, particularly the injunction and declaration, and their use in what might be called the 'public law' of the United Kingdom, the United States, Canada and Australia.

Attention first is given to the relationship between constitutional law and public or administrative law and the differing dimensions this provides for the application of equitable remedies. Consideration then is given to the advantages of equitable remedies, the need for an 'equity' to attract intervention, the position of the Crown, and the unconscientious exercise of statutory power as attracting equitable remedies.

The vantage point

Equitable remedies have a characteristic suppleness which makes them readily adaptable both in complex disputes between private parties and also where the cause of complaint is the exercise, or threatened exercise, of 'public power' by either or both of the other branches of government. That division of power may be explicit or implicit in a written and rigid constitution, or may be accepted as a method of government under the system associated with the United Kingdom.

Hence, I would, with respect, readily adopt the view of the editors of the current (the seventh) edition of *De Smith's Judicial Review*[1] that both the exercise of judicial review and the principles enunciated through judicial review have a constitutional basis. Further, as Professor Sykes

The writer is indebted to Professor David Feldman for his commentary at the presentation of the paper in its original form.

1 Lord Woolf, J. Jowell and A. Le Sueur, *De Smith's Judicial Review*, 7th ed. (London: Sweet & Maxwell, 2013), [1-013], [1-017]-[1-025].

observed over fifty years ago, in his essay 'The Injunction in Public Law',[2] every question of administrative law seems equally to be an issue of constitutional law, albeit the converse proposition perhaps cannot be maintained. This, thus, provides the vantage point from which to consider the role of equitable remedies in the modern administrative state.

Further, it surely would be to perpetuate conceptual myopia to continue to teach and practice 'administrative law' as a discrete discipline removed from its constitutional moorings. As to teaching, for too long that was the state of affairs, certainly in Australian law schools, and notwithstanding the conferral of jurisdiction by section 75(v) of the Constitution in matters in which a writ of mandamus or prohibition or an injunction 'is sought against an officer of the Commonwealth'. From the outset a federal minister was taken to be such an 'officer'.[3]

Federalism

This chapter also proceeds on the footing that it has come to pass that in the United Kingdom, as well as in the United States, Canada, and Australia, albeit by different means and processes, the modern state in which equitable remedies are in play has a federal character. The operation *inter se* of the components of those structures offers further scope for the use of equitable remedies.

With respect to the United Kingdom, one may recall the view of Sir William Wade that there comes a point, in debate about 'sovereignty' and related concepts, where the 'legal' and the 'political' intersect.[4] We have it on the authority of Windeyer J. that in a common law system the statement by the courts of constitutional principles, even those based on a written constitution, 'may vary and develop in response to changing circumstances' and that in so acting the courts have not 'transgressed lawful boundaries'.[5]

Hence, even without staying to consider the further significance of 'devolution' for Scotland, Northern Ireland, and Wales, I respectfully

[2] E.I. Sykes, 'The Injunction in Public Law' (1956) 2 U.Q.L.J. 114, 114–15.

[3] *Ferrando* v. *Pearce* (1918) 25 C.L.R. 241, 262, 289.

[4] H.W.R. Wade, 'The Bases of Legal Sovereignty' [1955] C.L.J. 172.

[5] *Victoria* v. *Commonwealth* (1971) 122 C.L.R. 353, 397. See also *Shaw* v. *Minister for Immigration and Multicultural Affairs* (2003) 218 C.L.R. 28, [12]; [2003] HCA 72.

would commend the opening passage in the speech of Lord Hope of Craighead in *R (Jackson)* v. *Attorney-General.*[6] His Lordship said:

> Our constitution is dominated by the sovereignty of Parliament. But parliamentary sovereignty is no longer, if it ever was, absolute. It is not uncontrolled in the sense referred to by Lord Birkenhead L.C. in *McCawley* v. *The King.*[7] It is no longer right to say that its freedom to legislate admits of no qualification whatever. Step by step, gradually but surely, the English principle of the absolute legislative sovereignty of Parliament which Dicey derived from Coke and Blackstone is being qualified.[8]

Lord Hope developed that proposition as follows:

> For the most part these qualifications are themselves the product of measures enacted by Parliament. Part I of the European Communities Act 1972 [(UK)] is perhaps the prime example. Although Parliament was careful not to say in terms that it could not enact legislation which was in conflict with Community law, that in practice is the effect of section 2(1) when read with section 2(4) of that Act. The direction in section 2(1) that Community law is to be recognised and available in law and is to be given legal effect without further enactment, which is the method by which the Community Treaties have been implemented, concedes the last word in this matter to the courts. The doctrine of the supremacy of Community law restricts the absolute authority of Parliament to legislate as it wants in this area. This plainly is how the matter would be viewed in Luxembourg.[9] Section 3(1) of the Human Rights Act 1998 [(UK)] has introduced a further qualification, as it directs the courts to read and give effect to legislation in a way that is compatible with the Convention rights. So long as it is possible to do so, the interpretative obligation enables the courts to give a meaning to legislation which is compatible even if this appears to differ from what Parliament had in mind when enacting it.[10]

In the passage from Professor Feldman's inaugural lecture to which Lord Hope referred, the author wrote that the courts have a duty to restrain the enforcement of the provisions of a statute which if enforced would place the United Kingdom in breach of immediately effective

[6] [2006] 1 A.C. 262; [2005] UKHL 56. See, further, the remarks of Lord Sumption J.S.C. in *R (Chester)* v. *Secretary of State of Justice* [2014] A.C. 271, [120]; [2013] UKSC 63.

[7] [1920] A.C. 691, 720.

[8] *R (Jackson)* v. *A.-G.* [2006] 1 A.C. 262, [104]; [2005] UKHL 56.

[9] See D. Feldman, 'None, One or Several? Perspectives on the UK's Constitution(s)' [2005] C.L.J. 329, 346–7; see also, for the practical effects in this country, *R* v. *Secretary of State for Transport, Ex p. Factortame Ltd (No. 2)* [1991] 1 A.C. 603.

[10] *R (Jackson)* v. *A.-G.* [2006] 1 A.C. 262, [105].

European Union law.[11] But, as Lord Reed J.S.C., in particular, recently emphasised,[12] very different (and constitutional) questions arise where an attempt is made to enlist the courts to prevent the presentation of a Bill to the Parliament on the ground that a White Paper has not been proposed in accordance with a Directive.

Save where, on a close reading, the provisions of a written constitution make the validity of a law depend upon there having been compliance with a procedure within the legislature, the settled practice is not to grant injunctive and declaratory relief in respect of such intra-mural proceedings.[13] However, with respect to the legislative 'competence' of the Assemblies for Scotland and Wales, the devolution legislation provides for Law Officers to 'refer' to the Supreme Court 'for decision' a Bill or provision of a Bill, which has been passed but not yet received the Royal Assent.[14]

This leads one to related distinctions between equitable intervention on an interim and final basis and between curial intervention to restrain administration of an allegedly invalid statute and to restrain abuses in the exercise of power conferred by valid legislation.

First, as to interim relief in cases of alleged statutory invalidity. The emphasis by Lord Goff of Chieveley in *Factortame*[15] upon the need for a strong prima facie case of statutory invalidity by reason of incompatibility with EU law may be compared with the similar (but earlier) statement by Mason A.-C.J. in *Castlemaine Tooheys Ltd* v. *South Australia*.[16] In dismissing interlocutory applications in the original jurisdiction of the High Court to restrain enforcement of the State law under

[11] See also D. Feldman, 'Public Interest Litigation and Constitutional Theory in Comparative Perspective' (1992) 55 M.L.R. 44, 59.

[12] *R (HS2 Action Alliance Limited)* v. *Secretary of State for Transport* [2014] 1 W.L.R. 324, [78]–[79], [116]; [2014] UKSC 3; see also at [203]–[208] (Lord Neuberger P.S.C. and Lord Mance J.S.C.).

[13] *Cormack* v. *Cope* (1974) 131 C.L.R. 432, 461, 464–6, 467, 472, 473; *Leung Kwok Hung* v. *President of the Legislative Council of the Hong Kong SAR (No. 1)* (2014) 17 H.K.C.F.A.R. 689, [30]–[38]; [2014] HKCFA 74.

[14] Scotland Act 1998 (UK), s. 33; Government of Wales Act 2006 (UK), s. 112; cf. Judicial Committee Act 1833 (UK), s. 4, considered by Jacobs J. in *Commonwealth* v. *Queensland* (1975) 134 C.L.R. 298, 322–3. See, further, *Agricultural Sector (Wales) Bill – Reference by the Attorney-General for England and Wales* [2014] 1 W.L.R. 2622, [5]–[6]; [2014] UKSC 43; *Re Recovery of Medical Costs for Asbestos Diseases (Wales) Bill* [2015] A.C. 1016; [2015] UKSC 3.

[15] *R* v. *Secretary of State for Transport, Ex p. Factortame Ltd (No. 2)* [1991] 1 A.C. 603, 664, 674.

[16] (1986) 161 C.L.R. 148, 155–6.

challenge, his Honour said that 'in the absence of compelling grounds' the duty of the judicial branch is to defer to the enactment of the legislature until the statute is adjudged invalid.[17]

But, secondly, there is a deeper question here, concerning the degree of interaction between the branches of government.

Differing dimensions

Both an injunction to restrain enforcement of an invalid statute and an injunction to restrain what would be a defective exercise of power conferred by a valid statute are expressions of the relationship between the judicial and the other branches of government. But there is an important difference in dimension.

A good starting point is supplied by the judgment of Marshall C.J. in *Marbury* v. *Madison*.[18] The immediate concern there was with questions of constitutional validity, but his grand scheme included as an essential characteristic of the judicature the determination and enforcement of the limits of power conferred by statute upon decision-makers.

The distinction this presents was expressed by a modern US scholar, in a passage adopted by the High Court in *City of Enfield* v. *Development Assessment Commission*.[19] The passage reads:

> '[T]here is in our society,' as Professor Jaffe says, 'a profound, tradition-taught reliance on the courts as the ultimate guardian and assurance of the limits set upon [administrative] power by the constitutions and legislatures.' But judicial review of administrative action stands on a different footing from constitutional adjudication, both historically and functionally. In part no doubt because alternative methods of control, both political and administrative in nature, are available to confine agencies within bounds, there has never been a pervasive notion that limited government mandated an all-encompassing judicial duty to supply all of the relevant meaning of statutes. Rather, the judicial duty is to ensure that the administrative agency stays within the zone of discretion committed to it by its organic act.[20]

Hence, the propositions in the Australian case law, that the merits of administrative actions are the subject of political not judicial control and

17 See, further, *Australian Broadcasting Corp.* v. *O'Neill* (2006) 227 C.L.R. 57, [65]–[72]; [2006] HCA 46.

18 (1803) 1 Cranch 137, 177; 5 U.S. 87, 111.

19 (2000) 199 C.L.R. 135, [43]; [2000] HCA 5.

20 H.P. Monaghan, '*Marbury* and the Administrative State' (1983) 83 Colum. L. Rev. 1, 32–3.

that, per se, there is no error of law in an incorrect finding of fact. These reservations as to the scope of judicial review may also respond to claims of the 'democratic deficit' of the judicial beside the 'popular' branches of government.

In the modern case law of other jurisdictions, the United States, Canada, and the United Kingdom, the relationship between the judicial and other branches of government has been seen rather differently and with marked contrasts between jurisdictions. This has a significant effect upon the use of equitable remedies.

Professor Feldman, in his oral commentary on the original version of this chapter, emphasised that the theory among administrative lawyers in England that all errors are errors of law and that any error of law makes a decision a nullity did not sit well with the discretionary nature of equitable remedies in public law.

In the United States, the enforcement of constitutional provisions, particularly obedience to section 1 of the Civil Rights Act of 1871,[21] has seen over the last fifty years the development by the federal courts of the mandatory injunction to effect the structural reorganisation of public and social institutions. In *Swann* v. *Charlotte-Mecklenburg Board of Education*[22] the Supreme Court observed that the distinguishing characteristic of equity has been adjustment and reconciliation between both competing private claims and between the public interest and private needs and went on: '[a]s with any equity case, the nature of the violation determines the scope of the remedy';[23] but the structural injunction cases have been criticised as crossing the line between the judicial branch and the legislative and executive branches.[24]

On the other hand, while equitable relief provides an important supplement to statutory review of federal agency action[25] (particularly that available under the Administrative Procedure Act enacted in 1946),[26] the *Chevron* doctrine[27] bespeaks 'deference' by the judicial branch if the statute administered by a federal agency or regulatory authority is susceptible of several constructions, each of which appears to be a reasonable representation of Congressional intent. The attendant risk of

[21] 17 Stat. 13; now 42 U.S.C. § 1983. [22] 402 U.S. 1, 15–16 (1971). [23] *Ibid.*, 16.

[24] An early but still instructive discussion is by R.F. Nagel, 'Separation of Powers and the Scope of Federal Equitable Remedies' (1978) 30 Stan. L. Rev. 661.

[25] R.J. Pierce, *Administrative Law Treatise*, 4th ed. (New York: Aspen, 2002), vol. 3, § 18.

[26] 5 U.S.C. § 706.

[27] After *Chevron USA Inc.* v. *Natural Resources Defense Council Inc.*, 467 U.S. 837, 842–4 (1984).

'delegalisation' of the administrative process occasioned criticism of *Chevron*.[28] More recent authority requires less deference in penalty cases, to reflect 'due process' considerations.[29] Further curtailment of *Chevron* is apparent in *Christopher* v. *Smithkline Beecham Corp.*,[30] which concerned the administration by the Department of Labor of the minimum wage and maximum hours provisions of the Fair Labor Standards Act of 1938 (US).[31]

The Supreme Court of Canada, expressly putting constitutional cases to one side, has gone even further than *Chevron*. Moved by the views of Professor Dyzenhaus,[32] the Supreme Court emphasises that legislatures create decision-making bodies to provide an alternative to court process and that legislative 'supremacy' limits the role of the courts and determines the 'deference' to be accorded to administrative bodies.[33]

The flow of judicial decision in the United Kingdom thus has been actively and strongly in the other direction to that of Canada. Australia and the United States are placed more or less mid-way. This state of affairs bears out the statement of Sir Owen Dixon, made in 1935,[34] that the idea of legislative supremacy has operated, in different places and different degrees, to modify the conceptions of the supremacy of the law; to Dixon it was the English common law which by a process of evolution had endowed the King in Parliament with 'supreme and unlimited legislative power', and, of course, the judges were the expositors of the common law.

In the present edition of *De Smith's Judicial Review*,[35] there is discussion of the need to 'reconcile' parliamentary sovereignty and 'the rule of law'. The editors refer to the statements in *AXA General Insurance Ltd* v. *HM Lord Advocate*,[36] to the effect that the Scottish Parliament not being 'sovereign' and its legislative competence being limited by section

[28] K. Werham, 'Delegalizing Administrative Law' [1996] U. Ill. L. Rev. 423, 457; T.W. Merrill, 'Judicial Deference to Executive Precedent' (1992) 101 Yale L.J. 969, 993–8.

[29] Pierce, *Administrative Law Treatise*, 4th ed., vol. 1, § 6.11.

[30] 132 Sup. Ct. 2156 (2012). [31] 29 U.S.C. §§ 206–7.

[32] Expressed particularly in his essay: D. Dyzenhaus, 'The Politics of Deference: Judicial Review and Democracy', in M. Taggart (ed.), *The Province of Administrative Law* (Oxford: Hart Publishing, 1997), 279.

[33] *Newfoundland and Labrador Nurses' Union* v. *Newfoundland and Labrador (Treasury Board)* [2011] 3 S.C.R. 708, [11]–[14]; 2011 SCC 62.

[34] O. Dixon, 'The Law and the Constitution' (1935) 51 L.Q.R. 590, 595.

[35] 7th ed. (2013), [1–024]–[1–026].

[36] [2012] 1 A.C. 868, [45]–[49], [51]–[52], [142]–[154]; [2011] UKSC 46. See also *A.-G.* v. *National Assembly for Wales Commission* [2013] 1 A.C. 792, [81]; [2012] UKSC 53.

29 of the Scotland Act 1998 (UK), in 'exceptional circumstances' the courts might look beyond section 29 to restrain implementation of decisions which abrogated such 'fundamental rights' as 'the rule of law'. In similar vein, the majority in *R (Lumba)* v. *Secretary of State for the Home Department*[37] appears to support the propositions that, even where an administrative decision is within the relevant statutory power,[38] the failure by that decision to realise the expectation of a favourable exercise of the power is an unlawful act, and that this attribution of illegality is required to maintain the constitutional relationship between the courts and the executive.

But some would say that observance of the rule of law involves more than the exercise of judicial authority, so that, for example, political accountability provides the ordinary means of constraint upon the exercise of power by the executive. Even with respect to the US Constitution, Chief Justice Earl Warren preferred to speak of a 'balancing of powers', that is to say, 'the diffusion of powers so that no one agency of Government could ever take to itself the full power of Government'.[39] Equitable remedies then find their place in a system of government outlined (albeit in an immediate Australian context) by Justice Gageler in a paper delivered when Commonwealth Solicitor-General. He said:

> You start with the notion that the Constitution sets up a system to enlarge the powers of self-government of the people of Australia through institutions of government that are structured to be politically accountable to the people of Australia. You recognise that, within that system, political accountability provides the ordinary constitutional means of constraining governmental power. You see the judicial power as an extraordinary constitutional constraint operating within that system not outside it. You see the judicious use of the judicial power as tailoring itself to the strengths and weaknesses of the ordinary constitutional means of constraining governmental power. You see judicial deference as appropriate where political accountability is inherently strong. You see judicial vigilance as appropriate where political accountability is either inherently weak or endangered.
>
> This will not give you the answer to a particular case: the possibilities are always richer, and the considerations which might legitimately be

[37] [2012] 1 A.C. 245 esp. at [170]–[175]; [2011] UKSC 12. Cf. the treatment of the distinction between law and fact as 'a matter of expediency' in *Jones* v. *First Tier Tribunal and Criminal Injuries Compensation Authority* [2013] 2 A.C. 48, [46]; [2013] UKSC 19.

[38] Here, the powers conferred upon the Secretary of State by the Immigration Act 1971 (UK).

[39] Chief Justice Warren, 'Commentary at the Twelfth Legal Convention of the Law Council of Australia' (1961) 35 A.L.J. 191, 192.

> taken into account are always more varied, than could be explained or predicted by any one theory. But it can give you a framework for understanding at a very broad level why a great deal of modern constitutional doctrine might take the form that it does and how aspects of that doctrine might possibly develop in the future.[40]

He continued:

> The point to be made for present purposes is that both for the Commonwealth and for each of the States there exists through the mechanism of responsible government something that can be described as 'the government' and which not only itself lacks sovereign status but which, through the need for the government constantly to maintain the confidence of a popularly elected legislature, can be seen to have an existence constantly contingent on it maintaining the confidence of the people. The government at each level is thus formally responsible to a head of state who can legally do no wrong yet in practice is politically responsible to and identifiable with the people.[41]

The advantage of equitable remedies

A starting point is provided by the response of a significant nineteenth-century equity judge, James L.J., to the submission that certiorari would be sufficient remedy for Lord Auckland to deal with the threatened depredations to his land in Belgravia by the Westminster Local Board of Works, acting beyond the powers conferred by the Metropolis Management Amendment Act 1862 (UK).[42] An appeal to the Court of Appeal in Chancery from an interlocutory injunction was, by consent, treated as a final hearing of the suit. James L.J. said:

> What is the case? A man files his bill with regard to a grievous wrong which is threatened to be inflicted upon him by a public body, and he has a right to see whether this body has the power to inflict this wrong upon him; or, at all events, to try and relieve his title from the cloud which is put upon it by this proceeding, which has been taken under a public Act of Parliament [*sc.* the Metropolis Management Amendment Act 1862 (UK)] by public functionaries intrusted with great and arbitrary powers. It seems to me to be the same kind of case as those well-known cases in which this Court has exercised its jurisdiction by restraining railway companies from proceeding to take and which they had power to take for one purpose, for

[40] S. Gageler, 'Beyond the Text: A Vision of the Structure and Function of the Constitution', in N. Perram and R. Pepper (eds.), *The Byers Lectures 2000–2012* (Sydney: Federation Press, 2012), 211–12.

[41] *Ibid.*, 205–6. [42] 25 & 26 Vict. c. 102.

> some other purpose for which they were not entitled to take it; or to take part of a house only, where the law obliged them to take the whole of it. In those cases the Court has stopped them at once and granted an injunction, because they were about to exercise their powers in a manner that was oppressive or in a manner that was illegal. I have no doubt therefore that this is a case within the jurisdiction of this Court, and that it is a case proper for this Court to decide once for all instead of obliging Lord *Auckland* to go before a magistrate and discuss before him the question of jurisdiction and the difficult construction of these Acts of Parliament [*sc.* the 1862 Act and the Metropolis Management Act 1855 (18 &19 Vict. c. 120) (UK)], and then to carry the case to the Court of Queen's Bench by *certiorari*, or to take some other step to get it finally decided.[43]

This passage illustrates the point that while an injunction may be refused if there be another and adequate remedy, the efficiency of the procedures in Chancery after the reforms of the 1850s[44] favoured equitable relief over that available at common law under the prerogative writs.

Chancery procedure, the influence of which remains apparent in modern Judicature systems, had distinctive characteristics. One of these remains the requirement that all persons interested in the subject matter of the suit generally[45] ought to be made parties so as to settle the controversy by binding those interested to the final decree.[46] Another is the ability of the court to tailor or mould relief to meet the particular circumstance of the case. A declaration may be made that, in a pending matter before it, a tribunal should not follow its earlier decisions on a point of statutory construction, leaving the tribunal otherwise at liberty to continue with the matter before it. The operation of an injunction may be suspended for a time to allow a public authority to get its house in order, and there may be liberty reserved to apply to discharge the order.[47]

A plaintiff may be put on terms which condition the grant of relief, thereby giving effect to the principle that a party seeking equity must be

[43] *Auckland (Lord)* v. *Westminster Local Board of Works* (1872) L.R. 7 Ch. App. 597, 603–4.

[44] See P.I. McMahon, 'Field, Fusion and the 1850s: How an American Law Reformer Influenced the Judicature Act of 1875', Chapter 22 of this volume, and M. Leeming, 'Five Judicature Fallacies', in J.T. Gleeson, J.A. Watson and R.C.A. Higgins (eds.), *Historical Foundations of Australian Law – Vol I: Institutions, Concepts and Personalities* (Sydney: Federation Press, 2013), 171–3.

[45] Special provision might be made for representative parties: *Wong* v. *Silkfield Pty Ltd* (1999) 199 C.L.R. 235, 261–2; [1999] HCA 48.

[46] *Wong* v. *Silkfield Pty Ltd* (1999) 199 C.L.R. 235, 261–2.

[47] See for example *Jones* v. *Llanrwst Urban District Council* [1911] 1 Ch. 393, 411; *Pride of Derby and Derbyshire Angling Association* v. *British Celanese Ltd* [1953] 1 Ch. 149, 154–5, 182.

prepared to do equity. More unusually, to achieve 'equitable adjustment', a price may be exacted for the defendant successfully maintaining against the plaintiff a discretionary defence. In *Hewson* v. *Sydney Stock Exchange*,[48] the Exchange succeeded on its discretionary defence that the application by the plaintiff, a stockbroker, to restrain the presentation by the Exchange of a bankruptcy petition against him be dismissed by reason of the unclean hands of the plaintiff; but Street J. did so on terms that the Exchange deliver up for cancellation certain deeds which had been executed by the plaintiff.

The declaration may be the only available remedy to vindicate the public interest in due administration where the misconduct is complete and for that or some other reason no prerogative writ is available. Three examples may be given of such an 'equity' in due administration. The report of the Criminal Justice Commission, a statutory body, which was in issue in *Ainsworth* v. *Criminal Justice Commission*[49] carried no immediate legal consequences of its own, and certiorari would not issue. But the High Court declared that in reporting adversely to the appellants, the Commission had failed to observe the requirements of procedural fairness. *Ainsworth* was followed and a declaration was made in *M61/2010* v. *Commonwealth*;[50] the Migration Act 1958 (Cth) did not require the minister to exercise the power in question, so certiorari and mandamus were unavailable where the minister denied procedural fairness in the course of actual exercise of the power; but the declaration vindicated the considerable public interest in the proper exercise of the power.

Further, the considerable interest in the due administration by the police force and law enforcement bodies of statutory powers to authorise 'controlled operations', to produce evidence admissible at trial under special provisions, supports the grant of declaratory relief where the statutory powers have been exceeded; this has been held to outweigh the deep reluctance to use this civil remedy to fragment the criminal process.[51]

48 (1967) 87 W.N. (Pt 1) (NSW) 432, 429–30.

49 (1992) 175 C.L.R. 564. The significance for certiorari of the removal of the legal consequences or purported legal consequences of the exercise of power is further considered in the joint reasons of the court in *Wingfoot Australia Partners Pty Ltd* v. *Kocak* (2013) 252 C.L.R. 480, [26], [29], [31]; [2013] HCA 43.

50 (2010) 243 C.L.R. 319, [99]–[104]; [2010] HCA 41.

51 *Gedeon* v. *Commissioner of the New South Wales Crime Commission* (2008) 236 C.L.R. 120, [22]–[25]; [2008] HCA 43.

What is your equity?

This is the question feared by counsel seeking to pursue an adventurous case for relief from an equity judge. It is one which has to be faced because it requires identification of the animating principles which drive the case for equitable intervention.[52] Is the conduct or threatened conduct of which the plaintiff complains against good conscience in the technical sense of that expression? Does the plaintiff have a sufficient interest in the matter to seek an equitable remedy? Does the plaintiff have available another remedy (including an interlocutory remedy) which equity regards as adequate?

Lord Wilberforce observed in 1984 that, typically, English law fastens upon remedies not upon principles.[53] But matters stand somewhat differently in equity. For example, the simple view that promises are to be kept may support the remedy of damages, but it cannot sufficiently explain those classes of cases in which specific performance is not available; some deeper analysis of the nature of contract law is required. It should be added that Lord Wilberforce went on to say that 'something resembling a system of public law' was being developed 'by an extension of remedies and flexible procedure'.[54]

So it was said by the High Court in *Cardile* v. *LED Builders Pty Ltd*:[55]

> [T]he injunctive remedy is still the subject of development in courts exercising equitable jurisdiction. Thus, whilst once there may have been an absolute requirement that, negative covenants aside, before an injunction might be granted in aid of a legal or statutory right, the right must be proprietary in nature, in modern cases, including, in this Court, *Bradley* v. *The Commonwealth*,[56] there has been no advertence to such a requirement. Again, in this Court, the view once taken that an injunction should issue to restrain breach of a negative stipulation, without weighing the usual discretionary considerations, has been discounted as an overstatement. The use of the anti-suit injunction, at least if granted in aid of contractual rights and obligations, is another example of development of traditional doctrine.
>
> ... [I]n England, it is now settled by several decisions of the House of Lords that the power stated in Judicature legislation – that the court may grant an injunction in all cases in which it appears to the court to be just and convenient to do so – does not confer an unlimited power to grant

[52] *Bateman's Bay Local Aboriginal Land Council* v. *The Aboriginal Community Benefit Fund Pty Ltd* (1998) 194 C.L.R. 247, [25]; [1998] HCA 49; see also *Australian Broadcasting Corp.* v. *Lenah Game Meats Pty Ltd* (2001) 208 C.L.R. 199, [8]; [2001] HCA 63.

[53] *Davy* v. *Spelthorne Borough Council* [1984] 1 A.C. 262, 276.

[54] *Ibid.*, 276.

[55] (1998) 198 C.L.R. 380; [1999] HCA 18.

[56] (1973) 128 C.L.R. 557.

> injunctive relief. Regard must still be had to the existence of a legal or equitable right which the injunction protects against invasion or threatened invasion, or other unconscientious conduct or exercise of legal or equitable rights.[57]

As early as 1838, Lord Cottenham L.C. referred to the exercise of powers by railway and canal corporations and other statutory bodies and said of them:

> If, under presence of an authority which the law does give them to a certain extent, they go beyond the line of their authority, and infringe or violate the rights of others, they become like all other individuals, amenable to the jurisdiction of this court by injunction.[58]

The rights of which the Lord Chancellor spoke in terms were not confined to proprietary rights, but that would have been the common understanding of the time; equity acted in the auxiliary jurisdiction to restrain injuries to proprietary rights where there was no adequate legal remedy. In more recent times, as noted in the passage from *Cardile* set out above, the insistence upon a proprietary character of the right of the plaintiff has weakened, if not disappeared. As long ago as 1923, in a case in which the plaintiffs sought injunctions to restrain deportation proceedings which were conducted by a statutory authority under the Immigration Act 1901 (Cth), Isaacs J. stated that no legal claim higher than that to personal liberty could be asserted, save that to life itself.[59]

Speaking in broad terms, the need for the Attorney-General's fiat unless, in the absence of infringement of a private legal right, the plaintiff can show special damage over and above that suffered by the public at large – a 'rule' associated with *Boyce* v. *Paddington Corp.*[60] – has been much relaxed, whether by rules of court or judicial decisions. Indeed, in *Ainsworth* v. *Criminal Justice Commission*[61] Mason C.J., Dawson, Toohey and Gaudron JJ. said that issues of adequacy of standing were determined 'by the considerations which mark out the boundaries of the judicial power', including the presence of a 'real interest' of the plaintiff, and the avoidance of abstract or hypothetical questions.[62]

57 *Cardile* v. *LED Builders Pty Ltd* (1998) 198 C.L.R. 380, [30]–[31].

58 *Frewin* v. *Lewis* (1838) 4 My. & Cr. 249, 255; 41 E.R. 98, 100. See also *A.-G.* v. *Bishop of Manchester* (1867) L.R. 3 Eq. 436, 455.

59 *R* v. *Macfarlane, Ex p. O'Flanagan and O'Kelly* (1923) 32 C.L.R. 518, 540. See also *Tait* v. *R* (1962) 108 C.L.R. 620, where officers of the executive government of Victoria were restrained from executing the applicant, pending the disposition of his application for special leave to appeal.

60 [1903] 1 Ch. 109. 61 (1992) 175 C.L.R. 564. 62 *Ibid.*, 581–2.

In Australia, it has been suggested that this relaxation of the requirements for sufficient standing to support direct action without involvement of the Attorney-General is a response to the acceleration in recent times of the process of the 'politicisation' of the position of the First Law Officer.[63]

The Crown

The correct form of injunctive order is directed to 'the defendant by himself his servants and agents', the latter not being parties to the suit.[64] (Of course, a third party who knowingly facilitates breach of the injunction may be in contempt.[65]) How does this apply where the public authority whose conduct is to be restrained is the Crown itself? The question becomes more acute where the conduct complained of (e.g. in administering a scheme or program) is not an exercise of authority conferred by statute, but is the expression of executive power (or the 'prerogative' as it often is put in the United Kingdom), albeit funded by parliamentary appropriation.[66] What, if any, remains in this setting of the maxim that the Crown can do no wrong and the principle (in the absence of statutory or constitutional provisions which qualify or remove it[67]) of the immunity of the Crown from suit in the royal courts of justice? Even after the Crown Proceedings Act 1947 (UK), the use of the injunction in public law was constrained by the proposition that to enjoin a Department of State or one of its officers would be to restrain the Crown.

At bottom, the problem in the United Kingdom appears to have been a failure in the common law to detach the notion that 'the King can do no wrong' and what Sir Owen Dixon described as 'the splendour of the

[63] *Bateman's Bay Local Aboriginal Land Council* v. *Aboriginal Community Benefit Fund Pty Ltd* (1998) 194 C.L.R. 247, [38]; D. Williams, 'The Role of the Attorney-General' (2002) 13 Public L. Rev. 232, 261–2; B. Selway, 'The Different Role of an Australian Attorney-General' (2002) 13 Public L. Rev. 263, 270–1.

[64] *Marengo* v. *Daily Sketch and Sunday Graphic Ltd* [1948] 1 All E.R. 406; *Colbeam Palmer Ltd* v. *Stock Affiliates Pty Ltd* (1968) 122 C.L.R. 25, 47–8.

[65] *A.-G.* v. *Newspaper Publishing Plc* [1988] Ch. 333, a sequel to the interlocutory injunctive relief granted in the *Spycatcher* litigation.

[66] Examples are the Criminal Injuries Compensation Scheme considered in *R* v. *Secretary of State for the Home Department, Ex p. Fire Brigades Union* [1995] 2 A.C. 513, and the National School Chaplaincy Program considered in *Williams* v. *Commonwealth* (2012) 248 C.L.R. 156; [2012] HCA 23.

[67] In Australia, section 75(iii) of the Constitution construed in *Commonwealth* v. *Mewett* (1997) 191 C.L.R. 471.

Crown' from 'the Crown as the legal expression of the sovereignty of the State'.[68] More specifically, this has remained so despite Lord Penzance (in 1876),[69] and Lord Diplock (in 1978)[70] having identified 'the Crown' with 'the Government', being the executive rather than the legislative branch, and comprising the Ministry and the administrative bureaucracy which attends to the business of the Departments of State. The practice seems to have developed – the *Factortame* litigation is an example – of seeking to enjoin a particular secretary of state, thereby rendering the minister directly accountable for any contempt.[71]

The decision in *In re M*[72] rests upon the holding that statute (section 31(2) of the Supreme Court Act 1981 (UK)[73]) conferred jurisdiction to enjoin ministers and other officials, on applications for judicial review. Professor Loughlin has regretted that the opportunity was not taken to effect the detachment referred to above.[74]

In a federal system such as in Canada and Australia (if not also today in the United Kingdom) it is necessary to confront these issues. To quote again from Sir Owen Dixon:[75]

> The Constitution sweeps aside the difficulties which might be thought to arise in a federation from the traditional distinction between, on the one hand the position of the Sovereign as the representative of the State in a monarchy, and the other hand the State as a legal person in other forms of government (see per Cairns L.J. in *USA* v. *Wagner*[76]) and goes directly to the conceptions of ordinary life. From beginning to end it treats the Commonwealth and the States as organizations or institutions of government possessing distinct individualities. Formally they may not be juristic persons, but they are conceived as politically organized bodies having mutual legal relations and amenable to the jurisdiction of courts upon which the responsibility of enforcing the Constitution rests.

In New South Wales, injunctions may be granted against the defendant-styled 'State of New South Wales'.[77] There is comparable legislation in

[68] Dixon, 'The Law and the Constitution', 593.
[69] *Dixon* v. *London Small Arms Co.* (1876) 1 App. Cas. 632, 651.
[70] *Town Investments Ltd* v. *Department of the Environment* [1978] A.C. 359, 380–1. See also at 400 (Lord Simon of Glaisdale).
[71] *In re M* [1994] 1 A.C. 377. [72] *Ibid.*
[73] See now Senior Courts Act 1981 (UK), s. 31(2).
[74] M. Loughlin, 'The State, the Crown and the Law', in M. Sunkin and S. Payne (eds.), *The Nature of the Crown: A Legal and Political Analysis* (Oxford University Press, 1999), 32, 59. See, further, *Sue* v. *Hill* (1999) 199 C.L.R. 462, [83]–[94]; [1999] HCA 30.
[75] *Bank of NSW* v. *Commonwealth* (1948) 76 C.L.R. 1, 363.
[76] (1867) L.R. 2 Ch. App. 582, 593–4. [77] Crown Proceedings Act 1988 (NSW), s. 5.

other states. However, in Tasmania[78] and South Australia[79] the legislation forbids the grant of mandatory injunctions against not only the state but also against ministers and agencies, instrumentalities, and persons prescribed by regulation.

The basis for equitable intervention

We are concerned here, as elsewhere in the world of equity, with the unconscientious exercise of legal power, in particular, power conferred by statute. One such exercise of power is that beyond its enabling terms, captured by the phrase *ultra vires*. The public law expression 'jurisdictional error' then comes to mind.

Another species of unconscientious exercise of legal power assumes that the activity was within the terms of the legal power but, particularly with respect to powers conferred upon trustees, stigmatises it as a fraud on the power.[80] Thus directors may act within the constraints of the constituent documents of the company but a particular exercise of the power to issue shares may be liable to attack in equity as a fraud on that power.[81]

Both ideas are captured in the identification by the US Supreme Court a century ago of two grounds for equitable relief in public law as 'a ruling in excess of jurisdiction' and 'an arbitrary exercise of statutory power'.[82] The Administrative Procedure Act[83] draws within the scope of review actions findings and conclusions which are 'arbitrary', 'capricious', or 'an abuse of discretion'. The development and retention in the United States of equity jurisprudence in public law is given detailed treatment in the chapter by Professor Henry E. Smith.[84]

Sir Anthony Mason, writing in the *Law Quarterly Review*,[85] observed that the regulation by the injunction and declaration of the exercise of fiduciary powers has guided the shaping of modern administrative law.

[78] Crown Proceedings Act 1993 (Tas.), ss. 4, 8.

[79] Crown Proceedings Act 1992 (SA), ss. 4, 7.

[80] Discussed in detail by Higgins J. in *Commonwealth* v. *Colonial Combing Spinning and Weaving Co. Ltd* (1922) 31 C.L.R. 421, 469–72.

[81] See, for example, *Harlowe's Nominees Pty Ltd* v. *Woodside (Lakes Entrance) Oil Co. NL* (1968) 121 C.L.R. 483, 492.

[82] *Degge* v. *Hitchcock*, 229 U.S. 162, 170–1 (1913).

[83] 5 U.S.C. § 706.

[84] H.E. Smith, 'Equity and Administrative Behaviour', Chapter 18 of this volume.

[85] A. Mason, 'The Place of Equity and Equitable Remedies in the Common Law World' (1994) 110 L.Q.R. 238, 238.

These remedies, as noted above, were concerned not merely with absence of power, but with abuse of power.

The administration of trusts has provided a fertile source of litigation. Charitable trusts, in particular, concern public not just private rights. It tends to be overlooked that the Statute of Charitable Uses of 1601,[86] to the preamble to which countless generations of law students have been referred and which countless cases have considered, was concerned to remedy certain abuses in administration.[87] At a higher level of abstraction, there was the notion that holders of public office were accountable to the commonweal for the use and exercise of their office.[88] In more recent times, in *Horne* v. *Barber*,[89] Rich J. remarked that, in dealing with transactions between private persons, courts of equity have looked strictly upon self-dealing by trustees and that this attitude applied 'with greater force to public affairs and the obligations and the responsibility of the trust towards the public implied by the position of representatives of the people'. The attributions to public officers of fiduciary responsibilities may be seen in *Reading* v. *R.*[90]

Two legislative developments associated with the growth of a recognisably modern state apparatus stimulated the nineteenth-century equity judges. Reference has been made above to the first, the conferral upon statutory bodies of powers injuriously to affect the rights of landowners.

The second development concerned local government. The Municipal Corporations Act 1835 (UK)[91] subjected borough funds to the control of the Court of Chancery, with the position of municipal corporations assimilated to that of trustees; this brought with it equitable remedies to prevent or redress breaches of trust. The essential issue was whether,

[86] 43 Eliz. I, c. 4.

[87] G. Jones, *History of the Law of Charity 1532–1827* (Cambridge University Press, 1969), 17–56.

[88] P.D. Finn, 'A Sovereign People, A Public Trust', in P.D. Finn (ed.), *Essays on Law and Government. Vol. 1: Principles and Values* (Sydney: Law Book Co., 1995), 9–14; S. Anderson, 'The Courts and the Crown; the Still-Birth of Public Law in England', in W. Cornish, S. Anderson, R. Cocks, M. Lobban, P. Polden and K. Smith (eds.), *The Oxford History of the Laws of England: Volume XI 1820–1914 English Legal System* (Oxford University Press, 2010), 366–9; Cf. *Tito* v. *Waddell (No. 2)* [1977] Ch. 106, 216.

[89] (1920) 27 C.L.R. 49, 501–2. See also G.W. Thomas, *Thomas on Powers*, 2nd ed. (Oxford University Press, 2012), [1.62].

[90] [1949] 2 K.B. 232 (C.A.); [1951] A.C. 507 (H.L.).

[91] 5 & 6 Will. IV, c. 76. See generally, S. Anderson 'Municipal Corporations', in *The Oxford History of the Laws of England: Volume XI 1820–1914 English Legal System*, 429–37; J. Barratt, 'Public Trusts' (2006) 69 M.L.R. 514, 521–6.

within the meaning of the statute, the challenged expenditure was 'for the benefit of the inhabitants and the improvement of the Borough';[92] in this way, there was a judicial assimilation of the trust law respecting the exercise of powers by trustees.

A court of equity might intervene by directing trustees to reconsider the exercise of their discretion (not being an absolute discretion)[93] or by making a declaration and leaving it to the trustees to act in accordance with that relief.[94] The causes of complaint included both action by the trustees that was corrupt, oppressive or otherwise improper or was irrational or perverse,[95] and also inaction by failure or refusal to exercise their power.

Against this background, it may be thought that in *Associated Picture Houses Ltd* v. *Wednesbury Corp.*,[96] Lord Greene M.R. had trust law principles in mind. Those principles emphasised that the court did not intervene by way of 'merits review'. (The plaintiff had sought a declaration that the conditions attached by the licensing authority were '*ultra vires* and unreasonable'.[97])

In *Pitt* v. *Holt*,[98] the Supreme Court, speaking through Lord Walker J.S.C., has cautioned against pressing too far the analogy between what the law requires of trustees in their decision-making and of decision-makers in the field of public law. That said, the analogy with the powers of trustee is consistent with the constitutional considerations indicated in the passage from *Enfield* set out earlier in this chapter. This suggests the need for caution in an expansion of judicial review into an appeal on the merits against what appears to be a hard result at the administrative level. The distinction, and contrast, between an appeal and a review in this field was recently discussed, with reference to Australian authorities and affirmed, by Gageler J. in *Minister for Immigration and Citizenship* v. *Li*.[99]

[92] *A.-G.* v. *Corp. of Norwich* (1848) 16 Sim. 225; 60 E.R. 860. See, more recently, *Bromley London Borough Council* v. *Greater London Council* [1983] 1 A.C. 768, 814–15 (Lord Wilberforce); *Porter* v. *Magill* [2002] 2 A.C. 357, [19]; [2001] UKHL 67 (Lord Bingham); *Westminster City Council* v. *Porter (No. 2)* [2003] Ch. 436, [15]–[16]; [2002] EWHC 2179 (Ch) (Hart J.).

[93] *Wain* v. *(Lord) Egmont* (1843) 3 My. & R. 445; 40 E.R. 170.

[94] *Cowan* v. *Scargill* [1985] Ch. 270, 296–7.

[95] *Re Manisty's Settlement* [1974] Ch. 17, 26. It was said in *Scott* v. *National Trust for Places of Historic Interest or Natural Beauty* [1998] 2 All E.R. 705, 717, to be clear beyond argument that trustees must act in good faith, responsibly and reasonably, and inform themselves of relevant matters before making their decisions.

[96] [1948] 1 K.B. 223. [97] *Ibid.*, 224. [98] [2013] 2 A.C. 65, [11]; [2013] UKSC 26.

[99] (2013) 249 C.L.R. 332, [105]–[111]; [2013] HCA 18.

Grounds for equitable intervention

Plainly enough these will include cases of *ultra vires*. In England, with the apparent merging of error of law and *ultra vires*, so that an error of law renders the decision one beyond power,[100] there will be scope for injunctive relief in circumstances not attracting review elsewhere.[101]

It should then be emphasised that there may be abuse of power, within the sense discussed above, without an absence of power. That is to say, there may be what a court of equity, from which an injunction is sought, regards in the technical sense as a fraud on the statutory power in question. When the court will so regard a particular case cannot be answered by setting up a system of closed categories.

It is said in the joint reasons in *Plaintiff S157/2002* v. *Commonwealth*[102] that 'injunctive relief would clearly be available for fraud, bribery, dishonesty or other improper purposes' and 'may be' available on grounds wider than jurisdictional error as understood with prohibition and mandamus. In *Abebe* v. *Commonwealth*,[103] Gaudron J. instanced the erroneous placement by a tribunal of limits on its functions or powers, and in *Muin* v. *Refugee Tribunal*,[104] her Honour saw a sufficient equity for injunctive relief in failure by the tribunal to take a procedural step which had it been taken might have affected the ultimate decision.

Conclusion

In the first edition of *Judicial Review of Administrative Action*, published in 1959, Professor de Smith noted[105] that in the United States the injunction had become the most important of judicial remedies in federal administrative law; in England, save for actionable civil wrongs committed by public authorities, the injunction remained 'relatively inconspicuous'. This was so, he observed,[106] even though there was a sense of greater freedom in the fields of equity after 'the labyrinthine by-ways of the common law'.

[100] *O'Reilly* v. *Mackman* [1982] 2 A.C. 237, 278; *R* v. *Hull University Visitor, Ex p. Page* [1993] A.C. 682, 696, 702.

[101] *Kirk* v. *Industrial Court of New South Wales* (2010) 239 C.L.R. 531, [65]; [2010] HCA 1.

[102] (2003) 211 C.L.R. 476, [82]; [2003] HCA 2.

[103] (1999) 197 C.L.R. 510, [107]–[108]; [1999] HCA 14.

[104] (2002) 76 A.L.J.R. 966, [47]; [2002] HCA 30.

[105] S.A. de Smith, *Judicial Review of Administrative Action*, 1st ed. (London: Stevens, 1959), 365.

[106] *Ibid.*, 323.

Perhaps the slower development in English public law may be a reflection of the apprehension that the discretion which attends the administration of equitable relief undermines the certainty which is desirable in public administration. Similar reservations have long been apparent in the Commercial Court, and, more recently, in what appears to be the concentration in England upon imposing a rigid taxonomy on principles of restitution, and resisting the imposition of the remedial constructive trust.[107]

An answer may be suggested in a letter written by Holmes to Pollock on 26 October 1919. Holmes wrote that he had just sent back a draft judgment by a colleague which was marred by an argument 'of the "where are you going to draw the line" type'; rather, as Holmes put it, all decisions are 'a series of points tending to fix a point in a line' and '[t]he admission of an antithesis between extremes necessitates it', as 'the North and South Poles import an equator'.[108]

At all events, Professor de Smith concluded:[109]

> One may reasonably predict that in the general field of administrative law the tendency will be for the role of the injunction and the declaratory order gradually to increase in importance, not only in those areas of administrative activity that lie within the ambit of certiorari, prohibition and mandamus but also in the areas that lie beyond.

He has been proved correct.

[107] *Sinclair Investments (UK) Ltd* v. *Versailles Trade Finance Ltd* [2012] Ch. 453, [37]; [2011] EWCA Civ 347; *FHR European Ventures LLP* v. *Cedar Capital Partners LLC* [2015] A.C. 250, [45], [47]; [2014] UKSC 45; cf. *Grimaldi* v. *Chameleon Mining NL (No. 2)* (2012) 200 F.C.R. 296, [574]; [2012] FCAFC 6.

[108] M. deW. Howe (ed.), *The Holmes-Pollock Letters* (Cambridge, Mass.: Harvard University Press, 1946), vol. II, 28.

[109] De Smith, *Judicial Review of Administrative Action*, 1st ed., 323.

17

Equity in the modern administrative state

A commentary

DAVID FELDMAN

Introduction

In his valuable chapter (Chapter 16), Professor Gummow provides us with a structure within which to consider the relationship between equitable remedies, in which he includes declarations, and public administration. The main features of his chapter seem to me to be these.

(a) Professor Gummow adopts a comparative approach, noting the significant differences between the ways in which judges in Australia, Canada, the United Kingdom, and the United States approach the task of reviewing administrative decision-making but arguing that there are certain features of equity which make it important in each of those systems.

(b) He distinguishes between constitutional review and administrative law review, while noting that administrative law is rooted in constitutional law. The constitutional context of the law is important: it sets the scope of and limits to the roles of judicial remedies. For example, in Australia, section 75(v) of the Commonwealth Constitution entrenches the availability of prerogative writs against officers of the Commonwealth, whereas in the United Kingdom, judicial review remedies have only common law protection against exclusion by way of principles of statutory interpretation, subject to the possibility that courts might refuse to give effect to legislation which fundamentally undermines the rule of law.[1] Another difference is between ways in which different jurisdictions have responded to the challenge to normal remedial structures which the notion of

[1] See for example *R (A)* v. *Director of Establishments of the Security Service* [2010] 2 A.C. 1, [21]–[24]; [2009] UKSC 12 (Lord Brown of Eaton-under-Heywood J.S.C.). I am grateful to Dr Peter Turner for drawing the significance of this to my attention.

the Crown (substituting for the State) represents in constitutional law.

(c) In relation to the substance of administrative law, he observes, with appropriate caution, similarities between the equitable obligations of trustees and other fiduciaries in private law and the obligations of holders of public office in administrative and constitutional law.

(d) He reveals how equitable remedies can fill gaps between administrative law remedies, providing effective redress where the prerogative writs (or as they are now known in the United Kingdom, orders) would be unlikely to achieve a satisfactory outcome.

Professor Gummow's conclusion is that the late Professor de Smith was a true prophet when he wrote in 1959 that the importance of equitable remedies to the development of administrative law was likely to increase. One could sum it up by saying that their role has increased, is increasing, and ought not to be diminished.

The comments which follow are concerned mainly with the constitutional roots of administrative law, the fiduciary obligations of public officials, and the capacity of equitable remedies to fill remedial gaps left by prerogative writs or orders.

Public-sector obligations and the constitutional roots of administrative law

Professor Gummow argues that the basis for equitable intervention in administrative settings is the unconscientious exercise of administrative power, particularly power conferred by statute. Exceeding the power and committing a fraud on the power (on the analogy of trustees or directors) – called in the United States an 'arbitrary exercise of statutory power' – are the grounds for equitable intervention in administrative law, and the use of injunctions and declarations has helped to shape it. In Australia, where flawed administrative decisions are regarded as void only if something of those kinds has occurred (other flaws making the decision voidable, i.e. valid until quashed), this analogy is consistent with broader constitutional principles: as political and administrative means of control are available to keep administrative decision-makers within their bounds,

> there has never been a pervasive notion that limited government mandated an all-encompassing judicial duty to supply all of the relevant

> meaning of statutes. Rather, the judicial duty is to ensure that the administrative agency stays within the zone of discretion committed to it by its organic act.[2]

Professor Gummow acknowledges that Lord Walker of Gestingthorpe J.S.C. in *Pitt* v. *Holt* has cautioned against taking the analogy between trustees and public-law decision-makers too far,[3] pointing out that the Court of Appeal in the same case had disapproved the analogy.[4] Nevertheless, Professor Gummow considers that there is a similarity between principles of equity and those of administrative law, and between the way in which equity and administrative law use injunctions and declarations. The link which Professor Gummow sees helps to explain several phenomena in English law that are otherwise hard to explain. One example is the use of what appear to be administrative law principles of procedural fairness in cases involving private parties where there is no pre-existing contractual relationship.[5] It is therefore worth considering the arguments against such an analogy. As Lord Walker observed in *Pitt* v. *Holt*, Lightman J. had previously 'identified three important differences as the discretionary nature of relief in judicial review, a different approach to nullity, and strict time limits'.[6]

With respect to Lightman J., I am not convinced that those differences are particularly significant, at least for our purposes. Remedies are discretionary in equity as well as in judicial review. (The only remedies which are not discretionary are common law damages and habeas corpus.) The discretion may be exercised according to somewhat different criteria in private law and public law settings, but when equitable remedies are used in judicial review, one can safely assume that the criteria will be those which are normally applicable to the exercise of remedial discretion in administrative law. The second difference, between approaches to nullity in equity and administrative law, may be more apparent than real. In Australia, as already observed, administrative law has developed in ways which leave the two close together. In England and Wales,

[2] *City of Enfield v. Development Assessment Commission* (2000) 199 CLR 135, [43]; [2000] HCA 5, quoting H.P. Monaghan, '*Marbury* and the Administrative State' (1983) 83 Colum. L. Rev. 1, 32–3.

[3] *Pitt* v. *Holt* [2013] 2 A.C. 108, [11]; [2013] UKSC 26.

[4] [2012] Ch. 132, [77] (Lloyd L.J.), [235] (Mummery L.J.); [2011] EWCA Civ 197.

[5] See the illuminating discussion by Dr Philip Murray, 'Natural Justice at the Boundaries of Public Law', *UK Const. L. Blog* (21 November 2013) (available at http://ukconstitutionallaw.org).

[6] *Pitt* v. *Holt* [2013] 2 A.C. 108, [11], referring to *Abacus Trust Co. (Isle of Man)* v. *Barr* [2003] Ch. 409, [29]; [2003] EWHC 114 (Ch) (Lightman J.).

a theory has developed among administrative lawyers that all errors are errors of law, and that any error of law makes a decision a nullity. But this seems to me to be simply wrong. If we look at what courts actually do in practice (and leave aside the lip service which judges often pay to the theory), we find that there are many, many cases in which flawed decisions are not nullities; they survive as a matter of law.[7] As for judicial review's strict time limits, it is not clear why they should affect the substance of a public officer's obligations.

The case for a link between equitable and public law obligations is, I suggest, strong. Professor Dawn Oliver has long argued that the same values are pervasive in private law and public law.[8] Even if one does not accept that the identity between the values of public law and private law is as complete as Professor Oliver suggests – there seem to me to be some values in public law, such as good administration, democratic accountability, and transparency, which are not replicated in private law – Professor Oliver's argument is persuasive at least to the extent that the values of private law can be seen operating in public law, though their effects might be affected by having to operate in a setting where public rather than private interests generally have priority. There are also methodological similarities between administrative law and equity, at least as equity was in the days before the first Lord Hardwicke L.C. turned it into a precedent-regulated field. When students of administrative law struggle to grasp any concrete rules underlying what often seems like a bewildering mass of single instances, particularly in areas such as natural justice, unreasonableness, and legitimate expectation, one is inclined to start murmuring about the length of the Lord Chief Justice's foot. Administrative law is governed by general principles rather than rules. The difference between its principles and those of equity is that administrative law is administered largely so as to secure the public good rather than private equity. Equity can therefore fit comfortably alongside administrative law, whether or not there are historical continuities between them.

This does not mean, however, that the equitable obligations of public officers are identical to those of private fiduciaries. Each of their respective sets of obligations is a result of the need to accommodate a number of principles which are in tension with each other. In the public sphere, the

[7] For full discussion, see D. Feldman, 'Error of Law and Flawed Administrative Acts' [2014] C.L.J. 275.

[8] D. Oliver, *Common Values and the Public-Private Divide* (London: Butterworths, 1999).

public good is a far weightier matter than it is in relation to private trusts or companies. If we forget this, we fall into serious error. Two cases in which the House of Lords fell into that error should always be in our minds, because they remind us what can go wrong if we treat public officers simply as if they were private fiduciaries. One is *Roberts* v. *Hopwood*,[9] in which the House of Lords prevented the electorally accountable, Labour-controlled Poplar London Borough Council from introducing an equal pay policy on the ground (among others) that it would breach the council's fiduciary duty to its ratepayers. The other is *Bromley London Borough Council* v. *Greater London Council*,[10] in which the House of Lords deployed a similar argument to prevent the electorally accountable, Labour-controlled Greater London Council from introducing subsidised fares on London Transport. In each case, the idea that local authorities had a fiduciary obligation to ratepayers was used to justify elevating individual over collective goods, ignoring the fact that public bodies exist for the collective rather than individual good. Nowadays, it is not respectable to cite either case, except as a dreadful warning.

Other cases which display similar, though not identical, flaws are those in which governments seek accounts of profit to discourage publishers from publishing confidential information about the behaviour of institutions of the state. For example, the newspapers which published extracts from *Spycatcher*, a memoir by former Security Service (MI5) officer Peter Wright of his time in MI5, eventually established that they should not have been prevented from continuing to do so, but were still required to account for their profits on the basis that they had been implicated in breaches of Wright's duty of confidence owed to the Government.[11] The implication was that it was in the public interest to publish the extracts, but that the publishers should not profit from having done so. The government received a windfall which was not compensatory, since the government had lost nothing of financial value; it was an expropriation of gains made by private publishers in a matter of public interest, but the private-law principles were applied in a way which did not recognise that this was a public-law matter. The later extension of restitutionary remedies to deprive George Blake, a former officer of the Secret Intelligence Service, MI6, of gains made by publishing a memoir of his treasonous activities in breach of his contract of secrecy with MI6 is an

[9] [1925] A.C. 578. [10] [1983] 1 A.C. 768.
[11] *A.-G.* v. *Guardian Newspapers Ltd (No. 2)* [1990] 1 A.C. 109.

example of the converse effect, when a perceived public interest was used to justify damagingly distorting the principles on which private law remedies are deployed by confusing account of profits with contractual remedies.[12]

Equitable remedies in public law

In relation to curial intervention, Professor Gummow reminds us that applications for equitable relief against the state refer us to a deep question concerning 'the degree of interaction between the branches of government',[13] as to which there are constitutional differences between jurisdictions. In Australia, the role of the court in administrative law is to ensure that other branches stay within the limits of their statutory powers. Once within them, political rather than legal controls operate in respect of the merits of administrative decisions. In the United States, Canada, and the United Kingdom, the relationship between branches is seen differently, leading to a difference in the way equitable remedies are used. In the United States' desegregation cases, injunctions were deployed inventively and intrusively. On the other hand, where a statutory scheme creates specific agencies to make decisions, courts respect decisions of those agencies, including decisions as to the interpretation of the statute if they are not unreasonable. In Canada, the Supreme Court has taken an even more deferential approach to agency decision-making.

In the United Kingdom, Professor Gummow considers that judicial decisions have flowed 'actively and strongly in the other direction'.[14] He points out that the rule of law requires more than judicial accountability. The primary form of accountability for institutions of government in a democracy is political, and judicial review operates as an extraordinary remedy within the democratic structure of the constitution (quoting Gageler J. in a paper delivered when Solicitor General).[15]

[12] *A.-G.* v. *Blake* [2001] 1 A.C. 268. See R. Buxton, 'How the Common Law Gets Made: *Hedley Byrne* and Other Cautionary Tales' (2009) 125 L.Q.R. 60, 60–1, 73–8.

[13] W. Gummow, 'Equity in the Modern Administrative State', Chapter 16 of this volume, text after n. 17.

[14] *Ibid.*, text after n. 33.

[15] S. Gageler, 'Beyond the Text: A Vision of the Structure and Function of the Constitution', in N. Perram and R. Pepper (eds.), *The Byers Lectures 2000–2012* (Sydney: Federation Press, 2012), 205–6, 211–12.

I agree with Professor Gummow that the rule of law requires more than judicial accountability, but, with great reticence, I have to express a doubt as to whether it requires political accountability for governmental institutions. One can imagine regimes in which political accountability is seriously defective yet the rule of law prevails. Pre-1993 South Africa might be an example. It might be said that there was political accountability there, but that shows how slippery the notion is. Does accountability to a legislature and electorate which are grossly unrepresentative qualify as effective political accountability? From another viewpoint, my characterisation of the country as having the rule of law might be questioned, but that shows how slippery the idea of the rule of law is. What can be said, I think, is that the rule of law requires (or even is the idea) that public officers must regard themselves as subject to the law and as being obligated to accept final rulings of independent tribunals on questions of law. They may change them prospectively by legislation or challenge them in later litigation, but if they cease to feel that it is proper to respect the law and the decisions of its independent arbitrators, there can be no effective legal accountability, and the rule of law is dead. The rule of law is, ultimately, an attitude of mind on the part of non-lawyers in government, or what Professor Sir Jeffrey Jowell has called an 'institutional morality'.[16]

The position in the United Kingdom seems to me to be as follows. Between 1979 and 1993 or so, and again between 1997 and 2010, political accountability was severely weakened by a combination of the breakdown of a middle-of-the-road political consensus and very large parliamentary majorities for the incumbent government. All sorts of issues were litigated because they could not be effectively resolved through political channels. Courts tried to develop principled responses to novel claims, and in the process significantly extended the common law obligations of public bodies. For example, review of the exercise of prerogative powers was largely assimilated to review of statutory powers, and the judicial armoury was reinforced with doctrines such as legitimate expectation, a duty to give reasons as an aspect of natural justice, and reviewable error of fact. This was facilitated by procedural reforms in 1976–78, introducing an Application for Judicial Review procedure in which for the first time the prerogative orders of certiorari, prohibition, and mandamus were available in the same proceedings as injunctions, declarations, and damages, from specialised public law judges.

[16] J. Jowell, 'The Rule of Law and Its Underlying Values', in J. Jowell and D. Oliver (eds.), *The Changing Constitution*, 8th ed. (Oxford University Press, 2015), 27.

The result, I suggest, has been to allow courts (and tribunals) increasingly to plug the accountability deficit which has existed in politics. The period of coalition government since the 2010 general election somewhat redressed the balance, but the severe financial and economic stringency of the period since 2008 simultaneously presented courts with new challenges concerning the way in which financial retrenchment has had effect. The pendulum might well swing back again following the 2015 general election in the United Kingdom. The 2015 general election produced a Conservative Party Government free from any coalition partner; but its overall majority is small, there are many new Conservative MPs, senior Tories are manoeuvring against each other to succeed Mr Cameron as Conservative leader in due course, and there are likely to be significant divisions within the Conservative Party over EU membership. These factors might improve the chance of the House of Commons being able to exercise rigorous scrutiny of the Government, rather than leave it to the relatively less powerful House of Lords. Yet the election also weakened the opposition, with an influx of Scottish National Party MPs who cannot vote on matters affecting only England, a collapse in the number of Liberal Democrats, and a Labour Party embarking on what may be a long period of internal conflict and instability. The likelihood is that on most important policy matters, the Government will get its own way in the Commons, unless Conservative back-benchers disapprove. At the same time, the capacity of the judiciary to provide accountability is being systematically reduced by Government initiatives, including restrictions on judicial review, cuts in the availability of legal aid, and plans to repeal the Human Rights Act 1998 without any clarity, at the time of writing (January 2016), about what will replace it. In these circumstances, it seems likely that the accountability gap will grow, and judges may be less able to redress the balance over the next few years than over the past thirty or forty.

Mention of the Application for Judicial Review procedure brings us back to remedies. Professor Gummow outlines the advantages of injunctions and declarations in equity over the prerogative writs at common law: speediness; flexibility; allowing remedies to be moulded to different circumstances; scope for imposing conditions for the grant of relief; and availability of declarations for the purpose of public interest adjudication.[17] This outline raises two intriguing questions.

[17] In this connection, it is interesting to note that the House of Lords in 1980 regarded the availability of a fuller range of remedies in the special Application for Judicial Review procedure, and removal of some of the procedural disadvantages faced by applicants for

First, why do we need anything other than declarations? If it were true to say that, in England and Wales, all errors are errors of law and all errors of law take bodies outside their jurisdiction, a flawed decision or rule would be void and a nullity without the need for any coercive order. Would a declaration not suffice? It depends both on public administrators and politicians being imbued with the sense of propriety which I described above as the essence of the rule of law and on there being no need to make binding decisions about consequential matters. There is authority for the proposition that, since a flawed order is void, nothing is gained by delaying a declaration that it is so.[18] In reality, that cannot be more than a weak fiction, because the discretionary nature of remedies would then be irrelevant, and cases in which flawed decisions, orders and rules are given full legal effects would be inexplicable.[19]

Secondly, what are the special problems of use of equitable remedies by or against public administration? The problem of giving injunctive relief against the Crown has been resolved in the United Kingdom partly by using declarations instead, relying on the government to act in accordance with the dictates of the rule of law, or (as Professor Gummow points out) by enjoining a natural person, such as a Secretary of State. There was a problem about interlocutory relief, in that an interim declaration was thought to be a contradiction in terms.[20] This, however, did not stop the Rules Committee from making the Civil Procedure Rules 1998 (UK) Part 25.1, which expressly allows a court to make an interim declaration. It has proved difficult, however, to find circumstances in which it is regarded as appropriate to make one, and so far as I have been able to discover none has ever been made against the Crown.

prerogative writs or orders, as justifying courts in treating it as an abuse of process to litigate public-law matters in a private-law procedure (*Cocks* v. *Thanet Urban District Council* [1983] 2 A.C. 286; *O'Reilly* v. *Mackman* [1983] 2 A.C. 237), though the practical problems of deciding what a public-law matter is, coupled with rule-of-law considerations, led to a rapid development of exceptions (*Davy* v. *Spelthorne Urban District Council* [1984] A.C. 262; *Wandsworth London Borough Council* v. *Winder (No. 1)* [1985] A.C. 461; *Roy* v. *Kensington and Chelsea and Westminster Family Practitioner Committee* [1992] 1 A.C. 624; *Boddington* v. *British Transport Police* [1992] 2 A.C. 143, etc.).

[18] *HM Treasury* v. *Ahmed (No. 2)* [2010] 2 A.C. 534; [2010] UKSC 5.

[19] There have been several attempts to explain the inexplicable, but none of them convinces me, and they would be unnecessary if we simply accepted reality instead of paying lip-service to unrealistic theories.

[20] *International General Electric* v. *Commissioners of Customs and Excise* [1962] Ch. 784, 790 (Diplock L.J.); *Riverside Mental Health Trust* v. *Fox* [1994] 1 F.L.R. 614; *St George's Healthcare NHS Trust* v. *S* [1998] 2 F.L.R. 728, 755.

Attempts by defendants or potential defendants to a criminal prosecution to obtain a declaration from a civil court that they are not guilty of an offence have not generally been successful, although there seems to be no rule entirely excluding them.[21] Whilst there are circumstances in which a court will conduct judicial review of a decision by a prosecuting authority to prosecute (or not to prosecute), the relief is not usually by way of injunction. But in cases involving directly applicable or directly effective EU law, courts are required to provide effective relief from domestic law which conflicts with it, even if that involves giving interim or final injunctions against the Crown.[22]

Where an enforcement agency, including the Crown, applies for an injunction to enforce a law, the position in England and Wales remains as it has long been. The Attorney General as guardian of the public interest has standing to seek such an injunction, as do local authorities under the Local Government Act 1972 (UK), s. 222(1) where they 'consider it expedient for the promotion or protection of the interests of the inhabitants of their area', but other people or bodies have no such power unless it is expressly conferred by statute or the person concerned has the Attorney General's consent to a relator action.[23] There is no rule against requiring the agency to give an undertaking in damages as a condition for granting the injunction; the court has discretion, though there will usually have to be special circumstances to cause the court to require an undertaking in damages.[24]

Conclusion

I fully and respectfully agree with the main thrust of Professor Gummow's contribution. Where I depart from his views, it is to add to

[21] *Imperial Tobacco Ltd* v. *A.-G.* [1981] A.C. 718. See D. Feldman, 'Declarations and the Control of Prosecutions' [1981] Crim. L.R. 25.

[22] See for example Case C-213/89, *R* v. *Secretary of State for Transport, Ex p. Factortame Ltd* [1990] 3 C.M.L.R. 1 (E.C.J.); *R* v. *Secretary of State for Transport, Ex p. Factortame (No. 2)* [1991] A.C. 603; *R* v. *HM Treasury, Ex p. British Telecommunications plc* [1994] 1 C.M.L.R. 621.

[23] *Gouriet* v. *Union of Post Office Workers* [1978] A.C. 435. See D. Feldman, 'Injunctions and the Criminal Law' (1979) 42 M.L.R. 369.

[24] *F. Hoffmann-La Roche & Co. AG* v. *Secretary of State for Trade and Industry* [1975] A.C. 295; *Kirklees Metropolitan Borough Council* v. *Wickes Building Supplies Ltd* [1993] A.C. 227; *Financial Services Authority* v. *Sinaloa Gold plc* [2013] 2 A.C. 28, [31]; [2013] UKSC 11, where Lord Mance J.S.C. pointed out that there is no general right to compensation for unlawful administrative action in English law.

the comparative law elements by offering some additional details about distinctive features of administrative law in the United Kingdom, and more particularly England and Wales, as I understand it (and there are those who would say that I do not). Professor Gummow's chapter justifies us in approaching our deliberations in the confident expectation that, where they overlap, equity can illuminate public administration as long as the particular functions of public administration are not forgotten.

18

Equity and administrative behaviour

HENRY E. SMITH

Introduction

Administrative law owes a debt to equity – one that is not always paid in full. Administrative law began its modern era just at the point that law and equity were being fused. As in so many other areas, the fusion of law and equity – despite its promises of rationalisation and transparency – has ironically obscured important functional questions about the design of decision-making institutions. Nowhere is this more so than in administrative law.

The equitable background to administrative law might at first glance appear to be of historical or even antiquarian interest only. I argue that this is false. Equity is a decision-making mode – or cluster of related decision-making modes – that was roughly (but only roughly) associated with traditional equity jurisdiction. The equitable tradition, tracing back to Aristotle, comes in wider and narrower versions. At its widest, we can label as 'equity' any intervention that corrects the law when it is defective owing to its generality. Flexibility and context-sensitivity are the order of the day. This tradition stands behind one variant of the 'equity of the statute', and it formed the backdrop to the desire for flexible expert administration in the early twentieth century.

There is another equitable tradition, especially associated with the actual operation of the doctrines and procedures of the old equity courts, that continues to shape pockets of the law in a half-understood fashion, especially in the United States, my main focus in this chapter. Here equity focuses on a special problem that general rules present: the problem of

For helpful comments and questions, I would like to thank Timothy Endicott, John Golden, Peter Turner and the participants at the seminar on Equity and Administration at Trinity College, Cambridge, in January 2014. All errors are mine.

opportunism. Formal law is vulnerable to efforts at evasion. For example, if a professional actress on the verge of majority invokes voidability to exit a contract for a better deal, a court of equity would refuse to enjoin interference by the forsaken contractual partner with the new contract.[1] Doctrines relating to clean hands and not profiting from one's own wrong implement a narrow version of basic morality aimed especially at people who take advantage of the law in hard-to-foresee ways. The domain of equity courts was 'near fraud': activity that might not be fully provable as fraud but that constitutes behaviour that is both undesirable and hard to specify *ex ante*. Equity in this sense is usually a safety valve, in the sense that it need only intervene for especially serious and elusive types of advantage taking (opportunism). On the spectrum of rules and standards, it is usually meant to be narrow and *ex post*.

Both equitable traditions – the wider and the narrower – find a place in fiduciary law, the most famous major outgrowth of equity.[2] The equity courts developed the trust, in which the settlor typically transfers legal title to a trustee but subject to equitable rights in one or more beneficiaries. The trustee is under fiduciary duties to manage the property in the interest of the beneficiary and more concretely is subject to duties of care and especially loyalty. Here the opportunism problem is presented in a stark form, given the beneficiary's vulnerability and the fiduciary's discretion. Policing for opportunism in this context takes the form of a combination of *ex post* interventions for hard-to-foresee kinds of opportunism and broad *ex ante* prophylactic rules like the no-profit and no-conflicts rules to head off the possibility of opportunism in a broad category of cases arising from the role of the fiduciary. Fiduciary law is equity that goes beyond an *ex post* safety valve. Where the problem of evasion cannot be handled by ever more fine-grained *ex ante* rules, equity may intervene in a tailored way *ex post* or in a broad way *ex ante*.

Equity needs to avoid being both broad and *ex post* – a combination which would lead to limitless discretion. In other words, equity is cabined by operating either as an *ex post* safety valve that will only be triggered by narrow proxies relating to the inadequacy of law and the strong suspicion of opportunism, or as prophylactic *ex ante* rules, at some cost of inaccuracy. Neither approach involves the unbounded discretion implied by

[1] *Carmen* v. *Fox Film Corp.*, 269 F. 928 (2d Cir. 1920).

[2] H.E. Smith, 'Why Fiduciary Law is Equitable', in A.S. Gold and P.B. Miller (eds.), *Philosophical Foundations of Fiduciary Law* (Oxford University Press, 2014), ch. 13.

broad *ex post* intervention. The danger in equity has always lurked in this direction and the fiercest critics of equity saw it as being indeed too broad and *ex post*. This critique is often associated with the rule of law, with equity cast as the threat to it.

Modern administration partakes of both these advantages and dangers of equity. Administrative law grew out of the same needs that equity courts did. As a mixture of executive and quasi-judicial expert decision-making, administration could be more flexible than regular courts. Administrative law was hailed as the new equity at the time.

This chapter will argue that equity as anti-opportunism provides an explanation for why devices originally thought adequate to keep agency opportunism in check are valuable but increasingly inadequate, in that the path of expansion of agencies has outpaced the tools of equity to deal with them. In our post-fusion world, the inadequacy of equity to combat opportunism is typically taken to one of two extremes: a celebration of flexibility at the expense of constraints, or a backlash that denies the value of discretion in the first place. The tradition of equity as anti-opportunism points to the possibility of constrained equity. In many contexts, a defined but not over-expansive version of equitable decision making may still be possible, and some version of it may be unavoidable some of the time.

Administrative law itself has partaken equally of the tradition of equity focused on anti-opportunism. Agencies themselves were meant to act as equity courts did, to prevent gaming and loophole finding by primary actors. But agencies themselves needed to be kept in line, just as trustees did. Traditionally courts relied on their equity jurisdiction to police administrators and afford remedies for those whose rights were violated by administrative action. In the United States, this general equity was partially displaced with the passage of the Administrative Procedure Act (APA) in 1946.[3] I will argue that in addition to non-statutory review, the APA itself incorporates certain strands of equity as anti-opportunism. Recent scholarship emphasises the notion of administrative agencies as fiduciaries, another equitable approach, but one which is hard to implement judicially. Something more is needed.

In the area of administration, the problem of a large administrative state pushes the opportunism problem to ever larger scales, where we

[3] 5 U.S.C. §§ 551–84, 701–6, 1215, 1305, 3105, 3344, 3502, 4301, 5335, 5372, 7521, 7532.

meet the problem of the rule of law.[4] Here we need equity on a macro-scale, on account of the problem of the opportunistic evasion of the criteria for the rule of law. Law can tick the boxes of Lon Fuller's rule-of-law criteria of generality, publicity, non-retroactivity, comprehensibility, non-contradictoriness, feasibility of compliance, stability and administrability,[5] and still be wicked law, as positivists are fond of pointing out.[6] Partly the problem is that no system can be completely formal, and one main reason is the potential for evasion. On this macro-level, though, the possibility of vindicating the rule of law through judicial decision-making can be partial at best. What is required is either a structure that limits the scale of opportunism and tolerates what's left, or a strong social consensus and culture of the rule of law that imposes costs internally and externally on actors at the macro-level for deviations from the rule of law not fully captured in the Fullerian criteria.

This chapter will argue that in its role as a counter to opportunism, equity has played an important role at three successively more general levels: administration, judicial review, and the rule of law. Seeing administrative law through the lens of equity suggests ways simultaneously to shore up and constrain judicial review of administrative decision-making. At the same time, it provides a more precise diagnostic for the dangers to the rule of law inherent in an expansive administrative state.

Equity and opportunism

Equity is not a unitary phenomenon, and it comes in versions varying greatly in their scope and strength.[7] Equity is a slippery concept in part because different strands of the equitable tradition have been more or less intertwined – especially after the fusion of law and equity. In this section, I sketch a theory of one major function of equity, one that is of particular relevance to administration, administrative law and the rule of law itself.

[4] H.E. Smith, 'Property, Equity, and the Rule of Law', in L.M. Austin and D. Klimchuk (eds.), *Private Law and the Rule of Law* (Oxford University Press, 2014), ch. 10.

[5] See L.L. Fuller, *Morality of Law* (New Haven: Yale University Press, 1964), 38–91.

[6] H.L.A. Hart, *The Concept of Law* (Oxford: Clarendon Press, 1961), 202 (arguing that rule of law principles are 'compatible with very great iniquity'); J. Raz, 'Rule of Law and its Virtue', in J. Raz, *The Authority of Law: Essays on Law and Morality*, 2nd ed. (Oxford University Press, 2009), 210, 215.

[7] For a discussion of the wide variety of equitable intervention, with a focus on business associations, see P.G. Turner, 'Equitable Doctrines in Business Associations', Chapter 8 of this volume.

Equity as anti-opportunism

Elsewhere, I have argued that equity can be thought of as a decision-making mode that aims to counter opportunism.[8] Some clue as to this narrower tradition comes from the traditional formulations of the domain of equity. Typically courts and commentators would invoke the triad of 'fraud, accident, and mistake'.[9] Or, in a more poetic version attributed to Thomas More, the first lawyer to serve as Chancellor, one can say that 'Three things are to be helpt in Conscience; Fraud, Accident, and things of Confidence'.[10] Fraud, accident and mistake are a good rough first cut at situations in which opportunism is a danger. Joseph Story, America's foremost commentator on equity, made equity's role in countering opportunism quite plain,[11] when he structured his account of equity jurisdiction by starting with the trust (and confidences), working outward to 'mistake, accident, and fraud', and then adding

> many cases of penalties and forfeitures; many cases of impending irreparable injuries, or meditated mischiefs; and many cases of oppressive proceedings, undue advantages and impositions, betrayals of confidence, and unconscionable bargains; in all of which Courts of Equity will interfere and grant redress; but which the Common Law takes no notice of, or silently disregards.[12]

[8] H.E. Smith, 'An Economic Analysis of Law Versus Equity', working paper (22 October 2010), available: www.law.yale.edu/documents/pdf/LEO/HSmith_LawVersusEquity7.pdf.

[9] 47 Am. Jur. 2d Judgments § 718 ('Generally, claimants seeking equitable relief from judgments through independent actions must meet three requirements [, the third of which is that] they must establish a recognized ground, such as fraud, accident, or mistake, for the equitable relief.') (footnotes omitted); see also W.F. Walsh, *A Treatise on Mortgages* (Chicago, IL: Callaghan, 1934), 6, 11 (relief from mortgages in equity on grounds of fraud, accident, or mistake); V.D. Ricks, 'American Mutual Mistake: Half-Civilian Mongrel, Consideration Reincarnate' (1998) 58 La. L. Rev. 663, 717 and n. 277 (speculating that Allen C.J. in *Swift* v. *Hawkins*, 1 Dall. 17 (Pa. 1768) 'considered "mistake" to be representative of all categories of equity').

[10] H. Rolle, *Un Abridgment des Plusieurs Cases et Resolutions del Common Ley* (London: printed for A. Cooke *et al.*, 1668), vol. 1, 374; see also *Coco* v. *A.N. Clark (Engineers) Ltd* [1969] R.P.C. 41, 46 (Megarry J. quoting More's couplet); A. Laussat, Jr., *An Essay on Equity in Pennsylvania* (Philadelphia: Desilver, 1826), 67 (stating that 'Sir Thomas More used to say that the following doggerel contained all the heads of chancery jurisdiction'). William Blackstone, more a fan of the common law than of equity, gets a little defensive in making the legitimate point that the triggers for equity were not ignored by the common law: W. Blackstone, *Commentaries on the Laws of England* (Oxford: Clarendon Press, 1772), vol. 3, 431.

[11] See nn. 32–3 below and accompanying text.

[12] See J. Story, *Commentaries on Equity Jurisprudence, as Administered in England and America*, 4th ed. (Boston: Little & Brown, 1846), § 29.

Again, I do not mean to make too much of the history of equity. Indeed, even as famous an opponent of expansive equity jurisdiction as Sir Edward Coke saw 'discretion [as] a science or understanding to discern between falsity and truth, between wrong and right, between shadows and substance, between equity and colourable glosses and pretences, and not to do according to their wills and private affections'.[13] As we will see, much of opportunism consists of 'colourable glosses and pretences', and the role of (functional) equity is to employ constrain discretion to defeat them.

Again, it is a functional account I am most interested in – but the overlap between historical equity and functional equity in both theory and practice is quite striking. And there are functional reasons for this convergence: the equity courts were faced with people manipulating the common law to subvert its justice, and at the same time the equity courts were endowed with powerful discretionary tools like the injunction that could easily be misused themselves.

Specifically, the proxies that equity courts used to intervene against potential opportunism are keyed to fraud, accident and mistake or confidence. In areas like unconscionability, courts would look to gross imbalance in knowledge or result (e.g. forfeiture) to scrutinise certain transactions, throwing the burden of justification on the advantaged party.[14] They would also use disproportionate hardship as a reason to withhold injunctions in building encroachment cases. Nevertheless, proxies relating to good faith would disqualify an actor from taking advantage of this reversal of the presumption for an injunction to prevent continuing trespass.

Consider a couple of familiar scenarios with which students used to start their study of equity. In the famous case of *J.R.* v. *M.P.*,[15] the obligee

[13] *Rooke's Case* (1597) 5 Co. Rep. 99b, 100a; 77 E.R. 209, 210.

[14] Smith, 'An Economic Analysis of Law Versus Equity'. A few modern American commentators are faithful to this tradition. See R.A. Epstein, 'Unconscionability: A Critical Reappraisal' (1975) 18 J.L. & Econ. 293, 293–301; J. Gordley, 'Equality in Exchange' (1981) 69 Cal. L. Rev. 1587, 1639; A.A. Leff, 'Unconscionability and the Code – The Emperor's New Clause' (1967) 115 U. Pa. L. Rev. 485, 532, 537, 539.

[15] (1459) Y.B. 37 Hen. VI, f. 13, pl. 3 (Court of Common Pleas). This was the first case in Ames's casebook: J.B. Ames, *A Selection of Cases in Equity Jurisdiction* (Cambridge, Mass.: Harvard Law Review Publishing Association, 1904), vol. 1, 1–2; see also Z. Chafee, Jr. and E.D. Re, *Cases and Materials on Equity*, 5th ed. (Brooklyn: Foundation Press, 1967), 26. See further *The Earl of Oxford's Case* (1615) 1 Ch. Rep. 1, 10; 21 E.R. 485, 487 ('[W]hen a judgment is obtained by Oppression, Wrong and a hard Conscience, the Chancellor will frustrate and set it aside, not for any error or Defect in the Judgment, but for the hard Conscience of the Party'); D. Ibbetson, '*The Earl of Oxford's*

on the debt was paid, but instead of cancelling or destroying the note, negotiated the instrument to a bona fide purchaser, who sued the debtor. The debtor sued in equity and obtained an injunction ordering the misdoer to reimburse the debtor. The equity court defeated the lender's opportunism, based on commercial morality, and did so by a personal order and not the alteration or revision of general rules or even the obligation itself.

A second starting point (and one even more interesting than usually thought) is *Riggs* v. *Palmer*,[16] the case of the murdering heir. For our purposes, the case is a good illustration of the different strands of equity, broader and narrower, and how these have become subsumed in larger debates about formalism and contextualism. Indeed, *Riggs* is one of the commonly discussed cases – if not the most commonly discussed case – in jurisprudence on the question of style of legal reasoning: positivism versus morality in law and formalism versus contextualism. In *Riggs*, grandson Elmer killed his grandfather to prevent him from changing his will to provide for his new wife (as promised in an antenuptial agreement). The majority per Judge Earl held that Elmer could neither take under the will nor as the grandfather's heir at law. The court arrived at this result through two routes. First, it invoked equity in what it called a 'common law' principle, that '[n]o one shall be permitted to profit by his own fraud, or to take advantage of his own wrong, or to found any claim upon his own iniquity, or to acquire property by his own crime'.[17] This is almost a restatement of equitable anti-opportunism, and, but for the court's confusion in the wake of New York's early version of the fusion of law and equity, probably should simply have led to the application of the constructive trust.[18] The court also applied the equity of the

Case (1615)', in C. Mitchell and P. Mitchell (eds.), *Landmark Cases in Equity* (Oxford: Hart Publishing, 2012), ch. 1.

16 22 N.E. 188 (N.Y. 1889) (Earl J.). For an excellent discussion of the case itself and the vast jurisprudential commentary to which it has given rise, see D.A. Farber, 'Courts, Statutes, and Public Policy: The Case of the Murderous Heir' (2000) 53 SMU L. Rev. 31.

17 22 N.E. 188, 190 (1889). Perhaps the court labelled the principle a 'common law' one in order to promote the fusion of law versus equity begun in New York in the Field Code in 1848. See Anon., Note, 'Can a Murderer Acquire Title by His Crime?' (1890) 4 Harv. L. Rev. 394, 395 (attributing decisions like *Riggs* v. *Palmer* to the confusion of law and equity as a result of their jurisdictional fusion).

18 Anon., Note, 'Can a Murderer Acquire a Title by His Crime?' (1894) 8 Harv. L. Rev. 170; Anon., Note, 'Can a Murderer Acquire a Title by His Crime?' (1896) 9 Harv. L. Rev. 474; J.B. Ames, 'Can a Murderer Acquire Title by His Crime and Keep It?' (1897) 45 Am. L. Reg. 225; Anon., Note, 'Constructive Trust Theory as Applied to Property Acquired by Crime' (1917) 30 Harv. L. Rev. 622. In *Ellerson* v. *Westcott*, 42 N.E. 540 (N.Y. 1896)

statute, a controversial method of statutory interpretation, to which we will return. The dissent, sounding themes of the rule of law and the primacy of statutes, would have held that under the statute Elmer could take, arguing that any punishment was solely a matter of criminal law.[19] *Riggs* combats a blatant form of opportunism, and much of this problem is now handled by statute. *Riggs* can thus be interpreted more narrowly than it usually is; it is typically taken as a paradigm case of non-formalistic, principles-based judging in discussions of jurisprudence – something like the fix-it version of equity magnified.[20]

More generally, doctrines of clean hands, estoppel, defences like laches, and, as we will see, the standards for injunctions, can all be read as aimed at combating opportunism. Many of the famous maxims of equity can be understood as signalling the trigger for equitable scrutiny for opportunism.

What is opportunism? Not all bad behaviour is opportunism. Certain branches of transaction cost economics have dealt extensively with opportunism, but the notion is controversial, for reasons similar to the scepticism about equity. Nobel laureate Oliver Williamson defines opportunism as 'self-interest seeking with guile',[21] but this only gets us part of the way. Self-interest per se is not a problem (especially to economists), so the problem must be guile. This is promising, as we will see with 'near fraud'. However, Williamson takes 'guile' so broadly that opportunism covers all sorts of rule breaking. But we are interested in the special kind of rule breaking that is not susceptible to control by tailored *ex ante* rules – the kind that functional equity and traditional equity courts largely focus on. Williamson's definition is too narrow in a different respect, if it requires full-blown deception. Other definitions are broad in precisely the way that common lawyers did not favour:

Andrews C.J. recharacterises *Riggs* as a case of equity and denies that the will was held void. On the fusion of law and equity in New York, see P.I. McMahon, 'Field, Fusion and the 1850s: How an American Law Reform Influenced the Judicature Act of 1875', Chapter 22 of this volume.

19 22 N.E. 188, 191 (1889) (Gray J., dissenting).

20 See, for example, B.N. Cardozo, *The Nature of the Judicial Process* (New Haven: Yale University Press, 1921), 40–1; R. Dworkin, *Taking Rights Seriously* (Cambridge, Mass.: Harvard University Press, 1977), 17–45; H.M. Hart, Jr. and A.M. Sacks, *The Legal Process: Basic Problems in the Making and Application of Law*, unpublished tentative ed. (1958), 75–110; R.A. Posner, *The Problems of Jurisprudence* (Cambridge, Mass.: Harvard University Press, 1990), 105–7.

21 O.E. Williamson, *The Economic Institutions of Capitalism: Firms, Markets, Relational Contracting* (New York: Free Press, 1985), 47.

opportunism is often said to be contravention of the spirit of the law or the defeating of a counterparty's legitimate expectations,[22] but what is the spirit of an agreement or of the law, and where do these expectations come from? Opportunism is advantage taking in a bad way, and sometimes the opportunity in question is simply unexpected. If conditions change in an unforeseeable way, it may make sense to disallow the opportunist from using the letter of the law or a contract to gain an unintended advantage at someone else's expense (More's 'accident').[23]

Opportunism would not be a special problem in the absence of our imperfect ability to detect it. Elsewhere, I have defined it as 'behavior that is undesirable but that cannot be cost-effectively captured – defined, detected and deterred – by explicit *ex ante* rulemaking . . . It often consists of behavior that is technically legal but is done with a view to securing unintended benefits from the system, and these benefits are usually smaller than the costs they impose on others'.[24] From an institutional point of view, the question is whether doing anything about it is worthwhile given the chilling costs and unfairness of some of the more draconian responses equity might employ against what it views as opportunists. Typically, equity responds to opportunism *ex post* but does so in a narrow way, based on various proxies and presumptions. It seeks to avoid being too broad, with commands like 'do the right thing or else'. Likewise, it can act *ex ante*, but almost definitionally, it cannot do so in a tailored way. As we will see, rules about fiduciaries categorically put entire categories of transactions off-limits – in a very untailored

[22] See, for example, G.M. Cohen, 'The Negligence-Opportunism Trade-off in Contract Law' (1992) 20 Hofstra L. Rev. 941, 957 (defining 'opportunism' as 'any contractual conduct by one party contrary to the other party's reasonable expectations based on the parties' agreement, contractual norms, or conventional morality') (footnotes omitted); T.J. Muris, 'Opportunistic Behavior and the Law of Contracts' (1981) 65 Minn. L. Rev. 521, 521 (opportunism is conduct that is 'contrary to the other party's understanding of their contract, but not necessarily contrary to the agreement's explicit terms'); see also, for example, S.W. Buell, 'Good Faith and Law Evasion' (2011) 58 UCLA L. Rev. 611, 623 ('In common parlance, the evasive actor is one whose project is to get around the law. She seeks to avoid sanction while engaging, in substance, in the very sort of behavior that the law means to price or punish.'). For a wider definition, see, for example, R.A. Posner, *Economic Analysis of Law*, 5th ed. (New York: Aspen, 1998), 103 (defining 'opportunism' in the contracting context as 'trying to take advantage of the vulnerabilities created by the sequential character of the contract').

[23] There is a tendency to call any nefarious behaviour with an element of concealment 'fraud', which includes breach of trust and underground mining. See *Livingstone* v. *Rawyards Coal Co.* (1880) 5 App. Cas. 25, 34 (Lord Hatherley), quoted in *Marengo Cave Co.* v. *Ross*, 10 N.E.2d 917, 923 (Ind. 1937).

[24] Smith, 'An Economic Analysis of Law Versus Equity', 10–11.

fashion – because the danger of opportunism is great enough and the chilled behaviour is worth paying as a price. Thus, in its various guises equity solves a specific problem stemming from the strategic interaction of legal decision-makers and primary actors.

I do not claim that this function of countering opportunism was the exclusive province of the equity courts, nor do I claim that rooting out and preventing opportunism was the only function of equity jurisdiction. Nevertheless, as I have argued elsewhere, there is a large enough overlap between the equitable decision-making mode and what these specialist courts were up to that it makes sense to examine the role that equity courts, equitable procedure and substantive equity have historically played in dealing with the problem of the evasion of the formal structures of the law. As we will see, this has been quite true in the area of administration and administrative law.

Opportunism and the traditions of equity

Despite its often being treated as a unitary phenomenon, the equitable tradition has many strains, and anti-opportunism is only one of them. It is an important strain and one that can be appealing even if one finds more expansive versions of equity too problematic for the rule of law.[25]

Although courts in the Anglo-American tradition tend to be thought of as pragmatic rather than deeply philosophical, like the Romans they were willing to invoke philosophy for practical purposes. Equity courts drew on notions of equity tracing explicitly back to Aristotle, who defined equity (*epieikeia*) as an invocation of justice where law fails on account of its generality.[26] The Aristotelian sources support both a broader and a narrower version of equity. The broader equity fixes the law because legislators could not do a perfect job; equity corrects flaws in the law that emerge *ex post* in the light of experience, thereby bringing the law closer

[25] See, generally, Smith, 'An Economic Analysis of Law Versus Equity'.

[26] Aristotle, *The Nicomachean Ethics*, trans. by D. Ross, rev. by J.L. Ackrill and J.O. Urmson (Oxford University Press, 1980), 133; T. Aquinas, *Summa Theologica* I–II, q. 96, art. 6; C. St. German, *Doctor and Student*, ed. by T.F.T. Plucknett and J.L. Barton, 91 Selden Society (London: Selden Society, 1974), 94–107; see also, for example, *Riggs* v. *Palmer*, 22 N.E. 188, 189 (1889) (quoting Aristotle on equity); E.G. Zahnd, 'The Application of Universal Laws to Particular Cases: A Defense of Equity in Aristotelianism and Anglo-American Law' (Winter 1996) 59 Law & Contemp. Probs. 263, 270–5 (documenting influence of Aristotelian equity on Anglo-American law); but cf. D. Shanske, 'Four Theses: Preliminary to an Appeal to Equity' (2005) 57 Stan. L. Rev. 2053 (arguing that Aristotle's equity was not primarily legal).

to its purpose. On the strain of equity focused on opportunism, the law fails on account of its generality because certain kinds of generality are open to exploitation by opportunists.[27] Again, I argue for anti-opportunism as a function of a defined decision-making mode, and more tentatively, I identify this strain in the historical operation of courts of equity. Anti-opportunism may well be the best interpretation of Aristotle's equity, as Dennis Klimchuk has shown.[28]

Before leaving Aristotle, consider how he likened equity to the leaden measuring rulers of the builders of the island of Lesbos.[29] A leaden rule would adapt itself to the shape of a stone, allowing builders to select another exactly matching stone to fit with it. Iron rules, by contrast, do not bend and cannot be used to fit one stone exactly upon another in this fashion. On one reading, this is a plea for using equity to get things exactly right through the use of *ex post* discretion. In a more focused fashion, flexible *ex post* measures exactly tailored to the situation aim to prevent the gap between the law and its purposes from being exploited in hard-to-foresee ways – opportunism. The problem of opportunism sometimes calls for a residuum of open-ended *ex post* intervention. This *ex post* intervention cannot be fully predictable, because, if it were, the well-informed opportunist could treat it as a narrow and avoidable *ex ante* rule.

What both equitable traditions take from Aristotle is the recognition that not every situation can be anticipated *ex ante*, thus making an elaborately, even perfectly, specified *ex ante* law an impossibility. The anti-opportunism strain of equity sees the necessity for targeted *ex post* standards to counter opportunism, and in some especially salient problematic situations, for broad *ex ante* untailored prophylactic measures. What the general fix-it version of equity *also* countenances is a roving *ex post* commission to adjust the law to serve its purposes better – a broad *and ex post* approach. It is the broad and *ex post* version of equity that raises concerns about the Chancellor's foot and more generally runs the risk of violating the rule of law.[30]

27 Smith, 'An Economic Analysis of Law Versus Equity'.

28 D. Klimchuk, 'Is the Law of Equity Equitable in Aristotle's Sense?', unpublished manuscript (June 2011), 4 ('Correction is sometimes necessary because all law is universal and, owing to its universality, can lead to error in particular cases.').

29 Aristotle, *The Nicomachean Ethics*, 133.

30 The most famous critique is Selden's humorous one (J. Selden, 'Equity', in *Table-Talk: Being the Discourses of John Selden, Esq.* (London: E. Smith, 1689), 18):

> Equity is a Roguish thing, for Law we have a measure, know what to trust to, Equity is according to the Conscience of him that is Chancellor, and as that is larger or narrower, so is Equity. 'Tis all one as if they should make

Historically, courts and commentators were well aware of the problem of opportunism, and specifically that the law cannot explicitly specify *ex ante* in a tailored fashion what would be opportunism. The problem of description and limited foresight here stems in large part from the strategic interaction between the opportunist and legal decision makers. A wholly *ex ante* approach tailored to the bad behaviour would not be able to keep up with strategic efforts at evasion. This problem is familiar in tax law and forms the basis for vague *ex post* 'anti-evasion' doctrines (like step-transaction, form-over-substance and the like).[31] This dynamic aspect of the strategic interaction between opportunists and legal institutions was familiar to older courts and commentators on equity. To return to Story, after noting that '[f]raud is infinite' given the 'fertility of man's invention',[32] he quoted one explicit judicial pronouncement about the nature of equity:

> Now equity is no part of the law, but a moral virtue, which qualifies, moderates, and reforms the rigour, hardness, and edge of the law, and is

---

> the Standard for the measure, we call a Chancellors Foot, what an uncertain Measure would this be? One Chancellor has a long Foot, another a short Foot, a Third an indifferent Foot: 'Tis the same thing in the Chancellors Conscience.

See also, for example, *Bisciglia* v. *Kenosha Unified School District No. 1*, 45 F.3d 223, 228 (7th Cir. 1995) (denying temporary injunction in suit over employment termination and stating: '[T]his court does not possess a roving commission to do good. It must make a decision based upon the record and the law.'); D. Laycock, 'The Triumph of Equity' (Summer 1993) 56 Law & Contemp. Probs. 53, 73 (denying 'that a court of equity has a roving commission to do good once it identifies a threshold violation of law that justifies its intervention'). See generally J.H. Baker, *An Introduction to English Legal History*, 4th ed. (London: Butterworths, 2002), 97–115.

[31] D.A. Weisbach, 'Formalism in the Tax Law' (1999) 66 U. Chi. L. Rev. 860; see also S.B. Lawsky, 'Probably? Understanding Tax Law's Uncertainty' (2009) 157 U. Pa. L. Rev. 1017, 1032 (arguing that tax law uses probabilistic doctrines because 'the essence of a tax shelter is that it technically complies with the law while nonetheless violating the substance or intent of the law, which is no easy thing to determine.'); S.S. Surrey, 'Complexity and the Internal Revenue Code: The Problem of the Management of Tax Detail' (1969) 34 Law & Contemp. Probs. 673, 707 n. 31; see also C. Stebbings, 'The Equity of the Executive: Fairness in Tax Law in Nineteenth Century England', Chapter 14 of this volume.

[32] Story, *Commentaries on Equity Jurisprudence*, 4th ed., § 186 n. 6 (quoting a letter from Lord Hardwicke to Lord Kames (30 June 1759)). Or, as Chancellor Ellesmere put the point: 'The Cause why there is a Chancery is, for that Mens Actions are so divers and infinite, That it is impossible to make any general Law which may aptly meet with every particular Act, and not fail in some Circumstances': *Earl of Oxford's Case* (1615) 1 Ch. Rep. 1, 6; 21 E.R. 485, 486.

> an universal truth; it does also assist the law where it is defective and weak in the constitution (which is the life of the law) and defends the law from crafty evasions, delusions, and new subtilties, invented and contrived to evade and delude the common law, whereby such as have undoubted right are made remediless; and this is the office of equity, to support and protect the common law from shifts and crafty contrivances against the justice of the law. Equity therefore does not destroy the law, nor create it, but assist it.[33]

Ex ante approaches are limited because the scrutiny they will later get from opportunists means they have to be nearly perfect: it makes no sense to bother closing nine loopholes if all the opportunists will simply get through the tenth, unclosed, one. Further, the strategic interaction here reinforces the inherent uncertainty in many of the situations equity has to deal with: true (or Knightian) uncertainty, in which the future cannot be sorted in probability distributions,[34] invites more strategic behaviour, because it will be difficult to sort out opportunism from mere accident.[35] Knightian uncertainty is the basis for the entrepreneurial function – the entrepreneur is relatively good at handling uncertainty – and the opportunist can be thought of as an entrepreneur in doing bad.[36]

Equity as opportunism offers an explanation for the contours of some major features of the functional decision-making mode I am calling equity, and to a lesser extent, the features of historic equity jurisdiction: equity's reliance on proxies and presumptions, its lack of tailored *ex ante* rules, its typically *ex post* operation, its open-endedness at the margin, and its grounding in morality, good faith and notice – all relate to the problem of countering opportunism. Equity has to thread the needle between being too broad *ex post* and therefore threatening to the rule of law and too narrow *ex ante*, at the risk of letting the opportunists have their field day.

Fiduciary law and avoidance of ex post *breadth*

One offshoot of equity, to which we will have reason to return, presents the problem of opportunism in a strong form.[37] Courts of equity early on

[33] *Dudley* v. *Dudley* (1705) Prec. Ch. 241, 244; 24 E.R. 118, 119, quoted in Story, *Commentaries on Equity Jurisprudence*, 4th ed., § 17. Story expresses some qualms about the broad identification of equity with virtue, but endorses this account of equity's function.

[34] F.H. Knight, *Risk, Uncertainty, and Profit* (Boston: Houghton Mifflin, 1921), 19–21, 197–232.

[35] Williamson, *The Economic Institutions of Capitalism*, 3–4, 56–9.

[36] Knight, *Risk, Uncertainty, and Profit*, 267–85, 369–73 (developing a theory of entrepreneurship based on an ability to deal with uncertainty).

[37] Smith, 'Why Fiduciary Law is Equitable', in Gold and Miller (eds.), *Philosophical Foundations of Fiduciary Law*, ch. 13.

were heavily involved in affording justice to those complaining about faithless proto-trustees.[38] Out of this grew the notion of a fiduciary relationship with its fiduciary duties of the trustee or other trusted party towards the beneficiary. Chief among these is the duty of loyalty. Under the duty of loyalty, the fiduciary is held to a high standard in which he must act in the sole interest of the beneficiary. This means categorically avoiding self-enrichment and conflicts of interest.[39] The duty of loyalty acts prophylactically, to prevent situations from arising in which it would be very difficult *ex post* to disentangle behaviour distorted in a self-interested direction from actions that are in the best interest of the beneficiary.[40] Generally, fiduciaries cannot even escape liability by proving good faith. Consider again the proxies and presumptions used in general equity. There the combination of state of mind and disproportionate hardship required for intervention varies by context. In the fiduciary context, the danger is so great that the state of mind is irrelevant and the proxy is not an invitation for an *ex post* evaluation but an outright ban.

These prophylactic rules come at a cost, and recently they have been tweaked in certain contexts, especially for investment trusts and in corporate law in order to be less over-inclusive. For example, a trustee

[38] A.W. Scott, W.F. Fratcher and M.L. Ascher, *Scott and Ascher on Trusts*, 5th ed. (New York: Aspen Publishers, 2006), vol. 1, § 1.5 ('Petitioners complained frequently to the chancellor … about faithless feoffees. Such breaches of faith naturally appealed strongly to the chancellor's sense of justice, and … the chancellor began to compel recalcitrant feoffees to do what they had undertaken to do.'); J.H. Langbein, 'The Contractarian Basis of the Law of Trusts' (1995) 105 Yale L.J. 625, 634 and n. 42 (citing as an example a petition to the Chancellor from the 1390s, see W.P. Baildon (ed.), *Select Cases in Chancery: A.D. 1364 to 1471*, 10 Seldon Society (London: Selden Society, 1896), 48–9.) Although equity developed the notion of trustee accountability, such accountability antedates the equity courts: J. Getzler, '"As If". Accountability and Counterfactual Trust' (2011) 91 B.U. L. Rev. 973, 979–80.

[39] See, for example, T. Frankel, *Fiduciary Law* (London and New York: Oxford University Press, 2011), 104; L.I. Rotman, *Fiduciary Law* (Toronto: Thomson Carswell, 2005), ch. 6; P.B. Miller, 'Justifying Fiduciary Duties' (2013) 58 McGill L.J. 969.

[40] See, for example, M. Conaglen, *Fiduciary Loyalty: Protecting the Due Performance of Non-Fiduciary Duties* (Oxford: Hart Publishing, 2010), 59–105; R. Cooter and B.J. Freedman, 'The Fiduciary Relationship: Its Economic Character and Legal Consequences' (1991) 66 N.Y.U. L. Rev. 1045, 1050, 1057; see also A.S. Gold, 'The New Concept of Loyalty in Corporate Law' (2009) 43 U.C. Davis L. Rev. 457, 498–9 (arguing that self-interest may cause directors' assessments of the best interests of the beneficiary to be less accurate); J.E. Penner, 'Is Loyalty a Virtue, and Even if it is, Does it Really Help Explain Fiduciary Liability?', in Gold and Miller (eds.), *Philosophical Foundations of Fiduciary Law*, 168–9; I. Samet, 'Guarding the Fiduciary's Conscience – A Justification of a Stringent Profit-Stripping Rule' (2008) 28 O.J.L.S. 763.

under current US case law is held to a prudent investor standard under which risky investments are allowed if undertaken as part of a diversified portfolio.[41] This rule supplanted the older prudent man rule under which investments would be evaluated individually and a more stringent approach to risk was applied – a rule which did not make much sense in terms of portfolio theory. In the corporate context, the importance of directors' and managers' not being second guessed by shareholders and courts has led to the development of the business judgment rule, which tempers scrutiny under the duty of care by applying a presumption that actions were taken for the benefit of the corporation.[42] The presumption can be overcome only by showing that those actions were undertaken irrationally or in bad faith. In some types of situation, a showing of conflict shifts the burden to the self-interested corporate fiduciary then to show entire fairness.[43] In corporate law, there is more scope for contracting out of fiduciary duties, but as long as the danger exists of a party acting opportunistically outside the domain of the contract, it is hard to see how one can do away with some residuum of equitable intervention against opportunism.[44]

Equity thus rests on proxies and presumptions, but it is important to realise how this both constrains equity and limits its effectiveness. The problem with opportunism is that it is hard to specify in any detail *ex ante*. We have to compare the varieties of institutions that can deal with opportunism. Transaction costs economics deals with a variety of such devices ranging from vertical integration to keeping hostages.[45] When it comes to the law itself, it is useful to consider legal norms

[41] See M.M. Schanzenbach and R.H. Sitkoff, 'The Prudent Investor Rule and Trust Asset Allocation: An Empirical Analysis' (2010) 35 ACTEC J. 314, 317–18; see also *Nestle* v. *National Westminster Bank plc* (1988) [2000] W.T.L.R. 795n, 802 (Ch.D.) (aff'd [1993] 1 W.L.R. 1260 (C.A.)); *Dominica Social Security Board* v. *Nature Island Investment Co. Ltd* [2008] UKPC 19, [30].

[42] See *Joy* v. *North*, 692 F.2d 880, 885 (2d Cir. 1982) (Winter J.) ('[T]he fact is that liability is rarely imposed upon corporate directors or officers simply for bad judgment and this reluctance to impose liability for unsuccessful business decisions has been doctrinally labelled the business judgment rule.').

[43] *Sinclair Oil Corp.* v. *Levien*, 280 A.2d 717 (Del. 1971); *Weinberger* v. *UOP Inc.*, 457 A.2d 701 (Del. 1983); see also *Nixon* v. *Blackwell*, 626 A.2d 1366, 1376 (Del. 1993).

[44] Smith, 'An Economic Analysis of Law Versus Equity'; Smith, 'Why Fiduciary Law is Equitable', in Gold and Miller (eds.), *Philosophical Foundations of Fiduciary Law*, ch. 13. In the trust context in England and Guernsey, see respectively *Armitage* v. *Nurse* [1998] Ch. 241 and *Spread Trustee Ltd* v. *Hutcheson* [2012] 2 A.C. 194; [2011] UKPC 13.

[45] See, for example, O.E. Williamson, 'Transactions-Cost Economics: The Governance of Contractual Relations' (1979) 22 J.L. & Econ. 233; O.E. Williamson, 'Credible Commitments: Using Hostages to Support Exchange' (1983) 73 Am. Econ. Rev. 519,

along two dimensions. First, they can be *ex ante* or *ex post*. In the literature on law and economics, this is sometimes cast as 'rules versus standards'.[46] Under a rule, the content needed to tell whether someone is violating is already in the rule *ex ante*. With a standard, more discretion is given to an *ex post* decision-maker to fill in content (which may result in a rule going forward). To take the familiar example, the choice between a numeric speed limit and a command to drive reasonably under the conditions is in part about the timing of legal decision-making. Another axis of variation is how tailored legal directives are. How large is the set of situations that fall under them? These two dimensions are separate but not unrelated. One might think rules are more tailored and standards are broader, but this is not necessarily true. The fiduciary rules are examples of *ex ante* rules that are broad. That is what prophylactic rules are: they are broader than the problem to be solved. Unlike standards they do not leave decisions about this tailoring for *ex post* application. They are indeed rules, in the sense in which legal economists use the term.

It is the broad *ex post* standard that poses the biggest problem. Such directives are conceptually possible. 'Do the right thing' would be an extreme example. But it is precisely this type of command if built into the law that prompts accusations of violating the rule of law. The idea of a roving commission to apply open-ended morality after the fact is exactly what has long motivated critics of the broad equitable tradition.[47] The common lawyers accused equity of being both broad and *ex post*. I have argued that the narrower anti-opportunism strand in equity is not as subject to these objections.[48] In most of its contexts, it is indeed *ex post*, but it employs a set of proxies and presumptions and draws on existing law and custom in order to cabin its effect and minimise the extent to which it chills behaviour. Sometimes when the opportunism problem is difficult and costly enough, one can find *ex ante* prophylactic rules that make sense. The question is whether the overbreadth is worth it given the amount of chilling involved. As with the *ex post* interventions, the less worthwhile the chilled transactions on average are, the less this is a problem. Fiduciary law relies on a combination of

526; B. Klein, R.G. Crawford and A.A. Alchian, 'Vertical Integration, Appropriable Rents, and the Competitive Contracting Process' (1978) 21 J.L. & Econ. 297.

46 L. Kaplow, 'Rules versus Standards: An Economic Analysis' (1992) 42 Duke L.J. 557.

47 See n. 30 above and accompanying text.

48 Smith, 'Property, Equity, and the Rule of Law', in Austin and Klimchuk (eds.), *Private Law and the Rule of Law*, ch. 10.

broad prophylactic *ex ante* rules and narrower proxy-triggered *ex post* standards.

As we will see, the general fix-it strain of equity does face a greater danger of being so broad and *ex post* as to violate the criteria for the rule of law. This can be a matter of injustice on this view, because the criteria of uniformity and non-retroactivity are being violated wholesale. Such broad *ex post* directives are also suspicious from an efficiency point of view in light of their chilling effect.

Unfortunately, the fusion of law and equity (possibly accentuated by its adoption by the Legal Realist movement) has made it even more difficult to tease these strands of equity apart and evaluate them separately. When law and equity were fused, one can say 'equity won' in two senses. First, in cases of conflict between their rules, equity would trump. And in general the new procedure applying after fusion looked like the older equity procedure (in terms of notice pleading, joinder, discovery and the like). Realists and their predecessors called the limits on equity into question as doctrines were mixed and matched.[49] Further, as equity was less a matter of specialisation, the language of equity (balancing of the hardships) and even 'equity' itself were susceptible to the broadest interpretation. At the same time, fusion in America culminated in the Legal Realist era, in which, at least at first, heroic judging with maximal attention to context and policy was celebrated. Thus, among Realists, there was enthusiasm for equity as long as it could be reinterpreted as general and *ex post*, shorn of its limits. Limits relating to proxies and presumptions like disproportionate hardship, especially, could be loosened or removed. Not coincidentally, the Realists did not take rule of law objections seriously and their successors saw them as roadblocks raised by opponents of the new order.[50] As we will see, this slipping of the

[49] See, for example, R. Pound, 'The End of Law as Developed in Legal Rules and Doctrines' (1913) 27 Harv. L. Rev. 195, 226 ('Equity sought to prevent the unconscientious exercise of rights; today we seek to prevent the anti-social exercise of rights.'), 227 ('Equity imposed moral limitations. The law today is beginning to impose social limitations.'). See O.M. Fiss, 'The Supreme Court, 1978 Term – Foreword: The Forms of Justice' (1979) 93 Harv. L. Rev. 1, 2 ('The structural suit is one in which a judge, confronting a state bureaucracy over values of constitutional dimension, undertakes to restructure the organization to eliminate a threat to those values posed by the present institutional arrangements. The injunction is the means by which these reconstructive directives are transmitted.').

[50] See B.Z. Tamanaha, *On the Rule of Law: History, Politics, Theory* (Cambridge University Press, 2004), 73–90.

bounds of equity in the Realist era is part of the rise of the modern administrative state and administrative law as well.

Administrative equity

At the dawn of the modern administrative state, notions of equity and even historical equity jurisdiction were invoked to illustrate the need (and precedent) for a dynamic, flexible expert version of law that would shore up the weaknesses of legislation. Mostly this appeal to equity was to the broadest versions, because those arguing for a greater administrative state believed in maximal responsiveness to context on the part of all organs of government. Although one motivation for expanding administration was to prevent evasion of the law's command by opportunists, concerns about opportunism both outside and inside agencies themselves were mostly treated as an organisational question.

Administration as the new equity

Early to mid-twentieth-century advocates for a larger role for administration saw the possibility of a 'new equity' in this function of government. Equity and administration were no strangers. The equity courts themselves grew out of the justice-dispensing activities of the Chancellor, who was in many respects an all-round administrator. And one of the functions of the equity court was to police actors that had taken on a private administrative function, especially trustees, guardians and other fiduciaries.

Arguments made for the necessity of a greater scope for administration hark back to the broad equitable tradition. Legislators could not possibly foresee every detail of a problem to be solved through legislation. It would take too much time and effort and overly tax legislators' expertise to try to solve these problems on an ongoing basis. And, as for opportunism, the constant worry was that the law would be caught flatfooted by highly informed private parties, who could only be kept in check by expert administrators with the time, knowledge and resources to keep up. For this reason, legislatures would need to delegate to administrators the task of curing the defects of law on account of its generality.

That the activities of equity courts were a precedent for the administrative state was seen by a pre-Realist like Harvard Law School Dean Roscoe Pound:

> Almost all of the problems of jurisprudence come down to a fundamental one of rule and discretion, of administration of justice by law and administration of justice by the more or less trained intuition of experienced magistrates. Controversies as to the nature of law, whether the traditional element or the imperative element of legal systems is the typical law, controversies as to the nature of lawmaking, whether the law is found by judicial empiricism or made by conscious legislation, and controversies as to the bases of law's authority, whether in reason and science on the one hand or in command and sovereign will on the other hand, get their significance from their bearing upon this question. Controversies as to the relation of law and morals, as to the distinction of law and equity, as to the province of the court and of the jury, as to fixed rule or wide judicial power in procedure, and as to judicial sentence and administrative individualization in punitive justice are but forms of this fundamental problem ... The power of the magistrate has been a liberalizing agency in periods of growth. In the stage of equity and natural law, a stage of infusion of moral ideas from without into the law, the power of the magistrate to give legal force to his purely moral ideas was a chief instrument. Today we rely largely upon administrative boards and commissions to give legal force to ideas which the law ignores.[51]

After setting out his theory of the administrative element in adjudication, for which Roman and English equity furnished examples, he discusses how societies typically veer between discretionary tailoring and mechanical laws.[52] He argues that partly because the administrative element goes missing in law, it flowers in an executive context, leading to the rise of the administrative state:

> Even more striking is the recrudescence of personal government, by way of reaction from an extreme of government of laws and not of men, which is involved in the setting up of administrative tribunals on every hand and for every purpose. The regulation of public utilities, apportionment of the use of the water of running streams among different appropriators, workmen's compensation, the actual duration and nature of punishment for crime, admission to and practice of professions and even of trades, the power to enter or to remain in the country, banking, insurance, unfair competition and restraint of trade, the enforcement of factory laws, of pure food laws, of housing laws and of laws as to protection from fire and the relation of principal and agent, as between farmers and commission merchants, are but some of the subjects which the living law, the law in action, is leaving to executive justice in administrative tribunals. To some extent this is required by the increasing complexity of the social order and

[51] R. Pound, *An Introduction to the Philosophy of Law* (New Haven: Yale University Press, 1922), 111–12.

[52] *Ibid.*, 114–35.

> the minute division of labor which it involves. Yet this complexity and this division of labor developed for generations in which the common-law jealousy of administration was dominant. Chiefly our revival of executive justice in the present century is one of those reversions to justice without law which are perennial in legal history. As in the case of like reversions in the past it is the forerunner of growth. It is the first form of reaction from the overrigid application of law in a period of stability. A bad adjustment between law and administration and cumbrous, ineffective and unbusinesslike legal procedure, involving waste of time and money in the mere etiquette of justice, are doing in our time what like conditions did in English law in the middle of the sixteenth century.[53]

Pound came to the view that the 'bad adjustment' between law and administration had led not just to administrative adjudication but the entire apparatus of the administrative state.[54] Interestingly, Pound also saw that the review by equity courts, in the early stage of the administrative state, 'was likely to have the incidental effect of substituting the discretion of the court for that of the administrative agency'.[55]

These themes become even more apparent in the Legal Realist era when the administrative state expanded greatly as a result of the New Deal. To take a prominent but typical example, James Landis, another Harvard Law School Dean and a leading advocate of the administrative state, saw in equity the historical antecedent for ongoing non-legislative policy-informed lawmaking outside legislatures. In addition to being an academic expert on administrative law, he was a member of the Federal Trade Commission, Chairman of the Securities and Exchange Commission, and Chairman of the Civil Aeronautics Board.[56] He (controversially) argued that historically from early on equity courts moulded the law, even statutory law, in order to serve policy ends.[57] One device for doing this was the equity of the statute, under which 'exceptions dictated by sound policy were written by judges into loose statutory generalisations, and, on the other hand, situations were brought within the reach of the statute that admittedly lay without its express terms'.[58]

53 *Ibid.*, 135–7.

54 R. Pound, 'The Challenge of the Administrative Process' (1944) 30 A.B.A. J. 121; R. Pound, 'Administrative Agencies and the Law' (1945) 31 Women Law. J. 6.

55 R. Pound, 'Administrative Law and the Courts' (1944) 23 B.U. L. Rev. 201, 203–4.

56 T.K. McCraw, *Prophets of Regulation: Charles Francis Adams, Louis D. Brandeis, James M. Landis, Alfred E. Kahn* (Cambridge, Mass.: Belknap Press, 1984).

57 J.M. Landis, 'Statutes and the Sources of Law', in *Harvard Legal Essays* (Cambridge, Mass.: Harvard University Press, 1934), 213, 215, reprinted in (1965) 2 Harv. J. on Legis. 7.

58 *Ibid.*, 215–16. For an argument that the equity of the statute, especially in the broad version argued for by its modern proponents, is incompatible with American separation

In this, Landis was arguing for the widest version of the equitable tradition, of equity as an all-purpose fix-it, or perhaps even more as an ongoing source of legislation where flexibility, fit and dynamism were required.[59] This is the function he and others would argue that administration should fill.

Here Landis was speaking for one strand of Legal Realism in endorsing the administrative process as a modern-day analogue of equity. Others made similar arguments about the equity of the statute.[60] Jerome Frank, while noting this revival among Landis and others,[61] had this to say about equity in general:

> I heartily endorse the fusion, procedurally, of 'law' and 'equity.' But 'substantive equity,' I think, should never be forgotten. And the retention of the word 'equity' I deem important. It instills in the judge a different mood, one of elasticity and fairness. Nothing is more absurd than the saying: 'A rose by any other name is just as sweet.' If the rose were called the 'bloody-nose flower,' it might well be odious.[62]

This is the broadest version of equity, based on elasticity and fairness, which Frank and others saw as the province of the administrative state.

Beyond the equity of the statute and closer to the theme of administration, Landis explicitly argued for the administrative state based on his reading of historical equity in a speech delivered in 1941 to the Mississippi State Bar Association.[63] After setting out the case for administration in terms of expert decision-making in light of rapidly changing conditions, he concluded by defending the administrative state against its naysayers by invoking the history of equity:

of powers, see J.F. Manning, 'Textualism and the Equity of the Statute' (2001) 101 Colum. L. Rev. 1, 22–3. See also J.D. Heydon, 'Equity and Statute', Chapter 12 of this volume.

59 Others disagreed. Prominently, Samuel Thorne argued that originally in the equity courts '[t]he strict, literal meaning of a statute may be extended, but only slightly extended, through use of the doctrine of the statute's equity': S.E. Thorne, 'The Equity of a Statute and Heydon's Case' (1936) 31 Ill. L. Rev. 202, 210.

60 See, for example, H.F. Stone, 'The Common Law in the United States' (1936) 50 Harv. L. Rev. 4, 13–14.

61 J. Frank, 'Civil Law Influences on the Common Law – Some Reflections on "Comparative" and "Contrastive" Law' (1956) 104 U. Pa. L. Rev. 887, 890–1 (discussing views of Landis, Stone, Crawford and Cardozo, and discussing the influence of the civilian tradition).

62 *Ibid.*, 895.

63 J.M. Landis, 'The Challenge to Traditional Law in the Rise of Administrative Law' (1941) 13 Miss. L.J. 724, 731.

> It seems plain that challenges of this character cannot be met simply by railing at the administrative process. For despite some of its patent defects that process is entering more and more into American life, and gaining more and more adherents. It does so only because it fills certain lacks. Just as in the seventeenth century the outcry of the common law judges and the common law bar against the new and dangerous system of equity failed to stem its advance, mere condemnation of administrative methods of dispensing justice, will fail to alter one of the truly great currents of legal history. Like the rise of equity, administrative law for the moment seemingly threatens to put alien hands upon the sacred ark of the covenant. But these hands seem alien, I believe, only because of our own inadequate and myopic vision. If we truly see the significance of this rise, we see it as a response to the desire of communities for more knowledge, more wisdom, more expertness in the handling of claims. That desire can no more be denied than could the revolt of the seventeenth century against the strict formalism of the common law with its insistance [*sic*] upon the reference of judgment to criteria of fairness and conscience instead of sterile precedent. And just as for decades resistance to this demand characterized the older common law, finally to give way to appreciation that both law and equity had their proper parts to play in a greater, more humane, legal system, we must speed rather than delay the period when understanding and mutual respect rather than distrust color the relationship between traditional law and administrative law. One is not the stepchild but the handmaiden of the other, pursuing its ends in somewhat different ways and with somewhat unfamiliar techniques, but devoted also, as law must be, to the endless task of shaping and applying those wise restraints which make men free.[64]

The assumption here is that equity was not a safety valve but a general method of breaking down formalism in the law – and that this is a good thing. Both equity and administration aimed at making law more responsive to human needs, which goes far beyond policing private opportunism. Fairness in its most general terms is contrasted with sterile precedent.

This generalised view of equity is consistent with Landis's general theory of administration and administrative law, set out in his classic book, *The Administrative Process*.[65] Landis saw administration as being both *ex ante* and *ex post* as well as maximally broad, transcending the traditional separation of powers:

> Viewed from this standpoint, it is obvious that the resort to the administrative process is not, as some suppose, simply an extension of executive

[64] *Ibid.*, 731.

[65] J.M. Landis, *The Administrative Process* (New Haven: Yale University Press, 1938).

> power. Confused observers have sought to liken this development to a pervasive use of executive power. But the administrative differs not only with regard to the scope of its powers; it differs most radically in regard to the responsibility it possesses for their exercise. In the grant to it of that full ambit of authority necessary for it in order to plan, to promote, and to police, it presents an assemblage of rights normally exercisable by government as a whole. Moreover, its characteristic is this concept of governance, limited, of course, within those boundaries derived from its constituent statutory authority. But administrative power, though it may begin as an effort to adapt and make efficient police protection within a particular field, moves soon to think in terms of the economic well-being of an industry. The creation of that power is, in essence, the response made in the light of a tripartite political theory to the demand that government assume responsibility not merely to maintain ethical levels in the economic relations of the members of society, but to provide for the efficient functioning of the economic processes of the state.[66]

When Landis speaks of the ethics of an industry, he is echoing the New Deal view of what constitutes unfair and harmful competition. He is also perhaps making an implicit comparison with traditional equity, which did enforce a kind of commercial morality (but until recently also implemented a classical liberal version of which he disapproved). The more far-reaching and expert administrative state he saw as necessitated not only by the Depression but by modern economic conditions in general. One reason for the far-reaching powers of an agency was to counteract the modern business's enhanced ability to act opportunistically. He gives the example of how, to prevent retaliation by companies, the Federal Trade Commission and other similar agencies were given the power to keep secret the names of those who complained to it of unfair business practices.[67] And the administrative state he had in mind goes beyond the wildest dreams of the Chancellors. In a similar vein, Landis sees the injunction and its limits as the background to understanding the remedial powers of administrative agencies. Particularly noteworthy is Landis's discussion of how the administrative state needed to wield hefty sanctions, the licensing power, and sometimes taxation to ensure compliance.[68]

One function of administrative agencies was adjudication, and here the parallel to equity was easy to draw, as it was long before by Pound. John Dickinson, an important theorist of judicial review of administration, saw equity as special among courts because it combined adjudicating and executing (unlike other courts), thus 'disclos[ing] the essentially

[66] *Ibid.*, 15–16. [67] *Ibid.*, 34–5. [68] *Ibid.*, 117–22.

"administrative" character of equity jurisdiction'.[69] Indeed, Dickinson noted that equity courts were attacked for being too administrative in combining executive and judicial functions.[70] In an article entitled 'A Century of the New Equity', Leonard Emmerglick, a Special Assistant to the Attorney General and former Secretary of the American Bar Association's Committee on Administrative Law, leads up to a justification of administrative courts by tracing the development of equity through the fusion era. Writing a year before the passage of the APA, he expresses concern about how fusion might actually dilute equity, again in its most expansive fix-it guise based on generalised fairness (complete with an invocation of Aristotle).[71] The need for separate courts for adaptation of the law that cannot be accomplished by the more ponderous device of legislation is likewise a justification of administrative justice:

> To perform its high office, equity must be administered as a check upon strict law and in opposition to it. This requires for equity a selfhood. The desirability of special courts to meet parts of the need for individualized justice has become well recognized in recent years. This has resulted in the creation of juvenile courts, domestic realtions [*sic*] courts, and many varieties of municipal and traffic courts. *The administrative court, found in both the federal and state legal systems, is a corresponding effort to meet the need for specialized judicial administration of equity.* There is much to indicate that in the endless alternation of discretion and rule, equity and law, we have entered upon a new phase. A specialized equity court, functioning under a court of last resort exercising supervisory and appellate functions, can be accommodated into a system of state courts without sacrifice of essential symmetry and efficiency. This demanding task confronts the administration of justice.[72]

Emmerglick is arguing that a function of keeping the law reformed on an ongoing basis requires separate courts and that administrative courts can serve this function.[73]

[69] J. Dickinson, *Administrative Justice and the Supremacy of Law in the United States* (Cambridge, Mass.: Harvard University Press, 1927), 24 n. 41 (citing Pound and Langdell).

[70] *Ibid.*, 33.

[71] L.J. Emmerglick, 'A Century of the New Equity' (1945) 23 Tex. L. Rev. 244, 253–4 (footnotes omitted).

[72] *Ibid.*, 255–6 (footnote omitted, italics added).

[73] In a variant of Realism, Emmerglick saw equity and administration as part of a whole system that could and should incorporate a morality that embraced a wide swath of policy:

In actual practice, administrative agencies often engage in decision-making that is reminiscent of both strands of traditional equity. In identifying 'administrative equity', Alfred Aman constructs a list of maxims reminiscent of the maxims of equity.[74] Many of these sound in granting exceptions in the name of hardship and preventing unfairness. Interestingly, many of them seem well designed to prevent opportunism, make exceptions that are robust to opportunism, or to assure regulated parties that they will not be treated opportunistically by the agency. Particularly interesting are maxims that seek to prevent disproportionate hardship as between regulated entities and allow exceptions to rules that would penalise a firm for action taken in good faith prior to the rule's existence.[75]

Fiduciary conceptions of administrative law

For situations of extreme discretion based on expertise and corresponding vulnerability, the equity courts developed fiduciary law, an outgrowth of the trust. Fiduciary notions have played an understandable role in describing the activities of administrative agencies. Recently, some public law scholars have revived this strand of thinking about administration in order to develop a fiduciary model of the duties of administrators.

Administrative agencies do pose problems similar to those of fiduciaries. Evan Criddle, in developing the fiduciary model, argues that the wide scope of discretion and expertise make administrative agencies like fiduciaries.[76] And, correspondingly, in the early days of the modern administrative state, proponents did talk in fiduciary terms.

> Today, law is not conceived to be a closed part of the field of morality, which is not to be extended beyond fixed boundaries. A system of statutes, common law, equity, courts, and administrative officers is designed to do something more than keep the peace. It exists to continually promote the condition of the citizen – to provide for him the highest possible measure of good. This is but a purpose to embrace as much of morals as can be assimilated.
>
> "L.J. Emmerglick, 'Legal Adoption of Equitable Principles' (1936) 2 N.J. L. Rev. Univ. of Newark 53, 62–3 (footnote omitted)"

[74] A.C. Aman, Jr., 'Administrative Equity: An Analysis of Exceptions to Administrative Rules' 1982 Duke L.J. 277. English administrative law also keys judicial review to triggers like pretext, absurdity and bad faith. See T.A.O. Endicott, *Administrative Law*, 2nd ed. (Oxford University Press, 2011), 47, 219–306.

[75] Aman, 'Administrative Equity', 309.

[76] E.J. Criddle, 'Fiduciary Foundations of Administrative Law' (2006) 54 UCLA L. Rev. 117.

As for the methods of controlling fiduciaries, Criddle identifies residual control, judicial review and socialisation.[77] There are reasons to think that courts are hardly in the position of policing fiduciary duties, in the manner of equity courts. Fiduciary law employs narrow but open-ended *ex post* standards and broad *ex ante* prophylactic rules. Outside of a few rules of thumb based on arbitrary behaviour, it is hard to see how courts can employ *ex post* standards, without usurping political and policy choices.[78] And unlike private fiduciaries, conflicts of interest and duty really do not get at what alarms us about administrative decision-making that has gone off the rails. Instead of implementing a fiduciary version of equity in administration, the narrower strand of equity as anti-opportunism suggests a strong but narrow and highly incomplete role for courts in policing for agency opportunism.

More promising is non-judicial equitable anti-opportunism, which includes what Criddle calls residual control and socialisation. Residual control refers to policing by the 'principals', here the more politically accountable branches (the legislature and the executive), and more remotely the public. Socialisation is the internalisation by officials of norms of proper behaviour. Both can be seen as reflections of an equity-oriented culture of the rule of law, to which I shall return at the end of the chapter.

Equity's role in administrative law

Equity has played an important role in administrative law, both historically and functionally. Functionally and historically, equity has countered opportunism by reining in agencies in a limited fashion. Courts in the United States have played an especially large role in reviewing the activities of agencies.[79] Functional equity extends beyond literal equity jurisdiction in that the APA adopts strands of functional equity and can be read against a background of functional equitable principles. A better understanding of the various types of equity, both historical and functional, can clarify descriptively and normatively the role of courts in

[77] *Ibid.*, 123–35.

[78] Some of the devices Criddle points to accord in a limited way with equity as anti-opportunism, in particular the 'arbitrary and capricious' standard of the Administrative Procedure Act (to which I return in the next section): *ibid.*, 154.

[79] T.W. Merrill, 'Article III, Agency Adjudication, and the Origins of the Appellate Review Model of Administrative Law' (2011) 111 Colum. L. Rev. 939.

preventing the grossest forms of agency abuses, especially in the area of remedies.

Equity and the development of administrative law

Before and during the early modern era of the administrative state, courts relied on their general equity jurisdiction to engage in judicial review of government actors engaging in administration. John Duffy has documented how federal courts relied on their general equity jurisdiction to develop judicial review of administration.[80] Notably, the US Supreme Court held in *Pennsylvania* v. *Wheeling & Belmont Bridge Co.*,[81] that federal courts through equity could enforce federal statutory rights without a specific grant of equity jurisdiction. Congress granted general equity power in federal question cases to the federal courts in 1875, which was understood to give federal courts general remedial powers in cases involving federal question jurisdiction.[82] Duffy goes on to show that this tradition persisted even after the enactment in 1946 of the APA. Courts often did not cite the APA and developed judicial doctrines even in contradiction of the statute, especially in the areas of exhaustion and mootness.[83] This approach reached its zenith with the era of the New Federal Common Law, in which courts were relatively unconcerned about being able to point to a specific source of authority as legitimation for the exercise of judicial review power over agencies.[84] Duffy argues that the APA should have displaced equity where the APA applies, and thus courts have no warrant to create 'common law' doctrines like exhaustion and ripeness that contradict the terms of the APA. He discerned an incipient tendency in the courts to become more oriented to the statute and more concerned with the source of their power.[85] In his view, the *Chevron* doctrine,[86] under which courts are to defer to an agency's reasonable interpretation of an ambiguous statute, was born of

[80] J.F. Duffy, 'Administrative Common Law in Judicial Review' (1998) 77 Tex. L. Rev. 113.
[81] 54 U.S. (13 How.) 518, 563 (1851).
[82] Act of Mar. 3, 1875, ch. 137, § 1, 18 Stat. 470, 470 (current version 28 U.S.C. § 1331).
[83] Duffy, 'Administrative Common Law in Judicial Review', 130–8, 152–81. See also W. Gummow, 'Equity in the Modern Administrative State', Chapter 16 of this volume.
[84] Duffy, 'Administrative Common Law in Judicial Review', 119–20, 130–8. The phrase 'New Federal Common Law' is associated with an article by Judge Henry Friendly celebrating this development: H.J. Friendly, 'In Praise of *Erie* – and of the New Federal Common Law' (1964) 39 N.Y.U. L. Rev. 383.
[85] Duffy, 'Administrative Common Law in Judicial Review', 181–211.
[86] *Chevron USA Inc.* v. *Natural Resources Defense Council Inc.*, 467 U.S. 837 (1984).

the common law method unmoored to the APA but has been refashioned towards greater concern with statutory authority.[87]

It is true that the APA displaces much of traditional equity jurisdiction. Duffy's argument is well taken, but it is consistent with some room for equity as anti-opportunism. First of all, Duffy does not deny that outside the APA courts retain equitable power. As Duffy argues, the APA did not displace all of the general equity jurisdiction (from the 1875 statute) from applying in an administrative context, which puts doctrines like non-statutory review on a sounder footing. From a functional point of view, these doctrines can be seen as reining in the opportunism of agencies. One might also add that retention of some equitable anti-opportunism is reflected in the APA, to which I now turn.

Equity and the statutory framework for judicial review

The functional view of equity as anti-opportunism allows for a different gloss on the APA itself. Consider the text of section 706 of the statute itself, which sets out the scope of judicial review of administrative agencies:

> Section 706. Scope of review
>
> To the extent necessary to decision and when presented, the reviewing court shall decide all relevant questions of law, interpret constitutional and statutory provisions, and determine the meaning or applicability of the terms of an agency action. The reviewing court shall–
>
> (1) compel agency action unlawfully withheld or unreasonably delayed; and
>
> (2) hold unlawful and set aside agency action, findings, and conclusions found to be–
>
> (A) arbitrary, capricious, an abuse of discretion, or otherwise not in accordance with law;
>
> (B) contrary to constitutional right, power, privilege, or immunity;

[87] Duffy, 'Administrative Common Law in Judicial Review', 189–211. See *United States* v. *Mead Corp.*, 533 U.S. 218 (2001); T.W. Merrill and K.E. Hickman, '*Chevron*'s Domain' (2001) 89 Geo. L.J. 833. Interestingly, Justice Stevens, the author of *Chevron*, can be seen as adhering to the common law approach: T.W. Merrill, 'Justice Stevens and the *Chevron* Puzzle' (2012) 106 Nw. U. L. Rev. 551. And as Duffy notes, two conceptions of *Chevron* have long been in competition with each other. *Chevron*'s deference to agencies is in tension with the command to courts to 'set aside' agency actions that are 'not in accordance with law', the determination of which is usually a judicial function. See S. Breyer, 'Judicial Review of Questions of Law and Policy' (1986) 38 Admin. L. Rev. 363.

> (C) in excess of statutory jurisdiction, authority, or limitations, or short of statutory right;
> (D) without observance of procedure required by law;
> (E) unsupported by substantial evidence in a case subject to sections 556 and 557 of this title or otherwise reviewed on the record of an agency hearing provided by statute; or
> (F) unwarranted by the facts to the extent that the facts are subject to trial de novo by the reviewing court.
>
> In making the foregoing determinations, the court shall review the whole record or those parts of it cited by a party, and due account shall be taken of the rule of prejudicial error.

Here one can see traces of equity that relate to its strand of anti-opportunism. First, the relief it contemplates is injunctive ('compel'), and, as we will see, the equitable standards for injunctions – or what the court takes to be the traditional equitable standards for injunctions – apply, even in review under a statute like the APA. I will argue that the (real) traditional equitable standards responded coherently to the problems of opportunism. Further, the triggers for review tend to be like those in equity – ones in which something is seriously out of whack, not a little off. One could even say that the standard of 'arbitrary, capricious, an abuse of discretion, or otherwise not in accordance with law' is not that different from the triggers (such as disproportionate hardship) that get an equity court interested in a problem like unconscionability. Accountability based on records, while not surprising, is consistent with the approach of equity courts to policing trustees and other fiduciaries (the duty to keep records and render accounts). There is also in section 706 a command to take a wide view of the record, which is reminiscent of the comprehensive anti-opportunism to which equity courts aspired.[88] When it comes to

[88] The record in question is the administrative record, and I do not suggest that defining what this record is and how to protect it from manipulation are easy tasks. Potential opportunism requires judicial vigilance in this regard. See *Citizens to Preserve Overton Park Inc.* v. *Volpe*, 401 U.S. 402, 418 (1971): ('[R]eview is to be based on the full administrative record that was before the Secretary at the time he made his decision. But since the bare record may not disclose the factors that were considered or the Secretary's construction of the evidence it may be necessary for the District Court to require some explanation in order to determine if the Secretary acted within the scope of his authority and if the Secretary's action was justifiable under the applicable standard.' (footnote omitted)); *Walter O. Boswell Memorial Hospital* v. *Heckler*, 749 F.2d 788, 792 (D.C. Cir. 1984) ('To review less than the full administrative record might allow a party to withhold evidence unfavorable to its case, and so the APA requires review of the "whole record"'.).

opportunism, a view of only part of the situation can make conduct look legitimate when if it is in fact anything but.[89] In addition to the maxim, 'equity loves to do justice and not by halves', we have functionally related anti-avoidance doctrines in tax (step-transaction doctrine, substance over form).

Moreover, one could argue more tentatively, based on these hints, that the APA was passed against a background understanding of courts' equitable powers to prevent opportunism, including abuse of its own processes. Consider the 'set aside' language of section 706. Duffy argues that the APA's clear command requires courts ('shall') to set aside an agency action when remanding.[90] By contrast, Ronald Levin argues that traditional equitable principles, at least in the area of remedies, would allow courts to remand without vacation.[91] A narrower version of the equitable approach is available, under which the traditional equitable principles should be read in light of the more specific function of countering opportunism. Thus, if a party helps manufacture the problem that requires remand, a court would be able to employ remand without vacatur as part of its equitable toolkit to prevent the opportunism. One need not see in the APA an acceptance (or non-displacement) of a general fix-it equity, nor of the free-floating unbounded caricature of equity that can be found in the more intemperate versions of Legal Realism.

The legislative history of the APA confirms that equity as anti-opportunism is part of the background adopted by the APA. The APA itself was the result of convergence and compromise between those who wanted to constrain the administrative state and those who wanted to entrench it.[92] Congress was in general ready to compare administrative hearings themselves to equity, when in the legislative history it noted, 'an administrative hearing is to be compared with an equity proceeding in the courts. The mere admission of evidence is not to be taken as pre-judicial error (there being no lay jury to be protected from improper

89 For further discussion, see Smith, 'An Economic Analysis of Law Versus Equity'.

90 Duffy, 'Administrative Common Law in Judicial Review', 165–6.

91 R.M. Levin, '"Vacation" at Sea: Judicial Remedies and Equitable Discretion in Administrative Law' (2003) 53 Duke L.J. 291, 323–4.

92 See McNollgast [*sc.* M.D. McCubbins, R.G. Noll and B.R. Weingast], 'The Political Origins of the Administrative Procedure Act' (1999) 15 J.L. Econ. & Org. 180; G.B. Shepherd, 'Fierce Compromise: The Administrative Procedure Act Emerges from New Deal Politics' (1996) 90 Nw. U. L. Rev. 1557.

influence).'[93] Perhaps most interestingly, the Senate Report notes the role of evasion, when it states that the provisions relating to judicial review to 'prevent avoidance of the requirements of the [Act] by any manner or form of indirection'.[94] The APA can be seen as providing for a judicial source of equitable anti-opportunism.

Returning to administrative law doctrines, it is now not out of the question that a very narrow version of the exhaustion doctrine could survive even under the APA. Duffy is right that the general form of the exhaustion doctrine, as a matter of the New Federal Common Law, contradicts section 706 of the APA, which directs that courts 'shall' provide review under the circumstances spelled out in the rest of the section. Nevertheless, if the APA incorporates the notion of equity as anti-opportunism, situations could arise in which a party acts deceptively to induce an action by an agency that would trigger review under section 706, even though the problem was either caused by or hidden from the agency by the party. Perhaps such a situation could fit under estoppel, but the point is that something like exhaustion – a requirement to pursue the administrative process further before obtaining review – could be invoked in order to prevent this form of opportunism. Such intervention would be far narrower than traditional exhaustion doctrine, but it could preserve the court's ability to protect the process from abuse.

Remedies

When it comes to remedies, there is at least a surface consensus that equity is still relevant. Some doctrines of remedies in the area of judicial review of administrative agencies trace back – at least in theory – to equity jurisdiction. Most prominent is the law of injunctions, which the Supreme Court has done much to confuse recently. It should be said at the outset that it is generally regarded as uncontroversial that the same standards for injunctions apply across substantive areas and that those principles draw on the traditions of equity. The problem is that in our post-fusion world, those traditions are subject to misinterpretation, by no less than the US Supreme Court.

[93] S. Doc. No. 79–248 (1946), 208 (statement of Sen. McCarran).

[94] S. Rep. No. 79–752 (1946), 31, reprinted in Staff of Senate Comm. on the Judiciary, Legislative History of the Administrative Procedure Act (1946), S. Doc. No. 79–248, 217 (statement of Sen. McCarran).

In *eBay* v. *MercExchange LLC*,[95] the Court invoking 'traditional principles of equity'[96] set out a four-prong test for injunctions. To get injunctive relief the moving party 'must demonstrate: (1) that it has suffered an irreparable injury; (2) that remedies available at law, such as monetary damages, are inadequate to compensate for that injury; (3) that, considering the balance of hardships between the plaintiff and defendant, a remedy in equity is warranted; and (4) that the public interest would not be disserved by a permanent injunction'.[97] This standard, however, which was unknown to equity, is taken from the test for preliminary injunctions, with a doubling up (irreparable injury and inadequacy of the legal remedy are not really distinct).[98] In the context of a preliminary injunction, it makes sense to act as if in equipoise: the moving party has not yet demonstrated injury. By contrast, at the stage when an injunction is sought, the moving party has typically established injury. Thus, a test like balancing of the equities is properly (and traditionally) based on disproportionate hardship, not equipoise.[99] The question is whether someone otherwise (presumptively) entitled to an injunction should not get one because the harm to the enjoined party would far exceed the benefit to the movant. As we have seen, disproportionate hardship is one of the most important proxies that equity used to identify possible opportunism. And courts of equity were worried that the availability of injunctions could be used opportunistically against others, especially those in good faith.[100] Crucially, the law of injunctions was keyed to good faith. For example, excusing doctrines like undue (disproportionate) hardship could not be invoked by those in bad faith. By contrast, at

[95] 547 U.S. 388, 391 (2006). [96] *Ibid.*, 394. [97] *Ibid.*, 391.

[98] M.P. Gergen, J.M. Golden and H.E. Smith, 'The Supreme Court's Accidental Revolution? The Test for Permanent Injunctions' (2011) 112 Colum. L. Rev. 203.

[99] *Ibid.*, 226–30, 246–9; see also D. Laycock, *Modern American Remedies: Cases and Materials*, 4th ed. (New York: Aspen, 2010), 426; H.L. McClintock, *Handbook of the Principles of Equity*, 2nd ed. (St. Paul, Minn.: West, 1948), 51 (observing that, when 'the award of specific relief would inflict a hardship on the defendant which is out of all proportion to the injury its refusal would cause to plaintiff[,] . . . the great weight of authority' holds 'equity still has discretion in adjusting the relief to be rewarded'); R.A. Epstein, 'A Clear View of *The Cathedral*: The Dominance of Property Rules' (1997) 106 Yale L.J. 2091, 2102; D. Laycock, 'The Neglected Defense of Undue Hardship (and the Doctrinal Train Wreck in *Boomer* v. *Atlantic Cement*)' (2011) 4 J. Tort L. 1; H.E. Smith, 'Institutions and Indirectness in Intellectual Property' (2009) 157 U. Pa. L. Rev. 2083, 2131–2.

[100] Gergen, Golden and Smith, 'The Supreme Court's Accidental Revolution? The Test for Permanent Injunctions', 239–40, 248.

least on its face, the *eBay* test makes no room for considerations of good and bad faith, or wilfulness.

The *eBay* test was understandable, if not advisable, as a compromise solution on what to do about so-called patent trolls – those who seek to use the leverage of an injunction to 'extort' large settlements for infringements of hard-to-detect, possibly bad patents that the owner is not practising. Ironically, the traditional equitable approach, dealing as it does with opportunism, is well suited to taking on the troll problem.[101]

Nevertheless, and more alarmingly, the Supreme Court has now applied the *eBay* test outside of intellectual property. Notably it did so in *Monsanto Co.* v. *Geertson Seed Farms*,[102] an administrative law case in the core area of the environment.[103] In *Geertson*, the Court held that the *eBay* four-prong test would apply to the availability of an injunction under the National Environmental Policy Act,[104] the administrative framework legislation for federal activity impacting the environment. Using the *eBay* test in the context of administrative law relating to the environment prevents the Court from using it with its traditional flexibility.[105] Unfortunately, the test is gaining ground in the federal courts.[106]

The traditional law of injunctions relied on proxies and presumptions that were attuned to a two-sided opportunism problem. The trigger for injunctions was irreparable injury.[107] Courts realised that injunctions could become a tool of opportunism and so were empowered to deny injunctions in cases of disproportionate hardship. One can read APA section 702 as incorporating these tests too.[108]

[101] *Ibid.*, 243–9; H.E. Smith, 'Property as Platform: Coordinating Standards for Technological Innovation' (2013) 9 J. Competition L. & Econ. 1057.

[102] 561 U.S. 139 (2010).

[103] See *ibid.*, 176 (Stevens J. dissenting) ('[T]he District Court's decision can be understood as an equitable application of administrative law.').

[104] 42 U.S.C. §§ 4321–70; 5 U.S.C. §§ 500–96. See L.A. Herrmann, 'Injunctions for NEPA Violations: Balancing the Equities' (1992) 59 U. Chi. L. Rev. 1263.

[105] D. Mach, 'Rules without Reasons: The Diminishing Role of Statutory Policy and Equitable Discretion in the Law of NEPA Remedies' (2011) 35 Harv. Envtl. L. Rev. 205, 246.

[106] Gergen, Golden and Smith, 'The Supreme Court's Accidental Revolution? The Test for Permanent Injunctions', 205.

[107] The irreparable injury required is in the context of a rights violation. The nature of a right is no less important in a public law than in a private law context. See J.N.E. Varuhas, 'The Reformation of English Administrative Law? "Rights", Rhetoric and Reality' [2013] C.L.J. 369.

[108] 5 U.S.C. § 702 ('Nothing herein (1) affects other limitations on judicial review or the power or duty of the court to dismiss any action or deny relief on any other appropriate legal or equitable ground.').

The limits of equitable administrative law

In the era when courts employed their equity jurisdiction in administrative matters and the APA was passed, the administrative state was not as far-reaching as it is today. The expansion of the administrative state has put strains equity, in a fashion parallel to other areas of law, but more so.

Equity could never be a complete answer to how to keep the administrative state in check, but the expansion of the administrative state shows the limits of equitable tools. Without necessarily endorsing any suggestions for the judicial policing of violations of fiduciary duties in administrative law, one can interpret Criddle's theory of a fiduciary administrative state as a diagnosis of the problem.[109] Administrative agencies present the extreme danger of opportunism that private fiduciaries do, but much more so. The discretion, expertise and corresponding vulnerability of the beneficiary give rise to a wide scope of opportunism. The principal in this principal-agent structure and the beneficiary of the fiduciary relationship (if that is what it is) is the public at large, possibly represented by actors from the political branches or various interest groups – all of whom have their own agendas.

Put differently, the state itself is the agent of the public. Yoram Barzel offers a theory of the state in which the public gives power to enforce contracts, but will not do so unless they retain a power to check the state itself.[110] Other theories of the state come at things from the other end. The state is a stationary bandit and only gives up power when it needs to elicit more effort from the people.[111] The question under either type of theory is how an organ as powerful as the state can ever forbear from using (and abusing) its power, and how to strike the trade-off between government flexibility and forbearance.[112] In other words, the opportunism problem is at its strongest here. That the administrative state has taken on a wide range of functions only compounds this problem.

The transaction cost literature offers a range of partial solutions to this problem. And the question of institutional design is: which

[109] See Criddle, 'Fiduciary Foundations of Administrative Law'.

[110] Y. Barzel, *A Theory of the State: Economic Rights, Legal Rights, and the Scope of the State* (Cambridge University Press, 2002).

[111] M. Olson, 'Dictatorship, Democracy, and Development' (1993) 87 Am. Pol. Sci. Rev. 567.

[112] T.W. Merrill and H.E. Smith, *The Oxford Introductions to US Law: Property* (New York: Oxford University Press, 2010), ch. 9 (describing general problem of government flexibility versus forbearance).

combination of these devices along with a decision about the scope of the state will be best (welfare-maximising on a strictly economic framework)? In a contracting context, the institutional economics literature tends to emphasise specific *ex post* contractual provisions to counter opportunism.[113] Alternatively, the scope of an activity (inside or outside the firm) can be altered to reduce the problem of opportunism. Competition can play a role here, but translates poorly to a public law context. What the transaction cost literature tends to downplay is *ex post* equitable-style intervention,[114] mostly because of the fear of the chilling effect.

Recall that the challenge for equity is to avoid being both broad and *ex post*. Is this possible in a public law context? The pressure from the problem of opportunism in administration pushes in the direction of broad and *ex post* intervention. The structural injunction can be regarded as a broad *ex post* measure that takes equity far beyond the countering of opportunism.[115] In implementing a 'roving commission to do good', it is subject to the criticism of judicial overreach, in that judges are likely to lack the legitimacy or the expertise to run large institutions like school systems or prisons, or to decide on levels of taxes and services. But putting aside controversies over the waxing and waning of the structural injunction, many of the arguments for administrative agencies were arguments against administration by judges. The question remains how an administrative state can be cabined if at all using either equity as anti-opportunism or broader notions of equity.

Equity as anti-opportunism calls for limited policing based on proxies like disproportionate hardship and bad faith. It does not and cannot furnish a more complete answer along the lines of fiduciary law. Recall that the difference between plain equity and fiduciary law lies in the extremity of the opportunism problem, from discretion and vulnerability. Where *ex ante* tailored rules are not effective, equitable

[113] See, for example, Williamson, *The Economic Institutions of Capitalism*, and the sources cited in n. 45 above.

[114] Williamson mentions the possibility of *ex post* intervention in O.E. Williamson, 'Cooperative Economic Organization: The Analysis of Discrete Structural Alternatives' (1991) 36 Admin. Sci. Q. 269, 273.

[115] See Fiss, 'The Supreme Court, 1978 Term – Foreword: The Forms of Justice', 2; but see *Bisciglia* v. *Kenosha Uniform School District No. 1*, 45 F.3d 223, 228 (1995), quoted n. 30 above; Laycock, 'The Triumph of Equity', 73 (denying 'that a court of equity has a roving commission to do good once it identifies a threshold violation of law that justifies its intervention').

anti-opportunism offers the choices of beefed up *ex post* tailored standards and *ex ante* untailored rules, both of which fiduciary law employs. Untailored 'rules' are threatening to the rule of law (to which we return in the next section). They are rightly criticised as 'palm tree justice'.[116] And much of what has gone under the heading of 'fiduciary duty' can be read as the substitution of the court's view of policy for that of other branches, as in the Court of Appeal decision (later reversed by the House of Lords) in *Roberts* v. *Hopwood*,[117] where fiduciary law was invoked to second-guess, in the name of protecting taxpayers, a local council's decision to pay above-market wages. In general, courts lack the democratic legitimacy to devise and enforce prophylactic rules or to use fact-based evaluation across the board to enforce strong duties. Pervasive fact-based evaluation would anyway run afoul of the rule of law, which is a serious problem that the administrative state faces.

Interestingly, the literature on administrative law has cycled through most of the candidates for devices for constraining administrative decision behaviour. These purported solutions mostly fall under the heading of denying the problem or allowing the equitable solution to expand beyond its traditional bounds. After the era of faith in expert flexible decision-making represented early by Wilson and later on by Landis,[118] theories of the administrative state posited that interests would compete

116 Judges 4:5. See, for example, *Pettkus* v. *Becker* [1980] 2 S.C.R. 834, 859 (Martland J. dissenting) ('[T]he adoption of this concept . . . would clothe judges with a very wide power to apply what has been described as "palm tree justice" without the benefit of any guidelines. By what test is a judge to determine what constitutes unjust enrichment? The only test [is] his individual perception of what he consider[s] to be unjust.'). A similar note was sounded decades earlier in W.S. Holdsworth, 'Unjustifiable Enrichment' (1939) 55 L.Q.R. 37, 49. See also E.J. Weinrib, 'The Structure of Unjustness' (2012) 92 B.U. L. Rev. 1067, 1067 n. 2.

117 [1925] A.C. 578. For an early criticism, see H.J. Laski, 'Judicial Review of Social Policy in England: A Study of *Roberts* v. *Hopwood et al.*' (1926) 39 Harv. L. Rev. 832, 846:

> No one suggests that the Poplar Council acted without good faith or proper care . . . And it is my submission that only at the point where it is demonstrable that fault may be imputed with general approval in judging of the exercise of a discretionary power is a judicial authority justified in seeking to overturn the acts of an elected body. In any other circumstances, the proper sources of control are the electorate on the one hand, or the appropriate legislature on the other . . . Nothing is more dangerous than [judges'] use of the authority committed to them to suppress views or experiments they happen to dislike.

118 W. Wilson, 'The Study of Administration' (1887) 2 Pol. Sci. Q. 197; Landis, *The Administrative Process*.

in the administrative arena.[119] Thus, administrative decision-making would have a sort of public legitimacy because affected interests had had their role in the process. The cynical version of this is capture theory, which points in the opposite direction (and for some to a greater role for judicial review).[120] More recently, commentators have offered descriptive theories and normative justifications for control of agencies by the president.[121] As the sole political actor elected by the entire country, the US President is said to possess democratic legitimacy and at the same time has (and should have) control over agencies. Problematic for this theory are the host of independent agencies, along with the fact that, like Congress, the President (or the White House) has limited time and attention to spend on policing agencies.

Here, the fiduciary theories of administrative law are of special interest. They are motivated by the inadequacies of control by the political branches, and the extreme discretion and vulnerability (of the public) presented by a large administrative state. The danger here, though, is the one equity always faces: how not to be both broad and *ex post*. On the anti-opportunism view, private fiduciary law supplements the *ex post* equitable safety valve with broad but untailored prophylactic rules against engaging in self-enriching transactions or entering into conflicts of interest. It is hard to see how such broad prophylactic rules can be implemented in judicial review of administrative agencies. Prophylactic rules are more likely to emerge directly from constitutions or legislation (if at all). Under a constitution or legislation, some subject matters might be treated as too dangerous for the government to handle. Thus, critics of campaign finance regulation might see the permanent bureaucracy as too interested in the political process to entrust with regulation of campaign speech. This danger has to be weighed against the purported benefits of campaign finance regulation in terms of the avoidance of corruption or the appearance of corruption. Or one might think that revenue raising, with all its attendant

[119] See R.B. Stewart, 'The Reformation of American Administrative Law' (1975) 88 Harv. L. Rev. 1667, 1760; see also E.J. Criddle, 'Fiduciary Administration: Rethinking Popular Representation in Agency Rulemaking' (2010) 88 Tex. L. Rev. 441, 451–2.

[120] T.W. Merrill, 'Capture Theory and the Courts: 1967–1983' (1997) 72 Chi.-Kent L. Rev. 1039.

[121] See, for example, S.G. Calabresi and C.S. Yoo, *The Unitary Executive: Presidential Power from Washington to Bush* (New Haven: Yale University Press, 2008), 208; Criddle, 'Fiduciary Administration: Rethinking Popular Representation in Agency Rulemaking', 452–3; J. Mantel, 'Procedural Safeguards for Agency Guidance: A Source of Legitimacy for the Administrative State' (2009) 61 Admin. L. Rev. 343.

control over information and enforcement authority, is incompatible with regulating political speech (or administering health care insurance). The point here is that such prophylactic 'off limits' rules cannot be expected to emerge from the case law in common law fashion. They must come from the political process or not at all.

I will argue that equity does have some continuing but limited role to play in containing administrative opportunism, but the same danger of describing fossils applies there too. Recall that the US Supreme Court managed to confuse the law of injunctions and mess up its function, presumably because equity is only half-recognised as a distinct decision-making mode whose phraseology can be misinterpreted as coextensive with more everyday notions. Examples include 'balancing of the equities', 'public interest' and 'equity' itself.

Fiduciary policing of administrative discretion might be possible if the administrative state were small and well defined enough or other mechanisms dealt with the opportunism of agencies well enough. The fact that most theories of administrative law start with the need for a large administrative state and work backwards is not a good sign.[122] The recent trend towards massive executive grants of waivers is not encouraging in this regard either.[123] What are other mechanisms to deal with agency opportunism? Competition is indirect at best, on the federal level. Political oversight has severe limits, at least for the type of administrative state ours has grown into. Indeed, this is the motivation in the first place for the fiduciary theory of administrative law. Procedural requirements such as notice-and-comment and reason-giving, coupled with court review, can cabin limited forms of opportunism. But they can become boxes to tick. There is reason to think they cannot completely substitute for a culture of the rule of law, to which it is time to turn.

[122] G. Lawson, 'The Rise and Rise of the Administrative State' (1994) 107 Harv. L. Rev. 1231, 1249–54 (critiquing theories that seek to justify the modern administrative state while not giving up on some form of constitutionalism).

[123] Cf. D.J. Barron and T.D. Rakoff, 'In Defense of Big Waiver' (2013) 113 Colum. L. Rev. 265, 267 (welcoming, despite risk, the rise of what they call 'big waiver' which 'gives agencies the broad, discretionary power to determine whether the rule or rules that Congress *has* established should be dispensed with. It is the delegation, in other words, of the power to waive Congress's rules. Or, put another way, it is the delegation of the power to unmake law Congress has made rather than to make law Congress has not.' (italics original)).

Equity, administration and the rule of law

Equity and the rule of law have a complicated relationship. At first glance, equity seems to be a threat to the rule of law. In its all-round fix-it version, it is open to criticism that it fails the criteria of generality, clarity, non-retroactivity and possibly non-contradiction, constancy as well. The snappy 'Chancellor's foot' put-down encapsulates this critique.[124] Indeed, in our post-fusion world, in many areas, including administrative law, we find a polarisation between a celebration of the most expansive version of equity or a formalist backlash.[125] The shift from the New Common Law to a new focus on statutes, including textualist approaches, is an example. Equity as anti-opportunism lies between these poles.

Elsewhere, I have argued that the strand of equity as anti-opportunism actually protects the rule of law.[126] Let me assume for purposes of argument a thin notion of the rule of law, but one that still can be evaded. Just as equity intervenes to prevent opportunists from subverting the law, a macro-version of equity is needed to prevent the evasion of the rule of law criteria themselves. It is indeed true that law can meet the criteria and still be wicked law. It is also true that the rule of law ideal can never be fully realised.[127] One brake on this type of opportunism (besides a more robust version of the rule of law incorporating swaths of natural law) is the anti-evasion principle.

At this macro-level, the problem of institutional enforcement becomes difficult. Yes, courts might enforce some outer limits on opportunism

[124] This critique is sometimes met head on. See, for example, T.A.O. Endicott, *Vagueness in Law* (Oxford University Press, 2000), 185–203 (arguing that vagueness and discretion are necessary to the rule of law in the sense of trueness of law's actions to its purposes); L.B. Solum, 'Equity and the Rule of Law', in I. Shapiro (ed.), *The Rule of Law* (New York University Press, 1994), ch. 6 (arguing for a theory of virtuous judging to reconcile equity and the rule of law). Note that one reason for law's actions not to be true to its purposes is evasion and abuse. See Endicott, *Vagueness in Law*, 191, 198, 203.

[125] This split can sometimes be seen in duelling opinions in the same case, while overlooking an intermediate approach based on anti-opportunism that accords better with historical equity. See P.G. Turner, '"Mending Men's Bargains" in Equity: Mortgage Redemption and Relief Against Forfeiture' (2014) 130 L.Q.R. 188 (analysing *Çukurova Finance International Ltd* v. *Alfa Telecom Turkey Ltd (No. 4)* [2015] 2 W.L.R. 875; [2013] UKPC 20); Smith, 'An Economic Analysis of Law Versus Equity', 51–2 (discussing *Grupo Mexicano de Desarrollo SA* v. *Alliance Bond Fund Inc.*, 527 U.S. 308 (1999)).

[126] Smith, 'Property, Equity, and the Rule of Law', in Austin and Klimchuk (eds.), *Private Law and the Rule of Law*, ch. 10.

[127] Endicott, *Vagueness in Law*.

through the kind of equity in administrative law I have argued for here. But the courts themselves need to be kept in check, especially when they are employing equity.

Ultimately, the rule of law rests on some very basic customs that require widespread acceptance. All law requires an equilibrium of mutual expectations of acceptance.[128] That goes as well for the rule of law.

The rule-of-law custom or norm can be reinforced by specific institutions. If equity doctrine is well specified (narrow trigger, or clear category), this makes monitoring by other branches easier. It increases the cost of deviation. If one accepts broad *ex post* intervention, there is less of a defined trigger for objection. The rule of law problem in administrative law can be seen as an example of macro-equity and its institutional limits.

Thus, some version of equity reinforces the rule of law at the macro-level. This could be interpreted as a fiduciary norm, in a loose sense. Even Criddle's fiduciary model depends on notions of fidelity operating through first-party enforcement – through internalisation of norms.[129] This happens through a process of socialisation. As Feldman and I have argued, equity as anti-opportunism may work on multiple audiences – or people in different modes.[130] The same legal command couched in moral terms can function as a threat against bad faith evaders and at the same time promote high performance by good faith actors who will hear the same command as in accord with and supportive of their moral notions.[131]

What is the morality in play here? Some would see all of public law as based in the state's role as a fiduciary, and the rule of law as gaining its content from this fiduciary relationship.[132] When we get to the type of procedural style of morality associated with narrow versions of the rule of law, courts are at most part of the solution. It is hard to see how courts can promote generality, certainty, non-retroactivity and the like, without a high degree of consensus and concern about such criteria among those

[128] For a model, see G.J. Mailath, S. Morris and A. Postlewaite, 'Laws and Authority', unpublished manuscript (February 1998, rev. April 2001), available www.princeton.edu/~smorris/pdfs/laws&authority.pdf.

[129] Criddle, 'Fiduciary Foundations of Administrative Law', 132–4, 161–3.

[130] Y. Feldman and H.E. Smith, 'Behavioral Equity' (2014) 170 J. Institutional & Theoretical Econ. 137.

[131] Criddle argues for something similar in his fiduciary model of administrative agencies: Criddle, 'Fiduciary Foundations of Administrative Law', 134.

[132] See, for example, E. Fox-Decent, 'The Fiduciary Nature of State Legal Authority' (2005) 31 Queen's L.J. 259; E.J. Leib, D.L. Ponet and M. Serota, 'Translating Fiduciary Principles into Public Law' (2013) 126 Harv. L. Rev. F. 91.

operating the legal system and those subject to its control. Moreover, nothing in the fiduciary model or general equity on its own solves the higher-order problem of what keeps the courts themselves from being opportunistic. Regarding the rule of law criteria as boxes to be ticked is easy enough in the absence of a consensus about the rule of law that is strong enough for people to feel embarrassed by such box checking in the service of causes they believe in. Can one get exercised about a decision that one agrees with on the merits? It is not clear such a consensus, minimal though it might seem, is possible. Again this brings us back to the set of conventions and overall culture of the rule of law.

Conclusion

Administrative law and equity go hand in hand. This is true historically but also functionally. Here I have defended part of the equitable tradition that aims at countering opportunism by serving as an important check on the excesses of administrative agencies. This can and should work at the level of administrative law, even, and in some cases especially, after the passage of the APA in the United States. The growth of the administrative state points to the need for equity as anti-opportunism at the macro-level, where the rule of law is the issue. Thus, administrative law does implicate the rule of law, but equity is not the problem. It can be part of the solution.

19

Equity and administrative behaviour

A commentary

TIMOTHY ENDICOTT

In a wide-ranging and penetrating account of connections between modern public administration and equity, and between administrative law and equity, Henry Smith outlines a 'narrower anti-opportunism strand in equity'.[1] Opportunism is 'behaviour that is undesirable but that cannot be cost-effectively captured – defined, detected, and deterred – by explicit *ex ante* rulemaking'.[2] In this sense of equity, an institution that imposes equity may be preventing an opportunist from unfairly taking advantage of the generality of a law. Narrow anti-opportunism equity is contrasted with 'a general fix-it equity'.[3] In this general fix-it equity, an institution that imposes equity is imposing fairness in general terms on the persons subject to the decision, in a way that may reform or depart from the law.

Professor Smith makes the case that the narrow (but not too narrow)[4] anti-opportunism strand can be seen at work in the history and current institutional manifestations and processes and remedies and substantive standards of equity in US administrative law. And that is a good thing, the argument goes, because if courts give effect to the narrower version of equity in hearing claims against administrative agencies, they can prevent opportunistic evasion of legitimate administrative regulation by private actors, and opportunistic evasion of the law by administrative agencies. And the courts will be doing so in a way that does not violate the rule of

[1] H.E. Smith, 'Equity and Administrative Behaviour', Chapter 18 of this volume, text to n. 48.

[2] H.E. Smith, 'An Economic Analysis of Law Versus Equity', working paper (22 October 2010), 10–11, available: www.law.yale.edu/documents/pdf/LEO/HSmith_LawVersusEquity7.pdf, quoted in Smith, 'Equity and Administrative Behaviour', text to n. 24.

[3] Smith, 'Equity and Administrative Behaviour', text after n. 91. [4] *Ibid.*, text after n. 21.

law. They will be resisting the temptation to take on the 'roving commission to apply open-ended morality after the fact [that] is exactly what has long motivated critics of the broad equitable tradition'.[5] The implication is that by taking on that roving commission, the judges would themselves be acting opportunistically.

Professor Smith has a compelling case against a general fix-it equity in administrative law, and there is indeed value in a narrower anti-opportunism equity in administrative law. As in other areas of the law, applying equitable principles in administrative law calls for moderation and for a cautious approach to the courts' capacity to use equitable principles to put things right.

Professor Smith is appropriately cautious about 'broad *ex post*' attempts to do justice; I will suggest that we can take the cautious approach somewhat further. I will argue that the core of English administrative law developed at common law not in Chancery;[6] that the fiduciary principle developed in Chancery does not have a general role to play in administrative law;[7] and that even Professor Smith's narrow anti-opportunism version of equity remains in tension with the rule of law.[8]

Those comments may at points seem to play down the role of equity in administrative law, so let me emphasise at this point the importance, in my view, of the deep insight at the heart of Professor Smith's argument: the genuine role of equity in administrative law lies in the provision and the evolution of institutions that can make the law true to its own reason. The risk – as with any equitable jurisdiction – is that public administration will be ruled, instead, by the reason of the judges.

The King's Bench and administrative law

It is striking for a lawyer from another jurisdiction to encounter the special role that courts of Chancery have played in US administrative law, for judicial review of the lawfulness of executive action in England developed primarily in the Court of King's Bench, and *not* in Chancery.[9] With the early modern development of administrative powers, the judicial role

[5] *Ibid.*, text to n. 47.
[6] See *ibid.*, section entitled 'Equity and opportunism' starting after n. 6.
[7] See *ibid.*, section on 'Administrative equity' starting after n. 50.
[8] See *ibid.*, section on 'Equity's role in administrative law' starting after n. 78.
[9] But note that the Chancellor had power to issue the writ of *habeas corpus*. I do not mean to say that the Court of Chancery played no important role in control of the executive.

emerged in actions in tort in Common Pleas and in the King's Bench and, more significantly still, the King's Bench developed administrative law through its jurisdiction to issue the prerogative writs.

Consider *Rooke's Case*.[10] The Commissioners of Sewers, those Tudor antetypes of the administrative state, had power to repair river banks, to charge landowners to cover the cost and to enforce their charges through distress of goods. The power was stated widely in the statute: 'and all those personnes and every of them to taxe assesse charge distreyne and punysshe, . . . as . . . shall seme moste convenient'.[11] Rooke owned seven acres of land along the Thames, where the commissioners made repairs to a bank to prevent flooding. It seemed most convenient to the commissioners to charge him for the entire cost of works that would also protect 800 acres of land away from the riverbank, which was owned by others. Rooke brought an action in King's Bench in replevin, and succeeded. Faced with the argument that the power granted by Parliament was wide enough to authorise the charge, Sir Edward Coke said:

> [A]nd notwithstanding the words . . . give authority to the commissioners to do according to their discretions, yet their proceedings ought to be limited and bound with the rule of reason and law.[12]

This was an early and significant instance of the judges' willingness to interfere with the substance of administrative decisions. It involves an obvious potential for them to curb opportunism by an administrative agency; also, you might say, an obvious potential for them to act opportunistically in turn, to order the administrative agency to do what the judges would prefer. Sir William Blackstone altogether lauded this development in the King's Bench. He noted that the Privy Council under James I had tried to prevent the bringing of claims against the Commissioners of Sewers in King's Bench:

> The pretence for which arbitrary measures was no other than the tyrant's plea of the *necessity* of unlimited powers in works of evident utility to the public, 'the supreme reason above all reasons, which is the salvation of the king's lands and people'. But now it is clearly held, that this (as well as all other inferior jurisdictions) is subject to the discretionary coercion of his majesty's court of king's bench.[13]

[10] (1597) 5 Co. Rep. 99b; 77 E.R. 209. [11] Statute of Sewers 1531, 23 Hen. VIII c. 5, s. 4.

[12] *Rooke's Case* (1597) 5 Co. Rep. 99b, 100a; 77 E.R. 209, 210.

[13] W. Blackstone, *Commentaries on the Laws of England* (Oxford: Clarendon Press, 1753), bk III, ch. VI, 74 (citations omitted).

The risk in this judicial power is latent, even in Blackstone's ringing endorsement of judicial review. It is true that unlimited powers are *not* necessary, even in works of evident utility to the public. But the doctrine in *Rooke's Case* creates a potential for unmerited interference with those works, by a reviewing court. It is a risk that the English courts gladly took on, as we can see from those other great actions in tort that have become staples of English public law, *Entick* v. *Carrington*[14] (a warrant of the secretary of state was not lawful authorisation for trespass to property and to Entick's papers) and *Cooper* v. *Wandsworth Board of Works*[15] (demolition of a building without a hearing was not authorised by a legislative provision that 'it shall be lawful for the . . . Board to cause such House or Building to be demolished'[16] when works were started without notice to the Board).

More importantly for the development of the judicial role, the Court of King's Bench took over the supervision of inferior tribunals, through its jurisdiction to issue prerogative writs – in particular, certiorari and mandamus, but also of course habeas corpus, quo warranto and prohibition. That was a common law jurisdiction, thoroughly knitted into the notion of the King's Bench as the court that had responsibility for causes that concerned His Majesty. As the modern administrative state developed, certiorari in the common law courts was the standard process for legal control of administrative agencies. Its successor, the quashing order regulated by the Civil Procedure Rules,[17] is still the standard process in the twenty-first century.

You may be tempted to say that this history shows that administrative law is a creature of law *and not of equity*. The central principle (I will call it 'the principle of legality') is to hold public authorities to the law, and not to interfere with administration on grounds of conscience. The distinctive American role of courts of equity arises from American peculiarities, such as the entrenched role of the jury in civil matters in the common law courts, and the obvious good sense in avoiding jury trials – or trials in general – in judicial review of administrative action.[18]

[14] (1765) 19 St. Tr. 1029; also reported 2 Wils. K.B. 275; 95 E.R. 807.

[15] (1863) 14 C.B. (N.S.) 180; 143 E.R. 414.

[16] Metropolis Local Management Act 1855, 18 & 19 Vict. c. 120, s. 76.

[17] Civil Procedure Rules 1998 (UK), Part 54.

[18] England solved the same problem through summary process in petitions for prerogative writs and, in the twentieth century, through legislative reforms of judicial review procedure by the Supreme Court Act 1981 (UK), s. 31 and Civil Procedure Rules 1998 (UK), Part 54.

Those conclusions would miss the central insight of Professor Smith's contribution. It is true that, in a system with courts of Chancery separate from the courts of common law, courts of Chancery need play no role in administrative law. But that does not mean that *equity* need play no role; even in a system of separate courts, equity is not *only* available in the courts of equity. The English system of separate courts, like the American, was a product of historical accidents partly generated by the pleas of parties who had suffered from the refusal of the judges in the common law courts to administer the law with equity. There never was any general rule that common law courts could not mitigate the rigour of their law, as Thomas More put it.[19] Even in More's classic, interventionist view of his jurisdiction as Chancellor, he was only to intervene where the judges of the common law failed or declined to mitigate its rigour. There was and is no general rule that the common law courts could not do equity, where equity is conceived in the Aristotelian sense of solving problems that arise from the generality of the law. And the reasoning in *Rooke's Case* shows the equitable aspect of the principle of legality: it is not merely a principle that the administration must not depart from the ambit of the power. It is also very patently what Professor Smith terms an anti-opportunistic principle. The agency may not take the opportunity of a wide power, to act in ways that are repugnant to its public role. *Cooper* v. *Wandsworth Board of Works* illustrates this form of narrow anti-opportunistic equity: when a statute does not specify that a power is to be used with due process, 'the justice of the common law will supply the omission of the legislature'.[20] Mr Justice Byles could just as well have said that equity will supply the omission of the legislature.

The principle of legality is an equitable principle in this Aristotelian sense, and in Professor Smith's narrow anti-opportunism sense. It is a technique for curbing opportunism by the agency in cases like *Rooke* and *Cooper*, where the agency is doing just precisely what the law ostensibly authorises in its generality. It is the judges' technique for ensuring that the legal power given to the agency is exercised in accordance with 'the rule of reason and law', as the Lord Chief Justice put it.[21]

[19] See the discussion in T.A.O. Endicott, 'The Conscience of the King: Christopher St German and Thomas More and the Development of English Equity' (1989) 47 U. Toronto Fac. L. Rev. 549, 567.

[20] *Cooper* v. *Wandsworth Board of Works* (1863) 14 C.B. (N.S.) 180, 194; 143 E.R. 414, 420 (Byles J.).

[21] (1597) 5 Co. Rep. 99b, 100a; 77 E.R. 209, 210.

And if it is a principle of the Court of Common Pleas, it is not the less an equitable principle, for in this respect law and equity were always fused. In fact, in *Rooke's Case*, Sir Edward Coke went on to say:

> For discretion is a science or understanding to discern between falsity and truth, between wrong and right, between shadows and substance, between equity and colourable glosses and pretences, and not to do according to their wills and private affections; for as one saith, *talis discretio discretionem confundit.*[22]

We will see that it is a dangerous principle. It suggests that the court is to determine what reason requires. A court applying this principle, even sincerely, might act opportunistically in exercising its power to determine the rule of reason and law.

The fiduciary model of administrative law

Administrative agencies may have fiduciary duties. An administrative agency could be made a trustee. The Public Trustee in the United Kingdom is a prime example.[23] A public agency that is authorised to take children into care incurs fiduciary duties when it does so. These examples show how different those fiduciary duties are from other duties to which administrative agencies are held in administrative law. For the fiduciary duties are imposed on public bodies when there is special reason for them to act with exclusive regard for particular, private interests.

In fact, I think that the legal and the moral duties of public authorities are very diverse and are not in general fiduciary duties. But I suggest this with some diffidence, as I do not have room here to respond to the sophisticated arguments that have been made for a fiduciary model of administrative law.[24] And you can see the attraction of the model. As Evan Criddle has put it, 'the fiduciary model emphasizes that agencies bear a solemn responsibility to honour the terms and spirit of their

[22] *Ibid.*, 210. The Latin can be translated as 'such a discretion confounds discretion'.

[23] Public Trustee Act 1906 (UK). See www.justice.gov.uk/protecting-the-vulnerable/public-trustee.

[24] Henry Smith cites E.J. Criddle, 'Fiduciary Foundations of Administrative Law' (2006) 54 UCLA L. Rev. 117 and E. Fox-Decent, 'The Fiduciary Nature of State Legal Authority' (2005) 31 Queen's L.J. 259. See also E. Fox-Decent, *Sovereignty's Promise: The State as Fiduciary* (Oxford University Press, 2011), and the bibliography listed in E.J. Leib, D.L. Ponet and M. Serota, 'Translating Fiduciary Principles into Public Law' (2013) 126 Harv. L. Rev. F. 91, 91 n. 2.

entrusted authority'.[25] There are, of course, similarities between fiduciaries and public authorities. But the differences are deep and significant. At its best, I will argue, the fiduciary model can only advance understanding of some particular duties of public authorities (i.e. those that are indeed fiduciary) and of the courts' role in enforcing those particular duties.

A trustee holding funds under a fiduciary obligation to the beneficiary of the trust must deal with the funds in a way that serves the interests of the beneficiary. We can say the same of an administrative agency holding funds on trust. But we most definitely cannot say this in general of an administrative agency holding funds. All we can say in general is that administrative agencies holding public funds must use them for public purposes and not for any purposes that are expressly or implicitly excluded by law. That general principle implies, of course, that the individuals acting on behalf of such an agency cannot use the funds for their own private gain, and this is the most important general similarity between duties of public authorities and duties of trustees. But the administrative agency's salient duty is to deal with the funds for public purposes, and the trustee's salient duty is to deal with the funds for the private benefit of beneficiaries. The agency's specific duties depend on the particular public purposes for which the power is held; a trustee's specific duties depend on the private purposes prescribed by the settlor.

There has been at least one serious effort to import the fiduciary principle into English administrative law, in a way that really did make a difference. I will argue that it was a mistake. The mistake reflects the unhelpfulness of fiduciary law as a general model for administrative law.

In *Roberts* v. *Hopwood*,[26] the socialist majority on the local council decided that the London Borough of Poplar should be a model employer, paying £4 a week as a minimum – and paying women the same as men. The auditor levied charges on the councillors personally for the resulting substantial excess of the local authority's salary bill above market rates for labour. The Divisional Court held that the councillors had violated a fiduciary duty:

> The Council are in a fiduciary position, not merely towards a majority who have elected them, but towards the whole of the ratepayers. A councillor is not entitled to follow the course which in his private capacity he might think it proper or advisable to pursue, but must confine

[25] Criddle, 'Fiduciary Foundations of Administrative Law', 137. [26] [1925] A.C. 578.

> his discretion within the limits imposed by law. He is not entitled to be unduly generous at the expense of those on whose behalf he is a trustee.[27]

The Court of Appeal overturned that decision, but the House of Lords restored it, and upheld the auditor's charges against the councillors. Lord Atkinson affirmed the lower court's view that the councillors were – at least 'somewhat' – in the position of trustees:

> A body charged with the administration for definite purposes of funds contributed in whole or in part by persons other than the members of that body, owes, in my view, a duty to those latter persons to conduct that administration in a fairly businesslike manner with reasonable care, skill and caution, and with a due and alert regard to the interest of those contributors who are not members of the body. Towards these latter persons the body stands somewhat in the position of trustees or managers of the property of others.[28]

The decision vividly illustrates the dangers of what Professor Smith calls a general fix-it equity: the judges imposed on local governance their fix for an ill that they saw, and the reason for counting it as an ill did not lie in the law, but in the judges' own model of local governance. Rather than the rule of law, local communities got the rule of judges, through Lord Atkinson's imposition of a fiduciary (or at least somewhat fiduciary) duty. The result was to require local governments to act in the private interests of their ratepayers rather than in the public interest of their localities. That requirement, justifiable only if the law's arrangements for local governance were a sham, was an injudicious interference with public administration.

You may say that the problem with *Roberts* v. *Hopwood* is just that the House of Lords got the beneficiaries wrong; they should have said that the beneficiaries are not the ratepayers, but the public to whose account the rates are received, and on whose account the council held the funds. Lord Atkinson was right, on this view, to treat the councillors as 'managers of the property of others'. But it was the property of Poplar Borough, not the property of the ratepayers. That would improve the fiduciary model, by reducing its impact. No one could justly put a fiduciary model of administrative law into effect, except insofar as it says nothing more than that administrative agencies owe a general duty to use public funds (and generally to exercise public power) for public

[27] *R* v. *Roberts* [1924] 1 K.B. 514, 522 (Sankey J. for himself, Lord Hewart C.J. and Salter J.).
[28] *Roberts* v. *Hopwood* [1925] A.C. 578, 595–6.

purposes, and may owe specific duties to use them for specified public purposes.

Professor Smith does not expressly endorse the fiduciary model of administrative law; it is enough for his purposes to point out that '[a]dministrative agencies do pose problems similar to those of fiduciaries',[29] and that some aspects of administrative law are similar to controls over fiduciaries. But his chapter shows the deeply significant differences between fiduciaries and administrative agencies. He points out the stringent enforcement of duties of trustees in the courts of equity.[30] How different that judicial role was, as the law of trusts developed, from the judges' role in controlling decisions of public authorities. And here I think it is actually significant that the stringent judicial enforcement of trustees' duties was developed in Chancery, while the King's Bench was developing its relatively restrained, deferential, discretionary enforcement of the much more diverse (and sometimes much less well defined) duties of public authorities. In the original paper on which Professor Smith's chapter is based, he wrote:

> The question arises, to what extent a fiduciary conception of administration helps define the courts' role in keeping agencies within their bounds and policing their exercise of discretion. The narrower strand of equity as anti-opportunism suggests a strong but narrow and highly incomplete role for courts in serving this function.[31]

I think that the answer to the question is that the fiduciary conception of administration does not help to define the courts' role in keeping agencies within their bounds, and that this is shown by the courts' 'highly incomplete' role in preventing opportunism by administrative agencies. As Professor Smith points out, '[f]iduciary law is equity that goes beyond an *ex post* safety valve'.[32] Its rules 'put entire categories of transactions off-limits . . . because the danger of opportunism is great enough and the chilled behaviour is worth paying as a price'.[33] It has special reasons for those rules, to give effect to the will of the settlor and to protect the beneficiary's interests. This view of fiduciary law points out (1) how deeply different the role of a fiduciary is, from the role of administrative agencies in general, and (2) how different the role of judges is in enforcing trustees' fiduciary duties, from their role in reviewing the lawfulness of administrative decision making.

29 Smith, 'Equity and Administrative Behaviour', text before n. 76.
30 *Ibid.*, text after n. 37. 31 See now *ibid.*, text after n. 78. 32 *Ibid.*, text after n. 2.
33 *Ibid.*, text after n. 24.

Perhaps you will think that the fiduciary principle simply needs to be specified very widely, so that *the people* are both settlors and beneficiaries in the trust relationship, and each public agency is a trustee on whom powers have been conferred by the public, for the benefit of the public. Evan Fox-Decent writes that 'anyone subject to legal authority, regardless of status, is an equal co-beneficiary of the rule of law' (and, therefore, of the fiduciary duties of public authorities).[34] This wide approach to the class of beneficiaries, it seems to me, does all that can be done to reconcile the fiduciary model with the open-ended diversity of the legal and moral duties of public authorities, and of the state. As a general model of the political obligations of the state, however, there is still an important objection. A good public agency ought to be prepared to deal decently with the interests of strangers (of asylum seekers, of foreign commercial competitors and foreign consumers, of foreign victims of domestic air pollution, of foreign states and international agencies, etc.). A good public agency will not set out to further those interests of strangers willy-nilly. It certainly does not have general fiduciary duties to foreign individuals or states.[35] But in a good system of state governance, public agencies will respect those outside interests (1) in a way for which they are accountable to their own citizens, and (2) with a view to the duties of their state towards human beings, in general, and towards other states and international agencies. In fact, when a public authority rightly gives asylum to an asylum seeker (or regulates domestic commerce in ways that benefit world trade, or refrains from predatory conduct in international economic affairs, or curtails domestic pollution because of its external impact, or, in general, abides by a treaty obligation that is contrary to a narrow national interest, etc.), it will be acting in the discharge of its people's duties. But acting in discharge of the people's duties is very remote from acting as a fiduciary of the people.

Think of the model of trust law: a trustee in English law has no lawful power to disburse the *res* of the trust for the benefit of non-beneficiaries. Suppose that a trustee did so, and claimed to have acted for the

[34] Fox-Decent, *The State as Fiduciary*, 40; cf. 'the set of candidate public beneficiaries may include some or all of the public (including some *and* all of the public in a single case)': at 152. Criddle offers a nuanced account in which the 'beneficiaries' may be the people as a whole, or some discrete set of persons. See Criddle, 'Fiduciary Foundations of Administrative Law', 138.

[35] Fox-Decent makes a provocative suggestion to the contrary: 'it is not too far a stretch to think that the state is under an obligation to exercise power over strangers on the same basis as it exercises power over its own subjects, which is to say, on the basis of their trust': Fox-Decent, *The State as Fiduciary*, 109.

beneficiaries in discharging their moral duty of concern for the good of others, and argued that the beneficiaries would have had a moral duty to spend the *res* for the purposes for which the trustee acted, if the beneficiaries had held the legal title to the *res*. None of this would be an answer to a complaint of breach of trust. Accept for the sake of argument that it is in the interest of persons (and in the interest of peoples) that they should discharge their duties; even then, the fiduciary model does not explain how it can be right for a state to use the people's funds for the benefit of others. The private law of fiduciary duty acts on a conception of interests that is blinkered and artificially restricted. It has to do so, of course, because judges are not in a position to impose on trustees an unblinkered, unrestricted view of what is good for beneficiaries. The resulting conception of the interests of beneficiaries yields an impoverished model for the diverse duties of public authorities.

The fiduciary model of administrative law could only be made fully sound if it were reduced to saying that public authorities cannot exercise public powers for their own private benefit, but only for public purposes. And then it seems to me that the differences between duties of public authorities and fiduciary duties in private law are deep and significant. Public authorities' duties are, in general, non-fiduciary duties that share one characteristic of fiduciary duties: the prohibition on private profit by the holder of a power.

Anti-opportunism: three layers

Opportunities for opportunism arise at all three levels, in an administrative scheme such as the sixteenth-century arrangement for the administration of riverbank improvements. Table 1 contains a list of examples.[36]

The striking, structural feature of judicial review in administrative law is that while there are opportunities for opportunism at all levels, the regression of anti-opportunism stops with the courts. The agency has lawful power to curb opportunism by actors. The court has jurisdiction to curb opportunism by the agency. But no other institution has jurisdiction to curb opportunism by the court.

I think that *Roberts* v. *Hopwood* was an example of opportunism by the courts. The decision reflects the challenge of equity – of the principle of

[36] Note that opportunities for criminality by actors and corruption by the agency or the court are not listed; criminality and corruption would not be opportunism in the relevant sense.

Table 1 *Anti-opportunism: three layers*

	Opportunism
Actors– the landowners	– evading charges for repairs, trying to free-ride on works paid for by the neighbours
Agency – the Commissioners of Sewers	– building an empire, making people pay for unproductive projects that make the Commissioners look good, cutting corners to make administration easy and keep costs down
Court – Common Pleas	– building an empire, increasing their court's business, ordering a result that promotes the policy that the judges prefer

legality – to the rule of law. If a reviewing court applies a general fix-it equity in reviewing the decisions of other public authorities, we will be ruled not by law, but by the judges' conception of the public purposes that are to be pursued. This is a central strand in Professor Smith's argument, and I agree with it. The prospect in Professor Smith's chapter is that if the courts, instead, hold to the narrower anti-opportunistic form of equity, administrative law will be achieving its potential to improve public administration, without substituting the judges' administrative decisions for those of the responsible agency.

It is evidently true that the narrower anti-opportunistic form of equity is a better basis for the development of administrative law by judges; it justifies the doctrines developed in *Rooke's Case* and in *Cooper* v. *Wandsworth Board of Works*. But reflect for a moment on the fragility of the distinction between anti-opportunism, and setting out to fix things in general. Professor Smith characterises opportunism very broadly, as 'behaviour that is . . . undesirable', but cannot be controlled by general rules.[37] Suppose that the judges in judicial review of administrative action take it as their legitimate role, not to engage in a general fix-it job, but only to interfere with behaviour that is undesirable but could not be captured by *ex ante* rules. We would still have a doctrine of judicial review that is very broad and is hard to distinguish from the basis on which *Roberts* v. *Hopwood* was decided.

[37] Smith, 'Equity and Administrative Behaviour', text following n. 1.

It is not generally for judges to decide what public decisions are undesirable in general. So even with Professor Smith's quite sound rejection of general fix-it equity as an engine of administrative law, there is still a tension between judicial review of administrative action, and the rule of law. The tension can only be resolved if the judges can distinguish between conduct that is undesirable (which is not their concern) and conduct which is undesirable in the particular sense that it takes advantage of the generality of the law to act contrary to the purpose of the law. It is a permanent tension, because it is permanently challenging for judges to draw this distinction. I think that this is the lesson of Professor Smith's chapter.

And with great respect for Sir Edward Coke, we should add something to his sound principle that the discretionary action of administrative agencies 'ought to be limited and bound with the rule of reason and law'.[38] We should add that it is not up to judges to decide what reason in general requires. The judges' role is to decide what reasons they – from their limited and partial perspective on the situation, and given their capacity to acquire and to digest information, and their remedial capacities and limitations – can justly and conveniently present to the agency, and to the community, as limits on a power that is in the discretion of the agency, and not of the judges. For government according to law, we need *both* administrative agencies and courts to discern, as Sir Edward Coke put it, 'between equity and colourable glosses and pretences, and not to do according to their wills and private affections'.[39]

[38] *Rooke's Case* (1597) 5 Co. Rep. 99b, 100a; 77 E.R. 209, 210. [39] *Ibid.*, 210.

20

Equity and human rights

ROBERT WALKER

Introduction

There are two fields of law in which equity can claim to have made a conspicuous contribution to the advancement of human rights. One is now no more than a matter of history: the property rights in England of married women before the Married Women's Property Acts of 1870,[1] 1874[2] and 1882.[3] This would be, to a modern human rights lawyer, the subject-matter of article 1 of the first protocol to the European Convention on Human Rights, the right to enjoyment of one's property. The other is the recent development, from the old equitable doctrine of breach of confidence, of our modern law of personal privacy. Its development has been extraordinarily rapid, and undoubtedly it has been influenced and accelerated by article 8 of the European Convention, which recognises the right to respect for one's private and family life, home and correspondence. The developing body of law is rooted in equitable doctrine, but it is being brought on in the hothouse of the Human Rights Act, and it is hard to predict how much further it has to grow.

This chapter is in three sections. The first discusses equity's intervention in relation to married women's property, which is still of interest though it is now past history. The second discusses the development of our modern law of personal privacy. The third contains some more general reflections, including some thoughts about the difference between rules and standards, and the suggestion that the practical realism and proportionality of equitable remedies have contributed to the right to

[1] Married Women's Property Act 1870, 33 & 34 Vict. c. 93.

[2] Married Women's Property Act 1874, 37 & 38 Vict. c. 50.

[3] Married Women's Property Act 1882, 45 & 46 Vict. c. 75. There were further amending Acts: Married Women's Property Act 1884, 47 Vict. c. 14; Married Women's Property Act 1893; Married Women's Property Act 1907; and Married Women's Property Act 1908.

a fair trial, under article 6 of the European Convention, in the determination of civil rights and obligations.

Married women's property

At common law, a married woman could not hold or acquire property independently of her husband. Her personal property vested in him outright. Any real property of hers vested in him for the duration of the marriage and continued in him as tenant by curtesy if she died first, unless the marriage had been childless. During the marriage she could not acquire any property in her own right, even savings from her own earnings.[4] These disabilities as to ownership of property were matched by other comparable disabilities in her personal and family life, well documented in a valuable body of work by scholars of English social and legal history.[5] A husband could physically chastise his wife. He could not be convicted of raping her. In the event of separation, whether judicial or informal, he could prevent her from having any contact with her children, whatever their ages. She could not obtain a divorce, in the modern sense, unless she could obtain a personal Act of Parliament. Much of this flowed from the grotesquely one-sided common law doctrine of the unity of husband and wife. John Stuart Mill described the position of married women in England as 'worse than that of slaves in many countries' and commented acerbically on the unity doctrine that it was used 'for the purpose of inferring that whatever is hers is his, but the parallel inference is never drawn that whatever is his is hers'.[6]

Another significant factor, which features in several of the authorities during the first half of the eighteenth century, was the prevalence of elopement and clandestine marriage, until this was effectively halted by Lord Hardwicke's Marriage Act of 1753.[7]

4 In 1865, some influential women presented a petition to Parliament protesting at the plight of a woman who 'worked from morning till night to see the produce of her labour wrested from her, and wasted in a gin-palace'.

5 There are some useful references in W. Cornish, 'Family Law, Family Authority', in W. Cornish, S. Anderson, R. Cocks, M. Lobban, P. Polden and K. Smith, *The Oxford History of the Laws of England: Volume XIII 1820–1914: Fields of Development* (Oxford University Press, 2010), 744–6, and bibliography at 1027–9; also L. Stone, *Uncertain Unions and Broken Lives* (Oxford University Press, 1995); C. Stebbings, *The Private Trustee in Victorian England* (Cambridge University Press, 2002).

6 J.S. Mill, *The Subjection of Women* (1867), reprinted in A. Ryan (ed.), *Mill: Texts and Commentaries* (London: Norton & Co., 1997), 157.

7 Marriage Act 1763, 26 Geo. II c. 33.

Equity's intervention did not in practice benefit all or even most married women. Its principal beneficiaries were women in the aristocracy or the gentry, because they were most likely to have ready access to attorneys and conveyancers and to have fortunes large enough to justify engaging their professional services. It was the Married Women's Property Acts which, in Dicey's much-quoted observation, extended the rules of equity, framed for the daughters of the rich, to the daughters of the poor.[8] But trade does occasionally appear in the reports. Just as statutory reform was getting under way, the Court of Appeal in Chancery considered the case of Mrs Outram[9] who, starting on a small scale in her own kitchen, had by her husband's death in 1874 built up a flourishing wholesale trade in preserved fruit. Her husband's personal representative then claimed the entire undertaking as part of his estate. The case was initially argued under the Married Women's Property Act 1870 but was eventually decided in favour of the wife by the old equitable doctrine of the separate use: a generous decision, as there were no trustees and no evidence of the creation of any express trust.

James L.J. said in the course of his judgment, after referring to the position at common law:

> But the Court of Chancery (a very great [c]ourt in its day, although it has now ceased to exist) invented that blessed word and thing 'the separate use of a married woman', and as that Court never allowed itself to be impeded or obstructed by mere technicalities, it provided that whenever it was necessary, and so far as it was necessary to give effect to that separate use of a married woman, the husband should be made a trustee of whatever property came to him in his marital right which ought to be so held.[10]

As this passage indicates, the separate use was at the heart of equity's intervention. It enabled property to be settled on a woman in such a way that, despite the common law rule, it remained in her beneficial ownership and at her disposal during her marriage. The property might be provided by someone else (typically her father, under the treaty for a marriage settlement) or by the intended wife herself, so long as she obtained the concurrence of her intended husband. (I shall come back to this important point.)

[8] A.V. Dicey, *Lectures on the Relation between Law and Public Opinion during the Nineteenth Century*, 2nd ed. (London: Macmillan & Co., 1962), 395.

[9] *Ashworth* v. *Outram* (1877) 5 Ch. D. 923. [10] *Ibid.*, 941.

The invention of the separate use cannot be dated with any accuracy, but there are signs of it before the end of the sixteenth century,[11] and by the early years of the eighteenth century, it was referred to as well-established law.[12] In *Bennet* v. *Davis*[13] in 1725, a grant of freehold land to a woman 'for her separate and peculiar use' was held to create a separate estate even though no trustees were appointed.

The separate use was essential to two subsidiary doctrines which equity developed: the wife's equity to a settlement and the restraint upon anticipation. If a husband was compelled to come to the Court of Chancery in order to obtain title to an asset of his wife's (for instance, to obtain payment of a legacy bequeathed to his wife which the executor was reluctant to pay to him), the Court of Chancery could make relief conditional on the husband settling some or all of the fund for the benefit of his wife and children. The trusts of the settlement were to be 'in analogy to what a prudent parent would probably have done in giving a portion to a daughter'.[14] The imposition of the condition was justified on the strength of the maxim 'he who seeks equity must do equity'.[15] The reports show that this jurisdiction was often attacked in argument by the husband's counsel as depending on the irrelevant procedural accident of the need for an application to the Court of Chancery. In a pensive judgment in *Sturgis* v. *Champneys*,[16] Lord Cottenham L.C. recognised the force of this argument. He seems to have felt some uncertainty as to whether it was the maxim about an equity-seeker doing equity, rather than the maxim about equity following the law, to which he should be giving most weight.[17] But he eventually concluded that it was not 'a case of difficulty or doubt'.[18]

The jurisdiction to direct a settlement was discretionary and often involved the court in enquiring into the conduct of the parties to the marriage. If a husband treated his wife cruelly, and refused or failed to maintain her, the court would be ready to grant relief. Examples are

[11] *Witham* v. *Waterhowse* (1595) Tothill 91; 21 E.R. 133; *sub. nom. Wytham* v. *Waterhouse* (1595) Cro. Eliz. 466; 78 E.R. 703.

[12] *Brown* v. *Elton* (1733) 3 P. Wms 202, 205; 24 E.R. 1030, 1031 (Lord King L.C.).

[13] (1725) 2 P. Wms 316; 24 E.R. 746.

[14] *Tidd* v. *Lister* (1854) 3 De G. M. & G. 857, 869; 43 E.R. 336, 340 (Lord Cranworth L.C.). There is a useful discussion of 'courts as settlors' by S. Anderson, 'Succession, Inheritance, and the Family', in Cornish, Anderson, Cocks, Lobban, Polden and Smith, *The Oxford History of the Laws of England: Volume XII 1820–1914: Private Law*, 12–18.

[15] *Brown* v. *Elton* (1733) 3 P. Wms 202, 203, 205; 24 E.R. 1030, 1030, 1031.

[16] (1839) 5 My. & Cr. 97; 41 E.R. 308. [17] *Ibid.*, 101–2, 107; 311, 312.

[18] *Ibid.*, 107; 312.

Oxenden v. *Oxenden*,[19] a case of cruelty by an aristocratic husband, and *Williams* v. *Callow*,[20] a case of cruelty by a husband much lower in the social order, who 'has wasted all, and has no fixed habitation, but goes from alehouse to alehouse'.[21] Professor William Cornish has summarised the position:

> The amount available, the wife's needs and that of their children, the conduct of the husband and that of the wife, all went into a moral melting pot; typically she could expect half the asset to be kept for her and the offspring. If the husband was living with his mistress while refusing to make a voluntary settlement on the wife, he could expect tough treatment. If she, however, committed adultery her hands were unequivocally sullied and she could expect no help.[22]

The facts of some of the cases are remarkable. *Barrow* v. *Barrow*[23] concerned the marriage between a twenty-nine-year-old bachelor and a widow who (on his evidence) 'acknowledged [herself] to be at forty-five years old, but [who believed] she was more'.[24] They spent a month's honeymoon abroad and separated as soon as they got home. The Court of Appeal in Chancery had no hesitation in directing the whole of the fund to be settled for the benefit of the wife, reversing the Vice-Chancellor's direction for a settlement of only a half.[25]

The wife's equity to a settlement gave her the benefit of a settlement to her separate use, but (just because her interest was at her free disposal) there was a risk of her husband 'kissing or kicking' her into an assignment in favour of himself or his creditors. *Pybus* v. *Smith*,[26] a case heard by Lord Thurlow L.C., was a notorious example. Lord Eldon L.C. referred to it in a later case:

> So, in *Pybus* v. *Smith* the Court, settling the property, in order to protect it, with all the anxious terms then known to conveyancers, in a day or two

[19] (1705) 2 Vern. 493; 23 E.R. 916; also reported *sub. nom. Rockingham* v. *Oxendon* (1705) Prec. Chan. 239; 24 E.R. 116.

[20] (1717) 2 Vern. 752; 23 E.R. 1091. [21] *Ibid.*, 753; 1092.

[22] Cornish, 'Family Law, Family Authority', in Cornish, Anderson, Cocks, Lobban, Polden and Smith, *The Oxford History of the Laws of England: Volume XIII 1820–1914: Fields of Development*, 743 (footnote omitted).

[23] (1834) 5 De G. M. & G. 782; 43 E.R. 1073. In his *Miscellany at Law* (London: Stevens & Sons, 1955), 112–15, Sir Robert Megarry reprinted much of the judgment of Knight Bruce L.J. as an example of judicial wit, but some will today find the humour heavy-handed and self-indulgent.

[24] (1834) 5 De G. M. & G. 782, 788; 43 E.R. 1073, 1076.

[25] *Ibid.*, 791–3, 794–6; 1077–8, 1078–9. [26] (1791) 3 Bro. C.C. 340; 29 E.R. 570.

> afterwards, while the wax was yet warm upon the deed, the creditors of the husband got a claim upon it by an informal instrument; and the same Judge [*sc.* Lord Thurlow], who had made such efforts to protect her, was upon authority obliged to withdraw that protection.[27]

Lord Eldon recounted how Lord Thurlow then invented the restraint upon anticipation by inserting into a settlement the words 'not to be paid by way of anticipation'.[28] The circumstances have been explained in a scholarly note by Walter G. Hart.[29] Lord Thurlow invented the new doctrine, not when sitting as Lord Chancellor, but when acting as a trustee for a Miss Watson. Such was Lord Thurlow's prestige that his extra-judicial innovation secured immediate acceptance. Restraints upon anticipation could not be imposed after 1935,[30] but existing restraints continued. After the Second World War, a personal Bill was introduced to remove (no doubt for the purpose of saving estate duty) restraints affecting the interests of the daughters of the Marquess of Reading. But Parliament decided instead to abolish all surviving restraints, and did so in 1949.[31]

By these three measures equity did much to protect married women who occupied privileged positions in society. But the protection was limited, and it was no more than that: protection of what was viewed as a disadvantaged class, without any recognition of women's human right to genuine equality with men. One scholar, Eileen Spring, has commented that '[equity] cannot be seen as a simple supporter of women's rights',[32] and another has pointed out that younger sons as well as daughters were disadvantaged by the strict settlement's emphasis on male primogeniture.[33]

The fact is that equity followed the law in its basic patriarchal assumption that a married woman was subservient to her husband so long as he kept his side of the bargain and provided for her. This comes out most

[27] *Jones* v. *Harris* (1804) 9 Ves. 486, 493–4; 32 E.R. 691, 693–4.

[28] *Brandon* v. *Robinson* (1811) 18 Ves. 429, 434–5; 34 E.R. 379, 381. See also *Jones* v. *Harris* (1804) 9 Ves. 486, 494; 32 E.R. 691, 694; *Parkes* v. *White* (1805) 11 Ves. 209, 221–2; 32 E.R. 1068, 1073; *Jackson* v. *Hobhouse* (1817) 2 Mer. 483, 487–8; 35 E.R. 1025, 1026–7.

[29] W.G. Hart, 'The Origin of the Restraint upon Anticipation' (1924) 40 L.Q.R. 221. Hart conjectures (at 226) that Miss Watson may have been married to Lord Carbery in 1792.

[30] Law Reform (Married Women and Tortfeasors) Act 1935 (UK), s. 2.

[31] Married Women (Restraint upon Anticipation) Act 1949 (UK).

[32] E. Spring, *Law, Land, and Family: Aristocratic Inheritance in England, 1300 to 1800* (Chapel Hill: University of North Carolina Press, 1993), 184–5.

[33] S. Staves, 'Resentment or Resignation? Dividing the Spoils among Daughters and Younger Sons', in J. Brewer and S. Staves (eds.), *Early Modern Conceptions of Property* (London: Routledge, 1995), 194–218.

clearly from equity's ready acceptance that it was fraudulent for an engaged woman to dispose of any part of her fortune without the concurrence of her intended husband. Lord Thurlow L.C. stated the position in *Countess of Strathmore* v. *Bowes*[34] in 1789:

> The law conveys the marital rights to the husband, because it charges him with all the burthens, which are the consideration, he pays for them; therefore it is a right, upon which fraud may be committed. Out of this right arises a rule of law, that the husband shall not be cheated, on account of his consideration.[35]

The circumstances of the case were, Buller J. said at an interlocutory hearing, 'such as probably never happened before, and may never happen again'.[36] Lady Strathmore became very wealthy on her husband's death in 1776. By the end of the year she was engaged to be married to Mr Grey, and on 9 and 10 January 1777 she granted valuable lands, with Mr Grey's knowledge and approbation, to trustees on trusts under which she had a power of revocation. Then on 16 January she met Mr Bowes, who claimed to have fought a duel in defence of her honour. (The duel was, it seems, a complete sham.) On 17 January, she married, not Mr Grey, but Mr Bowes. Shortly afterwards she revoked her settlement and later claimed to have done so under duress by Mr Bowes. The claim of duress was upheld, so Mr Bowes relied on the alternative argument that by the settlement he had been defrauded of his right.

Lord Thurlow dealt with this point in summary fashion: 'It is impossible for a man, marrying in the manner Bowes did, to come into equity, and talk of fraud.'[37] But the important point to take from the decision, I suggest, is that equity no less than the common law (indeed perhaps even more than the common law) accepted and supported the view of marriage as a distinctly one-sided commercial transaction. Equity might alleviate the consequences, but it did not challenge the premise.

The developing English law of privacy

As an introduction to the second part of my chapter I draw attention (as I have previously done[38]) to the close proximity, in the official law

[34] (1789) 1 Ves. Jun. 22; 30 E.R. 211. [35] *Ibid.*, 28; 214.

[36] *Countess of Strathmore* v. *Bowes* (1788) 2 Bro. C.C. 345, 349; 29 E.R. 194, 196.

[37] *Countess of Strathmore* v. *Bowes* (1789) 1 Ves. Jun. 22, 29; 30 E.R. 211, 214.

[38] In an unpublished paper, 'The Developing English Law of Privacy', given on 12 August 2008 at the University of Sydney, at a meeting chaired by the Hon. Justice William Gummow.

reports, of the decisions of the House of Lords in *Wainwright* v. *Home Office*[39] and *Campbell* v. *MGN Ltd.*[40] Their proximity is no doubt an accident of law reporting, but it serves to emphasise the speed with which English law has been developing a law of personal privacy.

Each case was concerned with an invasion of personal privacy. In *Wainwright* it took the form of humiliating strip-searches, carried out in breach of the Prison Rules, of Mrs Wainwright and one of her sons (who had learning difficulties) while visiting her other son in prison. In *Campbell*, it was a sensational news story printed in the *Daily Mirror* about the treatment for drug addiction of the celebrity model Naomi Campbell, accompanied by a photograph of her in the street after leaving a meeting of Narcotics Anonymous. But in every other respect, including the outcome, the cases were in striking contrast to each other.

The Wainwrights suffered indignities at the hands of the prison service in 1997. The Human Rights Act 1998 (UK) had not yet been enacted, so the fact that the prison service is a public authority for the purposes of that Act[41] did not assist the claimants. Judgment in their final appeal to the House of Lords was not given until October 2003, but it was decided under the law as it was before the Human Rights Act.[42] Ms Campbell, by contrast, issued her writ on the very day of the offending publication, 1 February 2001, when the Act had been in force for four months. Her case proceeded more speedily, and it was decided by the House of Lords in May 2004.

The fact that the Human Rights Act was in force in February 2001 might be thought not to assist Ms Campbell, since Mirror Group Newspapers, powerful though it is, is not a public authority. Nevertheless, the House of Lords, having dismissed the Wainwrights' appeal, allowed Ms Campbell's. She won by a narrow majority, but the difference of opinion in the Lords was largely as to whether the Court of Appeal had erred in departing from the evaluation made by the judge. The House was unanimous that equity's established doctrine of breach of confidence must be developed in order to protect the values embodied in article 8 of the European Convention, and that this protection should not be restricted to a statutory claim against a public authority.

[39] [2004] 2 A.C. 406; [2003] UKHL 53. [40] [2004] 2 A.C. 457; [2004] UKHL 22.

[41] Human Rights Act 1998 (UK), s. 6(3)(a).

[42] They subsequently obtained relief in Strasbourg: *Wainwright* v. *United Kingdom* (2007) 44 E.H.R.R. 40.

Lord Hoffmann was the only Law Lord who sat on both appeals.[43] In his opinion in *Campbell*, he did not acknowledge any inconsistency with *Wainwright*, which he referred to as authority for the proposition that English law does not have a general tort of invasion of privacy.[44] But some of Lord Hoffmann's reasoning does seem to have undergone modification, notably his observation in *Wainwright*:

> [T]his is an area which requires a detailed approach which can be achieved only by legislation rather than the broad brush of common law principle.[45]

and his further observation:

> [T]he coming into force of the Human Rights Act 1998 weakens the argument for saying that a general tort of invasion of privacy is needed to fill gaps in the existing remedies.[46]

In order to explore the change of direction in *Campbell* it may be helpful to look at some of the things that happened during the course of the Wainwrights' protracted litigation and the more rapid progress of Ms Campbell's claim. In 1999 and the first two-thirds of 2000, when the Human Rights Act had been enacted but was not yet in force, there was a good deal of academic discussion between what might be called 'verticalists' and 'horizontalists'. Both camps agreed that the Act operated vertically as between the state (and public authorities treated as emanations of the state), on the one hand, and the individual citizen (or some non-public body), on the other hand. The verticalists stopped there, relying on the limited class of potential defendants (that is public authorities) on which obligations were imposed by section 6 of the Act. The horizontalists, however, pointed out that the court is itself a public authority,[47] and that it is therefore arguably under a statutory obligation to maintain Convention rights even in disputes between private parties.

In the academic debate, the verticalists seem to have been in the majority, but the horizontalists had an eminently distinguished supporter in Sir William Wade. In the year 2000, successive issues of the *Law Quarterly Review* contained three relevant items: an article by Sir Richard

[43] On *Wainwright*, he sat with Lord Bingham, Lord Hope, Lord Hutton and Lord Scott, all of whom agreed with him; in *Campbell*, Lord Nicholls and he dissented as to the result, the majority consisting of Lord Hope, Lady Hale and Lord Carswell.

[44] *Campbell* v. *MGN Ltd* [2004] 2 A.C. 457, [43].

[45] *Wainwright* v. *Home Office* [2004] 2 A.C. 406, [33].

[46] *Ibid.*, [34].

[47] Human Rights Act 1998 (UK), s. 6(3)(a).

Buxton (then a Lord Justice of Appeal) challenging Sir William's views;[48] a reply, 'Horizons of Horizontality', by Sir William;[49] and a note by Anthony Lester and David Pannick disavowing support for the horizontalist cause.[50]

It might have been expected that this lively academic debate would soon be reflected in decisions of higher courts on disputes to which the Human Rights Act did (at least as a matter of timing)[51] apply. But in the event there has been surprisingly little judicial comment. The first notable reference was in the perceptive judgment of Sedley L.J. in *Douglas* v. *Hello! Ltd*,[52] which referred to the horizontality debate, but concentrated on the development of the action for breach of confidence:

> The law no longer needs to construct an artificial relationship of confidentiality between intruder and victim: it can recognise privacy itself as a legal principle drawn from the fundamental value of personal autonomy.[53]

There was then a gap, so far as I can see, until March 2002 when Lord Woolf C.J. (sitting with Laws and Dyson L.JJ.) gave the judgment of the Court of Appeal in *A* v. *B plc*.[54] It seems to have been the first reported case of an attempt by a celebrity (in that case a professional footballer) to prevent publication in the press of a news story about his marital infidelity. So far as we can tell from the report, there was no citation of the academic debate about the position of the court as a public authority (although the judgment did complain about the lengthy citation of authority on an interlocutory appeal). Nevertheless, the court took an explicitly horizontalist line:

> The court's approach to the issues which the applications raise has been modified because, under s 6 of the 1998 Act, the court, as a public authority, is required not to act 'in a way which is incompatible with a Convention right'. The court is able to achieve this by absorbing the rights which articles 8 and 10 protect into the long-established action for

48 R. Buxton, 'The Human Rights Act and Private Law' (2000) 116 L.Q.R. 48.

49 H.W.R. Wade, 'Horizons of Horizontality' (2000) 116 L.Q.R. 217.

50 D. Pannick and A. Lester, 'The Impact of the Human Rights Act on Private Law: The Knight's Move' (2000) 116 L.Q.R. 380.

51 For the temporal effect of section 4 of the Human Rights Act, in a dispute between private interests, see *Wilson* v. *First County Trust (No. 2)* [2004] 1 A.C. 816; [2003] UKHL 40, especially the speech of Lord Hope at [104]–[124]; and A. Burrows, 'Common Law Retrospectivity', in A. Burrows, D. Johnston and R. Zimmermann (eds.), *Judge and Jurist: Essays in Memory of Lord Rodger of Earlsferry* (Oxford University Press, 2013), 543–57.

52 [2001] Q.B. 967. 53 *Ibid.*, 1001. 54 [2003] Q.B. 195; [2002] EWCA Civ 337.

> breach of confidence. This involves giving a new strength and breadth to the action so that it accommodates the requirements of those articles.[55]

The judgment gave practical guidance to lower courts in no fewer than fifteen sub-paragraphs.[56] The guidance was perhaps over-detailed and over-prescriptive for that very early stage in the development of the law, reminiscent indeed of Clemenceau's comment on Woodrow Wilson's fourteen points: '*Le bon Dieu soi-même n'avait que dix.*' Not all of the guidelines have been followed, in particular as to the weight to be placed on the footballer's position as a 'role model'. Lord Phillips M.R. expressed doubt about this when the Court of Appeal allowed MGN's appeal in *Campbell*[57] in October 2002, and Sir Stephen Sedley commented on it in his 2006 Blackstone Lecture:

> [O]ne has to wonder what our moral custodians imagine goes on in young people's minds. Possibly – just possibly – a number of boys want to grow up playing football like Garry Flitcroft. Is the revelation in the family's Sunday paper that he has been sleeping with a lap dancer going to make them switch to, let us say, Wayne Rooney as their preferred role model? Or is it going to suggest to them that the great thing about being a professional footballer, or any other kind of media star, is that you can sleep with just about anyone?[58]

Rights under articles 8 and 10 (to respect for personal privacy and to freedom of expression) are not absolute, but qualified rights, and they may be in direct competition. The correct approach for the court to take in balancing such competing rights has now been authoritatively stated by Lord Steyn:

> First, neither article has *as such* precedence over the other. Secondly, where the values under the two articles are in conflict, an intense focus on the comparative importance of the specific rights being claimed in the individual case is necessary. Thirdly, the justifications for interfering with or restricting each right must be taken into account. Finally, the proportionality test must be applied to each.[59]

This is sometimes referred to as 'parallel analysis', but that expression may give a misleading impression of scientific precision. It is essentially

[55] [2003] Q.B. 195, [4]. [56] *Ibid.*, [4], [11].

[57] *Campbell* v. *MGN Ltd* [2003] Q.B. 663, [40]; [2002] EWCA Civ 1373.

[58] Published in S. Sedley, *Ashes and Sparks: Essays on Law and Justice* (Cambridge University Press, 2011), 314.

[59] *In re S (A Child) (Identification: Restrictions on Publication)* [2005] 1 A.C. 593, [17]; [2004] UKHL 47 (italics original).

an exercise in judicial evaluation of incommensurable interests made after close study of the facts of the particular case.

In practice, if asked to prohibit publication of a news story about sexual infidelity or other aberrant conduct on the part of a celebrity, the court is likely to attach weight, not to the claimant's supposed position as a role model, but to factors such as a professional footballer's appearing to be more concerned about his sponsorship contracts than about his family's feelings;[60] or a model's having acted hypocritically in publicly denying drug-taking;[61] or a prominent businessman's having misled the court on a without-notice application.[62] The degree of the threatened intrusion, in terms of lurid detail and photographs, is also relevant.

There is a useful discussion of the developing law in the judgment of Buxton L.J. in *McKennitt* v. *Ash*.[63] The claimant was a well-known Canadian folk-singer who guarded her privacy. The defendant, Ms Ash, had been a close friend of hers, but the friendship ended in acrimony. Ms Ash wrote a book containing a lot of personal and private material about Ms McKennitt, and accusing her of hypocrisy, for treating her friends badly while maintaining a warm public persona. There was a particular complaint about Ms McKennitt's involvement in the purchase of a house, and whether a substantial payment by her was a gift or a loan.

I have gone into the facts in a little detail because the authority is a good illustration of how real cases do not fit into convenient categories. In principle, defamation is one cause of action, with justification (i.e. truth) as a defence; invasion of personal privacy by publication of confidential material is another cause of action, to which truth is not a defence, though a public interest in publication may be. But in practice disputed issues of fact often arise in privacy cases, and Lord Steyn's 'intense focus' may require them to be resolved so far as that is possible on what is often a hurried interlocutory hearing, or a series of such hearings. It was, for instance, highly material, in Mr Max Mosley's proceedings against *The News of the World*,[64] whether his aberrant activities could be described as having a Nazi theme. I cannot therefore fully agree with the comment of Longmore L.J. in *McKennitt* v. *Ash* that in a case of misuse of private information, '[t]he truth or falsity of

60 *Terry* v. *Persons Unknown* [2010] E.M.L.R. 16, [95]; [2010] EWHC 119 (QB).

61 *Campbell* v. *MGN Ltd* [2004] 2 A.C. 457, [143], [149].

62 *Browne* v. *Associated Newspapers Ltd* [2008] Q.B. 103, [85]–[87]; [2008] EWCA Civ 295.

63 [2008] Q.B. 73; [2006] EWCA Civ 1714.

64 *Mosley* v. *News Group Newspapers Ltd* [2008] E.M.L.R. 20; [2008] EWHC 1777 (QB).

the information is an irrelevant inquiry in deciding whether the information is entitled to be protected'.[65] Life would be easier for judges if it were as simple as that.

That leads on to the rather vexed question of the rule in *Bonnard* v. *Perryman*.[66] When the Human Rights Act was enacted it had for over a century been settled law that in a libel action, if a defendant has pleaded, or intends to plead justification as a defence, an interlocutory injunction restraining publication will not normally be granted. As Lord Coleridge C.J. put it in *Bonnard* v. *Perryman*:

> Unless it is clear that an alleged libel is untrue, it is not clear that any right at all has been infringed; and the importance of leaving free speech unfettered is a strong reason in cases of libel for dealing most cautiously and warily with the granting of interim injunctions.[67]

This reluctance to impose prior restraint goes back to Blackstone.[68]

In *Greene* v. *Associated Newspapers Ltd*,[69] counsel for the claimant strenuously argued that the rule had become a 'sacred cow' which the Human Rights Act required to be culled,[70] but that argument was rejected by the Court of Appeal. If anything, the Act has in one respect reinforced the rule by section 12, which was added as a new clause and has some difficulties of construction.[71]

The decision in *Greene* v. *Associated Newspapers Ltd* has received some criticism.[72] Moreover, the rule in *Bonnard* v. *Perryman* applies only to cases in which defamation is the cause of action relied on, except possibly where a different (and less appropriate) cause of action is invoked in an attempt to circumvent the rule.[73] The degree of cross-over between libel and publication of private material suggests that the whole topic may

[65] *McKennitt* v. *Ash* [2008] Q.B. 73, [86]. [66] [1891] 2 Ch. 269.

[67] *Bonnard* v. *Perryman* [1891] 2 Ch. 269, 284.

[68] W. Blackstone, *Commentaries on the Laws of England* (Oxford: Clarendon Press, 1769), vol. 4, 151–2, quoted by Auld L.J. in his valuable account of the rule in *Holley* v. *Smyth* [1998] Q.B. 726, 737–8.

[69] [2005] Q.B. 972; [2004] EWCA Civ 1462. [70] [2005] Q.B. 972, 975–6.

[71] *Cream Holdings Limited* v. *Banerjee* [2005] 1 A.C. 253; [2004] UKHL 44.

[72] Notably in R. Clayton and H. Tomlinson (eds.), *The Law of Human Rights*, 2nd ed. (Oxford University Press, 2009), [15.28]; also M. Warby, N. Moreham and I. Christie (eds.), *Tugendhat and Christie: The Law of Privacy & the Media*, 2nd ed. (Oxford University Press, 2011), [7.65]–[7.84].

[73] See *Service Corp. International plc* v. *Channel Four Television Corp.* [1999] E.M.L.R. 83, 89–90; *Ajinomoto Sweeteners Europe SAS* v. *Asda Stores Ltd* [2011] Q.B. 497, [28]; [2010] EWCA Civ 609, in which Sedley L.J. observed, '[a] great many fact situations are able to be litigated through more than one cause of action, and the choice of them is as often tactical as jurisprudential'.

have to be revisited before long. If the topic is revisited by the Supreme Court it will undoubtedly look closely at the decision of the High Court of Australia in *Australian Broadcasting Corp.* v. *O'Neill*.[74] The facts of the case were very unusual. The claimant had been convicted in 1975 of the murder of one boy and had confessed to the murder of another boy, both crimes being committed in Tasmania. The alleged defamation, which the ABC sought to justify, was that he was also guilty of the murder of three children who had disappeared in South Australia in 1966. The relevant statute[75] provided a defence of truth, but only if publication was also in the public interest. The courts below had granted and upheld an interlocutory injunction primarily on the ground that 'trial by media' was not in the public interest. The High Court allowed the ABC's appeal and discharged the injunction. Kirby J. and Heydon J. dissented.

There are two joint judgments in favour of allowing the appeal. That of Gleeson C.J. and Crennan J. does not say much about the rule in *Bonnard* v. *Perryman*, but the rule is fully discussed in the joint judgment of Gummow J. and Hayne J., and in the two dissenting judgments. The joint judgment of Gummow and Hayne JJ. refers to Lord Cottenham L.C. in describing 'the reluctance by the courts of equity to participate in any indirect reinstatement of a licensing system by a method of prior restraint by injunctive order'.[76] It also observes,[77] with a reference to Lord Mansfield,[78] that the stance taken by the courts was not adopted in innocence of the malign influence, on occasion, which may be exerted by media of mass communication.

The dissenting judgments also contain much of interest. Kirby J. saw the rule as more flexible,[79] quoting Spry who said:

> [J]udges trained in a common law rather than an equitable tradition may misunderstand the nature of equitable discretions, and hence attempt to describe them in terms of inflexible rules.[80]

[74] (2006) 227 C.L.R. 57; [2006] HCA 46. [75] Defamation Act 1957 (Tas.), s. 15.

[76] *Australian Broadcasting Corp.* v. *O'Neill* (2006) 227 C.L.R. 57, [82], referring to *Fleming* v. *Newton* (1848) 1 H.L.C. 363, 376; 9 E.R. 797, 803. Lord Cottenham L.C. was himself speaking of the power of the Court of Session to grant an interdict against the publication of a libel.

[77] *Australian Broadcasting Corp.* v. *O'Neill* (2006) 227 C.L.R. 57, [87].

[78] *R* v. *Shipley* (1784) 4 Doug. K.B. 73, 170; 99 E.R. 774, 824, where Lord Mansfield spoke of the 'licentiousness of the press' as Pandora's Box.

[79] *Australian Broadcasting Corp.* v. *O'Neill* (2006) 227 C.L.R. 57, [142]–[146].

[80] I.C.F. Spry, *The Principles of Equitable Remedies*, 8th ed. (London: Sweet & Maxwell, 2010), 20.

Heydon J. gave what is, if I may respectfully say so, an account of the rule that is both scholarly and incisive. It does not admit of brief summary, but the following passage gives the flavour:

> If Pound is correct and Lord Halsbury is wrong, some most curious events took place between 1874 and 1894. On the one hand, by a gross misconstruction of the relevant legislation, the judges arrogated to themselves a power to grant interlocutory injunctions restraining public or defamatory matter which they had not hitherto had. On the other hand, they developed four limits regulating that power which were so restrictive that the power could hardly ever be exercised in favour of plaintiffs, and hardly ever has been.[81]

The contrast with the recent practice in the grant of interlocutory injunctions restraining publication of private and confidential matters is striking. About six years ago there was a sharp increase in the number of successful applications for what have come to be popularly called super-injunctions. An injunction prohibiting publication of the offending material would be reinforced by further satellite prohibitions designed to ensure secrecy for the whole proceedings. An example is *Terry* v. *Persons Unknown*,[82] to which I have already referred. Because Mr Terry's application failed, we know precisely what his lawyers were asking for, in addition to the principal injunction: first, a private hearing; secondly, anonymity for all concerned; thirdly, sealing of the court file; fourthly, prohibition of publication of the fact that the application had been made; and fifthly, prohibition of any third party served with the order from seeing the materials put before the judge.

Resort to such draconian measures in order to spare a celebrity from embarrassment may be thought obviously disproportionate. The administration of justice in public and public knowledge of the court's orders are matters of high constitutional principle. This was recognised by a committee formed and chaired by Lord Neuberger M.R. and the committee's prompt report[83] was accepted and endorsed by Lord Judge C.J. in

[81] *Australian Broadcasting Corp.* v. *O'Neill* (2006) 227 C.L.R. 57, [206]. The references are to R. Pound, 'Equitable Relief against Defamation and Injuries to Personality' (1916) 29 Harv. L. Rev. 640 and Lord Halsbury's judgment in *Monson* v. *Tussauds Ltd* [1894] 1 Q.B. 671, 688–9 (the 'Chamber of Horrors' case in which Lord Halsbury, sitting unusually in the Court of Appeal, took a broader view of the rule).

[82] [2010] E.M.L.R. 16.

[83] Committee on Super-Injunctions, *Report of the Committee on Super-Injunctions: Super-Injunctions, Anonymised Injunctions and Open Justice* (20 May 2011), available at www.judiciary.gov.uk/Resources/JCO/Documents/Reports/super-injunction-report-20052011.pdf.

May 2011.[84] There seems to have been a salutary fall in the number of super-injunctions granted.

The maxim that 'Equity does nothing in vain' may also be in point here. The court will not try to use injunctive relief to preserve the confidentiality of what is already in the public domain. The *Spycatcher* case[85] is a well-known illustration of that. When super-injunctions were granted, they were often notoriously ineffective because of disclosures made, either under the protection of parliamentary privilege or anonymously and untraceably through the Internet. None of this increases respect for the rule of law. We have certainly not yet reached the last chapter of this new development of equitable doctrine and equitable remedies.

General reflections

Two general points of similarity between equity and human rights law appear from time to time in the earlier sections of this chapter. The first common feature is that each is superimposed on an existing body of law as a modifying or ameliorating influence. In the case of equity the classic statement is that of Lord Ellesmere L.C. in the *Earl of Oxford's* case:

> The Cause why there is a Chancery is, for that Mens Actions are so divers and infinite, That it is impossible to make any general Law which will aptly meet with every particular Act, and not fail in some Circumstances.
>
> The Office of the Chancellor is to correct Mens Consciences for Frauds, Breach of Trusts, Wrongs and Oppressions, of what Nature soever they be, and to soften and mollify the Extremity of the law.[86]

Maitland referred to equity as 'supplementary law, a sort of appendix added on to our code, or a sort of gloss written round our code'.[87] But the cases in which equity modifies or overrides the common law, and those in which (in the words of the maxim) it follows the law, do not fall into a simple pattern. What can be said with some confidence is that equity always presupposes the existence of the common law. Even where it appears to contradict the common law, it does not ignore it.

[84] Judicial Communications Office Media Release, 'Committee Reports Findings on "Super-Injunctions"' (20 May 2011), available at www.judiciary.gov.uk/media/media-releases /2011/committee-reports-findings-super-injunctions-20052011.

[85] *A.-G.* v. *Guardian Newspapers Ltd (No. 2)* [1990] 1 A.C. 109.

[86] (1615) 1 Ch. Rep. 1, 6–7; 21 E.R. 485, 486.

[87] F.W. Maitland, *Equity: A Course of Lectures*, ed. by A.H. Chaytor and W.J. Whittaker, rev. by J. Brunyate (Cambridge University Press, 1936), 18.

In relation to human rights there is typically a Bill or Charter of Rights, or fundamental rights set out at the beginning of a constitutional instrument, which take precedence to other provisions of a state's existing legal order. But that precedence may be qualified, even when the nation's character as a sovereign independent state starts with the same constitutional instrument, as occurred with several former British colonies which attained full independence in the 1950s and 1960s.[88] Each of these territories had an existing body of statute law, parts of which (particularly as regards mandatory capital punishment for murder and corporal punishment) might be in conflict with fundamental rights. Constitutional provisions for the preservation of existing laws of that sort in the constitutions of Barbados, Jamaica and Trinidad and Tobago have produced some narrowly split decisions of the Judicial Committee of the Privy Council, with some dissenting judgments expressed in unusually robust terms.[89]

The degree to which human rights guarantees override a nation's general law is by no means uniform. In the United Kingdom, the Human Rights Act 1998 recognises the special potency of statutory rules, as representing the will of a sovereign parliament. Statutory rules are subject to the two-stage process in section 3 (by which statutes are to be interpreted consistently with Convention rights if possible) and section 4 (which establishes the fall-back possibility of a higher court making a declaration of incompatibility). Such a declaration does not invalidate the incompatible provision, but it sends to parliament a message that it should think again – a message that has never, so far, been ignored. Section 6(2) exonerates public authorities from liability for human rights infringements if acting in accordance with statute. That is a deliberately vague paraphrase because the full complexities of section 6(2) have not yet been fully explored, let alone definitively pronounced on, by the Supreme Court.[90]

The strength and reach of the interpretative obligation imposed by section 3 has been considered by the House of Lords and the Supreme

[88] See the monumental work by A.W.B. Simpson, *Human Rights and the End of Empire: Britain and the Genesis of the European Convention* (Oxford University Press, 2001).

[89] *Roodal* v. *State of Trinidad and Tobago* [2005] 1 A.C. 328; [2003] UKPC 78; *Boyce* v. *R* [2005] 1 A.C. 400; [2004] UKPC 32 (Barbados); *Matthew* v. *State of Trinidad and Tobago* [2005] 1 A.C. 433; [2004] UKPC 33; *Watson* v. *R* [2005] 1 A.C. 472; [2004] UKPC 34 (Jamaica). The last three appeals were heard together by a Board of nine which split five to four.

[90] *Manchester City Council* v. *Pinnock* [2011] 2 A.C. 104, [93]–[103]; [2010] UKSC 45 (Lord Neuberger of Abbotsbury M.R.).

Court in a number of cases. Well before the coming into force of the Human Rights Act, Lord Hoffmann observed that 'the principle of legality will be expressly enacted as a rule of construction in section 3'.[91] The obligation has been described as a 'strong adjuration',[92] at least as strong as the presumption that a statute transposing an EU measure should be construed consistently with that measure.[93] The most important cases are probably (in chronological order) *R* v. *A*,[94] *Re S (Minors) (Care Order: Implementation of Care Plan)*,[95] *R (Anderson)* v. *Secretary of State for the Home Department*,[96] *Bellinger* v. *Bellinger (Lord Chancellor intervening)*[97] and *Ghaidan* v. *Godin-Mendoza*.[98] These cases were discussed by the High Court of Australia in the important constitutional case of *Momcilovic* v. *R*.[99]

The single case that most repays study is *Ghaidan*, with full and thoughtful speeches by Lord Nicholls, Lord Steyn, Lord Millett (in dissent), Lord Rodger and Lady Hale. Several of the expressions used in these speeches were picked up by Lord Bingham in *Sheldrake* v. *Director of Public Prosecutions*:

> In explaining why a Convention-compliant interpretation may not be possible, members of the committee used differing expressions: such an interpretation would be incompatible with the underlying thrust of the legislation, or would not go with the grain of it, or would call for legislative deliberation, or would change the substance of a provision completely, or would remove its pith or substance, or would violate a cardinal principle of the legislation.[100] All these expressions, as I respectfully think, yield valuable insights, but none of them should be allowed to supplant the simple test enacted in the Act: 'So far as it is possible to do so.'[101]

In brief summary, there are two overlapping reasons why a statute may not be amenable to a Convention-compliant interpretation. The first is that it would be contrary to a fundamental aim of the statute, *Anderson*

91 *R* v. *Secretary of State for the Home Department, Ex p. Simms* [2000] 2 A.C. 115, 132.

92 *R* v. *DPP, Ex p. Kebilene* [2000] 2 A.C. 326, 373 (Lord Cooke). See also *R* v. *A (No. 2)* [2002] 1 A.C. 45, [44]; [2001] UKHL 25 (Lord Steyn).

93 *Litster* v. *Forth Dry Dock & Engineering Co. Ltd* [1990] 1 A.C. 546.

94 [2002] 1 A.C. 45.

95 [2002] 2 A.C. 291; [2002] UKHL 10.

96 [2003] 1 A.C. 837, [30]; [2002] UKHL 46, where Lord Bingham described the suggested construction as 'not judicial interpretation, but judicial vandalism'.

97 [2003] 2 A.C. 467; [2003] UKHL 21.

98 [2004] 2 A.C. 557; [2004] UKHL 30.

99 (2011) 245 C.L.R. 1; [2011] HCA 34, considering sections 32(1) and 36(2) of the Charter of Human Rights and Responsibilities Act 2006 (Vic.).

100 [2004] 2 A.C. 557, [33], [49], [110]–[113], [116].

101 [2005] 1 A.C. 264, [28]; [2004] UKHL 43.

being a very clear example. The second is that it would involve the court in an essentially legislative function: in *Bellinger*, precisely defining transgender status; in *Re S*, rewriting the balance of power between the family court and local authority social services when children are taken into care.

Thus, in the United Kingdom the general law, when embodied in statute, must yield and bend to comply with Convention rights so far as it can do so without reaching breaking point; but if the breaking point is about to be reached the interpretative obligation in section 3 is displaced by the possibility of a declaration of incompatibility. That is a prospect which normally brings little or no satisfaction to either side. The claimant fails to obtain relief, and the government (which normally intervenes, if not already a party, where there is any question of a declaration of incompatibility) is faced with the practical necessity for primary legislation or its equivalent.[102] Moreover, that legislation will have to be carried through against the background of some part of the body of statute law having been declared not to be Convention-compliant, which may cause political embarrassment.

Faced with a choice between the application of section 3 or section 4, lawyers representing the government are therefore inclined to opt for section 3 as the lesser of two evils. This was brought home to me forcibly by the experience of sitting in the Supreme Court on *R* v. *Waya*,[103] a case on the Proceeds of Crime Act 2002 (UK), a notoriously difficult statute concerned with the confiscation of the proceeds of crime. Mr Waya made false representations as to his financial position in order to obtain a 60 per cent mortgage on an up-market flat in London at a time when the market was rising rapidly. The mortgage lender lost nothing (indeed it got a bonus in the form of a premium on early repayment) and the judge sentenced Mr Waya not to imprisonment but to eighty hours' community punishment. Later a confiscation order was made against him in the sum of £1.54 m. The Court of Appeal (Criminal Division) reduced this to £1.11 m, and there was a further appeal to the Supreme Court on questions certified by the Court of Appeal. The scope of the appeal was later widened to take account of the Human Rights Act.

The appeal was not the Supreme Court's finest hour. It was heard twice, first in May 2011 by seven judges. In March 2012, it was reheard by

[102] Section 10 of Sch. 2 to the Human Rights Act, like section 2 of Sch. 2 to the European Communities Act 1972 (UK), enables changes to primary legislation to be made by Order in Council.

[103] [2013] 1 A.C. 294; [2012] UKSC 51.

nine judges, and judgment was given on 14 November 2012. A majority of seven reduced the confiscation order to just under £400,000, holding that that was not disproportionate but indicating (and this was much the most important point for the criminal justice system as a whole) that the statute must be read as if it included the words 'except in so far as such an order would be disproportionate and thus a breach of article 1, Protocol 1'.[104] Very distinguished leading counsel appearing for the Crown Prosecution Service as the respondent, and the Secretary of State as an intervener, joined in submitting that an order under the Proceeds of Crime Act must not be disproportionate. That must, I think, reflect a considered choice of the lesser of two evils. But I have to say, as one of the co-authors of the majority judgment, that the interpretation adopted under section 3 might be thought perilously close to going 'against the grain' of the legislation. That legislation had progressively been extended by Parliament from the most serious crimes, usually committed by gangs of professional criminals, to a much wider range of offences, with the original judicial discretion to mitigate the amount of the confiscation order virtually eliminated in the process.[105] The legislation was often described by the courts as 'draconian', a mantra which seems sometimes to have trumped the long-standing principle that penal statutes are to be construed strictly.

Manchester City Council v. *Pinnock*[106] is another case in which the Supreme Court may be thought to have come perilously close to going against the grain of the relevant legislation, in that case section 143D(2) of the Housing Act 1996 (UK), which appears to lay down an extremely summary form of procedure to be followed by the County Court.[107] Both these decisions can perhaps be described as pragmatic. In *Pinnock*, a declaration of incompatibility would have caused huge disruption in the field of social housing, just as a declaration of incompatibility in *Waya* would have caused huge disruption in the criminal justice system.

So much for statute law. As to non-statutory law, the horizontalist cause seems to have carried the day, almost without any struggle, in the rapid development of the law of confidence. But there is little sign of its having directly influenced the development of the common law, or

[104] [2013] 1 A.C. 294, [16].

[105] See the summary of the legislative background, *ibid.*, [3]–[5].

[106] *Manchester City Council* v. *Pinnock* [2011] 2 A.C. 104.

[107] Some will find the statement of the difficulty in *Manchester City Council* v. *Pinnock*, *ibid.*, [75] (which begins 'Much the more difficult question . . .') more convincing than the answer in [76]–[77].

equity, in other directions. It might have been thought that the Human Rights Act would also have influenced the development of the common law as to libel, but that task is, it seems, to be left to Parliament. The rule in *Bonnard* v. *Perryman* remains in place. In *Jameel* v. *Wall Street Journal Europe Sprl*,[108] the appellant's submissions had a horizontalist flavour, but they received little encouragement from the Supreme Court. Lord Hoffmann and Lady Hale did refer to article 10,[109] but the majority relied on the United Kingdom's margin of appreciation.[110]

That brings me to the second common feature of equity and human rights. When an added, ameliorative layer of law is superimposed on an existing body of legal rules, and to some extent takes precedence to existing law, it may be thought natural that it should modify (or in Lord Ellesmere's words, soften and mollify) those rules by reference to evaluative standards rather than by rigid counter-rules. In 1996, Professor Anthony Duggan of Monash University, in an interesting lecture entitled 'Is Equity Efficient?',[111] described, but by no means fully accepted, the 'standards' approach:

> An important difference between rules and standards is that a rule gives content to a legal command *ex ante*, whereas a standard gives it content *ex post*. Accordingly, rules are more costly to promulgate whereas standards are more costly to enforce.[112]

Justice Paul Finn was more positive in a paper 'Equitable Doctrines and Discretion in Remedies', which he gave in 1998:

> [T]he courts quite consciously now are propounding what are acceptable standards of conduct to be exhibited in our relationships and dealings with others ... A clear consequence of this emphasis on standards (and not on rules) is a far more instance-specific evaluation of conduct.[113]

On the other hand, the notion of redress against unconscionable conduct must not lead to an indiscriminate extension of equitable principles and remedies. As Viscount Simonds, a great master of equity, observed:

[108] [2007] 1 A.C. 359; [2006] UKHL 44. [109] [2007] 1 A.C. 359, [90]–[91], [152]–[158].

[110] *Ibid.*, [23]–[27], [98]–[104], [125]–[126].

[111] Published in an abbreviated version in (1997) 113 L.Q.R. 601; the second sentence of the quotation cites L. Kaplow, 'Rules versus Standards: An Economic Analysis' (1992) 42 Duke L.J. 557, 597.

[112] A. Duggan, 'Is Equity Efficient?' (1997) 113 L.Q.R. 601, 629–30.

[113] P. Finn, 'Equitable Doctrines and Discretion in Remedies', in W.R. Cornish, R. Nolan, J. O'Sullivan and G. Virgo (eds.), *Restitution: Past, Present and Future* (Oxford: Hart Publishing, 1998), 260. I quoted this in *Pitt* v. *Holt* [2013] 2 A.C. 108, [126]; [2013] UKSC 26.

> 'Unconscionable' must not be taken to be a panacea for adjusting any contract between competent persons when it shows a rough edge to one side or the other.[114]

Similarly, the preface to the fourth edition of *Meagher, Gummow and Lehane* refers, in relatively moderate language, to 'an indiscriminate and excessive reliance on "unconscionable" conduct as a test for intervention' as a notable exception to the generally satisfactory state of Australian equity jurisprudence.[115] This is mild fare in comparison to the learned authors' comments on Lord Denning's 'manufacture of novel equitable doctrines' in their discussion of the maxim 'Equity will not suffer a wrong to be without a remedy'.[116]

Standards, rather than rules, are the stuff of human rights. The notion of proportionality is of central importance to the weighing up of one qualified human right against another, as Lord Steyn made clear in *Re S (A Child) (Identification: Restrictions on Publication)*.[117] Proportionality is a relatively new concept in the United Kingdom's public law, now greatly influenced by the jurisprudence of the EU Court of Justice at Luxembourg and the European Court of Human Rights at Strasbourg. It has taken the coming into force of the Human Rights Act for it to start to displace the cruder *Wednesbury* test.[118] The slow process of evolution can be traced by comparing cases such as *R* v. *Secretary of State for the Home Department, Ex p. Brind*[119] in 1991 with *R* v. *Chief Constable of Sussex, Ex p. International Trader's Ferry Ltd*[120] in 1998 and *R (Daly)* v. *Secretary of State for the Home Department*[121] in 2001.

In equity, on the other hand, the evaluation of standards of conduct, often including issues of proportionality, is nothing new. It is at the heart of the discretionary nature of equitable remedies. It is also often close to the heart of whether equity recognises the claimant as having a good cause of action at all. I shall refer, by way of illustration, to a few aspects of the equitable remedies of specific performance and mandatory injunction, and to the cause of action based on undue influence.

114 *Bridge* v. *Campbell Discount Co. Ltd* [1962] A.C. 600, 626, echoing similar comments by Harman L.J. in the Court of Appeal: *Campbell Discount Co. Ltd* v. *Bridge* [1961] 1 Q.B. 445, 458–9.

115 R.P. Meagher, J.D. Heydon and M.J. Leeming, *Meagher, Gummow and Lehane's Equity: Doctrines and Remedies*, 4th ed. (Chatswood, NSW: LexisNexis, 2002), xi–xii.

116 *Ibid.*, [3–030].

117 *In re S (A Child) (Identification: Restrictions on Publication)* [2005] 1 A.C. 593, [17].

118 *Associated Provincial Picture Houses Ltd* v. *Wednesbury Corp.* [1948] 1 K.B. 223.

119 [1991] 1 A.C. 696, 750, 762–3, 766–7.

120 [1999] 2 A.C. 418, 439–40, 450, 452.

121 [2001] 2 A.C. 532, [19]–[23], [27]–[28], [32]; [2001] UKHL 26.

There are numerous restrictions, which could be described as rules of practice, as to when the court will decline to grant specific performance, or a mandatory injunction: notably when the order would compel the continuation of a contract for personal service, or some other personal relationship; or when compliance would require continuing superintendence by the court, subject to a well-defined exception for building contracts;[122] or where compliance would require the defendant to carry on business, employing a workforce, for the indefinite future.[123] But they are not wholly inflexible rules, and they are grounded, not in dogma, but in the practical realities of the situation, and the disinclination of the court ('Equity does nothing in vain') to involve the parties in pointless expenditure.

A particularly instructive case is *Co-operative Insurance Society Ltd* v. *Argyll Stores (Holdings) Ltd*,[124] in which Lord Hoffmann's admirable speech (with which the other Law Lords concurred) explained the good sense underlying the court's practice. Argyll had taken a lease of a supermarket in a prime location in a shopping mall and had covenanted to keep it open for business. When it made large losses, Argyll shut the store, admittedly in breach of covenant, and tried to find an assignee. The judge refused to order specific relief, leaving the landlord to its remedy in damages. The Court of Appeal took a very poor view of Argyll's commercial morality and ordered an injunction.[125] (Millett L.J., who dissented, was rather less censorious than Leggatt and Roch L.JJ.[126]) Lord Hoffmann's explanation of his reasoning on the further appeal merits citation at some length.

In holding that the injunction should be discharged, Lord Hoffmann allowed room for flexibility:

> A decree of specific performance is of course a discretionary remedy and the question for your Lordships is whether the Court of Appeal was entitled to set aside the exercise of the judge's discretion. There are well-established principles which govern the exercise of the discretion but these, like all equitable principles, are flexible and adaptable to achieve the ends of equity, which is, as Lord Selborne L.C. once remarked, to 'do

122 *Wolverhampton Corp.* v. *Emmons* [1901] 1 K.B. 515.

123 *Gravesham Borough Council* v. *British Railways Board* [1978] Ch. 379, a case about a loss-making ferry service between Gravesend and Tilbury: see Slade J. at 405.

124 [1998] A.C. 1.

125 *Co-operative Insurance Society Ltd* v. *Argyll Stores (Holdings) Ltd* [1996] Ch. 286, 295, 299, 306.

126 See *ibid.*, 294–5 (Leggatt L.J.), 295–6 (Roch L.J.), 304–6 (Millett L.J.).

more perfect and complete justice' than would be the result of leaving the parties to their remedies at common law.[127]

He mentioned[128] Lord Westbury L.C.'s reluctance (in *Isenberg* v. *East India House Estates Co. Ltd*[129]) to see a defendant delivered 'bound hand and foot' to the mercy of a plaintiff. He continued:

> A remedy which enables [the party entitled to performance] to secure, in money terms, more than the performance due to him is unjust. From a wider perspective, it cannot be in the public interest for the courts to require someone to carry on business at a loss if there is any plausible alternative by which the other party can be given compensation. It is not only a waste of resources but yokes the parties together in a continuing hostile relationship. The order for specific performance prolongs the battle. If the defendant is ordered to run a business, its conduct becomes the subject of a flow of complaints, solicitors' letters and affidavits. This is wasteful for both parties and the legal system. An award of damages, on the other hand, brings the litigation to an end. The defendant pays damages, the forensic link between them is severed, they go their separate ways and the wounds of conflict can heal.
>
> The cumulative effect of these various reasons, none of which would necessarily be sufficient on its own, seems to me to show that the settled practice is based upon sound sense.[130]

After referring to the Court of Appeal's view of Argyll's conduct, he observed:

> The principles of equity have always had a strong ethical content and nothing which I say is intended to diminish the influence of moral values in their application. I can envisage cases of gross breach of personal faith, or attempts to use the threat of non-performance as blackmail, in which the needs of justice will override all considerations which support the settled practice.[131]

But, taking a milder view of Argyll's conduct, he concluded:

> On the scale of broken promises, I can think of worse cases, but the language of the Court of Appeal left them with few adjectives to spare.[132]

127 *Co-operative Insurance Society Ltd* v. *Argyll Stores (Holdings) Ltd* [1998] A.C. 1, 9, quoting *Wilson* v. *Northampton & Banbury Junction Railway Co.* (1874) L.R. 9 Ch. App. 279, 284.

128 *Co-operative Insurance Society Ltd* v. *Argyll Stores (Holdings) Ltd* [1998] A.C. 1, 15.

129 (1863) 3 De G. J. & S. 263, 273; 46 E.R. 637, 641.

130 *Co-operative Insurance Society Ltd* v. *Argyll Stores (Holdings) Ltd* [1998] A.C. 1, 15–16.

131 *Ibid.*, 18. 132 *Ibid.*, 18.

A case in which the court's view of the merits seems to have been decisive was *Kennard* v. *Cory Brothers & Co. Ltd*,[133] the case of the 'moving mountain' which was a precursor (but without the tragic consequences) of the Aberfan disaster. The mine-owner's objections to a mandatory order to make safe its unstable spoil-tip were dismissed. On the other hand, there is equity's disinclination to act 'in vain' by ordering pointless expenditure. *Tito* v. *Waddell (No. 2)*[134] is a well-known example, where the court declined to make a mandatory order for the planting of trees on Ocean Island after its devastation by guano mining. A similar example is *Jordan* v. *Norfolk County Council*.[135]

Equitable remedies are therefore capable of giving relief of a precise and nuanced character, appropriate to the particular case. They can contribute significantly to the attainment of a just outcome to litigation, and to the fair trial rights set out in article 6 of the European Convention. Unfortunately, the shocking delays and formalism of the Court of Chancery during the first half of the nineteenth century, as vividly depicted in Dickens' *Bleak House*, have tended to obscure the valuable contribution that equity has made to the development of civil procedure.

Finally, I come to causes of action based on the unconscionable conduct of the defendant. The word 'unconscionable' is rarely used except by lawyers, and even among lawyers there seems to be a degree of aversion from it in New South Wales.[136] But some equitable causes of action do require the evaluation of the defendant's conduct, with close attention to all the relevant facts (including in particular any furnishing of competent independent advice) for the court to reach a judicial determination as to whether good conscience requires equity to intervene.

Undue influence is a good example. It is striking that in all the leading cases there is a marked reluctance, which cannot be coincidental, to define precisely the elements of the cause of action. Some of the more recent cases set out some simple categories (class 1, class 2A and class 2B).[137] But in the classic statements of the cause of action – Lord Eldon L.C. in *Huguenin* v. *Baseley*,[138] Lindley L.J. in *Allcard* v. *Skinner*,[139] Lord Hailsham L.C. in *Inche Noriah* v. *Shaik Allie bin Omar*[140] and Lord

[133] [1922] 2 Ch. 1. [134] [1977] Ch. 106, 326–7. [135] [1994] 1 W.L.R. 1353.
[136] And, I suspect, among scholars of unjust enrichment; a case of my enemy's enemy?
[137] *Bank of Credit and Commerce International SA* v. *Aboody* [1990] 1 Q.B. 923, 953.
[138] (1807) 14 Ves. 273, 300; 33 E.R. 526, 536. [139] (1887) 36 Ch. D. 145, 181–6.
[140] [1929] A.C. 127, 135.

Nicholls in *Royal Bank of Scotland plc* v. *Etridge (No. 2)*[141] – the language is flexible, tentative even, for fear that it should be too exclusive.

In *Allcard* v. *Skinner*, Miss Allcard, a pious unmarried woman in her thirties, joined a religious sisterhood and gave them a large part of her modest wealth. The Court of Appeal was unanimous in holding that it was a case of undue influence, but divided as to whether the plaintiff's inactivity had barred her right. Lindley L.J.'s classic statement is of a principle rather than a rule:

> Nor can I find any authority which actually covers the present case. But it does not follow that it is not reached by the principle on which the Court has proceeded in dealing with the cases which have already called for decision. They illustrate but do not limit the principle applied to them.
>
> The principle must be examined. What then is the principle? Is it that it is right and expedient to save persons from the consequences of their own folly? [O]r is it that it is right and expedient to save them from being victimised by other people? In my opinion the doctrine of undue influence is founded upon the second of these two principles.[142]

In *Etridge*, Lord Nicholls was even more reluctant to be prescriptive:

> Even this test [*sc.* whether one party has reposed sufficient trust and confidence in another] is not comprehensive. The principle is not confined to cases of abuse of trust and confidence. It also includes, for instance, cases where a vulnerable person has been exploited. Indeed, there is no single touchstone for determining whether the principle is applicable . . . None of these descriptions is perfect. None is all embracing. Each has its proper place.[143]

The reason, I suggest, is a recognition that the cause of action depends, not on the application of rigid rules, but on the judicial evaluation of conduct against an objective standard, with an 'intense focus' on the relevant facts. Essentially, the same approach should be taken, in my view, in cases of proprietary estoppel, and of rescission of a voluntary disposition on the ground of mistake. But I have had my say, and probably more than my fair share of expressing my views, in some well-known cases, culminating in *Pitt* v. *Holt*.[144]

141 [2002] 2 A.C. 773, [11]; [2001] UKHL 44.

142 *Allcard* v. *Skinner* (1887) 36 Ch. D. 145, 182.

143 *Royal Bank of Scotland plc* v. *Etridge* (No. 2) [2002] 2 A.C. 773, [11].

144 [2013] 2 A.C. 108, [124]–[128], citing *Ogilvie* v. *Littleboy* (1897) 13 T.L.R. 399, 400; *Gillett* v. *Holt* [2001] Ch. 210, 225; and *Fisher* v. *Brooker* [2009] 1 W.L.R. 1764, [63]; [2009] UKHL 41.

Conclusion

In conclusion, I have in this chapter taken a quick look at how equity achieved a limited improvement in the property rights of a limited class of women over a period of about two centuries during which women's rights were not a particularly popular cause. I have also taken a quick look at how equity has in the much more favourable climate of the Human Rights Act 1998 developed the law of confidence so as to protect personal privacy and has achieved a great deal in a very much shorter time.

These are important chapters in the history of equity, but they are, in the larger scheme of things, isolated episodes. Even the most devoted students of equity could not contend that its aims and principles are close to those of the contemporary human rights movement. The parallel between equity and human rights law as modifications of another body of law suggested in the chapter is, as Sir Philip Sales observes,[145] at such a high level of generality as to be of little practical interest. But equity and human rights law share a commitment to proportionality, and an intense focus on the facts of the particular case, in order to achieve the right outcome. Despite Sir Philip's disapproval I would respectfully suggest that equitable remedies can be seen as contributing to fair trial rights. Article 6 of the European Convention is supposed to be concerned with access to justice, not substantive law. But the borderline between substantive law and procedure is not clearly defined. Remedies, especially remedies of a discretionary and flexible nature, capable of being granted, varied and discharged in interlocutory proceedings, can make a valuable contribution, on the borderline of procedural and substantive law, to the fair disposal of civil cases.

[145] P. Sales, 'Equity and Human Rights: A Commentary', Chapter 21 of this volume.

21

Equity and human rights

A commentary

PHILIP SALES

In his elegant and informative chapter (Chapter 20), Lord Walker covers a great deal of ground. I highlight two topics which emerge from it: (1) similarities in the legal reasoning involved in the application of equity and human rights law[1] and (2) areas where the law of equity draws on human rights law directly.[2] I also comment on a case study chosen by Lord Walker – *Pitt* v. *Holt*[3] – which illustrates some of the points which arise.

Equity reasoning and human rights reasoning

Lord Walker emphasises two common features of equitable and human rights law: (a) 'each is superimposed on an existing body of law as a modifying or ameliorating influence'; and (b) their use of 'evaluative standards' rather than 'rigid counter-rules'.

Equity as a set of rules or principles grew out of the jurisdiction of the Lord Chancellor to modify and soften the stringent application of the common law to do justice in the circumstances of the individual case.[4] This is a reflection of Aristotelian thinking, employing his concept of *epieikeia* (equity) to supplement and work partial modification of legal rules at their point of application.[5]

[1] R. Walker, 'Equity and Human Rights', Chapter 20 of this volume, text between nn. 3 and 38, and text between nn. 85 and 145.

[2] *Ibid.*, text between nn. 37 and 86. [3] [2013] 2 A.C. 108; [2013] UKSC 26.

[4] *Earl of Oxford's Case* (1615) 1 Ch. Rep. 1, 6; 21 E.R. 485, 486.

[5] *Nicomachean Ethics*, V. 10. 1137b, 12–29; R.A. Wasserstrom, *The Judicial Decision: Toward a Theory of Legal Justification* (Stanford University Press, 1961), ch. 10.

The need for a separate body of law to achieve this weakens as the common law itself has come to be seen as the direct bearer of justice values and as something amenable to correction and modification through judicial legislation,[6] and also as increasing areas of activity come to be regulated by statute and by contracts subject to more purpose-oriented rules of construction.[7] The old idea of the equity of a statute – the capacity for a statute to be interpreted according to its spirit, to accommodate unexpected situations or to avoid unwelcome consequences – itself drawn from Aristotle's *epieikeia*,[8] has revived in this modern form. Something similar has happened with the common law. A sense of justice has increasingly come to be seen as something which infuses the law itself, and it has come to be accepted that the law can be adjusted to accommodate the perceived demands of justice without need to supplement it by appeal to separate doctrines of equity. Accordingly, the scope for development of distinct equitable doctrines has narrowed. Also, the relationship between equity and the common law has come under fresh pressure,[9] as each area of doctrine seeks to develop its own conception of just responses to particular fact situations. For example,

[6] In this regard, see, for example, the remarkable rediscovery of equity within the law itself as referred to by Lord Mansfield in *Moses* v. *Macferlan* (1760) 2 Burr. 1005; 97 E.R. 676 which has inspired the modern law of unjust enrichment and restitution and the protean, rights – and policy-infused development of the tort of negligence, among other areas: cf. R. Stevens, *Torts and Rights* (Oxford University Press, 2007). Compare *In re Hallett's Estate* (1880) 13 Ch. D. 696, 710 (Sir George Jessel M.R.):

> . . . it must not be forgotten that the rules of Courts of Equity are not, like the rules of the Common Law, supposed to have been established from time immemorial. It is perfectly well known that they have been established from time to time – altered, improved and refined from time to time. In many cases we know the names of the Chancellors who invented them. No doubt they were invented for the purpose of securing the better administration of justice, but they were still invented . . . . This now happens within the common law.

[7] For statute, see, for example, N. Duxbury, *Elements of Legislation* (Cambridge University Press, 2013), ch. 6. For contract, see, for example, Lord Steyn, 'Contract Law: Fulfilling the Reasonable Expectations of Honest Men' (1997) 113 L.Q.R. 433; *Investors Compensation Scheme Ltd* v. *West Bromwich Building Society* [1998] 1 W.L.R. 896; and the modern emphasis on interpretation in accordance with business common sense: *Re Sigma Finance Corp. (in admin.)* [2010] 1 All E.R. 571; [2009] UKSC 2; *Rainy Sky SA* v. *Kookmin Bank* [2011] 1 W.L.R. 2900; [2011] UKSC 50.

[8] Duxbury, *Elements of Legislation*, 179–86. Plowden was the key figure who drew on Aristotle and developed this way of looking at statutory interpretation. See J.D. Heydon, 'Equity and Statute', Chapter 12 of this volume.

[9] See, for example, A. Burrows, 'We Do This at Common Law but That in Equity' (2002) 22 O.J.L.S. 1; and for an example of an integrated doctrinal account of an area of law which

the law relating to mistaken payments, recently addressed in the Supreme Court judgment in *Pitt* v. *Holt*, is discussed by Lord Walker in his chapter and commented on below.

At the same time, the availability of recourse to an active legislature, combined with the increasing normative force of democratic ideology from the twentieth century, has also reduced the perceived legitimacy of an active court of equity to amend the application of the common law.[10]

A further factor is that equitable principles tended to build up as accretions around the law of property. This is an area in which there is a particularly pressing demand for legal certainty and predictability, so that individuals know where they stand and can plan their affairs. Accordingly, after an initial period of freedom in the development of doctrine in the courts of equity, emphasis came to be placed on precedent and settled rules equity itself resembled more closely the common law it supplemented. Decisions according to the length of the Lord Chancellor's foot met with disapproval.

The Convention rights under the Human Rights Act 1998 (UK) also operate to influence existing standards of domestic law, but they operate in a more active way and do so by a significantly different process, through a double filter. First, one tests whether the domestic legal rule (statutory, common law or equitable) operates at its point of application in a manner compatible with Convention rights. Secondly, if it does not, one has to assess whether domestic law should be modified in its application by reference to those rights, by applying section 6 of the Act (imposing a duty on public authorities to act compatibly with Convention rights) and section 3 of the Act (imposing on courts an interpretive obligation). If it is not 'possible' to interpret legislation compatibly with convention rights, the remedy is a declaration of incompatibility under section 4.

These filters allow for practical compromise between democracy and human rights in a pan-European context at the first stage (in particular, through the operation of the doctrine of the margin of appreciation)[11]

has arisen out of common law and equity, see B. McFarlane, 'Understanding Equitable Estoppel: From Metaphors to Better Laws' (2013) 66 C.L.P. 267.

[10] B. Cardozo, *The Nature of the Judicial Process* (New Haven: Yale University Press, 1921), 24, 60; Duxbury, *Elements of Legislation*, 33–5.

[11] P. Sales, 'Law and Democracy in a Human Rights Framework', in D. Feldman (ed.), *Law in Politics, Politics in Law* (Oxford: Hart Publishing, 2013), ch. 15.

and then for a balance between the authority of Parliament and the courts in a United Kingdom context at the second.[12]

At the second stage, the division between the use of section 3 and resort to section 4 is a sensitive one, which maps the courts' perception of the proper dividing line between law and politics specifically in the United Kingdom context. In broad terms, one can agree[13] that reasons why resort to section 3 is not considered appropriate are that an amended, Convention-compliant interpretation would be contrary to a fundamental aim of the statute or that it would involve the court in an essentially legislative function. But both reasons are complex. In assessing whether a section 3 interpretation would go with the grain of the statute, difficult questions arise regarding how one identifies 'the grain of the statute' as a purpose separate from its wording.[14] Issues arise regarding the level of abstraction at which it is appropriate to ask that question and the forms of evidence which are relevant. In assessing whether it is legitimate for the interpreting court to produce an amended, Convention-compliant interpretation, rather than leaving it to the government and legislature to produce a new compliant law, a range of factors come into play: democratic legitimacy, the range of persons who should have a right of access to the decision-making process, the polycentricity of the issues to be resolved,[15] the expertise appropriate to the subject matter, and the need for detailed regulation and provision extending beyond the resolution of the particular case.

It is by no means always the case that the government will wish to argue for use of section 3 rather than section 4, where a problem of incompatibility is found to exist.[16] To do so involves surrendering the initiative regarding the detail of the amendment required to render a statute compatible with Convention rights to the courts (which might be difficult to revise), rather than allowing the government to retain the power to produce a solution which satisfies its own policy objectives,

[12] P. Sales and R. Ekins, 'Rights-Consistent Interpretation and the Human Rights Act 1998' (2011) 127 L.Q.R. 217.

[13] Walker, 'Equity and Human Rights', text after n. 101.

[14] See, for example, the speech of Lord Nicholls in *Wilson* v. *First County Trust Ltd (No. 2)* [2004] 1 A.C. 816, [60]–[67]; [2003] UKHL 40; Sales and Ekins, 'Rights-Consistent Interpretation and the Human Rights Act 1998'; Duxbury, *Elements of Legislation*, 176–9, 233–40.

[15] See L.L. Fuller, 'The Forms and Limits of Adjudication', reprinted in K. Winston (ed.), *Fuller's Principles of Social Order* (Oxford: Hart Publishing, 2001), 101–40.

[16] Cf. Walker, 'Equity and Human Rights', text after n. 102.

using the Henry VIII power to revise legislation which comes with a declaration of incompatibility.[17]

It is also not really correct to say that a declaration under section 4 means that the claimant fails to obtain relief.[18] First, in almost every case where a declaration of incompatibility is made, Convention-compatible amending legislation is brought forward. Secondly, even if it is not, or where the amending legislation is not fully retrospective,[19] a declaration of incompatibility by the domestic courts provides a powerful platform for an individual application to the European Court of Human Rights. It is important to remember the international dimension, which lies behind and greatly increases the force of the Human Rights Act.

These differences mean that the parallel between equity and human rights as supplementary law can only really be drawn at a relatively high level of abstraction. The institutional and intellectual contexts in which they each operate are very different. What is common in their approach is that when the existing rules fail to give adequate respect to a set of values which may be partially reflected in them, but which in some sense provide a vantage point standing outside the rules themselves from which their application can be criticised, they provide in their different ways for modification of the existing rules by reference to that broader frame of reference. For equity, the framework is one of natural law or broad conceptions of justice, used to modify stricter, more rigid and reified common law norms. For human rights, the framework is that of formulated, partially determinate rights set out in the European Convention on Human Rights and informed in an increasingly specific

[17] Hence, in several cases in which the courts either were or might have been asked to exercise their power of interpretation under section 3, the government argued that section 3 did not allow for production of an amended, Convention 'rights' compatible interpretation, and that a declaration of incompatibility should if necessary be made: see, for example, *Re S (Minors) (Care Order: Implementation of Care Plan)* [2002] 2 A.C. 291; [2002] UKHL 10; *Bellinger* v. *Bellinger* [2003] 2 A.C. 467; [2003] UKHL 21; *R (Anderson)* v. *Secretary of State for the Home Department* [2003] 1 A.C. 837; [2002] UKHL 46; *R* v. *McLoughlin* [2014] 1 W.L.R. 3964; [2014] EWCA Crim 188.

[18] Walker, 'Equity and Human Rights', text to n. 102.

[19] As in the case of claimants in *A* v. *Secretary of State for the Home Department* [2005] 2 A.C. 68; [2004] UKHL 56 (the *Belmarsh Case*) and *A* v. *United Kingdom* (2009) 49 E.H.R.R. 29. The system of administrative detention which was found to be incompatible in the *Belmarsh* case was replaced by the system of control orders, but no relief was given under the new regime for past periods of detention. See Sales and Ekins, 'Rights-Consistent Interpretation and the Human Rights Act 1998', 230; A. Kavanagh, *Constitutional Review under the UK Human Rights Act* (Cambridge University Press, 2009); I. Leigh and R. Masterman, *Making Rights Real: The Human Rights Act in Its First Decade* (Oxford: Hart Publishing, 2008), 112–18.

and determinate way by the jurisprudence of the European Court of Human Rights.[20]

Similarity in the practical operation of equity and human rights law may be illustrated in relation to actions for possession of land. In the case of a mortgage, the borrower will be protected by the equity of redemption; in the case of a lease, by relief against forfeiture. Even prior to the Human Rights Act, a public authority seeking to recover land could be restricted by public law norms.[21] The duty under the Human Rights Act to act compatibly with Convention rights has opened up new scope for public law defences to be put forward against public authorities, based on breach of human rights in taking action to recover possession.[22]

Turning to the issue of standards versus rules, this is a tension which underlies wide areas of law.[23] As Lord Walker points out, a preference for resort to standards tends to be prominent in both equity and human rights law.[24] The reason is essentially the same, a desire to remain open to balancing a range of often incommensurate factors and moral considerations in specific contexts before arriving at the appropriate or just solution in the particular case, which is entailed by appeal to wider, more abstract principles than are encapsulated in rigid legal rules. For equity, Lord Walker gives a range of examples to illustrate this approach.[25] The court is required to make an evaluative judgment in application of a broadly framed norm of assessment of conduct. In making such judgments, courts draw on what they identify as standards of inter-personal and commercial morality, while also seeking to avoid creating power for unmerited exploitative behaviour by the relief granted.[26]

[20] See Sales, 'Law and Democracy in a Human Rights Framework', 231–2; G. Webber, 'Rights and the Rule of Law in the Balance' (2013) 129 L.Q.R. 399, 416–17.

[21] See, for example, *Wandsworth London Borough Council* v. *Winder* [1985] A.C. 461 (the tenant of a public authority could seek to plead public law unlawfulness as a defence to an action for possession).

[22] See, for example, *Kay* v. *Lambeth London Borough Council* [2006] 2 A.C. 465; [2006] UKHL 10; *Manchester City Council* v. *Pinnock* [2011] 2 A.C. 104; [2010] UKSC 45.

[23] Lord Reid, 'The Judge as Law Maker' (1972) 12 J.S.P.T.L. 22; F. Schauer, *Playing by the Rules: A Philosophical Examination of Rule-Based Decision-Making in Law and in Life* (Oxford: Clarendon Press, 1991); K.M. Sullivan, 'The Supreme Court 1991 Term: Foreword: The Justices of Rules and Standards' (1992) 106 Harv. L. Rev. 22. For discussion of some of the institutional issues which underlie this choice in the human rights context, see P. Sales and B. Hooper, 'Proportionality and the Form of Law' (2003) 119 L.Q.R. 426.

[24] Walker, 'Equity and Human Rights', text after n. 110.

[25] *Ibid.*, text between nn. 121 and 124, and text to nn. 133–5.

[26] Cf. *Co-operative Insurance Society Ltd* v. *Argyll Stores (Holdings) Ltd* [1998] A.C. 1; discussed Walker, 'Equity and Human Rights', text to nn. 124ff.

Although proportionality is a term which can be apt to describe what equity seeks to do in certain situations – in the sense that equity seeks to ensure that the remedies it gives are proportionate to the legitimate interests of the claimant – it is questionable whether this is comparable with proportionality in human rights analysis, which involves a structured method of seeking to balance public interest against private interest.[27] The proportionality framework of analysis employed in human rights litigation is directed to achieving a fair balance between collective public interests and private interests, and any attempt to introduce it into the operation of the law of equity (which is concerned with balancing competing private interests) would be likely to have a seriously distorting effect. So, again, the comparison between equity and human rights law can be made, but at such a high level of abstraction as not to provide helpful guidance for the development of doctrine to be applied in cases.

It is also difficult to regard the presence of an equitable overlay for the common law as contributing in itself to satisfaction of the fair trial obligation in article 6.[28] Generally, article 6 is neutral regarding the content of rights in domestic law, requiring only that there be a fair trial to apply such rights as domestic law provides.[29] Article 6 does not itself require that equitable standards be applied in domestic law.

For human rights law, it is primarily the margin of appreciation and proportionality which, in combination, provide for solutions which are sensitive to both institutional factors[30] and the precise balance of moral or social factors between claimant, state and third persons.

[27] Cf. Walker, 'Equity and Human Rights', text to nn. 121ff. Compare the account of proportionality analysis in K. Möller, *The Global Model of Constitutional Rights* (Oxford University Press, 2012), ch. 7, and see H. Collins, 'On the (In)compatibility of Human Rights Discourse and Private Law', in H.-W. Micklitz (ed.), *The Constitutionalization of European Private Law* (Oxford University Press, 2014).

[28] Cf. Walker, 'Equity and Human Rights', text between nn. 3 and 4, and text after n. 135. Lord Walker does not expand upon this point. No doubt at some level aspects of equitable doctrines contribute to satisfaction of article 6 requirements, such as by ensuring that remedies are prompt and effective, but it is difficult to see that substantive equitable rules are required to satisfy article 6.

[29] *Z* v. *United Kingdom* (2002) 34 E.H.R.R. 3; *Matthews* v. *Ministry of Defence* [2003] 1 A.C. 1163; [2003] UKHL 4. The experience of English law in seeking to adjust substantive rules by reason of article 6 has not been altogether happy: see the adjustment of the law of negligence in response to *Osman* v. *United Kingdom* (2000) 29 E.H.R.R. 245 before correction in *Z* v. *United Kingdom*, discussed in C. Booth and D. Squires, *The Negligence Liability of Public Authorities* (Oxford University Press, 2006), 121–31.

[30] Has the legislature created a rule within its margin of appreciation?

The complexity of these factors can lead the courts into decisions involving very fine-grained balancing of different factors.[31]

Use of standards rather than rules places a premium on the judgment in court, that is, at the point of application of the norm. A price is paid in terms of predictability when people plan their affairs; the ability of the parties to resolve their dispute without going to court; and the shifting of practical decision-making power from a legislature which promulgates clear rules to judges. Therefore, both systems of law face pressures in the opposite direction, in favour of a more rule-based approach, in the interests of rule of law values.

In the context of equity, the tension is particularly acute at the interface between commercial law (with its traditional emphasis upon the value of certainty) and equitable doctrine. There is a desire not to allow equity to create undue disruption of bargains freely made or settled property rights, around which persons have planned their affairs.[32]

The standards approach favoured by equity often has a particular association with the way in which the conscience of a defendant may be found to be affected in the context of a long-term relationship. Here again the connection with a sense of Aristotelian *epieikeia* comes through. The more remote a decision-point is from the particular circumstances plainly contemplated and legislated for by the parties to a contract or relationship, the easier it will be to say that a particular matter to be decided falls outside their real intentions and foresight and that the outcome should be governed by a more flexible, open-textured standard of justice or fair-dealing and that judgment is to be exercised by the court in light of all the circumstances of the case at the point its decision falls to be made.

The pressure for an outlet for *epieikeia* in a long-term relational context is such that in the paradigm case of the relationship between members in a company (especially a company which is characterised as a quasi-partnership), a standard-based control against exploitative behaviour and abuse of rights within the relationship amounting to unfairly

[31] See, for example, *Evans* v. *United Kingdom* (2008) 46 E.H.R.R. 34.

[32] *In re Goldcorp Exchange Ltd (in receivership)* [1995] 1 A.C. 74, 98; P.J. Millett, 'Equity's Place in the Law of Commerce' (1998) 114 L.Q.R. 214; Lord Neuberger of Abbotsbury, 'The Stuffing of Minerva's Owl? Taxonomy and Taxidermy in Equity' [2009] C.L.J. 537, esp. at 543; *Vercoe* v. *Rutland Fund Management Ltd* [2010] EWHC 424 (Ch), [352]; cf. Lord Cottenham's weighing up of the maxim that equity follows the law against broader fairness standards in *Sturgis* v. *Champneys* (1839) 5 My. & Cr. 97; 41 E.R. 308; Walker, 'Equity and Human Rights', text to nn. 16–18.

prejudicial behaviour has been created in various forms by the legislature.[33] Legislative intervention has expanded the narrow scope for relief in equity, based on the concept of fraud on a power[34] and fraud on the minority.[35] But in this context, again, one sees familiar pressure to try to constrain within reasonable limits what might otherwise be an overly wide and unpredictable judicial discretion.[36]

In the human rights context there is a similar tension between the values advanced by favouring a rule-based approach and a standards approach, but here it is also strongly affected by institutional factors relating to the proper balance of authority and practical decision-making power between the courts, the executive and Parliament.[37] The human rights provisions used to assess the acceptability of existing domestic law themselves use standards for evaluation. The application of those standards tends to require domestic law itself to use standards allowing for flexible application by the courts. But sometimes it may be found to be legitimate and compatible with Convention rights for Parliament to legislate to create a 'bright line' rule, notwithstanding that its application may produce harsh decisions at the margins.[38] In this way, the tension between rules and standards is sometimes manifest in the rhetoric of argument regarding the acceptability of a particular statutory rule as a 'bright line' rule (good) or a 'blanket' rule or prohibition (bad).

The balance between flexibility and predictability in application of a legal norm can be struck in different ways along a spectrum. In the human rights context, for example, the minority in *Kay* argued for a defence to possession actions on human rights grounds which would apply only in exceptional cases, while the majority held that there should be no scope for such a defence. Even the minority, therefore, wished to

33 See now section 994 of the Companies Act 2006 (UK).

34 See, for example, *Vatcher* v. *Paull* [1915] A.C. 372, 378 (Lord Parker of Waddington): the court will intervene if a power in a trust instrument is 'exercised for a purpose, or with an intention, beyond the scope of or not justified by the instrument creating the power'.

35 *Allen* v. *Gold Reefs of West Africa Ltd* [1900] 1 Ch. 656; *Greenhalgh* v. *Arderne Cinemas Ltd* [1951] Ch. 286.

36 *O'Neill* v. *Phillips* [1999] 1 W.L.R. 1092, 1098C–1099A: fairness depends on context and should be assessed primarily having regard to agreements made by the company members.

37 See, for example, Sales and Hooper, 'Proportionality and the Form of Law'.

38 P. Sales, 'The General and the Particular: Parliament and the Courts under the Scheme of the European Convention on Human Rights', in M. Andenas and D. Fairgrieve (eds.), *Tom Bingham and the Transformation of the Law: A Liber Amicorum* (Oxford University Press, 2009), ch. 12.

avoid a high degree of disruption of ordinary property rights of local authorities. In the dialogue with the Strasbourg court mapped in *Pinnock*, the European Court of Human Rights favoured the view of the minority in *Kay*, and that is where the domestic law has now ended up, through the operation of the Human Rights Act.

Equity appeals to moral standards worked out in a determinate way over time with an increasing degree of predictability. The format of reasoning for deciding whether, say, specific performance should be granted has become largely settled, with clearer identification of relevant factors. It still requires an evaluative judgment to be made by the court, but the specification of relevant factors makes it easier to predict the outcome. A broadly similar process of articulation of relevant factors is occurring in the human rights jurisprudence, but the sheer variety of situations in which human rights law falls to be applied and the wide range of incommensurable considerations which fall to be accommodated means that outcomes often remain more uncertain.

There is also a sense in which an appeal to broad standards of justice or fairness can contribute in some ways to rule of law values, in making the general operation of the law perhaps more accessible and predictable than might be the case if left to highly detailed, but hard to understand, rigid rules. As Jeremy Waldron notes in his essay, 'Thoughtfulness and the Rule of Law',[39] flexibility and appeals to widely shared moral standards may promote a level of general predictability of the operation of the law which allows individuals to plan their affairs with more confidence.

Ultimately, provided the standards of commercial and inter-personal morality that the courts will apply are reasonably determinate and are generally understood by those entering relationships, this sort of approach can provide greater practical support for predictability of likely outcomes as at the point of contracting or establishing binding legal instruments, and hence for party autonomy and ability to legislate for themselves which is at the heart of contract and the law of trusts. If there

[39] [2011] British Academy Review (issue 18), 1, 10–11. A similar point is made in R. Posner, *The Problems of Jurisprudence* (Cambridge, Mass.: Harvard University Press, 1990), 48, and in R.H. Fallon Jr, '"The Rule of Law" as a Concept in Constitutional Discourse' (1997) 97 Colum. L. Rev. 1, 48–50. See also R.E. Goodin, 'An Epistemic Case for Legal Moralism' (2010) 30 O.J.L.S. 615: the best way for the law to provide guidance for citizens is to track broad moral principles understood by them. As Fallon observes, 'In contexts marked by normative consensus, there might be broad agreement about how standards should be applied, and standards would permit both citizens and officials to be ruled by law . . . [T]he greater the normative consensus, the less the realization of Rule-of-Law values depends on the law being a law of rules' (97 Colum. L. Rev. 1, 49–50, citations omitted).

is rigid adherence to the literal text of a contract or trust instrument at a later point in time when action under the contract or trust is required or litigation occurs, there is a risk that capricious, unpredicted and (judged at the time the contract or trust was actually established) unintended outcomes might occur, simply because the parties did not foresee the way in which events happen to have turned out. So recourse to equity and business common sense/equitable interpretations is itself an appeal to a conception of legal certainty and predictability.

Waldron refers to Hayek's view, late in life, that he may have been wrong to think that clear codified legislation would always increase the predictability of the law. Rather, Hayek came to think that

> [J]udicial decisions may in fact be more predictable if the judge is also bound by generally held views of what is just, even when they are not supported by the letter of the law.

Waldron comments:

> Thinking through the abstract issue of what a fair order of mutually-adjusted intentions would involve so far as the settlement of the instant case is concerned may enable the judge to come up with a result more congruent to the expectations of the parties than his application of some enacted rule according to its terms.[40]

The same reasoning applies in relation to private legislation in the form of contracts and trust instruments.

Finally in this section, turning to the married woman's equity,[41] it is doubtful whether this history of equity's protection for women's property interests really represents an infusion of equity with human rights thinking. It appears more to have reflected the developing mores of the propertied classes, particularly in the context of the transition of a woman from the dominion of her family of birth to the dominion of her husband.[42] One strains to see a human rights dimension in this. Despite the agitation of J.S. Mill, to which Lord Walker refers, the rights afforded by equity to a married woman were not given in virtue of her status as a human being. Nor does this development of the law appear to have contributed to a wider acceptance of the rights of women in society or the

40 Waldron, 'Thoughtfulness and the Rule of Law', 11.

41 Walker, 'Equity and Human Rights', text between nn. 3 and 38.

42 Hence the focus of the equity upon safeguarding her property in the marriage by reference to a test of 'what a prudent parent would probably have done in giving a portion to a daughter': *Tidd* v. *Lister* (1853) 3 De G. M. & G. 857, 869; 43 E.R. 336, 340; Walker, 'Equity and Human Rights', text to n. 8.

law. However, what this history does illustrate is the relative openness of equity[43] to social influences and arguments by appeal to wider social standards in fashioning its doctrines and their application. This indicates a pattern of reasoning in the same family as that in relation to application of human rights standards, as human rights came increasingly to be accepted as legitimating social standards in the period after the Second World War.

Human rights as a ground for development of equity

There are three distinct processes by which human rights can provide a basis for the development of legal and equitable doctrine. First, section 6(1) of the Human Rights Act imposes an obligation on public authorities to act in a manner which is compatible with Convention rights. This obligation applies to courts pursuant to section 6(3). So if a court finds that to enforce legal rights in a particular way would involve a violation of Convention rights,[44] the court is obliged to refuse to enforce those rights. This is straightforward when the person seeking to enforce the rights is a public authority, where there is vertical enforcement of Convention rights by citizen (defendant) against public authority (claimant). Is there scope for horizontal enforcement of Convention rights between private persons, in such a way as will defeat the ordinary legal rights of one party?

I suggest that the answer lies in the law of positive obligations under the European Convention on Human Rights.[45] The court is a state authority, which is being asked to intervene in a dispute regarding the respective rights in private law of two private parties. If what is said to make the difference to the outcome of that dispute is the Human Rights

[43] At a time when the idea of legislation by judges to develop the common law, as opposed to the idea that they discovered and applied the common law as something already given and incapable of development, was not recognised, at any rate explicitly.

[44] And the case is not one in which section 6(2) disapplies the obligation under section 6(1).

[45] See, for example, Möller, *The Global Model of Constitutional Rights*, 5–10, 35–8, 147–9; M. Pitkänen, 'Fair and Balanced Positive Obligations – Do They Exist?' [2012] E.H.R.L.R. 538; D.J. Harris, M. O'Boyle, E.P. Bates and C.M. Buckley, *Harris, O'Boyle and Warbrick: The Law of the European Convention on Human Rights*, 3rd ed. (Oxford University Press, 2014), 21–4, 504–5; *R (Sheikh)* v. *Secretary of State for the Home Department* [2011] EWHC 3390 (Admin), [74]; and the detailed discussion of positive obligations by reference to each article of the European Convention on Human Rights in C. Grabenwarter, *European Convention on Human Rights: Commentary* (Munich: Hart Publishing, 2014).

Act, it seems reasonable to frame the conditions under which it *should* make a difference by reference to the jurisprudence of the European Court of Human Rights on positive obligations, where it holds that the state has a positive obligation to intervene in relations between private persons. A useful way of looking at this is to ask whether the values and interests protected by a Convention right are so strong as to justify disruption of ordinary patterns of rights and property in domestic law. Since property and contract rights are themselves protected interests under article 1 of Protocol 1, the margin of appreciation to refuse to override those rights is often likely to be wide, and where this is so the courts do not have legitimate authority to act to disrupt those rights. Therefore, in general, the scope to intervene may be expected to be narrow.

Where the court does intervene, relying on its obligation under section 6, does this involve development of ordinary domestic law, or just simple compliance with a supervening statutory duty? There is a curious ambiguity in the authorities about this. In *A* v. *B plc*,[46] the Court of Appeal responded to what it perceived to be a deficiency in protection of Convention rights under ordinary domestic law by modifying the action for breach of confidence to incorporate the requirements of articles 8 and 10. So perhaps the best analysis is that the courts have used human rights as external standards to inform and legitimate a change in domestic legal rules, inferring from section 6 that they have been given special licence by the legislature to modify the general common law.

Secondly, human rights may be treated as a type of a wider class of what Eisenberg calls 'social propositions',[47] that is, social standards which are capable of informing the development of the common law and equity as they adapt to changing demands and expectations in society. This seems to be the best explanation of what occurred in *Campbell* v. *MGN Ltd*.[48] The Human Rights Act's reference to human rights standards might be said to have unblocked a log-jam in the development of equity and the common law to recognise privacy interests as protectable in their own right apart from confidentiality. Some

[46] [2003] Q.B. 195, [4]; [2002] EWCA Civ 337.

[47] M.A. Eisenberg, *The Nature of the Common Law* (Cambridge, Mass.: Harvard University Press, 1988); cf. D. Oliver, *Common Values and the Public-Private Divide* (London: Butterworths, 1999).

[48] [2004] 2 A.C. 457; [2004] UKHL 22.

might say that this was a long over-due development of domestic law.[49] But this sort of approach is capable of wider use, as recent case law makes clear.[50] Convention rights can be used to inform the content of standards and rules in ordinary domestic law.

Thirdly, as a weaker form of the second point, human rights may be regarded as relevant considerations for the courts in the exercise of more discretionary choices or in the application of broad evaluative standards.[51] This is as yet an under-explored area of the law in relation to equitable doctrines, despite their relative openness to influence by wider social standards.

The case of *Pitt* v. *Holt*

This case[52] involved analysis of the controversial so-called 'rule in *Hastings-Bass*' (concerning the extent of legitimate equitable intervention for failure by trustees to take into account relevant considerations) and of the equitable jurisdiction to rescind a voluntary transaction for mistake. The Supreme Court corrected a mis-development of the law in relation to the former (significantly restricting the scope for transactions to be unwound on the grounds of mistake by trustees) and elucidated the ambit of the latter.

[49] Cf. the recognition of privacy interests in US law. See G. Phillipson, 'Privacy', in D. Hoffman (ed.), *The Impact of the UK Human Rights Act on Private Law* (Cambridge University Press, 2011), ch. 7; *Michael* v. *Chief Constable of South Wales Police* [2015] 2 W.L.R. 343, [124]; [2015] UKSC 2.

[50] See in particular *R* v. *Lord Chancellor, Ex p. Witham* [1998] Q.B. 575 (article 6 of European Convention on Human Rights used to inform the domestic principle of legality in interpreting the width of the power to make subordinate legislation requiring payment of court fees); *R (Osborn)* v. *Parole Board* [2014] A.C. 1115; [2013] UKSC 61 (article 5 of the Convention used to inform domestic judicial review standards of fairness in relation to access to rehabilitation programmes so as to have the opportunity of seeking release on probation); *Kennedy* v. *Charity Commission* [2015] A.C. 455, [45]–[47]; [2014] UKSC 20; cf. the possibility of naturalisation of human rights standards into ordinary domestic law referred to by Lord Reed J.S.C. in *R (Faulkner)* v. *Secretary of State for Justice* [2013] 2 A.C. 254, [29]; [2013] UKSC 23. This is part of a wider phenomenon, not unique to the United Kingdom and its relationship with the Convention: cf. the speech delivered by the Chief Justice of the High Court of Australia, the Hon. R.S. French A.C., 'International Law and Australian Domestic Law', speech to the Supreme Court of New South Wales Annual Conference, 21 August 2009, 33–5, at www.hcourt.gov.au/assets/publications/speeches/current-justices/frenchcj/frenchcj21aug09.pdf.

[51] Cf. *John* v. *MGN Ltd* [1997] Q.B. 586 (assessment of damages for libel informed by article 10).

[52] *Pitt* v. *Holt* [2013] 2 A.C. 108.

On the first issue, the decision is itself a salutary warning against over-ready recourse in private law to public law style analysis, which the statement of the rule in *Hastings-Bass* appeared to draw upon. The contexts are in fact very different. Unlike public officials, trustees are not charged with acting in the public interest,[53] but with acting within the scope of their duties to private persons; and unlike public officials, trustees have obligations to pay compensation or restore a trust fund if they have breached their duty. So the balance of interests is different in the two situations, and one cannot simply transpose the public law standard to the private.

On the second issue, an important feature of Lord Walker's judgment in *Pitt* v. *Holt* is his unwillingness to close off the cases in which equity might intervene where a mistake has been made in making a voluntary disposition by a rigid rule. Instead, very much in line with the traditional equitable approach, he leaves the question to be governed by an evaluative standard: a voluntary transaction will only be rescinded if the mistake is of sufficient gravity to make it unconscionable to deny relief.

This is an area where equity now finds itself in competition with the equity of the common law. The common law has developed its rules for reversing payments made by mistake, balancing an expansion of the basis for a claim in unjust enrichment[54] with a defence of good faith change of position to create what is perceived overall to be a just balancing of competing interests. The following question now comes into focus: what is the relationship between the equitable jurisdiction to set aside a voluntary transaction for mistake and common law claims in unjust enrichment, grounded on mistake?[55] Perhaps, it is the effect on third parties (in *Pitt* v. *Holt*, the tax authorities) which provides a basis for reverting to the (in some respects) narrower equitable jurisdiction: when what is sought is not just a repayment of money paid by mistake, but a more complete unwinding of the transaction so that it is treated as never having been made at all (to avoid a tax liability in that case), a narrower doctrine of mistake may be appropriate. But as in many areas, the relationship between equitable doctrine and common law rules continues to be hazy and unclear. A principled integration of equity and a dynamic common law remains elusive.

53 A responsibility which is undermined if there is a failure to take into account relevant considerations, calling into question the effectiveness of the rule of law in the public sphere.

54 To cover all forms of mistake, of law as well as of fact.

55 See the case note on *Pitt* v. *Holt* by S. Watterson, 'Reversing Mistaken Voluntary Dispositions' [2013] C.L.J. 501.

Perhaps we should be referring more explicitly to the idea of *epieikeia* as a potential important organising criterion across both common law and equity. From this perspective, there is a continuum across the two systems. The need for some sense of flexibility in application of rules to meet the particular justice of a case, while taking into account the institutional reasons why rules laid down by the law-giver (whether contracting parties, legislature or superior court) should be respected, is general across law. Where the parties have made a clear (private) legislative choice in a contract or other instrument, their decision governs.[56] But the further one moves from that paradigm case, the greater the scope there is for the law to supplement what the parties have provided for in order to do practical justice between them and to meet (in a residual and generalised sense) their expectations that fair outcomes will be achieved. So, the more open-textured and unspecific the language used in a contract, the more contractual interpretation will allow for operation of business common sense (according to norms of commercial expectations of fair-dealing). In relation to implied terms in contract, the scope for implication is narrower the more clearly the parties have made explicit provision to cover the situation which has arisen.[57] Where a contract governs a long-term relationship and provides for discretionary powers for one or other party to enable adaptation within the scope of the relationship to unforeseen events, good faith and reasonableness standards may be implied to govern the exercise of those powers.[58] Flexibility in the availability of equitable remedies,

[56] So, for instance, contractual agreement generally prevails over the background default law of unjust enrichment: see, for example, *Pan Ocean Shipping Co. Ltd* v. *Creditcorp Ltd (The Trident Beauty)* [1994] 1 W.L.R. 161, 166 (Lord Goff of Chieveley).

[57] See, for example, *Philips Electronique Grand Public SA* v. *British Sky Broadcasting Ltd* [1995] E.M.L.R. 472, 481–2. This is not to say that there is a wide role for implication of terms, just on grounds of reasonableness: that would detract too much from party autonomy.

[58] See *Socimer International Bank Ltd* v. *Standard Bank London Ltd* [2008] Bus L.R. 1304, [66]; [2008] EWCA Civ 116 (Rix L.J.):

> . . . a decision-maker's discretion will be limited, as a matter of necessary implication, by concepts of honesty, good faith, and genuineness, and the need for the absence of arbitrariness, capriciousness, perversity and irrationality. The concern is that the discretion should not be abused. Reasonableness and unreasonableness are also concepts deployed in this context, but only in a sense analogous to *Wednesbury* unreasonableness, not in the sense in which that expression is used when speaking of the duty to take reasonable care, or when otherwise deploying entirely objective criteria . . .

especially for particularly powerful ones such as injunctions and specific performance, allows for factors which may not have been foreseen or provided for to be taken into account in producing a just result overall. Where a contractual arrangement may have significant effects on third parties who have not had an opportunity to bargain for protection, a reasonable standard of care will be imposed.[59] Where a fiduciary relationship is created, so that a principal's property or affairs are managed by the fiduciary according to his discretion and outside specific rules stipulated in the governing instrument, the justification for equitable control according to open-textured standards becomes stronger still, but on a continuum from controls of contractual discretions according to these other techniques.[60]

At the same time, the law of unjust enrichment and equity operate to produce just outcomes where party agreement is subverted or incomplete in important respects. Here again, one is remote from or there is good reason not to treat as binding a rule legislated by the parties. *Pitt* v. *Holt* is illustrative of one dimension of this. Another area of equitable intervention is in relation to imperfect agreements concerning property, where the device of the constructive trust is important.[61] It is because both the law of unjust enrichment and equity have important roles to play in protection of property rights and reasonable expectations outside rules laid down in a contract that the relationship between them is somewhat fraught at the moment, and why their coherent amalgamation and integration is a pressing issue for the courts.

See also *Mid-Essex Hospital Services NHS Trust* v. *Compass Group UK and Ireland Ltd* [2013] B.L.R. 265; [2013] EWCA Civ 200; G. Newey, 'Constraints on the Exercise of Trustees' Powers', Chapter 2 of this volume.

59 Cf. *Henderson* v. *Merrett Syndicates Ltd* [1995] 2 A.C. 145.

60 Cf. J. Edelman, 'When Do Fiduciary Duties Arise?' (2010) 126 L Q.R. 302; *F&C Alternative Investments (Holdings) Ltd* v. *Barthelemy* [2012] Ch. 613, [222]–[225]; [2011] EWHC 1731 (Ch).

61 Agreements may be imperfect because of a failure to comply with legal formalities, or because of vagueness about the agreement made: see in particular *Jones* v. *Kernott* [2012] 1 A.C. 776; [2011] UKSC 53.

22

Field, fusion and the 1850s

How an American law reformer influenced the Judicature Act of 1875

PATRICIA I. MCMAHON

Introduction and overview

When the American law reformer David Dudley Field addressed a gathering of the Law Amendment Society in London on 18 November 1850, he created what one legal periodical called a 'sensation'.[1] He did so by talking about reforms he had recently helped to introduce in New York State. Those reforms eliminated the procedural distinction between law and equity and created a single superior court governed by a unified code of practice and procedure. Field thought England could benefit from similar changes, and after he spoke to members of the society, many reformers agreed.

I make two claims in this chapter. First, I suggest that David Dudley Field and his work in New York State – particularly his code of procedure – influenced the efforts of English law reformers in the 1850s. Secondly, although there is wide recognition that the reforms of this period laid the groundwork for fusion,[2] I contend that a number of these

[1] Anon., 'History of the New York Code and Its Applicability to This Country' (1851) 13 L. Rev. & Q.J. Brit. & Foreign Juris. 213, 214.

[2] See D.M. Kerly, *An Historical Sketch of the Equitable Jurisdiction of the Court of Chancery* (Cambridge University Press, 1890), 282; H.H. Fowler, 'A Psychological Approach to Procedural Law Reform' (1934) 43 Yale L.J. 1254, 1259–60; F.W. Maitland, *Equity: A Course of Lectures*, ed. by A.H. Chaytor and W.J. Whittaker, rev. by J. Brunyate (Cambridge University Press, 1936), 14–15; W.S. Holdsworth, *A History of English Law* (London: Methuen & Co., 1955), vol. 15, 102–4, 120–1, 134; G.W. Keeton and L.A. Sheridan, *Equity*, 3rd ed. (Chichester: Rose, 1987), 59–62; W.R. Cornish, 'England', in H. Coing (ed.), *Handbuch der Quellen und Literatur der neueren europäischen Privatrechtsgeschichte. Band III* (Munich: Beck, 1982), 2217, 2223–4; G. Watt, *Trusts and Equity*, 5th ed. (Oxford University Press, 2012), 7–8; R. Pearce and W. Barr, *Pearce and Stevens' Trusts and Equitable Obligations*, 6th ed. (Oxford University Press, 2015), 8–12.

statutes implemented core elements of procedural fusion well before it was adopted formally by the Judicature Act in 1875.[3] The real debate about the merits of procedural fusion occurred in the 1850s, not in the 1870s.

Field's influence during this time may be under-appreciated because it is overshadowed by the portrait of Chancery that Charles Dickens painted in *Bleak House*. Although the woeful tale of *Jarndyce* v. *Jarndyce* was set in the late 1820s, a time described as 'the very worst period of the Court of Chancery', the account is more commonly associated with the period between 1851 and 1853 in which it was serialised.[4] Additionally, discussions about fusion tend to be confined temporally to the context of the Judicature Act and to the 1870s, thus ignoring the serious reforms discussed and implemented twenty years earlier.[5]

Field's influence is apparent upon an examination of fusion through a broader lens. Michael Lobban has acknowledged Field's efforts and described the reforms of the 1850s as an 'important staging post on the way to the changes wrought by the Judicature Acts of 1873–5'.[6] Building on that work, I suggest that the reforms of the 1850s were nevertheless more than a staging post. Together, these reforming statutes of the 1850s achieved much of what Field accomplished by what became known as the Field Code[7] without the benefit and efficiency of a single set of procedures in a unified court.[8] Field's influence was

[3] Judicature Act 1875, 38 & 39 Vict. c. 77.

[4] W.S. Holdsworth, *Charles Dickens as a Legal Historian* (New Haven, CT: Yale University Press, 1929), 79. See also M. Leeming, 'Equity, the Judicature Acts and Restitution' (2011) 5 J. Eq. 1.

[5] See T.F.T. Plucknett, *A Concise History of the Common Law*, 5th ed. (London: Butterworth & Co., 1956), 73–5, 210–12, 381–2; J.H. Baker, *An Introduction to English Legal History* (London: Butterworths, 2002); F.W. Maitland, *Equity also the Forms of Action at Common Law*, ed. A.J. Chaytor and W.J. Whittaker (Cambridge University Press, 1909); W.S. Holdsworth, *A History of English Law*, 7th ed. (1956), vol. 1, 637; M. Weber, 'General Introduction to the Series', in New York (State), Commissioners on Practice and Pleadings, *New York Field Codes Series* (Clark, NJ: The Lawbook Exchange, 2011), vol. 1, ix; A. Reppy, 'The Field Codification Concept', in A. Reppy (ed.), *David Dudley Field: Centenary Essays* (New York University School of Law, 1949), 48.

[6] M. Lobban, 'Henry Brougham and Law Reform' (2000) 115 Eng. Hist. Rev. 1184, 1207. See also M. Lobban, 'Preparing for Fusion: Reforming the Nineteenth-Century Court of Chancery, Part 1' (2004) 22 Law & Hist. Rev. 389; M. Lobban, 'Preparing for Fusion: Reforming the Nineteenth-Century Court of Chancery, Part 2' (2004) 22 Law & Hist. Rev. 565.

[7] 1848 N.Y. Laws c. 379.

[8] For common law reforms, the key statutes were the Common Law Procedure Act 1852, 15 & 16 Vict. c. 76, the Common Law Procedure Act 1854, 17 & 18 Vict. c. 125, and the

apparent throughout the reform process of the 1850s, particularly through the activities of the Law Amendment Society, a law reform organisation that promoted procedural fusion and encouraged English reformers to adopt the approach of New York State. The Field Code blended practice and procedure in four key areas: the form and substance of pleadings; the treatment of multiple parties and issues; the rules governing fact-finding (both before and during trial); and the availability of equitable remedies. In reviewing each, I discuss Field's reforms, their influence on the recommendations of the Law Amendment Society and two royal commissions, and the legislative changes that followed. Although the reforms of the 1850s did not implement formal procedural fusion, they nonetheless reconciled many key procedural differences between law and equity, and did so almost a generation before the Judicature Acts.

The Law Amendment Society

Field's presentation at a meeting of the Law Amendment Society in November 1850 motivated members to pursue the procedural fusion of law and equity as a means of curing the twin ills of expense and delay that had plagued the English courts for generations.[9] English legal periodicals had discussed the reforms in New York State before Field came to England,[10] but Field's personal appeal seems to have been what inspired action. Within a month of Field's address, members formed a special committee to investigate the subject; within the year, they had formally endorsed fusion, drafted a model code and proposed legislation to implement it.

Common Law Procedure Act 1860, 23 & 24 Vict. c. 126. For Chancery reforms, the most important statutes were the Court of Chancery Procedure Act 1852, 15 & 16 Vict. c. 86, the Court of Chancery Examiners Act 1853, 16 & 17 Vict. c. 22, the Court of Chancery Act 1854, 17 & 18 Vict. c. 100, and the Chancery Amendment Act 1858, 21 & 22 Vict. c. 27.

9 Anon., 'History of the New York Code and Its Applicability to This Country', 214.

10 See Law Amendment Society, 'Reports and Papers of the Society for Promoting the Amendment of the Law' (1847) 6 L. Rev. & Q.J. Brit. & Foreign Juris. 300; Anon., 'Severance of Law and Equity' (1848) 8 L. Rev. & Q.J. Brit. & Foreign Juris. 62; Anon., 'Comparative Anatomy of Judicial Procedure – On the Recent Consolidation of the Courts of Law and Equity in New York' (1848) 8 L. Rev. & Q.J. Brit. & Foreign Juris. 387; Anon., 'The Code of Civil Procedure of the State of New York' (1850) 12 L. Rev. & Q.J. Brit. & Foreign Juris. 366; Anon., 'The Code of Civil Procedure of the State of New York' (1850) 13 L. Rev. & Q.J. Brit. & Foreign Juris. 65.

Field was more than a source of inspiration for reformers. He also provided tangible proof of the improvements in New York State brought about by his code and a concrete plan to implement similar changes in England. His experience was evidence that fusion was not just possible but beneficial, resolving many of the inefficiencies and expenses that accompanied different courts, different procedures and overlapping jurisdictions.

Created in London on New Year's Day in 1844,[11] the Society for Promoting the Amendment of Law – more commonly known as the Law Amendment Society – was the brainchild of Henry Brougham and a group of his friends.[12] A champion of law reform, Brougham was a long-time parliamentarian who had served as Lord Chancellor between 1830 and 1834. Frustrated by the difficulties he had encountered while trying to reform Chancery without public support, and with little chance of ever returning to cabinet, he helped to found the society to serve as a clearing house for reform ideas.

The society was 'a non-party organization designed to stimulate inquiry and investigation'.[13] Robert Stewart describes it as a 'fertilizing agency'.[14] It helped move discussions about reform forward in two ways. First, it filled a void left by Parliament and the absence of a Ministry of Justice. Lobban characterises the relationship between Brougham and the society 'as that of a quasi-Lord Chancellor with his quasi-ministry of justice'.[15] As Brougham's quasi-ministry of justice, the society studied legal problems, canvassed possible remedies and proposed legislative solutions.[16] Secondly, through its own periodical, the *Law Review*, the society actively supported and promoted fusion as

[11] Anon., 'The History of the Law Amendment Society from Its Institution, in 1844, Till the Present Time' (1853) 18 L. Rev. & Q.J. Brit. & Foreign Juris. 304, 306.

[12] Lobban, 'Henry Brougham and Law Reform', 1205. See also O.R. McGregor, *Social History and Social Reform* (London: Stevens and Sons, 1981), 18–19.

[13] Lobban, 'Henry Brougham and Law Reform', citing Anon., 'The History of the Law Amendment Society from Its Institution, in 1844, Till the Present Time', 305. See also Law Amendment Society, 'Proceedings of the Society' (1846) 4 L. Rev. & Q.J. Brit. & Foreign Juris. 446, 450–1.

[14] R. Stewart, *Henry Brougham 1778–1868[:] His Public Career* (London: Bodley Head, 1985), 349.

[15] Lobban, 'Henry Brougham and Law Reform', 1205. Campbell, a contemporary of Brougham's, was less positive about the society's efforts, calling the group 'comparatively obscure', and argued that the Social Science Society was more influential: J. Campbell, *Lives of Lord Lyndhurst and Lord Brougham* (London: John Murray, 1869), 588.

[16] Lobban, 'Henry Brougham and Law Reform', 1205–6.

a way to reduce the time and expense associated with judicial proceedings.[17]

Interest in law reform was the only requirement for membership; neither political affiliation nor national citizenship was relevant, and the founders hoped to attract a broad membership base.[18] They also wanted to make the society open to public participation and scrutiny. For example, newspapers published notices of meetings, and the society's annual meeting was a public event. Attendees elected the society's officers, including the president, vice-president, treasurer and secretary; they determined membership on the society's council and management committee; and they approved resolutions dealing with the society's general objectives. Anyone who wanted to speak at an open meeting was welcome to do so.[19]

General meetings were open to members and their guests, and outside speakers occasionally addressed 'special' meetings.[20] Attendees discussed various law reform issues and initiatives, usually after the presentation of papers prepared by the members of various committees, some standing and others created specifically to deal with a particular concern.[21] Among the first standing committees were those dedicated to dealing with procedural problems in equity and common law.[22] They took their instructions from the general meeting, investigated an issue, drafted a report and presented their findings to the general membership for discussion, which either approved or

[17] Founded by Brougham, the *Law Review and Quarterly Journal of British and Foreign Jurisprudence* ('the Law Review') published the society's proceedings and reports, along with articles about law reform efforts from other individuals and organisations, both English and foreign. These articles, especially those dealing with foreign courts, often included lengthy excerpts of speeches, pamphlets, or parliamentary reports on various initiatives.

[18] Anon., 'The History of the Law Amendment Society from Its Institution, in 1844, Till the Present Time', 306–8.

[19] Law Amendment Society, 'Proceedings of the Society' (1846) 4 L. Rev. & Q.J. Brit. & Foreign Juris. 446, 446–7; Anon., 'The History of the Law Amendment Society from Its Institution, in 1844, Till the Present Time', 308; Anon., 'The Public Meeting of the Society for the Amendment of the Law' (1848) 8 L. Rev. & Q.J. Brit. & Foreign Juris. 233, 241.

[20] Anon., 'The History of the Law Amendment Society from Its Institution, in 1844, Till the Present Time', 308.

[21] Law Amendment Society, 'Proceedings of the Society' (1849) 9 L. Rev. & Q.J. Brit. & Foreign Juris. 444, 445–6.

[22] Law Amendment Society, 'Proceedings of the Society' (1846) 4 L. Rev. & Q.J. Brit. & Foreign Juris. 446, 450; Law Amendment Society, 'Proceedings of the Society' (1847) 6 L. Rev. & Q.J. Brit. & Foreign Juris. 404, 411.

referred them back for additional consideration. Often, resolutions led to formal legislation.[23]

The need for Chancery reform was among the measures addressed by the society at its first public meeting in June 1846. A simple resolution calling for Chancery reform, proposed by Richard Bethell and seconded by George Spence, carried unanimously.[24] By the end of the year, members began to consider how foreign jurisdictions were trying to simplify and expedite equity proceedings.[25] Soon, they turned their attention to the masters' offices (which many regarded as a key source of expense and delay in Chancery),[26] a subject that sparked two and a half years of discussions and reports.[27] Then, in late 1850, Field addressed the special meeting.

[23] Anon., 'The History of the Law Amendment Society from Its Institution, in 1844, Till the Present Time', 309. Brougham claimed the society helped him with ninety reform bills between 1844 and 1857, forty of which became law: Lobban, 'Henry Brougham and Law Reform', 1205–6; McGregor, *Social History and Social Reform*, 19; J.E. Eardley-Wilmot, *Lord Brougham's Law Reforms Comprising the Acts and Bills Introduced or Carried by Him Through the Legislature since 1811* (London: Longman, Brown, Green, Longman and Roberts, 1860); R.K. Huch, *Henry, Lord Brougham[:] The Later Years 1830–1868* (Lampeter: Edward Mellen, 1993), 194. But see Campbell, *Lives of Lord Lyndhurst and Lord Brougham*, 587–8.

[24] Bethell, described as a 'legal radical' interested in civilian legal systems, served on the Chancery commission (1850) and the commission on taking evidence in Chancery (1858) before becoming Lord Chancellor (1861): R.C.J. Cocks, 'Bethell, Richard, First Baron Westbury (1800–1873)', in *Oxford Dictionary of National Biography* (2004) at www.oxforddnb.com/view/article/2305. Having published his two volume treatise on Chancery in 1846, Spence left the society in 1847 but returned by late 1849: Law Amendment Society, 'Proceedings of the Society' (1847) 6 L. Rev. & Q.J. Brit. & Foreign Juris. 404, 413; Law Amendment Society, 'Proceedings of the Society' (1850) 12 L. Rev. & Q.J. Brit. & Foreign Juris. 211, 213–16; Law Amendment Society, 'Proceedings of the Society' (1846) 4 L. Rev. & Q.J. Brit. & Foreign Juris. 446, 457.

[25] Law Amendment Society, 'Proceedings of the Society' (1847) 5 L. Rev. & Q.J. Brit. & Foreign Juris. 431, 432.

[26] *Ibid.*, 434 (incorrectly numbered 344 in the original); Law Amendment Society, 'Proceedings of the Society' (1847) 6 L. Rev. & Q.J. Brit. & Foreign Juris. 181; Law Amendment Society, 'Proceedings of the Society' (1847) 6 L. Rev. & Q.J. Brit. & Foreign Juris. 404, 407–8.

[27] Law Amendment Society, 'Proceedings of the Society' (1847) 5 L. Rev. & Q.J. Brit. & Foreign Juris. 431, 434 (incorrectly numbered 344 in the original); Law Amendment Society, 'Proceedings of the Society' (1847) 6 L. Rev. & Q.J. Brit. & Foreign Juris. 181, 182–3; Law Amendment Society, 'Proceedings of the Society' (1847) 6 L. Rev. & Q.J. Brit. & Foreign Juris. 300, 308–35; Law Amendment Society, 'Proceedings of the Society' (1847) 6 L. Rev. & Q.J. Brit. & Foreign Juris. 404, 412–14; Law Amendment Society, 'Reports of the Society' (1847) 7 L. Rev. & Q.J. Brit. & Foreign Juris. 55; Law Amendment Society, 'Reports of the Society' (1848) 8 L. Rev. & Q.J. Brit. & Foreign Juris. 87; Law Amendment Society, 'Proceedings of the Society' (1848) 8 L. Rev. & Q.J. Brit. & Foreign

Bethell, one of the most sought-after Chancery lawyers in England,[28] captured the sentiment of many who attended Field's talk when he complained that it was 'a burning shame that a party could recover a judgment on one side of Westminster Hall, and on the other side be branded as a fraudulent rogue for having recovered it!'[29] Field and his code provided a solution to this sort of problem, and his comments left a lasting impression on attendees. The *Law Review* reported that the conversation

> exceeded any thing that we remember connected with the amendment of the Law: and we are much mistaken if the results of the whole movement are not as lasting as they will prove to be important. We do not wish to be guilty of any exaggeration when we say that the public mind was in that peculiar state which often precedes the arrival of some great intelligence.

The writers gushed about their hopes for reform because of Field and his code. The two filled a gap: 'We feel that, in the New York Code, a great blow has been struck; it may be for the human race, but more especially for the Anglo-Saxon sept, whether they inhabit the Old or the New World.'[30]

New York State reforms

English reformers were interested in New York State for a number of reasons. For one, they liked the manner in which the Field Code simplified the collection of evidence.[31] More basically, the code showed reformers and parliamentarians alike that fusion could work.[32] Having come into force in July 1848, the Field Code offered a guide to reformers who thought not just about the content of reform, but also about how to implement it.

Juris. 221; Law Amendment Society, 'Proceedings of the Society' (1848) 9 L. Rev. & Q.J. Brit. & Foreign Juris. 215; Law Amendment Society, 'Proceedings of the Society' (1849) 9 L. Rev. & Q.J. Brit. & Foreign Juris. 444; Law Amendment Society, 'Reports of the Society' (1849) 10 L. Rev. & Q.J. Brit. & Foreign Juris. 107; Law Amendment Society, 'Reports of the Society' (1850) 12 L. Rev. & Q.J. Brit. & Foreign Juris. 93; Law Amendment Society, 'Proceedings of the Society' (1850) 12 L. Rev. & Q.J. Brit. & Foreign Juris. 211; Law Amendment Society, 'Report of the Equity Committee of the Law Amendment Society on the Master's Office' (1852) 15 L. Rev. & Q.J. Brit. & Foreign Juris. 432, 442.

[28] Cocks, 'Bethell, Richard, First Baron Westbury (1800–1873)'.

[29] H.M. Field, *The Life of David Dudley Field* (New York: Charles Scribner's Sons, 1898), 53.

[30] Anon., 'History of the New York Code and Its Applicability to This Country', 214.

[31] Anon., 'The Code of Civil Procedure of the State of New York' (1850) 12 L. Rev. & Q.J. Brit. & Foreign Juris. 366; Anon., 'The Code of Civil Procedure of the State of New York' (1850) 13 L. Rev. & Q.J. Brit. & Foreign Juris. 65, 66, 87.

[32] Anon., 'Comparative Anatomy of Judicial Procedure – On the Recent Consolidation of the Courts of Law and Equity in New York', 392, 401.

The Field Code flowed from constitutional changes in the state. Following several months of deliberations at a convention, the New York State Assembly adopted a new constitution in October 1846. That document required the use of oral testimony to collect evidence and combined the courts of law and equity into a single court of general jurisdiction.[33] It also required the appointment of a three-member commission 'to revise, reform, simplify, and abridge the rules and practice, pleadings, forms, and proceedings of the courts of record'.[34] Duly appointed, the commissioners reported their recommendations to the legislature in early 1848, and the New York Code of Civil Procedure – the Field Code – was born.[35]

Field led the fight to create the code and drafted most of the reports and legislation produced by the committee.[36] Born in 1805 to a prominent Connecticut family, Field had three brothers, including one who served on the Supreme Court of the United States for decades.[37] After three years of study, Field got his call to the bar in 1828 and developed a successful commercial and constitutional practice in New York City before his death in 1894.[38] His passion, however, was law reform.

Field came to believe the problems associated with parallel systems of practice and procedure in law and equity were the primary challenge facing the legal system, and began to think seriously about reform by the mid-1830s.[39] He considered the approach to be cumbersome, time-consuming and expensive, just as it was in England.[40] Worried about

33 N.Y. Const. (1846), art. VI, § 3, § 10. 34 *Ibid.*, § 24.

35 M.V. Coe and L.W. Morse, 'Chronology of the Development of the David Dudley Field Code' (1942) 27 Cornell L.Q. 238, 242.

36 Field, *The Life of David Dudley Field*, 50.

37 Stephen Johnson Field served on the Supreme Court of the United States from May 1863 to December 1897.

38 Field served as one of the petitioner's four counsel in *Ex p. Milligan*, 71 U.S. (4 Wall.) 2; 18 L.Ed. 281 (1866) persuading the Supreme Court of the United States that a Reconstruction-era military commission could not convict a civilian for actions taken previously as a confederate. In *Cummings* v. *The State of Missouri*, 71 U.S. (4 Wall.) 277; 18 L. Ed. 356 (1867) Field argued (alone) against a provision in the Missouri constitution that excluded former confederates from office. The opinion of the court was delivered by Field J. See also P.J. Bergan, 'David Dudley Field: A Life in the Law', in P.J. Bergan, O.M. Fiss and C.W. McMurdy, *The Fields and the Law* (New York: United States District Court for the Northern District of California Historical Society and the Federal Bar Council, 1986), 21–51; and more generally Field, *The Life of David Dudley Field*.

39 Field, *The Life of David Dudley Field*, 45; Reppy, 'The Field Codification Concept', in Reppy (ed.), *David Dudley Field: Centenary Essays*, 30–1.

40 Field repeatedly described the approach as being, 'unreasonably arbitrary, dilatory, and expensive': letter from Field to J.L. O'Sullivan, 1 January 1842 (printed as an Appendix to

general access to the courts, Field was inspired by Jeremy Bentham, John Romilly, Henry Brougham, Edward Livingston and Joseph Story.[41] He was also influenced by Livingston's report of a code for Louisiana and Sampson's discourse on the history and nature of the common law[42] and believed the law should incorporate notions of natural justice and be set out in easily understood language.[43] Codification of the common law, which many assumed would eliminate judicial discretion and expand access to the law, seemed like a natural fit.

Field's public campaign for law reform began in 1839 when he wrote to a member of the New York State Assembly, urging legislators to take bold action on law reform, which he called, 'the most important question of the next session of the Legislature'.[44] He then appealed to a legislative committee to support reform,[45] and even tried – unsuccessfully – to join the State Assembly in 1841 to promote the cause.[46] Undeterred, he tried to persuade a friend who was an assembly member to submit three Bills to the judiciary committee on his behalf.[47] The committee did not end up promoting the bills in the legislature, but they were later published as an appendix to the New York Report on

the Report of the Committee on the Judiciary in New York (State), Legislature, Assembly, *Documents of the Assembly of the State of New-York, Sixty-Fourth Session, 1842* (Albany, N.Y.: Thurlow Weed, 1842), vol. 5, No. 81, 19ff and as D.D. Field, 'First Principles of Reform', in A.P. Sprague (ed.), *Speeches, Arguments, and Miscellaneous Papers of David Dudley Field* (New York: Appleton and Co., 1884), vol. 1, 223, 225); D.D. Field, 'What Shall Be Done with the Practice of the Courts?', in Sprague (ed.), *Speeches, Arguments, and Miscellaneous Papers of David Dudley Field*, vol. 1, 226, 232; Anon., 'History of the New York Code and its Applicability to This Country', 222.

41 Reppy, 'The Field Codification Concept', in Reppy (ed.), *David Dudley Field: Centenary Essays*, 30.

42 E. Livingston, *Report Made to the General Assembly of the State of Louisiana, on the Plan for a Penal Code for the Said State* (New Orleans, LA: Levy, 1822). See also Louisiana Legal Archives, in W.H. Byrnes, E. Livingston, L.M. Lislet, P. Derbigny and J.H. Tucker, *A Republication of the Project of the Civil Code of Louisiana of 1825* (New Orleans: T.J. Moran's Sons, 1937), vol. 1; W. Sampson, *An Anniversary Discourse Delivered before the Historical Society of New-York Showing the Origin, Progress, Antiquities, Curiosities, and Nature of the Common Law* (New York: Bliss and White, 1824); Field, *The Life of David Dudley Field*, 44.

43 Field, *The Life of David Dudley Field*, 44; Reppy, 'The Field Codification Concept', in Reppy (ed.), *David Dudley Field: Centenary Essays*, 30.

44 D.D. Field, letter to G.C. Verplanck, 26 December 1839, printed as 'Reform of the Judicial System of New York', in Sprague (ed.), *Speeches, Arguments, and Miscellaneous Papers of David Dudley Field*, vol. 1, 219, 220. See also Field, *The Life of David Dudley Field*, 46.

45 Field, *The Life of David Dudley Field*, 46. 46 *Ibid.*

47 Field, 'First Principles of Reform', in Sprague (ed.), *Speeches, Arguments, and Miscellaneous Papers of David Dudley Field*, vol. 1, 223.

Legislative Reform.[48] That appendix became the template for the new Code of New York.[49]

In 1845, when the New York State legislature decided to schedule a constitutional convention for the following year,[50] Field saw another opportunity to promote reform. He published a series of articles for the *Evening Post* entitled 'The Reorganization of the Judiciary' in January 1846 in an effort both to join the commission and to influence other members.[51] Unable to secure a position at the convention, he had to settle for regular contact with participants.[52]

As the constitutional convention met over the summer of 1846, Field continued to publish articles in the *Evening Post* on different parts of the constitution.[53] When deliberations wrapped up in October, three provisions dealt with procedural reform. Two were immediately relevant to Field's objectives. The first created a single supreme court with jurisdiction over law and equity, thereby abolishing the Court of Chancery.[54] The second required the legislature to create a three-person commission to produce the new rules (subject to legislative approval) for the administration of judicial proceedings in this new court.[55] The people approved the constitutional changes in November 1846, and the reforms came into force on 1 January 1847. At that time, Field published an essay entitled, 'What Shall Be Done with the Practice of the Courts?'[56] Appealing to the profession and prospective commissioners to take a broad approach to implementing fusion, Field urged them to adopt a uniform code of

48 Field, *The Life of David Dudley Field*, 46. See Field, 'First Principles of Reform', in Sprague (ed.), *Speeches, Arguments, and Miscellaneous Papers of David Dudley Field*, vol. 1, 223; 'Report in Part of the Committee on the Judiciary, in Relation to the Administration of Justice', in New York (State), Legislature, Assembly, *Documents of the Assembly of the State of New-York, Sixty-Fourth Session, 1842* (Albany, N.Y.: Thurlow Weed, 1842), vol. 5, No. 81.

49 See Field, 'First Principles of Reform', in Sprague (ed.), *Speeches, Arguments, and Miscellaneous Papers of David Dudley Field*, vol. 1, 226.

50 1845 N.Y. Laws c. 252 ('An Act recommending a Convention of the People of this State').

51 D.D. Field, *Re-Organization of the Judiciary: Five Articles Originally Published in the Evening Post on that Subject* (New York: D.D. Field, 1846). See also Field, *The Life of David Dudley Field*, 46–7; Reppy, 'The Field Codification Concept', in Reppy (ed.), *David Dudley Field: Centenary Essays*, 31.

52 Reppy, 'The Field Codification Concept', in Reppy (ed.), *David Dudley Field: Centenary Essays*, 31–2; Field, *The Life of David Dudley Field*, 47.

53 Field, *The Life of David Dudley Field*, 47.

54 N.Y. Const. (1846), art. XIV, § 8.

55 *Ibid.*, art. VI, § 24.

56 Field, 'What Shall Be Done with the Practice of the Courts?', 226.

procedure.[57] The essay helped to create the framework that eliminated the distinction between law and equity.[58]

Field followed his essay with a petition to the legislature encouraging members to adopt 'radical reform' that included abolishing forms of actions and pleadings in common law, adopting uniform procedure regardless of whether a proceeding involved law or equity and eliminating all unnecessary forms and proceedings.[59] Two months later, the legislature appointed the commission to draft the new rules of procedure.

Originally, the commission included Nicholas Hill, Jr., David Graham and Arphaxad Loomis.[60] Field was not included because he was considered 'too radical' and 'the conservative feeling . . . too strong' for him to be named a member.[61] However, when Hill wanted a more moderate approach to reform than the other two commissioners, he resigned.[62] Ironically, Field replaced him.[63] The committee's first report, which included provisions for a draft Act to simplify and

[57] Field opposed using the bill and answer for examinations, and wanted parties to state their case more simply. Instead, he suggested that examinations, whether oral or written, be separate. He believed forms of action would not be necessary if pleadings were structured this way. Without forms, there would be no need for separate equitable relief. See Field, *ibid.*, 226, 227, 229, 256–60.

[58] Field, *The Life of David Dudley Field*, 47–8.

[59] D.D. Field, 'Memorial to the Legislature', in Sprague (ed.), *Speeches, Arguments, and Miscellaneous Papers of David Dudley Field*, vol. 1, 261. For a slight variation, see Reppy, 'The Field Codification Concept', in Reppy (ed.), *David Dudley Field: Centenary Essays*, 32.

[60] Hill, a prominent lawyer, had written notes for an evidence treatise, S.M. Phillipps, *Treatise on the Law of Evidence* (New York: Banks, Gould and Co., 1850). Graham was the author of numerous treatises on pleadings and practice in common law and equity. See, for example, D. Graham, *A Treatise on the Practice of the Supreme Court of the State of New York*, 3rd ed. (New York: Banks, Gould and Co., 1847). Loomis was also a well-known lawyer and reformer. He introduced Field's three reform bills to the legislature in 1842, served in Congress, held county judicial positions, and served as a member of the constitutional convention in 1846. See Anon., 'History of the New York Code and Its Applicability to This Country', 229; Field, 'First Principles of Reform', in Sprague (ed.), *Speeches, Arguments, and Miscellaneous Papers of David Dudley Field*, vol. 1, 225.

[61] Field, *The Life of David Dudley Field*, 49.

[62] See New York (State), Legislature, Assembly, *Journal of the Assembly of the State of New-York at Their Seventieth Session* (Albany, N.Y.: van Benthuysen, 1847), vol. 2, 1482; New York (State), Legislature, Senate, *Journal of the Senate of the State of New-York at their Seventieth Session* (Albany, N.Y.: van Benthuysen & Co., 1847), 679; Coe and Morse, 'Chronology of the Development of the David Dudley Field Code', 239.

[63] 'Joint Resolution Appointing a Commission on Practice and Pleadings', 1847 N.Y. Laws, vol. 2, 744; Coe and Morse, 'Chronology of the Development of the David Dudley Field Code', 239; Reppy, 'The Field Codification Concept', in Reppy (ed.), *David Dudley Field: Centenary Essays*, 33.

abridge practice and proceedings in civil cases, followed at the end of February 1848.[64]

The commissioners recommended abolishing all the forms of action,[65] and adopting equitable rules with respect to parties, which would permit one proceeding to resolve a single controversy.[66] For fact-finding, they supported the use of oral evidence and trial by jury, recommending the use of oral evidence and cross-examination in all cases, and that parties should have the option to waive jury trials.[67] The commissioners supported a uniform, albeit limited, right of appeal.[68] They introduced joint and several liability of judgment creditors,[69] and proposed greater flexibility for the award of damages so that plaintiffs could recover what they were entitled to, not just what they had pleaded properly in their complaint.[70] They encouraged streamlined suits by allowing submission of a legal question for determination[71] and providing cost consequences for rejecting a reasonable settlement.[72]

A mere five months elapsed between publication of the first report and the introduction of rules to govern proceedings in the new superior court. The code became law on 12 April 1848 and came into force on 1 July of that year. Containing 391 sections, it came to be known as the Field Code.[73] The commissioners produced three more

[64] By this time, the commissioners had decided to codify all procedure, both civil and criminal, and the rules of evidence: New York (State), Commissioners on Practice and Pleadings, 'First Report of the Practice Commission', 29 February 1848, in Sprague (ed.), *Speeches, Arguments, and Miscellaneous Papers of David Dudley Field*, vol. 1, 262–4.

[65] New York (State), Commissioners on Practice and Pleadings, 'First Report of the Practice Commission', 264–7 (Title I, Part II, 'The Forms of Civil Action').

[66] *Ibid.*, 267–8 (Title III, Part I, 'Parties to Civil Actions').

[67] *Ibid.*, 270–1 (Title VIII, Part II, 'Trial and Judgment in Civil Actions').

[68] *Ibid.*, 271 (Title VIII, Part II, 'Trial and Judgment in Civil Actions'), 275 (Title XI, Part II, 'Appeals').

[69] *Ibid.*, 274 (Note to § 230 'Judgment For or Against Any Party').

[70] *Ibid.*, 275 (Note to § 231, 'Relief Granted to Plaintiff'), 275 (Note to § 232 'Measure of Damages').

[71] *Ibid.*, 276 (Note to § 325, 'Submitting a Controversy without Action').

[72] *Ibid.*, 276 (Chapter IV, Title XII, Part II, 'Compromising an Action').

[73] 1848 N.Y. Laws c. 379 ['1848 Code']. On the development of the Field Code, see K.R. Funk, 'Equity Without Chancery: The Fusion of Law and Equity in the Field Code of Civil Procedure, New York 1846–1876' (2015) 36 J.L.H. 152; Field, *The Life of David Dudley Field*, 49; Coe and Morse, 'Chronology of the Development of the David Dudley Field Code', 238; S.N. Subrin, 'How Equity Conquered Common Law: The Federal Rules of Civil Procedure in Historical Perspective' (1987) 135 U. Pa L. Rev. 909; S.N. Subrin, 'David Dudley Field and the Field Code: A Historical Analysis of an Earlier Procedural Vision' (1988) 6 Law & Hist. Rev. 311; Reppy, 'The Field Codification Concept', in Reppy (ed.), *David Dudley Field: Centenary Essays*, 33–4.

reports on civil procedure the following year.[74] The first two justified amendments,[75] and the third contained complete codes of civil and criminal procedure along with a plea for continued attention to reform.[76] Although the 1849 amendments to the Field Code became law, the proposed 'complete' codes, introduced in 1850, did not.[77] Nevertheless, when English reformers turned their attention to the subject of procedural fusion, they had before them the reports of the New York State practice and pleadings commission along with the various versions of their code, whether enacted or not.

The Field Code was revolutionary, but there were reforms for which it could not take credit. Between 1846 and 1848, common law secured access to pre-trial discovery in New York courts. In fact, the Field Code actually limited pre-trial discovery and put more emphasis on simplifying pleadings and taking oral evidence at trial. As well, the code did not eliminate the distinction between legal and equitable remedies. That did not occur formally until 1852.[78]

[74] New York (State), Commissioners on Practice and Pleadings, 'Second Report of the Practice Commission', 29 January 1849, printed in Sprague (ed.), *Speeches, Arguments, and Miscellaneous Papers of David Dudley Field*, vol. 1, 280; New York (State), Commissioners on Practice and Pleadings, 'Third Report of the Practice Commission', 30, January 1849, printed in Sprague (ed.), *Speeches, Arguments, and Miscellaneous Papers of David Dudley Field*, vol. 1, 285; New York (State), Commissioners on Practice and Pleadings, 'Final Report of the Practice Commission', 31 December 1849, printed in Sprague (ed.), *Speeches, Arguments, and Miscellaneous Papers of David Dudley Field*, vol. 1, 290; New York (State), Commissioners on Practice and Pleadings, *The Code of Civil Procedure of the State of New-York Reported Complete by the Commissioners on Practice and Pleadings* (Albany, N.Y.: Weed, Parsons & Co., 1850) ['1850 Proposed Code'].

[75] New York (State), Commissioners on Practice and Pleadings, 'Second Report of the Practice Commission', in Sprague (ed.), *Speeches, Arguments, and Miscellaneous Papers of David Dudley Field*, vol. 1, 281–3. Amendments passed in April 1849: 1849 N.Y. Laws chap. 438 ['1849 Amended Code']; New York (State), Commissioners on Practice and Pleadings, 'Third Report of the Practice Commission', in Sprague (ed.), *Speeches, Arguments, and Miscellaneous Papers of David Dudley Field*, vol. 1, 287.

[76] 1850 Proposed Code; New York (State), Commissioners on Practice and Pleadings, 'Final Report of the Practice Commission', 31 December 1849, printed in Sprague (ed.), *Speeches, Arguments, and Miscellaneous Papers of David Dudley Field*, vol. 1, 291.

[77] Coe and Morse, 'Chronology of the Development of the David Dudley Field Code', 243; Funk, 'Equity without Chancery: The Fusion of Law and Equity in the Field Code of Civil Procedure, New York 1846–1876'.

[78] 1852 N.Y. Laws chap. 392, § 150; Coe and Morse, 'Chronology of the Development of the David Dudley Field Code', 240.

The Law Amendment Society, Field and Chancery reform efforts

Inspired by Field's presentation, members of the society met in London in December 1850 and appointed a special committee to investigate and make recommendations on Chancery reform. Its mandate, in language suggested by Bethell, expressly referred to the experience of New York State.[79] Within days, Parliament appointed a royal commission to do the same.[80]

Led by Robert Fane, a bankruptcy court judge,[81] the special committee included thirteen other members of varying prominence and expertise. Bethell joined the committee,[82] as did James Stewart, a former parliamentarian and editor of the *Law Review*. Others, including Edward Vansittart Neale,[83] William Nathaniel Massey,[84] Charles Francis Trower[85] and Edward Creasy,[86] had published books and pamphlets on law reform. Another, Matthew Hill, was both a bankruptcy commissioner and a friend of Brougham.[87] Robert Lowe, a former Australian

[79] The special committee was asked to investigate 'whether the principles of Law and Equity can be administered in the same Court and by the same form of procedure; and in making such inquiry the Committee are requested to have regard to the provisions and operation of the New York Code': Anon., 'Note (A.) to Art. I' (1851) 13 L. Rev. & Q.J. Brit. & Foreign Juris. 434, 436.

[80] A Royal Commission to investigate reforms in Common Law was appointed in June 1850. Another commission was appointed six months later to investigate reforms in Chancery.

[81] G.C. Boase (rev. H.J. Spencer), 'Fane, Robert George Cecil (1796–1864)', in *Oxford Dictionary of National Biography* (2004) at www.oxforddnb.com/view/article/9142.

[82] Cocks, 'Bethell, Richard, First Baron Westbury (1800–1873)'; E. Foss, *A Biographical Dictionary of the Judges of England* (London: John Murray, 1870), 88–9.

[83] E.V. Neale, *The Real Property Acts of 1845* (London: Stevens and Norton, 1845) and *Thoughts on the Registration of the Title of Land* (London: Stevens and Norton, 1849). See M. Lee, 'Neale, Edward Vansittart (1810–1892)', in *Oxford Dictionary of National Biography* (2004) at www.oxforddnb.com/view/article/19820.

[84] W.N. Massey, *Common Sense versus Common Law* (London: Longman, Brown, Green and Longmans, 1850). See R. Garnett (rev. by H.C.G. Matthew), 'Massey, William Nathaniel (1809–1881)', in *Oxford Dictionary of National Biography* (2004) at www.oxforddnb.com/view/article/18301.

[85] C.F. Trower, *The Anomalous Condition of English Jurisprudence* (London: Hatchard and Son, 1850). Trower's pamphlet was reviewed. See Anon., 'Severance of Law and Equity', 63.

[86] E. Creasy, *The Text-Book of the Constitution* (London: Bentley, 1848) and *The Rise and Progress of the English Constitution* (London: Bentley, 1853). See H.C.G. Matthew, 'Creasy, Sir Edward Shepherd (1812–1878)', in *Oxford Dictionary of National Biography* (2004) at www.oxforddnb.com/view/article/6660.

[87] P.W.J. Bartrip, 'Hill, Matthew Davenport (1792–1872)', in *Oxford Dictionary of National Biography* (2004) at www.oxforddnb.com/view/article/13286; R. Ashton, 'Society for the Diffusion of Useful Knowledge (act. 1826–1846)', in *Oxford Dictionary of National Biography* (2004) at www.oxforddnb.com/view/theme/59807.

politician who had helped abolish imprisonment for debt in Australia,[88] and Benjamin Hawes, a radical politician and merchant,[89] also joined the committee.

Although Field had provided various letters of reference from New York State judges in support of the reforms,[90] the committee wanted more information on how the code worked from people who had actually used it. With the assistance of Abbott Lawrence, the United States ambassador to London, the society circulated questions about the operation of the code to 'lawyers, merchants, and others residing in New York and other parts of the United States'.[91] Ultimately, twenty New York State legal professionals – nineteen lawyers and a judge – received the survey.[92] Signed by Lord Brougham, William Vizard and Arthur Symonds, the questionnaire asked for information on a series of topics that ranged from the general to the specific.[93]

The committee's report was delivered to and approved by members in May 1851.[94] Lowe, as chief drafter, explained the origins of the problem to readers by reviewing the differences between law and equity, and assessing the advantages and disadvantages of maintaining them.[95] The committee concluded that there was no reason to retain the distinctions and offered three ways to eliminate them: adopt equitable procedure for all cases, adopt legal procedure for everything or create an

[88] J. Parry, 'Lowe, Robert, Viscount Sherbrooke (1811–1892)', in *Oxford Dictionary of National Biography* (2004) at www.oxforddnb.com/view/article/17088.

[89] G. Martin, 'Hawes, Sir Benjamin (1797–1862)', in *Oxford Dictionary of National Biography* (2004) at www.oxforddnb.com/view/article/12643. The remaining four members were Mr Elliott, Mr D. Power, Mr John Pitt Taylor and Mr Alderman Salomons.

[90] See Anon., 'Note (A.) to Art. I'. The letters were included as a note to the article Anon., 'History of the New York Code and Its Applicability to This Country', 213. In the note, the *Law Review* published excerpts of letters from three judges.

[91] Anon., 'History of the New York Code and Its Applicability to This Country', 239–40.

[92] Anon., 'Evidence on the Operation of the New York Code' (1851) 14 L. Rev. & Q.J. Brit. & Foreign Juris. 284, 286–305. See also D.D. Field, 'A Law Reform Association', in *Law Reform Tracts No. 2, Evidence of the Operation of the Code* (New York: Voorhies, 1852), 3–4.

[93] Anon., 'Evidence on the Operation of the New York Code', 286–305; Field, 'A Law Reform Association', 3–4, 5–25.

[94] Anon., 'First Report of the Common Law Commissioners' (1851) 14 L. Rev. & Q.J. Brit. & Foreign Juris. 217, 231.

[95] The committee argued that the difficulties of maintaining the distinctions outweighed any benefits from developing expertise in one procedural area, particularly since those who practiced in one area had to know about the other given the opportunities for intermingling. They felt it was increasingly difficult to maintain the distinction between law and equity with consistency. See Anon., 'Progress of Union of Law and Equity' (1851) 14 L. Rev. & Q.J. Brit. & Foreign Juris. 143, 153–63.

entirely 'new' procedure that took the best of each.[96] Only the final option was viable, and the committee offered fusion and the Field Code as a model for English legislators. Several recommendations followed. Foremost was the creation of a single tribunal to administer law and equity, governed by a single code of procedure applicable to all forms of litigation. In the event of conflict, equitable principles would trump legal ones.[97] Writers at the *Law Review* approved, noting that five other states had adopted the Field Code in the three years since its introduction in New York State.[98] The message was clear: it was safe to adopt a uniform code of procedure, even in England.

In its second report (delivered shortly after the first), the committee provided a model code, which the society considered and approved. 'Many of the following rules are doubtless open to much discussion, and, collectively, they form the mere outline of a system',[99] Lowe wrote. 'The Committee, however, consider that this outline is amply sufficient to prove that the great legal reform sanctioned by the Society has no insuperable obstacles to encounter'.[100] The proposed code was simple, with only thirty-four sections.[101]

The special committee delivered its final report in December 1851. When the *Law Review* published it six months later, writers were optimistic about the prospect of Chancery reform. The writers explained, 'We might say much about it; but we shall now give the Third Report of the Law Amendment Committee on the subject, and leave the plant to grow of itself.'[102]

Following receipt of the report, the society formally endorsed procedural fusion and called for the appointment of a paid commission to create a uniform code of procedure, just as in New York State.[103] However, the special committee recognised that form was less important than substance and, in its third report, proposed ten separate statutes that would eliminate key differences between law and equity without the need for formal fusion or a code.[104] Lowe explained that this legislation would 'operate most beneficially in smoothing the way for the ultimate

96 Anon., 'Progress of Union of Law and Equity', 165. 97 *Ibid.*, 166.

98 Missouri, Mississippi, California, Kentucky and Iowa followed New York: Anon., 'Progress of Union of Law and Equity', 143–4.

99 Anon., 'First Report of the Common Law Commissioners', 231. 100 *Ibid.*, 231.

101 *Ibid.*, 231–6.

102 Anon., 'Fusion of Law and Equity' (1852) 16 L. Rev. & Q.J. Brit. & Foreign Juris. 184.

103 Anon., 'Fusion of Law and Equity – Proposed Equity County Courts' (1852) 16 Law Mag. 82, 83.

104 Anon., 'Fusion of Law and Equity'.

establishment of fusion', while providing 'material improvements in the present system'.[105] Many of the recommendations came from the model code contained in the special committee's second report and the Field Code. I discuss them in the relevant context below.

When Field returned to England in December 1851 – around the same time members were considering the committee's third report – he spoke in several forums: a dinner held in his honour, a hearing of the Chancery royal commission and a special meeting of the society.[106] When members of the society and local merchants attended the dinner for Field at the London Tavern on 20 December, the American law reformer promoted fusion as the only way to simplify judicial proceedings. Questioning how long England could endure parallel proceedings, Field spoke about the increased efficiency and decreased expense under his code in New York State.[107] Thanks to the code, he explained, 'what had formerly occupied a year in America was now settled in twenty days'.[108]

Field also gave evidence to the Chancery Commission on 22 December 1851, the final day of hearings. He was the only witness to provide information about any aspect of fusion: its conception, implementation or implications. Observers described the presentation as 'successful in removing difficulties and resolving doubts',[109] although the details of Field's evidence were not widely noted at the time.[110]

Sir John Romilly, as head of the commission, asked Field more than 170 questions about the code.[111] He asked for general information about the scope and structure of the code, along with how it dealt with specific issues like the taking of evidence and the use of juries. He wanted to know

[105] *Ibid.*, 187.

[106] Anon., 'The Law Amendment Society: Its Progress and Prospects' (1852) 15 L. Rev. & Q.J. Brit. & Foreign Juris. 409, 418; Field, *The Life of David Dudley Field*, 55–6.

[107] Anon., 'Fusion of Law and Equity – Proposed Equity County Courts', 82–3, 86.

[108] 'Law and Police', *The Guardian*, 31 December 1851, 901.

[109] Anon., 'The Law Amendment Society: Its Progress and Prospects', 418.

[110] For example, neither the *Law Review* nor the *Law Magazine* published details of Field's evidence, which is unexpected given their enthusiasm for Field, if not fusion. Field's evidence was not included in the evidence appended to the first report of the Chancery commissioners published in the official parliamentary record. See United Kingdom, Chancery Commissioners, *First Report of Her Majesty's Commissioners Appointed to Inquire into the Process, Practice, and System of Pleading in the Court of Chancery, &c.* (London: H.M.S.O., 1852), Appendix A. Field's evidence was later published: United Kingdom, Chancery Commissioners, *Supplement to Appendix to the First Report of Her Majesty's Commissioners Appointed to Inquire into the Process, Practice, and System of Pleading in the Court of Chancery* (London: H.M.S.O., 1852).

[111] Field, 'A Law Reform Association', 25–45.

about the structure of appeal courts and the breadth of their powers. Most importantly, Romilly asked about the efficiencies brought about by the code, particularly reductions in time and cost.[112]

Field explained to the commissioners how the code had simplified matters by making it easier to decide proceedings on their merits. He detailed the discretion it gave judges to deal with procedural issues, including the amendment of pleadings, and described how abolishing forms of action had streamlined pleadings, which in turn led to simpler, briefer proceedings. He talked about the benefits of adopting equitable practice with respect to parties. He discussed fact finding and explained that parties could waive their right to a jury, though juries retained responsibility for fact finding in actions involving claims for recovery of money or property. Field discussed how changes to the rules governing the competence of witnesses meant more individuals were able to provide testimony; how adversaries could now call parties as witnesses subject to oral examination at trial; and how either party could examine his adversary before a judge at any time before trial.[113]

Field concluded his evidence by lauding the results of the code. 'It has done an immense amount of good',[114] he explained. Acknowledging the original divisions within the legal profession over the need for a code, including the many who were downright 'hostile' to it, Field claimed the majority of judges and lawyers now supported it. 'I do not think that there is an intelligent lawyer or judge in the State of New York who thinks that there is any inherent difficulty in abolishing the distinction between law and equity; or that there has been any real difficulty in the working of that change',[115] he told the commissioners. Any problems with implementation were 'minor details'.[116]

Legislative change

Eighteen fifty-two was a pivotal year for English law reform. Law reform had captured the political imagination. 'No Session of Parliament ever opened under circumstances of greater interest to the particular cause which we represent', noted the writers at the *Law Review*.[117] At the beginning of the year, one month after Field's testimony, the Chancery commissioners issued their first report.[118] Parliament responded to this

[112] *Ibid.*, 25–40. [113] *Ibid.*, 27, 34. [114] *Ibid.*, 28. [115] *Ibid.*, 28. [116] *Ibid.*, 28.

[117] Anon., 'Postscript' (1852) 15 L. Rev. & Q.J. Brit. & Foreign Juris. 442.

[118] United Kingdom, Chancery Commissioners, *First Report of Her Majesty's Commissioners Appointed to Inquire into the Process, Practice, and System of Pleading in the Court of Chancery, &c.*

report and the first report of the common law commissioners from the previous year[119] with several serious legislative initiatives that summer. As *The Law Times* noted at the time, 'Law Reform, beyond all other reforms, is self-promoting. One change *compels* many more.'[120] The influence of Field and his code were apparent throughout.

After collecting evidence from more than thirty witnesses over a six-month period, the Chancery commissioners focused extensively on two subjects in their first report: procedure, particularly the collection of evidence and examination of witnesses, and the masters' offices.[121] They recognised the need to reconcile some of the differences between law and equity, but decided that formal fusion was as yet too drastic a solution. Something so 'radical' required more consideration, and the commissioners promised to discuss the subject more fully in a future report.[122] Instead, without eliminating the distinction between law and equity or their respective courts, the commissioners proposed to 'blend' the jurisdiction of the two in order to 'render each Court competent to administer complete justice in the cases which fall under its cognizance'.[123] The proposals were supposed to improve the court's efficiency while reducing expense and delay. Each was rooted in the work of the New York State commissioners, the contents of the Field Code and the efforts of the Law Amendment Society.

Over the next decade, Parliament enacted a series of statutes that implemented key components of procedural fusion, blending practice and procedure one step at a time. At common law, the most important of these statutes were the Common Law Procedure Acts of 1852, 1854 and 1860. In Chancery, significant legislation included the Court of Chancery Procedure Act of 1852, the Court of Chancery Examiners Act of 1853, the Court of Chancery Act of 1854 and the Chancery Amendment Act of 1858. Together, these legislative Acts introduced changes that achieved much of what Field had accomplished in New York State, though without the benefit and efficiency of a single set of procedures for use in a unified court.

[119] United Kingdom, Common Law Commissioners, *First Report from the Commissioners for Inquiring into the Process, Practice, and System of Pleading in the Superior Courts of Common Law* (London: Eyre and Spottiswoode, 1851).

[120] 'The Next Great Law Reform' (1852) 20 L.T. 1 (emphasis original).

[121] United Kingdom, Chancery Commissioners, *First Report of Her Majesty's Commissioners Appointed to Inquire into the Process, Practice, and System of Pleading in the Court of Chancery, &c.*, 11–14.

[122] *Ibid.*, 2. [123] *Ibid.*, 3.

Fusion under the Field Code led to changes in four areas: the form and substance of pleadings; the treatment of multiple parties and issues; the rules governing the collection of evidence before and during trial; and the availability of equitable remedies. I review each below, discussing Field's reforms and their influence on the recommendations of the Law Amendment Society and royal commissions, along with the legislative changes that followed.

Pleadings: forms of actions

Overly complex pleadings contributed to unnecessary expense and delay whether in New York State or in England. Over time, the common law had developed a rigid system of forms to plead a cause of action. The system was excessively technical and the forms did little to describe the actual dispute between the parties. For Field, abolishing the forms of action was key to achieving procedural fusion, and the Field Code did just that in 1848. In England, the Common Law Procedure Act of 1852 accomplished something similar.

The Field Code

Field had consistently supported abolishing all forms of action. He did so in his letter to the profession of 1847, his petition on behalf of the New York State bar, the first report of the New York State Practice Commission, and, ultimately, the legislation that became the Field Code.[124] When the code replaced forms of action with seven categories of action in 1848,[125] it required a claim to include a short statement of facts with a request for relief 'in such a manner as to enable a person of common understanding to know what is intended'.[126] Similar requirements were introduced for a statement of defence.[127] In 1849, the amended code introduced voluntary verification of pleadings by oath and gave judges more discretion to amend and refine pleadings over the course of proceedings.[128]

124 Field, 'What Shall Be Done with the Practice of the Courts?', 226, 240, 259–60; Field, *The Life of David Dudley Field*, 48; New York (State), Commissioners on Practice and Pleadings, 'First Report of the Practice Commission', 262, 263; 1848 Code, § 118. See also 1849 N.Y. Laws c. 438, § 140; 1850 Proposed Code, § 636.

125 1848 Code, §§ 118, 143. The categories were contract; injuries by force to person or property; injuries without force to person or property; injuries to character; claims to recover real property; claims to recover personal property; and claims against a trustee.

126 1848 Code, § 120; 1849 Amended Code, § 142; 1850 Proposed Code, § 639.

127 1848 Code, § 128; 1849 Amended Code, § 149; 1850 Proposed Code, § 645.

128 1849 Amended Code, §§ 157, 160.

The Law Amendment Society

In late 1850, members of the Law Amendment Society's common law committee recommended reforming the pleadings process in ways that were similar to those introduced by the Field Code. They urged Parliament to abolish all forms of action, modify pleadings and eliminate all special pleading. They wanted to abolish 'all technicality' from common law pleading and apply 'a plain and sensible rule to its natural operation'.[129]

Field and his work also influenced the society's special committee on Chancery reform. The committee's model code emphasised the use of plain language in pleadings, which was in obvious contrast to the forms of action used at common law, and gave priority to rules in equity over law where there was a conflict between the two.[130] The committee also recommended legislation to eliminate all objections to the form of pleadings (effectively abolishing forms in the process) and to allow verification of pleadings by simple oath, whether at law or in equity.[131] The Field Code had implemented similar changes in New York State.

Royal commissions and their recommendations

When the common law commissioners issued their first report in June 1851, they may have been less bold than members of the Law Amendment Society had been or the writers at the *Law Review* would have liked,[132] but they did recommend eliminating forms of action generally.[133] They explained, 'it shall not be necessary that the facts should be stated in any technical or formal language or manner, or that any technical or formal statements should be used'.[134] Judgments should be based on the 'right of the cause' and 'the matter in law appearing on the pleadings'.[135] Mere form should not be permitted to impede or invalidate proceedings.[136] Instead, the commissioners recommended that Parliament introduce a new categorical approach to common law pleading while at the same time retaining the existing system of special pleading.[137] Although such an approach was more akin to the Field Code

[129] Anon., 'Reform in Common Law Procedure' (1851) 13 L. Rev. & Q.J. Brit. & Foreign Juris. 327, 344.

[130] Anon., 'First Report of the Common Law Commissioners', 232, rr. 4, 8.

[131] Anon., 'Fusion of Law and Equity', 186. [132] Editorial, *The Times*, 2 January 1851, 4.

[133] United Kingdom, Common Law Commissioners, *First Report from the Commissioners for Inquiring into the Process, Practice, and System of Pleading in the Superior Courts of Common Law*, 2, 21–35, 44.

[134] *Ibid.*, 22. [135] *Ibid.*, 21. [136] *Ibid.*, 21–2. [137] *Ibid.*, 2, 21–35, 44.

than the proposals of the Law Amendment Society, the proposed replacement of rigid forms of action with more flexible equitable pleading would nonetheless improve proceedings for litigants.[138]

Without an equitable counterpart to forms of action, pleadings were less of a concern to Chancery commissioners. Instead, they worried about the administrative details associated with pleading: things like how to complete and file the abundant paperwork required in Chancery. They proposed to make it easier and less costly to authenticate pleadings and urged the court to be more vigilant about the length of pleadings. They recommended the use of copies in place of formal writs at more stages of the proceeding and proposed to streamline bills by including interrogatories for answer only where necessary.[139]

Legislative changes

Parliament adopted many of the commissioners' recommendations in the summer of 1852. The Common Law Procedure Act recognised the importance of substance over form,[140] and introduced five reforms that dramatically changed common law pleading. It abolished forms of action, eliminated the old formalities of pleading (including the need for colour and special traverses) and used simple terms to describe the structure of a pleading.[141] It made clear that imperfections, omissions, defects or lack of form were no longer grounds for terminating an action. Instead, the court was permitted to strike out pleadings only where they were intended either to prejudice or embarrass the parties or to delay the fair trial of the issues.[142] Proceedings were permitted to survive the death or marriage of a party.[143]

The reforms in Chancery were more administrative in nature. The Court of Chancery Procedure Act of 1852, enacted the day after the Common Law Procedure Act, reflected the need to simplify practice and pleading in that court. It prescribed fewer copies of documents, simplified the means of producing them and provided for the amendment of bills without having to re-start the proceedings.[144]

138 *Ibid.*, 22.

139 United Kingdom, Chancery Commissioners, *First Report of Her Majesty's Commissioners Appointed to Inquire into the Process, Practice, and System of Pleading in the Court of Chancery, &c.*, 24–6, 40–1.

140 For example, Common Law Procedure Act 1852, s. 74. 141 *Ibid.*, ss. 59–61.

142 *Ibid.*, ss. 50–2. 143 *Ibid.*, ss. 134–52.

144 Court of Chancery Procedure Act 1852, ss. 1–15, 53.

Multiple parties and issues

Separate courts brought distinct approaches to handling multiple parties and issues. In England, the common law courts required separate actions to deal with multiple parties and issues. In Chancery, multiple parties in a single suit were not merely encouraged, but required because the rules required that every individual with an interest in the outcome of the litigation be named as a party to the suit. New York State had faced similar differences.

The Field Code

New York State had different rules for different kinds of disputes before the introduction of the Field Code. In contract, all the parties with an interest in the contract were named as defendants. Where the complaint involved harm to real property, the plaintiff had to name all parties with an interest in the damaged property. Only disputes involving personal injury were governed by rules that permitted (but did not require) a plaintiff to name multiple defendants. Multiple causes of action could be joined only where they were of the same type; for example, a plaintiff could have an action involving several causes of action in contract, but could not combine a claim in contract and a harm in tort into a single action.[145]

The Field Code simplified these rules and allowed a proceeding to be brought by 'all persons having an interest in the subject of the action, and in obtaining the relief demanded'.[146] Correspondingly, a proceeding was properly defended by any person 'who has an interest in the controversy, adverse to the plaintiff'.[147] Only 'real parties in interest' joined suit.[148] However, a plaintiff could not bring a single action involving multiple 'classes' of dispute until 1852,[149] when the legislature amended the code to permit plaintiffs to join 'several causes of action, whether they be such as have been heretofore denominated legal or equitable, or both'.[150]

Law Amendment Society

Members of the Law Amendment Society promoted an approach to parties and issues that was a more relaxed version of the practice in

[145] C.L. Monnell, *A Treatise on the Practice of the Courts of the State of New York* (Albany, N.Y.: Gould, Banks and Gould, 1849), 9–24, 45–8.

[146] 1848 Code, § 97; 1849 Amended Code, § 117; 1850 Proposed Code, § 608.

[147] 1848 Code, § 98; 1849 Amended Code, § 118; 1850 Proposed Code, § 609.

[148] 1848 Code, § 91; 1849 Amended Code, § 111; 1850 Proposed Code, § 597.

[149] 1848 Code, § 143. [150] 1852 N.Y. Laws c. 397, § 167.

equity. Ordinarily, non-joinder and mis-joinder were fatal in Chancery, but, like the Field Code, the society's model code reduced the number of grounds for terminating a suit for improper parties and gave judges additional powers to add or remove parties as necessary.[151] The model code also recommended that judges at common law be permitted to order joinder of parties and issues, and to allow multiple causes, defences and replies in a single proceeding.[152] However, the special committee did not regard joinder as a legislative priority and proposed no stand-alone legislation on the subject.

Royal commissions and their recommendations

The common law commissioners recommended that Parliament relax the rules governing the termination of actions over improperly named parties. They wanted to give judges more discretion to amend pleadings, award costs and allocate liability where appropriate.[153] The Chancery commissioners also dealt with the problem of multiple parties, but in the context of addressing the cost of litigation by reducing expense and delay. In equity, 'all persons interested in the subject matter of the litigation should be parties to the suit; so that the Court may in the one suit make a final determination as between all parties'.[154] However, the rules governing parties were so cumbersome that the Chancery commissioners singled them out as the greatest source of expense and delay. 'They operate not merely by the multiplication of parties in the first instance, but by creating the necessity, upon every birth and every death, of making fresh parties by fresh proceedings'.[155] The commissioners proposed to give judges greater discretion to resolve technical problems involving the parties to a proceeding without terminating the suit.[156] They suggested that judges be allowed to add parties as necessary and proposed to limit the situations in which a defendant could object to missing parties. They also wanted to introduce a representative procedure to allow an individual to act on behalf of a group with the same interest in the litigation. They hoped such a procedure would make it easier to deal with disputes

151 Anon., 'First Report of the Common Law Commissioners', 234, r. 32.

152 *Ibid.*, 232, r. 5.

153 United Kingdom, Common Law Commissioners, *First Report from the Commissioners for Inquiring into the Process, Practice, and System of Pleading in the Superior Courts of Common Law*, 9–11.

154 United Kingdom, Chancery Commissioners, *First Report of Her Majesty's Commissioners Appointed to Inquire into the Process, Practice, and System of Pleading in the Court of Chancery, &c.*, 17.

155 *Ibid.*, 18. 156 *Ibid.*, 18–20, 39.

involving trusts or estates where the multiplicity of parties was legendary.[157]

Legislative changes

Parliament accepted many of the recommendations pertaining to parties and issues, as it did with pleading. The Court of Chancery Procedure Act of 1852 abolished non-joinder and mis-joinder as grounds for terminating litigation,[158] and gave judges the power to proceed without a deceased litigant or to appoint a representative for the proceedings in certain situations.[159] It also gave judges more flexibility to deal with questions that involved some but not all parties.[160]

Multiple parties and issues were a bigger problem at common law than in Chancery, and the Common Law Procedure Act of 1852 introduced a broad approach to joinder that covered both. As under the Chancery Procedure Act, the Common Law Procedure Act abolished errors and omissions relating to parties as grounds for terminating a proceeding. It gave parties greater flexibility to add parties prior to trial,[161] though the court retained the power to end proceedings with too many parties.[162] It also allowed parties to join causes of action and issues into a single proceeding.[163]

Fact-finding: pre-trial discovery and trial practice

Unifying the collection of evidence was at the heart of procedural fusion in New York State, and in England significant differences remained in its absence. In England, pre-trial discovery was available only in Chancery, so parties at common law had to start afresh in Chancery to obtain a bill of discovery for use in common law proceedings. There were also different approaches to the collection of evidence. Common law dealt primarily with oral evidence from live witnesses, using examination and cross-examination before judges. Juries engaged in fact finding. In Chancery, most evidence was in written form and judges tended not to deal directly with live witnesses. Oral evidence remained the domain of examiners and masters. During this period, there were two types of efforts to reform the collection of evidence and fact finding. The first

[157] *Ibid.*, 18, 38–9. [158] Court of Chancery Procedure Act 1852, ss. 42–3, 49.
[159] *Ibid.*, s. 44. The Act did not create a general representative procedure.
[160] *Ibid.*, s. 51. [161] Common Law Procedure Act 1852, ss. 34–8.
[162] See Common Law Procedure Act 1860, ss. 19, 21, regarding joinder and *res judicata*.
[163] Common Law Procedure Act 1852, ss. 41, 79.

tried to reconcile differences in the collection of evidence at law and in equity, and many of the legislative changes of this period helped to blend procedures in a way that allowed each to secure many of the most useful powers of the other. The second did not necessarily involve fusion, but tried to make the laws of evidence more reasonable.

The Field Code

New York State introduced documentary discovery to common law proceedings two decades before the Field Code based on practice and principles in Chancery.[164] The change gave defendants access to documentary discovery to secure admissions before finalising their pleadings, and either party could request it to help prepare for trial.[165] Parties were also able to depose witnesses without an interest in the outcome of the litigation who were unlikely to be available at trial.[166] Examiners or masters were involved in the examination of witnesses or the subpoena of documents, just as English Chancery officials were responsible for administering written interrogatories and collecting evidence. Parties in New York State could not attend examinations until 1817.[167] Even after that time, examiners still conducted and recorded the examinations on behalf of the solicitor. The judge, responsible for all factual and legal determinations involving examinations, was not directly involved in the collection of this evidence.[168]

The 1846 constitutional amendments changed the pre-trial collection of evidence by requiring that 'testimony in equity cases shall be taken in the like manner in cases at law',[169] and the Field Code implemented the process by which the court could order the production of documents or the examination of a witness.[170] Parties with a material interest in

[164] New York (State), *The Revised Statutes of the State of New-York* (Albany, N.Y.: Packard and van Benthuysen, 1829), vol. 2, 199–200, §§ 21–7.

[165] New York (State), Courts, Supreme Court, *Rules of Practice of the Supreme Court of the State of New York at Law and in Equity* (Albany, N.Y.: Gould, Banks and Gould, 1847), 14–15, rr. 27–8.

[166] New York (State), *The Revised Statutes of the State of New-York*, vol. 2, 392, § 34.

[167] *Remsen* v. *Remsen*, 2 Johns. Ch. 495, 502 (N.Y. Ch. 1817).

[168] J.W. Moulton, *The Chancery Practice of the State of New York* (New York: Halsted, 1829), 317–22.

[169] N.Y. Const. (1846), art. VI, § 10.

[170] 1848 Code, §§ 342, 346–7; 1850 Proposed Code, § 1853. In 1849, state rules of practice allowed plaintiffs to obtain documents for their initial complaint: New York (State), Supreme Court, *Rules of Practice of the Supreme Court of the State of New York at Law and in Equity*, 15–16, r. 8.

documents could examine them before trial.[171] They – or their counsel – replaced examiners for the conduct of oral examinations as at common law.[172] In Chancery, a bill for discovery had allowed the examination of parties prior to the close of proceedings in order to provide information for the answer and complaint. The Field Code adopted this approach in 1848.[173]

Prior to the constitutional amendments of 1846, juries were solely responsible for fact finding. Although the Field Code adopted common law procedure over equity in this respect,[174] it gave parties the freedom to choose a method of trial.[175] Thus, while jury trial remained the default mode of trial when a dispute involved the recovery of real property or monetary damages,[176] trials by judge alone became the norm in all other situations.[177]

The Field Code also set out the process for examining witnesses, including parties, and limited examinations at trial to adverse parties. However, it permitted broader examination of all witnesses and parties to occur before a judge prior to trial. A party could be compelled to attend an examination, and refusal to do so was subject to a finding of contempt. Parties were able to provide evidence on their own behalf, but only after examination by an adverse party, and they were limited to rebutting the original examination. Otherwise, the adverse party could offer himself as a responding witness.[178] The code permitted the examination of non-party witnesses with an interest in the outcome of the litigation subject to the same rules of examination that governed parties.[179]

Law Amendment Society

The special committee's model code gave judges the authority to order the production of documents in the custody or control of an opposing

[171] 1848 Code, § 354.

[172] Monnell, *A Treatise on the Practice of the Courts of the State of New York*, 164–8.

[173] H. Whittaker, *Practice and Pleading under the Code, Original and Amended, with Appendix of Forms*, 2nd ed. (New York: 1854, printed for the author), 627–30.

[174] 1846 Constitution, Art. VI, § 10. The constitution governed fact finding under the 1848 Code and 1849 Amended Code. The 1850 Proposed Code adopted detailed provisions for examinations at trial. See §§ 1837–51. (The numbering of § 1837 as '§ 137' in the 1850 edition is a misprint.)

[175] 1848 Code, § 221; 1849 Amended Code, § 266; 1850 Proposed Code, § 796.

[176] 1848 Code, § 208; 1849 Amended Code, § 253; 1850 Proposed Code, § 761.

[177] 1848 Code, § 209; 1849 Amended Code, § 254; 1850 Proposed Code, § 762.

[178] 1848 Code, §§ 344–7; 1849 Amended Code, §§ 390–4; 1850 Proposed Code, §§ 1853–4.

[179] 1848 Code, §§ 348–52; 1849 Amended Code, §§ 395–9. The 1850 Proposed Code allowed individuals with an interest in the outcome of the proceeding to serve as witnesses: §§ 1708–10.

party,[180] and the attendance of a party for cross-examination.[181] The committee also proposed specific legislation to give common law courts the power to order bills of discovery and substitute, in all cases, oral examinations for written interrogatories.[182] The model code also gave judges the power to decide all questions of law and fact, unless either party requested a jury to make factual findings.[183] The committee recommended two statutes to implement these proposals. The first gave judges at common law the power to try questions of fact absent a jury, and judges in Chancery the power to try questions of fact with juries of their own. The other allowed parties, in any action or suit, to refer questions of law or fact to a judge for decision as decisive of the merits of the cause.[184]

The society's model code also dealt with witnesses. It rendered parties competent as witnesses on their own behalf and compellable to give evidence on behalf of the opposing party.[185] It subjected witnesses to oral examination in open court (subject to narrow exceptions),[186] including witnesses examined under a commission, who provided oral testimony without written interrogatories unless otherwise directed by the judge.[187] Although the model code permitted the continued use of affidavits, it confined their use to *ex parte* interlocutory motions and special proceedings, and it gave judges the authority to summons affiants to testify and submit to oral examination.[188] The committee also wanted to give judges a greater role in the collection of evidence. There was a bill to require equity judges to take evidence directly instead of examiners, and another that abolished the prohibition in Chancery against publishing evidence (thus permitting examinations in open court).[189]

To improve fact finding in Chancery, the role of the masters' offices required clarification. Members of the equity committee debated the subject for more than two and a half years in the late 1840s before coming up with two options: empower the masters to make decisions about proceedings, or abolish the offices altogether and re-allocate their

[180] Anon., 'First Report of the Common Law Commissioners', 233, r. 14.

[181] *Ibid.*, 233, r. 13. [182] Anon, 'Fusion of Law and Equity', 186–7.

[183] Anon., 'First Report of the Common Law Commissioners', 233, r. 15. Rules 20 to 23 required judges to travel on circuit twice a year to try questions of fact.

[184] Anon., 'Fusion of Law and Equity', 186–7 Bills 4 and 7.

[185] Anon., 'First Report of the Common Law Commissioners', 233, r. 15.

[186] *Ibid.*, 233, r. 17 However, the witness was not required to submit to oral examination in open court at trial where a commission could be issued in an action at common law.

[187] Anon., 'First Report of the Common Law Commissioners', 233, r. 18.

[188] *Ibid.*, 233, r. 19. [189] Anon., 'Fusion of Law and Equity', 186–7.

responsibilities to clerks and judges. Initially, members supported the former. By 1852, they settled on the latter.[190]

Royal commissions and their recommendations

Even though the common law stood to benefit most from changes to pre-trial discovery, it was the Chancery commissioners who first dealt with the subject in January 1852. The common law commissioners did not discuss the handling of pre-trial discovery until they released their second report in April 1853, and then only briefly. By that time, Parliament had enacted the Common Law Procedure Act and the Court of Chancery Procedure Act.

The Chancery commissioners recognised the benefits of discovery to review documents. 'This right', they wrote, 'is indispensable to the due administration of justice.'[191] However, a party seeking a bill of discovery from Chancery also had to secure a stay of the original proceeding, a process that was open to abuse. It was, the commissioners explained, 'too often made an engine of mere oppression and vexation, involving the parties in litigation on points wholly beside the merits of the case'.[192]

Instead, the commissioners urged Parliament to give sufficient power to each court to 'administer complete justice in all matters within its cognizance, without resort to the aid of the other'.[193] They recommended that common law judges have the power to compel discovery, issue common injunctions to enforce orders for discovery and order document production from defendants even where the plaintiff might not require an answer. They also suggested that defendants be able to seek an order for production of documents in the possession of the plaintiff when the plaintiff had served a notice of motion for a decree. Finally, they recommended abolishing the common injunction in Chancery.[194]

Although the Common Law Procedure Act of 1852 gave common law judges the power to compel inspection of documents, that power pertained only to documents in the possession of an adverse party.

[190] See n. 27 above.

[191] United Kingdom, Chancery Commissioners, *First Report of Her Majesty's Commissioners Appointed to Inquire into the Process, Practice, and System of Pleading in the Court of Chancery, &c.*, 23.

[192] *Ibid.*, 23. [193] *Ibid.*, 38.

[194] They acknowledged there was no reason to deny common law judges the power to issue injunctions to stay proceedings on their merits if they could already issue special injunctions, and conceded the court should retain the power to deal with bills of discovery where key evidence might be lost, as where a party was gravely ill: *ibid.*, 23, 25, 40.

The common law commissioners complained about this in their second report, noting that a party would call an opposing witness only 'in the most desperate emergency'.[195] No one would call an adverse witness to testify at trial without first having the chance to question them. For all practical purposes, then, whether for facts or documents, parties to an action at common law still ended up in Chancery. For this reason, the common law commissioners recommended a streamlined approach to discovery at common law. They suggested that a party seeking discovery of documents apply to a common law judge, relying on an affidavit that specified the necessary documents and basis for their belief that the party had the documents in its possession or control. They also wanted to extend common law discovery beyond access to documents to 'all matters relating to the questions in dispute'.[196] The rationale for such broad pre-trial discovery was to permit the parties to reveal facts exclusively within the knowledge of the opposing party and to minimise the time and expense involved with producing evidence of facts that a party was willing to admit. Expansive pre-trial examination could clarify the true points in issue, and might even eliminate the need for a trial by exposing 'groundless actions' and 'unfounded defences' introduced only for the purposes of delay.[197]

Although the common law commissioners urged Parliament to permit greater use of written evidence in common law proceedings, they still wanted to test that evidence through oral examination and cross-examination. For example, they suggested that parties be able to test written interrogatories and written answers under oath through oral examination. They were also mindful of the possibility that unscrupulous parties could abuse the power of examination and urged that it be limited to the questions originally posed.[198]

Like their common law counterparts, the Chancery commissioners worried about the use and reliability of written evidence. Counsel, not the witness, prepared written interrogatories. Court examiners or commissioners – not a judge – heard the evidence. As part of their move to reform the use of written evidence in Chancery, the commissioners recommended abolishing interrogatories altogether.[199] Affidavits, widely

[195] United Kingdom, Common Law Commissioners, *Second Report of Her Majesty's Commissioners for Inquiring into the Process, Practice, and System of Pleading in the Superior Courts of Common Law* (London: H.M.S.O., 1853), 35.

[196] *Ibid.*, 36. [197] *Ibid.* [198] *Ibid.*, 36–7.

[199] United Kingdom, Chancery Commissioners, *First Report of Her Majesty's Commissioners Appointed to Inquire into the Process, Practice, and System of Pleading in the Court of Chancery, &c.*, 40.

used in suits brought by petition, claim or interlocutory application, were adequate where no facts were in dispute, but remained problematic. They could be too long and often contained hearsay evidence or introduced new, irrelevant issues. But the biggest problem with affidavits lay in their crafting because solicitors, not witnesses, drafted them. Thus, a witness did not provide his statement by affidavit, but merely approved it, albeit under oath.[200]

The Chancery commissioners suggested using oral examination and cross-examination to test affidavit evidence and simplify evidence collection. They wanted to let plaintiffs choose between proving their case orally or in writing at trial and recommended that parties be able to rely exclusively on affidavit evidence only by consent of the parties. They suggested that judges have the authority to order the examination of any witness, and parties be able to ask to examine or cross-examine any deponent. They proposed that Parliament eliminate having examiners take evidence in secret, and allow parties or their counsel to attend oral examinations which they would conduct before a competent person. They recommended a change in approach to recording the examinations, suggesting that examiners record the evidence in narrative form instead of question–answer format, which the witness would then review and sign in the presence of the parties. Examiners would record specific language only at the request of either party where the language was relevant to issues in dispute. A master or 'other competent person accustomed to the examination of witnesses and practically conversant with the laws of evidence' would preside.[201] The commissioners believed that the mere possibility of examination and cross-examination on affidavits would make their contents more reliable.[202]

By contrast, the common law commissioners opposed the use of affidavit evidence. 'This species of evidence is, of all others, the most unsatisfactory',[203] they wrote in their second report. They argued that affidavits avoided all the best elements of English procedure. There were no procedural safeguards. Affidavits were not subject to oral examination or cross-examination in open court before judge and jury, and thus a decision-maker had no opportunity to observe the demeanour of the

200 *Ibid.*, 21–2, 40. 201 *Ibid.*, 22.

202 Parties who decided to use oral evidence could still use affidavits on consent to adduce evidence from specific witnesses or to deal with particular facts: *ibid.*, 22–3, 26, 40–2.

203 United Kingdom, Common Law Commissioners, *Second Report of Her Majesty's Commissioners for Inquiring into the Process, Practice, and System of Pleading in the Superior Courts of Common Law*, 32.

witness. Similarly, the court could not compel the production of affidavit evidence, and the evidence itself was not the spontaneous statement of a witness.[204] The commissioners conceded that affidavits might be useful where new facts were alleged in a reply, but only where the witness was available for oral examination and cross-examination before a judge or master. They went so far as to recommend that the court be able to compel a person to provide such evidence, subject to cross-examination, before a master where a party required it and the person refused to provide it in an affidavit.[205]

The lack of juries in Chancery was also problematic because parties had to spend time turning to common law to access them. Instead of recommending juries in Chancery, the commissioners proposed to allow questions of fact that were sent to common law for determination by a jury to be handled by Chancery 'by means of an issue'.[206] There were also situations in which Chancery could not act until a plaintiff established his right in law, and so the Chancery commissioners proposed to abolish the practice and allow Chancery judges to determine the relevant questions of law.[207]

Finally, the Chancery commissioners complained about the masters' offices. They regarded the procedures associated with the office as 'obviously calculated to cause unnecessary delay and expense'.[208] For example, masters, not judges, obtained oral evidence and heard cross-examinations.[209] They believed the only solution was abolition. The commissioners proposed to have the Master of the Rolls and the vice-chancellors handle many of the masters' duties in chambers, particularly those related to pleadings or parties under a disability, while they maintained their regular business in open court. Clerks could take over the masters' other responsibilities.[210]

Legislative responses

If the goal was complete justice for litigants, then the Court of Chancery Procedure Act of 1852 and the Common Law Procedure Acts of 1852 and

[204] *Ibid.*

[205] *Ibid.*, 32–3. They recommended that the common law courts should adopt Chancery's procedure for affidavits; that is, drafted in the first person with numbered paragraphs each confined to a distinct subject.

[206] United Kingdom, Chancery Commissioners, *First Report of Her Majesty's Commissioners Appointed to Inquire into the Process, Practice, and System of Pleading in the Court of Chancery, &c.*, 24, 42

[207] *Ibid.*, 42. [208] *Ibid.*, 30. [209] *Ibid.*, 21. [210] *Ibid.*, 26–36, 42–3.

1854 did much to accomplish it. The former implemented many of the commissioners' recommendations with respect to pre-trial discovery and document production, giving equity judges greater powers to intervene in the cases before them, and expanding the availability of documentary discovery for both plaintiffs and defendants. It allowed any plaintiff – whether in law or equity – to seek an order to permit discovery of documents from the defendant prior to the close of pleadings, and it gave the court broad discretion to deal with those documents. Defendants obtained reciprocal access to the plaintiff's documents.[211] The Common Law Procedure Act of 1854 gave common law judges full powers to order documentary discovery.[212]

Parliament also adopted a number of the Chancery commissioners' recommendations involving witnesses and the collection of evidence. The Chancery Procedure Act increased the importance of oral evidence in Chancery and introduced greater choice for parties. As the commissioners had proposed, the Act allowed parties to choose between presenting their evidence orally or in writing, while permitting the continued use of affidavits to adduce evidence from certain witnesses or to present particular facts by consent or with court approval.[213]

Underscoring the importance of being able to test evidence orally, the Act allowed parties to cross-examine and re-examine affiants. Examiners remained in use, but the evidence they took was now subject to cross-examination. Parties were empowered to obtain subpoenas requiring any witness to appear for examination, and the Act gave the court authority to order oral examination of any witness, including parties, at the hearing. The Act recognised the potential for abuse and allowed judges to curtail examinations of witnesses 'without a sufficient interest in the matter in question'.[214] It introduced greater transparency to the collection of evidence by allowing parties and their counsel to attend the examination, cross-examination or re-examination of witnesses before an examiner.[215] Where a witness provided evidence before trial with the expectation that he would be abroad and thus unable to attend, the Act

[211] Court of Chancery Procedure Act 1852, ss. 18, 20.

[212] Common Law Procedure Act 1854, s. 50.

[213] Court of Chancery Procedure Act 1852, ss. 29–31, 36. [214] *Ibid.*, s. 30.

[215] Parliament changed the relationship between examiners, parties and the court: Court of Chancery Examiners Act 1853. After that Act, examiners worked for the court, not the party who hired them.

required examinations, cross-examinations and re-examinations to follow the same procedures as at common law.[216]

The Common Law Procedure Acts of 1852 and 1854 did even more to reform trial practice. The 1852 Act changed the jury process at common law[217] and permitted parties to tender documents directly to the court.[218] Common law judges secured the power to try questions of fact without the need for a jury two years later.[219]

The handling of witnesses changed, too. The Evidence Act of 1851 had already rendered parties competent and compellable as witnesses,[220] but the Common Law Procedure Act of 1854 expanded the powers available to counsel to impeach adverse witnesses.[221] In addition to giving judges the authority to require the oral examination of a witness before a judge or a master, the Act gave common law judges power to order discovery of documents, along with the delivery of written interrogatories on any matter that could be subjected to discovery and oral examination to clarify the responses contained therein.[222] Previously, the Evidence Act had provided only that opposing parties in common law actions were entitled to inspect or take copies of relevant documents as parties to suits in equity.[223]

Finally, a key reform to equitable trial practice involved the masters. Parliament agreed with the Chancery commissioners on the need to abolish the masters, and the Court of Chancery Act abolished them through attrition in 1852, with judges and clerks empowered to take over from the masters henceforth. The Act authorised judges to retain third parties to assist with issues like conveyancing and accounts and directed the Master of the Rolls and Vice Chancellors to deal with new business in chambers while maintaining their ordinary business in open court. To help the remaining masters complete their outstanding matters, the Act increased their powers.[224] Parliament expanded their powers again in 1854, though their duties were not fully discharged until the summer of 1860.[225]

216 Court of Chancery Procedure Act 1852, ss. 30–1, 38–40.

217 Common Law Procedure Act 1852, ss. 105–16.

218 *Ibid.*, ss. 117–19.

219 Common Law Procedure Act 1854, ss. 1, 4.

220 Evidence Act 1851, 14 & 15 Vict. c. 99, s. 2.

221 Common Law Procedure Act 1854, ss. 22–4.

222 *Ibid.*, ss. 46–7, 50–3, 56–9.

223 Evidence Act 1851, s. 6.

224 The Act left vacancies unfilled, gave the Lord Chancellor authority to release individual masters upon completion of their work, and provided for lifelong pensions upon retirement. On these and other relevant matters, see Court of Chancery Act 1852, 15 & 16, Vict. c. 80, ss. 1–2, 4–10, 14, 16–18, 21–7, 29–34, 36–7, 39, 41–3.

225 Court of Chancery Act 1854; Court of Chancery Act 1860, 23 & 24 Vict. c. 149.

Equitable remedies

Typically, parties sought compensation in damages when they brought an action. Yet money could not compensate for all harms, and over the course of the 1850s, most efforts to reconcile the different approaches to remedies at law and in equity occurred at common law. Although Chancery acquired some common law remedies, common law judges more actively sought the power to award equitable remedies in the name of providing complete justice. Perhaps because members of the Law Amendment Society were more focused on the need to make changes in Chancery than in common law, they made few recommendations with respect to remedies aside from injunctions. Instead, the common law commissioners made a number of recommendations that Parliament implemented.

The Field Code

The power to award remedies was limited before the Field Code: Chancery offered equitable remedies for claims pertaining to trusts, mortgages, corporations, divorce and guardianship matters, and the common law was restricted to providing remedies like damages for disputes in contract, tort and property.[226] Unification of the New York State courts in 1848 changed this because the code empowered a court to grant 'any relief consistent with the case made by the complaint'.[227] Under the code, judges could provide a range of remedies, even those not requested specifically by a plaintiff. Although it did not set out the relationship between specific claims and remedies, it included detailed procedures to secure injunctions and enter judgment.[228]

Law Amendment Society

The Law Amendment Society said little about the need to improve access to equitable remedies apart from injunctions and specific performance. Neither the model code nor the ten-point legislative plan that emerged from the special committee dealt with the subject.

226 Moulton, *The Chancery Practice of the State of New York; Graham, A Treatise on the Practice of the Supreme Court of New York*, vols I and II; Monnell, *A Treatise on the Practice of the Courts of the State of New York*; Whittaker, *Practice and Pleading under the Code, Original and Amended, With Appendix of Forms*, 2nd ed.

227 1848 Field Code, § 231; 1849 Amended Code, § 275; 1850 Proposed Code, § 751.

228 1848 Field Code, §§ 191–9, 230–7; 1849 Amended Code, §§ 218–26, 274–82; 1850 Proposed Code, §§ 714–22, 813–25. See, also, Monnell, *A Treatise on the Practice of the Courts of the State of New York*, 81.

Royal commissions and their recommendations

Having recommended that common law judges have the authority to order full discovery in addition to the inspection of documents, the Chancery commissioners urged that they also have power to issue common injunctions to ensure the proper administration of discovery.[229] Acknowledging that there was no reason to deny judges the ability to issue injunctions to stay legal proceedings on the merits if they could issue special injunctions to help enforce pre-trial discovery,[230] the Chancery commissioners recommended that injunctions on the merits be subject to the same procedure as governed special injunctions. Their concern was for the plaintiff who succeeded at law but faced a finding that the original action was improper when he turned to equity for enforcement.[231]

Acknowledging the possibility of fusion, the second report of the common law commissioners discussed the need to make equitable remedies available at common law. Apart from whether fusion would make Chancery more efficient, the commissioners argued that the common law courts needed to be able to grant equitable remedies 'to give all the redress necessary to protect and vindicate common law rights and to prevent wrongs, whether existing or likely to happen unless prevented'.[232] Chancery had sole responsibility for remedies in certain areas, but there were other areas in which the court 'either furnish[ed] a supplementary or more complete remedy in respect of common law rights, or actually restrain[ed] the exercise of such rights on what are termed equitable grounds'.[233] For this class, the commissioners wanted common law judges to have the power to provide a complete remedy. They believed that a party should be able to insist on the specific performance of acts giving rise to obligations between parties where it was possible to perform the activity and where money could not perfectly compensate for non-performance.[234] They wanted common law judges to be able to prevent injury, especially where monetary damages would not provide 'full and perfect redress',[235] recommending that they have

[229] United Kingdom, Chancery Commissioners, *First Report of Her Majesty's Commissioners Appointed to Inquire into the Process, Practice, and System of Pleading in the Court of Chancery, &c.*, 23, 40.

[230] *Ibid.*, 24, 40. [231] *Ibid.*, 23–4.

[232] United Kingdom, Common Law Commissioners, *Second Report of Her Majesty's Commissioners for Inquiring into the Process, Practice, and System of Pleading in the Superior Courts of Common Law*, 38.

[233] *Ibid.*, 39. [234] *Ibid.*, 39–40. [235] *Ibid.*, 40

the power to order specific performance and injunctive relief in their own right.[236]

Legislative change

Parliament had begun to reconcile practice and procedure for injunctions before the common law commissioners even discussed it. In the summer of 1852, the Court of Chancery Procedure Act modified the manner in which Chancery granted injunctions to stay proceedings at law, assimilating the practice with the procedure for special injunctions in equity,[237] while the Common Law Procedure Act gave common law judges authority to award injunctions in limited circumstances.[238] At the same time, masters at common law were given the power to calculate damages instead of requiring use of a jury via a writ of enquiry.[239] When Parliament amended the Common Law Procedure Act in 1854, it gave common law judges more authority to award injunctions and specific performance and allowed common law parties to plead equitable defences (including equitable replication), making them available after judgment.[240] The Act also gave common law judges the power to order writs of mandamus and impose the same limitations of liability for ship owners already available in Chancery.[241]

Reform to remedies came more slowly to Chancery, where judges could not award monetary damages until 1858. At that time, Parliament allowed Chancery judges to assess damages and make the necessary findings of fact with or without a jury in Chancery, which replaced the need for a party to adjourn the proceedings to seek the opinion of a jury at common law.[242] Parliament also continued to expand the availability of remedies in common law proceedings. By 1860, the legislature gave the common law courts the authority to award relief against forfeiture following the same practice as in Chancery, and of interpleader,[243] as well as the power to deal with liens, debts and other payments,[244] along with the costs associated with writs of mandamus and injunctions, and the procedures for enforcing injunctions against corporations.[245] It was not until the Chancery Regulation Act in 1862

[236] *Ibid.* [237] Court of Chancery Procedure Act 1852, s. 58.

[238] Common Law Procedure Act 1852, s. 226. [239] *Ibid.*, s. 94.

[240] Common Law Procedure Act 1854, ss. 82–5. [241] *Ibid.*, ss. 68, 70, 71, 88.

[242] Chancery Amendment Act 1858, ss. 2–3, 5–7.

[243] Common Law Procedure Act 1860, ss. 2, 12.

[244] Like bonds and writ of right of dower: *ibid.*, ss. 25, 26, 28, 29.

[245] Common Law Procedure Act 1860, ss. 32–3.

that Chancery finally acquired full powers to deal with all legal and factual determinations needed to award equitable remedies.[246] (Previously, many of these cases still had to be referred to common law courts for factual determinations before the award of equitable remedies.) That Act also gave judges in Chancery the same powers as their common law counterparts to deal with property remedies.[247]

Conclusion

In this chapter, I have outlined how David Dudley Field inspired English law reformers to enact core components of procedural fusion in the 1850s even though fusion did not occur formally until 1875. The experience of New York State proved to English reformers that fusion could work, and the Field Code provided a blueprint for implementing it. Field, along with his code, influenced reformers, particularly members of the Law Amendment Society, who worked actively to eliminate the procedural distinctions between law and equity in England. Accepting that substance was more important than form, reformers came to realise that they could implement components of fusion even without wholesale reform.

Over the course of a decade, following recommendations from members of the Law Amendment Society and two royal commissions, Parliament enacted a series of statutes that introduced many of the reforms associated with fusion in New York State. They abolished forms of action and simplified proceedings at common law. They streamlined the process to join parties and issues. They brought pre-trial discovery, previously the domain of Chancery, directly to the common law courts. They introduced oral evidence and cross-examination to Chancery as a check on written evidence, beginning to limit the use of affidavit evidence in the process. They abolished the masters' offices in Chancery, requiring judges to take a more direct role in proceedings. They also made it easier for judges in Chancery to make their own findings of fact without recourse to a jury at common law. Finally, Parliament made sure that the common law courts acquired the power to award many of the equitable remedies that allowed parties to obtain full justice. Although there was no single superior court or unified code of procedure, the changes blended the jurisdiction of law and equity in

[246] Chancery Regulation Act 1862, 25 & 26 Vict. c. 42, s. 1. [247] *Ibid.*, s. 4.

a way that reflected the approach to judicial proceedings of David Dudley Field and his code. By the time the Judicature Acts came into force in the 1870s, the debate about the merits of procedural fusion was long over. However, the discussion surrounding the wisdom of substantive fusion had just begun and, as Michael Lobban writes in his comment on this chapter, remains alive today.

23

Field, fusion and the 1850s

A commentary

MICHAEL LOBBAN

In Chapter 22, Patricia McMahon convincingly argues that David Dudley Field's visit to London in the autumn of 1850 put the question of fusion on the political map in England. His code of procedure for New York seemed to offer the English a road map for the fusion of law and equity which the members of the Law Amendment Society were only too eager to take up.[1] As she describes, the society appointed a special committee to look into the question, which soon reported in favour of both a code on Field's lines and a single tribunal which would administer both law and equity.[2] Their restless activity convinced many senior figures of the desirability of fusion. In the summer of 1851, *The Morning Chronicle* – which regarded fusion as 'a safe, practicable, and most salutary plan' – commented that 'the House [of Commons] was thoroughly inoculated with the opinions which the Law Amendment Society have recently disseminated on the subject'.[3] In July, Alexander Cockburn, the Attorney General, described the Evidence Bill as the thin end of a wedge, which he hoped would end in the 'fusion of law and equity'.[4] In the following year, he argued in favour of appointing 'a mixed Commission of the Common Law and Equity members of the profession – for the purpose of inquiring into the propriety of amalgamating

[1] Having met Field, the secretary of the Law Amendment Society, James Stewart, wrote to Lord Brougham in September 1850, 'Looking to the unsettled state of our own Procedure and that we have here a Code ready made and proved workable, is it not worth considering whether we are not ripe for the changes here?' Brougham manuscripts, University College London, MS 12683 (emphasis original).

[2] (1851) 17 L.T. 119 (28 June 1851). The special committee which drafted a code also proposed creating a single tribunal, divided into seven sections, composing twenty-eight judges.

[3] *The Morning Chronicle*, 12, 19 July 1851.

[4] United Kingdom, H.C. Deb., 16 July 1851, vol. 118, col. 847.

the two systems, and effecting a general codification of our laws'.[5] The enthusiasm provoked by the Law Amendment Society's promotion of Field's ideas seemed to many to be projecting England to an inevitable fusion.

At the same time, however, many eminent lawyers remained highly sceptical about calls for a united judicature. Most prominent among these was Lord St Leonards, one of the most eminent Chancery lawyers of the age. Newly appointed as Lord Chancellor, he fully endorsed the proposition that any court hearing a case should have the full power to give all the relief that the case demanded – but he was far less convinced by the broader concept of a fusion of the two systems. '[W]hat was popularly called the fusion of law and equity', he declared, 'could never be accomplished.'[6] Lord Campbell also felt that giving every judge a 'universal jurisdiction over all causes ... could only lead to confusion and mischief'.[7] Nor was such scepticism confined to these grandees. The Chancery Commissioners were also cautious when it came to the question of fusion. Instead of seeking to unite 'the Courts into one Court of universal jurisdiction', they argued that 'a practical and effectual remedy for many of the evils in question may be found in such a transfer or blending of jurisdiction ... as will render each Court competent to administer complete justice in the cases which fall under its cognizance'. They were not convinced that fusion could be effected by procedural changes alone, but noted that '[t]he abolition of this distinction [between law and equity], if advisable, could not be effected as an isolated measure, but must be accompanied by a revision of the whole body of our Laws'.[8] Its members included Richard Bethell, later nicknamed the 'Galileo of fusion', who had himself told the November 1850 meeting of the Law Amendment Society that the aim of the project was not to abolish the Court of Chancery, but to extend 'such jurisdiction as it exercised to every court', so that the equitable rights of parties would prevail in every case.[9]

[5] United Kingdom, H.C. Deb., 3 June 1852, vol. 121, col. 1430.

[6] United Kingdom, H.C. Deb., 14 February 1853, vol. 124, col. 68.

[7] United Kingdom, H.C. Deb., 14 February 1853, vol. 124, col. 74.

[8] United Kingdom. Chancery Commission, *First Report of Her Majesty's Commissioners Appointed to Inquire into the Process, Practice, and System of Pleading in the Court of Chancery, &c.* (London: H.M.S.O., 1852), 2.

[9] *The Standard*, 19 November 1850. Bethell later claimed to have been among the first to raise the issue of fusion when the Law Amendment Society was first set up but was mocked by elements of the legal press for his failure to put it into effect: 'Proceedings of Law Societies. Juridical Society' (1858) 32 L.T. 140, 141.

If it is clear that the movement which led to the union of the judicatures in 1875 was effectively kicked off by Field's visit of 1850, it is much less evident that the 'fusion' which was ultimately achieved was the kind of fusion that Field and his English friends had envisaged. For many in the 1850s and 1860s, the notion that each court should have the power to deal fully with all the cases before it was very different from the notion of a fusion of law and equity. There was widespread criticism of a system which required parties in the same litigation to go from one court to another in order to make use of the other court's procedures and remedies. But this did not mean that they thought that the courts of equity should deal with ordinary common law cases or that the common lawyers should handle the core jurisdiction of the Chancery, such as trusts. Where the common law courts needed the *auxiliary* assistance of the Court of Chancery, it seemed to make sense to confer the Chancery's powers on the common law courts to avoid the problem of parties' having to go from one court to another. But it only seemed to make sense to give these courts such powers for the protection of legal, as opposed to equitable rights.

As Dr McMahon has demonstrated, Field's code of procedure for New York's newly created court of general jurisdiction was strikingly different from the system which the English sought to reform. At its heart stood the abolition of the forms of action and their replacement by a simple form of procedure, allowing any claim to be brought before the court in plain language. Under the new code, claimants would only need to state 'facts constituting the cause of action', leaving it to the court to apply the correct law. Since fictitious pleadings would be abolished, parties were expected to swear to the truth of their allegations. With its accompanying new rules on the joinder of parties and issues and the new rules on discovery and party evidence, the Field Code seemed to herald the triumph of an equitable mode of procedure. For under this code, judges would have access in all cases to the kind of information which equity courts had long used to probe the parties' consciences, and they would be given the power to direct the conscience, through the award of equitable remedies such as specific performance.

Field himself had argued that the abolition of the forms of action would undermine the distinction between common law and equity and would thereby effect a fusion.[10] If this implied that the new system would

[10] D.D. Field, *Speeches, Arguments and Miscellaneous Papers* (New York: Appleton & Co., 1884), vol. 1, 234. Cf. at 240: 'The distinction between the two classes of cases is now

encourage a more 'equitable' approach to the settlement of cases, with judges free to settle them in a flexible manner as their consciences dictated,[11] it was not the vision which the English common law commissioners had in mind when they proposed the abolition of the forms of action in 1852. They did not see their reforms as heralding the triumph of an equitable approach. Indeed, they were more concerned with addressing the practical problems caused by the existing rules respecting the forms of action than in opening the way to a wider reform; and they had no intention of freeing the common law from its established doctrinal bearings. In their report, the commissioners made a clear distinction between the ancient *forms* of action (which could be dispensed with) and the underlying *causes* of action (which could not). They dismissed the argument that the forms of action kept distinct causes of action apart by pointing out that under the current system 'causes the most dissimilar' could be joined. They felt that little use was served by forms of action: the idea that one should test whether a cause of action existed by seeing whether it fitted a form of action was, in their view, unscientific.[12] The commissioners did not envisage abandoning the classification of different kinds of cause of action, but they argued that the 'difference will be, that the classification will be the natural result of the similarity of the facts, instead of being artificial and technical'.[13] In their Report (Appendix C), they set out specimen forms of pleadings, setting out the familiar categories of contracts and wrongs independent of contract.[14] Schedule B of the 1852 Common Law Procedure Act also gave forms of pleadings, setting out statements of causes of action in contractual and

merely a distinction in the forms of proceeding. The Court of Chancery has existed only in consequence of the narrow and fixed forms of the common law. If those forms had been abolished, and a natural procedure adopted, the court of the two Courts would long ago have been assimilated.'

11 Whether this was how Field himself saw it may be questioned: see S.N. Subrin, 'David Dudley Field and the Field Code: A Historical Analysis of an Earlier Procedural Vision' (1988) 6 Law & Hist. Rev. 311.

12 '[A]s the question, whether there is a cause of action or not, must depend upon the facts and not upon the form adopted, the decision of a cause on the merits is not helped by means of these forms of action': United Kingdom. Chancery Commissioners, *First Report from the Commissioners for Inquiring into the Process, Practice, and System of Pleading in the Superior Courts of Common Law* (London: Eyre and Spottiswoode, 1851), 32–3.

13 United Kingdom. Chancery Commissioners, *First Report from the Commissioners for Inquiring into the Process, Practice, and System of Pleading in the Superior Courts of Common Law*, 34.

14 They dealt separately with ejectment, proposing a new form of writ shorn of fictions for such cases.

tort actions. This arrangement led Bullen and Leake to comment in the first edition of their manual on pleading after the reforms that '[t]he effect of the recent alterations in pleading has not been to destroy the system or to change its essential principles'.[15] It merely preferred substance to form. The old categories lived on in the Rules of the Supreme Court introduced under the Judicature Act of 1875. Little wonder that Maitland could observe that the forms of action ruled us from their graves.[16] Indeed, so set were the common law categories that many early twentieth-century common lawyers, a generation after fusion, saw no space for a distinct concept of unjust enrichment, which was neither contractual nor tortious.

If Field's Code seemed to make the common law's procedures more like equity's, it conversely proposed modifications in equity's procedure which would make it look more like the common law's. It preferred the common law model of oral testimony evaluated by a jury to the equitable one of extensive written documentation gathered outside the courtroom. It was also structured around the adversarialism of the common law trial, rather than the inquisitorial procedure which was to be found in equity. Where common lawyers tended to find the procedural changes suggested by reformers of the 1850s to their tastes, as removing unnecessary technical forms without sacrificing substance, Chancery lawyers were much more worried by the potentially disruptive effect of the proposed procedural reforms on the culture of their court. Where the common lawyers manifested relatively little concern that their settled system would be undermined by an alien culture of discretionary equity, the Chancery lawyers were profoundly worried by the prospect that equitable matters would be dealt with by common lawyers, untrained in their doctrine and lacking the machinery needed to apply it.

Chancery men like St Leonards consistently argued that to allow common lawyers to handle the core matter of equity jurisdiction could only result in 'irremediable confusion'.[17] They therefore strove to ensure that the common lawyers would not be able to encroach. Where a power was purely 'auxiliary', it was regarded as safe enough to confer; but where

[15] E. Bullen and S.M. Leake, *Precedents of Pleadings in Actions in the Superior Courts of Common Law* (London: V. & R. Stevens & Sons, 1860), iv.

[16] F.W. Maitland, *The Forms of Action at Common Law*, in A.H. Chaytor and W.J. Whittaker (eds.) (Cambridge University Press, 1909), 1.

[17] United Kingdom, H.C. Deb., 23 May 1854, vol. 133, cols. 787ff. He again argued that if parliament wanted to give a single court full jurisdiction, it would first have to develop appropriate machinery and a single set of substantive rules.

a power might be used to tread on equity's territory, less was given. These concerns were clearly manifested in the 1854 Common Law Procedure Act. On the one hand, it gave a wide power to compel the discovery and production of documents, an auxiliary power which was extensively used by the common law courts in the 1850s and 1860s. On the other hand, the power to award specific performance was hedged. While the Act gave the common law courts power to issue a mandamus for the performance of any duty, and the power to order specific delivery of chattels, they were not given the power to order specific performance of sales of land, since they lacked the machinery to investigate the title of the vendor.[18] The power to grant injunctions was also limited: under the Act, a writ of injunction could only be used 'where the Party injured is entitled to maintain and has brought an action'.[19] An injunction could not be sought to restrain a *threatened* violation of a right.

The Act also hedged perhaps the most significant potential route to fusion, the power given to common law defendants to plead equitable defences. This proposal – which had formed one of the Law Amendment Society's initial suggestions[20] – was taken up by the common law commissioners in their second report, where they noted that rules of law and equity often conflicted, not because of any defect in procedure, but from 'a defective state of the substantive law itself'. While this ultimately needed legislative correction,[21] they felt that the inconvenience of having litigants use two courts – where one would uphold and the other deny the plaintiff's claim – could be overcome by allowing equitable pleas in common law courts. Two things were proposed: first, that defendants at common law should be able to plead equitable defences 'in every case in which the party pleading them would be entitled to unconditional relief by injunction'; and secondly, 'that in cases where such relief in courts of equity would be conditional or discretionary the courts of law should have power to give, in a summary way, the same relief against actions pending therein as might be obtained by resorting to a court of equity'. In the event, only the first of these was enacted in the Common Law Procedure Act of 1854 (s. 83), and it proved constraining. While the

[18] Common Law Procedure Act 1854, 17 & 18 Vict. c. 125, ss. 68–78; United Kingdom, H.C. Deb., 24 March 1854, vol. 131, cols. 1258–9.

[19] Common Law Procedure Act 1854, s. 79.

[20] 'Fusion of Law and Equity' (1852) 16 Law Mag. 84.

[21] United Kingdom, Common Law Commissioners, *Second Report of Her Majesty's Commissioners for Inquiring into the Process, Practice, and System of Pleading in the Superior Courts of Common Law* (London: H.M.S.O., 1853), 45.

common law courts were able to provide complete justice by entertaining equitable pleas in cases where it was self-evident what the Chancery would do,[22] in cases where the issue was more complex, courts of common law were reluctant to interfere[23] and so parties continued to have to go to the Chancery for redress.

In practice, the cautious nature of the 1854 Act meant that even the ambition of the reformers to allow a single court to deal with the complete case was undermined. Because of this, attempts were made in 1860 to amend the legislation, in order to give the common law courts power to issue injunctions to restrain threatened harms and to decide on equitable defences where the Chancery would only give conditional relief.[24] However, the proposal once again met with hostility from those Chancery lawyers who feared that this was a Trojan horse which might give common lawyers a power to hear matters within the exclusive competence of equity men. As the *Solicitor's Journal* put it, '[i]f this Bill passes, an equitable claim may be set up in an action or feigned issue; and a common law judge may make an order calling upon persons to appear and state the nature and particulars of their claims, and may, upon their appearance, adjudicate upon such claims as are of an equitable nature'.[25] Behind their objections were the continued arguments that the common lawyers lacked the necessary knowledge to deal with matters of pure equity and that their courts lacked the requisite machinery.

A decade after Field's visit and the Law Amendment Society's high-profile campaign, the promised fusion seemed to be fizzling out. The *Solicitor's Journal* pointed out that after the 1854 Common Law Procedure Act had passed, common lawyers had spent much time reading up on specific performance and injunctions, but before long, 'the

[22] For instance, in *Luce* v. *Izod* (1856) 1 H. & N. 245; 156 E.R. 1194, the court allowed the defendant to plead that a deed had inaccurately described the geographical area in which he had covenanted not to practise, and held that the issue should be decided by the judge alone, and not by a jury.

[23] For instance, when in *Hunter* v. *Gibbons* (1856) 1 H. & N. 459; 156 E.R. 1281, the plaintiff sued his adversary in trespass for digging his coal and attempted to make an equitable replication to the defendant's plea of the Statute of Limitations that he had concealed his activity until within the limitation period, the court refused the plea. This was not, the court held, an appropriate issue for a jury to determine; and the plaintiff's remedy was to go to Chancery for an account, in which the money due would be calculated on a different (and less generous) basis from what would be received in trespass.

[24] United Kingdom, Common Law Commissioners, *Third Report of the Commissioners Appointed to Inquire into the Process, Practice and System of Pleading in the Superior Courts of Common Law* (London: H.M.S.O., 1860), 12.

[25] 'The Law and Equity Bill' (1860) 4 Sol. Jo. 300, 300.

equitable jurisdiction of the [Act] became nearly a dead letter; and common lawyers, as a class, have long since relinquished their study of equity'.[26] The Chancery men's defence of their territory seemed successful. Nor were they keen to assume the powers of a common law court. Although they were given the power to use juries in 1858, it took over fifteen months before the first one was called. Where they did acquire new powers, the Chancery men developed them in new, specifically equitable directions. This can be seen from the power they acquired in 1858 to award damages. Like the common law reforms, this reform did not envisage the court encroaching on core common law business; for damages could only be awarded where the court had 'jurisdiction to entertain an application for an injunction' or for specific performance. Rather than seeking to 'fuse' the courts, it was only designed to allow the court to give the party damages to avoid the inconvenience of having to go to the common law courts. However, the Chancery judges developed a new kind of remedy, exclusive to equity, from this legislation. Since the Act allowed the court to award damages 'in substitution for' the equitable relief sought (as well as 'in addition to it'), it was soon apparent that judges could use it to grant damages in equity in situations where it would not be available at common law.[27] Rather than uniting legal doctrine on one common foundation, widening the powers of each court opened the way for distinct notions of 'equitable damages', on principles different from those of common law damages. While Sir Hugh Cairns's Act was itself repealed in 1883, the new powers that it gave remained in place.[28]

On the eve of the fusion of judicatures, then, common lawyers and equity practitioners showed little sign of wanting a *substantive* fusion of the sort envisaged in 1850. They were happy enough to have a simplified and uniform procedure which would allow all cases to start with a common form in the same court. The Chancery's bill and answer procedure was consigned to history, along with the forms of action. However, there was no fusion of substantive law. The Judicature Acts after all retained distinct divisions of the court. Section 34(3) of the Judicature Act 1873 confirmed that the Chancery Division would deal with the traditional exclusive subject matter of the Court of Chancery,

[26] *Ibid.*, 301.

[27] See *Eastwood* v. *Lever* (1863) 4 De G. J. & S. 114; 46 E.R. 859; see further J.A. Jolowicz, 'Damages in Equity – A Study of Lord Cairns' Act' [1975] C.L.J. 224.

[28] See *Sayers* v. *Collier* (1884) 28 Ch. D. 103, 107–8; *Leeds Industrial Co-operative Society Ltd* v. *Slack* [1924] A.C. 851, 861–3. See now Senior Courts Act 1981 (UK), s. 50.

including trusts, specific performance of contracts relating to land and the rectification of contracts. Moreover, the Chancery Division retained a distinct machinery, with the Chief Clerks who had replaced the Chancery Masters in 1852 continuing to handle much of the work in Chambers.[29] As the Esher committee of 1874 put it, '[t]he changes ordered by the Judicature Act of 1873 . . . are very slight. Existing officers are to be transferred with existing titles, rights, and obligations, to the High Court of Justice.'[30] Efforts were made to 'mingle the waters', by putting common law men on the Chancery side, and vice versa, as way of encouraging a convergence of doctrine.[31] However, far from being settled in 1875, the question of whether the reforms aimed to effect a fusion of law and equity remains a topic of lively debate to this day.

[29] See P. Polden, 'The Chancery Division', in W. Cornish, S. Anderson, R. Cocks, M. Lobban, P. Polden and K. Smith (eds.), *Oxford History of the Laws of England. Volume XI 1820–1914 English Legal System* (Oxford University Press, 2010), 839–40.

[30] Second Report of the Commissioners Appointed to Inquire into the Administrative Departments of the Courts of Justice, *HCPP* 1874 (C. 1107), XXIV.583, 596.

[31] See P. Polden, 'Mingling the Waters: Personalities, Politics and the Making of the Supreme Court of Judicature' [2002] C.L.J. 575.

24

Equitable protection of legal professional privilege

A distraction

ADRIAN ZUCKERMAN

Introduction

For a century judges and scholars have been grappling with the tension created by a pair of cases: *Calcraft* v. *Guest*,[1] which concerned admissibility at common law, and *Ashburton* v. *Pape*,[2] which concerned the protection of confidentiality in equity. In both cases, documents to which legal professional privilege attached fell into the hands of an opponent who wished to adduce them in evidence at trial. In *Calcraft*, the Court of Appeal decided that copies of privileged documents were admissible no matter how they were obtained. In *Ashburton*, the Court of Appeal held that a person whose privileged documents fell into the hands of another may obtain an injunction ordering the return of the documents and prohibiting the use of information derived from such documents for any purpose.

Much effort has been devoted to finding ways of resolving the tension between these apparently inconsistent positions. Yet, such efforts have done little to provide a coherent solution to the problem. Far from finding a clear solution to the tension, the solution has become to an extent fact-based, with the result that whether the use of otherwise privileged material would be allowed may involve considerable argument. This chapter argues that the use of the equitable jurisdiction in the present context is largely a distraction because it diverts attention from the real issue. The real issue concerns the nature of the protection that should be accorded to communications with lawyers for the purpose of obtaining legal advice and to materials prepared for litigation. It is by

[1] [1898] 1 Q.B. 759. [2] [1913] 2 Ch. 469.

now accepted that the purpose of advice and litigation privilege is to create a secure space within which persons may obtain legal advice and prepare for litigation free of fear that their communications within the secure space may later be used against them. This being so, it must follow that advice privilege and litigation privilege are not protected only by immunity from compulsory disclosure and by discretionary protection of confidentiality. These privileges are also protected by a rule of inadmissibility, which renders communications made for the purpose of obtaining legal advice or in preparation for legal proceedings inadmissible as evidence against the person for whose benefit the privilege exists. Simply put, legal privilege is also supported by a rule of inadmissibility. The inadmissibility of privileged communications makes good the guarantee that the privilege is meant to give: that clients may confide in lawyers free of the risk that what they say to their lawyers may be later used to their detriment, and that parties may prepare for litigation free of fear that their preparations may be used to undermine their case.

The Calcraft *and* Ashburton *decisions*

In *Calcraft*, the issue was whether a party may adduce in evidence a copy of an original document which was privileged. The Court of Appeal's answer was a clear 'Yes'. In support of this conclusion Lindley M.R. referred to Parke B.'s judgment in *Lloyd* v. *Mostyn*[3] where the latter said, in the course of argument, that a copy of an original would be admissible even where the copy was obtained by the theft of the original.

Admissibility of evidence at law is governed by one overarching principle: relevance. Evidence is admissible at trial if it is relevant to an issue that requires court adjudication. Relevance is not a legal concept. Rather, it is a notion of rational reasoning denoting the contribution that knowledge of one fact can make to the possibility of inferring the existence of another fact. Accordingly, an item of evidence is relevant to a fact in issue if it makes it more probable that the fact existed (or did not exist, as the case may be).[4] Parke B.'s remarks in *Lloyd* v. *Mostyn* were addressed to admissibility and nothing else. He is reported to have said that where 'an attorney intrusted confidentially with a document communicates the contents of it, or suffers another to take a copy, surely the

[3] (1842) 10 M. & W. 478; 152 E.R. 558.

[4] The US Federal Rules of Evidence, r. 401 states that 'evidence is relevant if: (a) it has any tendency to make a fact more or less probable than it would be without the evidence . . .'

secondary evidence so obtained may be produced. Suppose the instrument were even stolen, and a correct copy taken, would it not be reasonable to admit it?' Lord Abinger C.B. seemed to agree. The court in *Lloyd* v. *Mostyn* was not concerned with how confidentiality may be protected. Nor was the court concerned with the protection of confidentiality in *Calcraft*, where the Court of Appeal endorsed Parke B.'s view on the admissibility of copies of privileged documents.

In *Ashburton* v. *Pape*, the Court of Appeal was at pains to stress that it was not disputing the correctness of *Lloyd* v. *Mostyn* and of *Calcraft* but that these decisions were in no way concerned with the exercise of jurisdiction to protect confidentiality, which was the business of equity. Lord Ashburton resisted the discharge from bankruptcy of the defendant Pape. Pape obtained from Ashburton's solicitors privileged documents. On request by Ashburton, Pape returned them to him, but not before he made copies which he sought to adduce in evidence in the bankruptcy proceedings. Ashburton brought an action for an injunction restraining Pape from using information derived from the privileged documents for any purpose and ordering him to return all copies. The Court of Appeal accepted the authority of *Calcraft*, but Cozens-Hardy M.R. distinguished it because it concerned admissibility while Ashburton was seeking an injunction to restrain the use of a confidential document. Kennedy L.J. spelt out the difference between the *Calcraft* situation and the one under consideration in *Ashburton*:

> [A]lthough it is true that the principle which is laid down in *Calcraft* v. *Guest* must be followed, yet, at the same time, if, before the occasion of the trial when a copy may be used, although a copy improperly obtained, the owner of the original can successfully promote proceedings against the person who has improperly obtained the copy to stop his using it, the owner is none the less entitled to protection . . .[5]

Swinfen Eady L.J. said to the same effect:

> The fact . . . that a document, whether original or copy, is admissible in evidence is no answer to the demand of the lawful owner for the delivery up of the document, and no answer to an application by the lawful owner of confidential information to restrain it from being published or copied.[6]

There are two difficulties about this way of dealing with the tension between common law rule of admissibility and the equitable protection of confidentiality. The first is practical. The need for equitable

[5] [1913] 2 Ch. 469, 474. [6] *Ibid.*, 477.

intervention would require the party objecting to the use of confidential material in legal proceedings to commence proceedings in Chancery for an injunction. For a long time this meant that the protection of confidentiality would be a matter of chance; if the party discovered the escape of the confidential document and was quick enough to seek an injunction, confidentiality could be protected. But if the party was confronted with the documents only when they were adduced in evidence, it is too late for equity. Further, the need to commence fresh proceedings in Chancery, rather than simply to object at the trial to the use of confidential documents, would generate unnecessary expense, which only determined and well-endowed litigants could afford.

Although, as we shall presently see, it is no longer necessary to commence proceedings for an injunction, timing continues to be problematic. A more serious problem is the nature of the protection offered by the equitable jurisdiction. Its discretionary character renders the outcome of an application to restrain use of confidential communications somewhat unpredictable. This is a distinct disadvantage because the privilege is meant to provide clients consulting lawyers with certainty that client–lawyer communications will not be disclosable in any circumstances.

Ashburton was decided as if the only relevant aspect of legal professional privilege was its confidentiality. That is why the court in *Ashburton* focused on the general principles governing the protection of confidentiality; any confidentiality and not just that of communications with lawyers. Cozens-Hardy M.R. gave as instances of confidentiality that needed protection

> cases where a man, being in the employment of another, has discovered the secrets of the manufacture of that other person, or has surreptitiously copied something which came under his hands while he was in the possession of that trust and confidence, and he has been restrained from communicating that secret to anybody else, and anybody who has obtained that secret from him has also been restrained from using it.[7]

The Court of Appeal limited itself to holding that since it had a general jurisdiction to restrain breach of confidence, it could exercise it in order to forbid a stranger from using confidential communications between

[7] *Ibid.*, 472; the quoted passage was from *Lamb* v. *Evans* [1893] 1 Ch. 218, 235. For the jurisdiction to protect confidentiality, see also: *Goddard* v. *Nationwide Building Society* [1987] Q.B. 670 (May L.J.); *General Mediterranean Holdings SA* v. *Patel* [2000] 1 W.L.R. 272; *ISTIL Group Inc.* v. *Zahoor* [2003] 2 All E.R. 252; [2003] EWHC 165 (Ch).

client and lawyer.[8] In doing so it overlooked the fact that confidentiality on its own provides no excuse from compulsory process.[9] A person cannot refuse to testify or produce documents in legal proceedings on the grounds that the information or documents in question are confidential or private. A person will not be heard to say that she is under a legal duty to keep them secret. Advice and litigation privilege provide something that confidentiality on its own does not: immunity from compulsory disclosure in legal proceedings and other contexts. Legal privilege provides an exception.

The *Calcraft* decision too is unsatisfactory, at any rate by today's standards. True admissibility at common law is governed by relevance. Advice privilege and litigation privilege too are rules recognised at common law, yet the court in *Calcraft* gave no consideration to whether its decision on admissibility was consistent with the rationale that supported the privilege. Had it done so, it might well have concluded that the reasons that support advice and litigation privilege are inconsistent with the position that stolen privileged documents are admissible in legal proceedings.

The exercise of equitable jurisdiction to protect legal professional privilege

In *Goddard* v. *Nationwide Building Society*,[10] a solicitor acting for the plaintiffs in the purchase of a house also acted for the building society which provided mortgage. He wrote an attendance note in which he set out information received from the building society and the contents of a conversation which he had with the plaintiffs on the subject. When the plaintiffs sued the society for negligence, the society pleaded some matters contained in the attendance note and the plaintiffs applied to have them struck out and for an injunction preventing the building society from making use of the information. The Court of Appeal considered itself bound by *Ashburton* to protect confidentiality by injunctive relief. May L.J. explained:

[8] *General Mediterranean Holdings SA* v. *Patel* [2000] 1 W.L.R. 272; *ISTIL Group Inc.* v. *Zahoor* [2003] 2 All E.R. 252.

[9] *Parry-Jones* v. *Law Society* [1969] 1 Ch. 1, 9, Diplock L.J. said that a duty of confidence is subject to, and overridden by, the duty of any party to comply with the law of the land. The duty to testify overrides the duty of confidence: *D* v. *National Society for the Prevention of Cruelty to Children* [1978] A.C. 171; *Science Research Council* v. *Nassé* [1980] A.C. 1028; *British Steel Corp.* v. *Granada Television Ltd* [1981] A.C. 1096; *X Ltd* v. *Morgan-Grampian (Publishers) Ltd* [1991] 1 A.C. 1.

[10] [1987] Q.B. 670.

> If a litigant has in his possession copies of documents to which legal professional privilege attaches he may nevertheless use such copies as secondary evidence in his litigation: however, if he has not yet used the documents in that way, the mere fact that he intends to do so is no answer to a claim against him by the person in whom the privilege is vested for delivery up of the copies or to restrain him from disclosing or making any use of any information contained in them.[11]

To remove any doubt, Nourse L.J. added: 'The crucial point is that the party who desires the protection must seek it before the other party has adduced the confidential communication in evidence or otherwise relied on it at trial.'[12] It seems odd to hold that it is too late to obtain protection when the person in possession of the confidential information seeks to put it in evidence. May L.J. confessed that he did 'not find the decision in *Lord Ashburton* v. *Pape* logically satisfactory, depending as it does upon the order in which applications are made in litigation'. There is no sense in making protection conditional on whether the proceedings to recover the privileged information are taken before the information is tendered in evidence. If there is justification for preventing confidential communications from being adduced in evidence, the protection should not turn on the accident of the timing of the application for protection.

This point was accepted in *Guinness Peat Properties Ltd* v. *Fitzroy Robinson Partnership*,[13] which removed the need to commence proceedings for an injunction. The claimants in that case sued the defendants, a firm of architects, for the faulty design of a building. When the claimants communicated their complaints to the defendants, the defendants wrote to their insurers notifying them of the complaints and stating their own position ('the letter'), as they were bound to do under of the terms of their policy. The first issue in the case was whether this letter was covered by legal professional privilege. The Court of Appeal decided that it was. However, at the discovery stage the defendants' solicitors inadvertently failed to claim privilege for the letter and allowed the claimants' solicitors to inspect it. When they realised their mistake and that the claimants were relying on the letter, they sought an order restraining the claimants from making any use of the information. The Court of Appeal upheld the order restraining the claimant from using the letter in evidence.

[11] *Ibid.*, 683.

[12] *Ibid.*, 684–5. See also *English and American Insurance Co.* v. *Herbert Smith* [1988] F.S.R. 232, 236.

[13] [1987] 1 W.L.R. 1027.

Slade L.J. articulated three principles. First, where solicitors inadvertently fail to claim privilege, 'the court will ordinarily permit them to amend the list ... at any time before inspection of the document has taken place'.[14] Secondly, once a document has been inspected by another party, 'the general rule is that it is too late for the party who seeks to claim privilege to attempt to correct the mistake by applying for injunctive relief'.[15] However, this rule is subject to two qualifications:

> If ... [the opponent or his solicitor] either (a) has procured inspection of the relevant document by fraud, or (b) on inspection, realises that he has been permitted to see the document only by reason of an obvious mistake, the court has power to intervene for the protection of the mistaken party by the grant of an injunction ... Furthermore ... it should ordinarily intervene ...[16]

The great practical benefit of this decision was that it obviated the need to run to court with a fresh action for an injunction. Henceforth the entire business, of both legal admissibility and of equitable protection of confidentiality, was to be done in the same proceedings and at the same time. This position is now enshrined in the rules. Rule 31.20 of the Civil Procedure Rules 1998 (UK) states:

> Where a party inadvertently allows a privileged document to be inspected, the party who has inspected the document may use it or its contents only with the permission of the court.

This rule has the added advantage of creating a presumption of inadmissibility and transferring the burden of obtaining court assistance from the party entitled to privilege, who might be unaware that the documents have been disclosed, to the party seeking to use them. It is no longer possible for the party entitled to privilege to lose protection simply because it has been pipped to the post by the party adducing the evidence.

However, C.P.R. r. 31.20 does not cover the entire ground occupied by the equitable discretion. It only applies to situations where persons entitled to privilege have inadvertently allowed their privileged documents to be inspected. It does not apply to situations where privileged documents came into the hands of others by means other than accidental disclosure. This can be a source of difficulty because the recipient of the document may argue that it assumed that the disclosure was intentional rather than inadvertent, as the recipient successfully argued in *Breeze* v. *John Stacey & Sons Ltd.*[17]

[14] *Ibid.*, 1045. [15] *Ibid.* [16] *Ibid.*, 1045–6. [17] [2000] C.P. Rep. 77.

While C.P.R. r. 31.20 has removed some practical difficulties, others persist. *Guinness Peat Properties Ltd* continues to govern the exercise of discretion whether to permit the use of inadvertently disclosed documents.[18] The equitable jurisdiction complicates the process of discovery and reduces its efficacy. Prior to *Guinness Peat Properties Ltd* solicitors could assume that privilege had been waived where they were allowed to inspect otherwise privileged documents. Now solicitors can no longer be sure that they will be able to use all the documents that they have seen. In *Guinness Peat Properties Ltd* the claimants' experts prepared their opinions on the basis of the defendants' otherwise privileged letter, only to discover that they were not allowed to do so and that they must, presumably, produce new opinions.

Permission to use the document will be withheld not only where the inspecting solicitor realised that a mistake had been made but also if the solicitor should have realised the other's mistake; for otherwise the court would be rewarding negligence or sloppiness. It would therefore appear that a solicitor inspecting documents owes a duty of care to the party giving inspection to refrain from perusing documents which a reasonably competent solicitor would have understood to be privileged.[19] An inspecting solicitor must therefore ask why the disclosing party would have wished to waive privilege and must conclude that the disclosure was a mistake if the solicitor cannot find a reasonable explanation for waiver.[20]

The guidelines for the exercise of discretion laid down by Slade L.J. in *Guinness Peat Properties Ltd* were reviewed and elaborated by the Court of Appeal in *Al Fayed* v. *Metropolitan Police Commissioner*,[21] and govern the exercise of discretion under the C.P.R. r. 31.20. Clarke L.J. stated:

> (i) A party giving inspection of documents must decide before doing so what privileged documents he wishes to allow the other party to see and what he does not.
>
> (ii) Although the privilege is that of the client and not the solicitor, a party clothes his solicitor with ostensible authority (if not implied

18 See *ibid.*

19 *International Business Machines Corp.* v. *Phoenix International (Computers) Ltd* [1995] 1 All E.R. 413.

20 *Ibid.*, 430 (Aldous J.).

21 *Al Fayed* v. *Metropolitan Police Commissioner* [2002] EWCA Civ 780.

or express authority) to waive privilege in respect of relevant documents.

(iii) A solicitor considering documents made available by the other party to litigation owes no duty of care to that party and is in general entitled to assume that any privilege which might otherwise have been claimed for such documents has been waived.

(iv) In these circumstances, where a party has given inspection of documents, including privileged documents which he has allowed the other party to inspect by mistake, it will in general be too late for him to claim privilege in order to attempt to correct the mistake by obtaining injunctive relief.

(v) However, the court has jurisdiction to intervene to prevent the use of documents made available for inspection by mistake where justice requires, as for example in the case of inspection procured by fraud.

(vi) In the absence of fraud, all will depend upon the circumstances, but the court may grant an injunction if the documents have been made available for inspection as a result of an obvious mistake.

(vii) A mistake is likely to be held to be obvious and an injunction granted where the documents are received by a solicitor and:

(a) the solicitor appreciates that a mistake has been made before making some use of the documents; or

(b) it would be obvious to a reasonable solicitor in his position that a mistake has been made;

and, in either case, there are no other circumstances which would make it unjust or inequitable to grant relief.

(viii) Where a solicitor gives detailed consideration to the question whether the documents have been made available for inspection by mistake and honestly concludes that they have not, that fact will be a relevant (and in many cases an important) pointer to the conclusion that it would not be obvious to the reasonable solicitor that a mistake had been made, but is not conclusive; the decision remains a matter for the court.

(ix) In both the cases identified in (vii) (a) and (b) above[,]there are many circumstances in which it may nevertheless be held to be inequitable or unjust to grant relief, but all will depend upon the particular circumstances.

(x) Since the court is exercising an equitable jurisdiction, there are no rigid rules.[22]

[22] *Ibid.*, [16]. See also *International Business Machines Corp.* v. *Phoenix International (Computers) Ltd* [1995] 1 All E.R. 413; *Breeze* v. *John Stacey & Sons Ltd* [2000] C.P. Rep. 77; *ISTIL Group Inc.* v. *Zahoor* [2003] 2 All E.R. 252.

In *Al Fayed*, Clarke L.J. sought to ease the burden of inspecting solicitors and held that 'the test is one of obvious mistake and nothing less. Anything less would involve holding that the solicitor for the receiving party B owed a duty of care to the other party A, which he does not'.[23] However, the obviousness test is far from straightforward with the result that a receiving solicitor may not appreciate the need for an application to use a privileged document. Further, the mere assertion of a mistake made by the party giving inspection would oblige the receiving party to apply for permission, the consideration of which could necessitate extensive examination of the facts and lead to considerable argument.[24] This point is illustrated by the *Al Fayed* case, where after extensive consideration of the disclosure process the Court of Appeal observed that 'while a solicitor might have concluded that a mistake had been made, it was by no means obvious'.[25]

The exercise of the equitable jurisdiction places considerable emphasis on the state of mind (actual or implied) of the solicitors who have inspected privileged documents and thereby creates considerable scope for dispute. In *International Business Machines Corp.* v. *Phoenix International (Computers) Ltd*,[26] Aldous J. held that where discovery involving substantial numbers of documents had been carried out under a tight timetable and without due care, a reasonable solicitor would realise that there was a risk of mistakes being made, and therefore it would not be reasonable for the solicitor to conclude that a deliberate decision had been made to disclose the privileged documents that were given to him.

This decision may be contrasted with *Pizzey* v. *Ford Motor Co Ltd.*[27] The claimant sought an injunction to restrain the defendant from using an expert report obtained by the claimant under cover of legal professional privilege which was mistakenly handed over to the defendant and which was unfavourable to the claimant's case. The Court of Appeal proceeded from the assumption that the burden rested on the party seeking to suppress confidential information to show that it was, or should have been, obvious to the party who received the privileged documents that they were disclosed by mistake. It is hardly likely that

[23] *Al Fayed* v. *Metropolitan Police Commissioner* [2002] EWCA Civ 780, [23]. And see *Breeze* v. *John Stacey & Sons Ltd* [2000] C.P. Rep. 77.

[24] I. Grainger, M. Fealy and M. Spencer, *The Civil Procedure Rules in Action*, 2nd ed. (London: Cavendish Publishing, 2000), 91–2.

[25] *Al Fayed* v. *Metropolitan Police Commissioner* [2002] EWCA Civ 780, [74].

[26] [1995] 1 All E.R. 412. [27] [1994] P.I.Q.R. P15.

a competent solicitor would disclose a privileged document that was damaging her own client's case. Yet, speaking for the Court of Appeal Mann L.J. said:

> I am not satisfied on probabilities that the hypothetical solicitor would have realised that privilege had not been waived ... The hypothetical solicitor might have been surprised to receive the documents, but I am not persuaded on probabilities that she would have thought other than [that] her fellow professional had waived the privilege . . .[28]

On the face of it this view seems puzzling. But the puzzle disappears once we take into account the fact that whereas in *International Business Machine Corp.* the documents consisted of legal bills and legal advice, the document in *Pizzey* contained reliable expert evidence that undermined the plaintiff's case. It is inconceivable that a court would have allowed the plaintiff to suppress the report and advance a case inconsistent with it.

This kind of consideration was made explicit by Scott J. in *Webster* v. *James Chapman & Co. (a firm).*[29] The claimant brought an action against his employers. His solicitors commissioned an engineer's report which contained conclusions adverse to the plaintiff's case. The solicitors sought a revised report and inadvertently sent the original and unhelpful report to the defendant's solicitors. The plaintiff sought an injunction to suppress the first report since he wished to rely exclusively on a revised report which was favourable to his case. Scott J. held that the court had to balance the interest of a party to protect his privilege against the interest of the opponent in obtaining the evidence. In the circumstances he concluded that since the report had come into the defendants' possession through no fault of theirs and since their case would be seriously embarrassed if they were not allowed to make use of it, no restraint should be placed on its use.

In *Pizzey* v. *Ford Motor Co. Ltd*, the Court of Appeal disapproved of the notion that the exercise of the equitable jurisdiction required a balance to be struck between protecting privilege, on the one hand, and on the other the probative significance of the documents inadvertently disclosed.[30] Yet it is fairly clear that the court will not protect privilege where this may result in a judgment that is at odds with the true facts. Notwithstanding the reservation in *Pizzey*, the court is unlikely to

[28] *Ibid.*, P22. [29] [1989] 3 All E.R. 939.

[30] *Pizzey* v. *Ford Motor Co. Ltd* [1994] P.I.Q.R. P15. See also *Derby & Co. Ltd* v. *Weldon (No. 8)* [1990] 3 All E.R. 762.

refuse the use of otherwise privileged expert reports where the interests of the administration of justice demand that the information should be made available to the court, as happened in *ISTIL Group Inc.* v. *Zahoor*.[31]

Administration of justice considerations seem to have led the Court of Appeal to hold that where the inadvertent disclosure of a privileged document has taken place at the trial, its use in evidence will not be restrained.[32] The only possible reason for this ruling is that by excluding evidence that has come to its attention the court may be compelled to give judgment which it knows to be at variance with the facts. Much would depend on the stage at which the inadvertent disclosure was made and on the consequences of preventing the receiving party from using the information. In one case the prosecution was allowed to rely on a privileged document which was found on the floor of the court room even though it had not been adduced.[33] It is possible that the court was swayed by the consideration that public confidence in the administration of justice would be undermined if the court were to turn a blind eye to relevant evidence that came into the possession of the prosecution, albeit accidentally.

It has been held that it was too late to insist on privilege where at the trial counsel for the party entitled to privilege has introduced a privileged document into the record.[34] It has been said that in such a case the consequences of the disclosure cannot be eradicated,[35] and that it is too late to restore the status quo.[36] Such reasoning proves too much because the same can be said in every situation where privileged material has been seen by a person who was not entitled to see it; once gained, knowledge cannot be wiped clean. Perhaps a better explanation is that since the party entitled to privilege has introduced a privileged document into the record, it would be harmful to the interests of justice to require the court to decide the case as if the information had not come to its attention.[37]

[31] [2003] 2 All E.R. 252.

[32] *Great Atlantic Insurance Co.* v. *Home Insurance Co.* [1981] 1 W.L.R. 529.

[33] *R* v. *Tompkins* (1977) 67 Cr. App. Rep. 181.

[34] *Great Atlantic Insurance Co.* v. *Home Insurance Co.* [1981] 1 W.L.R. 529.

[35] *Ibid.*, 541.

[36] *Guinness Peat Properties Ltd* v. *Fitzroy Robinson Partnership* [1987] 1 W.L.R. 1027, 1046.

[37] While it is true that in some situations the trier of fact may be asked to ignore inadmissible evidence that has come to its attention, these are usually concerned with instances where the inadmissibility is due to some probative defects; as where a jury may be asked to ignore similar fact evidence because its prejudicial effect outweighs its probative value. Evidence may be excluded because it was obtained by improper means. The view in *Lloyd* v. *Mostyn* (1842) 10 M. & W. 478; 152 E.R. 558, that privilege documents may be

Knowledge of privileged information may be embarrassing not only where it comes out at the trial. Suppose that a solicitor has seen privileged documents which reveal facts that are entirely at variance with the pleaded position of the party entitled to privilege. This very inconsistency would tend to suggest that the documents were handed over by mistake and the solicitor would be bound to return the documents and refrain from disclosing their contents to his client. But a solicitor cannot erase the information from his own mind (no one can unknow something they know). The information that such a solicitor must withhold from his own client may make it difficult for the solicitor to continue representing the client.[38] However, the court may not ask a solicitor to cease representing a client where the solicitor has been shown a privileged document during the disclosure process, no matter how difficult it may be for the solicitor to refrain from using the knowledge gained from such disclosure.[39] Where a solicitor has communicated the contents of a privileged document to the client the court may find it difficult to restrain the use of such document. Clarke L.J. thought that protection might not be given where the receiving party's solicitor sends the documents to the party before considering them himself and the party learns a fact which it would be unjust to prevent him from using in the litigation, even though it would have been apparent to the solicitor that a mistake had been made.[40] If this were the position then the protection to accidentally disclosed documents could be bypassed by adopting a practice of sending the client for comment all the documents that have been provided by the disclosing party.

Legal professional privilege must be protected by a rule of inadmissibility as well as immunity and confidentiality

As will have become clear, the reason why the tension between *Ashburton* v. *Pape* and *Calcraft* v. *Guest* has given rise to so much difficulty has nothing to do with the conflict between law and equity. Nor is it due to the inherently discretionary nature of equitable remedies. The difficulty is

admissible notwithstanding that they have been stolen, is for this reason alone unlikely to be followed.

38 *Ablitt* v. *Mills & Reeve (a firm)*, *The Times*, 25 October 1995.

39 *R (Ford)* v. *Financial Services Authority* [2012] Lloyd's Rep. F.C. 461; [2012] EWHC 997 (Admin). Cf. *Webster* v. *James Chapman & Co. (a firm)* [1989] 3 All E.R. 939.

40 *Al Fayed* v. *Metropolitan Police Commissioner* [2002] EWCA Civ 780, [25].

due to a flawed understanding of the nature of the protection accorded to litigation privilege and its implications.

As we have seen, rule 31.20 of the Civil Procedure Rules provides that where 'a party inadvertently allows a privileged document to be inspected, the party who has inspected the document may use it or its contents only with the permission of the court'. 'Privilege' is defined in the Glossary as the 'right of a party to refuse to disclose a document or produce a document or to refuse to answer questions on the ground of some special interest recognised by law'. As the Glossary definition reflects, privilege provides immunity from compulsory disclosure, whether in the course of the disclosure process or in the course of testimony. At the same time, a person entitled to privilege is completely free to waive this immunity and disclose privileged documents and information. This feature of privilege has implications for the operation of rule 31.20 because the limitation on use does not arise where a person has waived privilege; it only arises where a person entitled to privilege has inadvertently allowed inspection, without any intention of waiving privilege.

Legal professional privilege has tended to be regarded as primarily a rule of immunity, not of admissibility. As a rule of immunity, it provides the client with an excuse to refuse compulsory disclosure.[41] It entitles the client (and the lawyer on the client's behalf) to refuse to disclose documents or information to which the privilege attaches.[42] The immunity applies not just to disclosure in legal proceedings but can also be invoked as an excuse from disclosing the information wherever there might otherwise be a legal duty to make disclosure, as where a public authority is empowered to obtain information from the citizen.[43]

Immunity from compulsory disclosure is by its very nature limited to situations where disclosure may be required by law. Immunity does not come into play in situations where documents covered by advice or

[41] *R* v. *Tompkins* (1977) 67 Cr. App. Rep. 181, 184; *R* v. *Governor of Pentonville Prison, Ex p. Osman* [1990] 1 W.L.R. 277, 310.

[42] *Comfort Hotels Ltd* v. *Wembley Stadium Ltd* [1988] 1 W.L.R. 872.

[43] Although in *Parry-Jones* v. *Law Society* [1969] 1 Ch. 1, 9 Diplock L.J. said that '. . . strictly speaking, privilege refers to a right to withhold from a court, or a tribunal exercising judicial functions, material which would otherwise be admissible in evidence', the privilege protecting lawyer–client communications extends to situations where disclosure is demanded by public authorities: *R (Morgan Grenfell & Co. Ltd)* v. *Special Commissioner of Income Tax* [2003] 1 A.C. 563; [2002] UKHL 21. See also *Baker* v. *Campbell* (1983) 153 C.L.R. 52, which concerned disclosure of documents protected by legal professional privilege to the Federal Police.

litigation privilege have been obtained otherwise than through a legal process. While it is clearly necessary to exempt privileged material from any process of compulsory disclosure, there is no reason why the protection of advice and litigation privilege should not extend further. This has already been accepted in equity where privileged communications are accorded the protection of confidentiality. However, this protection, too, falls short of what the rationale behind advice and litigation privilege requires.

Legal advice and litigation privilege share a core idea: that people should have a private and secure space in which to consult lawyers and in which to prepare for litigation. Without a secure space for taking legal advice, citizens would lack meaningful means of ascertaining their rights and obligations. Without a secure space for preparation, parties to legal proceedings would be denied a fair opportunity to present their case.[44]

In *AM&S Europe Ltd* v. *Commission of the European Communities (Case 155/79)*,[45] Sir Gordon Slynn, Advocate General, reviewed the protection of confidences imparted to lawyers across the member states of the European Community and observed:

> Whether it is described as the right of the client or the duty of the lawyer, this principle has nothing to do with the protection or privilege of the lawyer. It springs essentially from the basic need of a man in a civilised society to be able to turn to his lawyer for advice and help, and if proceedings begin, for representation; it springs no less from the advantages to a society which evolves complex law reaching into all the business affairs of persons, real and legal, that they should be able to know what they can do under the law, what is forbidden, where they must tread circumspectly, where they run risks.[46]

Similar reasoning is reflected in numerous decisions in England, which stress the public interest in affording citizens access to legal advice as a means of promoting the rule of law.[47] Relying on rule of law

[44] In *Three Rivers District Council* v. *Governor and Company of the Bank of England (No. 6)* [2005] 1 A.C. 610, [52]; [2004] UKHL 48 Lord Rodger said that 'each party should be free to prepare his case as fully as possible without the risk that his opponent will be able to recover the material generated by his preparations'. See also comments by Hoffmann J. on the importance of the confidentiality of communications in connection with preparation for litigation in *Chandler* v. *Church* [1987] N.L.J. Rep. 451, and by Lawrence Collins J. on the importance of enabling litigants to prepare for litigation in *ISTIL Group Inc.* v. *Zahoor* [2003] 2 All E.R. 252, [52]ff.

[45] [1983] Q.B. 878. [46] *Ibid.*, 913.

[47] *Three Rivers District Council* v. *Governor and Company of the Bank of England (No. 6)* [2005] 1 A.C. 610, [34]; *R (Prudential Plc)* v. *Special Commissioner of Income Tax* [2013] 2 A.C. 185, [120]; [2013] UKSC 1.

considerations in the present context does not require any sophisticated constitutional or jurisprudential argumentation. Rather, it simply suggests that it is in the interest of all (the public interest) that people should comply with the law and use its facilities. If citizens are to comply with the law and take advantage of the opportunities it offers, they should have unimpeded means of finding out what the law says. Access to knowledge of the law is particularly important given that ignorance of the law provides no excuse.

The imperative of a secure space for taking legal advice is reflected in the Police and Criminal Evidence Act 1984 (UK), s. 58(1), which states that a 'person arrested and held in custody in a police station or other premises shall be entitled, if he so requests, to consult a solicitor privately at any time'. The rationale for the right to private consultation in custody is the same as that supporting advice and litigation privilege generally.[48]

It should be noted that litigation privilege is not confined to lawyer–client communications. Self-represented persons have as much a right to a private and secure sphere for preparation. The opponent of a self-represented litigant cannot demand disclosure to the notes that the litigant made in connection with the case, nor would such notes be allowed to be used as evidence against him.[49] It must not be assumed, as Bingham L.J. pointed out, 'that a litigant in person is denied, in preparing for litigation, the protection of secrecy which is enjoyed by a litigant who instructs a lawyer'.[50]

To make communications for taking legal advice and for preparing litigation inviolable it is not enough to protect them by an immunity rule and by equitable protection of confidentiality. The secure space needs to be protected from other incursions besides the process of disclosure. Lord Hoffmann pointed out in *R (Morgan Grenfell & Co. Ltd)* v. *Special Commissioners of Income Tax*[51] that the concern that may inhibit frank communication by a client to his lawyer is not so much that the matter

[48] For discussion, see *McE* v. *Prison Services of Northern Ireland* [2009] 1 A.C. 908; [2009] UKHL 15.

[49] See *Ventouris* v. *Mountain* [1991] 1 W.L.R. 607; A.A.S. Zuckerman, *Zuckerman on Civil Procedure*, 3rd ed. (London: Sweet and Maxwell, 2013), [15.18].

[50] *Ventouris* v. *Mountain* [1991] 1 W.L.R. 607, 611. See also *R (Kelly)* v. *Warley Magistrates' Court* [2008] 1 W.L.R. 2001, [18], [21]; [2007] EWHC 1836 (Admin); *S County Council* v. *B* [2000] Fam. 76, 83. Lord Carswell's view in *Three Rivers District Council* v. *Governor and Company of the Bank of England (No. 6)* [2005] 1 A.C. 610, [105] that legal professional privilege 'is a single integral privilege, whose sub-heads are legal advice privilege and litigation privilege', may therefore be doubted.

[51] [2003] 1 A.C. 563.

communicated may be disclosed but that the matter may then be used to the detriment of the client. The very considerations that support the rule that the client and his lawyer must not be compelled to reveal these communications also support a principle that what the client tells his lawyer in private should not be used to the client's detriment in any legal context.

Security of communications for obtaining legal advice or for preparing for litigation can only be obtained by a rule that prevents protected communications from being used against the interests of the person entitled to a secure space. If the law tells persons that they have complete freedom to talk to their lawyers 'secure in the knowledge that protected documents and information will not be disclosed at all', as Lord Hoffmann put it,[52] it would be unfair to allow the client's statements made under such conditions to be used as evidence against the client, whether or not the information was extracted by legal compulsion, whether or not the contents of the client–lawyer communications have emerged by accident or intentional incursion.

The inadmissibility aspect of the protection that advice and litigation privilege deserve can be demonstrated by considering two hypothetical situations. Suppose that, in breach of his duty of confidentiality, a lawyer has publicly stated that the client admitted to him the commission of an offence. Suppose that a person suspected of a criminal offence sends his lawyer a letter containing incriminating admissions, and the letter accidentally falls into the hands of the prosecution. It is inconceivable that a court would allow the lawyer's statement or the client's letter to be adduced in evidence in order to establish the client's guilt. To accept such evidence would offend our sense of justice and fair play. It would amount to reneging on the guarantee that legal professional privilege is meant to offer clients in order to induce them to speak freely to their lawyers and freely prepare for litigation.

The notion of fairness that is invoked here is not peculiar to legal proceedings. A secure and private sphere of preparation is a basic requirement of fairness wherever persons are entitled to be judged by reference to the product of their labour. A person sitting an examination is entitled to be judged exclusively by the answers submitted, rather than by the jottings made in preparation. Architects, designers or town planners would have just cause to complain if they were judged not by the plans or designs that they have put forward for assessment but by

[52] *Ibid.*, [30].

reference to preparatory or experimental work which they had discarded. In the legal context, the relevance and probative value of such preparations is doubtful as it may simply disclose views that the client has rejected or dissociated himself from. Documents in which various legal positions were discussed may not accurately reflect the party's position.

This concept of fairness is reflected in the old rule concerning the parties' briefs and proofs of evidence, in relation to which James L.J. said in *Anderson* v. *Bank of British Columbia*[53] 'that as you have no right to see your adversary's brief, you have no right to see that which comes into existence merely as the materials for the brief'.[54]

Similarly, in *Wheeler* v. *Le Marchant*,[55] Cotton L.J. said:

> Hitherto such communications [between a solicitor and a third person] have only been protected when they have been in contemplation of some litigation, or for the purpose of giving advice or obtaining evidence with reference to it. And that is reasonable, because then the solicitor is preparing for the defence or for bringing the action, and all communications he makes for that purpose, and the communications made to him for the purpose of giving him the information, are, in fact, the brief in the action, and ought to be protected.[56]

In *Waugh* v. *British Railways Board*,[57] Lord Wilberforce referred to legal professional privilege and said:

> It is sometimes ascribed to the exigencies of the adversary system of litigation under which a litigant is entitled within limits to refuse to disclose the nature of his case until the trial. Thus one side may not ask to see the proofs of the other side's witnesses or the opponent's brief or even know what witnesses will be called: he must wait until the card is played and cannot try to see it in the hand.[58]

In the modern cornerstone case of *R* v. *Derby Magistrates' Court, Ex p. B*,[59] Lord Taylor C.J. said:

> The principle which runs through all these cases, and the many other cases which were cited, is that a man must be able to consult his lawyer in confidence, since otherwise he might hold back half the truth. The client must be sure that what he tells his lawyer in confidence will never be revealed without his consent. Legal professional privilege is thus much more than an ordinary rule of evidence, limited in its application to the facts of a particular case. It is a fundamental condition on which the administration of justice as a whole rests . . .

[53] (1876) 2 Ch. D. 644. [54] *Ibid.*, 656. [55] (1881) 17 Ch. D. 675. [56] *Ibid.*, 684–5.
[57] [1980] A.C. 521. [58] *Ibid.*, 531. [59] [1995] 3 W.L.R. 681.

> But it is not for the sake of the appellant alone that the privilege must be upheld. It is in the wider interests of all those hereafter who might otherwise be deterred from telling the whole truth to their solicitors. For this reason I am of the opinion that no exception should be allowed to the absolute nature of legal professional privilege, once established.[60]

Although these statements were made in relation to litigation privilege, the same must apply to legal advice privilege. It would be unjust to disappoint the litigant's legitimate expectation that what he said to his lawyer will not be held as evidence against him.

It follows that the protection given to legitimate communications within the secure and private sphere must extend beyond immunity from compulsory disclosure and should include a right not to be judged by reference to communications that were made on the understanding that they are protected by legal privilege.[61]

It would be unfair to allow use of privileged material where it was extracted by trick or fraud and therefore amounted to an infringement of the secure sphere that the law accords citizens for the purpose of obtaining legal advice or for preparing for litigation.[62] Nor should the court allow a defendant who finds a discarded draft of the particulars of claim to rely on it for the purpose of showing inconsistencies with the particulars that actually were served by the claimant. The current position that where a privileged document has been disclosed by mistake, it will be assumed to have been waived unless the mistake was obvious[63] is indefensible.

Recent decisions in this country and in Australia come close to recognising the inadmissibility aspect of privilege. In *R (Ford)* v. *Financial Services Authority*,[64] the Financial Services Authority obtained by compulsory process documents protected by legal professional privilege and relied on the privileged material in obtaining a Warning Notice. The court accepted that had the privileged material provided the basis of the decision, the decision would have had to be set aside. In the event, the court upheld the decision because the privileged material was not central to the outcome.

[60] *R.* v. *Derby Magistrates' Court, Ex p. B* [1995] 3 W.L.R. 681, 695, 696–7.

[61] *The Aegis Blaze* [1986] 1 Lloyd's Rep. 203.

[62] *Webster* v. *James Chapman & Co. (a firm)* [1989] 3 All E.R. 939.

[63] *MMI Research Ltd* v. *Cellxion Ltd* [2007] EWHC 2456 (Ch) where the court held that privilege had been lost in a draft pleading in a related German court proceeding, which had been disclosed by mistake during the disclosure process.

[64] [2012] Lloyd's Rep. F.C. 461.

The Australian High Court has limited the scope of discretion in the use of inadvertently disclosed privileged documents and came close to adopting the solution advocated here. In *Expense Reduction Analysts Group Pty Ltd* v. *Armstrong Strategic Management and Marketing Pty Ltd*,[65] the defendants mistakenly listed a number of privileged documents in the non-privileged section of their disclosure list and allowed them to be inspected by the claimants. The claimants refused to return the documents. Much attention was given by the lower courts to whether the court should exercise its equitable jurisdiction to restrain the use of the documents. The Australia High Court held that there was no need to resort to the court's equitable jurisdiction to restrain the use of privileged documents. It decided that if a privileged document is inadvertently disclosed during discovery, the court has all powers necessary to permit the correction of that mistake and to order the return of the documents. The High Court ruled that the lower court should simply have allowed the defendants to amend their list of documents and claim privilege for the documents which they accidentally left out of the privileged section. Such amendment, the court explained, should be allowed because the defendant had never intended to waive privilege:

> It may be accepted that a continuing intention to claim privilege is relevant to the question of whether there has been a waiver of the privilege. But it was not necessary to prove a continuing intention to show that a reviewer formed an intention with respect to each document at the time it was listed. It was sufficient to prove that the [appellants] intended to maintain their claims to privilege and that the reviewers were carrying out their clients' instructions. From that point, the fact of mistake in the incorrect listing of the documents could be inferred.[66]

Welcome though this decision is, the High Court's solution to the problem is technical rather than principled. It relies on the jurisdiction to permit an amendment of the disclosure list in order to give effect to the intention to claim privilege. Further, it preserves the discretion to permit use when the court considers it just to do so.[67] Nonetheless, since the

[65] (2013) 250 C.L.R. 303; [2013] HCA 46.

[66] *Ibid.*, [20].

[67] *Ibid.*, [49]:

> The courts will normally only permit an error to be corrected if a party acts promptly. If the party to whom the documents have been disclosed has been placed in a position, as a result of the disclosure, where it would be unfair to order the return of the privileged documents, relief may be

clear intention of the Australian High Court was to make orders to return inadvertently disclosed privileged documents almost automatic, it would take only a small step to hold that privileged documents are inadmissible.

The implications of legal professional privilege as an inadmissibility rule

Accepting the inadmissibility aspect of the privilege rule would resolve the difficulties encountered in relation to accidentally disclosed privileged communications. A party who has accidentally disclosed a privileged document to the opponent would not be at the mercy of the court's discretion whether or not the opponent would be allowed to use it: the document would simply be inadmissible as evidence against the party entitled to privilege.

A number of qualifications need to be made to the notion that client–lawyer communications should be inadmissible. First, such inadmissibility would be limited to the use of a statement made by the client as an admission of the truth of facts stated by the client to his lawyer. Secondly, the inadmissibility aspect of the privilege would remain coextensive with the privilege. Thus, since privilege does not attach to communications made in furtherance of crime, such communications would be admissible.

The same should go for preparatory work relating to litigation, such as draft pleadings, notes of argument or research of the legal position. The inadmissibility rule would only apply to preparatory notes made by the party and to communications made by the party. However, communications with non-parties made in preparation for litigation cannot be similarly treated. A few examples will illustrate the limitations. A party writes to a potential witness asking for information. The witness, who may have had no previous relationship with the party, is under no duty of confidentiality to the party and is free to disclose the communication so received. For, plainly, a person cannot unilaterally impose a duty of confidence on a stranger. If the witness provides the party with a statement of relevant events, the witness is free to provide the same information to others. The position is different where a party to litigation

refused. However, in taking such considerations (analogous to equitable considerations) into account, no narrow view is likely to be taken of the ability of a party, or the party's lawyers, to put any knowledge gained to one side. That must be so in the conduct of complex litigation unless the documents assume particular importance.

retains an expert, who is bound by a duty of confidentiality under the retainer.

In *ISTIL Group Inc.* v. *Zahoor*,[68] the claimants communicated with a non-party in preparation of their case. The non-party disclosed to the defendants the communications between him and the claimants. Lawrence Collins J. explained that once a privileged document had been disclosed, the privilege was lost and the court was merely concerned whether to exercise the equitable jurisdiction to restrain breach of confidence. He refused to restrain the defendants from using the communications because their disclosure in the proceedings was necessary in order to ensure that the claimants did not create a false impression by using only some of the communications that they received from the same source and on which they had earlier relied.[69] Since the non-party was free to communicate with the defendants, and could certainly be summoned to testify to his knowledge of the material facts, it is difficult to see on what grounds the defendants could be restrained from adducing the evidence. The court made clear that it would be reluctant to restrain the use of the communication when to do so would be likely to lead the court into error. However, this last point has no bearing on communications between client and lawyer for the purpose of obtaining legal advice, or on the material that a person creates in preparations for litigation. If we accept that what a client tells a lawyer must not be allowed to be used as evidence against the client, it should make no difference whether the disclosed privileged material is probative or not. A rule of inadmissibility would remove all room for argument where privileged material consists of communication between client and lawyer, or of notes made in preparation for litigation.

It is not suggested that under a rule of inadmissibility the outcome of cases such as *Webster* v. *James Chapman & Co. (a firm)*,[70] and *Pizzey* v. *Ford Motor Co. Ltd*,[71] would be different. In these cases the court allowed the use of otherwise privileged expert reports that were unfavourable to the party that retained the expert. I argue elsewhere that

[68] [2003] 2 All E.R. 252.

[69] I argue elsewhere that it may be doubted whether privilege attached to those documents. A witness statement taken from a non-party in preparation for trial is indeed privileged in the hands of the party preparing for litigation. But the witness is not under any duty of confidentiality, she is free to tell the same story to anyone else. Indeed, the witness is compellable to testify to the facts for the simple reason that no litigant owns the witness: Zuckerman, *Zuckerman on Civil Procedure*, 3rd ed. [16.79].

[70] [1989] 3 All E.R. 939. [71] [1994] P.I.Q.R. P15.

where a party relies on an expert report, earlier drafts of the report should be disclosed in order to enable other parties to test the strength of the report's conclusions and avoid misleading the court.[72]

In Chapter 25, Dr Mike Macnair questions how the principle that legal professional privilege is capable of being waived can be reconciled with a rule of inadmissibility. Once it is accepted that legal privilege is protected by three rules, it is not difficult to see how waiver fits in. The confidentiality of any information may be waived by the person entitled to keep it confidential. Accordingly, a person who has received legal advice is free to publish it or share it with others. A person is entitled to seek equitable relief against the use of confidential information (and not just of privileged communications) but is not obliged to do so. Similarly, a party is entitled to resist the introduction into the proceedings of inadmissible evidence, such as hearsay in criminal proceedings, but is not obliged to do so.

The following point bears stress: recognising that communications between client and lawyer are protected by an inadmissibility rule would not make the immunity principle redundant. Nor would such a rule reduce the value of the equitable protection of confidentiality. On the contrary, both immunity and confidentiality would remain essential safeguards of the secure space for taking legal advice and for preparing for litigation. A person who communicates with a lawyer in order to obtain legal advice and a person who generates documents in preparation for litigation are both entitled to have these screened from the prying eyes of others, regardless whether others seek to use such information in legal proceedings.

Finally, in his commentary on this chapter Dr Macnair draws attention to the danger that the secure space for legal advice may be used to cloak in secrecy matters which should be disclosable. As an example he mentions the fact that privilege was claimed for the advice given to the British government by the Attorney-General as to the legality of the 2003 invasion of Iraq. I agree with this concern and have argued elsewhere that advice privilege has been given too wide a scope. In particular, it is far from clear that there is justification for according advice privilege to corporations or to the public servants.[73]

[72] Zuckerman, *Zuckerman on Civil Procedure*, 3rd ed., ch. 21. In Queensland privilege has been altogether removed from communications with experts: Uniform Civil Procedure Rules 1999 (Qld), r. 212(2); *Mitchell Contractors Pty Ltd* v. *Townsville-Thuringowa Water Supply Joint Board* [2005] 1 Qd. R. 373, [13]; [2004] QSC 329.

[73] Zuckerman, *Zuckerman on Civil Procedure*, 3rd ed. [16.58]ff. and in particular [16.69].

Conclusion

The theme of this chapter, that advice and litigation privilege should be considered as including a rule of inadmissibility, as well as a rule of immunity, is not intended to derogate from the equitable jurisdiction to protect confidentiality. It merely suggests that on its own the equitable jurisdiction cannot adequately provide the protection that should be accorded to communications between lawyer and client and to the preparatory work for litigation. Advice privilege is supported by rule of law considerations. If people's conduct is to be governed by the law, people must have the means of acquiring knowledge of the law. To this end the law offers citizens a secure space in which they may consult lawyers free of fear that what they say could be later used as evidence to their detriment. The same is true of materials generated in preparation for litigation. The right to a fair trial implies a right to an adequate opportunity to prepare for litigation. To this end the law offers litigants a secure place in which they can prepare, free of fear that their preparatory work may be used as evidence to their detriment. The notion of a secure space requires that what has passed within this sphere should be inadmissible in evidence. Such protection must not depend on the exercise of equitable discretion.

25

Equitable protection of legal professional privilege

A commentary

MIKE MACNAIR

Professor Zuckerman's chapter (Chapter 24) discusses what is sometimes called a 'short point' but one which raises fundamental issues of principle. The short point is that there is a practical conflict (though not a *logical* conflict) between the rule in *Calcraft* v. *Guest*,[1] following *Lloyd* v. *Mostyn*,[2] that documents prima facie subject to 'legal professional privilege' but accidentally disclosed (or obtained by wrongdoing), or copies of them, are admissible in evidence, and the rule in *Lord Ashburton* v. *Pape*[3] that a party who becomes aware that such documents have been unintentionally disclosed can obtain an injunction to prevent their use in court under the equitable jurisdiction to restrain breaches of confidence.

The practical conflict that Professor Zuckerman identifies consists of two aspects. The first is that the combination of the two rules tends to produce wasteful satellite litigation (which in turn entails 'equality of arms' problems as favouring litigants with deep pockets). Though this is *mitigated* by the fact that it is no longer necessary formally to apply for an injunction, the potential increase in interlocutory applications and appeals has the same general effects.

The second and more fundamental aspect is that 'legal professional privilege' (more exactly its two aspects, 'litigation privilege' and 'advice privilege') is as of right, but the equitable protection of confidentiality by injunction is discretionary, and that the approach to the issue in modern cases creates uncertainty and threatens to under-protect the litigant's 'secure space for preparation of his case'.

1 [1898] 1 Q.B. 759. 2 (1842) 10 M. & W. 478, 481–2; 152 E.R. 558, 560.
3 [1913] 2 Ch. 469.

Professor Zuckerman argues that '[t]o make communications for taking legal advice and for preparing litigation inviolable it is not enough to protect them by an immunity rule and by equitable protection of confidentiality'.[4] Litigation privilege is demanded by the fundamental right to a fair trial (guaranteed by article 6 of the European Convention of Human Rights); advice privilege is required by the principle of the rule of law because the subjects cannot know the law without access to legal advice and they cannot take effective legal advice without disclosing to their lawyers *possible* adverse evidence of facts which might not, in reality, be found against them in a trial.

Professor Zuckerman proposes, in effect, to reverse *Calcraft* v. *Guest* and the broad statements in *Lloyd* v. *Mostyn*, and thereby return to the rule of *inadmissibility* of privileged communications stated by *Phillips on Evidence* in 1820 on the basis of the 1809 *nisi prius* ruling in *Fisher* v. *Heming* (1809) (which itself probably reflected settled eighteenth-century law).[5] Professor Zuckerman's proposed inadmissibility rule is more limited and is tightly crafted. It would apply only to 'the use of a statement made by the client as an admission of the truth of the facts stated by the client to his lawyer'.[6] And 'since privilege does not attach to communications made in furtherance of crime, such communications would be admissible'.[7]

Professor Zuckerman has clearly identified a real problem in the relation between the rules in *Calcraft* v. *Guest* and *Lord Ashburton* v. *Pape*.[8] His argument against a discretionary approach to legal professional

[4] A. Zuckerman, 'Equitable Protection of Legal Professional Privilege: A Distraction', Chapter 24 of this volume, text after n. 50.

[5] S.M. Phillipps, *A Treatise on the Law of Evidence*, 4th ed. (London: Butterworth, 1820), vol. i, 140–1; cited in *Lloyd* v. *Mostyn* from a later edition; this passage was not in editions earlier than the fourth. 'Settled eighteenth century law': the rule is also treated as an inadmissibility rule in J. Gilbert, *The Law of Evidence* (written shortly before 1711, here from 4th ed., London: Rivington et al., 1777), 136; Anon., *The Theory of Evidence* (Dublin: S. Cotter, 1761), 95–6, and F. Buller (ed.), *An Introduction to the Law of Nisi Prius*, 3rd ed. (London: C. Bathurst, 1781), 284. However, W. Nelson, *The Law of Evidence* (London: Gosling, 1717), 60–2, working from seventeenth-century authorities, treats the rule as involving exemption from compulsion rather than a prohibition on disclosure by the lawyer. On the late sixteenth- to early eighteenth-century law, see also M. Macnair, *The Law of Proof in Early Modern Equity* (Berlin: Duncker & Humblot, 1999), 224–7, 236–42.

[6] Zuckerman, 'Equitable Protection of Legal Professional Privilege: A Distraction', text after n. 67.

[7] *Ibid.*

[8] Cf. also the discussion in I. Dennis, *The Law of Evidence*, 4th ed. (London: Sweet & Maxwell, 2010), 425–33, especially the comment at 431 that '[l]ater authorities are in disarray, and the matter is ripe to be taken to the Supreme Courts'.

privilege – at least in relation to litigation privilege – on the basis that the grounds in the right to a fair trial demand stronger protection, is also persuasive. The narrow inadmissibility rule he proposes also seems justifiable, though I think there may be a case for narrowing it slightly further. The point here is simply that the exception for communications in furtherance of *crime* is inappropriately narrower than the existing exception to the privilege for statements in furtherance of crime *or fraud*, here including the broad pre-1850 conception of fraud.[9]

However, with all respect, I do not think that the proposal solves the problem posed because the problem posed is posed by the present *breadth* both of legal professional privilege and of the rule in *Lord Ashburton* v. *Pape*, that is, as covering forms of documentary evidence which are *not* offered as being admissions by the party. Documents of this sort pose the problem of 'embarrassing' the lawyers to whom inadvertent disclosure has been made, and are likely to continue, even if Professor Zuckerman's new rule is to be introduced, to give rise to satellite litigation of the sort seen in the modern cases.

To begin at the most abstract level, I think that the argument for 'advice privilege' from the 'rule of law' principle is weaker than the argument for 'litigation privilege' from the right to a fair trial (though the two are clearly intertwined). My reasons for saying this are, in the first place, that the 'rule of law' principle is itself debatable: this is a huge can of worms and I will say no more than that the course of events since the 1980s has in my view confirmed the case for J.A.G. Griffith's 'political constitutionalism' and the similar case more recently argued by Adam Tomkins.[10] 'Political constitutionalism', it seems to me, implies the *reduction* of the 'private sphere', in so far as this is taken to apply to government institutions, limited-liability companies, and so on, in favour of increased transparency; and this, in turn, implies a fairly restrictive construction of legal advice privilege. The most striking example of the point is the issue of the advice given to the British government by Lord Goldsmith as Attorney-General as to the legality of the 2003 invasion of Iraq, whose release was initially

[9] Dennis, *The Law of Evidence*, 419–20. On the old broad conception of fraud and its narrowing, see M. Macnair, 'Sham and Related and Unrelated Doctrines', in E. Simpson and M. Stewart (eds.), *Sham Transactions* (Oxford University Press, 2013), ch. 2.

[10] J.A.G. Griffith, 'The Political Constitution' (1979) 42 M.L.R. 1; A. Tomkins, *Our Republican Constitution* (Oxford: Hart Publishing, 2005). See also R. Hirschl, *Towards Juristocracy: The Origins and Consequences of the New Constitutionalism* (Cambridge, Mass.: Harvard University Press, 2004).

resisted on legal advice privilege grounds; this is merely the tip of a large iceberg.

But secondly, leaving this larger issue aside, the logical connection from rule of law to advice privilege seems to me to be problematic. Suppose that there is a general right that the law should be knowable. I agree to this. Suppose that this implies in its turn a right to have professional advice as to how the law impacts on actual or proposed activities. Why should this imply a right *that that advice and the basis on which it was given become the private property of the advisee*, to be disclosed to other actors or not according to the recipient's advantage or disadvantage? This is arguably to convert *the law itself* into a private business asset by way of the right of deep pockets to engage high-quality lawyers.

My second point is that the core of the privilege is clearly the ground covered by Professor Zuckerman's proposed rule: that statements to a person's lawyers in pursuit of legal advice should not be used as admissions against that person. Here there is *not only* an issue of fairness but *also* an issue of reliability, since the statement is quite possibly misleading because made as a hypothetical worst-case scenario, or in ignorance of material facts, or on the basis of an approximate memory of events which proves to be inconsistent with evidence later uncovered.

The polar opposite is the case which has always from the very earliest cases in the 1580s been held to be outside the privilege, that is, knowledge which the lawyer has otherwise than in his capacity as lawyer, or *could have* other than in this capacity: among the latter, for example, the date of execution of an instrument.[11] *Lloyd* v. *Mostyn* is, in fact, a case of this sort: the document claimed to be privileged was the actual contract (by specialty) on which the action was brought. It would be ridiculous if secondary evidence of this document could not be given because of advice privilege.[12]

[11] *Lloyd d. Fiennes* v. *Lord Saye and Sele, sub. nom. Lord Say and Seal's Case* (1710) 10 Mod. 40, 41; 88 E.R. 617, 617.

[12] *Lloyd* v. *Mostyn* (1842) 10 M. & W. 478, 478–9; 152 E.R. 558, 559. Why this instrument was in the hands of the defendant's father's attorney before his death is unexplained in the report. The underlying context is a family dispute over payment of a legacy due to younger children (the contract being a conditional bond to indemnify an executor who had paid the children's legacy to the father), so that the deed is likely to have come into the father's lawyers hands *qua* family attorney as trustee for the benefit of the younger children beneficiaries, rather than *qua* attorney for the father and hence for the elder son, his executor, the defendant. (Hence, it may be guessed, the prior judicial order, probably in Chancery, to the defendant's attorney to produce the document to be copied.) The ruling at trial that the original was privileged therefore seems questionable. In this

The borderland is unclear. Third-party documents may be protected by litigation privilege but not by advice privilege;[13] pre-existing documents merely collected by lawyers are not thereby privileged,[14] but *collections of extracts* made by lawyers as such are privileged as tending to disclose the advice.[15] *Calcraft* v. *Guest* itself involved not only the issue of inadvertent disclosure but also the decision 'once privileged, always privileged', that documents produced for litigation 111 years before were prima facie privileged, though the privilege could be lost by the inadvertent disclosure. It is very hard indeed to see what principle or public interest is served by this rule so that the outcome in *Calcraft* v. *Guest* must be right even if reached by the wrong route.

The existing broad scope of the litigation and advice privileges forms the basis of some of the more difficult cases Professor Zuckerman discusses – and he has suggested that drafts of expert reports, for example, should be disclosed, and that it is questionable whether corporations or public bodies should have advice privilege.[16] The breadth of the rule in *Lyell* v. *Kennedy* as to collections of extracts seems to have its basis in an extreme adversarialism which positively promotes ambush tactics, and several of the decisions should arguably be seen as inconsistent with the 'cards on the table' principle of the Woolf reforms. Reduction of the scope of privilege to what is *really justifiable* would reduce the problems identified by Professor Zuckerman.

My third and connected point is *Lord Ashburton* v. *Pape*, waiver, and laches. I start from the point that *Lord Ashburton* v. *Pape* itself is not in reality a simple case of carelessness on the part of the claimant's solicitor. This was a certain William Nocton, with whom – by the time *Lord Ashburton* v. *Pape* reached the Court of Appeal – Lord Ashburton was already in litigation alleging that Nocton had defrauded him in connection with getting him to borrow and lend £65,000 on a property development transaction in which Nocton was interested.[17] The bankrupt, Edward James Pape, was not any old bankrupt, but a financial and social

context, the strong statements of Parke B. and Lord Abinger C.B. may be merely intended to stop counsel wasting time on the privilege point.

13 *Wheeler* v. *Le Marchant* (1881) 17 Ch. D. 675.

14 *Ventouris* v. *Mountain* [1991] 1 W.L.R. 607.

15 *Lyell* v. *Kennedy* (1884) 27 Ch. D. 1.

16 Zuckerman, 'Equitable Protection of Legal Professional Privilege: A Distraction', text to n. 73.

17 *Nocton* v. *Lord Ashburton* [1914] A.C. 932, discussed by J. Edelman, '*Nocton* v. *Lord Ashburton* (1914)', in C. Mitchell and P. Mitchell (eds.), *Landmark Cases in Equity* (Oxford: Hart Publishing, 2012), ch. 16.

high-flyer,[18] and a 'heroic' bankrupt who owed over £225,000 in total (£78.4 m in 2012 money using average earnings),[19] including £139,000 to Ashburton, and had no visible assets.[20] In this context, which must have been present to the minds of the members of the Court of Appeal in *Lord Ashburton* v. *Pape*, the fact that Nocton did not claim privilege in the letters when they were subpoenaed, and the peculiar story of his clerk Brooks 'not feeling well' and handing over the letters to Pape, looks like dodgy dealing between Nocton and Pape at Ashburton's expense rather than mere carelessness. The context also meant that the bankrupt Pape was unrepresented in the appeal so that the decision was, *de facto, ex parte* as well as being *ex tempore*.

I make this point in a little depth because the expressions used in the case, and the subsequent use of *Lord Ashburton* v. *Pape* in the cases discussed by Professor Zuckerman, assume that mere careless errors of the lawyers of the party claiming relief, without any wrongdoing more than carelessness of the adverse party's lawyers, is sufficient to invoke the equity jurisdiction. But it is not at all obvious that this *should* be the case.

Legal professional privilege is in principle waivable by the client. This has been the law since before the point was made *obiter* by North C.J. in *Lea* v. *Wheatley* in 1679.[21] It should not change. There may well be perfectly good reasons to waive privilege even in communications which could be used as admissions, if they otherwise contain material which can strengthen one's own case. Equitable obligations of confidence must also in principle be waivable.

The question this poses is how far the privilege and the right of confidence should be treated, in the context of litigation, as waived by the client's lawyers' carelessness in failing to claim privilege. It might be argued that the situation of inadvertent disclosure falls within the old

[18] In the 1890s, an associate of the Marquess of Queensberry involved in advising on the Oscar Wilde affair: Linda Stratmann, *The Marquess of Queensberry: Wilde's Nemesis* (New Haven, Conn.: Yale University Press, 2013), 162–3.

[19] Calculated at www.measuringworth.com/ppoweruk/.

[20] *Spokesman-Review*, 14 July 1912, http://news.google.com/newspapers?nid=1314&dat=19120714&id=WsZVAAAAIBAJ&sjid=YeADAAAAIBAJ&pg=1991,155714; *Ashburton Guardian*, 4 July 1913, http://paperspast.natlib.govt.nz/cgi-bin/paperspast?a=d&d=AG19130704.2.56&dliv=&e=---10–1--0–.

[21] M. Bacon, *A New Abridgment of the Law* (London: Lintot, 1736), vol. iv, 230 (tit. *Privilege*, (C) 2.). Serjeant Maynard is there reported as saying that this was already law in 'his father's case, before the Lord Cecil, in the Court of Wards' which would place it before 1612, but Maynard was an extremely unreliable reporter of precedents in his favour.

broad 'accident' jurisdiction of equity. But common lawyers argued very early that broad use of this jurisdiction risked rewarding negligence;[22] and equity lawyers also accepted pretty early that an 'accident' which resulted from the party's own carelessness was not a ground for relief.[23] There is no doubt that the client *can* be bound by his lawyers' carelessness (lawyers' technical mistakes were regularly characterised as *laches* of the party in the seventeenth-to nineteenth- century common law):[24] a recent example is in Andrew Mitchell MP's libel claim against the *Sun*.[25] The arguments of the Court of Appeal in that case emphasise the disadvantages of lenience towards lawyers' carelessness.

Who should bear the costs risk involved? Professor Zuckerman objects to the emphasis, in cases on the discretion since *Guinness Peat Properties Ltd* v. *Fitzroy Robinson Partnership*,[26] on the state of mind of the *inspecting* solicitor.[27] His solution would mean that the inspecting solicitor's client always bears the risk. But the problems he discusses actually suggest that the 'least cost avoider' is the *disclosing* solicitor, which would imply abolishing rule 31.20 of the Civil Procedure Rules 1998 (UK) and restricting any inadmissibility rule – beyond the core case identified by Professor Zuckerman of statements offered as admissions – to cases of intentional misconduct (whether by the disclosing solicitor or by others).

I would suggest, therefore, that, first, while in the 'core' case covered by Professor Zuckerman's proposed rule of exclusion accidental disclosure should not make the client's statement to his lawyers admissible, outside this 'core' the client should be bound – except where, as on the facts of *Lord Ashburton* v. *Pape*, the client's lawyer appears to have actively betrayed him, or where the adverse party has engaged not in mere carelessness but in active wrongdoing.

[22] *Barry & Styles' Case* (1626) Latch. 24; 82 E.R. 256 (Jones J.).

[23] For example, *Norton* v. *Searl* (1675) 73 S.S. 152.

[24] For only a few examples, *Cotton* v. *Daintry* (1669) 1 Vent. 29; 86 E.R. 21; *R* v. *Kirk* (1699) 12 Mod. 304; 88 E.R. 1337; *Dickson* v. *Fisher* (1768) 4 Burr. 2267; 98 E.R. 183; *Grant* v. *Lord Sondes* (1776) 2 W. Bl. 1094; 96 E.R. 646; and *Ruston* v. *Hatfield* (1819) 3 B. & Ald. 204; 106 E.R. 636.

[25] *Mitchell* v. *News Group Newspapers Ltd (Practice Note)* [2014] 1 W.L.R. 795; [2013] EWCA Civ 1537.

[26] [1987] 1 W.L.R. 1027.

[27] Zuckerman, 'Equitable Protection of Legal Professional Privilege: A Distraction', text to nn. 13 ff.

26

Equity's role

MATTHEW CONAGLEN

It is worthwhile reflecting upon the role that equity has served, and continues to serve, in common law systems. The preceding chapters perform that function in specific contexts. This chapter offers reflections on the general role of equity, in the light of the more specific points that have been made in earlier chapters.

The very breadth of the subject matter of the various chapters contained in this volume emphasises the importance of equity's role, as well as its continuing vitality, as a source of principles for facilitating and regulating administration. Perhaps most famous among equity's contributions – 'the most distinctive achievement of English lawyers'[1] – is the trust, which provides a much more flexible, and therefore facilitative, mechanism for splitting property rights than the common law provided. The doctrine of estates and other common law rules limited the ways in which real property could be dealt with at common law. And the common law was even more restrictive as to how title to personal property could be divided between various people.[2] Equity's recognition that a legal owner could be bound, in good conscience, to use the owner's title for the benefit of another (or multiple others) generated equitable obligations which developed over time into a form of property right.[3] Equity thus provided rules which facilitated the administration of property (and funds of property) for a variety of persons in ways which could not, or could not easily, be done at common law.[4]

[1] F.W. Maitland, *Equity: A Course of Lectures*, ed. by A.H. Chaytor and W.J. Whittaker, rev. by J. Brunyate (Cambridge University Press, 1936), 23.

[2] C. Harpum, S. Bridge and M. Dixon, *Megarry & Wade's Law of Real Property*, 8th ed. (London: Sweet & Maxwell, 2012), [3-001].

[3] See *ibid.*, [5-009]-[5-013].

[4] T.W. Merrill and H.E. Smith, 'Optimal Standardization in the Law of Property: The Numerus Clausus Principle' (2000) 110 Yale L.J. 1, 17–18.

However, as Dr Turner's introductory chapter emphasises,[5] the concept of administration is a broad one, ranging across contexts such as the administration of property held in trust, the administration of property for the benefit of creditors of an insolvent person or company, the administration of justice by courts and the administration of government through the executive branch. As the chapters in this volume establish, as the common law has developed equity has made contributions in all of these areas, and indeed in many others.

Equity is thus deeply embedded in the history of the common law as that law developed in England, and then beyond those shores as the common law was exported to other jurisdictions which were administered by the British. The common law's methodology means it is inherently focused on history. Equity's contribution to that history has left an imprint across the wide span of the common law.

In saying this, it is important not to lose sight of the fact that equity's role has not been limited solely to its interaction with judge-made common law. Equity has also made important contributions to ensure that various statutory regimes operate effectively. An obvious example of equity's interaction with statute lies in the development of principles by which the conduct of company directors would be regulated. These became increasingly important with the advent of statutory schemes permitting voluntary incorporation of companies by registration without needing parliamentary intervention in each case. Common law doctrines – particularly, the law of contract – had an obvious role to play in facilitating and regulating the deal made between the company and the director for the director's services, but so too did equity in providing other principles by which the director could be held to account for conduct which was contrary to the needs of good administration of the company. Thus, for example, company directors were held to owe a duty of care to the company, at a time when the common law of negligence was still in a relative state of infancy compared with its current state, by reason of the similarity between their position of control over the company and its assets and the positions held by trustees and agents. That similarity was sufficient for the courts of equity to treat company directors as subject to fiduciary duties.[6] Such duties were – and remain today – important in facilitating the good administration of companies. Where

[5] P.G. Turner, 'Equity and Administration', Chapter 1 of this volume.

[6] See, for example, L.S. Sealy, 'The Director as Trustee' [1967] C.L.J. 83, 85–6, 91–103; L.S. Sealy, 'Fiduciary Relationships' [1962] C.L.J. 69, 71–3; P.D. Finn, *Fiduciary Obligations* (Sydney: Law Book Co., 1977), [7]; P.D. Finn, 'The Fiduciary Principle', in T.G. Youdan

those duties are now incorporated into statutory formulations of director's duties,[7] their equitable origins nevertheless remain relevant in a number of ways.[8]

The importance of equity's role

The influence of equity throughout the common law is thus both deep and wide. One consequence of this is that questions as to whether the common law system (meaning, in this context, the system of judge-made law and thus including equity)[9] could operate effectively, or indeed better, without equity are not particularly instructive. For example, it has been suggested that the specific return of assets could be better provided for without the use of a (constructive) trust mechanism.[10] It is, of course, possible, as a thought experiment, to design a legal system from the ground up without resort to equity or the equitable doctrines that we currently have. However, that would generate a system different from the one that we have.

Equity's role in the specific return of assets grew, like so many equitable doctrines, out of the inadequacies of the common law regime's ability to recover assets *in specie*. In general terms, common law judgments were determinations of right between the parties which were then executed using specific writs. Most of those writs were concerned with the recovery of money: 'the primary remedy at common law for the protection of property interests is not the compulsory return of the property to the claimant but rather damages'.[11] In contrast, Chancery decrees were a command addressed to the party to act (or not to act) in a certain way.[12] As such, a court exercising equitable jurisdiction could

(ed.), *Equity, Fiduciaries and Trusts* (Toronto: Carswell, 1989), 34–5; P. Birks, 'The Content of Fiduciary Obligation' (2000) 34 Israel L. Rev. 3, 3.

7 See, for example, Companies Act 2006 (UK), ss. 170–80; Corporations Act 2001 (Cth), ss. 180–5.

8 See M. Conaglen, 'Interaction between Statutory and General Law Duties Concerning Company Director Conflicts' (2013) 31 C. & S.L.J. 403, 411–12.

9 For discussion of the various different senses of the term 'common law', see *PGA* v. *R* (2012) 245 C.L.R. 355, [20]–[22]; [2012] HCA 21.

10 E. Bant and M. Bryan, 'Specific Restitution without Trusts' (2012) 6 J. Eq. 181.

11 M.G. Bridge, *Personal Property Law*, 3rd ed. (Oxford University Press, 2002), 47. This statement concerns personalty: real property was dealt with differently: see R.E. Megarry and H.W.R. Wade, *The Law of Real Property*, 5th ed. (London: Stevens & Sons, 1984), 1155–60.

12 See *Pearson* v. *Arcadia Stores Guyra Ltd (No. 2)* (1935) 53 C.L.R. 587, 590–1, 592.

order the defendant to return (or transfer) a specific asset.[13] Over time, as it became clear in what circumstances a court would make that sort of order, a (constructive) trust could be recognised as arising in such circumstances, as an application of equity's maxim that it considers as done that which ought to be done.[14] Such a trust, in turn, provides further protection to the plaintiff, in the sense that if the defendant does not return the asset when he should, the plaintiff's right to recover the asset can potentially be enforced against a third party (provided the third party cannot rely on a relevant defence, such as being a bona fide purchaser without notice).

Conceivably, all of this could potentially have been done without the intervention of equity and equitable principles. But, as a matter of history, it was not done that way. And to realise a legal system which achieves this result without resort to equity or equitable principle would involve a paradigm shift, given the way that common law systems develop by building upon principles established in previous cases rather than casting aside those principles and starting afresh. To discard equity and equitable principle is to discard part of the anchor which helps to maintain the stability of the common law. The 'reason for going back into the past is to come forward to the present, to help us to see more clearly the shape of the law of to-day by seeing how it took shape'.[15]

Nor is it clear that a legal system designed from the ground up, without resort to equity, would necessarily be a desirable system. As Lord Millett has said:

> Those who favour the fusion of law and equity might perhaps reflect that the three greatest systems of jurisprudence in the Western world have all been dual systems. Jewish law had its written and oral law; Roman law its civil and praetorian or bonitary law; English law common law and equity. In each case the duality served a similar function. One system provided certainty; the other the necessary flexibility and adaptability to enable justice to be done. But the common law and equity are not two separate and parallel systems of law. The common law is a complete system of law which could stand alone, but if not tempered by equity would often be productive of injustice; while equity is not a complete and independent system of law and could not stand alone. In the words of that fine

[13] '[I]t was not until the coming into operation of the Common Law Procedure Act, 1854, that specific recovery of chattels became possible outside equity': E.L.G. Tyler and N.E. Palmer, *Crossley Vaines on Personal Property*, 5th ed. (London: Butterworths, 1973), 17.

[14] *Muschinski* v. *Dodds* (1985) 160 C.L.R. 583, 613–14; P.W. Young, C. Croft and M.L. Smith, *On Equity* (Sydney: Lawbook Co., 2009), [3.610].

[15] *A.-G. for Victoria* v. *Commonwealth* (1962) 107 C.L.R. 539, 595.

> Australian judge Kitto J. it is 'the saving supplement and complement of the Common Law'.[16]

Equity's fundamental role was, as Lord Selborne L.C. said in *Wilson* v. *Northampton and Banbury Junction Railway Co.*, to 'do more perfect and complete justice'[17] than was possible under the common law. That justification betrays the origins of the equitable jurisdiction, lying in the Chancellor's ability to dispense the King's justice as a form of Aristotelian equity designed to deal with the inadequacies of the common law.[18] As all students of equity know, the development of this equitable jurisdiction over centuries has led to it becoming a form of legal doctrine, capable of being subject to rigorous analysis and statement alongside the common law. As Deane J. said:

> Long before Lord [*sic*] Seldon's [*sic*] anachronism [*sic*] identifying the Chancellor's foot as the measure of Chancery relief, undefined notions of 'justice' and what was 'fair' had given way in the law of equity to the rule of ordered principle which is of the essence of any coherent system of rational law.[19]

The ultimate ground on which equity intervenes is to prevent unconscientious conduct, but the relevant conscience is a 'properly formed and instructed conscience'.[20] That conscience is formed and instructed 'by reference to well developed principles . . . It is to those principles that the court has first regard rather than entering into the case at that higher level of abstraction involved in notions of unconscientious conduct in some loose sense where all principles are at large.'[21] However, the doctrine which contains those equitable principles continues to betray some of its

[16] Lord Millett, 'Proprietary Restitution', in S. Degeling and J. Edelman (eds.), *Equity in Commercial Law* (Sydney: Lawbook Co., 2005), 309. Similarly, see W.M.C. Gummow, 'Equity: Too Successful?' (2003) 77 A.L.J. 30, 43. Professor Finn, who is self-professedly neither a champion of equity nor an admirer of its separateness, considers that we could not do without 'the animating ideas of our equity jurisprudence': P. Finn, 'Common Law Divergences' (2013) 37 M.U.L.R. 509, 535.

[17] *Wilson* v. *Northampton & Banbury Junction Railway Co.* (1874) L.R. 9 Ch. App. 279, 284.

[18] Young, Croft and Smith, *On Equity*, [1.160]. The early concept of statutory interpretation, as espoused by Plowden by reference to the 'equity of the statute', involved a form of Aristotelian equity: see the discussion in J.D. Heydon, 'Equity and Statute', Chapter 12 of this volume, text between nn. 115 and 130.

[19] *Muschinski* v. *Dodds* (1985) 160 C.L.R. 583, 616.

[20] *Australian Broadcasting Corp.* v. *Lenah Game Meats Pty Ltd* (2001) 208 C.L.R. 199, [45]; [2001] HCA 63. See also *Australian Financial Services & Leasing Pty Ltd* v. *Hills Industries Ltd* (2014) 253 C.L.R. 560, [76]; [2014] HCA 14.

[21] *Tanwar Enterprises Pty Ltd* v. *Cauchi* (2003) 217 C.L.R. 315, [20]; [2003] HCA 57.

origins. Thus, for example, equitable principles are 'both specific and flexible in character'.[22] Their specificity reflects the fact that they are not a general – 'at large' – jurisdiction to cure all unfairness.[23] Their flexibility reflects their role in 'soften[ing] and mollify[ing] the Extremity of the Law'.[24] General notions of fairness are relevant, but only insofar as they are embodied within equitable principles.[25]

Modes of regulation

In seeking to achieve this end, equity naturally adopted different modes of regulation, appropriate to its objective. As Professor Smith has noted in Chapter 18, there are differences between *ex ante* forms of regulation and *ex post facto* regulation.[26] Equity grew out of a desire to soften the hard edges, and other inadequacies, of the common law. Those inadequacies arose, in part at least, because of the well-known difficulties that are inherent in formulating *ex ante* rules: human foresight being what it is, it is difficult to formulate rules which will be adequate to all future eventualities. Equity developed out of a concern to remedy those inadequacies, at times by providing further rules to deal with situations not comprehended by the common law's rules, and at others by intervening to soften the consequences of the application of the common law's rules. It was natural, given that role, for equity to adopt an *ex post facto* analysis, which applied broader standards, as distinct from the common law's more exact *ex ante* rules, in order to determine whether the defendant's conduct was acceptable: even although the defendant may have acted in accordance with its legal rights and obligations, equity could determine that the defendant's conduct was nonetheless contrary to good conscience and take action to remedy the situation.

It is not suggested that there is a rigid division between *ex ante* regulation and *ex post* regulation, the former being the sole province of

[22] *Ibid.*, [20].

[23] 'The mere fact that it would be unjust or unfair in a situation of discord for the owner of a legal estate to assert his ownership against another provides, of itself, no mandate for a judicial declaration that the ownership in whole or in part lies, in equity, in that other': *Muschinski* v. *Dodds* (1985) 160 C.L.R. 583, 616.

[24] *Earl of Oxford's Case* (1615) 1 Ch. Rep. 1, 7; 21 E.R. 485, 486.

[25] *Muschinski* v. *Dodds* (1985) 160 C.L.R. 583, 616; *Stephenson Nominees Pty Ltd* v. *Official Receiver* (1987) 16 F.C.R. 536, 556. See also P. Keane, 'The Conscience of Equity', in M. Cope (ed.), *Interpreting Principles of Equity* (Sydney: Federation Press, 2014), 259–60.

[26] See H.E. Smith, 'Equity and Administrative Behaviour', Chapter 18 of this volume, text after n. 44.

the common law and the latter being exclusively that of equity. The common law has doctrines which operate in an *ex post* fashion as well, perhaps most obviously in the assessment of the reasonableness, or otherwise, of past conduct that is required by the doctrine of negligence. Conversely, equity has *ex ante* rules as well, such as its mandatory rules regarding the formation and operation of trusts, and the broad *ex ante* proscriptions that comprise fiduciary doctrine's conflict and profit doctrines.[27] Furthermore, there is an element of interaction between these two modes of regulation when they are deployed within a common law system, in the sense that a collection of consistent *ex post* decisions can develop into an *ex ante* rule or principle.

Nonetheless, the distinction between *ex post* and *ex ante* regulation remains a useful way of thinking, in general terms, about the distinctions between common law and equity. It helps to bring into sharper relief the fact that a number of equitable doctrines involve *ex post* review of prior conduct. For example, while the doctrine of fraud on a power is concerned with the scope of a power,[28] it is different from the construction of the words used to confer the power.[29] An exercise of a power is made in fraud of the power where, although it 'was according to the letter of the power',[30] it was made for a purpose other than the purpose (or purposes) for which the power was granted. Those purposes are often only identified after the fact, because it is often impossible to state, *ex ante*, for precisely what purposes the power was initially granted. The court determines, after the power has purportedly been exercised, whether the purpose for which it was exercised was within, or outwith, the range of purposes for which the power could legitimately be considered to have been granted. As Professor Gummow says in Chapter 16, the question of when the court will regard a particular exercise of power as a fraud on the power 'cannot be answered by setting up a system of closed

[27] It is, however, noteworthy that even in the fiduciary context there is an element of *ex post* regulation, in the sense that outside of the settled categories of fiduciary relationships it is notoriously difficult to define precisely which relationships are, or are not, fiduciary. It is also interesting to note that the formulations of fiduciary doctrine in the United States adopt a more *ex post* form of regulation, with the court assessing the fairness of the impugned transaction: see, for example, *Broz* v. *Cellular Information Systems Inc.*, 673 A.2d. 148, 155 (Del. S.C. 1996); *Re Southern Peru Copper Corp. Shareholder Derivative Litigation*, 30 A.3d. 60, 86–7 (Del. Ch. 2011).

[28] *Vatcher* v. *Paull* [1915] A.C. 372, 378; R.C. Nolan, 'Controlling Fiduciary Power' [2009] C.L.J. 293, 297.

[29] *Henty* v. *Wrey* (1882) 21 Ch. D. 332, 353–4, 355.

[30] *Re Queensberry Leases* (1819) 1 Bligh 339, 398; 4 E.R. 127, 148.

categories'.[31] Similarly, equity's doctrine of undue influence involves an *ex post* assessment of whether the influence that was used in procuring a particular transaction or decision was undue in all the circumstances.[32]

Again, it would be possible to design a legal system which did not employ *ex post* modes of regulation, but the question remains: would we want such a system? As Mr Heydon writes, '[c]oherence has high claims. But so does richness'.[33] *Ex post* review provides part of that richness. It does, of course, generate concerns about certainty, but certainty is not the only legal value.[34] The concern about certainty does, however, explain why courts have sought to constrain this *ex post* mode of review so that it is not too broad. As Professor Smith observes, '[e]quity needs to avoid being both broad and *ex post* – which would lead to limitless discretion'.[35] Professor Smith's observations provide a further explanation for, and thus give greater subtlety to, the observation that equity has developed into legal doctrine, rather than remaining a free-ranging discretion of the sort Selden famously criticised. Equity has developed in that way, both as a natural consequence of the nature of its involvement in a common law system of reasoning and as a result of judges' exercising the equitable jurisdiction in a way that attempts to retain legitimacy for the role that equity plays within the legal system.

It is a matter of balance. The need for balance sometimes disappears from sight, particularly when the function served by equity's involvement in the legal system is underplayed or overlooked. Thus, for example, the High Court of Australia's decision in *Andrews* v. *Australia and New Zealand Banking Group Ltd*,[36] which held that equity's ability to give

[31] See W. Gummow, 'Equity in the Modern Administrative State', Chapter 16 of this volume, text after n. 101. Professor Gummow's point is made in respect of injunctive relief, but that does not mean that the mode of review applied is *ex ante*: injunctions can be sought after the fact, and even where they are sought on an interim basis, the nature of the review involved in assessing whether the exercise of power would be a fraud on the power is not in the nature of an application of clear *ex ante* rules regarding the scope of the power.

[32] *Royal Bank of Scotland plc* v. *Etridge (No. 2)* [2002] 2 A.C. 773, [7]; [2001] UKHL 44. This example also illustrates the point made earlier, that common law doctrines adopt the *ex post* mode of review as well, in that the common law doctrine of duress involves an assessment of whether pressure was used in an illegitimate fashion: *Universe Tankships Inc. of Monrovia* v. *International Transport Workers Federation* [1983] 1 A.C. 366, 384.

[33] See Heydon, 'Equity and Statute', text after n. 42.

[34] *Lac Minerals Ltd* v. *International Corona Resources Ltd* [1989] 2 S.C.R. 574, 666.

[35] See Smith, 'Equity and Administrative Behaviour', text after n. 2.

[36] (2012) 247 C.L.R. 205; [2012] HCA 30. cf. *Cavendish Square Holding BV* v. *Makdessi* [2015] 3 W.L.R. 1373; [2015] UKSC 67.

relief against penalties was not limited to situations involving a breach of contract, has been decried by some for the uncertainty that it creates.[37] In part, that uncertainty will be worked out as subsequent cases determine what constitutes a penalty,[38] which cases will themselves refer – in the nature of common law analysis – to earlier decisions, as the High Court itself did in *Andrews*.[39] But the point for present purposes is that the critique accords insufficient weight to the idea that uncertainty can itself be part of the point of the mode of regulation adopted in such cases: the possibility of such *ex post* review warns parties that their dealings may be undone if they fail to meet the standards of behaviour which courts exercising equitable jurisdiction expect of them.[40] The existence and knowledge of those standards of behaviour then inform the parties' dealings, encouraging them to deal with one another in a way that eschews the extremes of self-interested opportunism.[41] Those standards need to be stated publicly,[42] but that does not mean that they must necessarily be precise *ex ante* rules rather than *ex post* standards. As Professor Smith says, however, it is important that such standards not be so broad as to detract from the legitimacy of the function that equity serves by adopting and enforcing them. For example, the Privy Council's decision in *Çukurova Finance International Ltd* v. *Alfa Telecom Turkey Ltd (No. 4)*[43] has been compellingly criticised for having failed to

[37] J.W. Carter, W. Courtney, E. Peden, A. Stewart and G.J. Tolhurst, 'Contractual Penalties: Resurrecting the Equitable Jurisdiction' (2013) 30 J.C.L. 99.

[38] For example, *Paciocco* v. *Australia and New Zealand Banking Group Ltd* (2014) 309 A.L.R. 249; [2014] FCA 35; (2015) 321 A.L.R. 584; [2015] FCAFC 50.

[39] See P.S. Davies and P.G. Turner, 'Relief against Penalties Without a Breach of Contract' [2013] C.L.J. 20, 23–4.

[40] The critique also fails to accord due weight to the fact that it has been clear for a long time that where there is a conflict between law and equity, equity prevails: see, for example, Judicature Act 1873 (UK), s. 25(11). This provision continued the relationship between law and equity that had been established following James I's proclamation regarding the *Earl of Oxford's Case*: see J. McGhee (gen. ed.), *Snell's Equity*, 33rd ed. (London: Sweet & Maxwell, 2015), [1-017]. (For discussion of the genesis of section 25(11), see M. Leeming, 'Equity, the Judicature Acts and Restitution' (2011) 5 J. Eq. 199.) Indeed, the High Court's decision in *Andrews* is predicated on the fact that the equitable jurisdiction to relieve against penalties existed before the law of contract developed into its modern form.

[41] A former Chancellor of the Supreme Court of Delaware has made a related argument that ambiguity in the implied duty of good faith is itself useful, in that it can facilitate re-bargaining of long term contracts after unforeseen events: W.T. Allen and G. Levy, 'The Uses of Ambiguity in Commercial Contracts: On Facilitating Re-Bargaining', in S. Worthington (ed.), *Commercial Law and Commercial Practice* (Oxford: Hart Publishing, 2003), 163.

[42] L.L. Fuller, *The Morality of Law*, rev ed. (London: Yale University Press, 1969), 49–51.

[43] [2015] 2 W.L.R. 875; [2013] UKPC 20.

heed that advice, by failing to pay attention to the principles which give form to the equitable jurisdiction to give relief against forfeiture,[44] and which thereby constrain the manner in which equity's *ex post* regulation of forfeiture is implemented.

It is this concern which has led the High Court of Australia to emphasise, repeatedly, that equity is grounded in conscience, though not a free-ranging discretion to fix all unfairness.[45] Equity's resort to conscience involves recourse to a series of principles which have been worked out and applied, in the classic tradition of the common law, through thousands of cases over hundreds of years. Contrary to what Professor Birks said,[46] it has been clear since the time of Lord Nottingham (and indeed earlier)[47] that it is not a 'forum internum':

> With such a conscience as is only *naturalis et interna*, this Court has nothing to do; the conscience by which I am to proceed is merely *civilis et politica*, and tied to certain measures.[48]

Equity's maxims

In other words, if one is to understand the way in which equity relies on the concept of conscience, it is vital to understand the principles by which equity instantiates that conscience. In this regard, the maxims of equity are noteworthy, as these are effectively short-form encapsulations or reflections of some of equity's principles. One – that equity considers as done that which ought to be done – has already been mentioned in this chapter.[49] Others – including the maxim that he who seeks equity must do equity, that equity does not act in vain and that equity follows the law – are referred to in Lord Walker's chapter (Chapter 20) in this

[44] P.G. Turner, '"Mending Men's Bargains" in Equity: Mortgage Redemption and Relief against Forfeiture' (2014) 130 L.Q.R. 188, 189–91.

[45] See text to nn. 19–25 above.

[46] P. Birks, 'Equity in the Modern Law: An Exercise in Taxonomy' (1996) 26 U.W.A. L. Rev. 1, 17.

[47] M. Macnair, '*Coke* v. *Fountaine* (1676)', in C. Mitchell and P. Mitchell (eds.), *Landmark Cases in Equity* (Oxford: Hart Publishing, 2012), 57.

[48] *Cook* v. *Fountain* (1676) 3 Swans. 585, 600; 36 E.R. 984, 990. See further D.E.C. Yale, *Lord Nottingham's Chancery Cases: Vol. 1*, 73 Selden Society (London: Quaritch, 1957), xlv–xlvi; M. Macnair, 'Equity and Conscience' (2007) 27 O.J.L.S. 659, 680; D.R. Klinck, *Conscience, Equity and the Court of Chancery in Early Modern England* (Farnham: Ashgate, 2010), ch. 8.

[49] See text to n. 14 above.

volume.[50] Just some of the case law examples of the importance of equity's maxims in judicial reasoning can be found in the Privy Council's decision in *Attorney-General for Hong Kong* v. *Reid*,[51] and in the High Court of Australia's decisions in *Corin* v. *Patton*[52] and *Friend* v. *Brooker*.[53]

The idea that he who seeks equity must do equity underpins equity's approach to its remedies generally. Thus, for example, where rescission is sought in equity following a breach of fiduciary duty, the person seeking the remedy must be prepared to restore the other party to the position that party occupied prior to the transaction which is being rescinded.[54] Equity's flexibility in this regard is seen in circumstances where it is not possible to make complete *restitutio in integrum*, for example, because property was transferred pursuant to the impugned transaction and has since been sold, so that it cannot now be returned. A court can give effect to the maxim by ordering a transfer of the monetary value of the property,[55] instead of the property itself, in order that the plaintiff do equity.

The maxims of equity reflect the broad motivating themes of equity. 'In a given field, those themes and values may compete or clash and require resolution. That resolution may then be reflected in particular doctrines of equity which then apply in the future.'[56] As Mason C.J. and McHugh J. said in *Corin* v. *Patton*, speaking of the maxim that equity will not assist a volunteer:

> it would be a mistake to set too much store by the maxim. Like other maxims of equity, it is not a specific rule or principle of law. It is a summary statement of a broad theme which underlies equitable concepts and principles. Its precise scope is necessarily ill-defined and somewhat uncertain. It is subject to certain clearly established exceptions ...

50 See R. Walker, 'Equity and Human Rights', Chapter 20 of this volume, text to n. 15, and text after nn. 84, 87, 115 and 123. See also Heydon, 'Equity and Statute', text following n. 70, discussing the concept of equity following the law.

51 [1994] 1 A.C. 324, 336. See Lord Millett, 'Account of Profits (Book Review)' (2014) 130 L.Q.R. 681, 683.

52 (1990) 169 C.L.R. 540, 551, 556–8.

53 (2009) 239 C.L.R. 129, [38]–[39]; [2009] HCA 21. See also *Lavin* v. *Toppi* (2015) 254 C.L.R. 459, [44], [54]; [2015] HCA 4.

54 *Mayfair Trading Co. Pty Ltd* v. *Dreyer* (1958) 101 C.L.R. 428, 451–2; *Maguire* v. *Makaronis* (1997) 188 C.L.R. 449, 474–5. The requirement to do equity can also, at times, require the plaintiff to transfer property or money to a third party: see, for example, *Nelson* v. *Nelson* (1995) 184 C.L.R. 538, 571, 617.

55 See, for example, *McKenzie* v. *McDonald* [1927] V.L.R. 134.

56 Gummow, 'Equity: Too Successful?', 42.

> These exceptions have no bearing on the present case except in so far as they demonstrate that the maxim does not enunciate an inflexible or universal rule.[57]

This is characteristic of the way in which equitable principles operate.[58] Professor Edelman (as he then was) 'provocatively'[59] advocated, in *Snell's Equity*, the abolition of the equitable maxims altogether, on the grounds that the maxims often conflict and are sometimes used by judges as a substitute for transparent reasoning.[60] While it is to be expected that judges (and indeed counsel)[61] will be transparent in their reasoning, the fact that the maxims conflict is in the very nature of principles.[62] It is thus a natural consequence of equity's resort, at times, to standards (particularly *ex post* ones) rather than (*ex ante*) rules.

The maxims were deduced from earlier cases. Their formulation as maxims gave a fresh impulse to the development of equity.[63] As such, they are a repository of earlier learning, which 'represent, reflect and disseminate certain of the fundamental moral ideas and themes which lie at the heart of the equitable jurisdiction'.[64] As such, 'their practical value in a scheme of arrangement is immense'[65] and they 'are therefore of considerable importance for an understanding of equity'.[66] It would be a mistake to discard that learning. The immediately prior edition of *Snell's Equity* captured the position well:

> Owing to its haphazard origin, equity is not a complete system. Nevertheless, there are certain general principles upon which the Court of Chancery exercised its jurisdiction. Many of these have been embodied in the so-called maxims of equity. These are not to be taken as positive laws of equity which will be applied literally and relentlessly in their full width, but rather as trends or principles which can be discerned in many

57 *Corin* v. *Patton* (1990) 169 C.L.R. 540, 557.

58 Rules of statutory construction operate in a similar fashion: see *Maunsell* v. *Olins* [1975] A.C. 373, 382; *Bank Officials' Association (South Australian Branch)* v. *Savings Bank of South Australia* (1923) 32 C.L.R. 276, 299.

59 *Parkview Qld Pty Ltd* v. *Commonwealth Bank of Australia* [2013] NSWCA 422, [119].

60 See J. McGhee (gen. ed.), *Snell's Equity*, 32nd ed. (London: Sweet & Maxwell, 2010), [5–001].

61 *Parkview Qld Pty Ltd* v. *Commonwealth Bank of Australia* [2013] NSWCA 422, [119].

62 R. Dworkin, 'The Model of Rules' (1967) 35 U. Chicago L. Rev. 14, 25–7.

63 Yale, *Lord Nottingham's Chancery Cases: Vol. 1*, lxiii.

64 P. Loughlan, 'The Historical Role of the Equitable Jurisdiction', in P. Parkinson (ed.), *The Principles of Equity*, 2nd ed. (Sydney: Lawbook Co., 2003), 25.

65 H.G. Hanbury, *Modern Equity* (London: Stevens and Sons, 1935), 63.

66 J.D. Heydon, M.J. Leeming and P.G. Turner, *Meagher, Gummow & Lehane's Equity: Doctrines and Remedies*, 5th ed. (Sydney: LexisNexis, 2015), [3–005].

> of the detailed rules which equity has established. Further, no logical division of these maxims is possible. The maxims do not cover the whole of the ground and, moreover, they overlap, one maxim containing by implication what belongs to another ... For all that, each merits separate consideration, for each embodies some peculiar function of equity.[67]

Interstitial operation

The equitable perspective matters. It is necessary to have a full understanding of common law doctrine because of the way equity operates interstitially.[68] Equity follows the law, in the sense that it acknowledges the existence of the common law position and then supplies a gloss to that position in circumstances where it has been thought that good conscience so requires.[69] If the gloss is ignored, the statement of law is apt to mislead. A classic example lies in Mr Justice Holmes' argument that '[t]he duty to keep a contract at common law means a prediction that you must pay damages if you do not keep it, – and nothing else'.[70] This view 'takes no account of the existence of equitable remedies, like decrees of specific performance and injunction, which ensure or encourage the performance of contracts rather than the payment of damages for breach'.[71] Equity developed the jurisdiction to grant the remedy of specific performance as a gloss on the common law to do 'more perfect and complete justice'.[72] As Lord Erskine L.C. said of the doctrine of specific performance:

> This Court assumed the jurisdiction upon this simple principle; that the party had a legal right to the performance of the contract; to which the Courts of Law, whose jurisdiction did not extend beyond damages, had not the means of giving effect.[73]

[67] J. McGhee (gen. ed.), *Snell's Equity*, 31st ed. (London: Sweet & Maxwell, 2005), [5–01]. The call to abolish the maxims has been removed from the most recent edition: see McGhee (gen. ed.), *Snell's Equity*, 33rd ed. [5–001].

[68] Maitland, *Equity: A Course of Lectures*, 21. [69] *Ibid.*, 19.

[70] O.W. Holmes, 'The Path of the Law' (1897) 10 Harv. L. Rev. 457, 462.

[71] *Tabcorp Holdings Ltd* v. *Bowen Investments Pty Ltd* (2009) 236 C.L.R. 272, [13]; [2009] HCA 8. See also *Zhu* v. *Treasurer of the State of New South Wales* (2004) 218 C.L.R. 530, [128]; [2004] HCA 56.

[72] See text accompanying n. 17 above.

[73] *Alley* v. *Deschamps* (1806) 13 Ves. 225, 227–8; 33 E.R. 278, 279.

A statement of the law which ignores equity's jurisdiction to provide specific relief is based on 'a faulty analysis'.[74]

Like statutes,[75] equity cuts across other categorisations of common law analysis. In particular, equity cuts across the categories laid down in the taxonomical project, associated most famously with the work of the late Professor Birks. That is important because equity reflected, and reflects, a different value system from that adopted by the common law.[76] A further consequence of this is that something may be lost if equitable concepts are corralled into common law categories. To take just one example, Justice Edelman has argued (extra-curially) that a number of puzzles about fiduciary duties can only be explained once those duties are understood as voluntary undertakings.[77] This appears to involve an attempt to fold fiduciary duties into the 'consent' category in the Birksian taxonomy. The argument that the puzzles to which Edelman refers can *only* be resolved if fiduciary duties are conceived of in accordance with his 'deconstructionalist thesis'[78] is incorrect: viable alternative explanations exist.[79] More importantly, to fold the doctrine of fiduciary duties into the (non-existent) legal category of 'voluntary undertakings' runs a real risk of that doctrine being conflated with the common law of contracts in a way that could involve a drastic change in what is expected of fiduciaries. For example, whereas a fiduciary requires fully informed consent in order to alter the consequences of his or her fiduciary duties, a contractual obligation can be altered with a less exacting form of consent. The reason for this difference lies in the protective function that fiduciary doctrine serves, which differs markedly from the functions

[74] *Coulls* v. *Bagot's Executor and Trustee Co. Ltd* (1967) 119 C.L.R. 460, 504.

[75] P.D. Finn, 'Equitable Doctrine and Discretion in Remedies', in W.R. Cornish, R. Nolan, J. O'Sullivan and G. Virgo (eds.), *Restitution: Past, Present and Future* (Oxford: Hart Publishing, 1998), 254; J. Dietrich, 'What is "Lawyering"? The Challenge of Taxonomy' [2009] C.L.J. 549, 573, 577; M. Leeming, 'Theories and Principles Underlying the Development of the Common Law: The Statutory Elephant in the Room' (2013) 36 U.N.S.W.L.J. 1002, 1026–8.

[76] A. Mason, 'The Impact of Equitable Doctrine on the Law of Contract' (1998) 27 Anglo-Am. L. Rev. 1, 3.

[77] J. Edelman, 'The Fiduciary "Self Dealing" Rule', in J. Glister and P. Ridge (eds.), *Fault Lines in Equity* (Oxford: Hart Publishing, 2012), 107–8. See also J. Edelman, 'When Do Fiduciary Duties Arise?' (2010) 126 L.Q.R. 302; J. Edelman, 'The Importance of the Fiduciary Undertaking' (2013) 7 J. Eq. 128.

[78] Edelman, 'The Fiduciary "Self Dealing" Rule', 108.

[79] See, for example, M. Conaglen, 'Fiduciary Duties and Voluntary Undertakings' (2013) 7 J. Eq. 105, 107–19.

served by contract law.[80] Similarly, rescission operates *ab initio* where there has been a breach of fiduciary duty, assuming none of the bars to rescission applies. It does not operate that way where there has been a breach of contract.[81] As Professor Frankel has said:

> When we blur the distinctions between fiduciary and contract relationships, calling them by the same name, we tend to disregard the reasons for the different rules that govern them. Having forgotten these reasons, we are proposing seriously flawed rules that could come back to haunt us.[82]

Public law

The fact that equity intersects with, or cuts across, other legal categories is also important when addressing the debate as to whether fiduciary duties exist in public law contexts. Professor Endicott suggests, in Chapter 19 of this volume, that they do not. His reasoning seems, in essence, to be encapsulated in the passage where he says:

> [T]he administrative agency's salient duty is to deal with the funds for public purposes, and the trustee's salient duty is to deal with the funds for the private benefit of beneficiaries.[83]

This places a large amount of weight on the distinction between public and private, which is a very difficult division to draw coherently.[84] In addition to those difficulties, there is no doubt that public authorities can be trustees of funds (or other property) that they hold.[85] The courts will not treat a fund as held in that fashion merely because it is held by a public authority,[86] but where it is clear that a trust subject to the court's equitable jurisdiction is intended, such a trust can arise, notwithstanding that the authority holds the trust fund for public purposes. The trustee of such a fund will owe fiduciary duties. Similarly, charitable trusts are also

[80] See further *ibid.*, 116–17. [81] See further *ibid.*, 124–5.

[82] T. Frankel, 'Fiduciary Duties as Default Rules' (1995) 74 Oregon L. Rev. 1209, 1211.

[83] See T. Endicott, 'Equity and Administrative Behaviour: A Commentary', Chapter 19 of this volume, text between nn. 25 and 26.

[84] See C. Campbell, 'The Nature of Power as Public in English Judicial Review' [2009] C.L.J. 90.

[85] For example, *A.-G. for Ireland* v. *Dublin* (1827) 1 Bligh N.S. 312, 341; 4 E.R. 888, 899; *A.-G.* v. *Liverpool* (1835) 1 My. & Cr. 171, 201, 202; 40 E.R. 342, 352; *A.-G.* v. *Aspinall* (1837) 2 My. & Cr. 613, 622–3; 40 E.R. 773, 777. See also J. Barratt, 'Public Trusts' (2006) 69 M.L.R. 514.

[86] *Kinloch* v. *Secretary of State for India in Council* (1882) 7 App. Cas. 619, 625–6.

held for public rather than private purposes,[87] and yet trustees of these trusts (or the directors, if the charity is a corporation) will owe fiduciary duties. Fiduciary duties are not foreign to public law.

This should not be a cause for surprise, when it is borne in mind that the fiduciary concept was used to justify the application of duties recognised in the paradigm fiduciary relationship between trustee and beneficiary to other relationships where the parties were similarly situated and where the courts considered that similar forms of regulation were apposite.[88] There is no clear reason why that exporting function could not lead to fiduciary duties being owed by public actors as well as private actors. The mere fact that there is a difference between the purposes they serve does not itself show that the export is inapposite. Where a public authority stands in such a relationship with its constituents (or whichever person or group is argued to be the principal in the fiduciary relationship) that it is legitimate for the constituents to expect that the authority will act in their interest to the exclusion of the authority's own several interest,[89] a fiduciary expectation could legitimately arise and with it fiduciary duties. Nor is this affected by Endicott's further point that '[t]he agency's specific duties depend on the particular public purposes for which the power is held; a trustee's specific duties depend on the purposes prescribed by the settlor'.[90] Neither the source nor the content of the purposes is necessarily inconsistent with the application of fiduciary principles, if the fiduciary expectation makes sense in the circumstances. As the Supreme Court of the United States said in *United States of America* v. *Carter*, explaining why a public official could not retain a profit acquired in circumstances involving a conflict between his personal interest and his public duty, '[t]he disability results not from the subject-matter but from the fiduciary character of the one against whom it is applied'.[91]

The concern about fiduciary doctrines being applied in the public sphere mirrors, to some degree, similar concerns about the application

[87] Gummow, 'Equity in the Modern Administrative State', text to nn. 86–87; *Bateman's Bay Local Aboriginal Land Council* v. *Aboriginal Community Benefit Fund Pty Ltd* (1998) 194 C.L.R. 247, [28]; [1998] HCA 49; *Truth About Motorways Pty Ltd* v. *Macquarie Infrastructure Investment Management Ltd* (2000) 200 C.L.R. 591, [97]; [2000] HCA 11.

[88] See M. Conaglen, *Fiduciary Loyalty: Protecting the Due Performance of Non-Fiduciary Duties* (Oxford: Hart Publishing, 2010), 12–15.

[89] See Finn, 'The Fiduciary Principle', 54; *Grimaldi* v. *Chameleon Mining NL (No. 2)* (2012) 200 F.C.R. 296, [177]; [2012] FCAFC 6.

[90] See Endicott, 'Equity and Administrative Behaviour: A Commentary', text before n. 26.

[91] *United States of America* v. *Carter*, 217 U.S. 286, 306 (1910).

of fiduciary concepts in commercial contexts. Lord Millett said, extra-curially, that 'it is of the first importance not to impose fiduciary obligations on parties to a purely commercial relationship who deal with each other at arm's length and can be expected to look after their own interests'.[92] Similarly, Bramwell L.J. famously said:

> I do not desire to find fault with the various intricacies and doctrines connected with trusts, but I should be very sorry to see them introduced into commercial transactions, and an agent in a commercial case turned into a trustee with all the troubles that attend that relation.[93]

And yet, 'business relationships (leaving aside partnerships) clearly can attract fiduciary obligations',[94] even though the circumstances include the existence of a commercial transaction. Company directors act in a commercial context. They owe fiduciary duties to the company. Lawyers and agents frequently act in commercial contexts while owing fiduciary duties to their principals. Hence, as Mason J. observed, 'it is altogether too simplistic, if not superficial, to suggest that commercial transactions stand outside the fiduciary regime as though in some way commercial transactions do not lend themselves to the creation of a relationship in which one comes under an obligation to act in the interests of another'.[95] Fiduciary duties do not commonly arise in commercial settings because it is normally inappropriate to expect a commercial party to put its own interests aside and to act solely in the interests of another commercial party.[96] But if, in all the circumstances of the relationship between the parties, that expectation is appropriate, then fiduciary duties can and will arise notwithstanding that it is a commercial relationship. In the same way, there is no good reason for categorically denying the possibility that fiduciary duties could apply in a public law context: if the fiduciary expectation is appropriate in the circumstances, there is no *a priori* reason preventing equity from giving effect to it.

92 P. Millett, 'Equity's Place in the Law of Commerce' (1998) 114 L.Q.R. 214, 217–18.

93 *New Zealand & Australian Land Co.* v. *Watson* (1881) 7 Q.B.D. 374, 382. See also *Cobbe* v. *Yeoman's Row Management Ltd* [2008] 1 W.L.R. 1752, [81]; [2008] UKHL 55.

94 *News Ltd* v. *Australian Rugby Football League Ltd* (1996) 64 F.C.R. 410, 538. See also *South Australia* v. *Peat Marwick Mitchell & Co.* (1997) 24 A.C.S.R. 231, 266.

95 *Hospital Products Ltd* v. *United States Surgical Corp.* (1984) 156 C.L.R. 41, 100. See also *Re Goldcorp Exchange Ltd (in receivership)* [1995] 1 A.C. 74, 98.

96 See also J.R.F. Lehane, 'Fiduciaries in a Commercial Context', in P.D. Finn (ed.), *Essays in Equity* (Sydney: Lawbook Co., 1985), 98; *John Alexander's Clubs Pty Ltd* v. *White City Tennis Club Pty Ltd* (2010) 241 C.L.R. 1, [90], [2010] HCA 19.

Equity has, after all, made important contributions to the development of public law in other ways.[97] In particular, equity's ability to grant declarations and injunctions was particularly useful where other legal remedies were insufficient to give full effect to public regulation.[98] As Gaudron, Gummow and Kirby JJ. said in *Bateman's Bay Local Aboriginal Land Council* v. *Aboriginal Community Benefit Fund Pty Ltd*, '[i]n this field, equity has proceeded on the footing of the inadequacy . . . of the legal remedies otherwise available to vindicate the public interest in the maintenance of due administration'.[99] And, as Gummow J. pointed out in *Minister for Immigration* v. *Eshetu*, in a passage which also has resonance with the points made by Professor Smith[100] concerning the importance of controlling the reach of *ex post* regulation:

> What have come to be known as the principles of '*Wednesbury* unreasonableness' have developed by analogy to principles governing the judicial control in private law of the exercise of powers and discretions vested in trustees and others. The principles in question are now part of that body of administrative law which is concerned with the judicial review of abuse of discretionary powers. That is how '*Wednesbury* unreasonableness' has been understood on numerous occasions in this Court. A notable example is provided by the judgment of Mason J. in *Minister for Aboriginal Affairs* v. *Peko-Wallsend Ltd*. His Honour's discussion of *Wednesbury* occurred in the course of elaboration of the proposition that '[t]he limited role of a court [in] reviewing the exercise of an administrative discretion must constantly be borne in mind'. The point, reiterated by leading United States scholars, is that '[j]udicial review can be a source of excessive discretion as well as a means of limiting discretion'.[101]

The potential application of fiduciary duties in public law contexts does, however, raise important questions as to what it means to say that such

[97] See generally H.G. Hanbury, *Essays in Equity* (Oxford: Clarendon Press, 1934), ch. 6; *Bateman's Bay Local Aboriginal Land Council* v. *Aboriginal Community Benefit Fund Pty Ltd* (1998) 194 C.L.R. 247, [24]–[32], [78].

[98] See, for example, *A.-G.* v. *Mayor, Aldermen, and Citizens of the City and County of Newcastle-Upon-Tyne and the North-Eastern Railway Co.* (1889) 23 Q.B.D. 492, 497 (aff'd [1892] A.C. 568); *Trethowan* v. *Peden* (1930) 31 S.R. (N.S.W.) 183 (aff'd *A.-G. for the State of New South Wales* v. *Trethowan* (1931) 44 C.L.R. 394 and [1932] A.C. 526 (P.C.)); *A.-G.* v. *Sharp* [1931] 1 Ch. 121. See also A. Mason, 'The Place of Equity and Equitable Remedies in the Contemporary Common Law World' (1994) 110 L.Q.R. 238, 238.

[99] (1998) 194 C.L.R. 247, [25].

[100] See n. 35 above.

[101] *Minister for Immigration & Multicultural Affairs* v. *Eshetu* (1999) 197 C.L.R. 611, [124]; [1999] HCA 21. See also *SZFDE* v. *Minister for Immigration and Citizenship* (2007) 232 C.L.R. 189, [12]; [2007] HCA 35.

duties apply. That topic is not straightforward, partly because the fiduciary concept of loyalty remains a contested one,[102] but also because equity's very nature meant that it was applied to different situations in a way that took into account the differences in context.[103] However, it can be said with reasonable confidence that '[t]he expression "fiduciary duty" is properly confined to those duties which are peculiar to fiduciaries and the breach of which attracts legal consequences differing from those consequent upon the breach of other duties'.[104] Further, the recognition of fiduciary duties does not 'supply any proper foundations for the imposition upon fiduciaries in general of a quasi-tortious duty to act solely in the best interests of their principals'.[105] But it would, presumably, be expected that any public actor who is held to owe fiduciary duties would have to abide by equity's core proscriptions on fiduciaries acting with a conflict between their duty and interest and making unauthorised profits from the fiduciary position. While the context in which public actors operate clearly differs from that in which a private law trustee (or other private law fiduciaries) operates,[106] it is not clear that those differences render the core fiduciary proscriptions inapposite in a public law context.

It is common, in arguing against fiduciary duties in public law, to raise the decisions in *Roberts* v. *Hopwood*[107] and *Bromley London Borough Council* v. *Greater London Council*.[108] In each of those cases, a court overturned decisions, which the court appeared to consider were taken extravagantly by public authorities, on the basis that the decisions were inconsistent with fiduciary duties. These decisions are rightly a cause for concern,[109] although it is not clear that fiduciary doctrine was the true basis of the decisions: they could easily be rationalised on traditional administrative law grounds of irrationality or unreasonableness.[110]

[102] Compare, for example, Conaglen, *Fiduciary Loyalty* with L. Smith. 'Fiduciary Relationships: Ensuring the Loyal Exercise of Judgement on Behalf of Another' (2014) 130 L.Q.R. 608.
[103] See, for example, the differences in the way duties of care were applied to company directors as opposed to trustees: see Conaglen, *Fiduciary Loyalty*, 15.
[104] *Bristol & West Building Society* v. *Mothew* [1998] Ch. 1, 16.
[105] *Breen* v. *Williams* (1996) 186 C.L.R. 71, 137.
[106] See P. Sales, 'Equity and Human Rights: A Commentary', Chapter 21 of this volume, text after n. 19.
[107] [1925] A.C. 578. Mentioned in Endicott, 'Equity and Administrative Behaviour: A Commentary', text to nn. 26 ff.
[108] [1983] 1 A.C. 768.
[109] D. Feldman, 'Equity in the Modern Administrative State: A Commentary', Chapter 17 of this volume, text to nn. 9 ff.
[110] See Barratt, 'Public Trusts', 531, 533–4.

It depends on the terms on which the power has been granted,[111] coupled with an assessment of the purposes for which that power was granted. The former involves standard issues of construction. While the latter does bring in equitable concepts, it is not a peculiarly fiduciary concept: the doctrine of fraud on a power (or proper purposes, as it is often referred to in company law and administrative law contexts) is not limited to fiduciaries in its application.[112]

These points do not mean that application of the proscriptive fiduciary duties would make no sense in the public sector. For example, the expenses scandal in England could easily be conceived of as a series of breaches of fiduciary duties by MPs, taking unauthorised benefits which only came to them by reason of their fiduciary position. That in turn raises potentially difficult issues as to the justiciability of such an argument in court, and also as to Parliamentary privilege (although the latter was no shield against criminal charges in the expenses scandal).[113] Such difficulties are less pronounced where the relevant public actors are part of local government authority.[114] Thus, for example, in *Westminster City Council* v. *Porter*, Lady Porter was found to have acted in breach of duty vis-à-vis the Council, of which she was the leader, when she arranged a scheme under which the Council would sell housing it owned in areas where it was thought the purchasers would be more likely than the incumbent residents to vote for her political party in subsequent elections. Hart J. considered that it was inaccurate to describe her as a trustee of the Council's assets, but she did nonetheless owe it trustee-like duties.[115] Her conduct constituted a breach of this equitable duty,[116] which meant that the Council could sue her for its loss.[117] The standard description for an equitable

[111] See Gummow, 'Equity in the Modern Administrative State', text after n. 79.

[112] See Conaglen, *Fiduciary Loyalty*, 47–9.

[113] *R* v. *Chaytor* [2011] 1 A.C. 684; [2010] UKSC 52.

[114] See, for example, *Bowes* v. *City of Toronto* (1858) 11 Moo. P.C. 463; 14 E.R. 770.

[115] *Westminster City Council* v. *Porter* [2003] Ch. 436, [27]; [2002] EWHC 1589 (Ch). Similarly, see *A.-G.* v. *Wilson* (1840) Cr. & Ph. 1, 23–4, 26–7; 41 E.R. 389, 396–7, 397–8.

[116] The wrongfulness of what she had done is discussed in more detail in *Porter* v. *Magill* [2002] 2 A.C. 357; [2001] UKHL 67. It was not described in this way in the judgments, but it would not be difficult to describe her conduct in terms of acting with a conflict between her duty and her personal interest.

[117] The Council had other statutory remedies as well, but the claim for breach of trust (or fiduciary duty) was brought, and decided, separately on the basis that interest would be calculated differently: *Westminster City Council* v. *Porter* [2003] Ch. 436, [10].

duty which is like those owed by trustees, but where the person who owes the duty is not strictly a trustee, is a fiduciary duty.[118]

Breadth

The breadth of equity's role, in acting as a correction to the common law across a vast range of contexts, is sometimes lost sight of. For example, courses and books from England on equity frequently focus their attention on the law of trusts: even the older textbooks tend to 'resemble a sandwich – a thick filling of trusts law inserted between thin slithers of equity history and a miscellany of (mainly) remedial topics',[119] without much attention being paid to the numerous other equitable doctrines. There are, of course, legitimate reasons for this focus. As Maitland observed,[120] the trust has been an extremely important contribution to the common law. It is important that it be studied as rigorously as other functional vehicles for facilitating transacting (contracts, corporations, etc.). And the law of trusts is complex: detailed attention is required for a full understanding of it. The emphasis on trusts may also partly reflect professional qualification requirements in England and Wales.[121] The point being made here is simply that there is a risk, in focusing so closely on trusts, that the breadth of influence of equitable doctrine may be lost sight of. The reverse, of course, is also true: for example, Australian courses on equity tend to emphasise more the breadth of equity's role, which naturally means that it is not possible to offer the same detailed level of analysis of the operation of trusts as is possible in English courses. As in all things, an element of balance is necessary.

This point also prompts mention of differences in the ways that equitable doctrine has developed in different common law jurisdictions. 'The common law is no longer monolithic',[122] and it has not been so since at least 1967 when the Privy Council accepted that different

[118] *Re West of England & South Wales District Bank, Ex p. Dale & Co*. (1879) 11 Ch. D. 772, 778.

[119] M. Bryan, 'Book Review' (2013) 7 J. Eq. 82, 82.

[120] Maitland, *Equity: A Course of Lectures*, 23. [121] Bryan, 'Book Review', 82.

[122] *B* v. *Auckland District Law Society* [2003] 2 A.C. 736, [55]; [2003] UKPC 38. See also *Invercargill City Council* v. *Hamlin* [1996] A.C. 624, 640; *Cassell & Co. Ltd* v. *Broome* [1972] A.C. 1027, 1127.

Commonwealth jurisdictions could develop different rules suited to their own circumstances.[123]

By way of one example, the doctrine of unconscionable (or unconscientious) transactions has been embraced in Australia as an effective *ex post* form of control on freedom of contract and other dealings: if one party has unconscientiously taken advantage of the fact that the other party occupied some special situation of disadvantage, the court can grant relief.[124] As the authors of *Meagher, Gummow & Lehane* note, following the High Court of Australia's decision in *Commonwealth Bank of Australia Ltd* v. *Amadio*,[125] 'the decisions have been legion'.[126] In contrast, while the doctrine continues to exist in England, the courts have emphasised that 'a bargain cannot be unfair and unconscionable unless one of the parties to it has imposed the objectionable terms in a morally reprehensible manner, that is to say, in a way which affects his conscience',[127] and that the defendant's impropriety must be such that it 'shocks the conscience of the court'.[128] This contrasts with the Australian approach which 'contains none of the rhetoric about imposition of harsh terms in a morally reprehensible manner'.[129] The English doctrine is 'starkly different from doctrines of substantially similar juridical bases that are applied by the courts of Ireland, Australia, New Zealand and Canada'[130] and is largely moribund.

It may be, as Professor Finn has suggested,[131] that these differences are in part explained by the influence of broad statutory regimes prohibiting misleading and deceptive conduct, which he points out have no British counterpart.[132] While Finn correctly points to the lack of broad statutory regimes in England equivalent to those in other countries, it is also noteworthy that the statutory regimes that have been adopted in England have at times also required a very high threshold to be met

123 *Australian Consolidated Press Ltd* v. *Uren* [1969] 1 A.C. 590, 641, 644.

124 *Commercial Bank of Australia Ltd* v. *Amadio* (1983) 151 C.L.R. 447, 461–2. See also *Blomley* v. *Ryan* (1956) 99 C.L.R. 362.

125 (1983) 151 C.L.R. 447.

126 Heydon, Leeming and Turner, *Meagher, Gummow & Lehane's Equity: Doctrines and Remedies*, 5th ed. [16–005] n. 2.

127 *Multiservice Bookbinding Ltd* v. *Marden* [1979] Ch. 84, 110.

128 *Alec Lobb (Garages) Ltd* v. *Total Oil Great Britain Ltd* [1983] 1 W.L.R. 87, 95.

129 D. Capper, 'The Unconscionable Bargain in the Common Law World' (2010) 126 L.Q.R. 403, 410.

130 *Ibid.*, 416.

131 Finn, 'Equitable Doctrine and Discretion in Remedies', in Cornish, Nolan, O'Sullivan and Virgo (eds.), *Restitution: Past, Present and Future*, 253–4.

132 Finn, 'Common Law Divergences', 520.

before a court could intervene. For example, under the Consumer Credit Act 1974, before it was amended in 2006, a court could reopen a credit agreement only where it found the bargain to be extortionate,[133] which was only the case where the debtor was required to make '*grossly* exorbitant' payments or where the bargain 'otherwise *grossly* contravenes ordinary principles of fair dealing'.[134] As Justice Leeming says in his chapter,[135] to draw a connection between such statutory regimes and equitable doctrine is somewhat speculative, but it will be interesting to see whether changes in the Consumer Credit Act regime since 2008 (when the 2006 amendments came into effect) might lead to a lowering of the threshold that is required to be met before the unconscionable transactions doctrine is applied. The new statutory regime permits the court to exercise broad powers in respect of credit agreements if the relationship between the two parties is 'unfair'.[136] Some consider that the judicial attitude to this new statutory power will remain the same,[137] but it is difficult to see how that can be given that the new power clearly offers 'enhanced protection'[138] to consumers when compared with the earlier regime. However, the broader reach of the new statutory regime will presumably mean that there is less call to extend the application of the unconscionable transactions doctrine where the Act applies, although the issue remains a live one in respect of transactions to which the Act does not apply.

It is, therefore, important to be careful with accounts of equity which draw their sources from different jurisdictions without acknowledging the differences between those jurisdictions. That does not mean that comparative analysis of equity is futile: on the contrary, there is much to be learned by looking at how equity is done in other places. Professor Gummow's chapter (Chapter 16) in this volume shows the importance of such comparative analysis. And in *FHR European Ventures LLP* v. *Cedar Capital Partners LLC*, the Supreme Court's decision to recognise proprietary constructive trusts as a potential remedy in respect of unauthorised profits taken in breach of fiduciary duty appears to have

[133] Consumer Credit Act 1974 (UK), s. 137(1). [134] *Ibid.*, s. 138(1) (emphasis added).

[135] See M. Leeming, 'Equity and Statute: A Commentary', Chapter 13 of this volume, text to n. 13.

[136] Consumer Credit Act 1974 (UK), s. 140A(1).

[137] M.P. Thompson, *Modern Land Law*, 4th ed. (Oxford University Press, 2009), 440.

[138] *Scotland* v. *British Credit Trust Ltd* [2014] Bus. L.R. 1079, [25]; [2014] EWCA Civ 790. See also *Plevin* v. *Paragon Personal Finance Ltd* [2014] 1 W.L.R. 4222, [7]; [2014] UKSC 61.

been influenced by the consistency with which other common law jurisdictions had already recognised that form of remedy.[139] Consistently with the view taken in other jurisdictions, the Supreme Court considered that 'the proceeds of a bribe or a secret commission consists [*sic*] of property which should not be in the agent's estate at all'.[140] Also, consistently with another theme of this chapter, the Supreme Court considered its conclusion to be justified, in part, by reference to equity's role in facilitating administration:

> Secret commissions are . . . objectionable as they inevitably tend to undermine trust in the commercial world. That has always been true, but concern about bribery and corruption generally has never been greater than it is now.[141]

[139] *FHR European Ventures LLP* v. *Cedar Capital Partners LLC* [2015] A.C. 250, [45]; [2014] UKSC 45.

[140] [2015] A.C. 250, [45]. [141] *Ibid.*, [42].

INDEX

www.ingramcontent.com/pod-product-compliance
Lightning Source LLC
LaVergne TN
LVHW011533200926
848484LV00001B/254
9781107142732